Minnesota Mediterranean and East European
Monographs

XVI

FETTERED INDEPENDENCE
Cyprus, 1878–1964

*The author with Archbishop Makarios, the first president
of the Republic of Cyprus*

Minnesota Mediterranean and East European
Monographs

FETTERED INDEPENDENCE
Cyprus, 1878–1964

Volume Two: The Documents

compiled by
Stella Soulioti

MODERN GREEK STUDIES

UNIVERSITY OF MINNESOTA

MINNEAPOLIS, MINNESOTA

Number 16   2006

Minnesota Mediterranean and East European Monographs (MMEEM)

Theofanis G. Stavrou, general editor
Soterios G. Stavrou, associate editor
Elizabeth A. Harry, assistant editor

The objective of the MMEEM is the dissemination of scholarly information about the Mediterranean and East European region. The field is broadly defined to include the social sciences and the humanities. Even though the emphasis of the series is on the Greek and Slavic worlds, there are no thematic, geographical, or chronological limitations. Through the series we hope to encourage research in a variety of contemporary problems in their historical context. In this regard, special efforts will be made to accommodate proceedings from scholarly conferences as well as monographic studies with a diachronic approach.

Monographs in the MMEEM series are published by the Modern Greek Studies Program at the University of Minnesota as supplements to the *Modern Greek Studies Yearbook*. *Fettered Independence: Cyprus, 1878–1964* (two volumes) by Stella Soulioti is number 16 in the series.

The publication of this work was made possible by a subsidy from the A. G. Leventis Foundation.

The price for this two-volume work is $100.00, paperback. Make checks payable to:

Modern Greek Studies
325 Social Science Building
UNIVERSITY OF MINNESOTA
267—19th Avenue South
Minneapolis, MN 55455
Telephone: (612) 624-4526

Cover: A natural sculpture on the south coast of Cyprus photographed by Avo Mangoian. The sculpture has been moved to Arodaphnousa Home for Cancer Patients, Nicosia, Cyprus.

The UNIVERSITY OF MINNESOTA is an equal-opportunity employer.
Printed in the United States of America on acid-free paper

CONTENTS

Volume Two: Documents

*Maps in Appendices 1, 82, and 86 appear in a separate booklet
as a supplement to Volume Two.*

PREFACE

THE DOCUMENTS in this companion volume to Stella Soulioti's *Fettered Independence: Cyprus, 1878–1964*, come from the author's personal archive and are published here with her permission. They reflect the passion for details of the first minister of justice of the Republic of Cyprus. They also reflect her sense of history and her concern about preserving a record of the island's long struggle for independence, and the complex developments during the first years of the republic.

This is arguably the most indispensable critical mass of documents collected by a single individual and published in one volume. Besides documenting Stella Soulioti's narrative, these sources are now accessible to scholars interested in a variety of issues dealing with the Cyprus Question.

While all efforts were made to maintain the integrity of the texts, some modifications were made to the format of the original documents for consistency purposes. Similarly, to the extent possible, attempts were made to correct typographical errors and other apparent discrepancies. We wish to express our appreciation to Jessica Hopeman, Alyssa Johnson-Wells, Allison Lindberg, Sheila Puhl, Cassandra Rosine, and Elizabeth Stavrou, who helped with the preparation of the documents for publication.

Editor's Note

APPENDIX 1

Population Map of Cyprus

See Map Supplement.

APPENDIX 2(1)

MEMORIAL: Dealing with the Chief Grievances of the People of Cyprus Addressed to His Lordship the Secretary of the State for the Colonies by the Greek Elected Members of the Legislative Council, Nicosia, 20 July 1929*

Your Lordship,

1.　　We the respectfully undersigned Greek members of the Legislative Council of Cyprus, representing about the 5/6 of its population, have the honour to submit for your Lordship's kind consideration and earnest solicitude the following:

Expression of joy and congratulations of the people of Cyprus on the victory of the Labour party.

2.　　The victory of Labour party at the last general election in England and its consequent accession to power has been a source of particular gratification to the Greek people of Cyprus. The more so as having been exceptionally oppressed and greatly wronged by the Conservative party—the governing body of yesterday—they reasonably hope for a more humane treatment from a Government coming from a party, which was formed by the rousing of consciences against a bourgeois dictatorship, and in consequence better in a position to appreciate the righteous struggles of a people—such as the people of Cyprus—fighting against foreign oppression. The recent declarations of policy made by the Labour party during the last general election campaign and the ideology both of the present Government and its eminent Leader so officially proclaimed by him at the Socialist Meeting of Berne in 1919, afford the Cyprus people a cause for rejoining in the Labour Victory.

We, therefore, in their name and on their behalf request to be allowed to submit to the Labour Government and to its Leader on the occasion of their victory and their assumption of authority, the expression of the most cordial congratulations of this people.

The national desire and claim of the people of Cyprus to be united with Mother Greece.

3.　　A foremost and basic complaint of the Greek people of Cyprus is that, contrary to their expressed unanimous will and against all justice, they are being kept separated from their Mother country Greece, with whom sacred and unbreakable ties of blood, religion, language, traditions and national conscience link them together.

Cyprus was without the knowledge of its people subjected to British administration in virtue of the Treaty of

---

* Printing-Office "Nicosia", Chr. Nicolaou (Nicosia, Cyprus).

3

1878, which has been very rightly, declared by great British statesmen and famous English papers, to be a shame for British policy. This Treaty has confirmed an unconscientious and unprincipled act of purchase-sale of a people, by agree-ment between England and Turkey, without the knowledge of the Cyprus people themselves who were thus made like live-stock the subject-matter of a shameful dealing. This in accord-ance with the aforesaid Treaty, Cyprus has been administered by Great Britain and badly administered too and despite its persistent claims for national restoration it was kept by England and was made a British Colony in 1914, under the lively and strong protest of the Island which in written form was handed by the Archbishop and Ethnarch to the Governor on the occasion of the annexation official ceremony.

And all this on the morrow of the great war, during which the peoples in general and individuals in particular vol-untarily, shed their blood, having given faith to the sincerity of such Liberal promises as were held out and widely proclaimed by Great Britain and the Allies regarding the Liberty and self-determination of small nations. But as a result of all this sacrifice the world has seen again the "right of might" only pre-vail.

The bitter disappointment felt by the Greek people of Cyprus on the frustration of their hopes for a national settle-ment, far from disheartening them in pursuing their national aspirations has certainly caused in their minds a diminution of the prestige enjoyed by Great Britain, as a country proud of the strict adhesion to her promises, and a country where justice both internally and internationally reigns as law supreme.

The Ottoman minority in Cyprus a pretext for denial of national restoration.

4.   Great Britain in denying to satisfy the just national claims of this Island put forward only by way of excuse and cer-tainly not as a serious reason, her obligation to protect a small Turkish Minority which, it was alleged, would be wronged by the change of the political status of Cyprus.

It is, though, evident that in thus excusing herself Great Britain on the one hand disregards the principles of the law of nations and introduces a fallacious theory, (which, were it to be adopted would have to reverse many post-war international conventions,) and on the other hand on the pretence of doing justice to a small minority, exercises great injustice and oppres-sion on the large majority. England moreover in handing over Cyprus to Greece would have every opportunity and all means of protecting the rights of the minority by "convention", the observance of which would be amply guaranteed by her own power, though the great rights and the protection already en-joyed by the minorities in Greece would afford sufficient assur-ance.

In denying to do justice to Cyprus in respect of its national restoration England did not treat her justly on other points as well.

5.　　　Having denied justice to this Island as to its claim for a national settlement Great Britain has not acted in a fairer way in her treatment of Cyprus in other respects. The same unjust and imperialistic police of administration as was first established continues till this day and in a worse form.

The constitution in force today criticized.

A clear manifestation of such an autocratic administration and its chief cause and reason at the same time, is the socalled constitution of the Colony, which was granted to her by the Letters Patent of the 1/5/1925 and the Instructions attached thereto and by the Legislative Council Order of the 6th February, 1925. This constitution is exactly the same as, and in those respects where it differs of a still more restricted application than the pseudo-constitution which was granted to the Island, very soon after the British occupation (vide Order in Council 14th Sept., 1878 and 16th Febr., 1882).

a) The Legislative power.

According to the existing constitution there is no Legislating Assembly, but merely a Legislative Council. Its powers are very limited and where they are a little extended are so much restricted as to annihilate the voice of the whole people of the Island in general and of the large majority in particular. That is to say:

　　　a) The Legislative Council can introduce no vote, resolution or law for the appropriation of part of the public revenues or propose a bill imposing a tax without having previously obtained permission from the Governor.

　　　b) It has no control over the whole of the sums to be appropriated during the voting of the Budget, a great portion of them being beyond its control by virtue of existing Imperial Orders in Council and laws.

　　　c) It enjoys no substantive participation in the preparation of the Budget, nor is it entitled to exercise any control over the estimates of expenditure.

　　　In general its obtaining rights and privileges are further curtailed by the power reserved to the Governor or the King in the exercise of the prerogative of disallowance and they are completely annihilated by the King's right to legislate for the Colony by Order in Council not only where the circumstances are such as to call for such extraordinary measures but also in respect of current routine in the service.

Examples.

We cite the following most recent examples of this latter party:

    a)   The Budget of 1927 rejected by the vote of the elected members of the Legislative Council was nevertheless put into force in its entirety by an Order in Council from the King.

    b)   Connected with the Budget and for the purposes of covering a deficiency provided therein a new levy to the sum of £40,000 was also imposed in the same year without the advice and consent of the Legislative Council.

    c)   The Penal Law published in the Government Gazette as a draft bill in order to be later introduced into the Legislative Council as expressly stated in the preamble to the said bill, was imposed as law from London by Royal Order, without its being laid before the Legislative Council and the advice of its members thereon being obtained.

    d)   During the last session of the Legislative Council a Pensions bill, as proposed by the Government was rejected. The same measure has just been sanctioned from England as law, by means of a Royal Order in Council.

Criticism from the point of view of the majority of the inhabitants who are Greeks.

6.   But if by all these it is shown that the present constitution of the Island is nothing else than a mockery for the people of Cyprus as a whole, for the Greek people of Cyprus forming the 5/6 of the population, it constitutes a daring and unconcealed provocation, as, owing to the composition of the Legislative Council with 9 appointed officials, 3 Moslem and 12 Greek elected members under the chairmanship of the English Governor, the stifling of the voice of the 5/6 of the population is nearly secured, the majority in the country being thus turned into a minority, a form of tyranny is thereby established over the heads of the majority of the inhabitants of the Island.

b) The Executive Council.

The administration of the country is substantially in the hands of the English Governor and the English officials as his Executive Councillors. The Governor being in fact responsible and answerable to the Home Government in London only, has no responsibility towards the tax-paying people of Cyprus. That is to say:

    a) The Executive Council consisting of not more that four persons appointed from among the high English Officials is, like a Cabinet, only an Advisory body, the Governor not being bound by their advice.

    b) The Governor is not bound to nominate members of the Executive Council from among the native elements.

c) The additional three members who are in fact called to attend its meetings are not always and necessarily taken from among the elected members of the Legislative Council.

It should thus be observed that under (c), the most liberal of the above cited instances, the constitution of the Executive Council, gives to the 5/8 of the opinion therein to the foreign Government and reserves to the tax-paying inhabitants of the country the 3/8 only. Furthermore to the Greek element which forms the 5/6 of the population a 2/8 portion is granted. But it also should be pointed out that there always exists the possibility of either the one or both the native elements being absolutely excluded from the said Council or of their being un-evenly and disproportionately represented therein, in as much as it is not at all binding for the Governor to make his nomina-tion and selection of the additional members according to their actual numbers in the Island. In addition, the fact that the Governor is not bound to invite always the additional members to attend the meetings of the Council and to participate in its deliberations, should not be lost sight of.

The commission of transgressions by the allpowerful Governor very probable.

8.   Consequently the present constitution of the Executive Council allows of many serious transgressions either on the part of the all-powerful Governor alone or of the other official members, whereby foreign interest may be favoured or pro-moted to the grave prejudice of important interests of the country or of private individuals. Unfortunately the policy of the Government, during these last years, tends to give its wholehearted and unqualified support to British capital alone, thus endeavouring to facilitate its introduction and domination in the country to the detrimental prejudice of local capital and of the existing enterprises.

Examples do not lack to testify to this conduct of the local Government. On the one hand exemption from import duty allowed to English Companies in order to import foreign materials and goods abounding locally and on the other denial to grant similar privileges to Cypriot enterprises to import raw material not abounding in the country; facilities on the part of the Government to English Companies and imposition of diffi-culties in the way of Cypriot or Greco-Cypriot capital during these last years; these are sufficient evidence to support the statements made above.

The clashing of the Legislature with the Executive thus fatal.

9.   We wish to lay special stress on the constitutional mon-struosity created in Cyprus by the establishment of an Execu-tive Council, holding the place of Government yet complete in itself and entirely independent of the representation of the people in the Legislative Council.

This forms the main cause of continuous troubles, for on the introduction by the Government of any measures into the Legislative Council for its sanction in case of measures not approved by the Greek elected Members, either of the following things will occur, namely: The Government will either succeed in getting them past by the assistance of the votes of the Turkish elected Members, being added to the official votes, much to the displeasure and annoyance of the 5/6 of the population, or else the proposed measures will be rejected by the united votes of the elected Members, who having no voice in the formation of the Government and consequently not being connected with it by political programme or otherwise, will, as it is very natural, disagree with the Government in many cases and throw out its Bills. And though the Government has at its disposal the Royal Orders in Council in order to meet with any resulting difficulties, yet, it should be remembered, this policy is certainly not conducive to smooth relations between Government and people, and badly serves the regular function of the Government machine.

Evil results; deplorable state of the country.

10.   Under such conditions of Government for the last fifty years it is but a natural consequence that this place reached its present deplorable state. Agriculture, its principal source of wealth, is found in a primitive condition compared to other countries. There are no harbours, though we have been governed for the last fifty years by the first naval nation of the world. Local means of communication are in such a ruinous state that an estimate of £360,000 was made for their repair and restoration. And so long as the annual budget could not be charged with such an exorbitant burden, it became necessary to apply for the sanctioning of a big loan. Elementary education is but recently assisted by half measures, and secondary education is left entirely to itself and to the care of the Communities. The forests, or what still remains of this beauty and wealth of the Island in ancient times, are half destroyed, and very little has been done for reafforestation, while the Government has completed the destructive work of fires by cutting down large wooded areas for the needs of war.

Excessive the amount of taxation and its proportion to the gross production.

11.   And all these at a time when the burden of taxation has long since reached the highest possible limit of endurance of the Cypriot tax-payer. The total amount of taxation paid by him yearly is £750,000 approximately and his yearly gross production, mostly agricultural is computed according to official statistical elements at 3 1/2 million pounds, i.e. the proportion of taxation to the gross production is between 20 to 25%, which represents, if it does not exceed, the amount of capitalization.

Causes; bad appropriation of the public revenues.

12.   But why is this? Because a Government foreign to the country, a Government composed of officers in the public service—another form of constitutional monstruosity—a Government, the actions of which lie beyond the effective control of the representatives of the people, in as much as by Royal Orders in Council, a facile source of legislation, it can easily fill up any gap and get over the refusal of the elected Members to pass a legislative measure even the most injurious—such a Government will always prove to be, in its disposal of the revenues of the Island, unscrupulously and unreasonably lavish and also devoid of any correct scientific criterion of public finance.

a) In respect of the proportion of the administrative expenditure to the amount of expenditure for the welfare and advancement of the country.

13.   Thus in a country where no charge for war debts and the maintenance of an army and navy exists; in a country without any important and serious public works to maintain and with no considerable support for education and agriculture, the total amount of expenditure in the Budget of 1929 has, save the contribution to the Public Ottoman Debt, reached the amazing, figure of £735,000. Out of this sum, sufficient, according to certain authorative statements by non official English residents in the Island for the administration of a country with an area thrice or four times larger than Cyprus and with a population thrice or four times greater that the population of this Island, an amount of 0,57 is appropriated for expenditure in respect of purely administrative matters and a 0,27 portion only is assigned for the welfare of the country. The remainder being spent for the various other departmental services and the maintainance of the property of the state.

b) In the appointment of supernumerary personnel for the public service with excessive salaries.

Owing to the fact that the Government of Cyprus is composed of English officials from among those employed in the local public service, the waste of the Island revenues becomes altogether unreasonable, developing into a serious financial question, in respect of the very high figure, charged for public salaries due to a supernumerary personnel and to exorbitant emoluments.

Number of officers in 1913, 1920 and 1929.

The fact that there is supernumerary personnel in the service, is admitted even by the public officers themselves, can also be demonstrated by the number of the Government employees in 1913 by comparison to that in 1920 and 1929.
    Thus we have 925 permanent officers in 1913, about 1000 in 1920 and 1220 in 1929, i.e. their number was increased by 30% without an analogous increase of the work in the various departments.

The increase of
the personal
emoluments by
200% in 1929 as
compared to the
year 1913.

In order that the high increase of salaries should be well and clearly understood it is sufficient to note that while the number of men in the service increased from 1913 to 1929 by 30%, the amount appropriated for personal emoluments was increased by 200%. It should be further noted that the amount in the Budget of 1929 to be appropriated for personal emoluments covers the 0,477 of the total of the general expenditure therein, the share of Cyprus to the Public Ottoman Debt excepted. This is no doubt due to the fact that the Government, during the period between 1920 and 1921, when the cost of living reached its highest pitch, consolidated the war allowances into fixed salaries without making any provision for analogous reduction consequent upon the falling of the cost of living.

What regulations
prevailed in
England.

In 1920, as far as we know, in England after a determination of the cost of living for the year 1920, at 230, taking as basis 100 for 1914, the Government regulated the increase in respect of the salaries of public Officers as follows: For the first £91.5.0 of the salary an increase of 130% was allowed and for any salary exceeding that sum but being under £200.0.0 an increase of 65% was given and for any sum over and above £200.0.0 an increase of 45%. And it was decided also that for any future alternate increase and decrease in the cost of living by 5 units, an alternate increase and decrease by 1/26 should be effected.

And what in
Cyprus.

In Cyprus the same principle in respect of the increase of salaries was approximately followed. According to certain official data published in the Blue Book we have been able to come to the conclusion that the cost of living in Cyprus was raised from 100 in 1913–1914 to 230 in 1920–1921, the latter being the year of the consolidation of the salaries as explained above. It has fallen to-day to 130. Thus in Cyprus as in England approximately the same principle in respect of the increase of salaries prevailed, no provision whatsoever having been made for a proportionate reduction of the allowed increase consequent upon the falling in respect of the cost of living. Owing to this latter omission and the continuous changes both in respect of the classification and the scale of salaries in the service, it so happened that not only the above referred to salaries (small salaries exempted) were not reduced but in some cases further increases over and above the increased salaries of 1920–1921, were made. The following off hand instances may be taken to illustrate how the salaries would stand had the principle applied in England been made applicable to Cyprus as well.

	Salary 1913/4	Salary 1920/1	Salary 1928/9
Colonial Secretary	£800 (100)	£1200 (150)	£1400 (175)
The maximum increase should have reached			£1253
It ought to have been reduced to			£965
He draws to-day			£1400
1st Assistant	£400 (100)	£600 (150)	£675 (187.5)
The maximum increase should have reached			£673
He ought to be drawing to-day			£453
He takes in fact			£675
The Treasurer	£400 (100)	£900 (150)	£1000 (166)
He should have taken as maximum			£963
He should to be drawing to-day			£680
But he draws in fact			£1000
1st class clerk	£200 (100)	£360 (180)	£325 (162.5)
He ought to have taken as maximum			£383
He ought to be drawing to-day			£243
But he actually takes			£325
2nd class clerk	£120 (100)	£185 (154)	£200 (168)
He ought to have taken as maximum			£257
He ought to be drawing to-day			£152
But he actually takes			£200

14.   A further important reason, one of detail but essential, of the heavy salaries paid by Cyprus is the continuous appointment to high-salaried post of officers coming from England—who are in most cases supernumerary in their department, and sometimes prove to be completely inefficient and unsuitable for the post which they are appointed to fill—despite the fact that there are local persons adequately equipped and trained to occupy these posts. Any off hand investigation into the various departments can at once establish

that the main service is carried out by the native officers. That most of the English officials are supernumerary can be proved by the fact that many of them taking advantage of the provisions of the Colonial Regulations, they travel on leave to England without the regular functioning of the machine of the Government being in the least upset or interfered with. How much does the maintainance of such sumptuous personnel cost for the Budget of Cyprus, is evidenced by the official statistics namely: British Officers take to-day £48320.

The high salaries of the English conducive to the increase of the salaries of the native officers.

The English officers who form the Government in order to justify their luxurious salaries did not hesitate to suggest that the salaries of the native officers should be also increased disproportionately to the scale of salaries in force before the war, the financial endurance of the country and the cost of living.

In the appointment of officers the Government is proved to be partial in favour of the minority. Reasons for such conduct.

15.   Incidently and with reference to the question relating to the present position of the public officers in the Island, the fact that the local Government favours the Moslem and the other less significant minorities in the country in order that it should enjoy the support of their representatives in the Council should also be noted. This unjustifiable favoritism and partiality on the part of the Government has been the chief cause of the above referred to alliance and co-operation by means of which the Government has, even since the occupation, been imposing its will on the country against the expressed opinion and desire of the large majority of the Greek population. The following table conclusively proves the partial policy of the local Government:

STATISTICAL TABLE OF 1927 (a)

		Proportion in respect of the total of officers	In proportion to the population it should have been	Salaries in £	Proportion in respect of the total of salaries	Average per head
GREEKS	1101	0.56	0.80	123,820	0.481	112.9.0
TURKS	699	0.36	0.17	70,680	0.275	101.2.3
ENGLISH	76	0.04	)	48,320	0.190	635.0.0
CATHOLICS	56	0.03	0.03	10,792	0.042	192.0.0
ARMENIANS	21	0.01	)	3,180	0.012	159.0.0

a) NOTE.—In accordance with an official answer to a question by the Hon. Hadji-Eftychios HadjiProcopi M.L.C. for the Orini division. And it should further be noted that the sum of £256,792, the total amount of the salaries, does not agree with the sum as mentioned in the estimates for 1927–1928 published in the Blue Book of the year according to which the total is much higher in 1927. (The total of the personal emoluments together with the amount of pensions (£38,090) being £312,910, in 1928 the total of the personal emoluments together with the amount of pensions (£42,100) being £326,425).

16.   In addition to this partiality on the part of the Government it should also be noted that in pursuance on the same as above stated policy, it pays by way of compensation, since the time of the abolition of the tithe, and out of the public revenues a sum of £5,959, to the Evcaf, a Moslem institution, and to other Moslem private owners of tithe. This is done arbitrarily, against the existing laws and without a shadow of legal obligation for the Government, it being purely an act of grace as was admitted in Council by the Hon. the Attorney General himself.

Injustice against Cyprus on the part of England for the socalled tribute.

17.   If for the facts explained above the local Government is to a great extent to blame for the suggestions in each case made by it to the Colonial Office, the Central Government in England is wholly responsible for the grave injustice done to this country from 1878 till 1928 by means of yearly financial extortion on the ground of payment of the so called Tribute to Turkey or, as it was later called share of Cyprus of the Turkish debt charge. By virtue of the Treaty of 1878 and especially of the Appendices attached thereto, England undertook to pay to Turkey a sum of £92800 which was calculated to be the excess of revenues over the expenditure in the Island. But contrary to the clear provision of the Convention that England should pay this sum to Turkey, Cyprus was made to provide its payment unjustly out of its own privation; nor can this injustice be excused on the ground that the principal signatory to the terms of the Convention helped Cyprus to make its payments by means of the so-called grant-in-aid, which were yearly voted by the Imperial Parliament. During the whole of the 50 years that elapsed since the British occupation a sum of £2640000, apart from the aforesaid grants-in-aid went out of Cyprus and has served to secure the payment of interest to the bondholders of the Ottoman Loan of the Crimean war, which had been denounced by Turkey since 1881.

Surplus until 1914.

18.   From the sum thus yearly paid a sum of about £11,000 remained as a surplus after the payment of the interest on the above referred to bonds which has been invested, ever since, with the Bank of England and forms a separate fund.

A capital of £475,000 has accumulated until 1914, which though morally at least belonging to the financially oppressed and exhausted people of Cyprus is nevertheless retained by wealthy and prosperous England.

Unjust and illegal continuation of this charge after 1914.

19.   If, the act of England in thus retaining the said sum is from a moral point of view blamable, her conduct in charging Cyprus with the same sum in a new form and name i.e. share of Cyprus of the Turkish debt charge, is undoubtedly far more

reprehensible; the reason being that if, until 1914, in forcing Cyprus to make payment of this sum, England put forward the obligations arising from the Treaty of 1878, after the abolition and avoidance of that Treaty, by the annexation of Cyprus on the 5th of November 1914, no such justification could any more be pleaded. Because: a) in the Treaty of Lausanne, which settled all question with Turkey after the war, no reference whatsoever is made to Cyprus, as being in any way liable for a share in the payment of the Turkish Public Debt. b) The Loan of 1855 did not form part of the Turkish Public Debt since 1881, nor does it appear in the table attached to the said Treaty and c) no legal relation exists between this loan and the revenues of Cyprus—the surplus of the Tribute of Egypt and the revenues of the Ports of Smyrna and Syria being answerable for its payment.—It therefore becomes manifest how arbitrary was the act of the British Government in depriving Cyprus for 14 further years of these important sums, in order to relieve herself and France from the onus of providing as guarantors the amount of the interests payable to the bondholders of the Turkish loan of 1855. The sums so unjustly paid by Cyprus amount to £588,000.

20.   At long last Great Britain having felt the injustice of such payments tried to make amends by raising the annual grants in aid to £92,000 on condition however that the sum of £10000 be annually paid by the Island towards the Empire defence. But the charge for this same sum of £92,000 continues formally to be made on the estimates, for unknown future purposes, though outbalanced by an equal grant-in-aid. Yet the Island until 1922 still fully felt these burdens in their different manifestations.

21.   We have so far tried to explain in broad lines the anomalous and unfortunate state of the Island and its disastrous effects, due to the basic cause which is that this place is governed against its will by foreign rule, arbitrary and autocratic in its essence.

Claim by the Greek people of Cyprus for union with Mother Greece the only way of solution.

In laying these facts before your Lordship, we have the honour to request your Lordship's kind consideration and earnest attention to the matter, trusting that the Government, adorned by your Lordship and other eminent Leaders of the Labour party, will grant as the only real remedy and solution, which is Union with our Mother country Greece.
        We have to declare to your Lordship, to the British people, and to the whole world that the Greek people of Cyprus, being fully aware and conscious of their national rights, and desirous of the real and true advancement of their interests

in general, will never cease to demand and claim from the Ruling Power their national settlement, as an act of justice and a beneficial solution of their problems.

The Greek people of Cyprus, far from being inspired by any anti-British feelings and truly caring for the Imperial British interests, trust that Great Britain call in her power, grant the just claims of the people of Cyprus and at the same time safeguard her own interests by special Conventions. They further hope and are fully confident that the new Government, under the enlightened leadership of that great herald of the liberties of nations at the Socialist Meeting of Berne, will, during its life do justice to them, thus honouring the ideology of its party in particular, and England in general.

22.   In regard to the other questions explained in this present Memorandum, if the British Government is of opinion that nowise injures primely itself and its reputation and secondly the Cyprus people can and may leave the same political state. But, if it cares to preserve the prestige of the British name, it must and it is an imperative duty with it to:

A)   Grant to this Island a constitution by which:
    a) The representatives of the people in the Council will be vested with full and unlimited legislative power regarding all local matters; but making the necessary exemptions and reservations for matters affecting the general interest of the British Empire. The Members of the Council to be only elective the two elements, forming the population, to be represented therein in proportion to their numbers.
    b) In the Executive Council the majority will be given to persons elected by the Legislative Council from among its own Members or from outside persons, only three British born officials participating in the Executive i. e. the Colonial Secretary, the Attorney General, and the Treasurer of the Island.
    c) The Governor will have only the right of disallowance in the ratification of laws.
    d) The decision of the Executive will bind the Governor.
    e) The King in Council will not enact laws for the Island except in extraordinary cases provided for in the constitution.

B)   Have British born officials removed from Cyprus and leave only three the aforementioned i. e. the Colonial Secretary, the Attorney General, and the Treasurer.

C)   Have the rights of the minorities protected by a special clause in the constitution and also their appointment in the public service in proportion to their numbers.

D)   Discontinue the following payments:
   a)   Compensation to the Evcaf and to individual owners of Tithe now paid as an act of grace.
   b)   The taxes of conquest paid to the Evcaf.

E)   Return the following sums and place them at the disposal of the Cyprus Government:
   a)   The surplus of the Tribute as stated in paragraph 18 of the Memorandum amounting to £475000 and
   b)   The sums unjustly and illegally collected as stated in paragraph 19 of this Memorandum amounting to £588000. These two sums coming up to £1,063,000 would be sufficient if applied to the Island to supply its great and vital needs, and form the basis of its future prosperity.

It is desirable and necessary that a special Royal Commission should be sent to Cyprus for inquiries and investigations.

23.   We have, Your Lordship, endeavoured to describe in outline the miserable state of the Island in every respect, after 50 years of British administration, and to point out the chief causes of such a state, interpreting thus the aspirations and conceptions of the people we represent. But in order that the Honourable Ministry of State for the Colonies may be able to form a clear and responsible opinion thereon, from first hand information, it is most desirable and necessary that a special Royal Commission of Inquiry should be sent to Cyprus empowered to inquire into the matter and with full liberty of action both in respect of the questions to be investigated and of their mode of action all of which should be carried out independently of the opinion of the local Government and in an absolutely unbiased and free way. We ask for the envoy of such a Commission on behalf and in the name of the people whom we represent, and we feel certain that this Commission, on visiting the Island, will draw appalling inferences of the 50 years British rule, which must form a quite unique instance of British maladministration. In returning to England the Commission will be able to make to the Ministry such suggestions and recommendations as would enlighten it to do the best for the prosperity of the Island.

Nicosia the
20 July 1929.

We have the honour to be
Sir,
Your Lordships Most Obedient
Humble Servants

Bishop of Kitium Nicodemos
S. G. Stavrinakis
G. Hadjipaulou
K. P. Rossides
P. Cacoyiannis
M. H. Michaelides
Hj Eftychios Hj Procopi
Ph. Joannides
L. Z. Pierides
D. Severis
N. Nicolaides
G. Emphiedjis.

*The Right Honourable
the Lord Passfield p. c.
Secretary of State
Downing Street
London.*

APPENDIX 2(2)

Reply of the Right Honourable the Secretary of State for the Colonies to the Memorial Addressed to Him by the Greek Elected Members of the Legislative Council, London, 28 November 1929

CYPRUS.   DOWNING STREET,
No. 264.   28 November, 1929.

Sir,

I have had before me the Memorial signed on the 20th of July last by the Greek Elected Members of the Legislative Council of Cyprus in which they formulated certain requests for change in the political status and administrative system of the Island. This Memorial has now received my attentive examination: and I have had the opportunity of listening to the arguments urged in its support by the Bishop of Kitium, Mr. Stavrinakis, and Mr. Rossides during their recent visit to London. My reply to these representations is contained in the following paragraphs; and I should be obliged if you would communicate this despatch to the Greek Elected Members and then publish it.

2. The first request contained in the Memorial is a renewal of the demand that Cyprus should be ceded to Greece. My answer on this point can only be the same as that which successive Secretaries of State have in the past returned to similar demands, namely, that His Majesty's Government are unable to accede to it. This subject, in their view, is definitely closed and cannot profitably be further discussed.

3. In paragraph 22 of the Memorial the Greek Elected Members put forward certain requests for consideration in the event of the rejection of their major demand for union with Greece. The first of these, contained in subparagraph A, is the submission that the Island should be granted a form of responsible government. This is a request which has been given very careful consideration. The conclusion at which I leave arrived, not without regret, is that the time has not yet come when it would be to the general advantage of the people of Cyprus to make a trial of a constitutional experiment in this direction. Those institutions already established in the Island which are subject in varying degrees to popular control cannot be said to have attained that reasonable measure of efficiency which should be looked for before any extension of the principle is approved. The requests contained in sub-paragraphs B and C do not in these circumstances appear to arise. In sub-paragraph D it is represented that the payment to the Evcaf and to individual tithe-owners should be discontinued. I can only say in regard to this that the matter is, as the

---

GOVERNOR
SIR RONALD STORRS, K.C.M.G., C.B.E.,
&c., &c., &c.

Elected Members are aware, already occupying the attention of the Cyprus Government.

4. I will now refer to the so-called "Tribute." The points made by the Greek Elected Members with regard to this subject are contained in paragraphs 17-20 and in sub-paragraph E of paragraph 22 of the Memorial. Up to the Annexation in 1914, the payment of the Tribute was made in virtue of the Convention with Turkey of 1878. His Majesty's Government are unable to share the view advanced by the Memorialists that the payment of this sum from Cyprus revenues was contrary to the provisions of the Convention. It is true that Clause III. of the Annex to the Convention stipulated that England should pay the money to Turkey. But it is clear from that document and from the terms of the allied negotiations that the intention was that England should pay the money from the revenues of Cyprus, or in other words, that it should come from the same source as in the past. The effect of the arrangement was that Cyprus became liable to Great Britain for £92,800 a year and Great Britain became liable to the Ottoman Empire for the same annual sum. When the Ottoman Empire defaulted on the 1855 Loan, the interest on which had been guaranteed by the British and French Governments, Her Majesty's then Government was advised that the "Cyprus Tribute" formed part of the revenues of the Ottoman Empire and could be withheld from the Porte and used for the service of the Loan so long as the default lasted. The whole of the money was therefore and always has been devoted to the liquidation of a liability on which the Ottoman Empire had defaulted. The Greek Elected Members state that no legal relation exists between the 1855 Loan and the revenue of Cyprus. The 1855 Loan, however, was secured upon the whole revenues of the Ottoman Empire as well as specifically on the balance of the Egyptian Tribute and the Customs revenues of Syria and Smyrna. In these circumstances the British Government clearly had ample justification in diverting to the service of the Loan the payment for which they were liable to the Ottoman Empire under the Cyprus Convention. It has never been their contention that the 1855 Loan had any specific connection with Cyprus.

It is hardly necessary for me to point out that the liability of Cyprus to Great Britain for the annual payment of £92,800 was in practice greatly reduced by Grants-in-Aid from the Imperial Exchequer. After a period of fluctuation the Grant was definitely fixed at £50,000 a year in 1907, and remained at that figure until 1927. During that period Cyprus had therefore to find only £42,800 a year. On a purely material evaluation this sum cannot be considered an excessive price to pay for the practical benefits which accrued from the establishment of a British administration.

On the Annexation in 1914, the 1878 Convention was abrogated: and I agree with the Greek Elected Members that the payment of the Tribute then ceased to find any sanction in that Instrument. The payment was however continued as the share of Cyprus in the general Public Debt of the Ottoman Empire. It is contended that in accordance with the generally accepted principle of international law Cyprus, as a Succession State of the Ottoman Empire, could properly be charged with this liability. It is true that, as the Greek Elected Members state, no reference to the liability of Cyprus in respect of the Ottoman Public Debt is made in the Treaty of Lausanne, although under Article 20 of that Treaty Turkey recognised the annexation of the Island by Great Britain. The reason why the liability of Cyprus was not mentioned in the Treaty was that the Island was already paying the sum of £92,800 a year which had been appropriated for the service of the 1855 Loan. The matter was carefully considered at the time, and it was decided that this payment should be treated as the contribution of Cyprus to the Ottoman Public Debt, and that the matter did not therefore require to be dealt with in an international Instrument. Had it not been for this payment, Cyprus would no doubt have been required to take over a share of the Ottoman Public Debt on the same basis as the other territories detached from Turkey as a result of the War, and on that basis her contribution would have been substantially more than the gross amount of the Tribute.

In 1927 His Majesty's Government, with the desire of accelerating the progress of the Island, decided to increase the Grant-in-Aid to the same amount as the Cyprus contribution to the Ottoman Public Debt charge, namely, £92,800 a year. The only condition attached to this increased grant was that Cyprus should contribute £10,000 a year towards the cost of Imperial defence. The grant on this condition was accepted by the Legislative Council. In the reply to the offer of His Majesty's Government dated the 5th of September, 1927, and signed by the Elected Members, which was handed to you on your return from your visit to Rhodes in that month, they stated "The happy answer of the Imperial Government has fulfilled all Cypriot aspirations concerning this burden." His Majesty's Government therefore regard the settlement of 1927 as having finally closed the question of the Tribute: and it is one which they are not prepared further to pursue. They feel that after studying the facts set out above, all reasonable opinion in Cyprus will agree that Cyprus has been treated not ungenerously in the matter.

5. In paragraph 23 of the Memorial, it is suggested that a Royal Commission should be appointed to enquire into the condition of affairs in Cyprus. This proposal has received my consideration, but after careful reflection I have formed the view that the appointment of such a body would, at the present juncture, be of no real benefit to Cyprus. An enquiry of the character proposed would raise unprofitable issues, and could only distract attention from those more practical matters on which the progress of the Colony depends. There is much to be said for the view that what Cyprus needs at present are fewer occasions for political discussion and more occasions for constructive work.

6. Before concluding this despatch, I desire to make the following observations with respect to certain of the statements contained in the Memorial. His Majesty's Government do not wish to make any immoderate claims for the achievements of British rule in Cyprus. They are conscious that the material progress of the Island has not been so rapid as they would have hoped. This is in a large measure attributable to certain special causes. The first of these is the anomalous and uncertain position of the Island up to the Annexation in 1914. Cyprus was until that date a territory leased by Great Britain from the Ottoman Empire. Owing to this ambiguous situation, the Island was unable to attract the capital necessary for its development, and no Government loan for

that purpose was raised in the open market. After the Annexation, the War and the subsequent economic depression further retarded development.

7. A further cause is to be found in the peculiar nature of the Cyprus Constitution. Responsible observers lave contended that had Cyprus possessed an officially-controlled Legislature, its progress would have been more rapid. There is much weight in this contention. The divorce of power from executive responsibility is rarely conducive to efficient administration, however much unofficial control over the Legislature may be valued from other standpoints. Had the Executive Government had full control it could, for example, have paid salaries which would have attracted highly qualified experts to the service of its technical departments. The Greek Elected Members lave argued that salaries paid to the British officials in the Island have been too high. In doing so they are, to my mind, failing to take a long view of their own material interests. Until recent years the salaries paid have in my opinion been too low. Had they been nearer to the market rate for the best ability, the progress of the Island would have been accelerated and the extra outlay would have been more than repaid in the added wealth derived from the development of the Island's undoubted resources. I think it is desirable that the Greek Elected Members should realise that on this subject they have adopted a policy of false economy, which is responsible to no small extent for the lack of progress of which they now complain.

8. In spite of these admitted obstacles to the advancement of the country, I am unable to admit that the picture drawn in the Memorial of the British achievement in Cyprus is a fair one. No person who is correctly informed as to the condition of the Island in 1878 could refuse to recognise the very great advance which it has made in only fifty years of British rule. In 1878 the population was only 180,000. At the time of the British occupation the only road in the Island was a track of some 26 miles between Nicosia and Larnaca. Under the rule of the Ottoman Empire there were no hospitals; and the protection of public health was a matter which received no attention from Government. The encouragement of agriculture and the preservation of the forests were equally neglected. No effort was made to develop the Island's mineral resources. Taxation was abusive, and rates of interest were usurious. The administration of justice was defective, and access to the Courts difficult.

9. The Island to-day shows considerable improvement upon this state of affairs. The population has nearly doubled. There are, apart from village roads, a thousand miles of roads which can be traversed by motor. The revenue has increased from £176,000 to nearly three-quarters of a million: and the whole of this money is devoted to the public service, which was not the case under the rule of the Ottoman Empire. A railway has been built and harbours have been considerably improved. Regular post, telegraph, and mail services have been instituted. The development and protection of the forests has been taken in hand on scientific lines. The growing revenue from royalties attests the attention which is being paid to the Island's mineral resources. The spread of education, which has been largely assisted by Government grants, is illustrated by the fact that there are now over 46,000 children attending the schools, whereas in 1881 there were fewer than 7,000. Increasing regard has been paid to the important subjects of agriculture and irrigation. The co-

operative system has received every encouragement from Government, while credit has been made available to the farmers upon reasonable terms.

10. It is, however, broadly true to say that until recent years the main work of the Government has been not so much to develop the country by direct administrative action as to create conditions favourable to the natural growth of prosperity. For fifty years Cyprus has enjoyed the benefits of law and order, and the equitable and honest administration of justice. There has been no public disorder within, and there has been immunity from attack from without. During the War, while neighbouring countries were the scene of military operations, Cyprus remained secure and peaceful. In the economic dislocation which followed the War, the Island preserved the advantages of a sound currency and financial system. The inhabitants of the Island have enjoyed a wide liberty of speech and action which compares favourably with that permitted in adjacent territories. They have escaped the obligation of compulsory military service; the more prosperous classes have not been called on to bear the heavy direct taxation which has been a feature of other fiscal systems. These conditions have not only allowed energy and enterprise to reap their due rewards, but have also a moral value which cannot be computed in merely material terms.

11. I have not written this despatch in any narrow spirit. In many ways I welcome the high standards of achievement which the Greek Elected Members set in their criticisms of the British administration. These conceptions are in some sense a tribute to the change in outlook which has resulted from half a century of British rule. The anxiety of the Greek Elected Members for improvement in the conditions of the Island has my entire sympathy. I am confident that in the next few years considerable improvement in the equipment of the country and in the development of its resources is possible. Government can do much to assist the people of the Island to take advantage of their opportunities; and I trust that this frank interchange of views may do something to foster the spirit of co-operation and mutual understanding which is a desirable condition to the attainment of this common goal. If this spirit is forthcoming, it will meet with a generous response.

I have the Honour to be,
Sir,
Your most obedient, humble Servant,
(Signed) PASSFIELD

(M.P. 1076/29.)

APPENDIX 3

Letter from Eleftherios Venizelos, Prime Minister of Greece, to Andreas Michalakopoulos, Foreign Minister of Greece, 23 October 1931 (translation)

President of the Government*

23 October 1931

Dear President,**

The events in Cyprus are taking an unfortunate turn at an inauspicious time.

From verbal protests, which the British endure very philosophically, the Cypriots have moved to actions, burning down Government House in Nicosia. In this matter the British will show great severity and will begin prosecutions and convictions of the guilty persons. The unfortunate thing is that the Cypriots are in all probability ignorant of the fact that the Greek Government does not at all approve such actions.

Two days ago I received the visit of Mr. Louizou who assured me that Mr. Lanitis,*** who was here only twenty days ago and has returned to Cyprus, has let it be clearly known that the escalation of events, for which he has long been striving, has my personal approval. I did indeed receive Mr. Lanitis and kept him to lunch, for the specific purpose of endeavouring to indicate to him that the policy promoted by him is foolish.

Moreover, I am afraid that our representative in Cyprus, instead of acting in conformity with the government policy to avoid the exacerbation of the situation, has either rather favoured such exacerbation or at least adopted a lukewarm attitude; and the Cypriots are probably pushing matters without knowing exactly where we stand. Fortunately, I learn from the Ministry that a telegram has been received announcing that he was due to leave yesterday as a result of his being invited here by telegram.

In any case, I think it imperative, in view of the demarche made to me, as Foreign Minister, three months ago by the British Ambassador and the promise given to him that Mr. Kyros would be recalled after your return from Geneva, that we inform Mr. Ramsay that Kyros has been instructed to come to Athens and that he will not again return to Cyprus, being replaced by another person.

---

* The prime minister of Greece is usually referred to as the president of the government.

** Although the letter is addressed to the foreign minister, Andreas Michalakopoulos, it is customary in Greece to address anyone who has held any office (e.g. president of a political party) by the title of that office.

*** Mr. N. Cl. Lanitis was a well-known Greek Cypriot supporter of Enosis.

I have not the slightest doubt that we are entirely in agreement that no cause whatsoever should be given to the British Government to question the absolute sincerity of our policy on Cyprus.

Yours sincerely,

(Signed) ELEFTHERIOS VENIZELOS

APPENDIX 4

Communiqué to the Citizens of Athens and Others by the Prime Minister of Greece Eleftherios Venizelos, 31 October 1931 (translation)

THE PRESIDENT OF THE GOVERNMENT

31 October 1931

TO: The Citizens of Athens and the Governing Bodies of Professional, Civic, Labour and Reservists' Organizations,

In yesterday's newspapers the following notice appeared:

"The Cypriots of Athens, who are holding the day after tomorrow, Sunday, 1 November, at 11.30 a.m., in the Church of St. Constantine a memorial service for those who have fallen in Cyprus for freedom and Country, call upon the Greek people of Athens and the governing bodies of all the professional, civic, labour and reservists' organizations to attend the memorial service, carrying their banners, to honour in the name of the Greek nation the memory of the brave fighters for freedom."

It is obvious that the purpose of this invitation, which bears no signature, is not simply, or even perhaps primarily, the offering of prayers for the souls of the fallen Cypriots, but also the holding of an open air demonstration, in support of the Cyprus movement, which will then be asked to pass underneath a certain embassy.

If the intention was simply the holding of a memorial service, then the recommendation of the Government that this be held in a Church outside the city would have been followed.

Believing that the contemplated holding of such a demonstration in the open air and in the centre of the city does not serve the wider interests of the country, I have given appropriate instructions that its holding be prevented.

Therefore, the gathering of a crowd outside a Church situated in the centre of the town will not be permitted.

In any case, no-one either intends or has the right to obstruct the expression of sentiments by groups of people, provided these do not take the form of open air demonstrations, which may lead to improprieties usually going far beyond the intentions of even those who provoked them.

To this end, I wish to bring to the notice of the citizens that the Government, acting under a rudimentary duty, will not tolerate that those who are conducting political or national struggles outside the borders of Greece, by actions within the country, should seek to create friction between Greece and the states of which they are subjects, and with which the general interests of the country dictate the maintenance of absolutely friendly and harmonious relations.

Sections of the national family, which are outside the borders of Greece, cannot be allowed to create problems in the country's politics, which only its citizens have the sovereign right to regulate. And the views of the citizens are expressed through the constitutional organs, the Government today and the Legislative bodies to-morrow, when they convene on the 15 November.

Disregard of these principles would mean anarchy, unworthy of a sober nation.

The Prime Minister

(Signed) ELEFTHERIOS VENIZELOS

APPENDIX 5

Appeal of the Central Committee for Cyprus, Athens, 30 October 1931

At this moment, when the people of Cyprus are struggling for their liberties and sacrificing their all upon the altar of the Fatherland, we feel it to be our duty to declare that the whole Greek race is watching this manly effort with admiration and fraternal solicitude.

The people of free Greece are not forgetful of the strong bonds of gratitude and sincere friendship, which bind them to Britain, one of the Powers, which once guaranteed Greek independence. But they believe that the liberal traditions of the British nation demand the satisfaction of the legitimate national aspirations of an island—Greek by race, language and sentiment—which Great Britain 53 years ago took over as a mere inanimate pledge from another Power, an alien conqueror of the island.

For this reason the undersigned have met this day and formed a Committee of fifty members, for the sole purpose of enlightening by every means the public opinion of the civilized world, and especially that of the great British nation, as to the imperishable human rights, on which the Greek nation bases its plea, that the people of Cyprus be permitted to determine their own destinies.

We believe that, in so doing, we are but fulfilling an elementary duty of our race to our sorely-tried brethren of Cyprus. And we venture to trust that our effort, which but reflects the sentiments of the nation, shall not be in vain.

Long live Greek Cyprus!

Athens, 30 October 1931.

PAUL COUNDOURIOTIS, President

A. CANARIS, Vice-President   S. LOUVERDHOS, treasurer
TH. YPSILANTIS, Vice-President   PH. DRAGOUMIS, secretary general

D. ACRIVOS	M. GHEORGANDAS	J. PAPAFLESSAS
S. AGAPITOS	A. GRIVAS	G. PESMAZOGLOU
N. ALIVIZATOS	D. HADZISCOS	TH. PETIMEZAS
M. AVEROFF	T. ILIOPOULOS	TH. PETRACOPOULOS
A. BENAKIS	A. KYRIAKIDHIS	P. PIERRACOS-MAVROMICHALIS
A. BOTSARIS	N. LEVIDHIS	J. RALLIS
G. CAPODISTRIAS	P. MAVROMICHALIS	N. RANGAVIS
A. CHRISTOMANOS	C. MAZARAKIS-AENIAN	J. THEOTOKIS
C. CODZIAS	P. MAZARAKIS	D. TOMBAZIS-MAVROCORDHATOS
A. CORIZIS	M. P. MELAS	S. TRICOUPIS
A. CRIEZIS	G. METAXAS	J. TSAMADHOS
J. DAMVERGHIS	A. MIAOULIS	A. VALAORITIS
E. DELIYANNIS	P. NIRVANAS	G. VASSILIADHIS
S. EVGHENIDHIS	C. PALAMAS	C. VOULGARIS
A. FRANDZIS	D. PAPADHIAMANDOPOULOS	A. P. ZAIMIS

APPENDIX 6

The Tripartite Conference on the Eastern Mediterranean and Cyprus, Held by the Governments of the United Kingdom of Great Britain and Northern Ireland, Greece and Turkey, London, August 29–September 7, 1955*

CONTENTS

---

* Cmd. 9594, Misc. No. 18 (London: HMSO, 1955).

FOREWORD

On June 30, 1955, Her Majesty's Government issued the following invitation to the Greek and Turkish Governments:

> "Her Majesty's Government have been giving further consideration to the strategic and other problems affecting alike the United Kingdom, Greece and Turkey in the Eastern Mediterranean. They consider that the association of the three countries in that area based on mutual confidence is essential to their common interests.
>
> "Her Majesty's Government accordingly invite the Greek and Turkish Governments to send representatives to confer with them in London at an early date on political and defence questions which affect the Eastern Mediterranean, including Cyprus."

In announcing this invitation to the House of Commons on the same day, the Prime Minister said that the discussions would be without prior commitment by any party. It was the intention of Her Majesty's Government that there should be no fixed agenda and that discussions should range widely over all the questions involved.

The British invitation was accepted by the Turkish Government on July 2 and by the Greek Government on July 8. After consultation between the three Governments, it was decided that the Conference should open in London on August 29.

The Conference opened at Lancaster House at 4 p.m. on August 29, 1955, when questions of procedure were settled. Three further Plenary Meetings were held on the following three days, August 30, August 31 and September 1, at which the Foreign Secretary, the Greek Foreign Minister and the Turkish Foreign Minister each made statements setting out the points of view of their respective Governments.

It was then agreed between the three delegations that a summary of the opening statements should be drawn up and published immediately as a statement of the position adopted by each of the three Governments at the beginning of the Conference. The intention was that this document should sum up the proceedings so far and make clear the area of agreement which had already been reached, while at the same time defining those points on which further discussion might be necessary.

At a restricted meeting on September 2 it was agreed that the Conference should adjourn until September 6 to allow for study of the three opening statements.

When the Conference resumed in restricted session on September 6, the Foreign Secretary presented proposals on behalf of Her Majesty's Government for future constitutional development in Cyprus and for the future work of the Conference. The Greek Foreign Minister made certain interim comments on these proposals at that meeting and at the next meeting on September 7 he and the Turkish Foreign Minister made formal statements in reply to the proposals of Her Majesty's Government. In addition the Turkish Foreign Minister asked for elucidation of the attitude of Her Majesty's Government in the form of two questions to which the Foreign Secretary replied. It was agreed, after a final meeting for the preparation of a communiqué, to consider the Conference as suspended.

The Greek Foreign Minister made it clear that his reply made on September 7 to the British proposals was an interim one and that the final Greek reply could only be given after consultation in Athens with the Greek Government. Accordingly a *Note Verbale* which contained the Greek Government's answer to the British proposals was delivered to Her Majesty's Embassy at Athens on September 17, 1955.

Before the Tripartite Conference met, the Greek Government had already made application to the Secretary-General of the United Nations for the inscription on the agenda of the General Assembly of an item entitled "Application, under the auspices of the United Nations, of the principle of equal rights and self-determination of peoples in the case of the population of the island of Cyprus." The General Committee of the United Nations considered this question on September 21 and recommended that the item should not be included in the agenda. The Greek Delegation challenged this recommendation in the Plenary Meeting of the General Assembly on September 23, but the exclusion of this item from the agenda was agreed to by 28 votes against 22 votes with 10 members abstaining.

This White Paper contains the texts of the various statements and proposals mentioned above. The United Kingdom proposals regarding the future of Cyprus and the Greek Government's reply to these proposals are given in Appendices I and II. The text of the speech made by Her Majesty's Minister of State for Foreign Affairs in the Plenary Session of the General Assembly of the United Nations on September 23 is given in Appendix III.

Foreign Office, October 1955.

THE TRIPARTITE CONFERENCE ON THE EASTERN MEDI-
TERRANEAN AND CYPRUS HELD BY THE GOVERNMENTS OF THE
UNITED KINGDOM OF GREAT BRITAIN AND NORTHERN
IRELAND, GREECE AND TURKEY, LONDON, AUGUST 29–
SEPTEMBER 7, 1955

Text of Agreed Communiqué issued after the First Plenary Meeting on August
29, 1955

The Tripartite Conference on the Eastern Mediterranean and Cyprus
opened at Lancaster House this afternoon at 4 p.m.

In an introductory speech the British Foreign Secretary welcomed the
delegations from Greece and Turkey and expressed his regrets that the Secretary of State for the Colonies and the Minister of Defence were unable to be
present during the first stages of the Conference. Mr. Macmillan recalled the
terms of the invitation to the Greek and Turkish Governments to attend the
Conference and expressed Her Majesty's Government's satisfaction that the
other two Governments were able to accept.

The Foreign Minister of Greece expressed the thanks of the Greek
Delegation for Mr. Macmillan's words of welcome and said his Government
had accepted the invitation because they earnestly hoped that the Conference
would produce fruitful results which would satisfy all three countries represented, who for so long had been linked in friendship and alliance.

The Foreign Minister of Turkey also expressed his thanks for the welcome extended. He expressed the hope that the British Colonial Secretary and
the Minister of Defence would be able to be present at a later stage and help
the Conference in the accomplishment of its tasks; and he trusted that with
good-will the three Governments would be able to take another step towards
the strengthening of mutual relations in the Eastern Mediterranean to the
benefit of the free world.

Procedural questions were then settled. The Conference agreed that
Mr. Macmillan should be the permanent chairman of the Conference. It was
also agreed that while the proceedings of the Conference would be confidential, regular communiqués would be issued and every effort would be made to
make these as substantial as possible. It was decided to meet again at 11 a.m.
on August 30 and thereafter to meet daily at 11 a.m. except as otherwise
agreed.

STATEMENT MADE BY THE RT. HON. HAROLD MACMILLAN AT
THE SECOND PLENARY MEETING HELD ON AUGUST 30, 1955

Yesterday afternoon, when I had the honour of welcoming the delegates to this Conference on behalf of all the members of Her Majesty's Government, I reminded you of the close friendship which binds us all together.

The three Governments—aye, and the three peoples represented here,
are friends—close friends. They have common interests in the Eastern Mediterranean area. They are vitally affected by all that concerns the peace and
progress of that area. But we are more than merely friends; we are allies. We

are members of the most important alliance perhaps of all history—on which the peace and progress of the whole world may depend—the North Atlantic Treaty Organisation.[1] Here we have special responsibilities, not only to ourselves, but to our partners. These obligations, in a sense, override all others. They are links not merely of interest, but of honour.

I am therefore confident that we shall conduct our proceedings to-day, and on successive days, at this Conference, in an atmosphere both of informality and co-operation—as befits friends and allies. For this is what our friends and allies have a right to expect from us.

It was certainly not the intention of Her Majesty's Government in issuing the invitation to this Conference that we should take up and pursue throughout the Conference formal positions in opposition to each other like litigants in a law-suit. We must—and it is the purpose of these first few days to do this—we must of course each explain our own point of view, fully and frankly. But we must try to reach solutions, not through a battle of conflicting views and arguments, but as a result of a sympathetic understanding and a clear recognition of our respective and indeed our common needs and interests. I suggest that the method by which we proceed should be discussion rather than debate; the result at which we aim should be harmony; and the means by which we achieve it should be orderly progress and an ever widening expansion of the area of common agreement.

We are meeting at this Conference at a fateful time. The world is divided into two great groups of States. The events of the next few years will, I think, very likely decide the pattern of relations between these two groups for many generations to come. The fact that the Western Powers have been able to discuss in a somewhat more relaxed mood some of the great problems with the Soviet Union is certainly a promising sign. It is our hope that the negotiations which are to begin this autumn will result in some real progress. But there are two realities which we must never forget. First, it is our unity and common resolution which have brought us to the point where parley between East and West has become possible. Secondly we are only at the very beginning of what will certainly prove a long and perhaps a difficult and testing period of negotiation and strain. Throughout this coming phase, our unity will be no less vital—perhaps even more important—than before.

Our chain of nations will be like all other chains—no stronger than its weakest link.

This unity and our common strength have been built up in the last few anxious years through many trials and great sacrifices.

Our friends in Greece emerged triumphant from their arduous struggle against Communist invaders. Our Turkish allies stood staunchly in the face of every threat. Both of them have had the fullest admiration and support of the British people. Together, in company with other friends, we have built an alliance which has grown steadily in material strength. It has done more. It has grown in moral stature. It has established itself in the hearts and minds of our peoples as the foundation of peace. Working together in the North

---

[1] "Treaty Series No. 56 (1949)," Cmd. 7789.

Atlantic Treaty Organisation, we have found, all of us, a wider invigorating loyalty which has called forth great endeavours. There have been some delays and reverses but in general the alliance has met with success. But if this initial success is to be maintained and developed we must persevere in our loyalties and endeavours. In this we have a responsibility to ourselves and to our Allies. In this we are the guardians of the present and trustees of the future.

Greece and Turkey together form the right wing of our common front. The Eastern Mediterranean is the hinge to the European and Middle East defence systems. The British Government are vitally concerned in both; and in Cyprus lies the base upon which they must rely to bring their strength and influence to bear on this vital sector of our defences. That they should be able to do this effectively is—I do not think this can be disputed—in the real interests of us all; both the three friends and allies represented here in this room, and all our comrades in Europe, in the Middle East and all through the Free World.

It is, as you know, a basic principle of the policy of Her Majesty's Government that the internal affairs of Her Majesty's possessions cannot be discussed with Foreign Powers.[2] It is perhaps, hardly necessary to say this; for it is fundamental to the existence of any State that it should have full control over its internal policies. This principle lies at the basis of our present community of nations. It is enshrined in the Charter of the United Nations,[3] where it is stated that there shall be no interference (I quote the words) "in matters which are essentially within the domestic jurisdiction of any State." In convening this conference of their own initiative, I wish to make it clear that Her Majesty's Government are not in any way departing from this principle. Indeed, they take this opportunity to reaffirm it. The object of this conference is to find a means of reconciling the unhappy differences which, as we know and all want to remedy, are imperilling our co-operation and the smooth working of our common defence in the Eastern Mediterranean. These differences centre upon the island of Cyprus, a part of Her Majesty's territories; but they threaten to disturb the calm of a widening area far outside British authority. They must be considered within the wider framework of our joint and several interests in the Eastern Mediterranean. It is our common task, to which we must devote ourselves and for which no effort is too great, to find the means to overcome these difficulties, and to enable our three countries, each of which holds a vital position in the free world, to work together as befits loyal allies.

Her Majesty's Government have therefore felt it right that no aspect of the causes of our present difficulties, including the position in Cyprus, should be excluded from our friendly consideration. Of course, from the purely British point of view there are inconveniences and even dangers in the course we have followed.

Nevertheless, it has already been widely recognised that the willingness of Her Majesty's Government to talk over with her friends the position of Cyprus is a bold and constructive initiative, which will permit the whole area of

---

[2] See "United Nations No. 4 (1954)," Cmd. 9300.
[3] "Treaty Series No. 67 (1946)," Cmd. 7015.

differences to be considered freely and frankly. We believe that this initiative has been welcomed by our friends and by the friends of our friends.

At this conference we look forward to frank and free discussion. We shall try to explain our point of view; we look forward to hearing the views of our guests. I trust that in talking together we shall find, when we begin to analyse, that we are not so far apart as many may suppose—or as some would like us to be. Indeed, it would be strange if our long traditions of friendship, built up through adversity and strong to endure even in the days of utmost disaster, together with the vital interests which bind our three countries together to-day, should not be able to overcome our differences or disagreements, or at least reduce them to their true proportions.

Perhaps the best thing for me now to do will be to open this part of our discussions by telling you of the way in which Her Majesty's Government regard the present position in the Eastern Mediterranean, including Cyprus. As I suggested yesterday, I think we could best proceed, in order of rotation, if my friend, the Greek Minister for Foreign Affairs, would then explain to us the altitude of his Government in these matters. The Turkish position could then be set out by my friend, the Turkish Minister for Foreign Affairs. I feel sure that we do not want to consider this as being in any way a debate; still less, a rhetorical exercise. But in order that our discussion may be both businesslike and fruitful, it seems desirable that we should begin by defining the area of agreement and the area of difference, between us. Of this I am confident. Our differences will be found to bear no comparison with the large extent of our common ground; of our trust in one another and our determination to serve and share in the defence of the same ideals.

When we know more clearly the precise extent of our differences, and can analyse them, we can then fruitfully begin to discuss the means of reconciling them. As I have already observed, we do not wish to be bound by formal rules of procedure. This should be a discussion in which we all feel free to speak frankly and freely. Therefore, if you agree, I suggest that we should not go further in laying down our method of procedure at this stage, than the plan which I have put forward. After each of us has put forward his general position we can decide the best way to make progress.

I think it may be useful if I begin by setting out how Her Majesty's Government came to have vital interests in Cyprus and the Eastern Mediterranean. I do not propose to dwell upon the long and chequered story of Cyprus under its many sovereigns. Yet the long processes of history have given us all different and varying interests in Cyprus. Centuries of Hellenic culture, and they by inclusion in the East Roman and Byzantine Empires, have created undeniable links which no-one will deny between Cyprus and the Greek world. Then for nearly four centuries, this civilisation was further enriched by the culture of Western Europe, under the Lusignans dynasty of the Latin Kingdom of Cyprus and the Republic of Venice. For three centuries more, Cyprus formed part of the Ottoman Empire. Many Turks made their home in the island, which lies so close to Turkey itself, and has in turn been the homeland of so many persons who have distinguished themselves in Turkish public life.

It is now nearly eighty years since Great Britain assumed her responsibilities in Cyprus. None of us can to-day forget that Turkey is in the frontline of defence of the Western World. It is therefore significant to recall the circumstances of 1878, when the peace of the world seemed seriously threatened and Her Majesty's Government entered into a defensive alliance with Turkey which brought British rule to Cyprus. This alliance embodied in a document, commonly known as the Cyprus Convention,[4] contained the following article:

> "If Batoum, Ardahan, Kars or any of them shall be retained by Russia, and if any attempt shall be made at any future time by Russia, to take possession of any further territories of His Imperial Majesty, the Sultan in Asia as fixed by the Definitive Treaty of Peace, England engages to join His Imperial Majesty the Sultan in defending them by force of arms." . . . . "in order to enable England to make necessary provision for executing her engagements. His Imperial Majesty the Sultan further consents to assign the Island of Cyprus to be occupied and administered by England."

Now once again Great Britain is linked by treaty with Turkey, and with other nations, in defence of the free world. In 1878 it was necessary for Britain to occupy and administer Cyprus in order to execute her engagements towards Turkey.[5] So it is again to-day; but with even greater force. Indeed, Britain's engagements and responsibilities have been multiplied and diversified. May I add that in order to honour them very considerable resources are required and considerable sacrifices fall upon our people to bear, both in money and in service.

The arrangement with Turkey made in 1878 was mutually satisfactory; and partly no doubt owing to that arrangement there was no necessity for British intervention on the frontiers of Turkey. In law, though not in practice, the position was changed in 1914, when, following the outbreak of the first World War, His Majesty's Government annexed the Island, by an Order-in-Council of November 5, 1914.[6] It is true that, under the compelling pressures and desperate straits of war, the British Government looked anxiously for the active assistance of the Kingdom of Greece. To this end His Majesty's Government offered to cede Cyprus to Greece "on the sole condition that Greece gives Serbia her immediate and complete support with her army." This offer was made. It was not accepted. So it lapsed.

The annexation of Cyprus by Great Britain was recognised internationally by means of the Treaty of Lausanne signed on July 24, 1923.[7] The relevant text is Article 20. "Turkey hereby recognises the annexation of Cyprus proclaimed by the British Government on the 5th November, 1914." There were no reservations made in regard to this article. This treaty was signed by the Turkish Government. But it was also signed by the Greek Government. It was signed on behalf of His Majesty the King of the Hellenes by M. Venizelos and by M. Caclamanos.

---

[4] "Turkey No. 36," 1878, C. 2057.
[5] "Cyprus No. 1," 1879, C. 2229.
[6] "State Papers," Vol. 108, page 165.
[7] "Treaty Series No. 16, 1923," Cmd. 1929.

Article 21 of the Treaty specified *inter alia* that "Turkish nationals ordinarily resident in Cyprus on the 5th November, 1914, will acquire British nationality subject to the conditions laid down in the local law, and will thereupon lose their Turkish nationality." Other sections of the Treaty which dealt with islands formerly under Turkish sovereignty are Articles 12-16 inclusive. Article 12 confirmed Greek sovereignty over certain islands of "the Eastern Mediterranean" while Article 15 gave certain others to Italy. The text of Article 16 is as follows:

> "Turkey hereby renounces all rights and title whatsoever over or respecting the territories situated outside the frontiers laid down in the present Treaty and the islands other than those over which her sovereignty is recognised by the said Treaty, the future of these territories and islands being settled or to be settled by the parties concerned. The provisions of the present Article do not prejudice any special arrangements arising from neighbourly relations which have been or may be concluded between Turkey and any limitrophe countries."

I have described the provisions of the Treaty of Lausanne at some length because despite whatever arrangements may arise from neighbourly and friendly relations, it is necessary that we should be clear at the outset of these talks that the sovereignty over Cyprus rests wholly and exclusively with the British Crown. This is a fact—recognised and confirmed by the legal authority of a Treaty to which all these Governments represented in this room were willing and consenting parties.

I have already referred to the multiplication of our British engagements and responsibilities. This is the inevitable consequence of our widening system of mutual defence. We have great and peculiar responsibilities in the Middle East. The pledges given by Her Majesty's Government cannot be honoured if the resources are lacking by which alone they can be sustained. It is therefore essential that the British Government should retain in their own hands all the resources and facilities required for the fulfillment of these obligations. The most recent of these undertakings arose out of the accession of the United Kingdom to the Pact of Mutual Co-operation between Turkey and Iraq signed at Baghdad in February 1955.[8] Article I of this Pact is as follows:

> "Consistent with Article 51 of the United Nations Charter the High Contracting Parties will co-operate for their security and defence. Such measures as they agree to take to give effect to this co-operation may form the subject of special agreements with each other."

Effect is given to this article by the provision in Article 2 that "In order to ensure the realisation and effect application of the co-operation provided for in Article 1 above, the competent authorities of the High Contracting Parties will determine the measures to be taken as soon as the present Pact enters into

---

[8] "Miscellaneous No. 5 (1955)," Cmd. 9429.

force." Article 3 is, I think, also worthy of note. It states that "The High Contracting Parties undertake to refrain from any interference whatsoever in each other's internal affairs. They will settle any dispute between themselves in a peaceful way in accordance with the United Nations Charter." It is true that this particular agreement covers, at present, only Turkey, Iraq and Great Britain. But this is a good clause—and has a wide application. This surely is the right way for friends to approach and settle any differences which may arise between them from time to time. This is what we at this conference are now attempting to do. I do not think that anyone would dispute the wisdom of the undertaking "to retrain from any interference whatsoever in each other's internal affairs."

At the same time, arising out of Article 1 of the Pact which I have just quoted, Her Majesty's Government entered into a Special Agreement with the Government of Iraq.[9] The British Government undertook, among others, the following obligation. It is contained in Article 8 of the Special Agreement:

> "In the event of an armed attack against Iraq or threat of an armed attack which, in the opinion of the two Contracting Governments, endangers the security of Iraq, the Government of the United Kingdom at the request of the Government of Iraq shall make available assistance, including if necessary armed forces to help to defend Iraq. . . . ."

Another of the solemn engagements into which we have entered is the Treaty of Alliance between the United Kingdom and the Hashimite Kingdom of Jordan which was signed in March 1948.[10]

> "Should either High Contracting Party notwithstanding the provisions of Article 2 become engaged in war, the other High Contracting Party will . . . immediately come to his aid as a measure of collective defence.
> "In the event of an imminent menace of hostilities the High Contracting Parties will immediately concert together the necessary measures of defence."

Then, too, there is the Tripartite Declaration made by the Governments the United Kingdom, France and the United States of America in May 1950, regarding the whole Middle East Area. This Declaration, which has been referred to several times of late is still in full force. Its third paragraph states:

> "The three Governments take this opportunity of declaring their deep interest in and their desire to promote the establishment and maintenance of peace and stability in the area and their unalterable opposition to the use of force or threat of force between any of the States in that area. The three Governments, should they find that any of these States was preparing to violate

---

[9] "Treaty Series No. 50 (1955)," Cmd. 9544.
[10] "Treaty Series No. 26 (1948)," Cmd. 7404.

frontiers or armistice lines would, consistently with their obligations as members of the United Nations, immediately take action, both within and outside the United Nations, to prevent such violation."

I must excuse myself if I have gone into some detail, but I think that it is right that you should know the extent and variety of our engagements. These are only some of the obligations which we have assumed. They all rest on the basis of a firm position in the Eastern Mediterranean. They cover a very wide area, and offer protection and support to many countries. If they are to be effective in preserving peace, they must, I repeat, be firmly based. This, in effect, can only be the possession of the Island of Cyprus.

I must now refer to the vital and far-reaching obligations which Her Majesty's Government have as members of the North Atlantic Treaty Organisation. This alliance for peace is one on which, it is no exaggeration to say, the peace of the world depends. All these obligations the British Government share with the Greek and Turkish Governments. We are all partners in this great co-operative effort; and this aspect of our duty, to ourselves and to each other, demands our closest attention, and our sincere loyalty.

The N.A.T.O. military commands have been organised upon the twin basis of convenience and sovereign rights. Each of us is primarily responsible for a naval sub-area in the Eastern Mediterranean. The Greek naval sub-area extends over those islands which are Greek. The Turkish naval sub-area includes the islands under Turkish sovereignty. The British naval sub-area encloses the island of Cyprus. These areas are closely interdependent. They are all equally under the Supreme Allied Commander and his Deputy. The working of one affects the working of the others. Consequently the closest degree of practical co-operation is necessary. There must, for example, be joint exercises and manoeuvres. There must be complete mutual confidence.

The most disturbing manifestations in the Eastern Mediterranean recently have been signs that this vital and practical co-operation is being threatened as a result of differences centering on Cyprus. What, one asks, can have occurred to change the situation? Surely real and active co-operation is as necessary as ever. The deepest interests of our three countries require that we should pursue our mutual interests in harmony. If differences arise between us they should not be allowed to affect our fundamental co-operation. Yet it is precisely because such a danger has arisen that it has been necessary to convene this meeting.

What then are we to do? It is profitless to enter into recriminations on any side. No one can change recorded history—even the historians. The only value in the study of the past lies in the ability to learn and apply its lessons. Our task to-day must be a constructive one. What an opportunity lies before us! Instead of being a source of discord, Cyprus could be a symbol of progress and harmony. If we are to build enduringly, we must build with the materials at hand; and on the firm foundation of reality.

No one will deny that one of the fundamentals is the defence of the free world, and more particularly the obligations arising from Her Majesty's Government's commitments in the Middle East and Eastern Mediterranean. I have already told you of the serious nature of our engagements. It follows

indubitably that the United Kingdom must be possessed of the necessary facilities to carry this out. For a number of different reasons, geographical, historical and legal, the only satisfactory site for these facilities is Cyprus. If this was
true in 1878, it is even more true in 1955. It has sometimes been said that the
United Kingdom only needs a base in Cyprus. This, I think, can be misleading,
for the term "base" implies that our needs can be satisfied by some self-
contained unit, bounded, perhaps, by a perimeter of barbed wire. This may
serve for an airfield or harbour. But for our special needs and to carry out our
special duties this is not enough. Indeed, our generation has learned the painful lesson that war and defence are total. The whole idea and process of defence cannot and must not be dissociated from the general life of the community. This, together with the complexities of modern methods of defence—and
Cyprus is a headquarters as well as a base—make it essential that the United
Kingdom should possess not so much a base (in the old sense of the word) as a
whole complex of inter-related facilities. Cyprus is the heart of our defence
system in that part of the world; and for its proper functioning every artery of
the heart must play its part in full co-ordination. The facilities we require
ramify, as you know, geographically all over the island. They are inseparable
from the life of the population.

Nor can there be any doubt that it is right that the soldiers of our free
alliance should mingle closely with the population which they are defending
and which in turn is providing material for defence.

The recent and considerable increases in the military forces, and their
ancillary services stationed in Cyprus, have contributed significantly to the
steadily expanding prosperity of the island. It is a relationship which has been
found mutually beneficial. Her Majesty's Government deeply resent the irresponsible allegations which have been made to the effect that British forces
have been brought to Cyprus to create a reign of terror. Can any of my Greek
friends believe such a calumny? Of course not. Just eleven years have passed
since I saw British forces engaged in Greece, on a large scale, not to make, but
to overcome a reign of terror. I, for one, can never forget the comradeship of
those grim days.

Unhappily there *has* been violence in Cyprus—even something like
terrorism. A heavy burden rests on those who commit these outrages; a still
greater responsibility lies on those who have encouraged the perpetrators to
believe that their acts of barbarism are noble and heroic. No amount of sophis-
try can justify criminal actions. Her Majesty's Government are determined to
fulfill the first duty of any Government in maintaining law and order. Moreover, the terrorists and their supporters must inevitably defeat their own ends.
The opinion of free men throughout the world will not tolerate such shameless
recourse to violence, no matter what specious cloak it may be given.

Another of the fundamentals upon which we must build is the true realisation of the best interests of the peoples of Cyprus. This has always been a
primary concern of Her Majesty's Government. Those who have published the
slanderous accusations to which I have referred, have also pretended that Her
Majesty's Government was not sincere in its support of the Charter of the
United Nations. That is not true. Her Majesty's Government acknowledge
and support the Purposes of the United Nations, just as they support the Pre-

amble and the rest of the Charter. We have always borne firmly in mind the principles declared in the Purposes of the United Nations. They are, however, principles and not specific directions. As a glance at the history of our three countries will show, there are many ways in which the same principles can be given expression. The achievement of an ideal does not necessarily lead to identical institutions by which it is enshrined. If this were not so, there would be specific directions in the Charter itself as to how the principles were to be put into practice. But the authors of the Charter were wise. In the application of a principle all relevant circumstances must be considered.

In the application of the principles which are the basis of Her Majesty's Government's policy and which are shared, I profoundly believe, by our allies, Greece and Turkey, we must observe the circumstances peculiar to Cyprus. We are all agreed that the best interests of the Cypriot people lie in the tranquil and progressive exercise of the rights of free men developing as may seem most expedient and just, according to circumstances. Unhappily there have been interruptions in the constitutional progress of the people of Cyprus. We regret this. We hope that this conference will help us to restore this process. We wish to do so. Meanwhile a serious responsibility lies upon those both within and without, who have sought to prevent this normal and proper evolution. Certainly it is in no way the fault of successive British Governments that the Cypriot people have not yet achieved internal self-government. Had they done so, we might to-day have had elected representatives of the Cypriot Government sitting with us. At present, however, for reasons which Her Majesty's Government regret, the only legal and constitutional representatives of the Cypriot people present at this Conference are myself and my colleagues. We are honoured to have this trust, which symbolises the close and enduring connexion of the interests of the people of the United Kingdom with those of Cyprus. Nevertheless, it is an undoubted anomaly—and it is in our view wrong—that while so many other parts of the world have made steady progress in the art and practice of self-government, there has been no comparable advance in Cyprus. We wish to put this right. Internal self-government in Cyprus must be the first aim. We believe that it can be realised with proper regard for the rights of all concerned, if there is a common effort and obstruction ceases. Only when self-government has been progressively established by orderly, legal process, such as it is the purpose of the United Nations to safeguard, can we hope to see our way still further ahead.

I have put before you the considerations underlying the attitude of Her Majesty's Government to the problems which face us in the Eastern Mediterranean, including Cyprus. To-morrow I look forward to the pleasure of hearing my friend the Greek Minister for Foreign Affairs tell us about the attitude of his Government. I look forward with equal interest to hearing my friend the representative of the Turkish Government explaining to us the point of view of his Government. After that I hope we shall be able to recognise the point at which it would be best to begin the process of conciliation, and the most practical methods to adopt.

We, for our part, approach the problems which we shall have to consider in a friendly and constructive spirit. We shall not be backward in making whatever practical suggestions seem, in the light of our discussions, to meet our requirements and the special circumstances of Cyprus. Nor shall we be inflexible. We look forward to reaching agreement through discussion. No one I am sure will expect us to abandon British interests or responsibilities or those for which we are trustees. That we cannot and will not do. But it is our object to take account of and, if possible, reconcile any differences there may be between us.

Whatever procedure we decide to follow I am confident that we shall make progress if we remember the record of our long friendships and the great issues which depend upon our future co-operation. It is well known that there is in Britain a feeling of deep affection and comradeship for the heroic people of Greece. This link goes back over many years, and has stood the test—the acid test of war. Equally Britain has stood many times at the side of Turkey in face of common danger. The sterling qualities of the Turkish people have evoked our respect and admiration. We like to feel that all these ties are genuine and reciprocal.

It is therefore with the support of the British people as a whole that Her Majesty's Government express their earnest hope that means will be found at this Conference not only to remove present differences but to establish still closer co-operation with our two N.A.T.O. allies in the Eastern Mediterranean. We are all conscious of the needs of the Cypriot people whose welfare we shall attempt to forward in tranquility and order in accordance with the traditions of our common heritage. The extent to which we can foster speedy progress in Cyprus and at the same time widen our co-operation and strengthen our joint defence will be a measure of our wisdom. It is certain that political wisdom, as Aristotle taught, is not to be found in extreme measures.

STATEMENT MADE BY M. STEPHANOPOULOS AT THE THIRD PLENARY MEETING HELD ON AUGUST 31, 1955 (translation from French)

On behalf of the Greek Government I wish to express our warmest thanks to Her Britannic Majesty's Government for their invitation to the present Tripartite Conference and for giving us an opportunity of discussing the political and defence questions concerning the Eastern Mediterranean and also the Cyprus question.

It has always been the opinion of the Greek Government that international differences between friends and allies should be the subject of direct discussion between the countries concerned, and we are happy that such opinion has finally been adopted with regard to the matters with which we are dealing at present. The Greek Delegation will spare no effort in ensuring that our discussions take place in a spirit of friendliness and good-will, and that they lead to the fulfilment of the aims pursued by this Conference.

The object of the Conference, as set forth in the British Government's invitation, is to discuss political and defence matters affecting the Eastern Mediterranean as well as the Cyprus question.

Greece has always considered of paramount importance those questions of the defence of the Eastern Mediterranean which are of special concern to Turkey, Great Britain and Greece, and during recent years my country has made a direct contribution which must not be ignored. Not only did Greece resist, with her entire forces and with dogged determination, attacks made on her by Fascism and Nazism but did so without a moment's hesitation and at a time when one after the other the European countries had collapsed, and even though Greece was perfectly aware that, notwithstanding Great Britain's invaluable support, her resistance was certain to be overcome.

Later on, when her freedom and independence were menaced by the Cominform, Greece did not hesitate to make yet another stand against mortal danger and to crush the forces of evil, thereby rendering an undeniable service to the cause of her allies and of free people everywhere.

Greece does not for a single moment lose sight of the importance of our common security. On the contrary, we consider that the grave perils surrounding us, coupled with our participation in N.A.T.O. and the Balkan Alliance, impose upon us duties which are mutually complementary and which at the same time reinforce the effectiveness of the defence of the three countries of Greece, Turkey and Great Britain against these common perils.

Greece also fully recognises the fact that Great Britain, having assumed contractual obligations for the defence of certain countries in the Eastern Mediterranean such as Iraq and Jordan, must have a base in Cyprus. We go even further and consider that, in view of the withdrawal of British forces from Suez, the necessity for such a base is even more evident to-day than ever before. Not only has Greece never had any intention of weakening Britain's defensive positions in these regions but, quite the contrary, my country is fully conscious of the ties which bind us to Great Britain, and is fully aware of the requirements on which depend not only our own safety but that of our friend and ally Turkey. In sponsoring the Cypriot people's demand for their right of self-determination, Greece has never (and I emphasise never) for a single moment entertained the idea of a withdrawal from Cyprus of the British Forces.

Bearing the foregoing in mind, the Greek view is that the defence of Cyprus and of the Eastern Mediterranean (thanks to the maintenance of the British bases and military installations in Cyprus) has everything to gain from satisfying the legitimate aspirations of the people of Cyprus. A friendly population devoted to the common cause would strengthen the defensive value of these military bases and would enhance the strategic importance of the island of Cyprus.

I do not think it is necessary again to take up the argument as to whether territory necessary to the security and defence of a given country must live under the sovereignty of that country. Proof of this point is N.A.T.O., within the framework of which the system of collective defence has made considerable progress. We are all aware that similar problems arose within N.A.T.O. whenever the utilisation of territory belonging to one country for the defensive needs of another country or of other member countries was considered necessary. In such cases there has never been any question of sovereignty nor has sovereignty proved an obstacle in the way of the successful solution to problems of defence. Moreover, I might mention here by way of example the agreement concluded in 1953 under which Greece ceded military bases to the United States.

One might well ask why the question of sovereignty should arise with regard to the strategic aspect of the Cyprus problem. The concept of military bases as so many areas enclosed by barbed wire is assuredly out of date. The concept of defence can no longer be separated from the daily life of the community. That is what we mean when we claim that a military base cannot function effectively in the midst of hostile populations and that, on the contrary, the value and efficiency of a military base is enhanced if the surrounding population is helpful and co-operative.

We accordingly believe that our common defence in Cyprus and in the Eastern Mediterranean can only be effectively organised if the full and willing support of the entire population of Cyprus is first of all forthcoming. Such support can only be obtained on one condition, namely, the formal recognition of the right of the people of Cyprus to determine their own future and to choose, by the free expression of their sovereign will, that political system which suits them best.

We thus come to the next subject of this Conference, that is, the question of Cyprus. It has often been claimed that Greece desires to effect a change in the sovereignty of Cyprus, that she seeks to bring about the union of Cyprus with Greece and even an immediate such union. Allow me to say that all this is incorrect.

The policy followed by the Greek Government, and which they perseveringly follow, is clear and precise. Greece has never claimed the right alone to determine the future status of Cyprus. We have simply requested that the population of the island should be permitted freely to decide its own future. That is why I once again declare that Greece will accept and respect any decision which may duly be taken by the population of Cyprus, no matter what that decision may be.

The Greek Government consider that neither they nor their friend and ally Turkey have the right to take decisions on the future status of the island on behalf of the population of Cyprus. It must moreover be remembered that at the Bandung Conference Turkey (and this is to Turkey's credit) was instrumental in obtaining the recognition of the right of self-determination on behalf of all peoples without exception.

The fact that Greece and Turkey were invited to the present Conference does not confer upon us the right ourselves to determine the fate of Cyprus; our presence here is only due to the existence in Cyprus of a Greek national majority and a Turkish national minority. At this Conference we therefore cannot decide on the future régime under which the island shall live, as only the people of Cyprus have that right. It cannot be permitted that we should endeavour to act on their behalf.

History shows us many examples of peoples compelled by force to accept sovereignty to which they objected. Changes of sovereignty have taken place sometimes by conquest and sometimes by cession; there have even been cases where sovereignty has changed as a result of financial negotiation. Nowadays however, populations are no longer conquered or annexed by force. In this new world, built upon the ruins of Fascism, various new principles will henceforward govern the destinies of man. These principles, which appear in the Charter of the United Nations, have been compiled by the free countries of the world in mutual accord, and recognise that all people, both great and small, have equal rights based on the respect of freedom and the dignity of man. Among these rights, that of self-determination is one of the fundamental principles which govern this free world to which we all have the privilege of belonging; this principle is recognised by Article 1 of the United Nations Charter and appears in the Proclamation issued in Washington on June 29, 1954, by President Eisenhower and Sir Winston Churchill. More recently this same principle appeared in the S.E.A.T.O. Agreement.[11]

Collective international security, and consequently international peace, could not be safeguarded if this principle were no longer respected. It is the application of this fundamental right of self-determination that the population of Cyprus now claims under the terms of the Charter of the United Nations and it was precisely this same claim that the Greek Government last year submitted to the United Nations.

It is this same right which we to-day request on behalf of the Cypriot population. I must repeat here that in this connexion Greece in no way claims a right to intervene and impose its own will, nor does it recognise such a right in others. That, moreover, would be contrary to the international obligations which all three peoples have assumed.

Nor can we accept the argument that the Cyprus question is a domestic matter. We do not dispute that sovereignty over Cyprus at present belongs to Great Britain. However, from the moment that the majority of the Cypriot population put forward its request for self-determination, and from the time that the United Nations, while agreeing to include the Cyprus question on the agenda for the 9th Assembly, thereby recognising its competence to deal with the matter, we find ourselves faced with a new situation, as the Cyprus question has now acquired an international character.

Moreover, does not this invitation to the present Conference, in which we are participating in a friendly and constructive spirit of collaboration, clearly and indisputably mean that Her Majesty's Government have also accepted this new aspect of the question before us? I hope that I have sufficiently demonstrated that the attitude of the Greek Government cannot be regarded as either expansionist or imperialist. The expansionist idea long ago ceased to determine the foreign policy of Greece. Our frontiers with Turkey, as we have never ceased to proclaim, are for us final and unchangeable. It has never even occurred to us to put forward a claim to any part of Turkish territory.

It is not only on behalf of the present Government that I make this declaration, but I thereby also interpret the viewpoint of every Greek political party. That is our national policy finally and universally proclaimed, and it has the support of the entire Greek population.

Nor do we recognise the right of history alone to modify or disturb existing frontiers. Historical reasons are valueless when they conflict with reality as determined by the development of conceptions of popular and national conscience. With regard to the question of Cyprus, whose history is in general related to the eventful history of Greece, we will only invoke historical arguments

---

[11] "Miscellaneous No. 27 (1954)," Cmd. 9282.

as a secondary consideration, as its Greek character is generally recognised and was even admitted in 1907 by Sir Winston Churchill when he was Under-Secretary of State for the Colonies. We also recognise no such right in favour of geography. Geographical criteria can have no priority over the will and conscience of a people. Acceptance of a contrary concept would be the denial of the principle of respect of the dignity of man and freedom, a principle recognised by all democratic nations as a fundamental and indispensable prerequisite for the creation of a better world. As a consequence we do not ask for the annexation of Cyprus or its union with Greece.

All we ask is that the people of Cyprus be allowed to exercise a fundamental and internationally guaranteed right—the right of self-determination. Nor do we ask that this right should be granted immediately. We realise that a transitory period of "free government" would have to intervene during which Cypriots of Greek origin and those of Turkish origin could, proportionately to their numerical strength and on a footing of equity, administer their territory through their duly elected representatives. The duration of this period of "free government" which will precede the exercise of self-determination must be fixed in a reasonable and objective manner.

If we take into consideration the fact that the Cypriot people enjoy a high level of culture and civilization, and that the British Government—in similar cases involving far less civilised peoples—has fixed the period of self-government at three years I feel that we cannot meet with serious difficulties in the case of Cyprus.

The Greek Delegation also regrets the fact that "free government" has not yet been granted to Cyprus as should have been done a long time ago, this in the same advanced degree as that enjoyed by other territories of the British Empire. If that had been done, even from the viewpoint of Commonwealth procedure, the right of self-determination would now have been granted to the people of Cyprus. I do not think that it is necessary to comment here on the reasons for this delay. Let it suffice to say that the responsibility for this does not devolve entirely on the population of Cyprus. It was with this situation in mind that we approached Her Majesty's Government with the request that they hasten the time of application—in favour of the Cypriots—of this fundamental principle which gives them the right to decide upon their own future, a right which doubtless would already have been recognised if the well-known but regrettable events had not taken place.

The question has already been raised as to why the Cyprus question was raised at a time of great anxiety for the free nations.

But now let me establish a true fact: it was not the Greek Government which raised the Cyprus question.

That question was raised by the Cypriot people themselves, by a great majority which, in despair of witnessing the fulfilment of an oft-repeated promise, felt that the time had at last come to demand the exercise of a right which was solemnly recognised and confirmed after the second world war by the very Charter of the United Nations.

The Greek Government, in exercising its United Nations' prerogative, was and is convinced that it adopted the most peaceable and appropriate means of safeguarding peace and order in Cyprus.

My Government has repeatedly repudiated (and continues to do so) the use of violence and any other act contrary to the peaceful course pursued on deciding to submit the matter to the United Nations. Such condemnation of violence was, however, of no avail. Immediately the decision taken by the General Assembly of the United Nations to postpone discussion of the Cypriot request was made known, and immediately the Greek Government was no longer able to keep the Cyprus question within the framework of peaceful procedure, the matter passed into the hands of extremist elements with the well-known and regrettable consequences.

I think that you will now admit, in the light of subsequent developments, that the policy pursued by the Greek Government was dictated by prudence and was the best and least dangerous in the circumstances. The Cyprus question was consequently raised by the inevitable force of circumstances. It is now before us as a question which demands an immediate and final solution.

There are still more reasons why the Cyprus question simply had to be raised. First of all the right of a people to self-determination is closely linked to the ideal of freedom. The Greeks are particularly sensitive to that ideal—our British friends have proof of that. Whenever freedom has been in jeopardy—not merely the freedom of Greece but that of others as well—my country has never hesitated in campaigning to safeguard such freedom and in placing herself alongside Great Britain during such periods of great peril, this with a complete disregard of the sacrifices she might have to make. The Greeks have a sincere desire for peace, and aim at achieving economic progress through hard work. Nevertheless, they always set their love of freedom above peace and comfort, and for the sake of freedom no sacrifice is too great.

Furthermore, a claim to the right of self-determination was bound to be raised by Cypriots from the very moment that the free countries, including the three countries we represent here, signed the Charter of the United Nations, which solemnly promised such a right to all peoples of the world. For the people of Cyprus it was unthinkable that yet again, and after so many sacrifices, promises categorically made would not be kept. Especially under present circumstances it would certainly be very dangerous were we to fail in promises made to the various peoples concerned.

And lastly there is yet another reason why it was necessary to raise the question of the request by Cyprus for self-determination—the reason being that the application would be made to Great Britain. To us Greeks, as to all other free men, the British nation represents the very ideal of freedom and justice. It is for this reason that we refuse to believe that a request concerning the freedom of a people, and bound up with the most elementary concept of justice, will not ultimately merit the understanding of the great British nation which is so justly proud of its own freedom. Those are the reasons why we are very hopeful of the result which this Conference can and must achieve.

In conclusion, the Greek Government do not ask for the union of Cyprus with Greece, as they feel that they have not the right of deciding the future of the island and that the Cypriot people itself alone can exercise such prerogative.

In this matter Greece is acting as interpreter of the will of the Cypriot people, and hereby requests that Cyprus be granted her basic rights after a period of "free government." That, moreover, is an obligation we have all assumed by adopting the Charter of the United Nations.

The frank and generous solution proposed and supported by the Greek Government will safeguard the real and true interests of all parties concerned.

The United Kingdom, having moreover frequently applied this principle of self-determination in favour of other peoples whose destinies it controlled, would thereby fulfill its traditional role and would thus earn the eternal gratitude of the Greek nation. Its military bases would also be strengthened as a result, as they would be surrounded by a happy and contented populace. In addition Great Britain could in due course and under the terms of a mutual agreement, obtain the military bases she might require not only in Cyprus but also on Greek territory itself, this, naturally, being within the framework of the defensive policy of the democratic nations.

Our friend and ally Turkey will also benefit from this strengthening of our common defences and she will secure full satisfaction of her legitimate requests for the safeguarding of the rights of the Turkish minority in Cyprus. We are determined, when the time comes, to grant the Turkish minority a status of full equality and freedom in religious, educational and economic spheres in accordance with the long and unchangeable tradition of our country and even to introduce, if Turkey should so desire, a special régime in connexion with matters of nationality and military service. I am firmly convinced, Mr. Chairman, that our discussions will take place in a spirit of mutual friendship and understanding which will contribute to the finding of a satisfactory solution of the problem before us. We do not wish to take up a position against anyone whatsoever, as we believe that we can all find satisfaction in an equitable solution.

In my opinion we should avoid everything which might hamper the success of our deliberations or disturb our close relationship of friendship and alliance, as that could do no more than directly benefit our common foes. We are in fact quite sure that the security, independence and very existence of our countries depend entirely, under the present international situation, on the ties of friendship and alliance which I have just mentioned. That is why we offer you our sincere collaboration in an endeavour to find together a solution which would naturally be based on the fundamental principles of international morality recognised by the Charter of the United Nations. Such a solution would mean that the island of Cyprus, instead of being a source of division and discord, would become an even closer and stronger link between our three countries.

STATEMENT MADE BY M. ZORLU AT THE FOURTH PLENARY MEETING HELD ON SEPTEMBER 1, 1955

I would like to express our thanks to Her Britannic Majesty's Government and specially to Mr. Macmillan for having given us the opportunity to discuss political and military questions concerning the Eastern Mediterranean, including Cyprus, and for having made it possible for the experts of three Allied countries to have a frank and free exchange of views on such questions.

It is quite normal, and even necessary, that three Governments which are bound to each other by military defence Pacts und Alliances should, especially when they differ on certain points, meet and discuss all problems relating to an area which is of common concern to them. Consequently, the Turkish Government accepted the invitation to the London Conference with great satisfaction and attended it with a maximum of good will. We are fully confident that the exchange of views which we shall have with the outstanding statesmen of the two friendly and allied countries that we meet here will yield positive results, and that we shall understand each other better at the conclusion of these discussions. It is inconceivable that it should be otherwise; for the commitments which we share with Her Majesty's Government in the United Kingdom and with the Royal Hellenic Government are so firm, and our interests are common to such an extent, that it behoves us to converse in the language of men who are all devoted to the same ideal. I am very happy to say that the Turkish Delegation has attended the Conference with that conviction and confidence.

The invitation of Her Majesty's Government specifically mentions the Island of Cyprus among the questions of defence relating to the Eastern Mediterranean. When one considers the great importance of this island for Turkey the wisdom of such a specific inclusion becomes apparent. Indeed, as we shall fully explain in the course of our discussions, this is an island which, above all things, is of vital importance for the defence of Turkey, to such an extent that it is impossible to calculate the defence potential and capacity of Turkey in case of war without taking Cyprus into consideration. I can say these words to my distinguished colleagues, the representatives of two allied countries, without reticence or fear of contradiction.

Up to now we have considered the status of Cyprus as follows: at a time when the Turkish-Ottoman State was faced with the gravest of dangers from Russia and when, as a result of an unfortunate war, she was constrained to relinquish a few of her Eastern Provinces to Russia, she was in dire need of the help of a powerful ally, and consequently transferred the administration of Cyprus to her ally Great Britain, maintaining nevertheless the right of sovereignty on the island. The Treaty of Alliance which we concluded with Great Britain in 1878 stipulates that Cyprus is transferred to the occupation and administration of Great Britain, who undertakes to come to the aid of Turkey with all her might in the case of Russian aggression, in order that the British Government, I quote, "may be further enabled to carry out its commitments." This in itself is a clear indication of the importance of the Island of Cyprus in the defence of Turkey. Subsequently, when Turkey receded within the boundaries of her "National Pact" with the Treaty of Lausanne, the Turkish Government felt the need of specifically determining the fate of Cyprus and, by Articles 20 and 21 of that Treaty, determined the status of the Island. According to Article 20 of the Treaty of Lausanne, Turkish sovereignty on Cyprus lapsed on November 5, 1914, and Cyprus was legally annexed to Great Britain as from that date. Article 21 of the same Treaty contains definite stipulations as to the conditions under which the people of Cyprus, who were all Turkish subjects, would assume Turkish or British nationality. By the terms of this Article the signatories have agreed that those of the inhabitants of

Cyprus who do not opt to remain Turkish citizens could only become British subjects. In other words, the fate of the Island was exclusively a matter of concern between Turkey and Great Britain, it was thus agreed and consented to by all the signatories of the Treaty of Lausanne, and it was on those terms that the Island went to Great Britain.

Given these explicit terms, it would be inadmissible to consider Cyprus as an island, I quote, "the fate of which remains to be determined." To argue in that sense would be tantamount to demanding the revision of the Treaty of Lausanne.

Nor, in the face of the explicit provisions of the Treaty of Lausanne, is it appropriate to refer to any other article of that Treaty. Nevertheless, in order to show how definite is the status of Cyprus and how justified the interest of Turkey in the island, let us look at Article 16 of the Treaty of Lausanne which is often mentioned in connexion with this question.

Article 16 provides that the future of the territories detached from the Ottoman Empire are "settled or to be settled by the parties concerned." The phrase quoted above was not contained in the original draft submitted by the Allies. Instead, Article 16 contained as its second paragraph the following provision: "Turkey recognises and agrees to dispositions which have been or shall be made concerning the attribution, independence or any other régime of those territories or Islands." Turkey rejected this paragraph, and in the counter-proposal which she submitted to the Conference she completely deleted it. In explaining her objection to the paragraph in question the Turkish Delegation declared:

> "Turkey is being asked to recognise and to agree to dispositions which will intervene in the future. It is obvious that Turkey cannot commit herself to accept dispositions the nature and scope of which are not known to her."

This declaration clearly shows that Turkey not only finally determined the fate of certain territories, like Cyprus, which had been detached from her, but also that she refused to undertake any previously undefined obligations with regard to the future concerning territories the fate of which was as yet uncertain at the time of the signature of the Treaty. Thus we see that the Treaty of Lausanne is quite explicit. If in spite of these express stipulations it were sought to reconsider the future of Cyprus, this, as I have just said, would be equivalent to attempting a revision of the Treaty of Lausanne. In other words it would be seeking to modify Articles 20, 21 and 16 of the Treaty which I mentioned above.

The fate of the Island can only be determined between Turkey and Great Britain, for at the time of the signature of the Treaty of Lausanne the parties concerned in Cyprus were only and exclusively Turkey on the one hand and Great Britain on the other. One of these is the country that relinquishes sovereignty on the Island and the other the country that annexes it. There is no other party concerned as regards Cyprus. By the Treaty of Lausanne, Greece was a party concerned in the Islands mentioned in Article 12, just as Italy was a party concerned in the Islands referred to in Article 15.

Such is the legal status of Cyprus and it was on that ground that we refused to recognise the existence of a "Cyprus question." For we considered that if one is to embark upon the modification of the Treaty of Lausanne which is the foundation of a new political constellation and, from the point of view of Turkey, of a system of security, this would not be confined to Cyprus and that it would create a number of ponderous questions which would also enable Turkey to put forward certain demands. One cannot therefore help but be surprised that the Cyprus question has been created without due consideration of these grave consequences. We have always looked upon this problem, which it has been attempted to create in an artificial manner, as a domestic question of Great Britain. Yet, there must not be the slightest doubt that the limits of this conduct of Turkey will be determined by the turn of events. In other words, speaking frankly, so long as British sovereignty on Cyprus remains absolute there will be no change in our attitude based on commitments; but if there is any question of altering the status of Cyprus in this or that manner Turkey will consider herself primarily concerned, for, since the "abnegation" and "sacrifice" of Turkey in the matter of Cyprus was only in favour of Great Britain and under certain conditions, if there is any attempt to alter this situation, the Turkish Government will demand a return to the status prior to such abnegation.

By the Treaty of Lausanne, Turkey waived her rights in favour of Great Britain. She consented to this renunciation in view of certain security considerations and of political conditions. Consequently, any attempt to transfer sovereignty on the Island or to alter its fate would represent a change in those conditions. From the point of view of physical geography, Turkey's interest in the Island is unalterable, and there is nothing more natural than that Turkey should reserve the right to reassert her interest in the Island according to new conditions.

Turkey is not only in her rights in making such a demand but she is also in duty bound to do so. For the importance of Cyprus for Turkey does not arise from a single cause; it is a necessity which emanates from the exigencies of history, geography, economy and military strategy, from the right to existence and security which is the most sacred right of every State, in short from the very nature of things. May I be allowed to explain briefly the justification of this statement?

This Island, which, by its geographical structure, is a prolongation of the Anatolian Peninsula, of which the soil is Anatolian soil, of which the climate is Anatolian climate, has, ever since the time it came under Turkish sovereignty, been attached to the Motherland as any other province of Turkey, and has constituted an inseparable part thereof. Indeed, in all the course of history the fate of Cyprus has remained attached to that of the peoples settled in the Anatolian Peninsula and has, in return, affected the fate of the peoples living in Anatolia. If the Island was once part of the Hellenic world, it was only because at that time Anatolia was within the orbit of ancient Hellenic civilisation; if it once belonged to Byzantium, it was only because Byzantium held sway over Anatolia; if Cyprus was once under the dominion of the Latin Empires, it was only because at the lime the Latins aspired to rule over Anatolia. In the same manner, when, previously and subsequently, the Caliphs began to extend their rule over Anatolia, they also ruled over Cyprus. It was also thus that the Ottomans established their sway on Cyprus. It is not therefore admissible to try to consider the Island of Cyprus from the point of view of the present-day composition of its population. So long as Cyprus remained under Turkish sovereignty, the number of Turks on the Island was sometimes a majority and sometimes a minority of the Island population; and yet this was never taken as a criterion of whether or not the island was Turkish, and for three-and-a-half centuries Cyprus and the other parts of Turkey lived in a state of complete inter-penetration. Consequently, to-day as well, when we take into account the state of the population in Cyprus, it is not sufficient to say, for instance that 100,000 Turks live there. One should rather say that 100,000 out of 24,000,000 Turks live there and that 300,000 Turkish Cypriots live in various parts of Turkey. The economic structure of the Island as well attaches it to Anatolia. Cyprus has never been able to sustain itself economically without external aid. It owes its present standard of living to being a part of Great Britain and of the British Commonwealth; the foodstuffs which it needs are produced in abundance in Turkey; and when during the Second World War, the supply lines of Great Britain to the Island were severed Cyprus lived on the resources of Turkey.

I mentioned briefly above the extent to which strategic reasons bind Cyprus to Turkey. I would like to add here that Cyprus must of necessity, from the military point of view, belong either to Turkey proper or to a country which is as closely interested as Turkey in the fate of Eastern countries in the vicinity of Turkey. That is to say, if Turkey or one of the countries of the Middle East which are bound to Turkey by military commitments should be involved in war, Cyprus too should be at war along with them. The defence and the logistics of this area cannot be conceived otherwise. In the case of war, outside assistance to the war potential of Turkey can only come through her Western and Southern ports in the Mediterranean. The Western ports of Turkey are unfortunately within the effective operations area of the potential enemy and Turkey at war can only be supplied through her Southern ports. The Second World War made this situation quite clear.

It is with that in mind that the whole system of infrastructure which will supply Turkey has been given its bases in Turkish ports like Antalya, Mersin and Iskenderun, and even the fuel supply of Istanbul is provided by a pipe-line starting in the Southern ports. And all these South-Western ports are under cover of the Island of Cyprus. Whoever controls this Island is in a position to control these Turkish ports. If the Power that controls this Island is also in control of the Western Islands it will have effectively surrounded Turkey. No country should be allowed to leave its entire security at the mercy of any one country, no matter how great a friend and ally the latter may be.

I believe that the explanations I have given up to now have been sufficient to show why Turkey is so closely interested in Cyprus. In return, what is the argument advanced by those who deny Turkey's interest in the Island? They contend that, in so far as possession of the Island is concerned, historical, geographical, economic, military and contractual factors bear no weight whatsoever; and that the only thing that must be taken into consideration is that "peoples should be given the right to self-determination." Let us for a moment, for the sake of argument, assume that that is so, and see whether such a principle is applicable in the case of Cyprus.

One point must be stressed before all others: In the words of the well-known International lawyer Fanchille: "Whenever it has been attempted to apply the principle of self-determination without full comprehension and without the exercise of maximum care, it has always yielded harmful results and has been of no use other than contributing to international tension. Indeed, the misapplication of this principle may, on the one hand, bring about the creation of very small States and may, on the other hand, encourage certain unscrupulous States to covet the Provinces and Colonies of their neighbours. The principle of self-determination which in pure theory emanates from sublime thoughts and feelings, is very liable in practice to become a source of revolution and anarchy." Almost all international jurists are in agreement on that point. As Ch. Rousseau says: ". . . . but, even as its defenders confess, this right could only be analysed as a relative and conditional one. In fact, its legal construction comes up against the effect of economic, administrative and strategical obstacles which sometimes, and in certain border-line cases, necessitate territorial dispositions contrary to the wishes of peoples." Professor Ch. Crozat applying the above consideration to the legal status of Cyprus arrives at the following conclusion: "If the question should arise of the abandonment of sovereignty on the Island of Cyprus by Great Britain, the question of the security of Turkey shall prevail over all other principles, even over the principle of the self-determination of the Cypriot people." To those who rely on the fact that the principle of self-determination is contained in the United Nations Charter it would be possible to reply with the following words of Eagleton:

> "The term "self-determination" was crowded into Article 1 of the Charter without relevance and without explanation, and upon that basis delegates are to-day making fantastic claims. Their irresponsibility alienates Americans who have sympathized with the struggle of many peoples for independence.
>
> "The concept of self-determination is not a simple one and it has always defied definition . . . . There has never been a judge to pass upon its claims, indeed there has never been a law by which judgment could be issued. The textbooks of international law do not recognise any legal right to self-determination nor do they know any standards for determining which groups are entitled to independence."

There is no doubt that the concept of self-determination often clashes with that of the sovereignty of States. Since it is necessary to find the right balance between these two concepts, where is the point of equilibrium to be established? Since no case in point can constitute a conclusive precedent how is this point of equilibrium to be found in each particular case?

The deduction to be made is that the principle of the self-determination of peoples, whereas it served the noblest humanitarian aims of the late President Wilson of the United States, has also served the most nefarious purposes of Nazism and, as Sibert has said, sometimes the right of the "self-determination of peoples" becomes the right "to determine the fate of peoples." It is certainly impossible to set aside realities based on historical, geographical and military exigencies on the grounds of such a perilous and indistinct theory.

There are definite cases extant where, by international decisions, for instance, geographical and military considerations have been made to prevail over the concept of self-determination. One of the best known cases in point is that of the dispute over the Aaland Islands between two very friendly neighbouring countries, where, in spite of the fact that the majority of the population were of Swedish origin, the League of Nations awarded the Islands to Finland. May I also remind you that the assignment of Western Thrace to Greece by the Treaty of Lausanne was not made by way of application of the principle of self-determination, since the majority of the people there were Turkish.

Was it not Elephtherios Venizelos himself who said during the Lausanne Conference that the principle of self-determination was not one that should always receive primary consideration where it was a question of assigning a certain territory to a certain State?

We are not against the principle of self-determination. On the contrary we are all for it. If this is not sufficiently evidenced by the fact that we have solemnly affixed our signature to the United Nations Charter wherein this principle is enshrined, I would like to mention that we have reaffirmed that principle as a confirmation of the United Nations Charter in the final communiqué of the Bandung Conference only a short while ago.

What we are trying to avoid is that the principle of self-determination should become an element of injustice, unsafety, insecurity and trouble.

If one applies the above-mentioned considerations to the particular case of Cyprus, one arrives at the following conclusion: the application of the principle of self-determination in that island clashes, first of all, with the right of sovereignty of Great Britain derived from the Treaty of Lausanne and at the same time with the right of Turkey to ensure her own security; and, for the same reasons, in case British sovereignty comes to an end, Cyprus cannot be taken in hand as an entity separate from Anatolia.

As for the question of self-government, we cannot say that we are against that either. But here again we must point to the necessity of avoiding its heedless application from becoming a source of trouble.

There are at present two principal groups living together in Cyprus, one of which, namely the Turkish community, has for years been subjected to violence and intimidation incited by the Church of Cyprus which, by the way, is exerting all manner of pressure, including excommunication. over the Orthodox population of the island in order to drag them to political activities and to bring about Enosis. As a result of this an atmosphere of antagonism and hostility has been instilled between the two communities. Consequently, before thinking about giving the inhabitants of the island the right to share in internal government, it is obvious that one must wait for the return of absolute peace and quiet in Cyprus. For self-government can only be considered for communities and groups who get along well with each other and do not bear antagonism towards each other. What the people of Cyprus need, therefore, before self-government, is a period of stable peace and calm. Violence must be prevented. The Church must refrain from dabbling in politics. Otherwise we might be faced with an even more serious situation than to-day. We see many instances in the recent past where self-government granted inappropriately and inopportunely has brought bloodshed in its wake. What we are all trying to achieve is not the triumph of vague principles but, first and foremost, the safeguard of the destiny and even of the lives and property of a people living in a given geographical area in whom we are closely interested.

These remarks should not be taken in any way as casting an aspersion on the maturity of the people of Cyprus. Yet, one has to remember that noble principles that must be revered in the abstract, can lead one to grave international blunders when applied without regard for existing circumstances.

Even when the circumstances change in Cyprus and the climate eventually becomes suitable for self-government as explained above, it must still be borne in mind that, on such a small parcel of land where live two different communities who vary in so many ways, the guiding principle should not be the consideration of majorities and minorities, but rather the granting of full equality to the two groups.

The purpose of all this explanation that I have given is to bring about a clear understanding of the so-called "Cyprus question," and to make it possible for us openly to face our differences and to find the right road of agreement which will serve the real interests of all three countries.

The co-operation among three countries closely concerned with the Eastern Mediterranean, particularly with the Northern area of the Eastern Mediterranean, and who are all members of the peace front, has been disturbed. The "Cyprus question" is responsible for this. There is no sense in ignoring this fact. We have tried to expound the views of Turkey on this question along the lines of the statement made by my Prime Minister, which has been fully endorsed by the entire population of Turkey, including all political parties. Turkey believes that the *status quo* should be maintained in Cyprus. If this is to be upset then the island should revert to Turkey. It should be made quite clear that any attempt to change the *status quo* by roundabout means is not compatible with the desire to keep friendship with Turkey intact. Those who wish a change in the *status quo* should take that point into consideration. Otherwise the trust and confidence of the Turkish people will be shaken. The people of Turkey cannot conceive in any other way the fate of an island which is of vital importance for the defence of their own soil.

Greek-Turkish friendship, co-operation and alliance is based on a political agreement in principle established by the Treaty of Lausanne which has liquidated a whole past full of antagonisms. This agreement implies that Greece has once and for all abandoned her claims based on the "megali idea," and that in return Turkey has accepted the boundaries laid down by the Treaty of Lausanne. To-day as well, the Turkish Government, moved by the same strong conviction, deems essential the continuation of this friendship and its safeguard from all disturbances—not only for the common benefit of Greece and Turkey, but also for the peace and security of the world and of the Mediterranean. It is therefore loth to abandon moderation in its entire political conduct. The claims that are now being put forward in connexion with the Cyprus question cannot be reconciled with our mutual rights which we must all respect and with our common duty to maintain and safeguard friendship; and they are engendering grave misgivings as to the future. If I have given full vent to those misgivings before you, Mr. President, I do not doubt that you will attribute it to the importance that we attach to Greek-Turkish friendship.

TEXT OF AGREED COMMUNIQUÉ ISSUED ON SEPTEMBER 1, 1955

As previously agreed, the Tripartite Conference on the Eastern Mediterranean and Cyprus this morning heard a statement by the Turkish Foreign Minister. The three Foreign Ministers met again at Lancaster House in the afternoon, when they agreed to issue the following summaries of the points of view of the three Governments as they had been put forward in the three opening statements.

In explaining the point of view of Her Majesty's Government Mr. Macmillan had emphasised that this was a conference between friends and allies whose unity was vital to the free world. The three countries represented had special responsibilities, not only to themselves but to their partners, which overrode all others. It was their duty to explain their points of view in all frankness and then to seek the best means to reconcile their differences.

These differences centred on Cyprus. But they threatened allied harmony and the smooth working of common defence over a much wider area. Consequently the British Government had thought it right that all aspects of our present problems, including the position in Cyprus, should be embraced in a wider consideration of political and defence questions in the Eastern Mediterranean.

History had given each of the three countries special interests in Cyprus. For Great Britain, Cyprus was both a territory, indisputably under British Sovereignty, for whose progress and welfare Her Majesty's Government were responsible; and also the vital defensive position at the hinge of the North Atlantic and Middle Eastern defence systems. British responsibilities included those arising from the British Government's adherence to the Turco-Iraqi Pact, from the Anglo-Iraqi Agreement, from the Anglo-Jordanian Alliance and from the Tripartite Declaration of 1950. To discharge these responsibilities, Britain needed not merely a "base" but the possession and use of the whole island and its facilities.

Her Majesty's Government were determined to fulfil the first duty of any government in maintaining law and order in Cyprus. They had sought to promote self-government. A serious responsibility lay on those who had caused violence and had obstructed democratic evolution. But for this, elected representatives of the Cypriot Government might be taking part in the present Conference. Self-government must be the first aim. He believed it could be realised with proper regard for the rights of all, if there were a common effort.

Britain would abandon neither her interests and responsibilities nor those for which she was trustee. But it was the object of Her Majesty's Government to seek through conciliation a settlement which would meet British requirements and the special circumstances of Cyprus. They looked forward to reaching agreement through discussion, and would not be inflexible.

Following Mr. Macmillan, the Greek Foreign Minister, after expressing his thanks to Her Majesty's Government for their initiative in convening the Tripartite Conference, voiced the satisfaction of the Greek Government who had consistently held the opinion that political questions of common concern to friendly and allied States should be solved by direct discussions amongst them.

M. Stephanopoulos then proceeded to a statement of the Greek Government's views on the question of Cyprus and its strategic implications.

He said that Greece recognised the need for Britain's presence for defensive purposes in Cyprus in order to be able to meet British contractual obligations in the Middle East and the Eastern Mediterranean as well as in the interests of Greece's own security. However, the Greek Foreign Minister pointed out that the question of sovereignty did not prejudice nor was it bound up with questions of defence and he quoted the example of N.A.T.O., whose strategic requirements had been successfully met by the establishment of allied bases on various territories without regard to the question of sovereignty.

M. Stephanopoulos repeatedly emphasised that the military and defensive value of the British bases in Cyprus would be enhanced, were the present ill-feeling among the Cypriot population to be changed into a spirit of spontaneous and unqualified co-operation. This result, said M. Stephanopoulos, could only be achieved by granting to the Cypriot population the right of self-determination. This right constituted one of the fundamental principles of the United Nations Charter and could certainly not be denied to a people with the high moral and cultural standards of the Cypriots.

Greece, stated M. Stephanopoulos, had not claimed and did not claim the right to decide by herself on the future destiny of Cyprus. Similarly, she denied that right to any third party, for that was the exclusive prerogative of the population of Cyprus. The Greek Government's sole endeavour had been to secure to the people of Cyprus their right to self-determination within a reasonably short period of time, during which Cyprus would be given self-government.

Greece repudiated all use of violence, which was contrary to her peaceful policy.

Greece, concluded M. Stephanopoulos, was willing to subscribe to any guarantee Her Majesty's Government would wish to have with respect to their military bases in Cyprus as well as any guarantee Turkey would wish to obtain concerning the Turkish minority in Cyprus.

Greece was convinced that, by granting the right of self-determination to the people of Cyprus, the common defence would be strengthened and that Cyprus would thus become a point of further contact and closer union between the three friendly and allied Nations.

M. Zorlu, the Turkish Foreign Minister, in explaining the point of view of the Turkish Government, said that the administration of Cyprus had been transferred to Great Britain in 1878 in return for a commitment on the part of Great Britain to come to the aid of Turkey in case of Russian aggression. According to Article 20 of the Treaty of Lausanne, Turkish sovereignty over Cyprus had lapsed on November 5, 1914, and British sovereignty had been recognised as from that date. The question of the nationality of the inhabitants of the Island had been settled by Article 21, which provided that the inhabitants would acquire British nationality, except for those who opted for Turkish nationality. Hence Cyprus had been exclusively a "matter of concern" for Turkey and Great Britain, and it had been so recognised by all signatories, including Greece, and the fate of Cyprus had been definitely determined by the Treaty of Lausanne.

Consequently, to call for a change in the status of the Island was tantamount to seeking a *modification* of the Treaty. Such a course would upset a whole political settlement in the area based upon the abandonment of an expansionist policy by Greece in return for the acceptance by Turkey of the boundaries of the Treaty of Lausanne, and would create a number of grave questions, which would also enable Turkey to put forward certain demands.

Turkey looked upon the "Cyprus question" as a British domestic issue. Turkey would continue to regard it as such so long as Britain retained sovereignty and the *status quo* was maintained. If there was any question of the Island changing hands, then it should revert to Turkey.

Turkey's interest in Cyprus was based on history, proximity, economy, military strategy, and on the sacred right of all countries to existence and security.

Cyprus was a prolongation of the Anatolian mainland and in all the course of history its fate had followed that of Anatolia. As an integral part of Turkey, the make-up of its population had never been a matter of consideration. Likewise to-day, one could not speak of 100,000 Turks living on the Island without mentioning 300,000 Turkish Cypriots living in Turkey.

Economically too, the Island, which depended for survival on outside aid, was a part of Anatolia, where the food-stuffs it needed were grown in abundance.

Strategically, the vital interests of Turkey and the requirements of defence and logistics made it imperative that the Island should belong either to Turkey or to a country which was as closely interested as Turkey in the fate of Turkey's eastern neighbours.

In case of war, Turkey could only be supplied through her southern ports, and whoever controlled Cyprus was in a position to control those ports.

As a result of the foregoing factors the principle of self-determination could not be applied to Cyprus.

This principle itself, as most international lawyers agreed, was a vague and undefined concept which had often lent itself to exploitation for ulterior motives. It often clashed with the right of sovereignty of States. It could not prevail over realities based on historical, geographical, strategic and security requirements. In itself a noble principle, which Turkey advocated, it must not be allowed to become an element of injustice, insecurity and trouble. Likewise, Turkey was not opposed to self-government, but its undiscerning application must not be allowed to cause trouble.

The two communities now living on the Island had been driven to antagonism. Consequently, what Cyprus needed before self-government was a return to peace and quiet, where clerics refrained from indulging in politics.

Even when the climate became suitable for self-government, the guiding principle should not be a consideration of majorities and minorities, but that of granting full equality to the two groups.

The Cyprus question had been responsible for disturbing the co-operation of three allied countries closely concerned with the Eastern Mediter-ranean. The Turkish position had been clearly stated by Prime Minister Menderes and fully endorsed by the whole Turkish nation including all politi-cal parties. Turkey was extremely eager to maintain friendship and co-operation with Greece and hoped and expected that her friends and Allies, acting in the same spirit, would appreciate her position.

It was agreed that the Conference would be continued by restricted session. The next meeting would be to-morrow, Friday morning, at 11.30 a.m. at Lancaster House.

STATEMENT MADE BY THE RT. HON. HAROLD MACMILLAN AT THE RESTRICTED SESSION HELD ON SEPTEMBER 6, 1955

I think my colleagues of the Conference wish me to begin by welcom-ing to our councils Mr. Lennox Boyd, the Colonial Secretary. He has been on a long journey, he has journeyed 22,000 miles, but, nevertheless, during all this period of his travels—which were arranged a long time ago—I have kept him in close touch with all that we have been doing, and he is now fully apprised of the exact position that we have now reached.

Last Friday, my colleagues will remember, after the first phase of the Conference, when detailed and exhaustive statements of the position of the three Governments had been made by the various delegations, I undertook to search for common ground and to put on Tuesday, that is, to-day, the results of my researches before my colleagues.

M. Stephanopoulos and M. Zorlu were both kind enough to agree to this plan. Although they were not too sanguine as to the success of my endeav-ours, they were generous enough to admire my motives. During the week-end, we have had some agreeable and useful personal contacts, and I have also had the opportunity of full discussion with my colleagues in the British Govern-ment.

I shall now therefore try to fulfil my undertaking. I shall try to analyse the position as I see it, and to expose by this means if I can the common factor of agreement which runs as it seems to me like a vein of gold beneath a great overburden of misunderstanding and confusion. And I shall try to put forward certain proposals on behalf of Her Majesty's Government for the consideration of the Conference.

I must first repeat what I said in my opening speech. Her Majesty's Government feel it necessary to recall to the Conference that this Conference is itself something in the nature of an act of faith, for it is a basic point in the policy of Her Majesty's Government, as indeed I think of all other Gov-ernments, that the internal affairs of Her Majesty's possessions can not ordinarily be discussed with foreign Powers. And we also recognise that in the final analysis the full responsibility for what is done, for good or evil, in any part of Her Majesty's Dominions, lies upon the British Government. This responsibility is one which the British Government cannot escape. Nevertheless, because of the long friendship and firm alliance which binds us with our Greek and Turkish friends, we thought it right to call this Conference as an act of friendship, without any derogation of the principles that these matters are legally and juridically solely within the province of Her Majesty's Government.

If in the course of my proposals we should ask our allies—as we shall—to associate themselves with us in working out the detail of some of these problems, I must say once again that this action cannot be taken as any departure from this general principle.

Meanwhile, I must thank my colleagues for the patience which they have shown in giving us these few days for thought. I have noticed certain impatience, which is not unnatural, for we have, of course, quite consciously not hurried this affair, because, I think, the more we think about it, and the more we meet and talk together, the better it is, whatever the result. My friend, M. Stephanopoulos, has told me of his desire to return to his pressing duties, and my friend, M. Zorlu, I see, has made some public declaration to the same effect. He says that the results of the Conference should be formulated, and that we should "call it a day." Perhaps he will allow me to congratulate him upon his quick grasp of our idiom. I wish I had a Turkish proverb at my disposal, equally apt! However, I think we all feel that if it led to no other result the holding of this Conference has been of great value in getting to know each other's point of view. However, I should certainly not be content if we parted with nothing more accomplished than that. I believe that we can at least set in motion, if we cannot to-day or here complete, a fruitful and constructive line of concrete endeavour. In pursuance, therefore, of my undertaking, I propose to act upon my self-imposed task.

I think my task is threefold: first, to analyse the results of the Conference, secondly, to seek an area of common agreement, and thirdly, to make some specific proposals. As a matter of procedure, and in order to facilitate progress, my staff hope to be able in the course of the afternoon to distribute to you as a Conference paper, in English and in French, a document which will be based upon what I now have to say. You will forgive them if it takes them a little time to complete this, because it has to be brought into line with what I am trying to say now. This document will be a Conference document, and will represent formal proposals tabled by the British Delegation.[12]

I would suggest that you will wish to study it, and if, as I hope, you think these proposals require your careful consideration, I would suggest that we meet here to-morrow at eleven o'clock, when the Colonial Secretary and I would try to answer any questions that might arise out of your study of the document and what I have said to-day, and we will try to elucidate what was obscure, or elaborate what might be too abbreviated or compressed.

I hope that you will find yourselves in agreement. But I could not press my colleagues here to accept, unless they feel able to, these proposals without reference to their colleagues at home. We here, we British, have the

---

[12] See Appendix I.

advantage of the presence of our Prime Minister and all our Cabinet colleagues, and it is therefore quite natural that you may wish to discuss this with your colleagues and your own Governments. Nevertheless, I ask, and I hope you will feel that I am right to ask, that you should study them carefully and sympathetically, and make sure that they are fully understood, so that we can have the full advantage of all the help you obtain from your own Governments.

The exact machinery we could perhaps discuss to-morrow how best to operate it, but the Colonial Secretary and I will be ready, both morning and afternoon, ready to elucidate all points, placing ourselves at your service, and we will hope thereby to bring at any rate this phase of our journey to a satisfactory conclusion, hoping our work may lead on to further fields of co-operation.

I think the first stage of the Conference brought out the fact that, in spite of important differences of opinion all three delegations were agreed upon three vital decisions: first, they are absolutely agreed on the over-riding need, transcending every other consideration, of maintaining the friendship and co-operation and the ties which bind these three countries here represented in close alliance. Secondly, they are, I think, agreed in recognising the key strategic position of Cyprus and the vital contribution which the British with their allies have to make in the maintenance of peace and security. We have undertaken very heavy engagements, which are fully recognised by our colleagues, and it is our duty to carry them out. I think, thirdly, we all hope, we especially, that all of us in our different ways have a duty to the population, the people of Cyprus, to see that their progress and happiness is maintained, and that happy relations should exist between all sections of the population and all communities, that they should advance together in their own life and progress.

Those three things it seemed to me came out of our declarations and our conversations in our private and friendly contacts. I think we are all aware in this room that what we say and do in this building has great importance in this immense world problem. The eyes of our friends are upon us, and also perhaps the eyes of those who are not so friendly, and I think it would really be a disaster, I regard it as quite unthinkable, that this Conference should end in what the world would describe as a failure.

And so, after thinking very carefully—and I have studied very carefully all the declarations that you have made, in detail, and all the results of private conversations—I would put forward for your consideration a line of approach, and more than that, concrete proposals which I think should bring us, if not to a complete agreement on all these matters, at least to a point of mutual understanding between us on which action can be based and from which good can flow towards the cementing of our friendship and alliance.

I think everybody who has listened to these discussions must have reached the conclusion that there are two quite separate problems which we have been trying to tackle. The first really deals with the life of the Cypriot people themselves; the need for the people of great traditions, long and ancient civilisations, to be organised as the modern world demands, and as their traditions give them the right to expect, in a system or a constitution of internal self-government by which they can manage their own internal affairs. There are difficulties and problems confronting us even with this part of the question.

These populations have a different tradition and history, and therefore there must be a system which provides proper safeguards for each, above all one which calls into being a sense of real partnership between all the communities and interests of the people in Cyprus. For whatever legal or constitutional arrangements are made it can only be by the development of a central partnership and common loyalty to each other and themselves that real progress can be made.

This, then, is the first set of problems. The second is a problem, a question of the future international status of Cyprus. I will now deal with the first.

Her Majesty's Government feel—and we believe that the Turkish Government also feel—that if harmony and prosperous life is to be restored and developed in Cyprus, if the Island is to make real progress, then as I have said, in this modern world, there must be a real, genuine advance towards internal self-government, with proper regard, of course, as I have said, to the rights and interests of all concerned.

We believe that, as a result of our meetings here, and the spirit which has been created, there really is now a great opportunity for a new advance, and the British Government confidently call upon their colleagues to help them in this task. It is, of course, their duty—and the British Government will not seek to escape it—to make their proposals themselves. That is our task and our responsibility. In ordinary conditions we should have advanced—as the Colonial Secretary has great experience of doing, in other parts of the world—with our proposals on our own authority. But, in this special relationship that we have together, we do not feel there is any derogation of our dignity, and we certainly feel it to be in conformity with our alliance of friendship, if we should seek your aid and your help in the task which we are determined to undertake.

It is obvious that, if the Greek Government and the Turkish Government feel able to express their approval of and sympathy with the proposals which we shall make, the task of everybody in Cyprus is made easier, and the chances of happy collaboration of all concerned are correspondingly improved. The British Government therefore intend to use every effort at their command to set the people of Cyprus on the normal path of democratic development. There is no one who has more experience of this work, or more sympathy for it, than my friend and colleague, the Colonial Secretary, and I know that he will give all his efforts and imagination to strive towards this new development.

It is obvious, of course, that the strategic requirements which the present international situation demand make it necessary for a form of constitution to leave in the hands of the British Government certain vital powers, matters dealing with foreign policy, defence, security and the like. But, subject to those considerations, it is our hope and intention to see developed a new and liberal constitution, and to give the fullest measure of internal self-government which is compatible with these overriding considerations. We propose, therefore, that the constitution should provide for an Assembly with an elected majority. We propose that all the departments of the Cyprus Government should be progressively transferred to Cypriot Ministers responsible to the Assembly. As usual in these forms of constitutions, there will be the exception that I have said in the case of Foreign Affairs, Defence and Public Security, which are the responsibility of the British Government. There would, of course, be the proper safeguards for the integrity and independence of the Public Service. A Cypriot chief minister would be chosen by the Assembly, with the approval of the Governor, to head the new independent administration. In order to safeguard the true collaboration of all communities, arrangements will have to be made, in our view, for an appropriate quota of seats to be reserved in the Assembly for the Turkish-speaking community, as well as a proportion of ministerial portfolios to be reserved for those representatives in the Government itself.

All this is intended therefore to do two things, and two vital things: the development of true internal self-government among the Cypriot people and the creation and preservation of a true sense of partnership between the communities in Cyprus.

I have spoken, gentlemen, of partnership in the island of Cyprus. We propose a procedure for your consideration which would apply the same conception which we want to build up locally to our own work among the three allies. We propose therefore what I might call a partnership at the centre. We therefore propose a procedure which is none the worse, I think, for being novel and perhaps unique. We propose that this Conference here assembled should set up a Tripartite Committee, which would meet in London, and which would be, as it were, an extension of the collaboration that we have made here between us.

What would be the task of this committee, and what would be the relations between it and Her Majesty's Government? First, the British Government must of course undertake the responsibility of preparing, with my colleague, the Colonial Secretary, a series of proposals for the creation of a constitution. But the British Government would be willing and anxious to place these detailed proposals before our two friends and allies, and ask for their comment and assistance. Obviously one of the most important matters in which the community of advice would be valuable would be the proposals for guaranteeing the interests of the various communities and the proper methods of securing that those guarantees were effective. However, I should hope that the committee would go far beyond that, and it would certainly be open to it to consider other suggestions which might be raised for the general improvement of the cultural and legal status of all the citizens of Cyprus; for instance, we think—and I think rightly—that the people of Cyprus draw very substantial benefits not only from their association in Cyprus with the British community of nations, but also when they go overseas. We have in our Metropolis large numbers of Cypriots who have found it convenient to have the free right of entry into this kingdom, as they have to all other parts of the British Empire. It occurs to us that there may be corresponding arrangements for mutual benefit between the citizens of Cyprus and those of the other two countries here associated with us. All these and similar questions would be within the purview of the committee, and we would be glad to feel that we held the support of our colleagues in making the best possible arrangements that can be made, now and in the future, for the benefit of the people.

This, then, would be the initial task of the Tripartite Committee, to advise the Colonial Secretary and the British Government on the many details involved in setting about this new pattern of self-government for the internal affairs of Cyprus. But I do not regard it by any means as a body that, once the constitution had been launched, was *functus officio*; I regard it as a body that should be continually in being. It would act as the centre for discussing problems and differences arising out of the new developments. Some of these it might not be possible to settle locally, some would be better dealt with in the considerations of the control committee. It would thus represent a permanent, living proof of the world of the co-operation of the three Governments in their task, and particularly in the assistance of the two Governments with the British Government, which is primarily responsible.

I was very glad to see that on this first part of the Conference and its work there was a general measure of agreement. The Greek Government felt that a system of local self-government should be set up, a Cypriot Government. It was a part of their proposal, and indeed it was inherent in their proposal, that such an organism should come into being, because—I am coming to this next—in their proposal for self-determination it was an essential element that the Cypriot Government, representing the Cypriot people, and a Cypriot Assembly, should first be constituted. Therefore I think I can claim, and I hope rightly, that in this part at any rate we are really trying to fulfil, trying to make practical proposals to fulfil in the most sensible way what is the wish of the Greek Government, as well as ours. And I think our Turkish colleagues felt that the development of self-government on internal affairs in Cyprus was a proper and inevitable part of this general forward march of peoples. I think perhaps they would feel that it is entirely our affair to arrange it for ourselves, but I hope they will regard this as an invitation that they will assist us with their sympathy and collaboration in this task, because I feel certain that the difficult work—and we must face it, it is difficult—of bringing about real harmony and progress between the two communities will be enormously assisted if the two Governments would give us their sympathy and their help. With this part, then, the first division of the problem, I believe that we may count confidently on the support and help of the two Governments concerned.

With regard to the precise forms of the proposals, we should be most happy to receive suggestions to improve them and develop them, elaborate them, and make them more effective. All we want is to ask you to study them in the spirit in which I have set them forward, and to help us in making them a real instrument of useful co-operation.

I must now come to the second problem which confronts us. While I think I am right in claiming that on the first aspect of our difficulty, the development of self-government, there is general approval, it would be foolish not to admit that on the second there is not apparent at the moment any measure of agreement—there is serious disagreement. In our statements which were made on behalf of the three delegations, on Tuesday, Wednesday and Thursday of last week, I think we had the great advantage that these statements were made in absolute frankness. The Greek Government stated a proposition in the form in which they now wish to present their views. We all naturally sympathise with the feeling that they have, I was glad to observe—and I hope they will correct me if I am wrong—that the proposal they put forward was not that there should be an immediate transfer of sovereignty for the island of Cyprus from Great Britain to Greece, not that there should be something of the character of a plebiscite, nor indeed that there should be any necessary obligation upon any organisation of the Cypriot people to reach any conclusion in one direction or another. As I understood it, that is what makes it possible to go some way with them. It was their view that there should be set up an instrument and a government or an assembly in Cyprus which, after some period of time—it might be short or long—should have the power of what is ordinarily called self-determination; and this organisation should have the right to determine its international status.

The Turkish Government expressed clearly their view that if there was any question of the abandonment of the sovereignty by Great Britain, then it should revert whence it came, to the sovereignty of Turkey. They defended that position on two grounds: first, the juridical ground, and secondly the strategical necessities of the geographical situation.

The British position, which I have tried to state broadly in my opening speech, is really a simple one. We are very empirical people. We try to deal with facts as we see them. There is nothing permanent in the world, especially in the nuclear world, and in the long story of mankind—no one knows it more than the races and countries bordering on the Mediterranean—there are many changes and permutations which may take place. But we face the facts as they are. We accepted Cyprus as a trust in 1878, to meet certain strategical and political conditions of the world. These strategical and political conditions have reproduced themselves with melancholy and monotonous iteration; and indeed are present to-day to a far greater degree than ever before. Therefore, while we cannot look into the future at a very great distance, we cannot foresee conditions which would enable us to abandon either in one direction or another the trust which we undertook and which we must still carry out.

Then what are we to do? We are practical people here. It is evident that at the moment these three positions cannot be reconciled.

Might I make some observations which occur to me on this dilemma? First, and above all, it would be absolutely tragic if we allowed this situation to make a breach in the alliance and friendship between our three countries. The consequences of such a breach might indeed be formidable and fatal, a breach between the Turco-Greek alliance, a breach between Greece and Great Britain or between Turkey and Great Britain. Why, that is the one thing which would bring comfort to all the dangerous and subversive forces of the world. It would be an act of folly for which all of us would be held guilty by generations that are to come.

I would propose then—I and my colleagues would propose—that the Conference should take the practical and sensible course that is open to it. It should say and record that on this question of the problem of the future international status of Cyprus it is unable to agree. But it will record it in a spirit of saying that we, to use a well-known phrase, "agree to differ." Let there be a moratorium, let there be a period when we can give up any further discussion of this issue and, without abandoning any of our positions *in principle* on this question, that we should continue our collaboration and common action in practice on that part of the problem upon which we are in agreement. Let us then record that position, and say that each member of the Conference is in no way committed, he is not asked to change his position. It is recorded as what it is. For the moment it is not possible to reconcile the different views. As I say, we agree to differ.

I would like to repeat the second part of what I have said. I think it should be expressly recognised between the three Powers that the fact of their co-operation over the introduction of self-government, the first part of my proposal, the fact that they were willing to co-operate, in no way invalidated their respective attitudes over the question of sovereignty; their position in each case was absolutely preserved as a principle.

I would further suggest that when the new constitution has come into working order in Cyprus, and the progress that we hope for has been made towards the election of a representative assembly and government, this Conference should meet again; it should be regarded as adjourned and not wound up. We should meet again with the same terms of reference, to discuss all the military and political problems of the Eastern Mediterranean, including the position of Cyprus. Nothing should be barred, nothing out of order, at such a conference; it should be merely adjourned, and then absolute freedom to raise all these questions will be allowed. We cannot any of us individually probably expect, we do not know whether we expect ourselves, to be in our respective Governments for all time, and we cannot bind our successors, except to say this, that we would regard the Conference as adjourned, and meet, as progress was made in self-government, to take further counsel upon all the questions that we have been discussing here during this week.

I would add that at that next meeting of the full Conference, the Plenary Conference, we would hope to have the immense advantage, of which we are now deprived, we would have properly constituted, constitutionally elected representatives of the Cypriot people.

Finally, the existence of the Tripartite Committee which was watching over and helping in the development of the self-government would be proof that the Conference was really in continual being, for the creation of the Conference responsibility would be a method of permanent standing consultation between the three allied Governments on all these subjects.

Gentlemen, it only remains for me to thank you very much for your kindness to me personally and to my colleagues during these last few days, and to ask you carefully to study, as I am sure you will, the formal document which I hope we shall have ready to circulate in the course of the afternoon. I hope that you will agree that we should meet to-morrow morning to discuss further any points in our proposals, or any counter-proposals that you would wish to make. We shall be willing to consecrate, as I have said, all day to this work, and I do venture, if I may do so, sincerely to ask you to give your helpful thought to what we have tried to propose.

Ours has not been an easy task, but I feel that I can appeal to both of my colleagues to look beyond the more pressing difficulties, of which we are all conscious each in our countries, and to bear in mind in what we finally agree to do the immense responsibilities which lie upon us all, not only towards each other but towards all the other countries of the free world with whom we are associated.

Thank you very much.

SUMMARY OF STATEMENT MADE BY M. STEPHANOPOULOS AT THE RESTRICTED SESSION HELD ON SEPTEMBER 6, 1955, FOLLOWING THE STATEMENT BY THE RT. HON. HAROLD MACMILLAN INTRODUCING THE BRITISH PROPOSALS

M. Stephanopoulos, after welcoming the Colonial Secretary with expressions of pleasure, said that any discussion of the British proposals would be *ad referendum* to his Government, and that he would need certain explanations in regard to them. He did not think that he could offer any suggestions; but certain questions immediately came to his mind. Firstly, he was bound to ask whether any procedure for working out a constitution for Cyprus could be described as democratic if Cypriots were not associated with the task of working it out. Moreover the proposed tripartite committee was bound in his view to interfere with the working of the freely elected Cypriot Government and would thus conflict with the proper functioning of democracy. Secondly, he asked why the traditional British principles applied elsewhere in the Commonwealth, of allowing the ultimate exercise of self-determination by dependent territories could not equally apply in the case of Cyprus. He was not suggesting that Cyprus should be accorded any privileges only that it should not be denied the benefit of normal British policy. He concluded by saying that even if the British proposals were found to be unacceptable he was nevertheless grateful for the realism and tact which Mr. Macmillan had shown in attempting to find a solution.

STATEMENT MADE BY M. STEPHANOPOULOS AT THE RESTRICTED SESSION HELD ON SEPTEMBER 7, 1955

The Greek Delegation, having taken cognisance of the proposals put forward by the Secretary of State for Foreign Affairs on behalf of Her Britannic Majesty's Government at the restricted meeting of September 6, 1955, on the question of Cyprus, regret to find that the proposals in question have not taken at all into account the Greek Government's basic demand and the hopes the latter had founded on the results of the present Conference.

In effect all the Greek Government ask for is the recognition, in favour of the people of Cyprus, of the right to choose the regime they prefer, as well as the creation of the conditions which would make it possible for them to exercise that right in a democratic manner and within a reasonable period of time.

The Greek Delegation specially regret that, contrary to the invariable practice successfully pursued by the United Kingdom in dealing with its dependent peoples—a practice which may by now be regarded us constituting a traditional policy within the Empire—the British Government have chosen to pursue a policy of discrimination towards the people of Cyprus by not admitting in the particular case of Cyprus, that internal self-government shall lead to self-determination.

The Greek Delegation are convinced that, in the event of the question of Cyprus reaching the solution which accords with the internationally recognised principle, the bonds of friendship and alliance, as well as our joint defence, far from being weakened, would, on the contrary, be drawn closer and strengthened through giving satisfaction to the well conceived interests of the three friendly and allied peoples.

The Greek Delegation are pleased to note that Her Britannic Majesty's Government have, through the summoning of this Conference, and by the proposals they have brought forward, recognised the necessity for bringing about a change in the present situation and facing up to the problem of Cyprus.

The Greek Delegation, while already aware of the views of the Royal Government, which are shared by all the political parties and the whole of the Greek people, will not fail to submit the British proposals to the Hellenic Government for their final answer.

We have stated our position with complete frankness and much moderation despite the differences of point of view revealed, we shall part with the resolve to continue our joint efforts for the defence of the Free World and the preservation of Peace.

DISCUSSION REGARDING THE STATEMENT MADE BY THE RIGHT HON. HAROLD MACMILLAN AT THE RESTRICTED MEETING HELD 0N SEPTEMBER 6, 1955

Following this statement by M. Stephanopoulos, *M. Zorlu* said he had also prepared a statement but before making it he wished to put two very important questions to Mr. Macmillan in order to clarify the statement made the previous day on behalf of Her Majesty's Government.

The first was: "Does the British Government intend to maintain in the present and in the future the right of sovereignty on the Island of Cyprus, devolved upon Great Britain by the Treaty of Lausanne?" To this, *Mr. Macmillan* replied as follows: "The British position, which I have tried to state broadly in my opening speech, is really a simple one. We are a very empirical people. We try to deal with facts as we see them. There is nothing permanent in the world and especially in the nuclear world, and in the long story of mankind—no-one knows it better than the races and countries bordering the Mediterranean—there are many changes and permutations which take place; but we face facts as they are.

"We accepted Cyprus as a trust in 1878 to meet certain strategic and political conditions of the world. These strategic and political conditions have reproduced themselves with melancholy and monotonous iteration and indeed are present to-day in a far greater degree than ever before. Therefore, while we cannot look into the future at a very great distance, we cannot foresee conditions enabling us to abandon in one direction or another the trust we undertook and which we must still carry out.

"Perhaps, to put it in a slightly more succinct way, I might add this: in my statement of August 30 I stated British sovereignty over Cyprus was beyond dispute and I explained why Her Majesty's Government regarded it as essential that the United Kingdom should continue to remain in possession of Cyprus in order to enable her to carry out her obligations in the Eastern Mediterranean and in the Middle East. Nothing has since occurred in any way to modify that view and I am bound to say that there is no prospect of any change in the fore-seeable future."

M. Zorlu's second question was: "If the British Government is determined to maintain sovereignty on the Island, does it, for the present or for the future, accept any principle of self-determination which might ultimately lead to the independence of the Island or to its accession to another country?"

To this *Mr. Macmillan* replied: "I think I have already answered that question, M. Zorlu. We do not accept the principle of self-determination, as one of universal application. We think that exceptions must be made in view of geographical, traditional, historical, strategical and other considerations."

STATEMENT MADE DY M. ZORLU AT THE RESTRICTED SESSION HELD ON SEPTEMBER 7, 1955

First of all I would like to express my appreciation of your continuous efforts, ever since the beginning of this Conference, to bring it to a successful conclusion, sometimes by going to the extent of renouncing your rights, at least in form, or refraining from asserting them openly.

But, as I said on the very first day, the Turkish Government has sent me here to explain its views in the most frank and precise manner. You will doubtless realise that in a question such as this, which is of vital importance for the whole Turkish nation, no Turkish Government could have given other instructions.

As I had the occasion to point out before, this Island is of vital importance for Turkey for many reasons, the chief one being the requirements of military security; and it constitutes an integral part of the Turkish mainland from the point of view of geo-politics and physical geography.

The status of Cyprus acquires additional importance inasmuch as it forms a part of the compact of Lausanne to which new Turkey is sincerely attached. It is highly regrettable that this Island, which is a vital factor for the security of Turkey and of the Middle East, and of which the status has been determined by an international accord, should have become, through no fault of Turkey or of Great Britain, and as a result of unjustified claims and incitements, a source of discord between Greece on the one hand and those two countries which have assumed serious responsibilities in the Eastern Mediterranean on the other hand.

The persistence of Greece in her demands in spite of the sincere and friendly warnings made by Turkey during the three years prior to this Conference has brought us to this inextricable position to-day. That is why, in our opinion, the assumption of a clear and unequivocal position in the Cyprus question is not only a national duty for us but also a matter of international responsibility for all three Governments represented here.

The proposals which you have submitted to us have been studied with the greatest care by our Government, and you will doubtless allow me to review each one of the points contained therein. You mentioned yesterday that for the three Governments their alliance and their friendship was a question of vital importance, and it is obvious that Turkey has always attached importance to that alliance and to that friendship. This has been proved, I think, throughout. May I add that the great importance which Turkey has always given to that friendship and to that alliance has been continuously proved, and there is no doubt that the calm and the prudence with which Turkey has up to now handled the question of Cyprus proves how much my country is attached to that friendship and to that alliance.

But, as the Turkish Prime Minister had occasion to say very clearly in his exposé, and as I personally was able to state in my first declaration at this Conference, Turkey considers that the question of Cyprus is of such importance to her that it is extremely difficult to maintain and to safeguard the friendship and the alliance with Turkey while seeking at the same time in one way or another to arrive either at the union of Cyprus with Greece or the giving of self-determination to the Island of Cyprus. It is true that Turkish public opinion and the Turkish Government hold very dear the alliance which links Turkey to its partners, and the friendship which it has for Greece has for my Government and my people a great importance, but we consider that an equal and just as vital importance is attached by the people of Turkey to the question of Cyprus, and to the safeguarding of our interest in the Island of Cyprus.

As I had occasion to tell you, any kind of change in the *status quo* of Cyprus would indeed amount to a revision of the Treaty of Lausanne, because it would affect the vital interests of Turkey; indeed, it would imperil the whole equilibrium which had been set up by this Treaty, and it would certainly impair Greek-Turkish friendship, which has one of its durable bases in that very Treaty.

In your statement, and in the proposals you made yesterday, you indicated that this problem, this question of Cyprus, had two main aspects. According to your proposals, one aspect of the question was that of self-government for the Island of Cyprus, an aspect on which you stated that the three interested parties had reached a certain measure of agreement.

The second aspect was that of sovereignty over the Island or of self-determination or, in a word, as you defined in your statement, the international status of the Island of Cyprus. You very clearly stated, yesterday, that there was a divergence of views on this point between Great Britain and Turkey on the one hand and Greece on the other. Whilst noting this divergence of views, you proposed that we should leave on one side this point on which there was no agreement, and should seek agreement on the aspect of self-government or internal autonomy for the Island.

I regret to have to tell you, on behalf of the Turkish Government, that it is impossible for us to share this view.

It is clear that as long as the three partners are not agreed on this question of self-determination for the inhabitants of the island of Cyprus, it is impossible for them to go forward towards implementing or trying self-government for the Island. And I think, in order to reach agreement on so important a point, the three partners must have been able to reach a preliminary agreement. The partner who has raised the question of the self-determination of peoples should retract this request in order that we may co-operate harmoniously in setting up the proposed regime of self-government in the island, otherwise this partner might do everything in its power to slant self-government towards self-determination, and this would not only imperil the harmony of the island, but it might also produce further troubles which would impair our international life as a whole.

On behalf of the Turkish Government, I was already able in my first statement to set out the conditions under which self-government could be set up in the island. An essential condition of this was the giving up of any idea of self-determination. Another equally essential and vital condition would be the complete cessation of the present troubled conditions in the island, and of the present antagonism between the two communities living on the island. In order to fulfil these essential conditions, the Turkish Government considers that the Greek Government should give up its present demand for the application of the principle of self-determination.

It should not be said that the Turkish Government has not understood the point of view of and the aim pursued by Her Majesty's Government in dividing the problem of Cyprus into two, and seeking first a solution to the question of self-government; and the Turkish Government would like to pay tribute to the spirit of abnegation and self-sacrifice shown by our friend and partner, a spirit in which you have been led even to appear to renounce your legitimate rights, either by only making a passing reference to them, some-times by not referring to them but only allowing them to be understood. In fact, Her Majesty's Government have gone so far in this course, in their desire to reach an agreement, that my Government had some doubts as to the real purpose, the real intent of Her Majesty's Government, and that is why I felt obliged this morning to ask you certain questions. The British Government have certainly worked, they have done their best to bring about agreement and to maintain harmony between our three Governments, and if my Government has not been able to follow her partner along this path, it is because my Government does not think that it was the proper way in which we could reach agreement, in which we could put an end to and remove all the forces of conflict which at present exist between us.

Another reason which prevents the Turkish Government from following Great Britain along this path is that the question is really of greater and more vital importance for Turkey, since geo-physically speaking this island is a part of Anatolia, and Turkey happens to be in Anatolia. Consequently the fate of the island has a vital and national importance and interest for us.

On the other hand, the Turkish Government thinks that the British Government, faced by the very clear provisions of the Treaty of Lausanne, cannot entertain any outside claims, or accept the formulation of any such claims, on the Island of Cyprus. This is the legal, the juridical point of view. From the political point of view as well, in the opinion of the Turkish Government, the Greek Government should not raise any claim on the Island of Cyprus, if it prizes Greek-Turkish friendship. That is why the Turkish Government thinks it is much better, both in the national interests and in the interests of the free world, which aspires for peace, that the three Governments should express their positions clearly and frankly, stating their claims, their responsibilities, and the direction which they think should be given to the solution of this problem. It is the only frank, sincere and clear way in which we can solve the present question, which has unfortunately created events which are very far from uniting us. We have witnessed these events: we have seen that Turkey has had to proclaim martial law as a result of them. In Greece, the Turkish Embassy and Consulate are under the protection of police cordons, and in Cyprus British troops have been hard put to it to preserve order in the Island.

This shows us, Sir, how far this question has led us, and what results it has already produced.

I think that public opinion in our three countries must be informed, clearly and frankly, of just what the problem is, and be made to understand just where this problem might lead us. And it is only then, in full possession of all the facts, that they can assume their full responsibility in the matter. So long as we cannot do this we shall not get anywhere. The British Government, as we have seen to-day, while not pressing its rights or not making reference to them, cannot follow any other course. I think that by not making this clear, we shall end in a situation where the public opinion of one of the three partners, that is to say the one which has a divergence of views with us, will push its Government towards an ever-increasing intransigency and towards greater imprudence, in the ignorance of the real scope of their responsibilities. I think people should understand clearly the dangers which lie along such a path.

That is why my Government still considers our present Conference as having been useful and fruitful in making it possible for our three Governments to state clearly and definitely their points of view. Consequently, the Turkish Government, after a careful study of the British proposals, while respecting the motives which prompted these proposals is obliged to refer to the first statement which I had the honour to make in this Conference, and to state that the Turkish Government does not change its position as set out in that statement; and, on the subject of Cyprus and its *status quo*, feel, that this *status quo* was created by an international treaty to which we were all signatories, and it must be maintained. Furthermore, if any changes were to take place in the *status quo* of the Island, this Island should come back to Turkey. And my Government does not think that under present conditions self-government in the Island is possible. This will not be possible until the Greek Government has given up its claims either for the annexation of the Island of Cyprus, its union with Greece, or for the application of the principle of the self-determination of peoples to the Island, and also, as I have already said, there must be a return to calm in the Island before any self-government could be applied.

That is the position of the Turkish Government, its answers to the proposals which you made in the name of Her Majesty's Government. This is my Government's final answer, but I would like to add that I reserve the right for my Government, should it think fit and deem it necessary, to make some additions to this statement. Of course, such possible additions will not change the substance of this statement of views. I will have copies of my statement ready this afternoon.

TEXT OF FINAL AGREED COMMUNIQUÉ ISSUED ON SEFTEMBER 7, 1955

The Tripartite Conference on the Eastern Mediterranean and Cyprus held further restricted meetings this morning and this evening. At this morning's meeting the Greek Foreign Minister made an interim reply to the statement made yesterday by the British Foreign Secretary. The Turkish Foreign Minister made a full and definitive reply on behalf of his Government. The British Foreign Secretary, Mr. Macmillan, undertook, before making any further proposal, to study these statements and to await the full reply of the Greek Government and any additions which the Turkish Government might wish to make to their statement. Meanwhile the Tripartite Conference on the Eastern Mediterranean and Cyprus, which has been meeting in London since August 29, stands suspended.

The text of the British proposals put forward to the Conference on September 6 and of certain other relevant statements made at the Conference are being released to the press.

APPENDIX I

TEXT OF PROPOSALS PUT FORWARD BY THE RT. HON. HAROLD MACMILLAN ON BEHALF OF HER MAJESTY'S GOVERNMENT AT THE RESTRICTED SESSION ON SEPTEMBER 6, 1955

The first stage of the Conference has shown that, despite certain important differences of opinion, all three Delegations are agreed upon the overriding importance of maintaining their friendship and co-operation and the ties which bind them in alliance. They are also agreed in recognising the key strategic position of Cyprus and the vital contribution of the British military headquarters and base in the Island to the maintenance of peace and security in the areas of the Eastern Mediterranean and the Middle East. They also share the desire to further the welfare of the population of Cyprus, to put an end to the acts of violence which have recently been disturbing the community and to restore harmony between all sections of the population.

2. The British Delegation are convinced therefore that their colleagues will agree that it would be unthinkable that the present Conference should end in a failure, which would run counter to their common objectives and impair their friendship and alliance, which all recognise as essential in the present state of world affairs. Having made a careful analysis of the respective positions of the three Delegations as disclosed at the Conference, the British Delegation wish to offer the following observations and proposals as a basis for the common understanding which they are confident it will be possible to reach:

3. It is clear that there are two main problems in determining the future of Cyprus. The first of these comprises the introduction and operation of a new constitution leading to internal self-government by the Cypriot people, under the proper safeguards and guarantees required by the international situation and the protection of the interests of the communities concerned. The second of these is the future international status of Cyprus.

4. With regard to the first of these two problems, the British Delegation believe that their colleagues share the opinion of Her Majesty's Government that an essential element in the restoration of harmony in Cyprus and in the future progress of the island must be a progressive advance towards internal self-government, with proper regard for the rights and interests of all parties. The British Delegation are confident therefore that the way is open for the Conference to establish a large measure of agreement upon the necessary plans and procedures for attaining this end. It is the responsibility of Her Majesty's Government to introduce the necessary constitutional measures, but, in view of the close interest which the Governments of Greece and Turkey naturally take in the welfare of the Greek and Turkish communities within Cyprus, the British Delegation wish to put before their colleagues the following proposals and to discuss them with a view to reaching common agreement. Her Majesty's Government would hope to obtain the expressed approval of the Greek and Turkish Governments for this programme, since it is evident that this would be of the greatest importance in securing the full co-operation of the Cypriot people. In thus inviting the co-operation of the Greek and Turkish Governments in this task, the British Delegation are in no way departing from

the principle which has already been emphasised by the Foreign Secretary in his remarks to the Conference that Her Majesty's Government are solely responsible for the internal affairs of Her Majesty's possessions.

5. The proposals of Her Majesty's Government are intended to set Cyprus upon the normal path of democratic development. To this end Her Majesty's Government propose the introduction of a new and liberal constitution leading to the fullest measure of internal self-government compatible with the strategic requirements of the present international situation. The constitution would provide for an Assembly with an elected majority, a proportionate quota of seats being reserved for the Turkish community. All Departments of the Cyprus Government would be progressively transferred to Cypriot Ministers, responsible to the Assembly, with the exception of Foreign Affairs, Defence and Public Security, which would be reserved to the Governor. There would be proper safeguards for the integrity and independence of the Public Service. As part of the safeguards to be provided for the Turkish community, a proportion of the Ministerial portfolios would be reserved for that community. A Cypriot Chief Minister to head the new Cypriot administration would be chosen by the Assembly with the approval of the Governor.

6. Her Majesty's Government propose that a special Tripartite Committee should be set up in London by the present Conference, and should be responsible to it, in order to examine detailed proposals to be drawn up by Her Majesty's Government for new constitutional instruments for Cyprus. It would be the duty of this Tripartite Committee to consider a suitable system of guarantees for the interests of the communities in Cyprus and the appropriate method of their implementation. The Committee might investigate any suggestions for the further benefit of the Cypriot population from the point of view of the close links between Cyprus and the United Kingdom, Greece and Turkey, for example, questions concerning the status and rights of Cypriots within the other three countries.

7. After completing its initial tasks the Tripartite Committee might be kept in being in order to receive reports regarding the development of self-government in Cyprus, and to act as a centre for discussing problems or differences arising out of self-government which it had not been possible to resolve locally in Cyprus.

8. With regard to the second of these main problems a divergence of view is unfortunately apparent between the three Delegations. It is evident that these positions cannot at present be reconciled. But the British Delegation feel strongly that this fact should not be allowed to create a breach between the three countries with very unfortunate and incalculable consequences to their co-operation as friends and allies in all the many fields of common endeavour. Nor should failure to settle this aspect of the problem at this time be allowed to destroy the wide measure of agreement established in regard to the other main problem of internal self-government.

9. Consequently the British Delegation propose that the Conference should record that it is unable to agree upon the problem of the future international status of Cyprus. The Conference would at the same time agree that each Government retains the position which it has taken up at the Conference and is in no way committed by the proceedings of the Conference to change its

attitude. It would in particular be expressly recognised between the three parties that the fact of their co-operation over the introduction of self-government in no way invalidated their respective attitudes over the question of sovereignty.

10. When the new constitution has come into working order in Cyprus, Her Majesty's Government would be prepared to call the Conference together again to take counsel once more together on the military and political problems of the Eastern Mediterranean, including the situation in Cyprus. It is hoped that sufficient progress will have been made to allow elected representatives of the Cypriot people to be associated with the Conference. In the meantime the Special Tripartite Committee proposed in connexion with the programme of self-government will serve as a standing instrument of consultation between the three allied Governments.

APPENDIX II

REPLY OF THE GREEK GOVERNMENT TO THE UNITED KINGDOM PROPOSALS MADE ON SEPTEMBER 6, 1955

(Athens—September 17, 1955)

On September 17 the reply of the Royal Greek Government to the British proposals was delivered in a Note Verbale to Her Majesty's Embassy at Athens. The following is the text:

The Royal Greek Government have the honour to communicate to Her Britannic Majesty's Embassy the answer to the British proposals put forward at the recent conference in London to which the Minister for Foreign Affairs, M. Stephanopoulos, had reserved the Athens Government's reply.

The Royal Greek Government were glad to note during the Tripartite Conference in London that the British Government had departed, to a certain extent, from their original inflexible attitude over the Cyprus question.

Unfortunately, the good intentions and hopes with which the Royal Greek Government came to the London Conference failed to meet with a favourable response on two capital points; namely, the right of self-determination and the right of self-government, on both of which it was impossible to reach agreement.

As regards the right to self-determination of the Cypriot people, in support of which the Royal Greek Government had appealed to the United Nations and had succeeded in obtaining its inscription, discussion of the question having been deferred "for the time being," the Royal Greek Government met with an absolute refusal on the part of the British Government.

Regardless of the above-mentioned main position of the Royal Greek Government with reference to the principle of self-determination, and although Her Britannic Majesty's Government showed themselves disposed to make certain concessions as regards the right of self-government of the Cypriot people, by granting a constitution, however this constitution was of a type that could not be regarded as adequate for so highly developed and civilised a people as the Cypriots. Her Britannic Majesty's Government proposed the establishment of a Tripartite Commission which would have the right to intervene in the administration of Cyprus under the proposed self-government, thereby rendering the self-government so promised, purely theoretical.

For the reasons given above, the Royal Greek Government find themselves unable, to their great regret, to accept the British proposals.

APPENDIX III

TEXT OF SPEECH DELIVERED BY THE RT. HON. ANTHONY NUTTING IN THE PLENARY ASSEMBLY OF THE UNITED NATIONS ON SEPTEMBER 23, 1955

The Greek Foreign Minister has just asked that the Assembly should reject the recommendation of the General Committee against the inscription of an item on Cyprus on the agenda of the tenth session. I was sorry to hear him challenge that recommendation because I am convinced that the course of wisdom is to accept it. I believe we should all be wise to accept what is, I am sure, the general opinion in the Assembly that it is not appropriate for the Assembly to go into this matter.

I know that some delegations have held the view that as a matter of principle any item should be inscribed on the agenda at the request of any Member State. They may feel that they do not want to oppose inscription, but at the same time they are anxious to avoid discussion. But I would point out that you cannot in practice draw a distinction between inscription and discussion. Once an item is inscribed, it is down for discussion and it stays down for discussion until it has been disposed of by discussion. Therefore, I do suggest that, in wisdom and in prudence, we should consider each item proposed for our agenda, and therefore for discussion, on its merits. I do suggest that before we inscribe any item we should ask ourselves whether the inevitable discussion of that item will help or hinder.

I listened with great attention to all that the Greek representative said on Wednesday in the General Committee. But I could not fail to notice that he did not attempt to answer the basic argument upon which I presented the case against inscription and discussion of the Cyprus issue. Indeed, M. Melas said that I rested the burden of my argument on Article 2 (7), that is, on whether the Assembly is competent to discuss this issue or not. I would ask M. Melas to look at my speech. If he does so, he will see that whilst I reserved my Government's position on the issue of competence, my whole argument was addressed to the two practical and all important questions: first, whether inscription and discussion of this issue in a public forum would help to find a solution or whether a settlement could not better be found by quiet diplomacy conducted in private? Secondly, whether inscription and debate here would help to promote that period of calm which is so urgently needed by the Administration and by the people of Cyprus?

I also listened to M. Stephanopoulos to-day. He, too, failed to reply to my simple contention that private negotiation and not public debate is the way to try to settle this problem. M. Stephanopoulos repeated the claim that the General Assembly, by its resolution of last year (814 (IX)), prejudged its decision on inscription and discussion for this tenth session. But last year's resolution decided that it was not appropriate to go into the matter further.

I will therefore repeat, what I said in the General Committee on Wednesday, 21st September, that what last year's resolution does is to place the onus on the representative of Greece to show that it is now appropriate for the United Nations to debate, and to pass judgment on this issue. But he has not done so. Neither in the General Committee was it done, nor was the case proved or attempted to be proved here in the General Assembly.

M. Stephanopoulos talked about the London Tripartite Conference which he attended. I shall not repeat the very full account which I gave on Wednesday of that Conference; this is on record and is within the knowledge of the whole Assembly. But I must say that I was astounded to hear the assessment, given by M. Stephanopoulos to-day and by M. Melas yesterday, of that Conference. M. Stephanopoulos, if I heard him correctly, said to-day that the possibilities of negotiation were exhausted. M. Melas, speaking for the Greek Government in the General Committee on Wednesday, described the London Conference as a tragic intermezzo bound to fail even before it began.

I must say that I am not so pessimistic. I refuse to believe that a solution of this difficult problem could never have been found and cannot still be found by diplomacy. With goodwill, these problems can be solved. I did not claim, at the meeting of the General Committee on Wednesday, as M. Melas said, that the London Conference was an "achievement"; that was the word which he used. On the contrary, I made it clear that the Conference stood suspended in disagreement. The whole purpose of what I said about the Conference was to show that it could have been a good beginning, and I am still convinced that, following on the proposals that my Government made at that Conference, we can still make a start on the path to settlement. This can be done if our two friends, Greece and Turkey, not only share our aims but are prepared to work out with us the means to translate them into practice. These two aims, I repeat, are first, to foster the well-being of the population of Cyprus and to promote as rapidly as possible their constitutional development towards self-government and, secondly, to maintain and cement their friendship and alliance with Greece and Turkey.

M. Melas described the proposals which we made as unconstructive and unhelpful. That was the statement of the Greek representative in the General Committee. But let us look for a brief moment at what these proposals were.

Mr. Macmillan, to whom M. Stephanopoulos referred a moment ago, put forward proposals which made the most of a considerable area of common ground. He proposed that we should agree to agree on as much as we could, and agree, for the moment, to differ where we could not agree. Leaving on one side, therefore, the future international status of Cyprus, he put forward a set of proposals designed to set Cyprus on the road to self-government. He proposed the introduction of a liberal constitution designed to lead to the fullest measure of self-government compatible with the strategic requirements of the present international situation. There would be, from the outset, an assembly with an elected majority, a proportionate quota of seats being reserved for the Turkish community. All departments of the Cyprus Government would be progressively transferred to Cypriot Ministers responsible to the assembly, with the sole exception of foreign affairs, defence and public security. As part of the safeguards to be provided for the Turkish community, a proportion of the ministerial portfolios would be reserved for that community. A Cypriot chief Minister would head the new Cypriot administration. These are described by the representative of Greece as unconstructive proposals.

Mr. Macmillan also proposed a tripartite committee of the three Powers which would, among other things, act as a standing body for consultation and co-operation between the three Governments on Cypriot problems.

I was amazed to hear M. Melas describe this proposal as the negation of democracy. He even used, though he said that he did not wish to use it, the word "mockery." He depicted the tripartite committee as a group of overlords who would dominate the whole self-governing administration of Cyprus. M. Stephanopoulos a moment ago described, if I heard his words correctly, this tripartite committee as the three masters of the people of Cyprus.

But what, in fact, is the truth? What is this tripartite committee to do? This body would be a consultative body, not a governing body. In the first place, it was designed to enable my Government to have the benefit of the views of our Greek and Turkish allies on the actual form of the constitution. It is also designed to provide the means by which the three Governments could keep in continuous touch with one another about the affairs of Cyprus, to associate with the affairs of Cyprus the Governments of Turkey and Greece. And it was hoped to provide the means to reconvene the Tripartite Conference with the association of elected Cypriot representatives when the constitution was in full and working effect.

I was sorry, and indeed astonished, to hear two representatives of the Greek Government, including the Greek Foreign Minister himself, complaining in such bitter terms of a proposal intended to help his country to maintain contact with and interest in the future and the affairs of Cyprus. Such objections, springing from the representatives of Greece in this Assembly and accompanied by such a misleading picture of the true facts and real intentions of these British proposals, can only go to prove once more that the real aim of Greece—and I say this with a heavy heart about a friend—is the acquisition of Cyprus and not the development of constitutional self-government in the island.

This is the root of the matter. What we are here confronted with is not a colonial issue. This is a straight, if disguised, bid for Enosis—that is, for the union of Cyprus with Greece.

On Wednesday I said, and I repeat here to-day, that my Government is most anxious to press forward with the development of self-government in Cyprus. I said that my Government was ready to resume discussion of the Cyprus question with the Greek and Turkish Governments at any time. I repeat—at any time we are ready to resume discussion. Our proposals stand, but we are ready to consider amendments or counter-proposals. I do not honestly see what more can be expected of us. I am only sorry that I heard no answering echo in the speeches on Wednesday or to-day of representatives of Greece. Nor have I heard of any response to my offer to resume discussion. On the contrary, the representatives of Greece have both ignored my offer and insisted upon pressing this item for debate in public in the United Nations.

The General Committee took the course of wisdom in deciding against inscription, but to-day our Greek friends and colleagues seek to challenge that recommendation. I will not weary the Assembly with a repetition of all that I said on Wednesday about the dangerous precedents which the inscription of this item would set. I will say only that the Assembly must not admit that

Member States can use the United Nations to promote claims on a neighbour's territory or to set aside treaties to which they are parties. But what would be the consequences in this particular case of debating these inflammable issues in the United Nations? None of us can be in any doubt that tempers would run high. None of us can doubt that there would be a bitter debate. None of us can doubt that the debate would solidify existing differences, crystallise present positions and heighten existing tensions. Could this possibly help to produce a settlement? That is the problem. That is the sole and simple issue. That is the all-important question we must all decide.

The last thing which my Government wishes to do is to quarrel with an old friend and ally. Nothing is more painful. We want to settle this problem. We want to remove the only barrier between us—for I know of no other. We do not want to stifle freedom of discussion. All we ask, in the name of statesmanship and wisdom, is a chance to settle this problem in peace, in calm, in quiet, to give time for reflection, to allow patient diplomacy and negotiation to play their essential parts.

For my part, I pledge solemnly, on behalf of my Government, an unremitting endeavour to work out a solution to this tangled, difficult and delicate issue. I appeal, therefore, to this Assembly to uphold the judgment and recommendation of its General Committee. I trust that I shall not appeal in vain.

APPENDIX 7

Constitutional Proposals for Cyprus: Report Submitted to the Secretary of State for the Colonies by the Right Hon. Lord Radcliffe, G.B.E., December 1956*

CONTENTS

COVERING NOTE AND STATEMENT OF PROPOSALS

---

* Cmnd. 42 (London: HMSO, 1956).

COVERING NOTE

I have the honour to present to you my recommendations for a new Constitution for Cyprus. I have drawn them up in the form of a single continuous document instead of expressing them in a series of separate recommendations and I hope therefore that they will be capable of speaking for themselves to those who read the document as a whole. At the same time I think it desirable that I should preface them with a brief commentary indicating what have presented themselves to me as the main features of my proposals and the reasons why I have preferred them to other possible arrangements which were proposed to me or which suggested themselves during the course of my work.

2.   I am not attempting in this to present to you a formal Report. The conditions under which I have done my work and the general desire that I should make my proposals available within as short a space of time as circumstances allowed would have made that impossible, even if I thought that a comprehensive survey of the Cyprus problem could add much to what is already known and has been often said about its several intractable elements. My recommendations are, in effect, the best Report that I can make.

3.   There are one or two preliminary points that I ought to make clear, so that my proposals should not be in danger of being considered in a setting in which I have not intended to place them. The first point is that, though, as requested, I have used all speed in bringing my proposals forward, I have not assumed that the Constitution they envisaged could be put into operation in Cyprus as it is to-day. It is a Constitution appropriate to a state of affairs in which men may express their will by voting and their views by speaking without fear of terrorism or intimidation: in which, on the other hand, Government does not have to impose or maintain those emergency measures, distorting ordinary life, which are the unavoidable counterpart of terrorism itself. In other words, my proposals contemplate a Cyprus in which it has been possible to declare that the present emergency has come to an end. I have no views as to when that time may come. Organised murder and violence have thrown a shadow over the Island which with only lift with the goodwill of many people. But it is possible to hope that the prospect of a Constitution with its fruitful possibilities of peaceful self-government may do something to bring nearer the end of the emergency itself.

4.   The other point is that the Constitution which I am dealing with is the Constitution of a territory which is under the sovereignty of Her Majesty The Queen—that, in fact, is what is laid down in the first of my Terms of Reference. It is not therefore within the province of such a Constitution to provide for or to provide against the possibility of a change in the international status of Cyprus or to prescribe conditions or guarantees attendant upon the occurrence of such an event. On the contrary, I think it plain law that there is no power in the Legislature of a self-governing dependency to change the status of the territory by union under a different sovereign. Acts or resolutions directed to such a purpose would be null. If such changes were to come about, they would have to come about by other means and by instruments designed for the pur-

pose. The Constitution as to which I am to make proposals is not one of them and I do not refer to the matter further.

5.   It is convenient that at this stage I should set out in full my terms of reference which you communicated to me on the 13th day of September last.

> "To make recommendations as to the form of a new Constitution for Cyprus which shall be consistent with the following requirements:
>
> (a) that during the period of the Constitution Cyprus is to remain under British sovereignty;
>
> (b) that the use of Cyprus as a base is necessary for the fulfilment by Her Majesty's Government of their international obligations and for the defence of British interests in the Middle East and the interests of other Powers allied or associated with the United Kingdom;
>
> (c) that all matters relating to external affairs, defence and internal security are retained in the hands of Her Majesty's Government or the Governor;
>
> (d) that, subject to this, the Constitution is to he based on the principles of liberal democracy and is to confer a wide measure of responsible self-government on elected representatives of the people of Cyprus, but is at the same time to contain such reservations, provisions and guarantees as may be necessary to give a just protection to the special interests of the various communities, religions and races in the island."

6.   I have not thought it my duty under this Commission to present to you as my proposals a draft of the complete instrument or instruments which would be needed to bring a Constitution into immediate operation. It would be premature to do so, anyway; but, apart from that, I know by experience that the niceties of legal phrasing and the accumulation of details which, though necessary, are not illuminating, tend to obscure for the reader the true purport of the whole scheme. What matters at this stage is the general outline, and it has throughout been my wish to keep that general outline as clear and simple as possible. My proposals are therefore to be read as instructions for a draftsman, not as a draft itself. I am afraid that in the result I cannot put them forward as being simple, because the complexity of the various interests that have to be recognised and provided for does preclude simplicity. A diarchy itself, such as results from the reservation of certain powers, is a complicated conception. But I hope that I have found a form of expression which is reasonably clear. For that purpose I have avoided technical language as far as I can, I have been explicit at points where much past experience suggests that it might nevertheless be wiser to substitute vagueness for precision and, though my draft has in the end become a great deal more detailed than at the beginning I hoped to find necessary, it does, I think, include everything that a reader, having appreciated the main ideas, would wish to know by way of detail in order to see how they are intended to be applied.

7.   In constitutional proposals it is usual that two conflicting influences should weigh against each other. On the one hand there is the natural desire to define terms and to express meticulously the powers and limitations proposed. On the other hand, it is well to recognise that a written Constitution is no more than a legal framework for a political body in which there is inherent the capacity of growth and development. From the latter point of view too

rigid a formulation is a positive mischance. I recognise this, and indeed it is hardly necessary to say that no Constitution under which political power is divided can provide answers to all questions or solutions to all problems. But in the conditions under which a Constitution is to be proposed for Cyprus I am firmly of the opinion that the preponderating advantage lies in constructing as precise a framework as is reasonably possible.

8.   The conditions are so specific that I ought briefly to indicate them. For the last 25 years Cyprus has been governed without political institutions that can be described as responsible or elective, except so far as certain organs of municipal or local self-government have filled the void. The maker of laws and the chief of administration has been the Governor, assisted, of course, by the advice of a Council and of his permanent officials. More than that, if one looks further back into the history of the Island, one sees that no established political tradition has had the opportunity of forming itself in Cyprus. In that setting to undertake the responsibilities of democratic self-government is inevitably to undertake an experiment with but little data to work upon. It seems to me only fair to all those who may be concerned in carrying out the experiment that they should be presented at the outset with as clear a picture as pencil can draw of the range and limits of their respective functions, rather than that the frontiers should be felt to be defined by trial and error or constitutional convention. For I fear that under the stress of such day-to-day exploration the constitution itself might begin to crack.

9.   There is a second consideration which argues the same way. The new distribution of political power which is involved in the very granting of the Constitution is a matter of the gravest concern to the different communities which make up the people of Cyprus. Whatever recommendations I make, they are bound to be scrutinised with a suspicious care by those who feel with justice that their future is staked upon the form such recommendations assume. I would like to hope that what I put forward will meet those misgivings. But in any event I think that it is to everyone's advantage that the guarantees proposed should be framed in as rigid and as inflexible a manner as may be—and by guarantees I do not mean merely the expression of what I have called in my draft the "fundamental rights" but I mean also the various special provisions, such, for instance, as the placing of broadcasting under public institutional control or the setting up of a Public Service Commission, which I put forward as being no less essential to the preservation of the rights of separate communities than the defined rights themselves. Strictly speaking, it is impossible to set up a representative Legislature in a British colonial territory under a constitution which unalterably limits its powers, unless the constitution is enacted by law of the United Kingdom Parliament itself. But for all that I do put forward what I propose as being in effect a rigid constitution, and the conditions which I suggest should govern any move to vary it on the part of the popular Assembly are such that there seems no practical likelihood of any variation on a matter of substance which affects the interests of the different communities. Even so, a law which seeks to vary the constitutional powers of the Legislative Assembly is one of the very few cases in which, according to my scheme, assent would be reserved by the Governor for Her Majesty and would not be a local matter for him as Governor of Cyprus.

10.   There are two main problems involved in the framing of the Constitutional form. The first is, how to express the relationship between the control of external affairs, defence and internal security, which are reserved from the local Legislature, and the control of the other matters which will fall within the scope of that Legislature. The other is, how to impose such restrictions on the local Legislature as to secure effective protection—protection "with teeth"—for the minorities in the Island. When I use the word "minorities" I do not at all forget that the minorities are themselves racial communities which possess, though in varying degrees, historical traditions and religious, cultural and social bonds different from those of the majority race in Cyprus, the Greek Cypriot.

11.   As to the first, it results from the reservation of powers that Cyprus will be governed under a system of diarchy. There will be two law-making authorities, their fields distinguished according to their subjects, and two distinct forms of administrative control. The idea of diarchy is familiar enough in the history of the developing relationship between the United Kingdom as an imperial Power and the overseas territories which have come within or passed without her central control. There is great variety in the forms in which it has been expressed—by subjecting Bills in the popular Assembly to the necessity of the Governor's consent before they can be introduced, by the use of an official majority, by leaving the Governor free to withhold assent from numerous categories of Bills if he considers that anyone of them prejudices reserved or protected interests, by giving the Governor power to enact legislation on certain subjects in the name of the popular Legislature if the Legislature itself will not take the action required.

12.   In the present case I have come to the conclusion that the most suitable form is that which recognises most explicitly the existence of the diarchy and its consequences. Accordingly I have proposed to invest the Governor with full law-making and executive power for his reserved field, and to leave the local Legislature correspondingly full master in its own field. There will thus be two systems of law-making existing side by side but separated according to the difference of subject with which they deal. I regard this as the system of diarchy which is simplest to present as a conception and which is most easily understood by those not concerned with the niceties of its application. If a public emergency should arise that of course must be dealt with by special provisions but it is better that the Crown should not retain any further reserved or supplemental powers of making laws for Cyprus by Order in Council, except the unavoidable power to alter the Order in Council itself which sets up the Constitution. It is better, I think, that the Governor and the local Legislature should be able to feel that, between them, they possess the full law-making powers for Cyprus, so long as the Constitution is in being and is honoured by observance.

13.   I do not mean it as a hollow phrase when I say that under my proposals the local Legislature and, as a consequence, the Ministers responsible to it, are intended to be masters in their own, the non-reserved, field. It seems to me that a generous interpretation of my terms of reference in this respect is a fair exchange for the considerable reduction of the full possible scope of responsible self-government which results from the reservation of defence and internal

security. Self-government is not, of course, a phrase with a single precise meaning nor does it connote a single identifiable form of government. It has in fact been used to cover a wide gradation of limited political systems amounting to less than full self-government. But in considering the possible application of such measures to a Constitution for Cyprus I have deliberately rejected schemes of "phasing," the progressive release of selected departments by stages into the hands of the self-governing side, each stage measured by proved success in the responsible handling of its predecessor. I do not think such an approach, however appropriate in other circumstances, is appropriate to this Cyprus Constitution. The people of Cyprus, I have reminded myself, are an adult people enjoying long cultural traditions and an established educational system, fully capable of furnishing qualified administrators, lawyers, doctors and men of business. It is a curiosity of their history that their political development has remained comparatively immature. It is owed, I think, to a people so placed that, when they are invited to assume political responsibility, the offer should be generous in the sense that, within the field offered, no qualification or restriction should be imposed that is not honestly required by the conditions of the problem.

14.   Consistently with this I have pared away from my proposals a number of those features that are often present in colonial constitutions, even those which present a comparatively advanced stage of development. I have not proposed the introduction of any official members into the Legislative Assembly. I have proposed so restricted a number of nominated members, 6 out of a total of 36, that no one can suspect that they represent an obscure attempt to give the Governor a residual influence upon the elected body. On the other hand, nominated members do serve at least the convenient purpose of allowing the smaller minorities to obtain some representation without the formalities of separate communal rolls. In addition I propose that the categories of legislation as to which the Governor is to be free to reserve assent for Her Majesty's pleasure should be reduced to the bare minimum of four: Bills that seek to alter the Constitution in some respect, Bills affecting currency, coinage or foreign exchange, Bills affecting the Royal prerogative, and Bills affecting the trustee status of Cyprus Government stock. In all other matters that come within the self-governing field the Governor is to have the duty of a constitutional head of government to assent according to his Ministers' advice subject to reference to the Supreme Court for a judicial ruling upon any Bill that may appear to be itself repugnant to the various guarantees or restrictions which the Constitution imposes. Lastly, I have omitted altogether any provision for disallowance of Cyprus legislation by Her Majesty's Government except in the single case of legislation prejudicing the trustee status of Cyprus Government stock. In fact the retention of this particular power is needed for purely technical reasons in relation to such Government stock.

15.   It is a familiar experience that when different fields of legislative or executive power are separated by reference to subjects—as, for instance, in federal constitutions—there is on occasions a difficulty in deciding to which field a particular piece of legislation or executive act belongs. This difficulty will be liable to occur in Cyprus. Words such as "defence" or "internal security" do not carry a precise connotation. It is necessary therefore to face the

question whether the dividing line can be drawn with any adequate precision by a process of defining a list of particular matters that fall within the range of these subjects. It would certainly be a great advantage if this could be done: for, if it could be done with even reasonable completeness, it would be possible to get rid of one of the most troublesome of those causes of dispute which disturb the relationship between the authorities responsible for the two sides of government. At any rate, even if the disputes remained, a means of resolving them by reasonable discussion would be available. And that perhaps is as much as anyone can hope to provide.

16. I am satisfied, however, that no good will be done by trying to provide exhaustive definitions. The truth of the matter is that it is the aspect or context in which a particular question presents itself that determines its relation to such subjects as defence or internal security rather than the intrinsic matter with which it deals. This consideration is especially relevant in the case of the Island of Cyprus which contains several very large military and air installations, themselves dependent for effective operation upon some measure of co-ordination with the rest of the Island, including its road communications, its ports and harbours and its water and power supplies. If one were to begin to enquire what were the matters with which the authority responsible for defence and internal security might conceivably be concerned on some occasion or other, it would be very difficult to confine the list so as not to include quite a large number of those matters that are the normal preserve of internal self government. Some things are obviously the exclusive concern of defence and internal security, the control and discipline of the military forces or of the police force, for instance. Some things are likely for some purposes and on some occasions to touch upon defence and internal security, for instance compulsory acquisition of land and the importation of goods or immigration of persons. But it would not be easy to make any long list of those things of which it can certainly be said that they will not in any circumstance or for any purpose affect the interests of defence or internal security.

17. In that situation the balance of advantage turns against any further definition than is afforded by the description of the subjects themselves. For either external affairs, defence and internal security are defined by a long list of matters which covers all the things capable of coming within their range, even if ordinarily many of them will not: in which case the range of self-governing matters is materially reduced in order to take care of the exceptional occasion. Or, to avoid the inconvenience and unfairness of this, the interests of defence and internal security are to some extent jeopardised by tying them down to a limited range of matters which does not do justice to their possible legitimate range.

18. The solution which I propose involves three provisions which should be considered as interdependent upon each other.

(a) The Governor must be the final judge both upon the question whether action that he feels it necessary to take in the interests of any of his reserved subjects is properly within their range and upon the obverse of this, whether a Bill of the Legislative Assembly presented for assent does or does not trench upon his reserved field. It is not possible to provide for the reference of such questions to an outside referee, such, for instance, as the Supreme Court. Defence and internal security involve matters which cannot be reasonably exposed or debated in public proceedings: moreover, they generally require positive and effective action, and it is not good sense that the validity of such action should be in suspense during the pendency of judicial proceedings.

(b) There should be a consultative body, formed on the highest level, for the purpose of keeping each side—the reserved side and the self-governing side—currently informed as to what the other is doing and, perhaps more important, what it proposes to do and why. Such a body should meet under the chairmanship of the Governor himself and from the start it should aim to meet frequently and to discuss fully. The membership that I propose would consist of Governor and Deputy Governor, Chief Minister and another Minister nominated by him, Minister of Turkish Cypriot Affairs, a representative of the Defence forces, Legal Secretary and Attorney-General. In a body of this kind criticisms can be made and policies explained with a freedom and lack of reserve that could not be expected in an open deliberative Assembly. I have suggested that this body should be styled the Joint Council of Cyprus and I suggest that name in order to mark the importance that I attach to its existence and its functions. Given reasonable good will on the two sides I believe that such an institution could be effective to iron out the many possible causes of friction to which a diarchy gives rise and of which the greater part has its origin in each side's ignorance of what the other is up to and the suspicions and lack of confidence arising from such ignorance.

(c) It is only a development of the idea which lies behind the Joint Council of Cyprus to propose, as I do, that the Governor should have constitutional power to invite the Legislative Assembly to take over from him any particular piece of law-making which, though formally within his reserved field, he can conveniently commit to the self-governing side. A power of this kind seems to me a valuable one. It provides the flexibility along that difficult frontier between what is reserved and what not that everyone would wish to see so long as it is felt that no true interest of defence or internal security is prejudiced by looseness of definition. And it affords a means by which to avoid, again given good will, what might otherwise look like an unexpected inroad by the reserved side into the normal field of self-government. It is my hope that as confidence grows, this power might be increasingly resorted to.

19.   I have been critical to examine whether the scheme that I propose for regulating the relations between the reserved side and the self-governing side does in any true sense deny to the latter a generous opportunity of occupying the field of self-government. I am satisfied that it does not. It would be a distortion of the picture to allow the circumstance that at some places and on some occasions the Governor may have to deal with matters that would normally be self-governing matters to suggest that in most places or on most occasions the self-governing field will be invaded in this way. There is no reason why it should be. It will be the Governor's duty to promote the most harmonious relationship that he can achieve between the two sources of authority in

the Island, sources which unite him in his two capacities, in one capacity as constitutional head, in the other as autocratic delegate of the Imperial Government.

20. Perhaps the simplest test of the reality of self-government under the system I have envisaged is to recite the names of the Ministries which I have provided for on the self-governing side (apart from the Chief Minister's Office and the Office of Minister for Turkish Cypriot Affairs): Development, Interior and Local Government, Finance, Communications and Works, Social Services, Natural Resources. It is true that these do not correspond to the existing Departments of Government, though they provide convenient groupings of them. But, to translate them into the Departments or Branches of Government as known to the Cypriot to-day I have invited the Administration in Cyprus to draw up a provisional list of those departments or branches which under my scheme might be expected to pass into the self-governing field and so under the Ministerial control of persons responsible to the elected Assembly. I set it out accordingly in the Appendix to this Covering Note.

21. I turn now to the problems of the self-governing side itself, having explained my proposals as to its relationship with the reserved powers. One thing I can draw attention to at once. My general conception is that the Governor should withdraw from active intervention in the work of the self-governing side, assuming instead the important, but different, status of the constitutional "head" on Her Majesty's behalf. Generally speaking, therefore, he will act on the advice of his Ministers, he will not preside at or take part in meetings of the Cabinet or of the Legislative Assembly. Certain decisions must be taken and acts performed on his own authority, as in the case of any other constitutional head. They will all however be found explicitly identified in my proposed scheme. Thus only he can decide on such matters as proroguing and dissolving the Assembly, relieving a Chief Minister of his office, the making of certain appointments, the reference of doubtful Bills to the Supreme Court for advice, the power of pardon. These citations are not exhaustive, but the full list is not a long one.

22. With this said, the chief problem in finding a suitable framework for the powers of self-government is so to design them that on the one hand self-government becomes a means of reflecting truly the will and purpose of the people of Cyprus and on the other it does not become an instrument by which a majority drawn from one community overrides the legitimate claims of a minority community to maintain its own life and customs as an integral part of the life and customs of Cyprus.

23. Everyone knows that Cyprus is not homogeneous. Taking the figures of the 1946 Census (and I have no reason to suppose that since then there has been any substantial change in favour of minorities), the population of the Island is formed, as to about 80 per cent., of Greek Cypriots, as to about 18 per cent., of Turkish Cypriots, and the remaining 2 per cent. consists of smaller communities of British residents, Armenians, Maronites and others. Throughout I take no account of the British armed forces who will be present in the territory from time to time in connection with the base.

24. The influences that make for separation between the communities are strong—religion, language, education, tradition, and custom. They are

reflected in the towns by separate quarters for Greek and Turk: in the country by Turkish villages and Greek villages. On the other hand there is only a weak supply of unifying elements which would make for a general consciousness that all the communities are Cypriot communities. True all these statements are generalisations to which there are exceptions. The degree of separation between Greek and Maronite Cypriot must be small to-day. Not all education is special to its own community: there are one or two valuable institutions in which boys from all communities receive the same education side by side. There are mixed villages shared by Greek and Turk. Many Turks speak Greek as well as Turkish, and the English language is a potential instrument of common understanding. But communal separation remains the general factor.

25.   How far this separation would be reflected in ability of the Greek and Turkish Cypriot communities to work together politically, I could not say. I am conscious that I do not know enough about the problem. Their representatives have worked together in the past in the service of the Government, in municipal administration, in the activities of co-operative societies and of district improvement boards. In some cases the combination seems to have been happy and unresentful: in others there seem to have been recurring suspicions and complaints on the side of the Turkish Cypriots that discrimination has been practised against them. Whatever the truth of the matter, I have no doubt at all that the circumstances of the last 18 months and the pressure of the Greek Cypriot campaign for Enosis have done much to sharpen the sense of alienation between the two communities, and I think that any plan for the future must accept the fact of this alienation as present now and in the future.

26.   The problem comes down to the political relations between these two communities. The figures that I have given show that the remaining communities are too small in numbers for it to be reasonable that they should expect to have anything more than the right to have their voices heard in an elected Assembly and the right to share in the protection of any guarantees that limit the power of the majority in that Assembly. In fact the representatives of the Armenian community told me that they did not desire to have any special arrangements made for their representation as a community. Their best protection lay in good government for all rather than in separate identification of different interests.

27.   I have given my best consideration to the claim put before me on behalf of the Turkish Cypriot community that they should be accorded political representation equal to that of the Greek Cypriot community. If I do not accept it I do not think that it is out of any lack of respect for the misgivings that lie behind it. But this is a claim by 18 per cent. of a population to share political power equally with 80 per cent., and, if it is to be given effect to, I think that it must be made good on one of two possible grounds. Either it is consistent with the principles of a constitution based on liberal and democratic conceptions that political power should be balanced in this way, or no other means than the creation of such political equilibrium will be effective to protect the essential interests of the community from oppression by the weight of the majority. I do not feel that I can stand firmly on either of these propositions.

28.   The first embodies the idea of a federation rather than a unitary State. It would be natural enough to accord to members of a federation equality of

representation in the federal body, regardless of the numerical proportions of the populations of the territories they represent. But can Cyprus be organised as a federation in this way? I do not think so. There is no pattern of territorial separation between the two communities and, apart from other objections, federation of communities which does not involve also federation of territories seems to me a very difficult constitutional form. If it is said that what is proposed is in reality nothing more than a system of functional representation, the function in this case being the community life and organisation and nothing else, I find myself baffled in the attempt to visualise how an effective executive government for Cyprus is to be thrown up by a system in which political power is to remain permanently divided in equal shares between two opposed communities. Either there is stagnation in political life, with the frustration that accompanies it, or some small minority group acquires an artificial weight by being able to hold the balance between the two main parties. A third alternative, that the Governor should be given under the Constitution some sort of arbitral position as between the two communities, I have already excluded by what I have said above. I do not think that it will be advantageous to embroil the Governor in the internal controversies of the self-governing side. My conclusion is that it cannot be in the interests of Cyprus as a whole that the constitution should be formed on the basis of equal political representation for the Greek and Turkish Cypriot communities.

29. Does the second ground lead to a different result? I do not think so. To give an equal political strength in a unitary State to two communities which have such a marked inequality in numbers—an inequality which, so far as signs go is as likely to increase as decrease—is to deny to the majority of the population over the whole field of self-government the power to have its will reflected in effective action. Yet it might well be right to insist on this denial if the Constitution could not be equipped with any other effective means of securing the smaller communities in the possession of their essential special interests. Not only do I think that it can be equipped with such means by placing those interests under the protection of independent tribunals with appropriate powers and relying only to a limited extent on direct political devices, but I think that the "legalist" solution which this depends on is in fact better suited to provide the protection that is required, and it does not have the effect of denying the validity of the majority principle over a field much wider than that with which special community interests are truly concerned.

30. At this point I will set out the main features of my proposals which are designed to protect the special interests of the Turkish Cypriot community and its political status.

(a) There will be 6 seats in the Legislative Assembly reserved for members elected on a separate roll of Turkish Cypriot voters. This number is to be compared with 24 seats for members elected on a general roll, in effect a roll of Greek Cypriot voters, and is very slightly more than the proportion attributable to the respective numbers of the two communities. My proposal to introduce 6 nominated members in addition has no material bearing on this and their class must in any event take care of nominees to represent other communities, such as non-Cypriot British residents and Maronites.

(b) The consent of two-thirds of the Turkish Cypriot members will be necessary before the Assembly can pass any law which alters the existing
laws of Cyprus regulating Turkish Cypriot domestic affairs, marriage,
divorce, Évkaf and Vakfs, &c., or which deals with their educational,
religious, charitable or cultural institutions. On the other hand the
Turkish Cypriot community can invite the Governor to make a regulation amending any of those laws if there is no prospect of the Assembly
itself being willing to act.

(c) There will be a branch of the permanent administration styled the Office of Turkish Cypriot Affairs under a Minister appointed by the Governor from among the Turkish Cypriot members of the Legislative Assembly. It will be the Government organ for dealing with all the
special affairs of the community, including its separate schools and
educational system, and will have an allotted share of the Cyprus revenues appropriated for the purpose.

(d) The Minister for Turkish Cypriot Affairs will have a seat in the Cabinet
ex officio and will be a member of the Joint Council of Cyprus.

(e) All legislative acts of the Assembly and all executive and administrative
actions or decisions on the self-governing side will be subject to the
condition that they must not conflict with certain guaranteed rights relating to religion, education, charitable, religious and cultural institutions and use of languages. Further there must be no discrimination
based on birth, nationality, language, race or religion. The independent tribunals to whom complaints about violation of these rights can be
preferred will be the Supreme Court, in the case of legislative acts, and
the body which I have styled the Tribunal of Guarantees, in the case of
executive or administrative actions of Government. If a complaint
against a legislative act is upheld, the act, or at least the offending part
of it, becomes a nullity. If it is an executive or administrative action
that is successfully challenged, the Tribunal will have a discretion as to
how best to deal with it including a power to award compensation to a
person injured.

31.   These are the main, but not the only, provisions which I have proposed
for the safeguarding of the position of the Turkish Cypriot community. There
are others, minor in themselves, which yet make up in combination a system
under which the community is secure of its place in the conduct of public
affairs. It is my hope that together they will be thought to justify the view that,
even under a system which concedes an electoral majority to the Greek
Cypriots in the Legislative Assembly, the interests of the smaller community
can be effectively protected and that the safeguards that are offered are not
mere "paper" guarantees.

32.   I have passed over several points in setting out my conclusion, and I
return to those of them which need explanation. For instance, I do not propose that the Legislature of Cyprus should comprise a second Chamber.
While I have been conscious of what I may call some general expectation that
my proposals would include a recommendation of a second Chamber, I have
been much less clear what was the purpose that such a Chamber would be intended to serve. Yet there is no point in designing all the complications of a bi-

cameral Legislature unless the designer is clear what are the advantages to be secured by thus duplicating the legislative authority.

33.　　A second Chamber may serve various purposes. It may act as a substantive check on the activities of the first Chamber in the sense that nothing can become law that does not secure the support of a majority in each Chamber. But then the second Chamber must have a membership constituted on a principle different from that of the first Chamber. Otherwise the check is illusory. I have met suggestions that there should be a second Chamber for Cyprus formed on a functional principle of representation, comprising representatives of municipalities, religious, educational, and business organisations, trade unions, &c. So there might be, in theory. But the idea offers no solution in itself. First, the significance of such a Chamber in acting as an effective check upon the other Chamber depends entirely upon the weighting that is given to the different bodies represented as between the two opposed communities. In deciding on the weighting one transfers to the formation of the second Chamber just the same controversy on a matter of principle that I have been discussing with regard to the first. And an answer has to be given, one way or the other, to the same question—Is it right to deny validity to the will of the majority for general political purposes? Secondly, I am bound to say that a scheme of functional representation for a political body, though attractive to me in theory, is not one which I would be ready to recommend for introduction into Cyprus unless I had had much more opportunity than I have had for working out its actual composition with the help of Cypriot representatives on the spot. Certainly, I could not put it forward as a system of representation that is usual or widely used to-day.

34.　　But then a second Chamber can serve other purposes than that of being a full partner in the Legislative body. It can be designed to act as a limited check upon the first Chamber, either by exercising a power to delay, though not finally to prevent, the realisation of the will of the first or by acting as a revising agent, subject of course, to the readiness of the first Chamber to accept the revisions proposed. No doubt these are useful functions, though they may seem more attractive to the members of a second Chamber that has dwindled from the historical status of full partner than to the members of a new body created from the first to serve no wider purpose. But I do not think that their utility is sufficient to justify the introduction of two separate Chambers into the Legislature proposed for Cyprus. The political field must, after all, be a comparatively small one; and the advantage lies in looking for an arrangement which will concentrate all the best available talent in one deliberative and law-making body, rather than for an arrangement that will dissipate that talent among two separate bodies. Incidentally, the work of revision does not essentially require the existence of two separate Chambers. It can be carried out, not necessarily with less ultimate effectiveness, by a special committee of a single Chamber, with or without expert assistance from outside. On the whole, therefore, I came to the conclusion that no sufficient advantage would be gained by a bi-cameral structure, when there had to be set on the debit side the importance of simplicity, of facing a single Chamber squarely with the responsibility for its own decisions, of avoiding distracting controversies between the two Chambers, and, lastly, of bringing all the available political talent into a single responsible assembly.

35.   If a second Chamber is favoured as itself the means of protecting minority rights I can only say that I do not think that it would be likely to prove a good instrument for that purpose. Compared with a system that allows resort to a competent and independent tribunal, I think it a poor one. In fact it is difficult to see how it can avoid going too far or not far enough. Either it gives the minority a general political power more extensive than is required for its proper protection, thereby distorting the political distribution, or it makes the minority judge in its own cause as to what its special interests are and what is needed for their protection: or on the other hand, avoiding this, it gives the minority no more than a nuisance value and so fails to achieve even its legitimate intention.

36.   With regard to the franchise I recommend the simplest scheme that is possible. I believe this to be the best way to launch the Cyprus Constitution among all the controversies that will attend its birth. Accepting as I do the necessity of a separate communal roll for Turkish Cypriots, I have enquired whether it would be possible to propose some mitigation of the drawbacks of thus perpetuating communal separation by introducing into Cyprus some scheme for a common roll upon which both Turkish Cypriot and all other voters would have an additional vote for a limited number of candidates. Such candidates, it might be hoped, conscious of their dependence upon a mixed constituency of voters, would be less likely to pursue strictly communal policies than candidates elected on separate rolls. I think that perhaps they would, and the idea that lies behind such schemes may well commend itself to Cypriot statesmen of the future. If so, measures can be taken to introduce it if it has the necessary support. But there is little experience available as to how such schemes have worked out in practice, and any version of this double franchise would present the voter in Cyprus with a more complicated election issue than I think appropriate for the opening stages of popular self-government. Besides, theory is one thing and electoral management is another: and in the shortage of experience, I do not feel any sufficient confidence as to the results of such a scheme in practice. A similar conviction of the importance of insisting on all possible simplicity in the franchise arrangements has led me to propose that there should be no option for Turkish Cypriots to register on the general roll. It seems to me inconsistent with the plan of guaranteeing the community a number of seats proportionate to its total numbers that it should be possible for members of the community to leave the necessary minimum on the separate roll to cover those seats and transfer the residue of their voting power to the election on the general roll.

37.   In one matter I have departed on my own responsibility from the franchise rule which previously held good in Cyprus and which was, as I understand, proposed to be retained in more recent discussions on a new Constitution. I propose that women should be admitted as voters equally with men. I cannot think that this is any great innovation, since they already enjoy the vote for certain purposes of local government. Considering that female franchise is now so widely accepted and that it is in operation in the United Kingdom, in Greece, and in Turkey, I think that if I proposed adherence to the old rule of

male franchise I might be thought to be recommending a form of self-government for Cyprus that deliberately departed from liberal or progressive ideas. That would be an unfortunate misunderstanding.

38.   I hope that my proposals as to the position of the Supreme Court and the Tribunal of Guarantees speak for themselves. It is plain enough that I am attaching great importance to the contribution that the judicial power can make to the resolution of inter-communal disputes in Cyprus. And, if inter-communal disputes can be resolved, a large part of the political difficulties of self-government disappears with them. It is indeed a grave responsibility for a judicial tribunal to decide upon the validity of legislative acts or to confirm or annul the administrative acts of Government. But it is, after all, a judicial function that has been discharged acceptably by the Courts of many countries under many systems. The first great written Constitution of modern democracy, that of the United States, owes its interpretation and a large measure of its development to the claim asserted by its Supreme Court to be the final arbiter whether legislative acts of Congress were valid or invalid under the Constitution. And the judicial power has been allotted a similar responsibility under the federal Constitutions of Canada and Australia. But there is no necessary connection between a federal structure and a judicial power to decide whether legislative acts are repugnant to the Constitution. Indeed the Governor's power, which I propose, to refer a doubtful Bill to the Supreme Court for advice before giving assent is modelled fairly closely on a similar provision in the Constitution of the Republic of Eire.

39.   It may be said that Cyprus is a small stage when compared with these territories, and I have asked myself critically whether the duty that I seek to lay upon its Judges is not too heavy for the circumstances of the case. Can they not only achieve the detachment required but also obtain from the public the credit for that detachment? Both are necessary, if their responsibility is to be discharged. I can only say, after going into the matter, that I believe that both objects can be realised, provided that one condition is accepted. The Chief Justice himself must be appointed from outside Cyprus and the number of Supreme Court Judges from inside Cyprus must always be equally balanced between Greek Cypriot and Turkish Cypriot. Given a President of the Court who by virtue of his origin is uncommitted to either community in the eyes of the public, I do not feel any misgivings as to the confidence that will be placed in the Judges' impartiality. The Cyprus judiciary enjoys a high reputation for conscientious performance of its duties and I think that, so formed, the Supreme Court can safely be entrusted with the responsibility that I propose.

40.   The Tribunal of Guarantees is, so far as I know, a novelty in any Constitutional scheme derived from British sources, though it may be recognised as a reflection on a very small scale of the Conseil d'Etat in France. I think that it will be a useful institution. I was impressed by the point reiterated to me that, if there is a tendency by members of one community to discriminate at the expense of the members of another, it is at least as likely that the discriminating will be found in the administrative as in the legislative field. I agree with this and while I do not assume that discrimination has been an abuse in Cyprus in the past—though I am aware of complaints on the matter—nor do I assume that it will be the more present in the future, I think that it is advantageous to

provide for a tribunal to which all complaints can be preferred and impartially investigated. The reason why I do not regard this as work altogether suitable for the Supreme Court is partly that it would be unfortunate to risk overloading that Court with a number of inquiries that are not legal matter in the strict sense and partly that the experience and, I think, the practice and procedure which best suits such a tribunal is rather different from that appropriate to a regular Court of Law. But the need for an independent Chairman remains the same.

41.   I have now completed my brief commentary on the main outline of my proposals. But there are two activities for which the Government of Cyprus is either responsible or with which it is directly concerned that I have not found it possible to fit into my general scheme of self-government without imperilling the basis of equitable protection for each community upon which it is constructed. One of these activities is broadcasting, the Cyprus Broadcasting Service being at present a branch of Government itself: the other is those educational activities, either conducted by Government or aided by it, which are not reserved for individual communities.

42.   To explain the problem raised by these two activities I must clear the ground by stating my general assumptions as to the control of education and information under self-government. The present Department of Education provides out of public funds the major part of the cost of all elementary education, which is carried on in separate schools and under separate systems according to the community concerned. Secondary education, with the exceptions that I have referred to above, is also the separate concern of each community, Greek and Turkish Cypriot. Virtually no Greek Cypriot secondary school is in receipt of Government grant at present; on the other hand grants are received by Turkish Cypriot secondary schools. With the institution of self-government it is to be supposed that governmental relations with Greek Cypriot education will be handled by a department of education under a Greek Cypriot Minister, while Government relations with Turkish Cypriot education will come under the Office of Turkish Cypriot Affairs and its Minister. Information and public relations in general will pass to the self-governing side; but that will not preclude the Governor from setting up independently whatever office for information and public relations relating to his reserved matters he may think necessary for their presentation.

43.   Broadcasting does not fit into such a scheme of division. It is as much a normal internal service for the use of Cyprus as, say, electric power and water and, as such, should fall among self-governing matters. On the other hand, it is most important for the future happiness of the island and its people that broadcasting should be kept secure from the impact of party or political controversies and, above all, from any tendency to favour one community at the expense of another. Yet no one who has had experience of the problems of controlling the output of a medium such as broadcasting could suppose that impartiality could be effectively enforced by an outside tribunal, as the Tribunal of Guarantees, or by any form of external reference. *Semel emissum volat irrevocabile verbum.* The essential things, balance, allocation of times, impartial presentation, depend on a right system at the source. I do not think, therefore, that it affords a proper protection for the minority communities that

broadcasting should be treated merely as one of the normal incidents of self-government and should pass accordingly under the control of a Minister responsible to the elected majority in the Legislative Assembly.

44.   Is there then an acceptable alternative? It would be possible, in theory, to place broadcasting under the control of the Governor himself, not as a reserved or security matter but as a special inter-communal service which he should hold as an impartial trustee for all communities. Yet I cannot bring myself to favour this as a solution. It runs counter to the general line of policy which I recommend, that of withdrawing the Governor from active embroilment in the controversies which may divide the two main communities. Fortunately there is an alternative arrangement which presents itself as much to be preferred.

45.   What I recommend is that broadcasting should be turned into a chartered public institution, on the lines of the B.B.C., charged with an independent public responsibility so to conduct the service as to hold a fair balance between the interests and claims of the different communities. I do not think that one can define the duty except in some vague general terms such as these. The important thing is that those in control of the service should be and should be recognised as being independent of external control or pressure as to all matters relating to the content and handling of the output. For this purpose the composition of the governing board needs rigid definition. My proposal is that it should be so formed that Greek and Turkish Cypriots have equal representation upon it and that, if a difference has to be weighed in the scales, the vote of an independent Chairman should decide between them. It does not seem to matter in this case whether he comes from inside or outside the Island, so long as he is not thought to be committed to either side. But I do not think that a member of the public service in Cyprus would be suitable for the appointment.

46.   There are two points that I ought to stress before leaving the subject of broadcasting. One is that my proposal does not merely involve that the conduct of broadcasting as an independent public institution would be a good way of starting off under a self-governing Constitution. It is much more than that. It involves that this method of treating broadcasting as an essential feature of the distribution of powers under the Constitution is in its own way as much a guarantee of minority rights as other more obvious provisions. The other is that I do mean that those who conduct the service should be genuinely free from outside control as to its content: and that this applies to the Governor as much as to any other political authority. This principle does not exclude reasonable provisions in the Charter regulating access to the service for the dissemination of official notices and information.

47.   My second problem is concerned with inter-communal education. This rather uncouth phrase denotes those activities in the Cyprus educational system which are not confined to any one community. As they stand they can be set down on a very short list—the English School for boys at Nicosia, the American Academy for boys at Larnaca, the American Academy for girls at Nicosia, the Teachers' Training College for men, the Teachers' Training College for women. In addition plans are now maturing for certain commercial and technical schools to be conducted by Government: and an impressive

Technical Institute is nearing the completion of its layout at Nicosia. The current cost to Government of its part in the whole activity is of the order of £150,000. It is envisaged that it may rise to £500,000 when present plans are completed, but there are capital sums of some £1 1/2 million that will need to be found apart from what is already earmarked in the Cyprus Development Fund.

48.　　　Certain things can be said without argument about these activities. The English School is not a school for the English any more than the American Academy is a school for Americans: they are schools in which Greek, Turkish, Armenian and other Cypriot boys are educated together. Nor is the English School or the American Academy a place for administering English or American educational systems to young Cypriots or for trying to impose upon them any new national loyalties. What they do is to provide a different curriculum from that in force in the separate Greek and Turkish Cypriot secondary schools and an approach to education which, just because they are inter-communal, is based on a rather wider and more general conception of its purpose. It is one of the admirable characteristics of the people of Cyprus that they have a sincere appreciation of the importance and value of education. The education offered by the inter-communal schools is, so experience shows, much sought after by parents, as are the opportunities afforded by Government scholarship grants to obtain the advantages of higher education outside Cyprus. Such a system of education cannot honestly be regarded as a challenge to the separate systems which are followed in the Greek and Turkish Cypriot secondary schools or as a threat to bring about "dehellenisation" in the Greek schools—a threat to which members of the Greek Cypriot community have been sensitive during the period of direct Governor's rule. But the inter-communal system and all its intangible advantages arising from the mixing of the children of the different communities at the formative period of education do provide a valuable supplement to the other, separate, systems of education. Taking a reasonably long view, such a means of education provides, as I see it, one of the most hopeful paths toward a mitigation of the racial separations which are at the bottom of the problem of Cyprus. And it is a path which no one is compelled to take. Those who enter on it enter by their parents' free choice.

49.　　　What then is to become of inter-communal education under the new Constitution? It does not fit into the pattern of the Greek Cypriot department of education or the office of Turkish Cypriot Affairs. It is by its nature a service that bridges the two without belonging to either. If it passes, as a general subject of self-government, into the control of a Minister responsible to an elected majority in the Legislative Assembly, I think that it may well be putting too heavy a burden upon him to expect him to support it and to further its possible developments in the face of hostile opposition from those who can see good only in the traditional curriculum of Greek Cypriot separate education. So either we must face the possibility or the probability that this activity, however beneficial to Cyprus, will be allowed to fail through lack of the means of support, or an exception must be made to secure its continuance by placing the instruments of inter-communal education under a special board responsible to the Governor, not to the Legislative Assembly. A board formed for this purpose should in my view invite the assistance of Greek and Turkish Cypriot members interested in education, but should have an independent Chairman. This is the expedient that I propose. I will mention later what I regard as the financial implications of such an arrangement.

50.   It only remains for me to give such explanations as seem called for with regard to the financial provisions which are set out in Section P of the constitutional proposals. I have left it to the last to deal with these points, since I take it to be an uncontroversial principle that the financial arrangements should be adjusted to suit the substantive proposals rather than that those proposals should themselves be subordinated to some fixed financial conceptions which may be ill-suited to the very special circumstances in which a new Constitution for Cyprus would have to be set on foot.

51.   The diarchy which is involved in the reserved powers over defence and internal security involves in my view that there will be two separate public funds for Cyprus, one controlled by the Governor for the purpose of those fields of administration which are retained in his charge, the other being the produce of the Cyprus revenues which will be available to be raised and appropriated according to the decisions of the self-governing Assembly and Ministers.

52.   The monies needed for the purpose of defence in Cyprus will be provided, I assume, from United Kingdom funds and will not be regarded as a charge upon the revenues of Cyprus except to the extent of the sum of £10,000 which is its standing annual contribution to Imperial defence. I am not concerned to express a view upon the question whether £10,000 or some larger sum is the right figure for this purpose, but I think it almost obvious that the very large sums which are being expended in Cyprus over a period of years towards its full equipment as a base are not expended for the defence of Cyprus itself regarded in the limited sense as a territory unconnected with the British defence system as a whole. It is relevant that these large demands on labour and material and the consumption demands of the troops stationed on base duty do, and will, bring considerable prosperity to the Island out of the United Kingdom money spent there, even though most of it is not an expenditure economically productive. This may be a good reason for increasing the fixed charge of £10,000 which for my purposes I have assumed as the contribution figure. But I do not think that anyone would suppose that it alters the general principle that Cyprus revenues cannot properly be charged with the creation and development of the defence base.

53.   The next item is the cost of internal security, which in substance is the cost of the Police Force and the prison service. What difficulties there are in providing for this cost can be discussed in terms of the Police and I will confine my explanation to this. The question that I have had to face is this: Should the cost of the Police Force be met out of the revenues of Cyprus, although the control of that force, including its strength, equipment, rates of pay, &c., is a reserved matter and not therefore within the range of self-government? I think that a question of this sort is peculiar to the special system which is proposed for Cyprus under which the police power is a reserved power. Internal security is, of course, a necessary service to civilised government. That means that self-government in Cyprus could not exist without some police force and

the expenditure needed to maintain it: and I deduce from that that it would be wrong that nothing should be required from Cyprus revenues to pay for Police, even though the control of the force is not on the self-governing side. But does it follow from that that the whole cost of the force should be found by Cyprus? That conclusion is a very big jump from the first and I have not been able to persuade myself that it would be just to impose this charge when the special circumstances that affect the Cyprus police force are understood. In my view the only fair thing is some sharing arrangement.

54.   What is happening is that the Cyprus Police force is undergoing a thorough reorganisation. The outbreak of the emergency in April 1955 is thought to have shown up serious deficiencies in numbers, training and organisation. The scheme of reorganisation is only now getting under way and it will be years before it will be completed according to the new scale that is designed for it. One or two figures will show the measure of the change. In 1954 the Police expenditure was about £600,000. The establishment authorised at the close of that year was Officers 51, Other Ranks 1,363. The total strength as recommended by the recent Report of the Cyprus Police Commission, 1956, and accepted by the Government is approximately 3,000 all ranks, rather more than double. Disregarding special expenditure which will not recur when the emergency is over, the future level of recurrent expenditure planned for Police is some £2,625,000 to £3,125,000 and that on Prisons is in the region of £125,000. To this must be added a very considerable capital expenditure on rehousing the police and on new buildings, which plan, if fully implemented, will require another £5 million over the next five years.

55.   None of this expenditure will be controllable by the Legislative Assembly. No doubt Police matters will be canvassed in the Joint Council of Cyprus, but the responsibility for the strength and organisation of the Force will remain with the Governor. I do not think that the situation would be improved if an official representative were to attend the Legislative Assembly and answer questions relating to the Police. It could be done, but where there is neither control of finance nor control of policy I doubt if question and answer are a useful expedient.

56.   The total Cyprus revenue for 1956 was about £12 million, itself representing a remarkable advance over recent years due largely to the pressure of defence expenditure. Even if £12 million* is taken as a representative annual figure, it looks as if about 25 per cent. of it would be needed to be appropriated for Police costs, if the whole burden were to be thrown on Cyprus.

57.   My conclusion is that it would be unjust to Cyprus to make such a requirement, whatever the future level of Cyprus revenues. I ought to say, though, that I have not detected any reason for supposing that they will show

---

* The figure of 12 million was taken from the official Estimates for 1956, presented by the Governor to the Executive Council on 27th March, 1956. After the submission of this report it was brought to my notice that Cyprus revenue for 1956 is now estimated as likely to amount to about £13.5 million; on the other hand the expenditure for the same period is expected to increase still more, above the previous estimates. These facts should be recorded; but the point that paragraph 56 is dealing with remains the same.

much increase in the next few years, while one item of importance may well decline. I think that it would be a bad thing to try to start constitutional self-government on a financial basis that is itself unfair. Internal security and defence are separate subjects, but they are not entirely distinct. It seems to me only reasonable to say that the necessity to create and to maintain a thoroughly effective police force in Cyprus is in part a recognition that we must be secure in the use of our base. What I recommend therefore is that a sum should be fixed as an annual contribution from the Cyprus revenues towards the total cost of Police and Prisons, to be paid into the Defence Fund, and that the balance should be provided by Her Majesty's Government out of United Kingdom funds. I thought it reasonable, if a formula had to be found, to turn to 1954, the year before the emergency broke out, to find a "normal" basis for police expenditure in Cyprus and then to write the figure up to the higher scales prevailing in 1956. That has produced the figure of £750,000 for Police and Prisons that I use in my proposals. I ought to add that, though I am firmly committed to the principle of sharing, I am not committed to the actual figure. Considering how deficient even the 1954 establishment (it was not filled) may be thought to have been shown to be in the light of what has happened since, my figure may be rather too favourable to Cyprus.

58.   With regard to broadcasting I do not find that the same difficulties arise. It is a service for the people of Cyprus in the full sense: and the mere fact that the need to safeguard the different interests of the various communities has led me to propose that its content should not be placed under the elected Assembly does not provide any good reason why the finance for it, so far as it is not self-financing out of licences and advertisements, should not continue to be met out of Cyprus revenues. I have no right to suppose that it will at any time be self-financing. It runs at a deficit of some £100,000 at present. When a planned extension of facilities has been completed, as it shortly will be, it is hoped to reduce the annual deficit to a figure in the region of £50,000. What I propose is that the annual estimates should be approved by the Governor in consultation with the Minister of Finance and the Minister for Turkish Cypriot Affairs. He should then be empowered to send a precept to the Finance Minister for the amount required to meet the estimated deficit and the sum so certified will thus become a charge on Cyprus revenues. I recommend also that the Broadcasting Corporation's annual accounts should be laid before the Legislative Assembly with a report on them by the Auditor-General.

59.   There remains the financing of inter-communal education. Valuable as such education is, it is not nor is it likely to be a major item of anyone's budget. As I have said, even allowing for planned developments, its annual cost to Government is not expected to be more than £500,000. And the enquiries that I have made do not suggest that, with the shortage of suitable teachers and facilities, any large-scale development could be undertaken in any near future. But what fund ought to bear the charge of it? It is in the same situation as broadcasting in the sense that it is purely a Cyprus service for the benefit of Cypriots: on the other hand, unlike broadcasting, and *pro tanto*, the police, it is not a necessary service, since it merely supplements other systems of education for the benefit of those parents who wish their children to be educated in this way. For reasons that I have explained I am proposing that inter-communal educa-

tion should be placed under the Governor, with the help of an education board on which Greek and Turkish Cypriots will be equally represented. Neither its maintenance nor its possible development will therefore be under the control of the Legislative Assembly or the Cabinet of Ministers. The position is anomalous, and I think that the best thing is to look for a practical solution rather than to try to apply some general principle which has no real application to the case. My recommendation is that the necessary funds should be found by Her Majesty's Government out of United Kingdom resources as a supplement to the monies already provided or promised for the economic development of Cyprus. It will be a worthwhile gift from the people of this country to the people of Cyprus, and at a time when such large expenditure has to be incurred in the island for the more general purposes of defence it is not a bad thing that this and other development monies should be visibly expended at the cost of the British taxpayer for the direct benefit of the internal purposes of Cyprus.

60.   My proposals therefore call for financial contributions from the United Kingdom to two special purposes—to pay for part of internal security and to pay for inter-communal education. I think that the reasons why these contributions are called for are valid independently of the rise or fall of Cyprus revenues in general or the taxing policy pursued by the Cypriot Government, because these reasons arise out of the constitutional structure itself. On the other hand, it is my view that, if these contributions are measured and provided as I have proposed, they close any question of further contributions from United Kingdom sources in general aid of the Cyprus budget. Cyprus is not, so far as any investigations of mine have led me, one of those territories which should require or expect a grant in aid in supplement of general administration. Nor do I think that such a system, with the attendant complications of more or less detailed Treasury inspection and approval of each year's budgetary position, is consonant with the conception of free and independent control of self-governing matters which I have made the basis of my constitutional proposals.

61.   I could not finish this covering memorandum without acknowledging gratefully the help that I have received during the course of my work. Before I do so I may take the opportunity of stating without qualification upon what authority my proposals rest, since I would prefer them to be criticised for the merits or demerits of what they in fact contain rather than for not being what they have at no time purported to be. The sole responsibility for the proposals is mine. They are not the outcome of negotiations, since negotiations have not taken place: nor do they represent suggestions which have been made to and worked out with any or all of the parties principally concerned. The reasons that prevented the holding of any round-table conference are familiar and do not need enlargement from me. On the other hand it would be misleading to allow the impression to prevail that my proposals have been produced in ignorance of the main attitudes and positions of these parties. Those are not difficult to ascertain for anyone who has the opportunity, as I have had, to study something of the history of Cyprus since 1878, of its constitutional controversies, and of the successive sets of proposals and discussions that are recorded from time to time up to the present day. Moreover, during the two visits to Cyprus that I have paid in the last four months I have not lacked means of

Cyprus that I have paid in the last four months I have not lacked means of learning at first hand of the attitude of the Turkish Cypriots, which has been presented to me officially, or something at first or second hand of the points of view of the Greek Cypriot and of the other communities in Cyprus.

62.   I have received sincere and generous assistance from the Governor of Cyprus, His Excellency Sir John Harding, his staff and all members of the administration in Cyprus, British, Greek and Turkish, with whom I was brought into contact. They spared no effort to make my visits informative or to make it possible for me to see and hear what I could during the time that I was there. The members of the Colonial Office in London whom I have called upon for advice have always been ready to let me draw upon their fund of knowledge and experience. Lastly, I can put on record my grateful appreciation of the services rendered by the two secretaries of my Commission, Mr. Geoffrey Cassels in Cyprus and Mr. Derek Pearson of the Colonial Office, without whose able co-operation my work would have been much longer and even more difficult.

(Signed) RADCLIFFE

London,
12th November, 1956

APPENDIX TO COVERING NOTE (see paragraph 20)

PROPOSED DEPARTMENTS AND FUNCTIONS ON THE SELF-GOVERNING SIDE

CHIEF MINISTER

C.M.'s Functions
Cabinet Office, District Administration, Ceremonial, London Office

Ministry for Development
Development Programme

OFFICE FOR TURKISH CYPRIOT AFFAIRS

Turkish Cypriot Affairs including Turkish Education and Relations with Turkish Religious Bodies

MINISTRY FOR FINANCE

Financial Affairs
Budget, Estimates, Inland Revenue, Treasury, Audit

Economic Affairs
Economic Policy, Banking, Customs and Excise, Commerce and Industry, Grain Commission, Co-operative Development

MINISTRY FOR THE INTERIOR AND LOCAL GOVERNMENT

Legal and Judicial Affairs, Official Receiver and Registrar, Local Authorities, Planning and Housing, Information Services and Public Relations, Touring, Antiquities, Printing

MINISTRY FOR COMMUNICATIONS AND WORKS

Public Works, Roads, Road Transport, Ports, Airports, Port Administration, Civil Aviation, Posts, Relations with Electricity Authority, Relations with C.I.T.A.

MINISTRY FOR SOCIAL SERVICES

Greek Education, Medical, Labour, Welfare, Relations with Religious Bodies

MINISTRY FOR NATURAL RESOURCES

Agriculture and Veterinary, Forests, Water Development, Lands and Survey, Geological Survey, Mines

STATEMENT OF PROPOSALS

INDEX

A.I.—PURPOSE OF THE CONSTITUTION
    The purpose of the Constitution is to provide for and to regulate the exercise of political power in the Island of Cyprus as a territory which is under the territorial sovereignty of Her Majesty The Queen.

A.II.—GOVERNOR AND LEGISLATIVE ASSEMBLY
    (1) There will be a Governor and Commander-in-Chief in and over Cyprus who will have the powers and duties prescribed by the Constitution. He shall perform those duties in accordance with the Constitution and will exercise his powers in accordance with any instructions that may be given to him from time to time by Her Majesty either by Royal Instructions or through a Secretary of State.
    (2) The Governor will be appointed by Her Majesty's Commission. There will be a Deputy Governor appointed by the Governor.
    (3) There will be a Legislative Assembly for Cyprus and a Cabinet of Ministers responsible to that Assembly, who will have the powers and duties provided in the Constitution. They shall exercise those powers and perform those duties in accordance with the Constitution.

B.—GENERAL DISTBIBUTION OF POWERS
    (1) The power to make laws and to conduct all aspects of executive administration in respect of the following matters:
    (a) external affairs;
    (b) the defence of Cyprus, either directly or indirectly as involved in the fulfilment by Her Majesty's Government of their international obligations and the defence of British interests in the Middle East or the interests of other Powers allied or associated with the United Kingdom;
    (c) internal security;
will be retained in the hands of the Governor. These matters (a), (b) and (c) are called "Governor's matters."
    (2) Subject to the retention of Governor's matters, the general power to make laws for the good government of Cyprus will be exercised by the Legislative Assembly. No such law will he valid as a law until the Governor has signified assent to it, but except in special cases which are provided for in the Constitution the Governor will signify that assent if a Bill has been duly passed by the Legislative Assembly.
    Matters which come within the competence of the Legislative Assembly under the Constitution are called "self-governing matters."
    The power of the Legislative Assembly to make laws on self-governing matters will be subject at all times to:
    (a) the provisions of the Constitution which safeguard the special interests of the various communities, religions and races in Cyprus and guarantee certain fundamental rights to all persons in Cyprus;
    (b) the provisions of the Constitution which except the subjects of broadcasting and inter-communal education, and accord them special treatment in the interests of the different communities in Cyprus;
    (c) the provisions of the Constitution which prescribe the Governor's duly to withhold or reserve assent to a Bill on the ground that it falls within

a certain class or deals with certain matters, as later set out, or to make an Ordinance prevailing over other laws if he is of the opinion that the Ordinance is necessary in the interests of foreign affairs, defence or internal security;

(d) the provisions of the Constitution which allow for the making of Emergency Laws during a period of public emergency.

(3) Subject to the same restrictions, so far as relevant, the administration of government and the executive power in respect of self-governing matters will be exercised by the Governor through Ministers chosen from the Legislative Assembly. It will be his duty to act on their advice in such matters, except in those cases where the Constitution provides that he shall act at his discretion or after some prescribed form of consultation or recommendation.

(4) The provisions of the Constitution cannot be altered or revoked by Ordinance of the Governor or by Law of the Legislative Assembly except as follows:

(a) where the Constitution explicitly provides that a particular matter can be dealt with or altered by the Legislative Assembly, then it may be dealt with or altered accordingly so long as any prescribed conditions are properly observed;

(b) without prejudice to (a) any provisions as to the constitution, powers and procedure of the Legislative Assembly may be altered by it by law passed for the purpose if such law is concurred in by—

(i) a majority of the members of the Legislative Assembly elected on the General Roll;

(ii) a majority of the members of the Legislative Assembly elected on the Turkish Cypriot Communal Roll;

(iii) a majority of the nominated members of the Legislative Assembly.

C.—SELF-GOVERNING MATTERS

C.I.—RESTRICTIONS AND GUARANTEES

(1) The provisions contained in the following paragraphs are fundamental restrictions on the powers of self-government to be granted by the Constitution, and no law, regulation or official action can conflict, interfere with or prevail over them.

(2) *Religion.*—All persons will be entitled to the free exercise in public or private, of any creed, religion or belief, the observance of which is not incompatible with public order and good morals.

(3) *Institutions and Schools.*—All persons acting individually, in association, or as a community, will be entitled to establish, maintain, manage and control at their own expense any charitable, religious and cultural institutions, and any schools and other instructional establishments, provided that such institutions, schools and establishments are so conducted as to be compatible with public order and good morals, with the right to use their own language and to exercise their own religion freely therein.

(4) *Language.*—All persons will be entitled to the free use of any language in private intercourse, in commerce, religion, in the press, or in publications of any kind or at public meetings.

(5) *Non-discrimination.*—There shall be no discrimination against any person on account of birth, nationality, language, race or religion. For this purpose discrimination means any action prejudicial to an individual which is based on his birth, nationality, language, race or religion as the case may be, and is not justly required by the circumstances of that birth, nationality, language, race or religion.

(6) *Expropriation*

 (i) No person shall be deprived of any property, movable or immovable, by compulsory power unless it be for public purposes and unless just compensation is provided for the deprivation, to be made available with all reasonable expedition.

 (ii) Any law authorising such deprivation of property shall secure to every claimant for compensation the right of access to the Supreme Court of Cyprus for the determination of the amount (if any) to be paid.

 (iii) This guarantee will not extend to action taken for the divesting or taking possession of property in any case to which the duty to make compensation would not normally be regarded as applicable.

(7) *Access to the Courts of Law.*—There shall be equality of access to the Courts of Law for all persons, whether individuals, associations or corporations. This guarantee is subject to the rules of law concerning proceedings by enemy aliens in time of war.

(8) *Turkish Cypriot Affairs.*—It shall not be lawful for the Legislative Assembly to make—

 (a) any law which repeals or alters the provisions of any of the following enactments, viz.:

  The Turkish Family (Marriage and Divorce) Laws (1951 and 1954).
  The Turkish Religious Head (Mufti) Law (1953).
  The Turkish Family Courts Law (1954).
  The Evkaf and Vakfs Law (1955), or

 (b) any law which deals with Turkish Cypriot educational, religious, charitable and cultural institutions or activities or any other matter which is exclusively of Turkish Cypriot concern (all of which matters are hereinafter referred to collectively as "Turkish Cypriot affairs"),

unless such law is supported by the votes of not less than two-thirds of the members of the Assembly elected by voters on the Turkish Cypriot communal roll.

C.II.—THE LEGISLATIVE ASSEMBLY

(1) There will be a *Legislative Assembly* consisting of a Speaker, a Deputy-Speaker and 36 other members.

(2) Six members will be elected by voters on a Turkish Cypriot communal roll, 24 will be elected by voters on a general roll, six will be nominated by the Governor. The Turkish Cypriot roll will be reserved exclusively for members of the Turkish Cypriot community: no member of this community may be entered as a voter on the general roll. All other persons qualified to vote will be entered on the general roll.

(3) *Qualifications for Voting*
   (i)   Sex: Male or Female.
   (ii) Age: 21 years or upwards.
   (iii) British subject born in Cyprus or otherwise legally a "native" of Cyprus if ordinarily resident in Cyprus.
   (iv) Any other British subject ordinarily resident in Cyprus for two preceding years except persons not domiciled in Cyprus who are in the armed service of the Crown.
   (v)   Freedom from such disqualifications as mental incapacity, imprisonment, conviction for a previous electoral offence, as may be prescribed by the electoral law for the time being in force.
(4) *Qualifications for election as member*
   (i)   The same qualifications as those required as qualifications for voting, except that a member must be at least 25 years of age at date of election;
   (ii) must not be under any acknowledgment of allegiance to a Foreign Power;
   (iii) must not, unless specially excepted, be holder of Public Office or member of Civil Service or otherwise in service of Her Majesty;
   (iv) must not be undischarged bankrupt;
   (v)   must not have any responsibility for compilation or revision of any electoral register, or any connection with the conduct of the election.
(5) *Nominated members* will be appointed by the Governor in his discretion. It will, however, be his duty to try to secure that at all times one at least of the nominated members is a British subject resident in Cyprus who belongs to the non-indigenous British community and that of the others one at least belongs to the Maronite community. A Nominated Member's qualifications will be the same as those required of an elected member.
(6) *Vacation of seats*. A member's seat will be vacated by:
   (a) resignation;
   (b) death;
   (c) failure to retain all the qualifications required of a member as set out in (4) above;
   (d) dissolution of the Legislative Assembly.
(7) *Constituencies*
   (i)   There will be 30 Constituencies, 24 General (excluding Turkish Cypriot) and six Turkish Cypriot, each constituency providing one seat in the legislative Assembly.
   (ii) Every voter will be entitled to one vote, to be exercised in his appropriate constituency.
   (iii) There will be six Electoral Districts, namely Nicosia, Kyrenia, Famagusta, Larnaca, Limassol and Paphos. These districts will be divided into the 30 General and Turkish Cypriot Constituencies according to the scheme of division set out in Appendix A.

(iv) Prior to the first election that takes place under the Constitution the physical boundaries of the constituencies will be determined by a person appointed by the Governor to act as Commissioner for this purpose.

(8) *The Speaker and Deputy-Speaker*

(i) There will be a Speaker and a Deputy-Speaker who will be appointed by the Legislative Assembly at the beginning of each new Assembly according to the majority votes of the members. They may be chosen from the members of the Assembly or from outside the Legislative Assembly provided that if an elected member becomes Speaker or Deputy-Speaker, the seat in his constituency shall be declared vacant and a by-election shall be held to appoint a new member in his place. If at any time the Speaker is a Greek Cypriot, the person chosen to be Deputy-Speaker must be a Turkish Cypriot: if a Turkish Cypriot, the person chosen to be Deputy-Speaker must be a Greek Cypriot. But no Turkish Cypriot may be chosen to act as Speaker or Deputy-Speaker unless he is approved for that purpose by at least two-thirds of the members of the Legislative Assembly elected by voters on the Turkish Cypriot communal roll.

(ii) The duty of the Speaker will be to preside at the sittings of the Legislative Assembly, to regulate and conduct the business of the sittings, and in all things to be the guardian of the order and dignity of the proceedings of the House.

(iii) The Deputy Speaker shall exercise the duties of Speaker in the absence of the Speaker.

(iv) Neither the Speaker nor the Deputy Speaker will be entitled to vote in the Legislative Assembly or to take any part in its proceedings except in his capacity as such Speaker or Deputy Speaker.

(9) *Language*

(i) Members will be entitled to address the Legislative Assembly in the English, Greek, or Turkish language as they please, provided that an immediate oral translation of the speech into either or both of the other languages must be made available if any member so requests and the Speaker so directs.

(ii) There is to be a printed record of speeches affording translations of each speech into the other two languages.

(iii) All Bills and records are to be printed in English, Greek and Turkish. In case of doubt the English text is to be accepted as definitive.

(10) *The Privileges and Immunities* of members shall be such as may be prescribed by any Law passed for that purpose by the Legislative Assembly, provided that no more extensive privilege or immunity on any matter may be enjoyed by a member than that enjoyed by a member of the House of Commons of the United Kingdom.

(11) Each member of the Legislative Assembly before taking his seat shall take an oath or make an affirmation to the effect that so long as he is a member

of the Assembly he will faithfully discharge his duties as a member of the Assembly and conduct himself as a loyal subject of Her Majesty.

(12) *Standing Orders.*—Prior to the first meeting of the Legislative Assembly the Governor will cause to be prepared a set of Standing Orders to govern the proceedings of the Legislative Assembly. These will be laid before the Legislative Assembly and shall be operative as its Standing Orders until any part of them is amended or revoked by resolution of the Legislative Assembly and except so far as they are so amended or revoked, provided that no such amendment or revocation shall be effective unless the majority voting in favour of it includes a majority of the Turkish Cypriot and nominated members combined. No Standing Order shall preclude the right of a member to address proper questions to a Minister.

(13) *Sessions of the Legislative Assembly.*—There must be at least one session of the Legislative Assembly in the course of each year. The Governor will have power to prorogue or dissolve the Legislative Assembly at his discretion provided that he will not exercise such powers on any occasion without previous consultation with the Chief Minister.

(14) Ten members shall constitute a quorum for the transaction of business in the Legislative Assembly. Unless otherwise provided in the Constitution the decisions of the Assembly will be by majority vote.

(15) *Frequency of Elections.*—A Legislative Assembly shall not be capable of remaining in being for a longer period than four years from the date of the preceding general election. It may be dissolved by the Governor before that time, but, unless so dissolved by him it shall stand dissolved automatically by the expiration of that period.

(16) *Salaries and Allowances.*—Members will be entitled to receive a salary and allowances in respect of their membership. An initial scale will be drawn up and published by the Governor before the date of the first general election under the Constitution, but the Legislative Assembly will have power to alter the scale at any time by a law passed for this purpose.

(17)–(i) There is to be a Clerk of the Assembly, who will be responsible for the preparing and circulating of Daily Orders and Notices of Motion, the custody of records, and the recording of votes. He will also be charged with the supervision of the administrative work incidental to the business of the Legislative Assembly.

(ii) The Clerk will be a Member of the Public Service. He will be appointed by the Speaker after consultation with the Chairman of the Public Service Commission, provided that the Governor may make a temporary appointment of a Clerk prior to the meeting of the first Legislative Assembly.

(iii) The Clerk shall be subject to retirement at the age prescribed for the retirement of Public Officers in Cyprus, but shall not be removable except on a resolution of the Legislative Assembly requiring his removal on the ground of misconduct or infirmity of body or mind, provided that no resolution shall be effective unless the majority voting in favour of it includes a majority of the Turkish Cypriot and nominated members combined. His salary shall be fixed by the Governor.

(iv) There shall be a Deputy Clerk whose appointment and conditions of service will be the same as those of the Clerk. If the Clerk is a Greek Cypriot the Deputy Clerk is to be a Turkish Cypriot, and if the Clerk is a Turkish Cypriot the Deputy Clerk is to be a Greek Cypriot.

(18) There shall be an official publication entitled *The Government Gazette*. Every Bill which is intended to be brought before the Legislative Assembly shall be published in the *Gazette* at a reasonable interval of time before it is to be brought forward unless the matter appears too urgent to admit of the delay involved.

(19)–(i) The Legislative Assembly will have power at any time to pass an Electoral Law altering as it thinks fit all or any of the provisions set out above which relate to:

Qualifications or disqualifications for voting.

Qualifications for election as member.—Sex and age.

Constituencies.—Division and boundaries, but not so as to affect the total number of members.

Frequency of elections.—Duration of the Assembly, provided that the term shall not in any case exceed four years.

(ii) No such alteration which is intended to apply to voters on the Turkish Cypriot Communal roll, or to members elected by such voters, or to Turkish Cypriot constituencies, shall be operative unless it is supported by at least two-thirds of the members elected by voters on the Turkish Cypriot Communal roll.

C.III.—THE EXECUTIVE

(1) There will be a Chief Minister to act as the Head of the Government in self-governing matters. He will be appointed by the Governor according to his discretion but it will be the Governor's duty to select for this purpose the person who appears to him to command the largest measure of general support among the members of the Legislative Assembly.

(2) The Governor will appoint such other persons being members of the Legislative Assembly to act as Ministers as shall be recommended to him by the Chief Minister.

(3) Apart from the Chief Minister and the other Ministers there will be a Minister for Turkish Cypriot Affairs who will be responsible for an Office dealing with Turkish Cypriot Affairs. He will be appointed by the Governor at his discretion from among the members of the Legislative Assembly elected by voters on the Turkish Cypriot communal roll.

(4) The Chief Minister, the Minister for Turkish Cypriot Affairs and the other Ministers appointed by the Governor shall constitute the Cabinet.

(5) There will be a Secretary of the Cabinet who shall be present as secretary at all its meetings. It will be his duty to ensure that meetings are summoned with due notice of the business proposed, that proper records are kept of all business done and decisions made, and that such decisions are duly communicated to the departments of Government concerned.

(6) The following will be the Departments of Government apart from the Chief Minister's Office and the Office for Turkish Cypriot Affairs: Ministry of

the Interior and Local Government, Ministry of Finance, Ministry of Communications and Works, Ministry of Social Services, Ministry of Natural Resources, Ministry of Development. It will be within the power of the Legislative Assembly at any time by law passed for the purpose to add to or reduce the number of departments or to change their responsibilities and functions.

(7) There will be a Permanent Secretary for each Department and Office, who will be a public officer. Subject to the general direction and control of his Minister and to his instructions on matters of policy the Permanent Secretary will exercise supervision over the department for which his Minister is responsible.

(8) The Governor may at any time in his discretion relieve the Chief Minister of his office: but he will not do so unless he is satisfied either that the Chief Minister does not enjoy the general support of the majority of the members of the Legislative Assembly or that his removal is urgently required by the public interest. If at any time he is so satisfied he shall so inform the Chief Minister, whereupon the latter will be entitled to request the Governor to dissolve the Legislative Assembly with a view to testing the views of the electorate. Unless the Governor decides that for some special reason which bears upon the public interest it would not be right for him to accede to this request, of which special reason he shall inform the Chief Minister, he will dissolve the Legislative Assembly accordingly.

(9)–(i) The Governor may at any time in his discretion, but only after consultation with the Chief Minister, relieve any of the other Ministers (except the Minister for Turkish Cypriot Affairs) of his office and appoint in his place a successor recommended by the Chief Minister.

(ii) Upon the office of Chief Minister becoming vacant all other Ministers except the Minister for Turkish Cypriot Affairs shall be deemed *ipso facto* to have resigned their respective offices, provided that until a successor is appointed in his place each Minister will remain responsible for carrying out the normal duties of his office.

(iii) The Governor may at any time in his discretion relieve the Minister for Turkish Cypriot Affairs of his office and appoint another member of the Legislative Assembly similarly qualified in his place.

(10) It will be the duty of the Chief Minister to keep the Governor currently informed upon all matters relating to the policies of the Cabinet and to report to him accordingly. In addition, the Secretary of the Cabinet shall send to the Governor copies of all Cabinet papers at the time when they are circulated to members of the Cabinet.

D.—GOVERNOR'S MATTERS
(1) The Governor will have power whenever he thinks necessary to make laws with respect to Governor's matters. Such laws shall be called Ordinances. Each Ordinance shall be prefaced by a declaration to the effect that the Governor is of opinion that it is necessary for the purposes of external affairs, defence or internal security, as the case may be, to make the legislative provisions that it contains: and an Ordinance so made shall have the full force of law not-

withstanding that it is in conflict with any other laws or enactments in force in Cyprus and to the extent necessary shall prevail over such laws.

(2) If an Ordinance is made by the Governor in the form prescribed neither his power to make it nor its validity shall be capable of being questioned in any Court of Law.

(3) Unless the Governor decides to the contrary because of the urgency of the matter prior notice of an intended Ordinance will be given in the Government Gazette. All Ordinances will be published in the Gazette as soon as they are made, and duly recorded. The publication will be in three languages, English, Greek and Turkish, and in case of doubt the English text is to be accepted as definitive.

(4) The following matters are enumerated as matters which in some cases it will always and in other cases it may sometimes be necessary to treat as included within the range of Governor's matters by virtue of the fact that they involve external affairs, defence or internal security, provided that the list is not to be taken as being exhaustive of the range of those subjects nor does it connote that there will not be aspects of some of those matters which have no bearing on the retained subjects and thus do not come within the scope of Ordinances:

  (a) the control and discipline of naval, military, air and police forces and the control and regulation of naval vessels and of air navigation and aircraft;
  (b) the compulsory acquisition of land and buildings as required in connection with Governor's matters, for example for naval, military, air force or police purposes or for purposes connected with air navigation or aircraft;
  (c) all forms of communication ancillary to naval, military, air force or police operations or air navigation;
  (d) lands, buildings, docks, harbours and waters used for naval, military, air force or police purposes or for the purposes of any of the Governor's matters;
  (e) prisons and the prison service;
  (f) importation of goods;
  (g) immigration, naturalisation of aliens, issue and visa of passports;
  (h) postal and telegraphic censorship;
  (i) shipping, air, telegraphic and wireless services between Cyprus and other countries;
  (j) relations with foreign States, with any other part of Her Majesty's Dominions, or with the United Nations or Specialised Agencies of the United Nations.

(5) The Governor will maintain such secretariat and will maintain or create such departments as he may think requisite to carry out the powers and duties of Government with regard to Governor's matters.

(6) The Governor's executive authority in respect of Governor's matters will extend to the giving of instructions to public officers in any department of the public service in Cyprus, if the Governor considers that these instructions are necessary for the execution of his retained powers. If any such order is

given on any occasion the Governor must at the same time inform the Minister concerned.

(7) There will be a Legal Secretary to the Governor who will be responsible for advising him on all legal questions relating to the making of Ordinances and the exercise of power over Governor's matters or his duties as Governor. The Legal Secretary will also be responsible for initiating, conducting and if necessary discontinuing prosecutions for criminal offences arising under any Ordinance or otherwise relating to defence and internal security.

(8) There will be a Defence Committee under the presidency of the Governor for the purpose of advising him with regard to Governor's matters. The Committee will consist of the Deputy Governor, the Legal Secretary, representatives of the naval, military and air forces in Cyprus and such other persons as the Governor may invite to be members.

(9) In the making of any Ordinance and in authorising or requiring any executive act in respect of Governor's matters, the Governor must have regard to the Restrictions and Guarantees which have been set out above and will conduct his own administrative policy in conformity with what they require.

(10) The Governor shall comply with any instructions that may be given to him from time to time either by Royal Instructions or through a Secretary of State requiring him to submit any proposed Ordinance for approval before it is made. Apart from that any Ordinance made by the Governor may be disallowed by Her Majesty through a Secretary of State and shall cease to have effect as soon as the fact of disallowance has been made public.

(11) The Governor's power to make Ordinances will not extend to a power to raise money by taxation.

E.—JOINT COUNCIL OF CYPRUS

(1) There will be a body to be known as the Joint Council of Cyprus which will have for its primary purpose the consideration and discussion of matters of common concern to the retained side and the self-governing side of Government.

(2) The Council will meet from time to time as summoned by the Governor. He will preside at its meetings; in his absence the Deputy Governor will preside.

(3) The Council will consist of the following members: the Deputy Governor, the Chief Minister, one other member of the Cabinet appointed on his recommendation, the Minister for Turkish Cypriot Affairs, one of the service members of the Defence Committee designated by the Governor, the Attorney-General and the Legal Secretary. Members of the Council shall take a prescribed oath of secrecy.

(4) The Council shall endeavour to harmonise the relations between the two sides of government and to eliminate occasions of conflict by anticipating and discussing them. For this purpose the Council shall be kept informed, so far as may be reasonably practicable, as to legislation proposed by either side and as to proposed administrative action, and shall take such matters into its consideration.

(5) The Governor will invite the views of the members of the Council on matters discussed and will give due weight to the views expressed, but he will

not be under obligation to act in accordance with them or in accordance with any particular preponderance of views.

(6) There will be a Standing Legal Sub-Committee of the Council, consisting of the Legal Secretary and the Attorney-General. One of its functions will be to settle which prosecutions for criminal offences are to be conducted by the Legal Secretary as affecting Governor's matters and which by the Attorney-General as affecting self-governing matters. For this purpose an officer to be known as the Director of Public Prosecutions may be set up to act as a channel between the Police and the Legal Sub-Committee with authority to act under the general instructions of the Committee.

(7) If at any time it shall appear to the Governor that some matter which he has power to deal with by way of Ordinance as being within the Governor's matters can with equal advantage be dealt with by a law of the Legislative Assembly, he may authorise and invite the Legislative Assembly to make a law for the purpose as if the matter were a self-governing matter and therefore within its powers. The authority will be conveyed by a special Ordinance, which shall specify any necessary limitations and conditions upon the authority conferred.

F.—ASSENT TO LEGISLATION

(1) No Bill passed by the Legislative Assembly shall become law unless and until the Governor has signified assent to it.

(2) The following conditions will apply to the Governor's action in giving his assent:

(a)–(i) If he is of opinion that a Bill either deals in whole or in part with any matter that is one of the Governor's matters or includes provisions relating to such matters going beyond those which he has by Ordinance authorised the Legislative Assembly to enact, he will withhold his assent.

(ii) The Governor's decision to give or withhold assent will not be capable of being challenged, and if he signifies assent to a Bill the assent shall be conclusive of the question whether the Bill deals with Governor's matters or self-governing matters.

(iii) If the Governor withholds assent in any case it will be open to him, if he so decides, to return the Bill to the Legislative Assembly with an intimation that he can only signify assent if specified alterations are made to it with a view to taking it outside the range of Governor's matters. If the Bill is so amended he will signify assent accordingly.

(b)–(i) If it appears to the Governor that a Bill or any part of a Bill is or may be repugnant to the provisions of the Constitution which guarantee certain rights or otherwise limit the legislative power of the Legislative Assembly (except those provisions which relate to the division between Governor's matters and self-governing matters, as to which he shall be the sole judge) he may refer the Bill to the Supreme Court for a decision on the question whether the Bill or any specified parts of it are so repugnant.

(ii) An appeal shall lie from the decision of the Supreme Court to the Judicial Committee of the Privy Council.

(iii) No assent may be given pending the pronouncement of the decision of the Court or, if there is an appeal, pending the determination of the appeal.

(iv) The decision of the majority of the Judges of the Supreme Court shall be the decision of the Court and shall be pronounced in open Court by a single Judge, and no other opinion, assenting or dissenting, shall be pronounced or its existence disclosed.

(v) The Governor will not signify assent to a Bill which, or any part of which, has been decided to be repugnant to the Constitution. But if part only is held to be repugnant, he may return the Bill to the Legislative Assembly with an intimation that an amended Bill may be submitted.

(3) The fact that the Governor has signified assent to a Bill without referring it for advice to the Supreme Court will not preclude any person interested from subsequently challenging the validity of the law in legal proceedings on the ground that it is repugnant to the Constitution (except that the assent is conclusive on the question whether a law deals with Governor's matters or self-governing matters).

(4) *Reservation of Assent.*—The Governor will not, without having previously obtained Her Majesty's instructions through a Secretary of State, signify assent to any Bill which in his opinion falls within any of the following classes:

(i) a Bill altering the Constitution, powers and procedure of the Legislative Assembly;

(ii) a Bill affecting the currency of Cyprus or its coinage or affecting foreign exchange or its control;

(iii) a Bill affecting the Royal prerogative;

(iv) a Bill affecting the Trustee Status of any Cyprus Government Stock, and any such Bill after enactment will be capable of being disallowed by Her Majesty.

(5) *Turkish Cypriot Affairs.*—No Bill shall be presented to the Governor for assent unless it is accompanied by a certificate signed by the Attorney-General to the effect that it does not affect Turkish Cypriot affairs or, alternatively, that if it does affect Turkish Cypriot affairs it was passed with the concurrence of the necessary two-thirds of the members of the Legislative Assembly elected by voters on the Turkish Cypriot communal roll.

(6) *Public Officers.*—No Bill which affects the position of a Public Officer shall be presented to the Governor for assent unless it is accompanied by a certificate signed jointly by the Attorney-General and the Chairman of the Public Service Commission to the effect that its provisions do not involve the breach of any contractual obligation or, where no contract is involved, that they satisfy the standard of obligation of a good employer.

(7) Subject to the foregoing, the Governor will signify assent to a Bill duly presented to him.

G.I.—THE JUDICATURE

(1) There shall be a Supreme Court of Cyprus.

(2) The Court shall consist of a President who shall be the Chief Justice of Cyprus and two other Judges. The Legislative Assembly shall have power to

increase the number of Judges from time to time provided always that the total number of members of the Court must always be an uneven number, that there shall at all times be an equal number of Judges belonging to the Greek Cypriot and the Turkish Cypriot communities respectively, and that the Chief Justice shall always be a person who is not native of Cyprus or resident therein at the time of his appointment.

(3) The Chief Justice shall be appointed by the Governor at his discretion after consultation with the Chief Minister. The other Judges of the Supreme Court shall be appointed by the Governor at his discretion after consultation with the Chief Justice.

(4) Judges of the Supreme Court shall retire at the age of 65 or such greater age as the Legislative Assembly may prescribe but shall be eligible for reappointment by the Governor for a further period of twelve months.

(5) A Judge of the Supreme Court will hold office during good behaviour, and will be removable only by the Governor. The Governor will not be entitled to remove a judge on the ground of misconduct unless a recommendation to that effect has been made by a judicial tribunal expressly appointed by a Secretary of State for the purpose of enquiry into complaints of such misconduct and the recommendation has been confirmed by the Judicial Committee of the Privy Council.

(6) The salaries of the Chief Justice and of Judges of the Supreme Court shall in the first place be on the scale in force at the date when the Constitution comes into force. No Judge's salary shall be diminished during his term of office, nor shall his right to pension be altered to his disadvantage. Subject to that the salary of the Chief Justice will be such as may be fixed by the Governor from time to time and the salaries of other Judges such as may be determined by the Legislative Assembly.

(7)–(i) The Supreme Court shall have original jurisdiction in all proceedings in which the validity of any law of the Legislative Assembly is called in question as being repugnant to the provisions of the Constitution which limit the legislative power of the Legislative Assembly (except those provisions which relate to the division between Governor's matters and self-governing matters, as to which the Governor shall be the sole judge).

(ii) A question of repugnancy may be raised by any person interested and in any proceedings if such a question arises in a Court of Law other than the Supreme Court the issue shall be transferred to the Supreme Court for decision.

(iii) If a law or any part of it is so adjudged to be repugnant, it shall be treated as having had no legislative effect whatever unless the Supreme Court shall affirmatively decide that such parts of the Bill as are not repugnant are capable of being accorded independent legal operation.

G.II.—THE JUDICIAL SERVICE COMMISSION

(1) There shall be a Judicial Service Commission for the purpose of advising the Governor in relation to the appointment, promotion, termination of

appointment, dismissal and disciplinary control of Judges (except the Judges of the Supreme Court) and judicial officers.

(2) The members of the Commission shall be as follows:
- (i) The Chief Justice.
- (ii) The Attorney-General.
- (iii) The Chairman of the Public Service Commission.
- (iv) Two persons appointed by the Governor in his discretion being in each case either a judge or retired judge of the Supreme Court or a President or retired President of a District Court, or the Legal Secretary.

(3) The appointment, promotion, termination of appointment, dismissal and disciplinary control of judges (except the Judges of the Supreme Court) and judicial officers shall be vested in the Governor acting on and in accordance with the recommendation of the Judicial Service Commission, provided that:
- (a) it shall be the duty of the Commission at all times to hold a fair balance between the claims of members of the different communities to opportunities of judicial service so far as the needs of the service allow;
- (b) other things being equal a candidate of local origin shall be preferred when recruitment is being considered.

(4) The Chief Justice shall be responsible for transfers of judges and judicial officers and shall have general responsibility with regard to the administration of the courts and the conduct of judicial business.

H.—BROADCASTING

(1) Broadcasting for reception by the public in Cyprus by sound or television shall be a public monopoly service conducted by a Corporation to be known as the Cyprus Broadcasting Corporation.

(2) The Corporation will be constituted by charter with the appropriate exclusive rights and the Charter will charge it with the duty of conducting the broadcasting service with impartial attention to the interests and susceptibilities of the different communities in the island and with due regard to the interests of minorities. Services will be required to be provided in English, Greek and Turkish, and it will be the Corporation's duty at all times to keep a fair balance in the allocation of hours and in other matters between the claims of the communities concerned.

(3) The right to determine the policies and to direct the management of the Corporation and the ownership of its assets will be vested in a Board of Trustees consisting of five persons, of whom two must be Greek Cypriots, two Turkish Cypriots and one, who will be Chairman, must be neither Greek Cypriot nor Turkish Cypriot. Questions before the Board will be decided by a majority of votes and in the event of an equality of votes at any meeting the Chairman will have a second or casting vote.

(4) Trustees will be appointed by the Governor in his discretion after consultation with the Chief Minister, and will hold office for a fixed term of years. The remuneration of the Chairman and the other Trustees will be fixed by the Governor.

(5) The Corporation will be entitled to accept advertisements for broadcasting, if the Trustees so decide, provided that the advertisements must not conflict with its general duty of preserving impartiality and fair balance. It will also enjoy the revenue arising from the issue of wireless licences.

(6) The Trustees shall present an annual report to the Governor on the Corporation's activities, which shall be laid before the Legislative Assembly.

I.—INTER-COMMUNAL EDUCATION

(1) There shall be a Board for inter-communal education which will be charged with the following functions:

(a) to maintain and develop facilities for education and instruction on the basis that such facilities are available to members of the different races and communities without distinction;

(b) to supervise the curriculum followed in the schools, colleges and institutes coming within their jurisdiction, to engage and dismiss staff, to supervise discipline and generally to be responsible for the superior management of such establishments;

(c) to appoint such Boards of Management for the various schools, colleges and institutes as may seem to them appropriate;

(d) to give financial or other support to any schools, colleges or institutes in Cyprus which, though not maintained by the Board, are affording such inter-communal education;

(e) to institute and further schemes for scholarships or other forms of assistance for higher education outside Cyprus;

(f) to advise the Governor on matters concerned with inter-communal education.

(2) There shall be three members of the Board, who will be appointed by the Governor at his discretion. Provided that suitable persons are available, one must be a Greek Cypriot, one a Turkish Cypriot, and the third, who shall be Chairman, must be neither Greek Cypriot nor Turkish Cypriot. They will be entitled to receive such salaries as the Governor shall determine.

(3) Subject to the Governor's approval the Board will have power to co-opt additional members.

(4) Questions before the Board will be decided by a majority of votes.

(5) The Board will be responsible to the Governor alone. He will be entitled to give them such general instructions with regard to matters of policy as in his discretion he may think requisite.

(6) As soon as may be after the Constitution has come into force the Board shall take over responsibility for the control and administration of the following establishments:

(a) the Cyprus Technical Institute;

(b) the Teachers' Training Colleges;

(c) the English School at Nicosia and any other secondary, technical or commercial schools then conducted by the Government.

K.—PUBLIC SERVICE AND THE PUBLIC SERVICE COMMISSION

(1) There shall be a Public Service Commission for the purpose of considering and recommending appointments, promotions, transfers when involving

increase of salary, terminations of appointment, dismissals and action affecting the disciplinary control of public officers. A public officer means for this purpose anyone who is in paid employment in the Public Service other than Her Majesty's armed forces or the police or prison service; but the functions of the Public Service Commission shall not extend to a number of excepted cases, such as the Deputy Governor, judges and judicial officers, the Attorney-General, the Auditor-General and the holders of certain excepted posts designated by the Governor as being special or security posts.

(2) The members of the Public Service Commission will be appointed by the Governor after consultation with the Chief Minister and the Governor in his discretion will nominate which member shall be Chairman. They shall serve for a fixed term of years and will be eligible for reappointment.

(3) No one who is a member of the Legislative Assembly or is a public officer shall be qualified to act as a member of the Public Service Commission.

(4) The members of the Public Service Commission will be paid such salaries as the Governor may determine.

(5) The appointment, promotion, transfer, termination of appointment, dismissal and disciplinary control of public officers within the range of the Public Service Commission shall be vested in the Governor acting on and in accordance with their recommendation, provided that the Governor may act at his discretion with regard to any question of terminating the appointment of or dismissing any public officer if he decides that the interests of defence or internal security are involved in the matter.

(6) The Governor, after consultation with the Chief Minister and the Chairman of the Public Service Commission, may make general regulations for the Public Service Commission as to the manner in which it shall exercise its functions, provided that:

(a) it shall be the duty of the Public Service Commission at all times to hold a fair balance between the claims of members of different communities to opportunities of public service, so far as the needs of the public service allow;

(b) other things being equal, a candidate of local origin shall be preferred when recruitment is being considered.

(7)–(i) The Deputy Governor will be appointed by the Governor on the instructions of the Secretary of State.

(ii) Holders of special posts, that is the Secretary of the Cabinet, Permanent Secretaries to Government Departments and holders of other posts of comparable importance designated by the Governor as special posts will be appointed and be removable by the Governor after consultation with the Chief Minister and the Chairman of the Public Service Commission.

L.—AUDITOR-GENERAL AND ATTORNEY-GENERAL

(1)–(i) There shall be an Auditor-General for Cyprus.

(ii) The Auditor-General will be appointed by the Governor, after consultation with the Chief Minister, and shall not be removable except by the Governor on an address of the Legislative Assembly carried by not less than three-quarters of its members praying for his removal on the ground of misconduct or infirmity of body or mind.

(iii) The Auditor-General will be subject to retirement at the age prescribed for the retirement of public officers in Cyprus.

(iv) The accounts of all Departments and Offices of Government, except those concerned with Governor's matters, shall be audited by the Auditor-General, and for this purpose all books, records and vouchers shall be open to him and his assistants for inspection.

(v) The Auditor-General shall report annually to the Legislative Assembly on the exercise of his functions.

(2)–(i) There shall be an Attorney-General for Cyprus.

(ii) The Attorney-General will be appointed and will be removable by the Governor on the recommendation of the Chief Minister.

(iii) He will be responsible for advising the Cabinet and the Ministers on all legal questions relating to self-governing matters, and for the initiation, conduct and, if necessary, the discontinuance of legal proceedings relating to them. He shall also advise the Governor when so requested.

(iv) The Attorney-General may be a member of the Legislative Assembly.

(3) The salaries of the Auditor-General and the Attorney-General shall be fixed by the Governor.

M.—TRIBUNAL OF GUARANTEES

(1) For the purpose of investigating any complaints of discrimination or other violations of fundamental rights guaranteed by the Constitution there shall be constituted a Tribunal which will have authority to enquire into any acts of Government alleged to be in violation of such rights.

(2) The jurisdiction of the Tribunal will not extend to laws of the Legislative Assembly, the validity of which may be determined by the Supreme Court alone, or to Ordinances made by the Governor but will extend to Orders and Regulations having the force of law as well as to executive acts.

(3) Complaints may be preferred to the Tribunal by individuals, associations or corporations. The Tribunal, while governing its procedure generally by the rules of equity and natural justice and paying regard to its own precedents in the course of its decisions, will have power to determine its own procedure.

(4) Unless the Tribunal sees special reason to the contrary in any particular case its decisions shall be announced in open Court and shall be accompanied by reasons. There will be no appeal from its decisions. The decision of a majority of the members sitting will be the decision of the Tribunal and only one decision is to be announced which will have effect as the decision of all.

(5) The Tribunal will be equipped with all necessary powers of summoning and examining witnesses and of requiring the production of documents, either from departments or offices of Government or from other sources.

(6) If the Tribunal finds a complaint well-founded it will have power, in its discretion, either to make a declaration of right alone or to annul the act of Government complained of or to refer it to the department or office of Gov-

ernment concerned with a recommendation as to the remedial action to be taken. The Tribunal will have the power to award compensation out of public funds.

(7) The jurisdiction of the Tribunal will extend to acts of Government relating to Governor's matters unless in any particular case the Governor files a declaration with the Tribunal to the effect that the complaint involves a subject which cannot be investigated without prejudice to the interests of defence or public security. Upon the filing of such a declaration the jurisdiction of the Tribunal will be withdrawn.

(8) The members of the Tribunal will be appointed by the Governor after consultation with the Chief Minister and the Chief Justice. They will serve for a fixed term of years, subject to re-appointment, at a remuneration which will be fixed in the first instance by the Governor, but will thereafter be such as may be determined by the Legislative Assembly, provided that no member's salary shall be diminished during his term of office nor shall any member be removable except by the Governor on an address of the Legislative Assembly carried by not less than three-quarters of its members praying for his removal on the ground of misconduct or infirmity of body or mind.

(9) The membership shall be so arranged that it includes an equal number of Greek and Turkish Cypriots and that the Chairman is neither Greek Cypriot nor Turkish Cypriot. The members will be selected so as to include persons of legal and administrative experience, provided that no Minister and no person holding a post in the Public Service (excluding the Judicature) can at the same time act as a member of the Tribunal.

(10) There shall be a Registrar of the Tribunal, who will be responsible for the administration of its office, and the proper record of all decisions. The Registrar will be a public officer within the scope of the Public Service Commission. His salary will be fixed by the Governor.

(11) The Tribunal shall present an annual Report to the Legislative Assembly upon the course and results of its work.

N.—AMENDMENT OF SPECIAL TURKISH LAWS

If at any time a petition is presented to the Governor on behalf of not less than two-thirds of the members of the Legislative Assembly elected by voters on the Turkish Cypriot Communal Roll and of not less than two-thirds of the members of the Evkaf Council praying for any specified amendments of or additions to any of the following laws, viz.:

    (i) The Turkish Family (Marriage and Divorce) Laws (1951 and 1954).
    (ii) The Turkish Religious Head (Mufti) Law (1953).
    (iii) The Turkish Family Courts Law (1954).
    (iv) The Evkaf and Vakfs Law (1955).

and the Governor is satisfied (a) that such amendments or additions relate exclusively to matters of Turkish concern and (b) that it is not reasonably likely that a Bill to enact such amendments or additions in the Legislative Assembly would receive sufficient support to become law, he will have power to make a Regulation enacting such amendments or additions and thereupon the Regulation shall take effect as if it were a law duly passed by the Legislative Assembly and assented to by the Governor.

O.—GOVERNOR'S POWERS OF PARDON

(1) The power of pardon is reserved to the Governor. He may:

(a) grant to any person concerned in or convicted of any offence a pardon, either free or subject to lawful conditions; or

(b) grant to any person a respite, either indefinite or for a specified period, of the execution of any sentence; or

(c) substitute a less severe form of punishment for that imposed; or

(d) remit the whole or any part of any sentence or of any penalty or forfeiture otherwise due to Her Majesty on account of an offence.

(2)–(a) Whenever a person has been sentenced to death the Governor will call upon the judge who presided at the trial to make a written report, and will cause this to be considered at a meeting of the Joint Council before deciding whether to exercise the power of pardon in accordance with his own discretion.

(b) Whenever a person has been sentenced to a penalty other than death, the Governor may cause the Joint Council to consider the case before deciding whether to exercise the power of pardon in accordance with his own discretion.

P.I.—FINANCE: SPECIAL PROVISIONS

(1) *Cyprus Broadcasting Corporation.*—The financial affairs of the Cyprus Broadcasting Corporation will be regulated as follows:

(i) The Corporation is to maintain a fund into which shall be paid the receipts from broadcasting licences and its advertising revenue. Against these receipts will be charged the Corporation's annual expenditure (including necessary charges on any monies borrowed) together with any necessary expenses of collecting licences. The Corporation will have power to raise loans subject to the Governor's approval.

(ii) The Corporation is to keep proper accounts. They shall be audited by the Auditor-General who shall report on them to the Governor.

(iii) The Corporation must prepare and submit to the Governor each year estimates of its revenue and expenditure for the succeeding year. These estimates must show what (if any) deficit is anticipated on the year's working. Estimates may include a reasonable provision for contingencies, provided that the amount of this provision is not to be expended without the Governor's sanction.

(iv) The estimates will be subject to the Governor's approval. For the purpose of considering them he will invite the assistance and observations of the Minister of Finance and the Minister for Turkish Cypriot Affairs. In so far as he has approved them and a deficit is involved, he will be empowered to send a precept to the Minister of Finance certifying the amount required. This amount will then constitute a charge upon the Cyprus Consolidated Fund.

(v) The Corporation's annual accounts shall be laid before the Legislative Assembly together with the Auditor-General's report on them.

(2) *Inter-Communal Education Board*

   (i) The Inter-Communal Education Board will maintain a fund into which shall be paid all sums received by it in respect of its operations and such other monies as may accrue to it by way of subvention from Her Majesty's Government, or from other sources. Against these receipts will be charged the Board's annual expenditure.

   (ii) The Board's accounts shall be audited annually by the Auditor-General who shall report thereon to the Governor.

(3) *Police Force and Prisons*

   (i) The cost of providing the Police Force and the prison service will be shared between the self-governing side and the Governor's side.

   (ii) For this purpose the self-governing side shall raise and provide annually the sum of £750,000, being approximately the equivalent at present cost of the expenditure of the approved establishment of the police and prison services in the year 1954, and the balance will be found by the Governor's side. The £750,000 will be charged upon the Cyprus Consolidated Fund.

   (iii) At any time not less than 5 years after the Constitution has come into force the sum of £750,000 may be reviewed and a sum larger or smaller may be substituted in its place if the Governor and the Chief Minister so agree.

(4) *Turkish Cypriot Affairs*

   (i) There shall be raised and provided annually a sum sufficient for the establishment of the Office of Turkish Cypriot Affairs and the discharge of its functions. This sum shall be ascertained under three separate heads, (a) establishment, (b) Turkish Cypriot education, (c) other functions.

   (ii) The sum raised and provided for Turkish Cypriot elementary education in any year shall not be in less proportion to the sum raised and provided for Greek Cypriot elementary education in that year than that which the number of pupils receiving instruction in Turkish Cypriot elementary schools bears to the number of pupils receiving instruction in Greek Cypriot elementary schools at the close of the previous year.

   (iii) The minimum sum raised and provided for Turkish Cypriot secondary education in any year shall not be less than the amount expended on such education in the last completed year before the coming into force of this Constitution.

   (iv) The sum to be provided for Turkish Cypriot Affairs shall be discussed in the first instance by the Chief Minister and the Minister for Turkish Cypriot Affairs. If they fail to agree the matter shall be referred to the Governor, whose decision shall be final; and, the decision being given the Governor will send a precept to the Minister of Finance specifying the amount required. The sum so ascertained shall be a charge on the Cyprus Consolidated Fund.

P.II.—FINANCE: SELF-GOVERNING MATTERS

(1) There shall be a Cyprus Consolidated Fund into which are to be paid all receipts and revenues arising in connection with self-governing matters and such other monies as may properly become available for appropriation by the Legislative Assembly. Provided that:

    (a) Receipts from the issue of wireless licences shall be paid direct into the revenues of the Cyprus Broadcasting Corporation, and

    (b) Receipts arising from the activities of the Inter-Communal Education Board shall be paid direct into the revenues of that Board.

(2) The Minister of Finance shall have annual estimates of revenue and expenditure on self-governing matters prepared. The estimates, when approved by the Cabinet, are to be laid before the Assembly.

(3) The proposals for all expenditure contained in the estimates shall be submitted to the Legislative Assembly by means of an Appropriation Bill.

(4) When additional expenditure on existing services or any new service is incurred or is likely to be incurred during the year a supplementary Appropriation Bill shall be prepared. But this is not to exclude provision being made for meeting urgent expenditure that may not have been foreseen.

(5) The following specific items will constitute a permanent annual charge on the Cyprus Consolidated Fund:

    (a) the salaries and remuneration of—

        (i) the Chief Justice and other Judges;

        (ii) members of the Tribunal of Guarantees;

        (iii) members of the Public Service Commission;

        (iv) the Attorney-General;

        (v) the Auditor-General;

        (vi) the Clerk and Deputy Clerk of the Legislative Assembly;

        (vii) the Registrar of the Tribunal of Guarantees.

    (b) the sums required to pay the salaries of the Governor and Deputy-Governor and the expenses of their official establishments;

    (c) the sum of £10,000 as the contribution of Cyprus to Imperial Defence;

    (d) the sums mentioned in the Special Provisions which relate to the Cyprus Broadcasting Corporation, the Police Force and Prisons, the Turkish Cypriot Affairs;

    (e) the sums required to meet contractual obligations to Public Officers (excluding members of the Police and Prison service and officers employed in the Governor's secretariat and departments), to pay their salaries and allowances and to pay superannuation benefits to retired Public Officers and their dependants.

(6) Any of the foregoing sums which are charged on the Cyprus Consolidated Fund may be paid in case of necessity on the authority of a warrant from the Governor.

P.III.—FINANCE: GOVERNOR'S MATTERS

(1) There will be a fund to be known as the Defence Fund into which will be paid all monies received in respect of Governor's Matters, and all other monies properly receivable by the Governor for appropriation by Ordinance.

(2) The Governor will make an Appropriation Ordinance in respect of annual expenditure. Before doing so he will prepare and submit estimates for the approval of a Secretary of State and as directed by him.

(3) No monies are to be paid from the Defence Fund except on warrant from the Governor duly executed in accordance with such instructions as may from time to time be issued by a Secretary of State.

(4) The Defence Fund will be audited in accordance with such directions as may be received through a Secretary of State.

Q.—EMERGENCY LAWS

(1) Notwithstanding anything that has gone before Her Majesty will be entitled by Order-in-Council at any time:

(a) to declare that a public emergency exists in Cyprus;

(b) to make provision for such measures as may appear necessary for dealing with the emergency security of public safety or order and of supplies and services in Cyprus during the period of such an emergency.

(2) An Order-in-Council made for this purpose may suspend all or any of the provisions of the Constitution during such period or empower the Governor so to do: in particular it may grant him power to make laws generally in self-governing matters and to take executive action in respect of them.

APPENDIX A

1. Electoral District	2. Urban or Rural	3. Number of Constituencies	
		General roll (all voters not included in the Turkish Cypriot communal roll)	Turkish Cypriot
Nicosia	Town	2	
	Rural		} 2
Kyrenia	Town }	7	
	Rural		
Famagusta	Town	1	
	Rural	4	} 1
Larnaca	Town	1	
	Rural	2	} 1
Limassol	Town	1	
	Rural	3	} 1
Paphos	Town }	3	1
	Rural		
		24	6

APPENDIX 8

Cyprus Constitution, despatch dated 7th May, 1948, from the Secretary of State for the Colonies to the Governor of Cyprus*

THE CHURCH HOUSE,
GREAT SMITH STREET, S.W.1.
7th May, 1948.

My Lord,

His Majesty's Government have given careful consideration to the future of constitutional development in Cyprus. The results of their study of the question are embodied in this despatch. I should be grateful if a copy of the despatch may be communicated to the Chairman of the Consultative Assembly, so that its contents may be brought before the Assembly for consideration without delay.

2. His Majesty's Government have had under review the outline of a constitution given to the Consultative Assembly by its Chairman, Sir Edward Jackson, on 7th November, 1947, and also the statement addressed to me by eight Greek members of the Assembly which was enclosed with the Chairman's letter of 26th November, 1947, and forwarded to me under the Acting Governor's despatch No. 170 of the same date. I intimated in the House of Commons on 28th January that His Majesty's Government saw considerable difficulties in the way of accepting the proposals of the eight Greek members, which embodied the principle of fully responsible government in the internal affairs of Cyprus. Further consideration of those proposals since that date has confirmed His Majesty's Government in the view that they are unacceptable and that the interests of Cyprus at this juncture will best be served by the adoption of a form of government which, without entailing any violent break with the existing administrative structure, will, nevertheless, provide for the active participation of the people of Cyprus in the conduct of their internal affairs, both through the normal processes of debating and voting by their elected representatives in the Legislature and through a close association between the Legislature and the executive side of Government.

3. In considering how this general conception may be translated into concrete terms, my colleagues and I have turned to the tentative outline laid before the Consultative Assembly by its Chairman on 7th November, 1947. We find ourselves in general agreement with this and consider that within its framework is to be found the proper line of advance in the shaping of a constitution for Cyprus. This being so His Majesty's Government now put forward proposals for filling in that framework which will be found to reflect the broad features of the outline which the Chairman commended to the Assembly, though in certain respects they go beyond it.

---

* Colonial No. 227 (London, HMSO).

4. These proposals are being laid before the Consultative Assembly so that its members, and the people of Cyprus, may have a clear view of the general form of Constitution which His Majesty's Government would be willing to see introduced in Cyprus if the people desire it. The proposals have, therefore, been set out with a fair degree of detail. While His Majesty's Government would be unable to give their approval to a Constitution which fundamentally exceeded these proposals in the direction of full self-government, they do not wish to limit the freedom of the Consultative Assembly unnecessarily, and it will be observed that a considerable number of points are left open for further discussion. I should make it clear that the language used in the following paragraphs is not in all respects the precise legal language, which would have to be employed in the eventual constitutional instruments embodying the new Constitution. It will also be understood that this despatch does not refer to all the provisions which, in common with other constitutions, would be required in those instruments.

5. The outline which follows is set out under four main headings: the composition of the Legislature, the functions and powers of the Legislature, the Executive Council and certain subsidiary matters.

COMPOSITION OF THE LEGISLATURE

Franchise

6. Every male British subject of 21 years or over, who is resident in the Colony, should have one vote. Provision should also be made to enfranchise non-British subjects who have appropriate residence and other qualifications. I would suggest that, as before 1931, residence in the Colony for five years would suffice, unless the Assembly see grounds for increasing the period required.

7. It will be for the Assembly to consider whether or not the franchise should be extended to women. If the Assembly favour this course, His Majesty's Government will be willing to accept it.

Frequency of Elections

8. Elections to the Legislature should be held at intervals of not more than a stated period—either four or five years. It will be for the Assembly to determine which of these two periods is to be preferred.

Form of Elections

9. The colony should be divided into constituencies for this purpose. In view of the presence in Cyprus of the substantial Turkish minority community, with its own religion, language and customs, I consider that at this stage it would be necessary that the Turkish community should elect their own representatives in the Legislature. Communal constituencies would be defined for that purpose and Turkish voters would register on a communal electoral roll. For representation of the general population, voters would be registered in each constituency on a general electoral roll. If any person qualified to be registered as a Turkish voter preferred to be registered on the general electoral roll for the appropriate constituency, he could so choose. The compilation of

the registers of voters would be undertaken by persons appointed by the Governor.

Number of Elected Members

10. His Majesty's Government take the view that there should be a clear and substantial majority of elected members in the Legislature, and that only the minimum number of officials whose presence is essential for the conduct of business should be members of the Legislature. The latter are dealt with in the next section.

11. I would therefore propose that there should be 22 elected members, that is to say, approximately one per 20,000 of the present population of Cyprus. Of these, again in approximate proportion to the respective population figures, 8 members should be elected on the general electoral register and four members on the Turkish communal electoral register.

12. The total figure of 22 elected members is put forward as a basis of discussion, and it will be for the Assembly to consider whether this number is appropriate or whether there are good grounds for modifying it. It appears, however, that to increase the number substantially would make the size of the electorate in each constituency undesirably small, while to decrease the number substantially would create a Legislature too small to reflect adequately all aspects of public opinion. I should make it clear that, if the Assembly should wish to suggest a modification in the total number of elected members, I should attach great importance to retaining the principle that the number of seats allotted for election on the Turkish communal register should be proportionate to the numerical strength of the Turkish community in the Island, as is the case with the proposal above for allotting them four seats out of 22.

Official Members of the Legislature

13. In accordance with the principles stated in the previous section, His Majesty's Government would wish to see provision made for a small number of senior officials to have seats in the Legislature. This requirement would be met if there were four official members, namely, the Colonial Secretary, the Attorney-General, the Treasurer and the Senior Commissioner. The presence of these officials would ensure that the Legislature is properly informed on executive subjects and on the policy of the Government, both by speeches and by answers to members' questions, and would also ensure that the members of the Legislature themselves, as the representatives of public opinion in the Island, would be able to make their views known directly and in the free exchange of debate to the most senior officials.

Chairman

14. His Majesty's Government take the view that, with a Legislature of the form now contemplated, it would be undesirable for the Governor himself to preside over its deliberations, and that the interests of the Legislature itself would be best served by the appointment of the Chairman by the Governor from among persons who are not members. He would thus be in an entirely independent and impartial position. It is my hope that a person of distinction would be found to accept the Governor's appointment to this post.

15. It is clear that a Chairman appointed in this manner should not have an original vote in the proceedings of the Legislature. I should welcome the views of the Assembly on the question whether there would be an advantage in giving the Chairman a casting vote. They may hold that, as long as the Chairman is not selected from among members, it would be inappropriate for him to exercise even a casting vote. In that event, it would be necessary to provide some other method of resolving the situation created when the votes on a matter before the Legislature are equally divided; for example, by providing that, when the vote is equal, the motion shall be deemed to be lost.

FUNCTIONS AND POWERS OF THE LEGISLATURE

16. It is the intention of His Majesty's Government that the field of debate and legislation should be restricted as little as possible. The Constitution must provide that the Legislature may not discuss the status of Cyprus within the British Commonwealth; but apart from this no subject need be *ipso facto* excluded.

Powers of Legislation, and Reservations

17. Subject to the above, the Legislature will thus be free to legislate on any subject in accordance with the procedure and necessary limitations set out below.

18. I consider it necessary to prescribe that the Governor's prior consent should be obtained, through the Chairman of the Legislature, before the introduction of any Money Bill or Resolution, any Bill which in the opinion of the Governor affects defence, external affairs, or the special interests of minorities, or any Bill amending the Constitution. Apart from this, I do not think it necessary for any limitation to be placed on freedom to introduce legislation, including private members' Bills.

19. It would be necessary to give the Governor the usual reserve legislative power; that is to say, power to declare a Bill or motion to have effect as if it had been duly passed, if (a) he considers that it is expedient in the interests of public order, good faith or good government that it should have effect, and (b) has been rejected by the Legislature or passed in a form which is unacceptable. The Governor should also be empowered to return Bills to the Legislature with his recommendations for amendments.

20. Bills passed by the Legislature would of course require the assent of The King or of the Governor in The King's name. The Governor, who would have the normal authority to reserve Bills which have been passed by the Legislature for the signification of His Majesty's pleasure, should be required by the Constitution to exercise this power of reservation in respect of certain classes of Bills, including in particular any Bill which he is satisfied affects defence or external affairs, or discriminates against minorities, or amends the Constitution. The usual provision would also be made in the Constitution for disallowance of laws by His Majesty.

21. The Consultative Assembly will, I hope, recognise that the provisions described in the preceding three paragraphs are not intended to circumscribe the freedom of the Legislature unnecessarily; and occasions on which it

might be necessary to invoke some of them, in particular the "reserve power," should be very rare. These provisions should, therefore, be regarded only as safeguards which His Majesty's Government consider necessary and not as evidence of any desire on the part of His Majesty's Government to interfere with the freedom of action of Legislature in the normal domestic affairs of the Island.

Questions

22. Standing Orders of the Legislature should recognise the normal right of legislative bodies to obtain information by means of questions, which would be addressed to the appropriate members of the Executive Council who would be sitting in the Legislature. This method of bringing public opinion to bear on day-to-day policy is of considerable value and would, I feel, meet a definite need in the circumstances of Cyprus to-day.

Reserved Civil List

23. I consider that provision should be made for a small reserved civil list covering the salaries of the Governor and of the Judiciary. The effect of this reservation would be that, while the Legislature might, if they thought fit, vote additional sums under any or all of these heads, they would not be in a position to reduce the sums provided, save by an amendment to the Constitution. The Assembly will, I think, recognise the desirability of placing these matters beyond day-to-day controversy.

Standing Orders

24. The Legislature will require Standing Orders for the conduct of its business. These should be prepared in the first instance by the Governor, so that the Legislature would have a code of procedure ready to hand as from its first meeting. Afterwards the Legislature would be entitled to amend the Standing Orders if occasion were seen to do so, but amendments should require the Governor's approval before they take effect.

THE EXECUTIVE COUNCIL

The Governor

25. In accordance with normal practice, general responsibility for the Executive would remain vested in the Governor as the representative of The King. He would be assisted, as at present, by an Executive Council. The Constitution should provide that the Governor would not be bound to take the advice of his Executive Council, but he would be required to inform the Secretary of State of any instance where he acted contrary to its advice.

Composition of Executive Council

26. With a Legislature of the type proposed, composed largely of elected representatives of the people, it would clearly be inappropriate for the Executive Council to remain a body composed almost entirely of officials. Close cooperation between the Legislature and those responsible under the Governor for the formation and execution of policy would be essential. One

way of providing this link has already been mentioned, namely, the proposal that four officials should have seats in the Legislature. It will be equally, if not more, important, however, for the elected members of the Legislature to be closely connected with the direction of affairs in the Executive Council. To this end, His Majesty's Government propose that certain of them should be appointed to membership of the Executive Council. Moreover, it is the view of His Majesty's Government that non-official members of the Executive Council should not be found otherwise than from among members of the Legislature.

27. In the Constitutional instruments, it would therefore be provided that the Executive Council should consist of the four officials who have already been named as official members of the Legislature, and of such other persons, being elected members of the Legislature or other officials, as His Majesty may from time to time direct through a Secretary of State.

28. The exact number of members of the Executive Council would not be laid down in the Constitution itself (except for the four officials already mentioned), in order to leave the greatest possible measure of flexibility. The number of non-official members appointed could vary as experience might show to be desirable. It would also be possible for other officials in addition to the four already mentioned to be made members of the Council if it were thought that the Council would benefit from their presence. Since an Executive Council does not proceed by the method of resolution or voting, which is inappropriate to a body of that nature, the question whether officials or non-officials are in the majority at a particular moment becomes of small significance.

29. While the formal position in the constitutional instruments would be left as indicated above, I think it desirable for me to state clearly now that it would be the intention of His Majesty's Government that, in the first instance, four non-official members should be appointed to the Council. Of these, three would be Greek members chosen from the majority party in the Legislature, and one a Turkish member chosen from among the Turkish representatives in the Legislature.

Functions of Councillors

30. It would, moreover, be the intention to associate these four non-official members of the Council (and any others who may be added in future) with certain specific Departments, in the manner already suggested to the Consultative Assembly by its Chairman. They would be known as Councillors for those subjects. The decision on the distribution of Departments would lie with the Governor, who would also prescribe the precise relationship between the Councillors and the Departments assigned to them. This procedure would be experimental, and no doubt in the initial stages there might be uncertainties and difficulties, but with good-will on both sides there is no reason why these should not be easily overcome. Councillors would take part in the formulation of general Government policy in Executive Council, with all the authority derived from their position as elected representatives of the people and leaders of the Legislature. More particularly, through their knowledge of the issues involved, they would be able to shape policy regarding the Departments with which they were individually associated. It would clearly be suitable for them

to speak and to answer questions in the Legislature on the work of the particular Departments associated with them. It is impossible to forecast exactly how an arrangement of this sort will work until it has been tried; but in the view of His Majesty's Government it opens up a wide and promising field of experience and one into which I trust the Consultative Assembly will be ready to enter.

SUBSIDIARY MATTERS

31. There are certain subsidiary matters on which His Majesty's Government do not feel it necessary at this stage to express a firm view, but which it is desirable to bring to the attention of the Consultative Assembly in this despatch.

Qualifications of Members of the Legislature

32. Members should be British subjects; and it is clear that, in accordance with normal practice, their qualifications should otherwise not be less than the qualifications of voters. The Assembly may wish to consider whether further qualifications for members, such as a higher age limit, should be imposed. I should be prepared to consider any such recommendations, though I do not myself feel that further restrictions would be necessary, apart from the normal disqualifications such as insanity and imprisonment.

Payment of Members of the Legislature

33. It is common practice in most democratic countries for members of the Legislature to be remunerated for their services. The Assembly will no doubt wish to consider this point, and, if they endorse the principle, to suggest an appropriate figure. Unless the rate of remuneration of members were written into the Constitution itself (which I should not consider desirable), the recommendations of the Assembly on this point would, of course, require confirmation by the Legislature when it comes into existence.

34. The Assembly may also wish to consider whether members of the Legislature who are from time to time also holding the position of members of the Executive Council, should be remunerated at a higher rate.

Name of the Legislature

35. For the sake of simplicity this body has been referred to throughout my despatch as "the Legislature," but a suitable title will be required. Members of the Consultative Assembly may feel that there would be advantage in marking the advance on the Constitution of 1882-1931 by a change in terminology; if so, I shall be most willing to hear their views.

36. I commend these proposals to the members of the Consultative Assembly. While they stipulate limits beyond which His Majesty's Government is not prepared to go, they have been shaped with the single purpose of affording, within those limits, the maximum advance in constitutional liberty. His Majesty's Government, always solicitous for the welfare of Cyprus, earnestly trust that the members of the Consultative Assembly will recognise the sincerity and singleness of purpose with which the proposals are put forward.

If they will rise to it they have now a great opportunity to enlarge the liberties of the people of Cyprus and to make them partners and helpers in that social and economic progress which it is the wish of His Majesty's Government to see the Island achieve. There have been many delays in the setting up and the work of the Consultative Assembly. I trust its members will now recognise the wisdom of pressing forward so that Cyprus may have its Constitution at an early date.

I have, etc.,
LISTOWEL
(for the Secretary of State)

Governor,
The LORD WINSTER

APPENDIX 9

The Ballad of Gregory Afxentiou

Gregory Afxentiou, the twenty-nine-year-old second-in-command to Colonel Grivas, the EOKA terrorist leader, fought sixty British troops today from a cave in the Troodos mountains. When the battle was over his body lay among flames. . . .

The Governor of Cyprus, Sir John Harding, has sent a message to the men of the Duke of Wellington's Regiment congratulating them on their success.—*The Times*, 4 March 1957

Come out, come out, young Gregory,
    There's guns all round your cave.
The sun's rising over the mountains
    And you've only one life to save.

Your price is paid young Gregory
    While you sleep deep underground,
For the man that brings the soldiers
    Shall have five thousand pound.

Can't you hear their officer calling?
    He speaks your language plain,
So lift your hands and meet him.
    And you'll see the sun again.

Five men lay down together,
    Five men last night were brave,
But four went to the daylight
    And one stayed in the cave.

You're all alone, young Gregory,
    Your friends have gone from you,
They chose a life in prison
    And you may choose it too.

Come in, come in, he shouted,
    For I am but one man,
One man and his gun are waiting,
    Come fetch me if you can.

They are sixty in the daylight,
    And one in the dark within,
But the one will not surrender
    And the sixty daren't go in.

So the guns begin to crackle
    And fast the bullets fly
And the sun young Gregory cannot see
    Is soon high in the sky.

You bleed, you bleed, young Gregory,
　　Now come out without shame,
A wounded man may save his life
　　And there'll be none to blame.

But still young Gregory's shooting
　　And the soldiers have no rest
And the hours pass in darkness
　　And the sun goes to the west.

Machine-guns go to fetch him,
　　Grenades are next to try,
Tear-gas is sent to blind him,
　　The man who will not die.

Then the petrol barrels lumber
　　Out of the soldiers' sight
And the bullets set them burning
　　And the cave is blazing bright.

But still the gun is speaking
　　And the sixty hear the one
And the light is grey with evening
　　And the battle is not done.

Now the engineers are busy,
　　They lay their charge and train,
And the sixty men stand silent
　　Who need not shoot again.

And dynamite and petrol
　　Are piled among the rocks,
For when the hounds are wearied
　　All's fair to kill a fox.

And the village on the hilltop
　　Is shaken with the din,
And when the cave is silent
　　The sixty men go in.

And the Governor came to tell them
　　How bravely they had done,
For the regiment gained new honour
　　When sixty men killed one.

But when brother speaks to brother
　　And father to his son,
In the memory of his people
　　Young Gregory lives on.

ANON

APPENDIX 10

Interview with Melih Esenbel, Secretary-General of the Foreign Ministry of Turkey at the Time of the Zurich Agreements and Ambassador in Washington during the 1974 Turkish Invasion of Cyprus, *Tercuman*, 30 July 1983 (translation)*

Interview conducted by: Taylan Sorgun
Title of the Interview: "The Zurich-London Agreement which Recognised the Right of Armed Intervention to Turkey."

Taylan Sorgun:
Recently we commemorated yet another anniversary of the Cyprus intervention. Besides, the Cyprus problem is always on the agenda. Obviously, Turkey's armed intervention in Cyprus was an important happening in the world politics. Before that we had witnessed an air operation and an attempt for intervention. The basis of Turkey's armed intervention in Cyprus went beyond the right in moral intervention and rested upon the legal right obtained at the Zurich-London agreements.

If we recall the period of the conclusion of this agreement in our recent history we will see that this agreement was materialized after passing through highly difficult conditions. It is also common knowledge that one cannot come across to another such agreement [in the world]. You were on duty at the Foreign Ministry at the time.

If we cast a glance on the phases through which this agreement passed which fundamental developments will come to our attention?

Melih Esenbel:
With the Lausanne Agreement Turkey had left to Britain Cyprus' sovereignty which was already de jure and de facto in the possession of that country. However, this situation continued only for some period. When after the Second World War Britain initiated a policy of granting independence to her colonies and to the territories under her protection, the Greek Cypriots' desire for Enosis too were excited. The Deputy-Foreign Minister of Greece, Venizelos, made a statement in this direction in the beginnings of 1951. However, the issue became an international problem in 1954.

In 1954 I and the late Prime Minister, Menderes, had gone to the USA for economic talks with Eisenhower. On our return from Washington we stopped in Athens. A meeting was planned there. Our Ambassador there, Cemal Husnu Taray, told us that during this planned meeting to be held with Papagos the Greek Prime Minister would raise the Cyprus problem.

---

* The author directs particular attention to italicized sections on pages 148, 149, 151, 153, 154 and 155.

Taylan Sorgun:
Menderes' reply was:

"If they are going to raise this question I won't stay here; I'll continue my trip this evening."

The purpose behind this was to make it explicit that Cyprus was a very important problem for Turkey and its discussion in this manner could have damaged the Turkish-Greek friendship. Thus, Papagos did not raise this issue during the meetings. However, after our return to Turkey, Greece made a recourse to the United Nations despite the objections from America. The United Nations with a resolution adopted in 1954 declared that it will not debate the problem; so no debate was held.

Taylan Sorgun:
Thus the problem came before the international forum for the first time in 1954 though the result was negative. Well, how the developments leading to Zurich and London agreements commenced?

Melih Esenbel:
As you indicated the problem came before the international platform in 1954. However, before that Britain's afore-mentioned decision had excited certain ambitions. Whereas, the road leading to Zurich and London agreements was opened as a result of Turkey's growing interest in the problem.

After Turkey's interest in the Cyprus problem increased and after Turkey openly and gradually indicated that she will protect her own strategic interests and that at the same time the Turkish community there must have a healthy existence, Turkey was accepted as one of the sides to the problem and idea arose to solve the problem by reconciling with Turkey too. This development took a lot of time. *Enormously patient work was done both on government and diplomatic levels in order to register the position of Turkey which had no right of say at all at the beginning. It required sustained and painstaking work to achieve results.* As you know these efforts also passed through various stages.

First the London Conference was convened in 1955 and Turkey was invited there as a side. Greece reacted to this strongly saying that "Turkey has no place here" but in the final analysis accepted Turkey's presence. But, the conference gave no positive result. Turkey's Foreign Minister the late Fatih Rustu Zorlu, represented Turkey at this conference convened in 1955.

Taylan Sorgun:
You just brought out two separate and important points concerning Cyprus. One was the defence of the rights of the Turkish community there and the other was the protection of Turkey's strategic interests. After the agreement concerning Cyprus, a new and a strategic situation emerged for Turkey both in the Aegean and with Mediterranean.

Melih Esenbel:
The Turkish community in Cyprus is a matter of great importance for Turkey. If we consider the problem in terms of strategy, Cyprus is not of great impor-

tance to Greece for them the problem is one of imperialism. The issue for Greece is to put her feet on yet another island, just like she jumped to the other islands. *Whereas, for us, Cyprus represents an important strategic location in the approaches of Iskenderun and Mersin. For us, Cyprus is a problem which concerns our national interests;* it is not a position for jumping and expansion.

Another important, very important point besides this is our community there. Once upon a time the Turks there were in majority. Later as a result of the policy followed, they gradually dispersed. Whatever the case, since 1570 they were living there as the remnants of the Turkish sovereignty. It was not possible for us to leave them alone. It was necessary to ensure their security and to enable them to live on their own territories as free human beings. If you recall the problems which have taken place between us and the Greeks, you will see that Turkey could not have allowed these people to come under Greek Cypriot sovereignty and to live as a simple minority. As I said it was Turkey's obligation to secure their existence as free human beings. So, from this point of view too great duties fell on Turkey.

Taylan Sorgun:
What difficulties Turkey faced during the period of the conclusion of the Zurich-London agreements? As far as I could recall the agreement passed through very difficult phases?

Melih Esenbel:
You know, as I said before the first London conference failed. After that Turkey exerted efforts particularly to force Britain accept Turkey's rights. As a result, Britain put forward a series of slightly different yet similar plans. The essence of these plans were: To recognize autonomy to the communities for a period of time and then to accept the discussion of the self-determination issue. But no precise date was fixed for this. Though this view was first put forward during the talks with Harding, actually it was the Radcliff plan of 1956.

This means that in a short period from 1955 to 1956 we covered an important distance. This is indicative by the fact that in Radcliff's plan the principle that the communities must have separate assemblies was accepted. In addition the two communities were to be represented in the administration under the Governor and that [this administration] was also to cooperate with representatives of Turkey and Greece. Here let me draw your attention to the following fact. Not only a separate identity was recognized to the [Turkish] community, it also provided that the Turks and Greek Cypriots should solve their problems within a council, and it also brought about a working system whereby under the presidency or the British Governor, Turkey and Greece were to work in cooperation. Turkey reached this point from 1954 when it had no right or say at all and thus acquired the authority or say in the form of a solution. From this, the process started towards recognizing a separate identity to Turkish community and towards the establishment or independent municipalities.

This plan reached its high point with the statement of the then Secretary of colonies, Lenox Boyd, during the unveiling of this plan at the British

House of Commons in December of 1956. This statement was at the same time the first indication of the form of the future solution of the Cyprus problem. In explaining Radcliff's plan, Boyd in his statement disclosed that the right of exercise of self-determination that is, when peoples exercise the right to determine their own destiny, should not be recognized, solely to a unit called the Cypriot people, that a solution could be achieved by recognizing this right separately to the Turkish and the Greek Cypriot communities and that such a final solution is also necessitated by the confusing situation in Cyprus and by Turkey's interests.

Taylan Sorgun:
What was the position of the other countries in the face of this statement which enormously boosted the problem forward?

Melih Esenbel:
It did not suit Greece because it prevented Enosis. Lenox Boyd statement that the Turkish community could have used this right separately and independently was in a way a road leading to taksim. It was also preventing Enosis. Upon this Makarios and Greece instigated terrorism both against the British and the Turks. After Radcliff's plan was put forward in this manner, the government in the island was replaced and Foot was appointed as the governor of the island. He too produced a plan inspired by these principles but in his plan the road leading to taksim was a bit closed. So we assumed a negative stance against this [plan]. Greece again took the problem to the UN but again got no results.

      After 1957 Macmillan became the Prime Minister in Britain and revived this problem. The late Prime Minister, Menderes's relations with him were very correct and they were holding tête-à-tête and secret talks. These talks were not being divulged to the press.

Taylan Sorgun:
What do you known about these talks?

Melih Esenbel:
These talks were put in minutes. During these talks Macmillan gave some kind of assurance to our Prime Minister. According to this, the period of autonomy was to be reduced to 7 years and the Turkish and Greek Cypriot representatlves were to be on the Governor's administration. But to placate Greece they were given "advisory" duty. Before it was described as "cooperation". And when Macmillan also gave assurance that after these 7 years the right of self-determination will be used within the framework of Lennox Boyd's statement and thus the road to taksim too would be opened, we assumed a positive stance from then on.

      The second factor opening the road to Zurich was Macmillan's plan. Britain said it would implement this plan as from 1958 without consulting the parties concerned. This plan envisaged the withdrawal of Britain from Cyprus, would only keep sovereign bases, a system of autonomy would be set up under the Governor for 7 years, the two communities would have two separate assemblies and if at the end of this 7-year period the sides desired, a tripartite administration was to be set up; that is, an administration made up of Britain, Turkey and Greece. If this solution too were unacceptable then Britain would give independence to Cyprus and under the then existing conditions the sides were going to use their right to self-determination. This naturally meant that the issue would have ended in taksim. Britain declared that she would "start implementing the new system starting with 1st of October regardless whether or not the Greek Cypriots and Greeks accept it." That was the first step.

Makarios, who failed at the United Nations and at the bi-lateral talks and who realizing that he will not be able to achieve Enosis, changed policy. He put forward the thesis of independence. In the meantime, the Priest-Grivas-Athina trio continued the terrorism.

While on the one hand Makarios put forward this independence issue, on the other hand Greece again took the self-determination problem to the United Nations in 1955 to see if it could obtain any results. She failed there too. What's more, the previous United Nations resolutions had spoken about the "solution of the problem through negotiation", whereas the term "sides" was used in the 1958 resolution. Who the sides were was clear; they were Turkey, Britain, Greece and the two communities. This was an open defeat for Greece.

Taylan Sorgun:
In those days quite intensive work was done at the United Nations and difficult days were experienced. . . .

Melih Esenbel:
Of course. . . . Excellent work was done. Separate work was done on each State and this successful resolution was obtained. Later, Greece started to soften its stance.

At the time I was not in New York. At the NATO meeting in December in Paris I met with the late Zorlu. Zorlu briefed me about his talks with Averoff and told me that there are possibilities of agreeing on a middle way. Here I'll reveal a point because this point has not been properly made public so far. Before going to the United Nations meeting the late Zorlu was called by the late Prime Minister Menderes who told Zorlu: "*Find a middle way solution to this Cyprus problem in such a way that the interests of both the [Turkish] community and of Turkey are protected.* But, let us act with more flexibility because its prolongation is making us uncomfortable both at home and abroad. If we are going to protect our interest we must stop this issue from being a matter of dispute and we must upgrade it to a higher plane as a solved problem."

Zorlu told me about this encounter. Half an hour later the late Prime Minister Menderes also called me in and repeated the same things and said to me: "I told Zorlu I am going to tell you too. Being at the head of the administration of the Foreign Ministry you are aware of the problems; find a solution to this problem. *It is becoming obvious that at this stage we will not be able to achieve taksim.* Find another formula which will ensure the possibilities for our security and for the community's survival".

Taylan Sorgun:
Thus the road to Zurich and London agreements were opened in this manner....

Melih Esenbel:
Yes, that's how it was opened. Greece's last defeat at the United Nations also led the way there. . . .

Taylan Sorgun:
That is, they [the Greeks] were forced to accept this. . . .

Melih Esenbel:
Yes, she could not obtain any results from the talks with Britain; what else could she have done? Given the unsuccessful continuation of the struggle it was also to their interests to approach to a middle way solution. However, we worked and struggled very hard to bring the affair to this stage. The late Prime Minister, the government and the late Zorlu worked hard. The late Prime Minister was quite sensitive on the issue. Zorlu knew the details of the affair and was constantly feeding the Prime Minister with his views.

Taylan Sorgun:
How were the interests of Turkey and of the community to be secured permanently? . . . I think here the issue of Turkey's right for armed intervention comes into fore.

Melih Esenbel:
Yes, it was agreed to conclude a treaty of guarantee against the possibility of violation of the existing system. The protectors of the system to be established were to be Britain, Turkey and Greece. If the existing system was violated anyone of these three guarantors could have even intervened alone; of course after consultations between them. If they disagreed during these consultations each could have used the right of separate intervention. The meaning of this is explicit.

Taylan Sorgun:
Certain arguments had taken place at the time concerning this article. . . .

Melih Esenbel:
Yes, in the Parliament criticism was leveled to the effect that a provision for a joint action under any situation with Britain was not included in the agreement. The point is that if we had inserted the condition of being together with Britain under any situation then we couldn't act if Britain did not act. The late Zorlu had explained the issue in this manner at the Parliament. What we achieved by this? If the Greek Cypriot administration attempted to upset the internal situation, then the intervention would have been considered as an Imperative action. Well, who was going to do this intervention? Britain had acquired the two bases and had no more intention for intervention and Greece would not have sent troops to the island against Makarios if the latter upset the order. . . .

This meant that in this manner the road was opened for Turkey's right of direct intervention.

Taylan Sorgun:
This was a provision on paper. However, there was another important factor which would have enabled the implementation of this provision: that is, the sending of troops. . . .

Melih Esenbel:
Yes, the issue of sending a unit was resolved by the alliance agreement. The articles of all these were defined in Zurich. It was then decided to insert these articles into the Constitution and a provision was included to the effect that these things are unalterable.

There was no difficulty where the principles were concerned but difficulties cropped up on the details. I was negotiating as the general-secretary [of the Foreign Ministry]. At the highest level were the prime ministers but they had left the issue to their foreign ministries: At this point a difficulty arose on the issue of troops. The issue was the following:

Averoff had insisted that only 150 Turkish troops could go to Cyprus and had added: "I cannot agree to more than that, otherwise I'll face charges of allowing Turkey to occupy Cyprus." Mr. Zorlu conveyed this to us and then went to see the late Menderes who, in a separate room in the hotel, was being briefed about the progress of the negotiations. The situation was explained to him. He was extremely nervous and enraged. He told Zorlu "to continue the negotiations." After Zorlu left his room he [Menderes] called me in and said: "Prepare the airplane, we are returning to Turkey."

I conveyed the situation to the private secretary, Muraffer Bey.

Taylan Sorgun:
This was probably an act meant to convey that we were abandoning the negotiations. . . .

Melih Esenbel:
Yes. . . . He [Menderes] said exactly the following things:

"We have no intention of sending a detachment there. Our intention is the following: The conditions in Cyprus are obvious, both sides will have units there, but because of the conditions in Cyprus, the Turkish unit must be militarily influential. *The unit which we will send will prove that Turkey has gained a foothold in Cyprus.* If a dispute arises later this unit in Cyprus will be an assurance that the agreement has not remained on paper. For that reason we will not send just a small unit there but a unit which will have the ability to operate. If this is not accepted I will not conclude the agreement".

Upon this Zorlu met with Averoff. They said: "We are unable to solve this issue, let it be taken up at prime-ministerial level." So the late Prime Minister and Karamanlis met alone for 45 minutes and Karamanlis acceded to Menderes' demands. The meaning which could be derived from this is the following: If there is good-will an agreement does work, if one side has no good-will that agreement does not work. Yet, we knew in concluding this agreement that Makarios lacked and would lack the good-will. In any case Makarios would not have adhered to this and would not have given up Enosis. *However, by sending our troops there, Turkey would have put its foot there.* Thus, the balance achieved by the Zurich agreement gave the legal right to Turkey to intervene. Of course a nation could protect its interest under any conditions but if it is done through legal means that country gains more justification before public opinion. What's more, this agreement was also registered at the U.N. Thus our right to intervene was also registered at the U.N.

Taylan Sorgun:
Did anyone at the United Nations oppose this right of intervention at the time?

Melih Esenbel:
Nothing happened at the time; no problems arose. Everything was decided upon in Zurich. The meeting in London was a matter of formality. As you know before going there a disaster happened, the airplane crashed, we lost many colleagues. I too was on that plane. . . .

Taylan Sorgun:
Mr. Esenbel, is there any other such agreement signed after the First World War which recognized the right of an armed intervention to a State to protect the rights of a community outside its borders?

Melih Esenbel:
I cannot recall any other such agreement. This is a sort of agreement which is exclusive to a particular case, what the Europeans call suo jure. As such it is unique. Already this is the reason for the importance of the agreement.

Taylan Sorgun:
How do you assess Greece's present actions?

Melih Esenbel:
I do not give much importance to these actions. These are obvious actions. Henceforth, upsetting the situation in Cyprus is not possible. There is a de facto situation. And according to the de facto situation it is clear on the territory itself and not on the paper as to how the Cyprus problem will be solved. The important point is that Turkey has finally reached this point. As you know this process passed through a few stages. As we had expected from the start Makarios tried to trample upon this agreement in 1963. At the time we launched an air operation. Makarios could not go further.

Another thing is that the attempt to intervene in 1967 was an important event. At the time a really serious decision was taken and even a clash with Greece was taken into account. At the time I was Ambassador in the U.S. The idea had developed with the Americans that not another Johnson-type letter could be written to Turkey. Come what may Turkey would reject it and things could go out of control. And in fact a hair's breadth remained for our intervention and as a result 10,000 Greek soldiers were forced to withdraw from

Cyprus. Of course this too was done in line with that [Zurich] agreement. And as you know the situation finally led to the 1974 intervention.

Taylan Sorgun:
You just said that you were with the late Prime Minister on the plane accident. . . .

Melih Esenbel:
Yes, at that moment first there was a silence. . . . Later, I and a colleague opened a hole in the airplane's body and came out. . . . The plane started to burn. The late Prime Minister jumped off the plane and came near us. . . . He had a few scars on the face. He reclined on a tree and said: "pity our friends are perishing inside, yet we are alive here!" . . .

Taylan Sorgun:
Do you have any memories concerning the agreement?

Melih Esenbel:
I am not telling this for political purposes, rather because it is an interesting memory. In 1957 the late Prime Minister wanted a reception organized for the 10th anniversary of the Turkish-American cooperation at the Ankara Palace. He said: "also invite the leader of the opposition Mr. Inonu." As the Foreign Ministry we were very pleased. It would have been good for the ruling party and the opposition to appear united on such an important issue. When I disclosed this view of mine to the late Prime Minister he replied: "that's why I wanted it this way." Inonu came, they met in a separate place. The aim was to jointly receive the American Ambassador. At Ankara Palace, there was a small room called the Green Room. The late Prime Minister showed extreme respect to the late Inonu. He kissed Inonu's hand who acknowledged the favor. Menderes told him: "My Pasha we need your guidance." He replied: "No, the turn now is with you, the young ones. You run the country better". . . . *At the time the objective was to explain the taksim thesis to Inonu.* . . . He was told: "The American Ambassador will come; will you support us?" Inonu replied: "I'll do it with pleasure. You already know that in Lausanne, because of the conditions existing then, Cyprus' sovereignty was handed over to Britain. *Therefore, whatever you can get back is acceptable for me.*" Then the American Ambassador arrived. Both Mr. Menderes and Mr. Inonu spoke in English. From time to time Inonu indicated that he supports Mr. Menderes. The American Ambassador was extremely happy that the ruling party and the opposition were united to this extent. The American Ambassador, F. Warren said: "The real major issue which I'll report [to Washington] is this partnership existing between the two great leaders of Turkey."

Taylan Sorgun:
What was the attitude of the Soviets . . . who want to descend to warm seas . . . towards this agreement which recognized such a right to Turkey?

Melih Esenbel:
They opposed this. They made propaganda to the effect that Cyprus is becoming a NATO base; but their propaganda did not work because the agreement got endorsement and enormous appreciation in world diplomacy.

Taylan Sorgun:
Mr. Esenbel at this period when there is too much talk on the Cyprus problem, you shed light on the materialization of an agreement. Thank you.

APPENDIX 11

Cyprus: Correspondence Exchanged between the Governor and Archbishop Makarios, 1956*

I

The following is the text of Her Majesty's Government's statement of policy on Cyprus, which was given by the Secretary of State for the Colonies in his statement in the House of Commons on 5th March, 1956.

Her Majesty's Government adhere to the principles embodied in the Charter of the United Nations, the Potomac Charter and the Pacific Charter, to which they have subscribed. It is not therefore their position that the principle of self-determination can never be applicable to Cyprus. It is their position that it is not now a practical proposition on account of the present situation in the Eastern Mediterranean.

Her Majesty's Government have offered a wide measure of self-government now. If the people of Cyprus will participate in the constitutional development, it is the intention of Her Majesty's Government to work for a final solution which will satisfy the wishes of the people of Cyprus, be consistent with the strategic interests of Her Majesty's Government and their allies and have regard to the existing treaties to which Her Majesty's Government are a party.

Her Majesty's Government will be prepared to discuss the future of the island with representatives of the people of Cyprus when self-government has proved itself capable of safeguarding the interests of all sections of the community.

II

The following are the texts of the correspondence with Archbishop Makarios.

SIR JOHN HARDING'S LETTER OF 28TH JANUARY, 1956

Your Beatitude,

I am taking the earliest opportunity of confirming what I told you yesterday about my visit to London and of asking you to consider earnestly

---

* Cmd. 9708 (London: HMSO, 1956).

whether, in the light of this letter, a basis for your co-operation in the development of constitutional government in Cyprus has now been established.

The purpose of my visit to London was to discuss the political problems of Cyprus with Ministers and in particular to avail myself of the opportunity for discussion with the Prime Minister before he left for his visit to the United States. I described to the Ministers concerned the course which our previous conversations have taken and the views expressed by you.

As a result of my conversations in London Her Majesty's Government are now prepared to make a statement in the form of the first enclosure to this letter, in which you will notice that certain amendments have been made. This readiness on their part is on the understanding that you on your part would then be prepared to indicate that you accept this statement as providing a basis for the co-operation of yourself and your fellow-countrymen in the development of constitutional government, and that you will use all your influence to put an end to violence and disorder. I must emphasise that in the view of Her Majesty's Government the statement of their position as contained in the first enclosure is so very reasonable as to be certain to command wide support not only in the United Kingdom but elsewhere also.

I suggest that the form which your statement might take should be as in the second enclosure to this letter. Whilst Her Majesty's Government are content to leave the wording of the statement of agreement to Your Beatitude they regard it as essential that the substance should be as indicated in the draft.

With regard to the questions you raised in the course of our discussion about the form of constitution which Her Majesty's Government have in mind, I must repeat that I cannot, at this stage, add to the statements that have already been made at different times by Her Majesty's Ministers. The details of the constitution must be a matter for discussion with representatives of all sections of the community at the appropriate time, and it is therefore open to Your Beatitude and your Council to reserve your position on that point, if you should wish to do so, in your reply to this letter.

I need not point out to you the grave consequences of a failure to reach agreement on the basis now proposed. Her Majesty's Government consider that they have now taken every possible step to meet the views you have expressed during our conversations regarding the form which their statement should take. It is in the interests of everyone, and not least of the people of Cyprus, that the uncertainty which has surrounded the question of our reaching an agreement should not be prolonged. Her Majesty's Government are of the opinion that, without any undue delay, an announcement of their position in this matter must be made so that opinion here and abroad can judge the efforts which they have made to reach an agreement—efforts which, they feel sure, will commend themselves to fair-minded people everywhere. I would therefore ask Your Beatitude to let me know as soon as possible whether you are now able to accept Her Majesty's Government's statement as a basis for co-operation and whether in informing me of your acceptance you will undertake to issue a statement on the lines I have suggested.

If, within the terms of this letter and of the enclosures, you consider that there is any matter which requires further explanation, I shall be very ready to arrange another meeting with Your Beatitude. But I must make it clear that, as far as the substance of the statements are concerned, I am not in a position to make any further changes.

I feel sure that Your Beatitude will share the view of Her Majesty's Government and myself that it is desirable to bring these discussions to a conclusion with the least possible delay. If, therefore, you should wish for a further discussion, I must ask that it should take place very soon.

I am, Your Beatitude,
Yours faithfully,
JOHN HARDING, *Governor*.

FIRST ENCLOSURE TO SIR JOHN HARDING'S LETTER OF 28TH JANUARY, 1956

This enclosure was the text of the statement of policy given in Section I of this Paper.

SECOND ENCLOSURE TO SIR JOHN HARDING'S LETTER OF 28TH JANUARY

His Beatitude, Archbishop Makarios of Cyprus, having taken note of the statement of policy which is being made by Her Majesty's Government on the future of Cyprus, has told the Governor that he finds this statement acceptable as a basis on which he will co-operate with the Government of Cyprus in the introduction of a constitution and in the development of self government and that he will advise his fellow countrymen to do the same.

He has further informed the Governor that he agreed that the framing of a constitution and the development of self-government cannot proceed in an atmosphere of violence and disorder. He has therefore assured His Excellency that he will use all his influence to bring an end to acts of violence and lawlessness so that constitutional government may be introduced in an orderly manner.

ARCHBISHOP MAKARIOS'S LETTER TO SIR JOHN HARDING OF 2ND FEBRUARY

Your Excellency, we have received and considered very carefully Your Excellency's letter of the 28th January as well as the accompanying text of the statement of policy which Her Britannic Majesty's Government intend to make regarding the future of Cyprus. In view of the seriousness of the decision we were called upon to take, we deemed it necessary to communicate with our Counsellors and with representatives of all sections of the Greek people of Cyprus before giving you this reply.

As we already pointed out during our last meeting, the text of the statement which Her Britannic Majesty's Government intend to make is not satisfactory to the Greek people of Cyprus, whose only claim is self-determination. The text in question recognises indirectly the principle of self-determination and states that its application in Cyprus is not being permanently ruled out. This application, however, is made dependent on conditions so general and vague, subject to so many interpretations and presenting so many difficulties as to the objective ascertainment of their fulfilment, as to create reasonable doubt about the positive nature of the promise which is given regarding the final solution of the question in accordance with the wish of the people of Cyprus. For that reason we would never put our signature under the above-mentioned text if it were to take the form of a bilateral agreement. In spite of this, considering that it is simply a statement of British policy on Cyprus, and since we earnestly desire the pacification of the island, we are prepared to exhaust every effort to find a way of reducing the present tension, while maintaining at the same time our reservations on the text of the statement intact, and our demand for an early application to Cyprus of the right of self-determination unchanged. We accept, therefore, the invitation of Your Excellency to co-operate with you and representatives of the minority in the framing of a constitution for the transitory regime, after the afore-mentioned Statement of Her Britannic Majesty's Government has been made.

As, however, no elucidation has been given to us on the meaning of the "wide measure of self-government" which, according to the text of the statement that was sent to us, "Her Majesty's Government have offered now" and as Your Excellency was not in a position to define the fundamental principles of such a constitution of self-government, in spite of the desire we expressed so persistently during our last meeting, we wish to inform Your Excellency that in order that our co-operation be effective, an official British assurance should be given now that this constitution will establish a regime of genuine self-government. To this effect the following general principles of the constitution should be made clear, if possible, simultaneously with the above-mentioned statement:

(1) All Legislative Executive and Judicial powers, with the exception of those expressly exempted, will originate from the people of Cyprus and will be exercised by them through their elected representatives and other organs.

(2) Responsibility for the defence and external political relations of the island will be excepted from the above principle and will be vested in the Governor in his capacity as representative of Her Britannic Majesty's Government.

(3) The Governor, beyond the powers mentioned in the previous paragraph (2) will exercise the normal duties of a constitutional head of State; thus he will sign, without having the right to veto, laws which are enacted by the Assembly within the framework of the Constitution, including the budget, and will sign the decrees which are lawfully issued by the Government. He will entrust the duty of forming the Government to the person enjoying the confidence of the House, and will dissolve the House on his advice. Ministers will be chosen by the Prime Minister and will, like him, be responsible only to the Assembly.

(4) Representation in the Assembly will be proportional to the composition of the population. Otherwise there will be absolute equality of all citizens and everyone will be eligible to any public Office. Exceptions to this rule may be provided for only in the case of special offices which are exclusively connected with the religious and educational rights of the island's communities. Such rights will be fully safeguarded and protected by the Constitution.

(5) A procedure will be defined for the impartial settlement of any difference arising out of the interpretation of constitutional provisions, in particular on questions of disputed authority between the Governor on the one hand and the Assembly or the Government on the other.

These fundamental principles which, in our view, constitute the only reasonable and acceptable interpretation of the meaning of the term, "A wide measure of self-government" should be defined in advance. They cannot be considered equal in importance to the details which Your Excellency rightly relegates for thorough discussion at a later stage.

Agreement on the above points will create the pre-requisites for the allaying of the present tension and will permit the soonest possible elaboration and operation of the constitution of self-government in an atmosphere of calm. To this pacification we shall contribute, naturally, in full measure of our powers by making the appropriate statement. However, such pacification will be brought about, more quickly than by anything else, by the policy to be followed simultaneously by Your Excellency. This should be a policy of appeasement capable of inspiring the citizens with a feeling of freedom and safety. Thus, emergency military measures and emergency legislation should be revoked and an amnesty should be granted for all political offences.

We are firmly convinced that our conciliatory altitude will be appreciated by all fair-minded people both in Great Britain and elsewhere.

We assure you of our readiness to give any explanation which Your Excellency may deem necessary on the above and remain, praying God's blessing upon you.

(Signed) ARCHBISHOP MAKARIOS OF CYPRUS

SIR JOHN HARDING'S LETTER OF 14TH FEBRUARY

Your Beatitude,

Your letter of the 2nd February has now been considered very carefully by Her Majesty's Government. It is with satisfaction that they have received Your Beatitude's assurance of your desire for the pacification of the island and of your readiness to exert every effort to find a way of reducing the present tension. They welcome your acceptance of my invitation to co-operate with me and with representatives of all sections of the community in the framing of a constitution and have followed with interest reports of your consultations which seem to confirm that there exists a widespread desire for a new and constructive approach to the island's political and constitutional problems.

2. With regard to Your Beatitude's request for the clarification of certain points regarding Her Majesty's Government's views about a constitution for Cyprus, I must make it clear that the form of any constitution must arise out of full discussions with representatives of all communities. This of course does not preclude private discussions which will doubtless be of great benefit, but they cannot be a substitute for consultation about the manner in which the daily lives of all Cypriots will be governed. Nevertheless I am authorised to say that Her Majesty's Government consider that the following points should be taken as a basis for discussion:

(a) Her Majesty's Government offer a wide measure of democratic self-government now. To this end a new and liberal constitution would be drawn up in consultation with all sections of the community.

(b) The constitution would enable the people of Cyprus through responsible Cypriot Ministers to assume control by a suitably phased process over the departments of Government except those relating to foreign affairs and defence which would be reserved to the Governor and to public security which would also be reserved to the Governor for as long as he deems necessary.

(c) The constitution would provide for an Assembly with an elected majority.

(d) A Cypriot Premier to head the new administration would be chosen by the Assembly with the approval of the Governor. Ministerial portfolios would be allocated by the Premier (subject to (e) below).

(e) The constitution would provide for Turkish membership in the Council of Ministers.

(f) There would be proper safeguards for the rights of individual citizens, the interests of all sections of the community, and the integrity and independence of the public service.

3. The points set out in my preceding paragraph constitute the broad objectives that Her Majesty's Government have in view. Elaboration of precise constitutional arrangements are matters of crucial importance to everyone and must be pursued by means of consultation and discussion on a widely representative basis. You will understand that Her Majesty's Government could not enter into commitments about the position of separate communities under the constitution before discussions have taken place at which representatives of those communities have expressed their views. It will, of course, be open to Your Beatitude to put forward your own views when the details of the constitution are being worked out.

4. It must be recognised that persistent violence and disorder have increased the difficulties of introducing constitutional government. Fear of intimidation has stifled free expression or opinion. The minorities are more concerned than before about the possible consequences for them of the advent of self-government. Nevertheless, as stated above, the proposals now put forward by Her Majesty's Government will constitute their objective. The speed at which they can be realised will depend on the response of the general public and their leaders to their new responsibilities.

5. I welcome the statement in your letter that Your Beatitude will contribute to the full measure of your powers in bringing peace to the island. I

trust, therefore, that as soon as Her Majesty's Government make their statement of policy you will on your part make the appropriate statement as indicated in your letter and take active steps to use all your influence to bring an end to violence and disorder. I shall be glad to receive an early assurance from Your Beatitude on that point.

6. I will then the more easily be able to relax the Emergency provisions without endangering public security. As an earnest of my desire to see peace and normality restored I intend to take steps to repeal certain of the Emergency Regulations as soon as there is positive evidence of a genuine response to Your Beatitude's appeal against violence. I shall be prepared to repeal other parts of these Regulations progressively as conditions in the island revert to normal.

7. In anticipation of a return to more peaceful and happy conditions I have submitted to Her Majesty's Government recommendations on the procedure to be adopted to sound all shades of opinion on the form the constitution should take, and I hope their decision on that subject will be published shortly. I trust that you will agree to participate in these deliberations which will set the stage for the political future of Cyprus.

I am, Your Beatitude,
Yours faithfully,
JOHN HARDING, *Governor*.

NOTE SENT TO THE ARCHBISHOPRIC BY THE GOVERNOR'S OFFICE ON 24TH FEBRUARY, 1956

Summary of the explanations given to Mr. Kranidiotis re the constitutional proposals.

1. Mr. Reddaway furnished the following explanations to Mr. Kranidiotis on the 19th February on certain points which Mr. Kranidiotis had raised on the 16th February re the terms of the Governor's letter of the 14th February.

2. The Governor was not asking the Archbishop to commit himself on the form of the constitution. He was asking that the Archbishop should co-operate in constitutional discussions and as part of that co-operation should denounce violence. It would be open to the Archbishop to reserve his position about the form the constitution should take.

3. The Governor wished to stress the need for mutual confidence if any basis for co-operation was to be established. Unless such confidence could be established there could be no hope of truly effective and sincere co-operation.

4. The Governor wished to assure the Archbishop that Her Majesty's Government were absolutely sincere in their desire to see a wide measure of self-government established in Cyprus. He felt that there could be no progress unless the Archbishop were prepared to accept this assurance.

5. As regards the use of the phrase "basis for discussion" in paragraph 2 of the Governor's letter, the Governor had repeatedly emphasised that the form of the constitution must be a matter for consultation and discussion on a

widely representative basis. However, his letter contained in paragraphs 3 and 4 a clear assurance that the proposals outlined in his letter would constitute the objective of Her Majesty's Government. He could assure the Archbishop that Her Majesty's Government hoped to see these objectives embodied in the constitution.

6. As regards the phrase "a suitably phased process", the Governor was authorised by Her Majesty's Government to assure the Archbishop that there was nothing in this phrase which implied deliberate delay on their part. But it was obviously necessary that there should be an orderly process for the transfer of powers to Cypriot Ministers. Once the constitutional machinery had been satisfactorily established and peace and order had been restored, there was no reason to apprehend any delay in the transfer of powers.

7. As regards the phrase "an elected majority", the Governor clearly could not tie the hands of the Constitutional Commissioner, as to the manner in which this elected majority should be constituted. He considered, however, that the Archbishop ought to have confidence in the wisdom and fair-mindedness of the Constitutional Commissioner, and should rely on the strength of the arguments which he could produce to the Constitutional Commissioner on this point.

8. On the matters which Mr. Kranidiotis had described as of secondary importance arising from the constitutional proposals, the Governor confirmed that:

(a) The Cypriot Ministers would be responsible to the Assembly;

(b) the intention of paragraph 2(b) of the Governor's letter was that Cypriot Ministers should exercise the legislative and judicial powers appertaining to the Departments of Government for which they were responsible;

(c) the decision as to how long responsibility for public security should be reserved to the Governor would have to rest with the Governor;

(d) the nature of the approval required of the Governor for the appointment of the Premier was a matter which ought to be raised with the Constitutional Commissioner.

ARCHBISHOP MAKARIOS'S LETTER TO THE GOVERNOR OF 15TH FEBRUARY, 1956

Your Excellency,

In our letter of the 2nd February we informed Your Excellency that although we do not agree with the preconditions on which, in the statement they intend to make, Her Britannic Majesty's Government make the application of the principle of self-determination in Cyprus depend we would nevertheless in the interest of the pacification of the country agree to co-operate in the framing and operation of a constitution of self-government as a transitional stage towards self-determination which ever remains our sole and final aim. However we made it clear that such co-operation would be possible for us only in so far as the fundamental democratic principles which we described in our previous letter were clearly established now as a basis of the constitution which is offered.

2. We have noted the contents of Your Excellency's letter of the 14th February as well as the explanations given thereon which make it clear:

(1) That the meaning of the words "suitably phased process" in paragraph 2(b) is that the transfer of powers to the constitutional organs of the people will be effected as soon as the constitution is put into operation excepting only the transfer of executive responsibility for questions of public security which as we understand will be effected as soon as order is restored, and

(2) that the meaning of the word "responsible" in the same paragraph is that Ministers will be responsible to the Assembly. Nevertheless your letter and the explanations which have been given do not cover the other points we have raised.

As regards the substance of the general principles of the constitution a number of basic points remain unclear. Thus:

(a) It is not made clear that all powers Executive (except those expressly reserved to the Governor in the spheres of defence and foreign affairs), Legislative and Judicial originate from the people and are exercised exclusively by them through their elected representatives and their other constitutional organs.

(b) It is not made clear that the representation in the Assembly will be proportionate to the composition of the population.

(c) No assurance is afforded that the Governor's approval as to the person of the Prime Minister will be entirely formal.

3. We have noted what is stated in paragraphs 3 and 4 of your letter regarding the incorporation in the constitution of the general principles set forth; nevertheless no adequate assurance is given on this point.

4. In my letter of the 2nd February we made it clear that for the purpose of restoring peace and order—to which we too wish to contribute with all our powers—the repeal by Your Excellency of the emergency laws now in force and the granting of an amnesty for all political offences are indispensable. Your reply contains no adequate assurance concerning the early repeal of all the above laws; furthermore there is no mention whatsoever regarding the granting of an amnesty for all political offences. Both these points however constitute an indispensable precondition for the normalisation of the island's political life.

5. In conclusion we feel obliged to emphasise that in our desire that the island should spend in peace the period up to the application of the principle of self-determination we have proceeded to make every possible concession beyond which our national conscience and natural dignity do not permit us to go. We remain, praying God's blessing upon you.

(Signed) ARCHBISHOP MAKARIOS OF CYPRUS

III

STATEMENT MADE BY THE SECRETARY OF STATE TO ARCHBISHOP MAKARIOS ON 29TH FEBRUARY, 1956

I am very glad to have this opportunity of making to Your Beatitude a statement on behalf of Her Majesty's Government. The undertakings that I am prepared to give are on the understanding that you on your part will assure me that you will co-operate in the framing of a constitution, that you will encourage your fellow countrymen to do the same, that you will make an appeal for the cessation of violence and that you will thereafter use all your influence for the restoration of peace and order.

2. Now as to the undertakings that I am prepared to give you. First, I can tell you that when law and order has been re-established there will be an amnesty for all those convicted of offences under the Emergency Regulations (or of comparable offences prior to their enactment) which were committed before (date to be settled) except those involving violence against the person or the illegal possession of arms, ammunition or explosives which would come up for review in accordance with the normal rules. The release of detainees would begin at the same time. As the Governor has already told you he is prepared to repeal all Emergency Regulations at a pace commensurate with that of the re-establishment of law and order.

3. Secondly, you raised certain questions in your letter of 25th February concerning our intentions in the constitutional field. I feel that the best way of replying is to restate to you in person our position on these points. Her Majesty's Government's objectives have been set out in paragraph 2 of the Governor's letter of 14th February. They propose to send a Constitutional Commissioner to Cyprus who would draw up a liberal and democratic constitution in consultation with representatives of all sections of opinion in the island. It would reserve to the Governor all powers in the fields of foreign affairs and defence. Public security would also be reserved to the Governor as long as he thinks necessary. Control of all other departments would be handed over to Cypriot Ministers responsible to a Legislative Assembly representing the people of Cyprus as quickly as is consistent with an orderly transfer. The constitution would provide for an elected majority in the Legislative Assembly and would safeguard the interests of all sections of the community. It would be for the Constitutional Commissioner to recommend what arrangements should be made for this purpose including the precise composition of the elected majority which he would define in accordance with normal liberal constitutional doctrine.

APPENDIX 12

Savingram from the Acting Governor of Cyprus to the Secretary of State for the Colonies, 13 November 1957

Parliamentary Questions in the
House of Commons

Original in File No. S/25/54/IV
Original from Acting Governor,
Extracted on 23.1.58

Ped 35
Dated 13.11.57
by S.A.S. (A)

No. 1740 SECRET Telegram.
Your telegram No. 1905
Parliamentary Question.

For our study on partition an estimate was made of proportion of land owned by main communities. This showed Crown 28%, Greeks 58%, Turks 12%, Others 2%.

2.   This was at best a very rough estimate and was not directly based on any published figures or on a census. Estimate if quoted is sure to be challenged locally by Turks and could not be convincingly supported.

3.   Accurate figure could only be obtained by consulting each individual registration of land since separate registers for each community are not kept. This would be a long task and would considerably disrupt activities of Lands and Surveys Department. I recommend that reply be given that accurate and reliable information is not available, and that any estimate would be conjectural and might be misleading. However, such meagre information as is available would seem to suggest that the extent of land owned by the two communities may be roughly proportionate to their numerical size.

Acting Governor.

APPENDIX 13

Rauf R. Denktash, "Cevdet Sunay ve Kibris Turkleri" (Cevdet Sunay and the Cyprus Turks), *Belge*, 19 June 1982 (translation)

One of the former Presidents, Cevdet Sunay, who on May 22, 1982 died at the age of 82, was a soldier who contributed to the Cyprus cause. His grandson was married in Cyprus. When the Head of State, Rauf Denktash, a few times invited him to visit Cyprus, Sunay Pasha replied: "God willing we will come . . . We could be considered Cypriots, our grandson is there."

"I have known Cevdet Pasha since 1958. We had just set up the TMT. In those early days there were colleagues who did not want to involve Turkey in the organisation. They used to argue: 'It will be enough only if Turkey supports us!' According to them we had to speedily collect money from the people, had to buy arms and we had to train the organisation . . . Even a list (of the wealthy people) was prepared. They were going to ask for a certain amount of contribution from the wealthy and those who refused to give money were going to be punished. I opposed this idea. I believed that if we resorted to such means in a short time the TMT would become an even worse terrorist organisation than EOKA. With their plan the Cypriots would have ruthlessly oppressed their own rivals; the people would have become annoyed. It was also impossible to train TMT members within a small community surrounded by the Greek Cypriots! We were short of trainers. Besides, the steps which we would have taken inside Cyprus in accordance with our own possibilities could have put Turkey in a very difficult position. To collect money from the people and then not to give account to the people by simply telling them that 'we have bought arms with the money' would have meant giving a death blow to the Organisation. . . . In the final analysis my other friends accepted my views. In those days I was going to pay my first visit to Ankara together with Dr. Kutchuk. I was going to ask for responsible support and trainers from the Turkish Government. The TMT was not going to be the organisation of certain individuals. It was going to be a national defence Organisation, the defence shield to be given to Turkey by a people whose cause was to prevent Enosis and to protect the Turkish people against EOKA terrorism! . . .

For the first time I was face to face with Fatin Rustu Zorlu in Ankara. Fatin Bey had a profound love and sympathy towards Dr. Kutchuk. Dr. Kutchuk introduced me to him. I had already left my position at the Attorney General's office and was elected as the President of the Federation of the Cyprus Turkish Societies. I briefed Fatin Bey about the people, the villages and the EOKA activities. I told him that we have already and set up the TMT but in order to prevent it in the future from turning into an organisation that might put Turkey into trouble we wanted to place it under the responsibility of Turkey. I also informed him about our shortages. In the years 1955-58 the Cyprus resistance and struggle was waged with 13 pistols. The British government had confiscated our shot-guns. The guns made out of water pipes were ineffective and did more harm than good. There were people who died in attempting to make bombs. Greece had found a retired Cypriot Colonel, had sent him to Cyprus and had thus founded EOKA. All the guns and support came from Greece. The activities of EOKA were planned at the Greek Chief-of-Staff and Grivas was directly taking orders and directives from the Chief-of-Staff. Contrary to what some think, EOKA was not a national organisation set up by the Greek Cypriots to liberate Cyprus from colonial rule. EOKA was a terrorist organisation set up by Greece through the Cyprus Church with the aim of annexing Cyprus to Greece. The objective was to make Britain speed up the granting of autonomy in Cyprus and at the same time to take the future into secure hands! How? Like this: Greek Cypriot terrorism would have subdued the Greek Cypriot communists and the Turkish Cypriots and thus would have enabled the EOKA-Church (that is Greece) front to be the only armed force to bargain with the British about the future of Cyprus! Thus the assistance and support we asked from Turkey was also necessary from the viewpoint of Turkey's national interests. This is more so in the face of Greece's intention to resort to terrorist methods to subdue the Turkish community (as in Crete) to get control of the island and threaten Turkey from the south."

After these contacts I returned to Nicosia . . . Efforts continued to organise the TMT island-wide. I went to Ankara again a few months later. It was then that I met Cevdet Sunay Pasha. I and Karabelen Pasha engaged him much on the issue of TMT. They gave their most select experts to us so that we could organise the TMT in the best manner possible. Riza Vurushkan was the most distinguished amongst them! The first members of the TMT were going to meet Cevdet Sunay under different conditions. Cevdet Sunay was first deputy Chief-of-Staff, later he became the Chief-of-Staff and finally became President!

During every position he occupied, Cevdet Sunay had exciting memories of Cyprus. . . . He used to see TMT as a defence organisation to protect peace! . . . He used to say: 'Makarios can commit every conceivable recklessness but he cannot annex Cyprus to Greece. . . . It will be insanity for him to try this. . . . They are the only ones who will be harmed by such a move! We want peace in the region, Greece is our ally. . . . We want to be on good terms with Greece. . . . We need each other. . . . Their attempts to annex Cyprus are harming our relations. . . . This too is to their disadvantage. . . . Sooner or later Greece will see this reality."

In those days of fear Cevdet Sunay gave hope to Cyprus. . . . Because of the strong support he gave the TMT he will live forever in the hearts of the Turkish Cypriots."

APPENDIX 14

Fazil Kutchuk, "The Cyprus Question: A Permanent Solution," 1957, Cover Page

The
Cyprus Question

A Permanent Solution

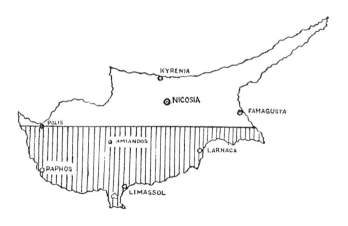

By Dr. Fazil KUCHUK

NICOSIA — CYPRUS

1957

APPENDIX 15

Panel discussion between Hayrettin Erkmen, Minister of Commerce at the Time of the Zurich Agreements and Foreign Minister of Turkey 1979–80, Orhan Eralp, Permanent Representative of Turkey at the UN in 1964 and at NATO during the 1974 Turkish Invasion of Cyprus, and Melih Esenbel, Secretary-General of the Turkish Foreign Ministry at the Time of the Zurich Agreements and Ambassador in Washington during the 1974 Invasion of Cyprus, Chaired by Taylan Sorgun, *Tercuman*, 21 July 1984 (translation)

Taylan Sorgun:
Turkey intervened in Cyprus based on the London-Zurich Agreement and under the conditions which have developed since, the North Cyprus Turkish Republic was formed. At present there exists a de facto situation based on a legal foundation. In this panel discussion we will debate the conditions leading to the landing and the present and the future of the North Cyprus Turkish Republic. To begin with I'll ask Mr. Erkmen to tell us about the government's work during London and Zurich Agreements.

Hayrettin Erkmen:
The issue had from time to time been brought to the attention of the government following an extensive work. This is the procedure in every foreign policy issue. Turkey's posture on Cyprus might appear variable, but actually it adheres to a specific line. In the past the Republic governments had continuously monitored the moves directed against the British in Cyprus and the actions that compromised the future of the Turks. However, the governments adhered to the policy that no initiative should be undertaken as long as the status quo continues. The Foreign Minister of the government set up by the Democrat Party had formulated the issue in the following terms: 'As long as the status quo is maintained we cannot think about an operation on these lands which belong to Britain. However, if there arises a question of changing the status-quo, then we have a right of say on Cyprus in accordance with the agreements signed during the Ottoman Empire; we cannot remain indifferent.' Here, a change of line is obvious; the governments walked along this line. First, we came out with the thesis that in accordance with the provision in the 1878 Agreement the whole of Cyprus should be returned to Turkey—later the idea of Taksim was debated and upheld. And later we came upon the formula of a Cyprus Republic which was a kind of Taksim. An essential point here is that Cyprus is important from the viewpoint of the security of our southern coasts; the second point was the problem of the Turks living in Cyprus. Moved by these two considerations the governments followed the principle that Turkey should never end its presence in Cyprus. Taksim was materialized by the London and Zurich agreements; that did not work, so landing was made.

Taylan Sorgun:
Just now you used a phrase of principle to the effect that 'if there is to be a change of status we cannot remain indifferent.' I presume that this explanation has been inserted into the clause relating to Cyprus at Lausanne.

Hayrettin Erkmen:
Yes there are two points, one of them is the explanation of Sultan Hamid in the agreements of that time to the effect that 'we cannot give up the domination over Cyprus' and the second is the decision which is in conformity and is parallel to the first [point] and mentioned by you and which was put into the agreement in Lausanne.

MY REPLY TO THE STATEMENT ON BBC

Taylan Sorgun:
Mr. Eralp during the landing you were a permanent delegate at NATO. What incidents did you live through when Turkey decided to land in Cyprus?

Orhan Eralp:
At that time I was at Tuzla on holiday. As soon as I received the news of the Nicos Sampson coup in Cyprus I went to Ankara to receive orders. Two days later a message to the effect that 'Mr. Ecevit is going to London to discuss the Cyprus issue and wants you to be at the airport within two hours' and we traveled to London together. There were also some ministers on the trip. This was a 24-hour lightning journey and its aim was to convince Britain of the necessity of intervention and if possible to secure joint intervention. There was a long meeting in Britain and Mr. Ecevit stated the necessity and the realities of this, that is of the intervention. But the British Prime Minister tried to dissuade Turkey from this, we even knew that they were in contact with America [USA]. While we were about to return to Turkey Sisco arrived [Deputy Secretary of State] and met with Ecevit at the Turkish Embassy. Sisco wanted to come to Ankara for talks and he was told to come to Ankara on Saturday, whereas on Saturday the landing was starting. When the landing happened everyone including Soviet Russia were of the opinion that this was a justified intervention. However when the second operation started they opposed us. . . . Even Callaghan made a statement to the BBC that 'today Cyprus is the hostage of the Turkish army, tomorrow the Turkish army will be hostage of Cyprus'. I reminded him of his statement during the meeting of the permanent delegates of NATO and said to him 'to the extent that the British army is a hostage in Northern Ireland so will the Turkish army be a hostage in Cyprus to the same extent'. Intervention happened under these conditions and necessitated great sacrifices, but this was unavoidable. The situation in Cyprus was so bad that whether or not agreements existed Turkey could not have accepted such a situation.

LONDON-ZURICH AGREEMENT

Taylan Sorgun:
Mr Esenbel, you were the Ambassador in America during the Cyprus landing. During this landing what incidents were you faced with?

Melih Esenbel:
First I want to refer to the following point: The London-Zurich Agreements created a new situation in Cyprus; the most important factor of the new situation was the 'right of intervention'. To think of a Zurich Agreement and yet to believe that one day there would have been no intervention would have rendered that agreement worthless. In concluding the Zurich Agreement we knew that the necessity would arise for an intervention. This is because we believed Makarios would not be willing to uphold the federal system in its legal form. Our intervention was executed bit by bit. In 1964 it was done from the air; in 1967 10,000 Greek soldiers were evicted from the island, but the real intervention took place in 1974. However, the intervention made in 1974 was the intervention thought about while concluding the 1958–1959 London-Zurich Agreement; this intervention only became possible in 1974. Another important point is the landing of the Turkish troops after the [London-Zurich] agreement; that too was one of the important objectives pursued by the London-Zurich Agreement. When the intervention happened I was in Washington. It was obvious that there would be a reaction but the whole question in everyone's mind was whether as in 1964 [at the time there was the question of the 6th fleet and the warning that we could be left alone face to face with the Soviets] they [West] would choose this road again or whether things would develop differently. But I personally did not see this as probable. Because in 1967 also a possibility for such an intervention had arisen and at that time the American officials were told not to adopt an attitude similar to their previous one and eventually 10,000 Greek troops were taken out of the island which was a great defeat for Greece. We more or less knew that America after seeing our reaction in 1967 would not show excessive reaction as in 1964.

WASHINGTON AND INTERVENTION

Taylan Sorgun:
What happened when the news of the intervention came?

Melih Esenbel:
That news came and the message said 'a long telegram is on the way'. I waited for this telegram to come before I sent a telegram to the U.S. government. This point is very interesting because it reflects the atmosphere of the time. At the time the deputy Secretary of State was Hartman who is now the Ambassador to Moscow. They [presumably U.S. officials] were constantly at their office and he [Hartman?] told me 'both the Ambassador [not clear which Ambassador] and I are awake but it appears that this message will take a long time to come'—already more or less they know what we would say—he went to his home after sending a message stating 'let him come at 9:30 in the morning'.

The meaning of this message was that 'the delivery of the message was not urgent. . . .' In the morning a phone call came before I went to the U.S. State Department. They said that 'the American Secretary of Defence wants the Ambassador'. It occurred to me that they may voice the opinion that 'you intervened there and you are using NATO arms; as such this is inappropriate stop it'. So I passed on the following message to them: 'The Ambassador is now going to the State Department, he also has other engagements, he may come at 1:30 in the afternoon'. . . . I did this for the following reason: The longer I delayed an engagement with them and so our actions in Cyprus would have progressed in the meantime. It was to my benefit for him [U.S. Secretary of Defence] to tell me belatedly what he wanted to say.

I met with Hartman at the State Department he told me that the affair may be dangerous and things like that, but he mentioned nothing like 'you are using American arms'.

Another point which surprised me is: When I went to the appointment at the Defence Department at half past one the Secretary of Defence did not refer to the Cyprus issue. Some time later he said to me [details are confidential] 'there are some arrangements relating to NATO and concerning Greece and Turkey, we have communicated with Greece, we are changing that approach, we want the same things from you, but still no positive reply has been received from you, so therefore you inform Ankara and implement this because this is an issue to which America gives extreme importance'. He did not utter a word concerning Cyprus. We sat for half an hour and spoke of this and that. He was continuously checking the telex and finally he said the following: 'There is no need for you to send a telegram because Ankara has accepted it'. While coming out he looked at me and smiled. After some time he left the government and during one of our chance meetings he said: 'You understood didn't you why we acted in a friendly manner towards you'.

Taylan Sorgun:
Your contacts with Kissinger?

Melih Esenbel:
Though he said don't do this or that he assumed no clear-cut stance, he found our position justified. . . . This also could be understood from his reactions.

Taylan Sorgun:
At this point I want to ask a question to Mr. Erkmen. Mr. Esenbel a while ago said that the Zurich-London Agreement was placed on a foundation of intervention. When you were in the cabinet what views were being expressed on this issue?

Hayrettin Erkmen:
I had already made a note of what Mr. Esenbel said. I fully share his assessment. We too discussed the issue in the Cabinet. Both deceased Prime Minister Menderes and the Foreign Minister Zorlu, in assessing and explaining the agreement, also stressed this point. They said: 'The right of intervention is a major gain for us and here lies the vital point of the agreement'. As a result

certain doubts existing amongst the Cabinet members were erased. In addition, the landing of a Turkish army unit on the island was yet another important point.

UNSINKABLE AIRCRAFT CARRIER

Taylan Sorgun:
Mr. Eralp, just now mention has been made of Turkey being left face to face with the Soviets. What is your assessment on this issue?

Orhan Eralp:
This point is highly important. The main worry of Russia concerning the Cyprus issue is Cyprus becoming part of NATO. How can this be realized? Either Turkey takes the island, or ENOSIS takes place, or it is divided between the two NATO members and in their view 'it becomes an unsinkable aircraft carrier'. In any case when we intervened they were sure of our goodwill. They knew we did not enter the island for Taksim. They even encouraged us for an intervention. Today the climate is the same. You can see the AKEL party, which is the main support of Kyprianou, is slowly turning against him due to his intransigent policy. Even AKEL Communist Party which leans on the Russians does not approve the ENOSIS policy. Today Russia trusts the goodwill of Turkey. Because of this it does not show much activity. Also the efforts of Greece on this issue have not given a result.

Taylan Sorgun:
At this point I would request an assessment from honorable Erkmen. You took part in a meeting in Cyprus. Could there be a question of turning back from the present situation in Cyprus, could this status be easily altered henceforth?

Hayrettin Erkmen:
The present situation is not merely a de facto one; it has at the same time a legal basis. What is this legal situation? Two communities live in Cyprus. The Turkish side wants the preparation of a partnership status for these two communities so that they [the communities] could live within this status. Whereas Greece favors Cyprus to come under Greece's sovereignty and to accord a minority treatment to the Turks. Faced with these two views en agreement does not seem possible. They [the Greek Cypriots] say that there is one people and it should decide its self-determination. We are saying that there are two peoples and therefore either we partition this place or we conclude an agreement which would separate the status of both sides. While this argument was continuing the intervention took place and as a result the territorial separation was realized. Now, the two peoples have separate territories and when the two peoples have separate territories, then the Turkish people residing on the territory belonging to the Turkish people have the right to set up a state and decide on their self-determination and set up their state. Therefore, this is a legal situation and there is no possibility of turning back from this. It is not possible to give up this status not merely from the point of view of prestige alone but

because the waving of the rights by the people who have used their rights could engender an unexpected result in international law in particular.

Taylan Sorgun:
Mr. Eralp what is your assessment?

Orhan Eralp:
I don't believe that today Kyprianou would abandon certain things and would be willing to share this sovereignty with the Turks. Now there will be meetings in Vienna between 6–7 August; Turks will attend this meeting with concessionist proposals whereas they, by mumbling and grumbling, will reject all of these. I am not optimistic on the issue of an agreement with the Greek Cypriots. They will say 'let us wrest Varosha and then let everything go on like this'. Today in North Cyprus there is a state and an assembly, an army and a government. Its elections and constitution will be realized. And in time this state will make its appearance in the international scene.

ATTITUDE OF USA
Taylan Sorgun:
Mr. Esenbel to what extent were the U.S.A. officials informed of the incidents during the Cyprus landing, do you have certain observations?

Melih Esenbel:
They knew of the military developments and certainly they were following them closely. Even during my contacts with Kissinger he was giving information to me also. In certain cases he was receiving through his own channels the information that came to us through our own channels. He was able to know the position of our detachments. Kissinger even phoned me one morning from Los Angeles and said: 'I am phoning you in the presence of the President. An initiative was launched with you in the morning, please inform Ankara that this operation must stop and please inform me of Ankara's reply'. When I asked him when I should convey Ankara's reply he told me 'you inform me when I arrive in Washington'. In this statement there was no implication that they wanted an urgent reply. That is through their stance and action they were accepting the justness of our position.
        Let me state the following: I don't think that the Greek Cypriots and Greeks wanted to reach an agreement from the very start, because there is an ongoing de facto situation and putting a signature under an agreement would mean the acceptance of that de facto situation and thus the existing situation is registered. I don't think that henceforth a legal solution could be achieved in Cyprus. Today there exists the declaration of independence based on legal grounds and this will continue as it is.

Taylan Sorgun:
Mr. Erkmen how do you assess U.S.'s stance?

Hayrettin Erkmen:
One must distinguish between the congress and the administration over there. I don't think that henceforth, as in the past, the United States would assume an offending stance and therefore I don't see a change in the attitude of the U.S. administration. Some speeches will be made in the U.S., some words will be uttered for electioneering purposes but I am not perturbed by these.

Orhan Eralp:
I can say the following on this issue: Because of my extensive work at the UN I'll look at the issues from that perspective. As you know at the Security Council the U.S. abstained on 552 resolution. For this reason it faced criticism. That decision was calling for the withdrawal of the Turkish troops from the island. The U.S. regarded this resolution as undermining the reconciliation between the two sides. The U.S. government is also working to pacify certain actions in Congress. The long-term thinking of the U.S. is that NATO's Southeastern wing could be weakened because of this. As you see because of this reason they are supporting both sides.

Taylan Sorgun:
Mr. Esenbel your assessment?

Melih Esenbel:
They are in no position to bicker with us. However whenever Congress enters into the issue the situation changes in particular in an election year. The U.S. Congress always thinks about the financial problem and the Greeks make constant suggestions in this direction. There could not be a question of an embargo but small irritations might crop up. One should not expect the recurrence of the former difficulties. There could be a possibility of pro-Greek Senators creating an irritation but as I said there is no possibility of an irritation within a general framework. Of course another important thing is also how the government applies itself to prevent this issue. . . . To what extent will it be able to resist this.

Taylan Sorgun:
You were in America during the landing. Was the U.S. giving probability to this landing or was she thinking of other things?

Melih Esenbel:
There was an issue of destruction of a state there and I think they had taken into account that this situation would give rise to the possibility of intervention by Turkey. It was not a surprise for them.

Orhan Eralp:
The meeting of Sisco with Ecevit is a proof of the fact that they guessed the landing.

DENKTASH AND INDEPENDENCE

Taylan Sorgun:
Mr Erkmen, had there been any question of the declaration of independence during your term of office as the Foreign Minister? Of course in the face of the Greek side's evasion from an agreement. . . .

Hayrettin Erkmen:
During my term of office the situation in Cyprus was as follows: There was the Turkish Federated State. This State was not even able to confirm its own identity. It was in a transitional status as a legal structure set up to enter a federation. At that time too Mr. Denktash had put forward the idea of turning it into independence. But, I advised him to wait a little bit more. I told him: 'With this trend this will happen one day, but at present I don't think the time is favorable for it'. The conditions existing in the days of the declaration of the independence were more favorable than in the days when I gave him this advice. Today even if it is not recognized it is able to say 'I am a State'. There is a State, Turkey, which has recognized it; there are also States which will recognize it. The Greeks always wanted the whole of the island. Someone who wants the whole of something might lose everything. That's what happened. It is hereforth impossible for these territories to come under the Greek Cypriot sovereignty.

Taylan Sorgun:
I thank the sides for participating in this open debate.

True translation.
Translated by Sureya Hami,
Director, Press and Information Office
(K. Psyllides)
24.2.1987

APPENDIX 16

Governor's Statement and Findings of the Commission of Inquiry into the Incidents at Geunyeli, Cyprus, on 12th June, 1958*

GOVERNOR'S STATEMENT
ON THE REPORT OF THE GEUNYELI ENQUIRY

Following on the events near Geunyeli village on the 12th June this year I appointed a Commission of Inquiry, and Sir Paget Bourke, Chief Justice of Cyprus, was good enough to accept my invitation to carry out the Inquiry.

The Commission's report was received early in July but I was advised that publication of the findings should not be made until the Court cases had been disposed of. I also had in mind that the publication of the report should be postponed until inter-communal tension had decreased. I have now given instructions for the findings of the Commission to be published.

The main reason which led me to appoint the Commission of Inquiry was that a terrible suggestion was made and repeated that members of the Security Forces had intentionally contributed to the death of the unfortunate victims. I knew that that suggestion must be untrue. But so serious was the allegation that I considered that it should be immediately investigated by an impartial authority.

The Inquiry has supported my confidence that the suggestion made was utterly unfounded. The Chief Justice has found as follows:

"There had been no instance of any clash or conflict between members of the communities occurring in the open fields and countryside. Such had been confined to the villages and towns. It is a fact that all concerned acted in the genuine belief that once the prisoners were on their way across country leaving Geunyeli, which was anyway under observation, behind, they ran no risk or danger and the worst they had to suffer was the weariness of the walk home. There was no intention to make these people, so to speak, run the gauntlet, or deliberately to expose them to risk or danger in making their way back; and indeed before this tribunal it has been stated by Counsel appearing for the survivors and heirs of the deceased members of the party that they did not associate themselves with any such wild and horrible suggestion. It has been submitted, however, that there was reckless indifference to the fate of these prisoners. I reject that submission on the evidence. There is no justification for it whatsoever. And I have no doubt at all that the impact of the terrible event that ensued came with almost as great a surprise, shock and horror to the members of the Security Forces engaged as it did to this unfortunate band of released prisoners themselves."

---

* (Nicosia: Cyprus Government Printing Office, 1958).

I myself visited the scene on the following day. I heard on the spot the accounts given by the Military and Police Officers concerned and saw how shocked they were by the dreadful events of the previous evening. I also know very well that at that time of communal strife their ceaseless patrolling for days and nights on end and their prompt and effective action over wide areas saved hundreds of lives.

Had it not been for their efforts carried out with the greatest zeal the loss of life and damage to property would have been far heavier. I greatly admire the courage and resolution and tireless energy with which they carried out a task of the utmost difficulty and I am very glad that the Inquiry has wholly disproved the "wild and horrible" allegation made against them.

GOVERNMENT HOUSE,
6th December, 1958.

FINDINGS OF THE COMMISSION OF INQUIRY INTO THE INCIDENTS AT GEUNYELI, CYPRUS ON 12TH JUNE, 1958

To: His Excellency Sir Hugh Foot, G.C.M.G., K.C.V.O., O.B.E.,
       Governor and Commander-in-Chief of Cyprus.

From: Sir Paget Bourke, Chief Justice of Cyprus.

PART I

Sir,

1. I have the honour to submit the Report of the Commission of Inquiry which, by an Order published in *Cyprus Gazette* (Extraordinary) No. 4144 dated 16th June, 1958, Your Excellency appointed under sections 2 and 3 of the Commissions of Inquiry Law, Cap. 64 of the Laws of Cyprus, with the following terms of reference:

To investigate and determine the facts concerning the incidents which occurred at and near the village of Geunyeli on Thursday, 12th June, 1958, in the course of which certain persons lost their lives and others were injured.

2. I was the sole Commissioner appointed by Your Excellency.

3. On the 16th June, at Government House, Nicosia, Your Excellency administered to me the Oath prescribed by law.

4. Taking into account the state of the Colony at that time I decided to exercise my power under the law to exclude the public and the press from the meetings of the Commission, and on 17th June the following notice was issued to the press and to the Cyprus Broadcasting Service:

"Commission of Inquiry into the Geunyeli Incidents.

It is hereby notified for the information of the public and all concerned that the Commission will hold its first meeting at 9 o'clock a.m., on Friday, 20th June, 1958, at the English School, Nicosia.

2. Any persons desiring to give evidence relevant to the subject matter of the Inquiry are informed that they should notify the Commissioner without delay at the Chief Justice's Chambers, Law Courts, Nicosia.

3. I have received information from His Excellency the Governor that inflamed communal feelings now prevail in the Island, and further—

    (1) that there is a risk of these feelings becoming more inflamed if the proceedings of the Inquiry are made known to the public as the Inquiry goes forward, and this might lead to further disturbances and loss of life;

    (2) that there is a danger that reprisals might be taken against witnesses who come forward to testify in public at the Inquiry;

    (3) that there is a probability that witnesses might be deterred by fear from coming forward to speak the truth in public, and as a result the object of the Inquiry would be frustrated.

After due consideration I have come to the conclusion that in the public interest the Inquiry should be held in private, and accordingly members of the public and the press will be excluded from its meetings.

4. His Excellency the Governor has further informed me that it is his intention to publish the findings of the Commission in due course.

PAGET J. BOURKE,
Commissioner."

5. On the 20th June the following notice was issued to the Press and the Cyprus Broadcasting Service:

"*Commission of Inquiry into the Geunyeli Incidents.*

It is hereby notified for the information of the public and all concerned that any persons desiring to give evidence relevant to the Inquiry should inform the Secretary to the Commissioner at the Chief Justice's Chambers, Law Courts, Nicosia, or at the English School, Nicosia, by Wednesday 25th June at the latest.

PAGET J. BOURKE,
Commissioner."

6. On the 20th June the Commission held its first sitting in the hall of the English School, Nicosia, which had kindly been placed at the disposal of the Commission by the Principal of the School, Mr. P. Griffin.

7. Counsel for interested parties appeared as follows:

The Attorney-General (Sir James Henry, Bart., Q.C.) and Mr. J. Ballard, Crown Counsel, appeared on behalf of the Government.

Mr. G. N. Chryssafinis, Q.C., Mr. J. C. Clerides, Q.C., Mr. S. Pavlides, Q.C., Mr. X. J. Clerides, Mr. L. Demetriades, Mr. C. Fanos, Mr. G. Ladas and Mr. M. A. Triantafyllides, appeared on behalf of the survivors and the heirs of the deceased.

Colonel J. C. Hamilton, Deputy Director of Army Legal Services, G.H.Q. Middle East Land Forces, represented the Military Authorities.

Mr. R. R. Denktash and Mr. Ergun Munir appeared on behalf of Inspector Errol Mehmet Assim, Auxiliary Policeman Hassan Hussein, Hassan Omer Mulla Ali, and Ismael Ali Hji Hassan.

8. During the course of the hearing, which occupied eight days, thirty-seven witnesses were brought by Counsel before the Commission and were examined on oath, cross-examined, and re-examined. One witness was allowed to give evidence by affidavit. One person applied to the Commission independently to give evidence and was allowed to do so. A list of witnesses is attached as an Appendix to this Report.

9. On the 25th June I visited the scenes of the occurrences at Skylloura, Yerolakkos and Geunyeli, which had been described to me. I was accompanied by Counsel engaged in the Inquiry, and by members of the Police Force and of the Army.

10. The last sitting of the Commission was held on the 28th June.

11. In the narrative of my findings which follows, the words "Greek" and "Turk" have for convenience been used to mean respectively "Greek Cypriot" and "Turkish Cypriot".

PART II
FINDINGS

12. The village of Skylloura lies in the Nicosia District on the main Nicosia-Myrtou road and at about 12 miles from Nicosia. About 3 1/2 miles further on to the north-west along the same road lies the Greek village of Kondemenos. Roughly about half way on the road between Skylloura and Nicosia is the larger village of Yerolakkos. Skylloura is a mixed village containing a Greek quarter and a Turkish quarter. The Turks are in a minority, the population consisting of roughly 550 Greeks to 300 Turks. Slightly over a mile from Skylloura on the road to Nicosia is the village of Ayios Vasilios, which also has a mixed community of Greeks and Turks; the 1946 census disclosed that there were 436 Greeks to 94 Turks. Skylloura is connected to the south by a dry weather road with the village of Philia five miles away; and Ayios Vasilios is similarly linked to the village of Mammari which is about 3 1/2 miles away and also to the south.

13. At the material time, that is, the 12th June, 1958, Police Sergeant Gill was stationed at the Greek village of Yerolakkos. He was responsible as the senior police officer in the locality for quite a large area including the villages of Yerolakkos, Skylloura, Ayios Vasilios, Ayia Marina, Dhyo Potami, and Kanli. He estimated the population of the area within which he carried out his police duties to be about 5,000 persons and the area itself to be 43 square miles.

For some days prior to the 12th June, in fact from the 7th June, inter-communal feeling was running very high in the Island and there had been many instances of attacks by Turks, particularly in Nicosia, upon members of the Greek community and upon Greek property. Things were very tense in and around the area for which Gill was responsible. In his own words in evidence "the situation was very tricky," and as a result he was obliged to carry out frequent patrols and take steps to investigate a number of alarms and complaints as to expected trouble in various places.

The Regiment of the Royal Horse Guards based on Camp Elizabeth, Nicosia, was responsible for keeping order in the Nicosia rural area, which included the section policed by Gill, and involved an area of about a 1,000 square miles. There can be no doubt that were it not for the magnificent work carried out by the Horse Guards, events in the Nicosia District countryside would have been dire indeed. The comparatively few police available could not have coped. As incidents arose it fell to the military to be on or get to the spot to investigate or restore the situation. As Major Medlen, the Acting Commanding Officer of the Regiment, said in evidence, the work being done by his officers and men was tremendous. They had been working intensely and non-stop from the 7th June. In the 24 hours leading up to the 12th June the tension greatly increased and the number of threatened incidents also increased—"I can best describe it as fantastic; a fantastic group of rumours, unconfirmed reports, amazing reports coming in through the police net. Through my net often came reports from civilians, and in every case we had to investigate these. If I say that my Regiment is still motoring 6,000 miles a day, the majority of that motoring is to confirm that the report was either completely exaggerated or unfounded." Replying to a question concerning the 12th June, Major Medlen said—"I think you have got to realise that this was a particularly trying day for my Regiment, we were trying to get out of one problem to get ready for the next".

14. Just after midnight on the 11th June, Gill was on patrol in Skylloura where a number of Greek and Turkish people were standing about armed with sticks and clubs and other weapons. The Turkish mukhtar of the village told the police officer that his people were very alarmed as they anticipated an attack upon them by Greeks. Gill set out with Auxiliary Policeman No. 3845 in his Land Rover to search in the vicinity of the village. At a distance of about 200 to 300 yards along the road to Philia he came upon 175 Greeks armed with clubs, sticks, knives and pitch forks. They were crouching in the dried up bed of a stream. By the side of the road were parked at least 10 motor buses and lorries with the headlights switched off. Gill kept most of these persons in the light of his car lamps and sent the auxiliary policeman back to the village to inform the military scout cars. Some of the armed persons started to run away and the police officer called on them to halt, and threatened to shoot, but did not do so. About 50 escaped. The military patrol that was sent for then arrived. The Greeks were disarmed and inquiry revealed that most of them had come from Philia village. This party was girded for attack and the only reasonable inference is that it was to be launched upon the Turkish minority in Skylloura. They were arrested and taken by Gill with the weapons under military escort to the Assistant Chief Constable at Nicosia Central Police Station. Their names were taken and they were later released, being, according to the recollection of Assistant Chief Constable Rice, allowed transport to get back to their village. Gill returned and searched the scene of the arrests and found three long knives of the "panga" type and a hatchet.

15. Police Sergeant Gill got back to Skylloura intending to return to his Police Station at Yerolakkos when he was approached by two Turks in a very agitated state who informed that their community in the village of Ayios Vasilios was going to be attacked. It was about 5.30 a.m. on the 11th June. The officer at once went to this village accompanied by three military scout cars. When approaching the village he saw two buses of what he took to be the "attacking party" turning round and going fast in the direction of Mammari: the scout cars pursued the buses. They contained 60 men and youths mostly from Mammari village and armed with pitch forks, sticks, clubs and knives. In all, five vehicles were rounded up, and the whole party numbered 250 Greek persons who were "all armed with some sort of weapon or other." It was considered that there were too many persons to take to a Police Station. They were all disarmed and, being kept under observation, were made to walk the 1 1/2 miles to Mammari from the spot where the vehicles were stopped. These vehicles were driven on ahead of them. Having regard to the number of persons involved, the proximity of their village, the fact that Security Forces in the area were stretched to the utmost, and the quite inadequate accommodation available at rural police stations, it would seem that this was a sensible course to pursue in the circumstances.

16. I have thought fit to make these findings as to happenings around Skylloura on the 11th June, because a certain pattern will emerge relevant to an appreciation of the occurrences of the 12th June. It is evident that this intrepid and indefatigable police officer, Police Sergeant Gill, was working under

considerable strain. As he said in cross-examination when asked as to why he did not charge the 250 people made to walk back to Mammari—"We were awfully busy, and I was awfully tired, having worked for nights and nights . . ."

17. At 3.30 p.m. on the 12th June, Police Sergeant Gill was at the Police Station at Yerolakkos when he was informed by Turks arriving by taxi that their community in Skylloura had been attacked. Gill asked for military assistance over the police radio and drove at once to Skylloura with Greek Police Sergeant Costas Charalambous. There he spoke with the Turkish mukhtar and discovered that there had been an alarm but no actual attack. A number of Turks were armed with sticks and about double that number of Greeks were similarly armed. They were facing each other from their respective community sections of the village. The mukhtar feared an attack from Philia or Kondemenos, and Gill decided that his best line of action was to go towards Kondemenos village, which he did. Meanwhile in response to the call for assistance, Lieutenant Legge-Bourke, in command of No. 4 Troop of B. Squadron of the Royal Horse Guards, arrived with two armoured scout cars and effectively controlled the situation in the village.

18. About 350 yards outside Skylloura on the Kondemenos road, Gill, accompanied by Charalambous, came upon 35 Greek men. They had come from Kondemenos and were standing in the defile of a dry river bed; it was a natural entrenched position. By the side of the road were two empty motor lorries facing Kondemenos. They were all carrying some sort of weapon such as sticks, short shovels and pitch forks, (there were about three pitch forks), and there were stones and a few iron bars in the vehicles. Some of these persons began to run away but stopped when Gill shouted "Halt" and threatened to shoot. He formed the impression that they were an attacking party, not only because they had weapons and were drawn up in formation in a concealed position, but also because they were in a very aggressive mood. They were close to a flank of the Turkish quarter, which began to the left of the main road intersecting the village about 350 yards away. The Greek side of the village begins at the same distance to the right of the road. In the circumstances to which he deposed, and which I accept, Gill felt justified in rejecting the explanation offered that they were there to protect any Kondemenos people returning from work outside their village. I believe it to be the fact that they were there either to launch an attack upon the Turkish quarter a little distance away, or else to join their compatriots in the village, and come to their assistance if an intercommunal fight was started there.

19. With the help of Squadron-Leader Smith of the R.A.F., who was passing, Gill completed the arrest of the 35 Greeks. I am satisfied that the arrest was lawful. Gill intended to bring them to Yerolakkos and charge them with the offence of having offensive weapons under the Offensive Weapons (Prohibition) Law, 1955. They were put into their two vehicles with the weapons and taken into Skylloura, where Legge-Bourke provided an escort of two scout cars under Sergeant Taylor and Corporal Straker while he, Legge-Bourke, remained to keep the peace at Skylloura. With Gill in charge of the prisoners the convoy, as it has been called, moved off towards Yerolakkos. Thus began the journey that was to end in such tragic circumstances.

20. At this time Assistant Superintendent of Police Trusler was at his station at the Central Police Station, Nicosia. He was in charge of the Nicosia Rural Sub-Division which included the area for which Gill was responsible. He received the news of the trouble at Skylloura (which went out over the military radio network and reached the Operations room at Nicosia Central Police Station and the Operations room at Camp Elizabeth) and set out in that direction with Inspector Assim. On the way he met the convoy and proceeded with it into Yerolakkos. There Gill told him of his intention to charge the 35 persons under arrest with the offence of carrying offensive weapons. While the two police officers were talking a crowd gathered around giving indications of hostile feeling. It was considered, obviously with good reason, that it would be unsafe and indeed impracticable to take such a large number of prisoners into the small Police Station in the circumstances and the decision was arrived at to bring them on to the Central Police Station at Nicosia. Acting upon the instruction of his superior, Gill set off with the convoy which was of the same composition as before: Police Sergeant Charalambous remained at his Police Station at Yerolakkos and was replaced by Auxiliary Policeman Hassan Hussein, who accompanied Gill. On the way the convoy was overtaken by Assistant Superintendent Trusler who went on to the Central Police Station at Nicosia with his companion Inspector Assim. It appears that both Inspector Assim and Auxiliary Policeman Hassan Hussein have suffered accusation from Greek sources that in some way they were involved in engineering or assisting the dreadful events that took place later that day in the Geunyeli lands. I am wholly satisfied that any such accusations are false.

21. When he arrived at the Central Police Station Assistant Superintendent Trusler found a serious riot in progress outside the Police Station. There was a considerable disturbance being caused by Turkish men and women, but it is not necessary to go into details which anyway are revealed by the record of evidence. In Trusler's words as a witness—"There was a vast number of army and police officers and a great number of policemen running about and general confusion ensued." Assistant Superintendent Trusler's first thought was to stop the convoy of Greek prisoners from Skylloura being brought into the centre of Turkish riot and commotion. Very sensibly he telephoned at once to the Duty Police Officer, Sergeant Deighton, in the Operations room at the Central Police Station and asked that the convoy should be stopped immediately. This message could be conveyed through the Military Liaison Officer in the Operations room operating the military radio network linking up with the escort scout cars accompanying the prisoners. According to Trusler, after a few minutes he received the reply from Sergeant Deighton that the convoy had in fact stopped outside Ayios Dhometios, which is a suburb on the outskirts of Nicosia. He thereupon instructed that it should be sent to Ayios Dhometios Police Station. He waited on the telephone and was then told that the prisoners had been released, and he understood that this had been done at Ayios Dhometios. Satisfied that all was well so far as the convoy was concerned he donned his riot kit and went out of the Police Station where he met the Assistant Chief Constable and the Chief Superintendent, Nicosia Division, and told them that he had prevented the convoy from coming into Nicosia. He was assured that this was satisfactory. Later that evening, he discovered that the

convoy had not been stopped but had gone on to Geunyeli village and he was "very puzzled indeed" as to how this had occurred.

22. Returning for a moment to the convoy, it was proceeding through Ayios Dhometios when Sergeant Taylor in his escort vehicle received a wireless message from his Control, Major Redgrave, at Camp Elizabeth, directing that the prisoners should not be taken to the Central Police Station but were to be taken to Geunyeli village and dropped there. On getting this message, which I have given in his words in evidence, he drove on and overtook the other four vehicles opposite Wolseley Barracks. There he informed Gill and, following the instruction, the convoy went on to Geunyeli on the Kyrenia Road. At the time Gill thought that the order had come from Police Control at the Central Police Station, Nicosia, over the military radio system.

23. It is obvious that there had been a misunderstanding or mistake and that Assistant Superintendent Trusler had been misled as to what had occurred. The convoy had not been stopped and the prisoners had not been brought to Ayios Dhometios Police Station and they had not been released there. Instead the convoy had been diverted to a place to the north of Geunyeli. No instruction to carry out this movement had issued from the Operations room at the Central Police Station and no message was received informing that the convoy was proceeding to Geunyeli with the intention of making the prisoners walk home from there. It was at 5.12 p.m. that the first message came in as to a fire at Geunyeli. Messages followed at short intervals concerning happenings near the village; but, on the evidence of Captain Wilson, it was only at 5.55 p.m. that Central Operations realised that the convoyed people were implicated—"It was only at 17.55 when we got this report from the Royal Horse Guards that we even married up the Skylloura incident and the Geunyeli incident. We did not know that it was one and the same thing."

24. In the endeavour to discover how things had gone wrong, that is, why Assistant Superintendent Trusler's instructions did not get through to the convoy, it is necessary to look into the Control or Operations room at the Central Police Station described in evidence by Major Medlen as "the nerve centre for the functioning of the Security Forces in the whole (Nicosia) rural area." It was a joint Police and Military (50 Brigade) Operations room and at the material time there were at least three army officers and three police officers working to send out and receive signals or messages over the army wireless network and the police wireless network. Police Sergeant Deighton testified that he was in charge generally on the 12th June. Captain Wilson was one of the officers operating on the army network and was the Military Duty Officer. All personnel were extremely busy. The room was small and, as Captain Wilson said in evidence, not ideal for the job. He described how persons were constantly coming in and out from another Operations room used "by other Battalions" so that one got, in the words of the witness, "quite a mêlée of people" in the room. He also told of the difficulties in getting messages through and that "the traffic on the command was very heavy indeed." And as Major Medlen said, "We have the picture of an enormous number of messages coming in by radio about the emergency outside"—a reference to the riots that were taking place at the time outside and in the vicinity of the Police Station.

According to Assistant Chief Constable Rice, it was a highly unsatisfactory Operations room, and he made a complaint to higher authority on the 8th June with the result that arrangements for other accommodation are now being carried out.

I make these references to the difficult conditions in the Operations room because it seems to me that herein may lie some explanation as to why Superintendent Trusler's specific instructions were not passed through to his subordinate officer, Sergeant Gill, in charge of the convoyed prisoners, and as to why Trusler was given to believe that action had been taken as he directed. A blunder suggesting some confusion had occurred: to what, if any, extent it was due to lack of proper liaison between police and military, I cannot say. Had Gill received Trusler's instructions at Wolseley Barracks instead of the order that did come to him through Sergeant Taylor, there can be no doubt that he would either have stopped there, and informed that he had passed Ayios Dhometios and enquired what he should do, or else he would in all probability have returned with the persons under his arrest to Ayios Dhometios Police Station; the disturbances were taking place inside the Old City and there was nothing to prevent him turning round and going back to the suburb he had passed through on the way into Nicosia. Alternatively, had the Central Operations room been advised of what was in fact being done with the convoy, it is likely that Trusler or Rice would have been informed and that they, having regard to their evidence, would have interfered to prevent it.

25. From approximately 3.0 p.m. signals had been coming in over the military (Royal Horse Guards) network informing of the trouble at Skylloura and at 3.50 p.m. the report arrived that the 35 persons arrested were being brought to the Central Police Station at Nicosia. Assistant Superintendent Trusler when he arrived was therefore by no means the only person at Nicosia who knew what was going forward. Major Medlen, for instance, was at the Central Police Station when the disturbances in Nicosia were brewing up and he was promptly alert and anxious as to the fate of the convoy. As he said in evidence, "When it became quite obvious that the city could easily reach a state of turmoil, I remember seeing the Assistant Chief Constable, Mr. Rice. We did not have a conversation, we talked maybe 30 to 40 seconds and we all realised that they (the Skylloura prisoners) mustn't come in here (to Nicosia) at any cost . . . my main fear was the trucks and escort coming round the corner of Kyrenia Gate and driving straight into the procession of Turks."

26. It is a fact that acute solicitude was felt by the members of the Security Forces immediately concerned who were at the Central Police Station as to the safety of the Greek prisoners on their way from Skylloura. It was fully appreciated that they must be kept away from the centre of Turkish disturbance and the danger involved. Steps were taken towards that end.

27. The action taken by Assistant Superintendent Trusler has already been observed. According to Police Sergeant Deighton, about 4.35 p.m. Trusler spoke to him on the telephone and asked "if we could have the convoy stopped and the prisoners taken to Ayios Dhometios Police Station." In fact the time that Deighton was so approached must have been very shortly before 4.20 p.m., which was the time the first instruction was sent out concerning the convoy. The order had to go out through the military wireless network linking

up with the escort vehicles attached to the convoy. Deighton said in evidence that he spoke to Captain Wilson, and "relayed to him Mr. Trusler's instructions." About ten minutes later Trusler again telephoned Deighton and asked what was the position regarding the convoy. Deighton says that he enquired of Captain Wilson what had happened and the latter informed him that the convoy had been stopped. This information was passed back to Trusler who enquired what had happened to the prisoners. According to Deighton he put the question to Wilson and got the reply that they had been "turned loose" but he did not know where: this was passed back by Deighton to Trusler who was still holding the telephone.

Captain Wilson said in evidence that at 4.20 p.m. a message was passed "to the Royal Horse Guards (at the Operations room at Elizabeth Camp) telling them not to bring them (the convoyed prisoners) into the Central Police Station." According to the Central Operations room log (Exhibit 3) at 4.16 p.m. a message was sent out to "N 11"—"Stop 2 armoured cars bringing Greeks at Pedias Bridge." Wilson stated that he did not take down the actual words of the message transmitted outwards, and he did not remember who instructed the sending of the message. He remembered no conversation with Deighton and no instruction from him that the convoy should be stopped and the prisoners be taken to Ayios Dhometios. But at 4.21 p.m., or "probably a bit later," the information was received by the witness that "the prisoners had been let go away from Skylloura." This presumably was intended to mean that the prisoners from Skylloura had been let go away. In evidence Captain Wilson added that—"According to our log it (this information) is from the police net, but I should say possibly it is a mistake; it may be from the Blues in fact." This may well be a reference to the message sent, according to the evidence of Lieutenant Eyre, Signals Officer of the Royal Horse Guards at Camp Elizabeth, confirming, in reply to a query from Brigade, that the convoy was not coming into the Central Police Station. Wilson agreed that every message received was passed out to Sergeant Deighton on the police side. His final account of the message sent was that it instructed the convoy to be stopped outside Nicosia and not come into Nicosia. It will be seen later that according to the evidence of Major Redgrave, who was in charge, so to speak, at the receiving end at Camp Elizabeth, the message was not simply to stop the convoy outside Nicosia and not let it in to the Central Police Station, but was an instruction to send the prisoners out of town into the country and make them walk home.

28. Assistant Chief Constable Rice was in the Operations room around 4.20 p.m. when he first learned of the convoy of arrested persons coming from Skylloura. His recollection is that Deighton was his informant and that he told him that "a convoy of the Royal Horse Guards had been stopped on the outskirts of the town—I believe at Wolseley Barracks—and they were seeking instructions." He was apparently given to understand that the convoy had been stopped and said in evidence that "the matter was then referred to me by Sergeant Deighton." Major Medlen was present, and the witness had a conversation with him which was necessarily hurried, as the noise of the demonstrations outside the Police Station "was quite unbelievable at the time." Beyond doubt the occasion is that referred to in paragraph 25 above. Rice gave evidence to

the effect that he enquired of Major Medlen as to what offence the convoyed prisoners had committed. He deposed that he was told of what had happened at Skylloura and then said—"Look, we do not want them here, or anywhere else for that matter. They do not appear to have committed any offence. Take them away again." He went on to say that to the best of his knowledge Major Medlen subsequently issued orders to that effect.

29. That brings me back to the evidence of Major Medlen, who said when asked what action he took after speaking with Rice, and realising that the convoy must not be brought into the centre of the disturbances going on, "I certainly took some action a little later on; but I know that our officer in the Brigade H.Q.—it could have been me, it could have been the Duty Officer—a message was passed: 'Do not bring them here.' The message went out on the Brigade Command net. It would be picked up by my own command position at Camp Elizabeth and rebroadcast on another frequency to the Squadron Leader of the armoured car squadron who in fact was operating in the area for that day."

Major Medlen then decided that he should avoid getting held up as a result of the trouble developing in the city and he made his way out in a Land Rover. He said in evidence that—"When I got clear of the city I was starting to look, I can't remember towards where, towards Camp Elizabeth. I thought I saw, in fact I did see, the pennants, that is, the red flags, on one or two of my scout cars and I saw a truck with men in it in white shirts. That was an impression. There was a lot of traffic. I got hold of my own radio in the Land Rover and I passed a flank communication to the Squadron Leader Major Redgrave. One has to realise that the situation was tense, very tense. I don't know what I said to him but I know what I conveyed to him—'For goodness sake, I have seen a truck which I think is the one from Skylloura. It must not come into the city at any cost. Get it out into the country, tell the occupants to be good boys'—I do remember saying that 'and tell them to go home to their villages.' After that, knowing the Squadron Leader as well as I do, I forgot the incident and got on with my other jobs." It was some time between 5.30 p.m. to 6.0 p.m. that the witness came to know that in fact the prisoners had been put down north of Geunyeli village.

30. It has been seen that according to Major Redgrave the order he got from the Central Operations room was to send the Skylloura prisoners out of town into the country and let them walk home. Despite the unsatisfactory nature of the evidence as to what went on in the Operations room and the inference arising that there was some bungling, I do not credit that Deighton, Wilson, Medlen and Rice can all be wrong as to the action decided upon there, or the substantial nature of the message sent out to stop the convoy outside Nicosia and not let it into the Central Police Station. Redgrave gave evidence that he was "almost sure" that he heard the voice of his Commanding Officer, Major Medlen, over the wireless. I think that the probabilities are that Major Redgrave's recollection is at fault and that he got the message spoken of in evidence by Captain Wilson from Central Operations, followed very shortly afterwards by the flank communication from Major Medlen referred to in the preceding paragraph. I have no doubt that the impression left upon his mind was that he was under instruction to stop the convoy going into the neighbour-

hood of the Central Police Station, and to send it into the country and allow the prisoners to walk home to their village. In the best of good faith he took steps to carry out that instruction. It is unfortunate that no message was sent back to Central Operations informing of the precise course he proposed to take, and that Operations were simply told that the convoy was not coming into the Central Police Station (Lieutenant Eyre) or that "the prisoners had been let go away from Skylloura" (Captain Wilson).

31. It was a time for quick decision and Major Redgrave made up his mind that the best plan to adopt was to have the prisoners taken to the north of Geunyeli village and made to walk home from there. No particular spot was specified—"that was for the man on the ground." The order was passed to Sergeant Taylor who was spoken to on the radio network as he was passing through Ayios Dhometios and again as the convoy was approaching Wolseley Barracks. Major Redgrave has given his "main reasons" for deciding upon a place to the north of Geunyeli village. They are—(1) the road to Geunyeli (the Kyrenia Road) was the first turning away into the country having regard to the route being taken by the convoy at the time; (2) the prisoners were known to come from the north of Skylloura and a diversion by Geunyeli "was therefore taking them towards their homes"; (3) "Once they were clear of Geunyeli village to my knowledge there was no other source of trouble on their route. On the map it can be seen that this is a clear cross-country route"; (4) it was an area in which during the whole time that the Regiment had been in charge of the rural district nothing, (apart from a minor incident when stones were thrown at a Greek bus), had ever happened to disturb the peace; (5) "I also knew that my own troops were in that area and had been on and off, and that everything was quiet there and that it was as safe as houses. To my knowledge there was no threat in that area."

Asked why he did not think of sending the prisoners back the way they had come the witness was emphatic that he would not have "dreamed" of sending them back to the place where the original trouble had taken place. (They were going back anyway, but on foot across country). He added—"It would not have been reasonable to send them back to the place where we had already arrested them. I realise now that it would have been even worse from the point of discipline and in the eyes of the local people. They had been bad boys—and not for a moment would I have taken them back to the place I had arrested them." Again, according to Major Medlen, it would involve "a certain loss of dignity to the Security Forces" if prisoners were taken back the same way to the scene of an incident in which they had been engaged. Lieutenant Legge-Bourke, who was keeping in touch on the radio network from Skylloura, offered the opinion in evidence that such a course would have "involved loss of face on the part of the Security Forces. It would not have reduced the attitude of mind of these people in the least. They would if anything be more likely to cause trouble by realising that we were going to do nothing with them . . ."

Those are points of view and I make no comment. It was evidently considered inappropriate or inadvisable that these prisoners who had to be released should be taken out of the town along the route they had been brought and at some point there be set down to walk home, if it was considered that there was good reason for depriving them of the use of their vehicles.

32. That brings me to the consideration of what has been referred to in evidence as a "practice" of causing persons arrested in this time of Emergency for offences in breach of the peace, or for anticipated breach of the peace, to be brought off some distance and caused to walk back to their homes. I think it necessary to find out something about this in order to understand why these particular prisoners were compelled to start on a walk back to Kondemenos from the vicinity of Geunyeli village. It is roughly 10 miles across country from Geunyeli to Skylloura and Kondemenos is 3 1/2 miles further on from Skylloura.

Police Sergeant Gill had heard of this "accepted practice"—"I had heard of people being taken away from their villages when there was trouble and possibly being made to walk a few miles to get home again." There were no orders or general instructions as to such a procedure but it was resorted to as an effective measure to give troublesome persons "a little exercise" so that they should behave themselves and have "time to meditate upon their doings." It was a way of teaching people a "lesson." Neither Assistant Chief Constable Rice nor Assistant Superintendent Trusler had heard of the practice prior to the Geunyeli happening, and they deprecated any such method of dealing with people. Rice told in evidence that as a result of his enquiries into the Geunyeli incident he was informed by military officers that it was a fairly common practice. He surmised that neither he nor Trusler had learned of it previously because—"I think irregularities of that nature would not be brought to our attention, that is the reason."

Lieutenant Legge-Bourke said in evidence that what was done with the Skylloura prisoners—"was a very normal habit of Security Forces when dealing with people who are very excited—to drop them some miles away from home and make them walk back . . . We were doing what a very large number of Security Forces do to cool them down. Because once you walk five miles or so you do not feel like causing trouble. It is in fact a normal practice of the Security Forces . . . It is a good thing to let (them) walk home and cool off . . . I have seen it done (i.e. compulsory walks across country) and I know a lot of companies do it."

Major Medlen said in evidence that if the Police for good reason cannot take in persons who have committed an offence or caused a breach of the peace—"we have alternatives; we either drive them back to their front doors, back home to their villages or on occasions we may take them in the direction of their villages and tell them to walk home—that puts them to an inconvenience. It is not a punishment and I might also add it makes them a little tired and they normally do not pick up sticks and start that day." The witness thought that it would be wrong to describe these forced walks as a "practice"; but in his short stay in Cyprus he had become aware that from time to time such a course was followed—not regularly but occasionally. Asked the object of such a procedure the witness replied with the candour and frankness that characterised his evidence, and indeed that of all the Army witnesses,—"I think to be perfectly honest, it is an unlawful practice, but it is done to teach people a very small lesson because perhaps the commander on the spot did not think it worth taking such people to a Police Station and having them charged—but it was felt that the throwing of stones at a car, say, should not be overlooked, so a compromise was reached which might teach them not to do such things again."

Major Redgrave made it clear through his evidence that when he understood his instructions to be that the Skylloura prisoners should be taken out into the country and made walk home to their village, he recognised that—"It was quite a normal thing and I knew what was meant." The officer regarded it as a routine and salutary measure.

33. It emerges as a fact that whatever about the rights and wrongs of the practice spoken of, the treatment of the Skylloura prisoners in being brought to a particular place and being forced to walk back across country to their village was no isolated matter, but was an instance of a measure which, though it had no sanction in law, was not uncommon and had been employed upon other occasions in not dissimilar circumstances.

34. Geunyeli is a Turkish village situated four miles from Nicosia on the Kyrenia road. On the same road lying two miles from Nicosia is the smaller Turkish village of Orta Keuy. At 2 1/2 miles to the west of Geunyeli lies the Turkish hamlet of Kanli: To the south-west of Geunyeli at a distance of 3 1/2 miles is the Greek village of Yerolakkos which has already been mentioned. From Geunyeli there is a wide view across fairly flat land and Yerolakkos can be seen.

35. The convoy was last observed making its way from Wolseley Barracks towards Geunyeli following the instruction received by Sergeant Taylor from Major Redgrave to take the prisoners north of the village and make them walk back to their own village from there. As they went through Orta Keuy the Greek prisoners were singing and shouting and one of them threw stones at some Turkish villagers but hit no one. Meanwhile Redgrave was instructing Lieutenant Baring, who was patrolling in an armoured car about two miles away from Geunyeli, to come and assist Sergeant Taylor and "to secure the area." Baring had some Grenadier Guards at his disposal as mobile infantry and they were to be brought up also. Taylor kept in touch over the radio network with both Redgrave and Baring.

The convoy went through Geunyeli and stopped at a point on the road about 400 yards from the village which was in clear view. The choosing of a place to put down the prisoners was left "to the men on the spot." Further on there was a rise in the road and the country became somewhat rougher. Taylor said in evidence that he stopped the convoy because "it was pretty flat country", while Gill's evidence is that he was leading the convoy and he decided to stop at what he considered was a reasonable distance from Geunyeli. Anyway they both obviously agreed on the spot. The place was pin-pointed back to Major Redgrave by grid reference on a map and the latter said in evidence that he thought the place was "perfectly suitable." He directed Taylor to "carry on" there with the dismounting and despatch of the Greeks across country.

36. The 35 prisoners were ordered down from their vehicles by Gill and were lined up in two rows on the edge of the field by the road. Gill spoke to them through one of their number who knew English and informed them that they would have to walk to their village on foot. He added that by the time they had walked to their village they would be too tired to think of attacking any other Turkish village that day, and that they would be too tired to think of

attacking Skylloura again that day. The prisoners did not appear to be frightened and did not protest against being made to run any risk or danger; they gave the impression that they were not displeased at being released. Another reason that Gill gave in evidence as to why he thought the place chosen was a good one was that the prisoners would be able to get across the 3 1/2 miles to Yerolakkos and the main road leading to Kondemenos. In fact, as soon as they were left on their own, this was precisely what they set out to do. I do not believe that Gill uttered any words of threat or of an ominous character to the prisoners or that he said to them as they were lined up by the road—"You went to attack the Turks at Skylloura, why are you now afraid? Wait and see." I thought Gill was an honest and trustworthy witness and I accept it from him that it never struck him for a moment that the Greeks might be running into danger from the Turkish villagers, and that if he had the slightest doubt he would never have permitted them to be put down there.

37. I am fully satisfied and find that all concerned with ordering and carrying out this operation acted with the utmost good faith and for the best on their appreciation of the situation. It is true that inter-communal feelings were known to be tense and as much so in the Geunyeli area as in any other part of the Nicosia rural district in which Major Medlen's Regiment was working. It was plainly appreciated that some trouble might be anticipated due to the proximity to the Turkish village and steps were taken towards maintaining security. Thus Baring was called up and the infantry to carry out Redgrave's order "to secure the area." It was Redgrave's view, and that of the officers in charge on the ground, that "once they (the prisoners) were clear of Geunyeli village . . . there would be no other source of trouble on the route." The existence of the Turkish hamlet of Kanli on the route seems to have been overlooked. In pursuance of the instructions received Lieutenant Baring and Sergeant Taylor kept watch on the village and road leading west from it. Corporal Straker in his scout car was moved closer to the village along the main road and, as Baring reported back to Redgrave, the Grenadiers, after completing their first duty of escorting the prisoners some distance on their way across the fields, were "to keep an eye on Geunyeli."

There had been no instance of any clash or conflict between members of the communities occurring in the open fields and countryside. Such had been confined to the villages and towns. It is a fact that all concerned acted in the genuine belief that once the prisoners were on their way across country leaving Geunyeli, which was anyway under observation, behind, they ran no risk or danger and the worst they had to suffer was the weariness of the walk home. There was no intention to make these people, so to speak, run the gauntlet, or deliberately to expose them to risk or danger in making their way back; and indeed before this tribunal it has been stated by Counsel appearing for the survivors and heirs of the deceased members of the party that they did not associate themselves with any such wild and horrible suggestion. It has been submitted, however, that there was reckless indifference to the fate of these prisoners. I reject that submission on the evidence. There is no justification for it whatsoever. And I have no doubt at all that the impact of the terrible event that ensued came with almost as great a surprise, shock and horror to the members of the Security Forces engaged as it did to this unfortunate band of released prisoners themselves.

38. I have been invited by Colonel Hamilton, representing the Military, to find not only that everyone acted in good faith, which I have had no difficulty in doing, but also that the order given and action taken upon it were reasonable. I am unable to do so. There is no question of being wise after the event. I do not say for a moment that anything like what did occur was reasonably to be anticipated. I do not propose to speculate upon the possibilities. The fact is that a party of Greeks arrested as intending attackers upon Turks was put down and compelled, at a time of great tenseness of inter-communal feeling, to walk across Turkish property, away from a Turkish village, but in the general direction of a Turkish hamlet, and out of the sight of the Security Forces remaining on the Kyrenia Road. Both Assistant Chief Constable Rice and Assistant Superintendent Trusler considered such a course unwise and they were also guarding themselves from being discerning merely after the event.

39. When Police Sergeant Gill lined up his prisoners in the field by the side of the road, he caused the stones and weapons in their two vehicles to be deposited in the bordering ditch. Later, when the prisoners were walking across the Turkish lands, the two vehicles were sent off under escort of Corporal Straker towards Kyrenia to take the northern road back to Myrtou and Kondemenos, a distance of about 40 miles. After going some distance Straker returned. About 10 minutes after the prisoners had been lined up, Lieutenant Baring arrived followed a few minutes later by Lieutenant Corkran and about 15 soldiers. At this stage things were taken out of Gill's hands and Baring was regarded as being in command. He directed Corkran "to set the party of Greeks marching to their village Skylloura across the country". The soldiers were formed up with fixed bayonets behind the prisoners. It was at Gill's request that this escort was provided. Corkran told the prisoners through their interpreter that they were going to walk back home. They did not appear to be frightened but, according to Corkran, "they did not seem frightfully pleased and the interpreter chap complained that it was 15 miles". They set out on the walk in the western direction fixed between Baring and Taylor, with Corkran in the centre of the semi-circle of soldiers following up behind. I am satisfied that the prisoners were not compelled to run and were not treated roughly by the troops. After going 300 to 400 yards from the road the section of troops was stopped and Corkran came back to inquire of Baring whether he wanted them to go farther. Baring said it was far enough and the soldiers were withdrawn as soon as the last Greek was seen to disappear over the sky line—the crest of a rise about a mile away.

40. Before Baring and Corkran had arrived on the scene a Turkish R.A.F. Auxiliary Policeman had approached the spot from Geunyeli on a motor-cycle. He was curious and Gill spoke to him sharply and told him to go back. Four Turkish cyclists also came out and viewed the proceedings. Gill chased them back into Geunyeli in his Land Rover. After the Greeks had walked about a mile, Gill went away. He was in Orta Keuy when he got tidings of a fire on the Geunyeli lands and he returned there at once.

41. As to the conditions in and around Geunyeli village, the evidence is to the effect that all was peaceful and no one was seen to leave the village and go

off in a western direction either before or immediately after the party of Greeks had started walking home. The Greeks were seen, from the spot where they had commenced their journey and where the army personnel and vehicles remained, to reach a slight dip before the slope upwards about a mile away from the Kyrenia Road. Some of them stopped for a moment there and then all were observed to run up this rise and they disappeared from view. About 4 or 5 minutes later the army watchers on the road saw heavy smoke and flames rising from beyond the crest of the slope. The time was shortly after 5.0 p.m. The first impression was that the Greeks had set crops afire. A large number of people began to pour out of Geunyeli along the road heading west from the village and marked 'A'—'B' on the map, Exhibit 1. They were armed "with clubs, sticks, pieces of iron and every possible weapon" (Baring). Lieutenant Baring acted promptly on seeing the fire. Having reported the happening back to Major Redgrave, he took his armoured car out along the road mentioned and got ahead of the people coming from Geunyeli. He had ordered the Grenadier Guards to follow. They did so and formed a road block against the oncoming crowd. There can be no doubt, and the evidence of Greek survivors goes also to support this, that the immediate action taken by Baring averted a very much worse tragedy than did in fact take place; any delay would most probably have resulted in the wholesale massacre of the Greek party. As the survivor witness Christos Tsikkos said in evidence—"If it had not been for the armoured car we would all have been slaughtered."

42. Arriving near a fork in the road marked 'B' on the map Exhibit 1, Baring came upon a motor-cyclist riding towards Geunyeli with a pillion passenger who threw a large club covered with blood to the ground. They were both Turks and he arrested them. He came upon the body of a man he took to be dead—"He was cut everywhere and you could not find a piece of flesh that was not". About 12 or 15 persons then came towards him in a bunch, one was wounded holding his side and another had his hands up. There were Greeks and Turks in the party and later the Police took charge of them. Baring then concerned himself with attending to the wounded on the ground. In a commendably short space of time, as a result of his radio messages, ambulances and helicopters were upon the scene to recover the dead and succour the injured.

43. I take up the broad story of what occurred as it comes from the witnesses who were among the party of 35 Greeks released near Geunyeli. The party had run up the slope as they wished to get home quickly; they were making for Yerolakkos. They passed the field of crops on the top of the rise that in a few minutes went up in flames, and were descending the slope some little distance away on the other side looking towards Yerolakkos. Two motor-cyclists and a pillion rider were observed coming on the village road from Geunyeli; they fired at the Greeks and some were hit. The Greeks made to go back and then suddenly found themselves encircled by a number of Turks, estimated at 50 and 100, armed with sticks, axes, pieces of wood and knives, who attacked them and cut and bludgeoned some of them down. The Greeks scattered in a desperate attempt to escape. As some of them were running back the way they had come the field of crops went on fire. The witness Tsikkos had been "running in all directions", and then he and those of the party who were

with him noticed the armoured car and they ran towards it "to save ourselves"; according to the witness some of the attacking Turks had thrown away the weapons when the armoured car was observed on the scene and also came up to the vehicle. The witness Charalambos Andrea was chased by an attacker holding a "piece of wood" but he managed to escape by concealing himself in bushes in a river bed, whence he emerged at 6.35 p.m. and went up to the soldiers present. Christoforos Andrea, aged 14, described how he was being shot at by the pillion rider, but he managed to get away under cover and make for Yerolakkos. Christos Agathocleous told in evidence how after the shooting began by the motor-cyclists and the sudden encirclement of armed Turkish attackers, he immediately turned back, and ran left and right to save his life. On his way back "as soon as the fight started" he saw the fire by the route over which they had passed. Then he saw the armoured car and "immediately ran there with my hands up" and was "rescued". Others of his co-villagers, he said, were with him and one man was wounded in the side; some Turks of the attackers threw their weapons away when the armoured vehicle came up.

44. It is a fact that this party of 35 unarmed Greeks walked into an ambush laid by Turks who had concealed themselves and went in to the attack when the motor-cyclists started shooting. As a result 4 Greeks died on the spot and 4 died later in hospital; five were severely wounded but survived. The attack was of a most savage nature and the injuries inflicted indicate an extraordinary blood lust.

45. I am unable to say with any degree of certainty where these attackers came from. There is every indication that it was not a haphazard affair but was arranged in anticipation of these Greeks passing along by where the killers were concealed. I do not accept the evidence of some of the survivor witnesses that, in addition to the attackers who sprang up from concealment, more arrived armed in trucks and cars from Geunyeli direction and jumped down to join in the attack. One such witness testified that this took place when the armoured car was a matter of 200 yards from the vehicles. Such trucks etc. would certainly have been observed by the Security Forces keeping watch. I prefer to think that these witnesses, who had gone through an awful experience, are blurred in their recollection and may be confused over the vehicles that did come out along the west road from Geunyeli after the fire was seen. The Grenadiers, for instance, came out in vehicles described in evidence as "trucks". One point is clear, that the attackers who had laid their plan must have gleaned or surmised what was going forward earlier close to Geunyeli village—that the Greeks were going to walk across these lands towards the west or north-west. There is some evidence by survivor witnesses going to identify a Turkish motor-cyclist said to have followed the convoy from Skylloura; and also that the motor-cyclist ordered back by Gill into Geunyeli was dressed similarly to a motor-cyclist who started the shooting. I do not conceive it to be my duty for the purposes of this Inquiry to go into such detailed questions, which may be the subject matter of investigation in proceedings elsewhere.

If the assailants came from Geunyeli, then it means either that the vigilance of the Security Forces watching on the Kyrenia Road was lacking, or that there was a way out to the place of ambush that offered concealment from watchers on the main road. The dry weather road leading west from the village can be seen from the spot on the Kyrenia road where the convoy halted. It may be that the Turks went out to their positions before Baring arrived and that they were reinforced from Kanli. There is the mystery of the two motor-cyclists, but no evidence that they were seen actually to emerge from Geunyeli village. It is fruitless for me to conjecture on the material afforded.

46. There is, however, one thing that I desire to touch upon, which comes more into the realm of fact, and that is as to the cause of the fire burning about 4 acres of "bearded wheat". Such a crop when dry would, if set alight, burst quickly into flames along its length and can be very easily ignited. In the opinion of Assistant Divisional Fire Officer Ball, who has had 22 years of experience, the fire started from the side of the field away from Geunyeli and was carried through with great rapidity by the prevailing wind from the west. Accident is unlikely. For myself, I would also think it unlikely that the party of unarmed Greeks would risk setting fire to the crop with Geunyeli a mile away on one flank and Kanli a lesser distance away on the other, and mobile military units also only a matter of a mile away, who would be bound to see the blaze and take action. There is the evidence of Ismael Ali Hji Hassan of Kanli who said that he was passing the spot at the material time cycling towards Geunyeli. He said that he saw some of the Greeks crouching down by the crop and then it went on fire. He concluded they had set fire to it. But he saw nothing of the attack upon the Greeks. He said he cycled on to give the alarm in Geunyeli about the fire and did not learn that any Greeks had been killed or wounded until the sun was about to set. He was an unimpressive witness and I do not believe his testimony. It will be recollected that about 4 to 5 minutes elapsed after the Greeks dropped out of sight over the crest of the slope, when the fire was observed from the Kyrenia Road. (Baring put it at three seconds but, having regard to the other evidence as to this by military witnesses, I believe him to be mistaken). The field is right on top of the slope, and if it was set on fire when the Greek party got there one would expect only the passage of a few seconds. The time lapse in fact occurring suggests to me that they had, as some survivors have testified, got beyond it and down the slightly descending slope on the other side before the fire started. Persons who stage a murderous ambush such as that which took place are not likely to stop short of firing a crop if it should serve a purpose. The setting on fire of this crop could serve two purposes—(a) to cut off a line of retreat by the intended victims; and (b) to serve as some excuse by suggesting a provocative act by the persons attacked. I think the survivor witnesses were speaking the truth about this, and that the fact is that just after the encirclement and attack, and when some Greeks ran back to escape, the field went up in flames more or less in their rear and along the route they had taken in walking forward from Geunyeli. I think it is the reasonable inference that the attacking Turks were responsible for the fire.

47. At 6.30 p.m. on the 12th June the following communiqué on the incidents at Geunyeli was issued from the Office of the Chief of Staff to the Director of Operations, to the press and to the Cyprus Broadcasting Service, and was broadcast in the radio news that same evening at 7.0 o'clock. The communiqué read as follows:

"At 17.10 hours today (12th June) some 300 Greek Cypriots who were marching on the Turkish village of Geunyeli from the Skylloura area were directed northwards from the village by Security Forces patrol in the area.

"A clash occurred between elements of the Greeks who were marching on the village, and the Turks in the area of HADJI BATAKJI CHIFTLIK. Some shots were fired and two Greeks were reported to have been killed and three are known to have been wounded.

"A Security Forces helicopter has been sent to the area to evacuate the two of the more seriously wounded."

This communiqué has since been officially acknowledged as inaccurate. The reason it was inaccurate appears to be that it was compiled, in too great haste, from a number of unconfirmed reports received from army and police units operating in the area of Geunyeli shortly after the incidents had taken place.

48. The first report of 200-300 people in the area of Geunyeli came from the pilot of a light aircraft, and this is likely to have become confused with the reports sent previously to the Operations room at the Nicosia Central Police Station to the effect that a group of prisoners were being brought in from Skylloura, to produce the garbled version of the true facts which came into the hands of Sergeant Deighton in the Operations room at the Nicosia Central Police Station at 5.27 p.m. This message, according to Deighton, was: "300 Greeks marched from Skylloura towards Geunyeli. They were diverted by the Royal Horse Guards northwards. Some shots fired, believed by Turks. One Greek dead, two wounded. Fire at farm west of Geunyeli, put out by Fire Brigade, Force Headquarters informed". In his evidence Deighton stated that he received this message from the Military Duty Officer in the Operations room, who was "either Mr. Wilson, or one of the other officers who was there; but which one I can't say for certain". It has not been possible to establish how and from whom Deighton received the false report, but what is known is that Deighton passed it on to the Operations room at Police Force Headquarters at Paphos Gate, from where it was in turn passed to the Office of the Chief of Staff to the Director of Operations. Here, at about 5.30 p.m., the message came into the hands of Major Gordon-Wilson, one of the officers responsible for compiling statements for issue to the press and to the Cyprus Broadcasting Service through Army Public Relations. In his evidence Gordon-Wilson stated that he was under great pressure from Army Public Relations in the Chief of Staff's Office to release information about the incidents at Geunyeli, but he was unwilling to do so, as he could not be certain of the accuracy of the report he had received. At 6.30 p.m., however, Gordon-Wilson received instructions that a statement should be issued based upon such information as was available, in order to quieten the wild rumours which had been circulating about the incidents at Geunyeli since they had occurred one and a half hours previously. The first, and inaccurate, communiqué was therefore drafted by Gordon-Wilson from the information at his disposal, and issued. Another, and almost equally inaccurate, communiqué was issued in time to be included in the Cyprus Broadcasting Service's news at 11.0 o'clock that night, and it was not until after midnight that the first true reports of the incidents at Geunyeli began to come to the various Operations rooms, and the first inaccurate com-

muniqués could be corrected. I am satisfied and find that these first communiqués were issued in good faith in the sincere belief that they afforded a substantially accurate account and in order to meet the clamour for news and allay the effect of irresponsible and dangerous rumours.

49. Such, as best I can find them, are the salient facts concerning the incidents which occurred at and near the village of Geunyeli on Thursday, 12th June, 1958. I trust it will be found that I have ranged sufficiently far over the events of that day.

I have the honour to be,
Sir,
Your Excellency's obedient servant,
PAGET J. BOURKE

2nd July, 1958.

Appendix

LIST OF WITNESSES IN THE ORDER IN WHICH THEY APPEARED BEFORE THE COMMISSION

Friday 20th June.
1. SHARPE, P. J.   Assistant Superintendent of Police.
2. LEGGE-BOURKE, W. N. H.   Cornet, Royal Horse Guards.
3. GILL, A. J.   Police Sergeant.

Saturday 21st June.
4. CHARALAMBOUS, C.   Police Sergeant.
5. TAYLOR, T. R.   Corporal of Horse, Royal Horse Guards.
6. BARING, C. P.   Cornet, Royal Horse Guards.

Monday 23rd June.
7. CORKRAN, R. S.   Second Lieutenant, Grenadier Guards.
8. STRAKER, M. L.   Lance-Corporal, Royal Horse Guards.
9. WOOD, W. J. N.   Lieutenant, Royal Military Police.
10. ROSE, G. T.   Corporal, Royal Military Police.
11. TRUSLER, M. G.   Assistant Superintendent of Police.

Tuesday 24th June.
12. DEIGHTON, K. R.   Police Sergeant.
13. WILSON, R. G.   Captain, Suffolk Regiment.
14. MEDLEN, A. C. N.   Major, Royal Horse Guards.
15. REDGRAVE, R. M. F.   Major, Royal Horse Guards.
16. RICE, A. P.   Assistant Chief Constable.

Wednesday 25th June.
17. FORSYTHE, G.   Assistant Superintendent of Police.
18. WARD, H.   Detective Superintendent.
19. YIANGOULLIS, O.   Schoolmaster.
20. ASSIM, E. M.   Police Inspector.
21. SMITH, N. F.   Squadron-Leader, Royal Air Force.
22. BALL, E.   Assistant Divisional Officer, Fire Service.
23. HUSSEIN, H.   Auxiliary Policeman.
24. SANERKIN, N. G.   Acting Government Pathologist.

Thursday 26th June.
25. JOSEBURY, J.   Senior Aircraftman, Royal Air Force.
26. HASSAN OMER MULLA ALI   Grocer.
27. ISMAEL ALI HAJI HASSAN   Stonemason.
28. SHEFTALIS, SAVVAS S.   Driver.
29. TSIKKOS, CHR. N.   Labourer.
30. CHARALAMBOS ANDREA   Gardener.
31. CHRISTOFOROS ANDREA   Apprentice mason.

Friday 27th June.

32.	AGATHOCLEOUS, CHR.	Labourer.
33.	GORDON-WILSON, N. F.	Major, Parachute Regiment.
34.	CUMMING, A. E.	Superintendent of Police.

Saturday 28th June.

35.	LADAS, G.	Advocate.
36.	SAVVA, A.	Driver (by Affidavit).
37.	BUSHBY, P. E.	Sergeant, Royal Artillery.
38.	EYRE, J. A. C. G.	Lieutenant, Royal Horse Guards.
39.	WARMAN, R. S.	Major, Royal Military Police.

APPENDIX 17

Cyprus: Statement of Policy, 1958*

CYPRUS

Aims of Policy

The policy of Her Majesty's Government in Cyprus has had four main purposes:

    (a) to serve the best interests of all the people of the Island;

    (b) to achieve a permanent settlement acceptable to the two communities in the Island and to the Greek and Turkish Governments;

    (c) to safeguard the British bases and installations in the Island, which are necessary to enable the United Kingdom to carry out her international obligations;

    (d) to strengthen peace and security, and co-operation between the United Kingdom and her Allies, in a vital area.

2. These are the aims which Her Majesty's Government have consistently pursued and which have guided their efforts in recent months to find common ground on which an agreed settlement might be reached. It is deeply regretted that all attempts in this direction have hitherto proved unsuccessful.

3. In view of the disagreement between the Greek and Turkish Governments and between the two communities in Cyprus, and of the disastrous consequences for all concerned if violence and conflict continue, an obligation rests with the United Kingdom Government, as the sovereign Power responsible for the administration of the Island and the well-being of its inhabitants, to give a firm and clear lead out of the present deadlock. They accordingly declare a new policy which represents an adventure in partnership—partnership between the communities in the Island and also between the Governments of the United Kingdom, Greece and Turkey.

4. The following is an outline of the partnership plan:

The Plan

I. Cyprus should enjoy the advantages of association not only with the United Kingdom, and therefore with the British Commonwealth, but also with Greece and Turkey.

II. Since the three Governments of the United Kingdom, Greece and Turkey all have an interest in Cyprus, Her Majesty's Government will welcome the co-operation and participation of the two other Governments in a joint effort to achieve the peace, progress and prosperity of the Island.

III. The Greek and Turkish Governments will each be invited to appoint a representative to co-operate with the Governor in carrying out this policy.

IV. The Island will have a system of representative Government with each community exercising autonomy in its own communal affairs.

---

* Cmnd. 455 (London: HMSO, 1958).

V. In order to satisfy the desire of the Greek and Turkish Cypriots to be recognised as Greeks and Turks, Her Majesty's Government will welcome an arrangement which gives them Greek or Turkish nationality, while enabling them to retain British nationality.

VI. To allow time for the new principle of partnership to be fully worked out and brought into operation under this plan in the necessary atmosphere of stability, the international status of the Island will remain unchanged for seven years.

VII. A system of representative government and communal autonomy will be worked out by consultation with representatives of the two communities and with the representatives of the Greek and Turkish Governments.

VIII. The essential provisions of the new constitution will be:
- (a) There will be a separate House of Representatives for each of the two communities, and these Houses will have final legislative authority in communal affairs.
- (b) Authority for internal administration, other than communal affairs and internal security, will be undertaken by a Council presided over by the Governor and including the representatives of the Greek and Turkish Governments and six elected Ministers drawn from the Houses of Representatives, four being Greek Cypriots and two Turkish Cypriots.
- (c) The Governor, acting after consultation with the representatives of the Greek and Turkish Governments, will have reserve powers to ensure that the interests of both communities are protected.
- (d) External affairs, defence and internal security will be matters specifically reserved to the Governor acting after consultation with the representatives of the Greek and Turkish Governments.
- (e) The representatives of the Greek and Turkish Governments will have the right to require any legislation which they consider to be discriminatory to be reserved for consideration by an impartial tribunal.

IX. If the full benefits of this policy are to be realised, it is evident that violence must cease. Subject to this, Her Majesty's Government intend to take progressive steps to relax the Emergency Regulations and eventually to end the State of Emergency. This process would include the return of those Cypriots at present excluded from the Island under the Emergency Regulations.

X. A policy based on those principles and proposals will give the people of the Island a specially favoured and protected status. Through representative institutions they will exercise authority in the management of the Island's internal affairs, and each community will control its own communal affairs. While the people of the Island enjoy these advantages, friendly relations and practical co-operation between the United Kingdom, Greece and Turkey will be maintained and strengthened as Cyprus becomes a symbol of co-operation instead of a cause of conflict between the three Allied Governments.

The Future

5. Her Majesty's Government trust that this imaginative plan will be welcomed by all concerned in the spirit in which it is put forward, and for their part they will bend all efforts to ensuring its success. Indeed, if the Greek and Turkish Governments were willing to extend this experiment in partnership

and co-operation, Her Majesty's Government would be prepared, at the appropriate time, to go further and, subject to the reservation to the United Kingdom of such bases and facilities as might be necessary for the discharge of her international obligations, to share the sovereignty of the Island with their Greek and Turkish Allies as their contribution to a lasting settlement.

APPENDIX 18

Conference on Cyprus: Documents Signed and Initialled at Lancaster House on February 19, 1959*

CONTENTS

Note: The documents were either signed in full or initialled, as shown in the texts.

---

* Cmnd. 679, Misc. No. 4 (London: HMSO, 1959).

I

MEMORANDUM SETTING OUT THE AGREED FOUNDATION FOR THE FINAL SETTLEMENT OF THE PROBLEM OF CYPRUS

The Prime Minister of the United Kingdom of Great Britain and Northern Ireland, the Prime Minister or the Kingdom of Greece and the Prime Minister of the Turkish Republic,

Taking note of the Declaration by the Representative of the Greek-Cypriot Community and the Representative of the Turkish-Cypriot Community that they accept the documents annexed to this Memorandum as the agreed foundation for the final settlement of the problem of Cyprus,

Hereby adopt, on behalf of their respective Governments, the documents annexed to this Memorandum and listed below, as the agreed foundation for the final settlement of the problem of Cyprus.

On behalf of the Government of the United Kingdom of Great Britain and Northern Ireland	On behalf of the Government of the Kingdom of Greece	On behalf of the Government of the Turkish Republic
HAROLD MACMILLAN	C. KARAMANLIS	A. MENDERES

London,
        February 19, 1959.

List of Documents Annexed

A.—Basic Structure of the Republic of Cyprus.

B.—Treaty of Guarantee between the Republic of Cyprus and Greece, the United Kingdom and Turkey.

C.—Treaty of Alliance between the Republic of Cyprus, Greece and Turkey.

D.—Declaration made by the Government of the United Kingdom on February 17, 1959.

E.—Additional Article to be inserted in the Treaty of Guarantee.

F.—Declaration made by the Greek and Turkish Foreign Ministers on February 17, 1959.

G.—Declaration made by the Representative of the Greek-Cypriot Community on February 19, 1959.

H.—Declaration made by the Representative of the Turkish-Cypriot Community on February 19, 1959.

I.—Agreed Measures to prepare for the new arrangements in Cyprus.

II
ENGLISH TRANSLATION OF THE DOCUMENTS AGREED IN THE FRENCH TEXTS AND INITIALLED BY THE GREEK AND TURKISH PRIME MINISTERS AT ZURICH ON FEBRUARY 11, 1959

(a)
Basic Structure of the Republic of Cyprus

1. The State of Cyprus shall be a Republic with a presidential régime, the President being Greek and the Vice-President Turkish elected by universal suffrage by the Greek and Turkish communities of the Island respectively.

2. The official languages of the Republic of Cyprus shall be Greek and Turkish. Legislative and administrative instruments and documents shall be drawn up and promulgated in the two official languages.

3. The Republic of Cyprus shall have its own flag of neutral design and colour, chosen jointly by the President and the Vice-President of the Republic.

Authorities and communities shall have the right to fly the Greek and Turkish flags on holidays at the same time as the flag of Cyprus.

The Greek and Turkish communities shall have the right to celebrate Greek and Turkish national holidays.

4 The President and the Vice-President shall be elected for a period of five years.

In the event of absence, impediment or vacancy of their posts, the President and the Vice-President shall be replaced by the President and the Vice-President of the House of Representatives respectively.

In the event of a vacancy in either post, the election of new incumbents shall take place within a period of not more than 45 days.

The President and the Vice-President shall be invested by the House of Representatives, before which they shall take an oath of loyalty and respect for the Constitution. For this purpose, the House of Representatives shall meet within 24 hours after its constitution.

5. Executive authority shall be vested in the President and the Vice-President. For this purpose they shall have a Council of Ministers composed of seven Greek Ministers and three Turkish Ministers. The Ministers shall be designated respectively by the President and the Vice-President who shall appoint them by an instrument signed by them both.

The Ministers may be chosen from outside the House of Representatives.

Decisions of the Council of Ministers shall be taken by an absolute majority.

Decisions so taken shall be promulgated immediately by the President and the Vice-President by publication in the official gazette.

However, the President and the Vice-President shall have the right of final veto and the right to return the decisions of the Council of Ministers under the same conditions as those laid down for laws and decisions of the House of Representatives.

6. Legislative authority shall be vested in a House of Representatives elected for a period of five years by universal suffrage of each community separately in the proportion of 70 per cent. for the Greek community and 30 per

cent. for the Turkish community, this proportion being fixed independently of statistical data. (*N.B.*—The number of Representatives shall be fixed by mutual agreement between the communities.)

The House of Representatives shall exercise authority in all matters other than those expressly reserved to the Communal Chambers. In the event of a conflict of authority, such conflict shall be decided by the Supreme Constitutional Court which shall be composed of one Greek, one Turk and one neutral, appointed jointly by the President and the Vice-President. The neutral judge shall be president of the Court.

7. Laws and decisions of the House of Representatives shall be adopted by a simple majority of the members present. They shall be promulgated within 15 days if neither the President nor the Vice-President returns them for reconsideration as provided in Point 9 below.

The Constitutional Law, with the exception of its basic articles, may be modified by a majority comprising two-thirds of the Greek members and two-thirds of the Turkish members of the House of Representatives.

Any modification of the electoral law and the adoption of any law relating to the municipalities and of any law imposing duties or taxes shall require a simple majority of the Greek and Turkish members of the House of Representatives taking part in the vote and considered separately.

On the adoption of the budget, the President and the Vice-President may exercise their right to return it to the House of Representatives, if in their judgment any question of discrimination arises. If the House maintains its decisions, the President and the Vice-President shall have the right of appeal to the Supreme Constitutional Court.

8. The President and the Vice-President, separately and conjointly, shall have the right of final veto on any law or decision concerning foreign affairs, except the participation of the Republic of Cyprus in international organisations and pacts of alliance in which Greece and Turkey both participate, or concerning defence and security as defined in Annex I.

9. The President and the Vice-President of the Republic shall have, separately and conjointly, the right to return all laws and decisions, which may be returned to the House of Representatives within a period of not more than 15 days for reconsideration.

The House of Representatives shall pronounce within 15 days on any matter so returned. If the House of Representatives maintains its decisions, the President and the Vice-President shall promulgate the law or decision in question within the time-limits fixed for the promulgation of laws and decisions.

Laws and decisions, which are considered by the President or the Vice-President to discriminate against either of the two communities, shall be submitted to the Supreme Constitutional Court which may annul or confirm the law or decision, or return it to the House of Representatives for reconsideration, in whole or in part. The law or decision shall not become effective until the Supreme Constitutional Court or, where it has been returned, the House of Representatives has taken a decision on it.

10. Each community shall have its Communal Chamber composed of a number of representatives which it shall itself determine.

The Communal Chambers shall have the right to impose taxes and levies on members of their community to provide for their needs and for the needs of bodies and institutions under their supervision.

The Communal Chambers shall exercise authority in all religious, educational, cultural and teaching questions and questions of personal status. They shall exercise authority in questions where the interests and institutions are of a purely communal nature, such as sporting and charitable foundations, bodies and associations, producers' and consumers' co-operatives and credit establishments, created for the purpose of promoting the welfare of one of the communities. (*N.B.*—It is understood that the provisions of the present paragraph cannot be interpreted in such a way as to prevent the creation of mixed and communal institutions where the inhabitants desire them.)

These producers' and consumers' co-operatives and credit establishments, which shall be administered under the laws of the Republic, shall be subject to the supervision of the Communal Chambers. The Communal Chambers shall also exercise authority in matters initiated by municipalities which are composed of one community only. These municipalities, to which the laws of the Republic shall apply, shall be supervised in their functions by the Communal Chambers.

Where the central administration is obliged to take over the supervision of the institutions, establishments, or municipalities mentioned in the two preceding paragraphs by virtue of legislation in force, this supervision shall be exercised by officials belonging to the same community as the institution, establishment or municipality in question.

11. The Civil Service shall be composed as to 70 per cent. of Greeks and as to 30 per cent. of Turks.

It is understood that this quantitative division will be applied as far as practicable in all grades of the Civil Service.

In regions or localities where one of the two communities is in a majority approaching 100 per cent., the organs of the local administration responsible to the central administration shall be composed solely of officials belonging to that community.

12. The deputies of the Attorney-General of the Republic, the Inspector-General, the Treasurer and the Governor of the Issuing Bank may not belong to the same community as their principals. The holders of these posts shall be appointed by the President and the Vice-President of the Republic acting in agreement.

13. The heads and deputy heads of the Armed Forces, the Gendarmerie and the Police shall be appointed by the President and the Vice-President of the Republic acting in agreement. One of these heads shall be Turkish and where the head belongs to one of the communities, the deputy head shall belong to the other.

14. Compulsory military service may only be instituted with the agreement of the President and the Vice-President of the Republic of Cyprus.

Cyprus shall have an army of 2,000 men, of whom 60 per cent. shall be Greek and 40 per cent. Turkish.

The security forces (gendarmerie and police) shall have a complement of 2,000 men, which may be reduced or increased with the agreement of both the

President and the Vice-President. The security forces shall be composed as to 70 per cent. of Greeks and as to 30 per cent. of Turks. However, for an initial period this percentage may be raised to a maximum of 40 per cent. of Turks (and consequently reduced to 60 per cent. of Greeks) in order not to discharge those Turks now serving in the police, apart from the auxiliary police.

15. Forces, which are stationed in parts of the territory of the Republic inhabited, in a proportion approaching 100 per cent., by members of a single community, shall belong to that community.

16. A High Court of Justice shall be established, which shall consist of two Greeks, one Turk and one neutral, nominated jointly by the President and the Vice-President of the Republic.

The President of the Court shall be the neutral judge, who shall have two votes.

This Court shall constitute the highest organ of the judicature (appointments, promotions of judges, &c.).

17. Civil disputes, where the plaintiff and the defendant belong to the same community, shall be tried by a tribunal composed of judges belonging to that community. If the plaintiff and defendant belong to different communities, the composition of the tribunal shall be mixed and shall be determined by the High Court of Justice.

Tribunals dealing with civil disputes relating to questions of personal status and to religious matters, which are reserved to the competence of the Communal Chambers under Point 10, shall be composed solely of judges belonging to the community concerned. The composition and status of these tribunals shall be determined according to the law drawn up by the Communal Chamber and they shall apply the law drawn up by the Communal Chamber.

In criminal cases, the tribunal shall consist of judges belonging to the same community as the accused. If the injured party belongs to another community, the composition of the tribunal shall be mixed and shall be determined by the High Court of Justice.

18. The President and the Vice-President of the Republic shall each have the right to exercise the prerogative of mercy to persons from their respective communities who are condemned to death. In cases where the plaintiffs and the convicted persons are members of different communities the prerogative of mercy shall be exercised by agreement between the President and the Vice-President. In the event of disagreement the vote for clemency shall prevail. When mercy is accorded the death penalty shall be commuted to life imprisonment.

19. In the event of agricultural reform, lands shall be redistributed only to persons who are members of the same community as the expropriated owners.

Expropriations by the State or the Municipalities shall only be carried out on payment of a just and equitable indemnity fixed, in disputed cases, by the tribunals. An appeal to the tribunals shall have the effect of suspending action.

Expropriated property shall only be used for the purpose for which the expropriation was made. Otherwise the property shall be restored to the owners.

20. Separate municipalities shall be created in the five largest towns of Cyprus by the Turkish inhabitants of these towns. However:

(a) In each of the towns a co-ordinating body shall be set up which shall supervise work which needs to be carried out jointly and shall concern itself with matters which require a degree of co-operation. These bodies shall each be composed of two members chosen by the Greek municipalities, two members chosen by the Turkish municipalities and a President chosen by agreement between the two municipalities.

(b) The President and the Vice-President shall examine within four years the question whether or not this separation of municipalities in the five largest towns shall continue.

With regard to other localities, special arrangements shall be made for the constitution of municipal bodies, following, as far as possible, the rule of proportional representation for the two communities.

21. A Treaty guaranteeing the independence, territorial integrity and constitution of the new State of Cyprus shall he concluded between the Republic of Cyprus, Greece, the United Kingdom and Turkey. A Treaty of military alliance shall also be concluded between the Republic of Cyprus, Greece and Turkey.

These two instruments shall have constitutional force. (This last paragraph shall be inserted in the Constitution as a basic article.)

22. It shall be recognised that the total or partial union of Cyprus with any other State, or a separatist independence for Cyprus (*i.e.*, the partition of Cyprus into two independent States), shall be excluded.

23. The Republic of Cyprus shall accord most-favoured-nation treatment to Great Britain, Greece and Turkey for all agreements whatever their nature.

This provision shall not apply to the Treaties between the Republic of Cyprus and the United Kingdom concerning the bases and military facilities accorded to the United Kingdom.

24. The Greek and Turkish Governments shall have the right to subsidise institutions for education, culture, athletics and charity belonging to their respective communities.

Equally, where either community considers that it has not the necessary number of schoolmasters, professors or priests for the working of its institutions, the Greek and Turkish Governments may provide them to the extent strictly necessary to meet their needs.

25. One of the following Ministries—the Ministry of Foreign Affairs, the Ministry of Defence or the Ministry of Finance—shall be entrusted to a Turk. If the President and the Vice-President agree they may replace this system by a system of rotation.

26. The new State which is to come into being with the signature of the Treaties shall be established as quickly as possible and within a period of not more than three months from the signature of the Treaties.

27. All the above Points shall be considered to be basic articles of the Constitution of Cyprus.

E. A.-T.		F. R. Z.
	S. L.	
†A. M.		F. K.

ANNEX I

A

The defence questions subject to veto under Point 8 of the Basic Structure are as follows:
    (a) Composition and size of the armed forces and credits for them.
    (b) Appointments and promotions.
    (c) Imports of warlike stores and of all kinds of explosives.
    (d) Granting of bases and other facilities to allied countries.

B

The security questions subject to veto are as follows:
    (a) Appointments and promotions.
    (b) Allocation and stationing of forces.
    (c) Emergency measures and martial law.
    (d) Police laws.
(It is provided that the right of veto shall cover all emergency measures or decisions, but not those which concern the normal functioning of the police and gendarmerie.)

(b)

Treaty of Guarantee

The Republic of Cyprus of the one part, and Greece, the United Kingdom and Turkey of the other part:

I. Considering that the recognition and maintenance of the independence, territorial integrity and security of the Republic of Cyprus, as established and regulated by the basic articles of its Constitution, are in their common interest;

II. Desiring to co-operate to ensure that the provisions of the aforesaid Constitution shall be respected;

HAVE AGREED AS FOLLOWS:

ARTICLE 1

The Republic of Cyprus undertakes to ensure the maintenance of its independence, territorial integrity and security, as well as respect for its Constitution.

It undertakes not to participate, in whole or in part, in any political or economic union with any State whatsoever. With this intent it prohibits all activity tending to promote directly or indirectly either union or partition of the Island.

ARTICLE 2

Greece, the United Kingdom and Turkey, taking note of the undertakings by the Republic of Cyprus embodied in Article 1, recognise and guarantee the independence, territorial integrity and security of the Republic of Cyprus, and also the provisions of the basic articles of its Constitution.

They likewise undertake to prohibit, as far as lies within their power, all activity having the object of promoting directly or indirectly either the union of the Republic of Cyprus with any other State, or the partition of the Island.

ARTICLE 3

In the event of any breach of the provisions of the present Treaty, Greece, the United Kingdom, and Turkey undertake to consult together, with a view to making representations, or taking the necessary steps to ensure observance of those provisions.

In so far as common or concerted action may prove impossible, each of the three guaranteeing powers reserves the right to take action with the sole aim of re-establishing the state of affairs established by the present Treaty.

ARTICLE 4

The present Treaty shall enter into force on signature.

The High Contracting Parties undertake to register the present Treaty at the earliest possible date with the Secretariat of the United Nations, in accordance with the provisions of Article 102 of the Charter.[1]

E. A.-T.   F. R. Z.

S. L.

†A. M.   F. K.

(c)

Treaty of Alliance between the Republic of Cyprus, Greece and Turkey

1. The Republic of Cyprus, Greece and Turkey shall co-operate for their common defence and undertake by this Treaty to consult together on the problems raised by this defence.

2. The High Contracting Parties undertake to resist any attack or aggression, direct or indirect, directed against the independence and territorial integrity of the Republic of Cyprus.

3. In the spirit of this alliance and in order to fulfil the above purpose a tripartite Headquarters shall be established on the territory of the Republic of Cyprus.

4. Greece shall take part in the Headquarters mentioned in the preceding article with a contingent of 950 officers, non-commissioned officers and

---

[1] "Treaty Series No. 67 (1946)," Cmd. 7015, page 21.

soldiers and Turkey with a contingent of 650 officers, non-commissioned officers and soldiers. The President and the Vice-President of the Republic of Cyprus, acting in agreement, may ask the Greek and Turkish Governments to increase or reduce the Greek and Turkish contingents.

5. The Greek and Turkish officers mentioned above shall be responsible for the training of the Army of the Republic of Cyprus.

6. The command of the tripartite Headquarters shall be assumed in rotation and for a period of one year each by a Cypriot, Greek and Turkish General Officer, who shall be nominated by the Governments of Greece and Turkey and by the President and the Vice-President of the Republic of Cyprus.

E. A.-T.   F. R. Z.

S. L.

†A. M.   F. K.

III
DECLARATION BY THE GOVERNMENT OF THE UNITED KINGDOM

The Government of the United Kingdom of Great Britain and Northern Ireland, having examined the documents concerning the establishment of the Republic of Cyprus, comprising the Basic Structure for the Republic of Cyprus, the Treaty of Guarantee and the Treaty of Alliance, drawn up and approved by the Heads of the Governments of Greece and Turkey in Zurich on February 11, 1959, and taking into account the consultations in London, from February 11 to 16, 1959, between the Foreign Ministers of Greece, Turkey and the United Kingdom
Declare:

A. That, subject to the acceptance of their requirements as set out in Section B below, they accept the documents approved by the Heads of the Governments of Greece and Turkey as the agreed foundation for the final settlement of the problem of Cyprus.

B. That, with the exception of two areas at

(a) Akrotiri–Episkopi–Paramali, and

(b) Dhekelia–Pergamos–Ayios Nikolaos–Xylophagou, which will be retained under full British sovereignty, they are willing to transfer sovereignty over the Island of Cyprus to the Republic of Cyprus subject to the following conditions:

(1) that such rights are secured to the United Kingdom Government as are necessary to enable the two areas as aforesaid to be used effectively as military bases, including among others those rights indicated in the Annex attached, and that satisfactory guarantees are given by Greece, Turkey and the Republic of Cyprus for the integrity of the areas retained under British sovereignty and the use and enjoyment by the United Kingdom of the rights referred to above;

(2) that provision shall be made by agreement for:

(i)　　the protection of the fundamental human rights of the various communities in Cyprus;

(ii)　　the protection of the interests of the members of the public services in Cyprus;

(iii)　　determining the nationality of persons affected by the settlement;

(iv)　　the assumption by the Republic of Cyprus of the appropriate obligations of the present Government of Cyprus, including the settlement of claims.

C. That the Government of the United Kingdom welcome the draft Treaty of Alliance between the Republic of Cyprus, the Kingdom of Greece and the Republic of Turkey and will co-operate with the Parties thereto in the common defence of Cyprus.

D. That the Constitution of the Republic of Cyprus shall come into force and the formal signature of the necessary instruments by the parties concerned shall take place at the earliest practicable date and on that date sovereignty will be transferred to the Republic of Cyprus.

SELWYN LLOYD.
ALAN LENNOX-BOYD.

E. A.-T.　　　　　　　　　　　　　　　　　　F. R. Z.

†A. M.　　　　　　　　　　　　　　　　　　　F. K.

ANNEX

The following rights will be necessary in connexion with the areas to be retained under British sovereignty:

(a) to continue to use, without restriction or interference, the existing small sites containing military and other installations and to exercise complete control within these sites, including the right to guard and defend them and to exclude from them all persons not authorised by the United Kingdom Government;

(b) to use roads, ports and other facilities freely for the movement of personnel and stores of all kinds to and from and between the above-mentioned areas and sites;

(c) to continue to have the use of specified port facilities at Famagusta;

(d) to use public services (such as water, telephone, telegraph, electric power, &c.);

(e) to use from time to time certain localities, which would be specified, for troop training;

(f) to use the airfield at Nicosia, together with any necessary buildings and facilities on or connected with the airfield to whatever extent is considered necessary by the British authorities for the operation of British military aircraft in peace and war, including the exercise of any necessary operational control of air traffic;

(g) to overfly the territory of the Republic of Cyprus without restriction;

(h) to exercise jurisdiction over British forces to an extent comparable with that provided in Article VII of the Agreement regarding the Status of Forces of Parties to the North Atlantic Treaty,[2] in respect of certain offences committed within the territory of the Republic of Cyprus;

(i) to employ freely in the areas and sites labour from other parts of Cyprus;

(j) to obtain, after consultation with the Government of the Republic of Cyprus, the use of such additional small sites and such additional rights as the United Kingdom may, from time to time, consider technically necessary for the efficient use of its base areas and installations in Cyprus.

IV
ADDITIONAL ARTICLE TO BE INSERTED IN THE TREATY OF GUARANTEE

The Kingdom of Greece, the Republic of Turkey and the Republic of Cyprus undertake to respect the integrity of the areas to be retained under the sovereignty of the United Kingdom upon the establishment of the Republic of Cyprus, and guarantee the use and enjoyment by the United Kingdom of the rights to be secured to the United Kingdom by the Republic of Cyprus in accordance with the declaration by the Government of the United Kingdom.

S. L.   E. A.-T.   F. R. Z.
         †A. M.   F. K.

V
DECLARATION MADE BY THE GREEK AND TURKISH FOREIGN MINISTERS ON FEBRUARY 17, 1959

The Foreign Ministers of Greece and Turkey, having considered the declaration made by the Government of the United Kingdom on February 17, 1959, accept that declaration, together with the document approved by the Heads of the Greek and Turkish Governments in Zurich on February 11, 1959, as providing the agreed foundation for the final settlement of the problem of Cyprus.

E. AVEROFF-TOSSIZZA   FATIN R. ZORLU
                          S. L.
         †A. M.   F. K.

---

[2] "Treaty Series No. 3 (1955)," Cmd. 9363.

VI
DECLARATION MADE BY THE REPRESENTATIVE OF THE GREEK-CYPRIOT COMMUNITY ON FEBRUARY 19, 1959

Archbishop Makarios, representing the Greek Cypriot Community, having examined the documents concerning the establishment of the Republic of Cyprus drawn up and approved by the Heads of the Governments of Greece and Turkey in Zurich on February 11, 1959, and the declarations made by the Government of the United Kingdom, and by the Foreign Ministers of Greece and Turkey on February 17, 1959, declares that he accepts the documents and declarations as the agreed foundation for the final settlement of the problem of Cyprus.

†ARCHBISHOP MAKARIOS.

S. L.   E. A.-T.   F. R. Z.

F. K.

VII
DECLARATION MADE BY THE REPRESENTATIVE OF THE TURKISH-CYPRIOT COMMUNITY ON FEBRUARY 19, 1959

Dr. Kutchuk, representing the Turkish Cypriot Community, having examined the documents concerning the establishment of the Republic of Cyprus drawn up and approved by the Heads of the Governments of Greece and Turkey in Zurich on February 11, 1959, and the declarations made by the Government of the United Kingdom, and by the Foreign Ministers of Greece and Turkey on February 17, 1959, declares that he accepts the documents and declarations as the agreed foundation for the final settlement of the problem of Cyprus.

F. KUTCHUK.

S. L.   E. A.-T.   F. R. Z.

†A. M.

VIII
AGREED MEASURES TO PREPARE FOR THE NEW ARRANGEMENTS IN CYPRUS

1. All parties to the Conference firmly endorse the aim of bringing the constitution (including the elections of President, Vice-President, and the three Assemblies) and the Treaties into full effect as soon as practicable and in any case not later than twelve months from to-day's date (the 19th of February, 1959). Measures leading to the transfer of sovereignty in Cyprus will begin at once.

2. The first of these measures will be the immediate establishment of:

(a) a Joint Commission in Cyprus with the duty of completing a draft constitution for the independent Republic of Cyprus, incorporating the basic structure agreed at the Zurich Conference. This Commission shall be composed of one representative each of the Greek-Cypriot and the Turkish-Cypriot community and one representative nominated by the Government of Greece and one representative nominated by the Government of Turkey, together with a legal adviser nominated by the Foreign Ministers of Greece and Turkey, and shall in its work have regard to and shall scrupulously observe the points contained in the documents of the Zurich Conference and shall fulfil its task in accordance with the principles there laid down;

(b) a Transitional Committee in Cyprus, with responsibility for drawing up plans for adapting and reorganising the Governmental machinery in Cyprus in preparation for the transfer of authority to the independent Republic of Cyprus. This Committee shall be composed of the Governor of Cyprus, the leading representative of the Greek community and the leading representative of the Turkish community and other Greek and Turkish Cypriots nominated by the Governor after consultation with the two leading representatives in such a way as not to conflict with paragraph 5 of the Basic Structure;

(c) a Joint Committee in London composed of a representative of each of the Governments of Greece, Turkey and the United Kingdom, and one representative each of the Greek Cypriot and Turkish Cypriot communities, with the duty of preparing the final treaties giving effect to the conclusions of the London Conference. This Committee will prepare drafts for submission to Governments covering *inter alia* matters arising from the retention of areas in Cyprus under British sovereignty, the provision to the United Kingdom Government of certain ancillary rights and facilities in the independent Republic of Cyprus, questions of nationality, the treatment of the liabilities of the present Government of Cyprus, and the financial and economic problems arising from the creation of an independent Republic of Cyprus.

3. The Governor will, after consultation with the two leading representatives, invite individual members of the Transitional Committee to assume special responsibilities for particular departments and functions of Government. This process will be started as soon as possible and will be progressively extended.

4. The headquarters mentioned in Article 4 of the Treaty of Alliance between the Republic of Cyprus, the Kingdom of Greece and the Republic of Turkey will be established three months after the completion of the work of the Commission referred to in paragraph 2(a) above and will be composed of a restricted number of officers who will immediately undertake the training of the armed forces of the Republic of Cyprus. The Greek and Turkish contingents will enter the territory of the Republic of Cyprus on the date when the sovereignty will be transferred to the Republic.

S. L.   E. A.-T.   F. R. Z.

APPENDIX 19

Agreements of London for the Final Settlement of the Cyprus Question, February 19, 1959*

MEMORANDUM SETTING OUT THE AGREED FOUNDATION FOR THE FINAL SETTLEMENT OF THE PROBLEM OF CYPRUS

The Prime Minister of the United Kingdom of Great Britain and Northern Ireland, the Prime Minister of the Kingdom of Greece and the Prime Minister of the Turkish Republic,

Taking note of the Declaration by the Representative of the Greek-Cypriot Community and the Representative of the Turkish-Cypriot Community that they accept the documents annexed to this Memorandum as the agreed foundation for the final settlement of the problem of Cyprus,

Hereby accept, on behalf of their respective Government, the documents annexed to this Memorandum and listed below, as the agreed foundation for the final settlement of the problem of Cyprus.

On behalf of the Government of the United Kingdom of Great Britain and Northern Ireland	On behalf of the Government of the Kingdom of Greece	On behalf of the Government of the Turkish Republic
Harold Macmillan	C. Karamanlis	A. Menderes

London
February 19, 1959.

---

* Ministry of the Prime Minister's Office, Direction General of Press, Foreign Press Division (Athens, 1959).

LIST OF DOCUMENTS ANNEXED

A.   Basic Structure of the Republic of Cyprus.

B.   Treaty of Guarantee between the Republic of Cyprus and Greece, the United Kingdom and Turkey.

C.   Treaty of Alliance between the Republic of Cyprus, Greece and Turkey.

D.   Declaration made by the Government of the United Kingdom on February 17, 1959.

E.   Additional Article to be inserted in the Treaty of Guarantee.

F.   Declaration made by the Greek and Turkish Foreign Ministers on February 17, 1959.

G.   Declaration made by the Representative of the Greek-Cypriot Community on February 19, 1959.

H.   Declaration made by the Representative of the Turkish-Cypriot Community on February 19, 1959.

I.   Agreed Measures to prepare for the new arrangements in Cyprus.

STRUCTURE DE BASE DE LA REPUBLIQUE DE CHYPRE

1.   L'état de Chypre est une république au régime présidentiel dont le Président est un grec et le Vice-Président un turc, respectivement élus par les communautés grecque et turque de l'île, au suffrage universel.

2.   Les langues officielles de la République de Chypre seront le grec et le turc. Les actes et documents législatifs et administratifs doivent être rédigés et promulgués dans les deux langues officielles.

3.   La République de Chypre aura son propre drapeau de couleur et de dessin neutres choisis en commun par le Président et le Vice-Président de la République.

Les autorités et les communautés auront la faculté d'arborer aux jours feriés les drapeaux grec et turc en même temps que le drapeau de Chypre.

Les communautés grecque ét turque auront le droit de célébrer les fêtes nationales grecques et turques.

4.   Le Président et le Vice-Président seront élus pour une période de 5 ans.

En cas d'absence, d'empêchement ou de vacance de leurs postes, le Président et le Vice-Président seront respectivement remplacés par le Président et le Vice-Président de la Chambre des Représentants.

En cas de vacance des postes respectifs on procèdera à l'élection de nouveaux titulaires dans un délai maximum de quarante-cinq jours.

L'investiture sera accordée au Président et au Vice-Président par la Chambre des Représentants, devant laquelle ils prèteront serment de fidélité et respect à la Constitution. Pour ce faire la Chambre des Représentants se réunira dans les vingt-quatre heures après sa constitution.

5.   Le pouvoir exécutif sera assuré par le Président et le Vice-Président. Pour ce faire ils auront un conseil de ministres composés de 7 Ministres grecs et 3 Ministres turcs. Les Ministres seront désignés respectivement par le Président et le Vice-Président qui les nommeront par un actc signé en commun.

Les Ministres pourront être choisis en dehors de la Chambre des Représentants.

Les décisions du Conseil des Ministres seront prises à la majorité absolue.

Les décisions ainsi prises devront être promulgués immédiatement par le Président et le Vice-President, par publication au journal officiel.

Toutefois, le Président et le Vice-Président auront le droit de veto définitif et le droit de renvoi sur les décisions du Conseil des Ministres, dans les mêmes conditions que celles établies pour les lois et décisions de la Chambre des Répresentants.

6.   Le pouvoir législatif sera exercé par une Chambre de Représentants élus pour une période de cinq ans au suffrage universel (par chaque communauté séparément) à proportion de 70% pour la communauté grecque et 30% pour la communauté turque, proportion fixée indépendamment des données statistiques.

(N.B. Le nombre des Représentants sera fixé d'un commun accord par les communautés).

La Chambre des Représentants sera compétente pour toutes les autres questions que celles réservées expressément aux Chambres Communales. En cas de conflit de compétence, ce conflit sera tranché par la Court Suprême Constitutionnelle, qui sera composée d'un Grec, d'un Turc et d'un neutre, nommés conjointement par le Président et le Vice-Président. La Cour sera presidée par le juge neutre.

7.   Les lois et décisions de la Chambre des Représentants seront adoptées à la majorité simple des membres présents. Elles seront promulguées dans un délai de quinze jours si le Président ou le Vice-Président ne les renvoient pas pour un nouvel examen ainsi que prévu au point 9.

La loi constitutionnelle, en dehors de ces articles fondamentaux, pourra ètre modifiée par une majorité composée des deux tiers des membres grecs et des deux tiers des membres turcs de la Chambre des Représentants.

Toute modification de la loi électorale, ainsi que l'adoption de toute loi relative aux municipalités et toute loi instituant des impôts ou taxes, réquiert une majorité simple des membres grecs et turcs de la Chambre des Représentants, participant au vote et considérés separément.

En ce qui concerne l'adoption du budget, le Président et le Vice-Président pourront faire usage de leur droit de renvoi à la Chambre des Représentants au cas où ils jugeraient qu'il y a discrimination. Dans le cas où la Chambre persisterait dans ses décisions, le Président et le Vice-Président auront le droit de recours à la Cour Suprême Constitutionnelle.

8.   Le Président et le Vice-Président auront séparément et conjointement le droit de veto définitif sur toute loi ou décision se référant aux affaires étrangères sauf la participation de la République de Chypre à des organisations internationales et pactes d'alliance dont la Grèce et la Turquie font toutes deux partie, à la défense et à la sécurité telles que définies dans l'annexe I.

9.   Le Président et le Vice-Président de la Republique auront séparément et conjointement le droit de renvoi pour toutes les lois et décisions qui pourront être renvoyées à la Chambre des Représentants dans un délai maximum de quinze jours, pour un nouvel examen.

La Chambre des Représentants devra se prononcer dans un délai de quinze jours sur l'objet du renvoi. Dans le cas où la Chambre des Représentants persisterait dans ses décisions, le Président et le Vice-Président devront promulguer la loi ou décision en question dans les délais fixés pour la promulgation des lois et décisions.

Les lois et décisions qui seront considérées par le Président ou le Vice-Président comme discriminatoires pour l'une des deux communautés, seront soumises à la Cour Suprême Constitutionnelle qui pourra casser, ratifier ou renvoyer cette loi ou décision à la Chambre des Représentants pour un nouvel examen en tout ou en partie. Cette loi ou décision n'aura pas force exécutoire jusqu'à ce que la Cour Suprême Constitutionnelle ou la Chambre des Représentants, en cas de renvoi, en aient décidé.

10.   Chaque communauté aura sa Chambre Communale composée d'un nombre de représentants qui sera fixé par elle-même.

Les Chambres Communales auront le droit d'imposer des impositions et des droite personnels aux membres de leur communauté pour subvenir à leurs besoins ainsi qu'aux besoins des oeuvres et institutions dont le controle leur incombe.

Les Chambres Communales seront compétentes pour toutes les questions religieuses, d'éducation, de culture et d'enseignement, ainsi que pour le statut personnel. Elles seront également compétentes pour les questions où les intérêts et institutions sont de nature purement communale, telles que les fondations, oeuvres et associations de bien-faisance et sportives, coopératives, créées dans le but de promouvoir le bien-être de l'une des communautés.
(N.B. Il est bien entendu que les dispositions contenues dans le para. présent ne pourront ètre interprétées de maniere a empêcher la création d'institutions mixtes et communes là où les habitants le désireraient).

Ces coopératives de production et de consommation ou établissements de crédit, qui seront régiés par les lois de la République, révéleront en ce qui concerne leur contrôle des Chambres Communales.

Les Chambres Communales seront aussi compétentes pour promouvoir les buts poursuivis par les municipalités à compositions uniquement d'une seule communauté. Ces municipalités, qui réléveront des lois de la République, seront supervisées quant à leur fonctionnement par les Chambres Communales.

Au cas où l'administration centrale devra de s on côté procéder à un contrôle des institutions, etablissements ou municipalités, mentionnés dans les deux paragraphes précédents, en vertu de la législation en vigueur, ce contrôle devra etre éfectue par des fonctionnaires appartenant à la même communauté que l'institution, établissement ou municipalité en question.

11.   L'administration sera composée d'un pourcentage de 70% de grecs et de 30% de turcs.

Il est bien entendu que cette répartition quantitative sera appliquée autant que cela sera pratiquement possible dans tous les grades de la hierarchie administrative.

Dans les régions où localités à majorité de l'une des deux comnunautés se rapprochant du 100%, les organes des administrations locales dépendant de l'administration centrale seront composés uniquement de fonctionnaires appurtenant à cette communauté.

12.   Les adjoints du Procureur de la République, de l'Inspecteur Général, du Trésorier et du Gouverneur de la Banque d'Emission ne pourront pas appartenir à la même communauté que leurs chefs. Les titulaires de ces postes seront nommés d'un commun accord par le Président et le Vice-Président de la République.

13.   Les Chefs et les Sous-Chefs de Forces Armées, des Forces de Gendarmerie et de la Police seront nommés d'un commun accord par le Président et le Vice-Président de la République.

L'un de ces chefs sera turc et là où le chef appertiendra à l'une des communautés, le sous-chef devra appertenir à l'autre.

14.   Le service militaire obligatoire ne pourra ètre institué qu'après accord du Président et du Vice-Président de la République.

Chypre aura une armée de 2000 hommes dont les 60% seront Grecs et 40% Turcs.

Les forces de sécurité (gendarmerie et police) auront un contingent de 2000 hommes qui pourra être diminué ou augmenté d'un commun accord du Président et du Vice-Président. Les forces de sécurité seront composées de 70% de Grecs et de 30% de Turcs. Toutefois, pour une première période ce pourcentage pourrait être elevé à un maximum de 40% pour les Turcs (et par conséquent de se réduire à 60% pour les Grecs) dans le but de ne pas licenser les Turcs qui servent aujourd'hui dans le corps de police, sauf la police auxiliaire.

15. Les forces stationnées dans les régions du territoire de la République habitées dans une proportion s'approchant de 100% par les membres d'une seule communauté, devront appartenir à cette communauté.

16. Une Haute Cour de Justice sera instituée qui sera composée de deux Grecs, un Turc et un neutre, nommés conjointement par le Président et le Vice-Président de la République.

La Cour sera présidée par le juge neutre, qui disposera de deux voix.

Cette Cour constituera le conseil suprême de la magistrature (nominations, avancements des juges, etc.).

17. Les différends en matière civile, dens le cas où le demandeur et le défendeur appartiennent, à la même communauté, seront jugés par un tribunal composé de juges appartenant à cette communauté. Si le demandeur et le défendeur appartiennent à des communautés différentes, la composition du tribunal sera mixte et fixée par la Haute Cour de Justice.

Les tribunaux connaissant des differends en matière civile relatifs au statut personnel et aux affaires religieuses, reservés à la compétence des Chambres Communales en vertu du Point 10, seront composés uniquement de juges appartenant à la comnunauté respective. La composition et instances de ces tribunaux seront déterminées selon la loi établie par la Chambre Communale et ils appliqueront la loi établie par la Chambre Communale.

En matière pénale, le tribunal sera constitué par des juges appartenant à la même communauté que celle de l'accusé. Si la partie lésée appartient à une autre communauté, la composition du tribunal sera mixte et fixée par la Haute Cour de Justice.

18. Le President et le Vice-Président de la République ont séparément le droit de faire grâce aux condamnés à mort appartenant à leurs communautés respectives. Dans le cas où les délinquants et les lésés appartiennent à les comnunautés différentes, le droit de grâce, doit être exercé d'un commun accord par le Président et le Vice-Président. Dans le cas d'un désaccord la voix de la clémence l'emportera. En cas de grâce la peine capitale sera commutée à l'emprisonnement à vie.

19. En cas de réforme agraire, les terres ne pourront être distribueés qu'à des personnes appartenant à la même communauté que le propriétaire exproprié.

En ce qui concerns les expropriations effectuées par l'État, aussi bien que par les municipalités, celles-ci ne pourront être effectuées que contre une juste et équitable indemnité fixée, en cas de contestation, par les tribunaux. Le recours aux tribunaux aura effet suspensif.

Les biens expropriés ne pourront être utilisés que dans le but dans lequel l'expropriation a été faite. Dans le cas contraire, les biens seront restitués à leurs propriétaires.

20.   Des Municipalités séparées seront créées dans lea cinq plus grandes villes de Chypre, par les habitants turcs de ces villes. Toutefois

a) dans chacune de ces villes un organe de coordination sera créé qui pourvoira aux travaux devant s'effectuer en commun et s'occupera des matières qui nécessitent une certaine coopération. Ces organes seront composés de deux membres choisis par les municipalités grecques, deux membres choisis par les municipalités turques et en Président choisi d'un commun accord par les deux municipalités,

b) le Président et le Vice-Président examineront dans quatre ans si cette séparation des municipalités dans les cinq plus grandes villes devra ou non continuer.

Quant aux autres localités, des dispositions spéciales devront être prises pour la constitution des organes des municipalités, selon—autant que possible—la règle de la représentation proportionnelle de deux communautés.

21.   Un traité garantissant l'indépendance, l'intégrité territoriale et la constitution du nouvel état de Chypre sera conclu entre la République de Chypre, la Grèce, le Royaume-Uni et la Turquie. Un traité d'alliance militaire sera également conclu entre la République de Chypre, la Grèce et la Turquie.

Ces deux actes auront force constitutionnelle. (Ce dernier paragraphe sera inséré dans la constitution comme article fondamental).

22.   Il sera reconnu que l'union intégrale ou partielle de Chypre avec n'importe quel Etat ou l'indépendance séparatiste seront exclues.

23.   La République de Chypre accordera la clause de la nation la plus favorisée à la Grande-Bretagne, la Grèce et la Turquie pour tous les accords quelle que soit leur nature.

Cette disposition ne s'étend pas aux traités entre la République de Chypre et le Royaume-Uni concernant les bases et les facilités militaires accordées au Royaume-Uni.

24.   Les Gouvernements grec et turc auront le droit de subventionner les institutions d'éducation, de culture, d'athlétisme et les oeuvres de bienfaisance appartenant aux communautés respectives.

Egalement, dans le cas où l'une des communautés jugera qu'elle n'a pas le nombre nécessaire de maîtres d'école, de professeurs ou de prêtres pour le fonctionnement de ses institutions, les Gouvernements Grec et Turc pourront leur fournir respectivement le strict nécessaire pour faire face à leur besoins.

25.   L'un des Ministères suivants: soit le Ministère des Affaires Etrangères, le Ministère de la Défense, le Ministère des Finances, sera confié à un Turc. Si le Président et le Vice-Président tombent d'accord, ils pourront substituer à ce système un système de rotation.

26.   Le nouvel État qui naîtra par la signature des Traités devra être constitué aussi rapidement que possible et dans un délai ne surpassant pas les trois mois après la signature de ces Traités.

27.   Tous les points mentionnés ci-dessus seront considérés comme articles fondamentaux de la Constitution de Chypre.

ANNEXE I

A

Sont questions de défense sujettes au véto en vertu du point 8 de la structure de base les questions suivantes:

a) Composition et volume des forces armées et des crédits les concernant.

b) Nominations des cadres et leurs avancements.

c) Importation de matériel de guerre et aussi de toutes sortes de matières explosives.

d) Cession de bases et d'autres facilités à des pays alliés.

B

Les questions de sécurité sujettes au véto sont les suivantes:

a) Nomination et avancement des cadres.

b) Répartition et stationnement des forces.

c) Mesures d'exception et loi martiale.

d) Lois de police.

(Il est spécifié que entre dans le droit de véto toute mesure ou décision exceptionnelle mais pas celles concernant le fonctionnement normal de la police et de la gendarmerie).

TRAITE DE GARANTIE

LA REPUBLIQUE DE CHYPRE
D'UNE PART

LA GRECE, LE ROYAUME UNI, ET LA TURQUIE
DE L'AUTRE

I.   Considérant que la reconnaissance et le maintien de l'indépendance, de l'intégrité territoriale et de la sécurité de la République de Chypre établies et regies par les articles fondamentaux de sa Constitution sont dans leur intérêt commun.

II.   Soucieux de coopérer pour assurer le respect de l'état de choses créé par la dite Constitution

SONT CONVENUS DE CE QUI SUIT

ARTICLE 1.

La République de Chypre s'engage à assurer le maintiem de son indépendance, de son intégrité territoriale et de sa sécurité, ainsi que le respect de sa constitution.

Elle assume l'obligation de ne participer intégralement ou partiellement à aucune union politique ou économique avec quelque État que ce soit. Dans ce sens elle déclare interdite toute activité de nature à favoriser directement ou indirectement tant l'union que le partage de l'île.

ARTICLE 2.

La Grèce, le Royaume Uni et la Turquie, prenant acte des engagements de la République de Chypre etablis dans l'article 1er, reconnaissent et garantissent l'indépendance, l'intégrité territoriale et la sécurité de la République de Chypre, ainsi que l'ordre de choses, établi par les articles fondamentaux de sa Constitution.

Ils assument également l'obligation d'interdire pour ce qui dépend d'eux toute activité ayant pour bot de favoriser directement ou indirectement tant l'union de la République de Chypre avec tout autre État que le partage de l'île.

ARTICLE 3.

En cas de violation dos dispositions du présent traité, la Grèce, le Royaume-Uni et la Turquie promettent de se concerter en vue des démarches ou mesures nécessaires pour en assurer l'observation.

Dans la mesure où une action commune ou concertée ne serait pas possible, chacune des trois Puissances garantes se réserve le droit d'agir dans le but exclusif du rétablissement de l'ordre établi par le présent traité.

ARTICLE 4.

La présent traité entrera en vigueur le jour même de sa signature.

Les Hautes Parties contractantes se réservent de procéder le plus tôt possible à son enregistrement au Secrétariat des Nations Unies conformément aux dispositions de l'article 102 de la Charte.

TRAITE D'ALLIANCE ENTRE LA REPUBLIQUE DE CHYPRE, LA GRECE ET LA TURQUIE

1. La République de Chypre, la Grèce et la Turquie coopéreront pour leur défense commune et s'engagent par ce traité à se concerter sur les problèmes que pose cette défense.

2. Les Hautes Parties Contractantes s'engagent à repousser toute attaque au agression, directe ou indirecte, dirigée contre l'indépendance et l'intégrité territoriale de la République de Chypre.

3. En expression de cette Alliance, et afin de réaliser le but mentionné ci-haut, un Quartier-Général tripartite sera établi sur le territoire de la République de Chypre.

4. La Grèce participera au Quartier-Général mentionné à l'article précédent avec un contingent de 950 officiers, sous-officiers et soldats et la Turquie avec un contingent de 650 offieiers, sous-officiers et soldats. Le Président et le Vice-Président de la République de Chypre pourront d'un commun accord demander aux gouvernements Grec et Turc l'augmentation ou la diminution des contingents grec et turc.

5. Les officiers grecs et turcs ci-haut mentionnés pourvoieront à l'entraînement de l'armée de la République de Chypre.

6. Le commandement du quartier-général tripartite sera assumé à tour de rôle et pour une période d'un an par un officier général chypriote, grec et turc qui sera désigné par les gouvernements de la Grèce et de la Turquie et par le Président et le Vice-Président de la République de Chypre.

APPENDIX 20

Record of a Meeting Held at the Foreign Office at 4 p.m. on Thursday, February 12, 1959

Foreign Office (Secret) and Whitehall (Secret) Distribution
Copy No. 13

Present:

The Foreign Secretary	M. Averoff	M. Zorlu
Lord Perth	M. Seferiades	M. Birgi
Mr. Profumo	M. Palamas	M. Tepedeten
Sir John Martin		
Mr. Melville		
Mr. Mothershead		
Mr. Addis		
Mr. Lackey		
Mr. Wade-Gery		

Cyprus

The Secretary of State, after welcoming the Greek and Turkish Foreign Ministers to the meeting, read out the text of the Parliamentary Answer which he had just delivered in the House of Commons. He explained that he had not yet studied the documents of the Zürich Conference sufficiently to be ready for an exhaustive discussion. But he had a number of questions he would like to ask; these were largely technical, and were not a sign of any hesitation on the part of Her Majesty's Government. He hoped to have a meeting with his colleagues on the morning of February 13, and that by that afternoon he would be in a position to say both what Her Majesty's Government were able to accept and Her Majesty's Government's requirements. If agreement between the Three Powers could be reached in this way on February 13, it should then be possible to invite the Greek and Turkish Cypriot Delegations to London for a Conference. Sir Hugh Foot had already been asked to come back and the Colonial Secretary would probably interrupt his travels and return also.

Mr. Averoff said that his Prime Minister had explained the Zürich agreement to Archbishop Makarios, whose reaction had been favourable. It was, however, important to pin him down to the actual documents, which he would be seeing that evening. M. Averoff hoped to be able to report the Archbishop's final reaction that night or the following morning. The current attitude of the Greek community in Cyprus itself was that they would agree to anything which the Archbishop accepted. *The Secretary of State* said that he thought the Archbishop's latest statement, as reported in the Press, had been helpful.

In answer to a question from the Secretary of State, *M. Averoff* and *M. Zorlu* confirmed that the documents would not be published yet. When they were, it would be simultaneously in both the Greek and Turkish Parliaments. Publication would never, in any case, extend to the "Gentlemen's Agreements" which would remain permanently secret.

The Secretary of State then said that he would prefer for the moment not to discuss British requirements for military bases. This was a technical matter, and one on which all three delegations were in any case agreed in principle. He therefore turned to the Zürich documents beginning with the Treaty of Guarantee. Was the second paragraph of Article 1 intended to preclude Cypriot membership of all international associations, as for example the Free Trade Area if that ever came into existence?

M. Zorlu explained that the paragraph was intended to prohibit partition and Enosis (either with Greece or with any other country). *M. Averoff* agreed; he explained that the wording was specifically designed to exclude possible Greek devices in the direction of Enosis, such as personal union of Cyprus and Greece under the Greek crown. *M. Zorlu and M. Averoff both made it clear that there would be no objection to Cypriot membership of international associations of which both Greece and Turkey were members; e.g., the Postal Union, and any Free Trade Area.** Nor did they exclude either Commonwealth membership for Cyprus or membership of the Sterling Area. They would, indeed, welcome Commonwealth membership, and had already so informed Mrs. Barbara Castle and Mr. Francis Noel Baker. Article 1 of the Treaty of Guarantee could be amended if necessary to make clear that neither Commonwealth nor Sterling Area membership were excluded. But the final decision on such memberships would, of course, rest with the Cypriots themselves.

In answer to the question from the Secretary of State, *M. Averoff* and *M. Zorlu* confirmed that the "basic articles" of the constitution referred to in Article 2 of the Treaty of Guarantee were all the articles set out in the document on the Basic Structure of Cyprus.

Turning to the Treaty of Alliance, *the Secretary of State* said that the United Kingdom would have to share in the external defence of Cyprus, partly because of her need to defend the immediate neighbourhood and the British bases, and partly because in practice the United Kingdom alone would have the necessary forces on the spot. *It would be advisable for the British commanders to have a common defence plan worked out in concert with the commanders of the other military forces in the island. M. Averoff said that if the island were ever invaded, the interests of Britain, Greece and Turkey would alike be in danger.* He recognised that in practice the British forces would need to defend their bases and the neighbourhood of their bases. It should be possible to arrange the necessary co-ordination between the proposed tripartite Headquarters and the British forces, and for the tripartite Headquarters to make it known that a common plan worked out with the British would be necessary. But he would prefer not formally to include the United Kingdom in the tripartite Headquarters, which for presentational reasons it would be better to keep entirely "in the family."

After further discussion *M. Averoff* and *M. Zorlu* promised on behalf of their Governments that the Greek and Turkish representatives in the tripartite

---

* Author's emphasis.

Headquarters would state that defence co-ordination with the British forces would be necessary. It was generally agreed that a British share in the responsibility for the Island's external defence was in any case established by the Treaty of Guarantee, under which Britain would be pledged to ensure the independence, territorial integrity and security of the Republic of Cyprus.

M. Averoff said that joint defence planning would follow naturally if Cyprus became a member of NATO. Cypriot membership of NATO was foreseen in the "Gentlemen's Agreements" and was very strongly desired by Greece for three reasons:

(a) It would discourage the extremists in Cyprus, who might at some future date be tempted to agitate against the maintenance of the present settlement.

(b) It would help to bind Cyprus securely to the West.

(c) It would encourage the development of Cypriot national consciousness (M. Averoff admitted that M. Zorlu was less enthusiastic than himself about this last point).

The Secretary of State said that he was not opposed in principle to Cypriot membership of NATO. But was it really likely that the other members of NATO would all agree? *M. Averoff* and *M. Zorlu* said that NATO agreement ought not in their view to be unobtainable; M. Zorlu added that he personally expected even the Scandinavian members to be amenable.

In reply to a question from M. Averoff, *the Secretary of State* said that he was not yet in a position to say what bases and facilities the United Kingdom would need to retain. In addition to the British areas, there would have to be provision for such matters as freedom of access. For reasons of administrative convenience alone these requirements would naturally be kept to the minimum.

M. Averoff said that the question of the extent of British requirements was not really a matter of great concern to his Government. The essential basis of the Greek-Turkish discussions had been that whatever sovereign bases and other facilities the United Kingdom required would have to be provided. For practical reasons, they hoped that the British bases and installations would be as geographically concentrated as possible. Greece would naturally prefer, if possible, not to see as many as 20 separate British bases in Cyprus; but if as many as 12 were required that should be quite possible. *M. Zorlu* agreed, while adding that it would be important for Britain not to demand so much as to arouse the suspicions of the emergent Cypriot State.

The Secretary of State said that an indispensable prerequisite for the United Kingdom in any agreement would be that the British bases and facilities must not only be accepted by the Cypriot Government, but must also be guaranteed by the Governments of Greece and Turkey. Otherwise, there would be a danger that the Cypriots might seek to repudiate their agreement with the United Kingdom. *M. Averoff* and *M. Zorlu* agreed that this British requirement should be met and that if necessary extra articles should be added to one or other of the Treaties.

In answer to a question from the Secretary of State, *M. Averoff* and *M. Zorlu* said that the Greek and Turkish Governments would be represented in Cyprus by Ambassadors. *Lord Perth* suggested that the United Kingdom might appoint a representative to be associated in some way with the internal administration of Cyprus, to provide for practical co-ordination. *M. Averoff* replied that something could be worked out in practice once the alliance had been established. It would not be a good idea to have a British representative actually playing a role in the internal administration of the Republic. But he agreed with a suggestion of M. Zorlu's that administrative co-ordination could be handled through the proposed tripartite Headquarters.

Turning to questions of timing, *the Secretary of State* said that on the assumption that a basic understanding was reached between the Three Powers on the following day and between them and the Cypriots at a formal conference in the following week, there would be much technical preparation to be done by the British authorities. The transfer of sovereignty in a Colony always took time. An Act of Parliament would be necessary and there would, for example, be problems connected with nationality. *Sir John Martin* said that it would be necessary for the new State to be born, as it were, fully grown-up. For this purpose, parliamentary elections would have to be held first, under the auspices of the present British administration, so that the new State was fully equipped to take over when British sovereignty was withdrawn.

M. Averoff agreed that this would have to be arranged, and that a transitional period might be necessary. It had just occurred to him that it might, for instance, be possible to hold elections under a special Commission with Greek and Turkish members; he did not like the idea of all the preparatory steps being taken under British control.

M. Zorlu drew attention to the provision for drafting the Constitution set out in paragraph 5 of the "Gentlemen's Agreements." The committee there proposed would endeavour to see that under the Cypriot Constitution the powers of the President and the Vice-President were as wide as possible and that the power of the Assemblies were as small as possible. Large multi-member constituencies and electoral lists would be used in order to keep Communist representation to a minimum.

The Secretary of State and *Lord Perth* suggested that there might be a British adviser on the committee for drafting the Constitution. There were also technical problems connected with the competence of Cypriots to sign international agreements before the termination of British sovereignty.

M. Averoff and *M. Zorlu* said that they would discuss this whole problem further between themselves. *M. Zorlu* said that the basis of the whole of the proposed settlement was that there would be a unilateral declaration by the United Kingdom that, provided the Greek and Turkish Governments and the Greek and Turkish Cypriots were agreed, she would hand over sovereignty outside her bases to the Cypriot people.

In answer to a question from the Secretary of State, *M. Averoff* and *M. Zorlu* said that they hoped that the amnesty and the lifting of the emergency, envisaged in the "Gentlemen's Agreements," could take place at the end of the Conference to be held the following week. This would naturally be on the assumption that EOKA did not seek to oppose the settlement. The amnesty would, of course, exclude non-political criminals. *M. Averoff* pointed out that it would be fatal to the success of the agreement if the British Security Forces were to capture Colonel Grivas after the Conference had been successfully held. In the unlikely event of any continued violence in Cyprus it would be the responsibility of the Greek Government and Archbishop Makarios to denounce it.

The Secretary of State and *Lord Perth* said that it would be impossible to promise a complete amnesty and a complete end to the emergency for the coming week. But as much as possible would be done in this direction. The Governor would be consulted on his return to London. *M. Averoff* pleaded for some announcement about relaxations to be made straight away if possible.

Turning to the documents on the "Basic Structure" of Cyprus, the *Secretary of State* asked what would be the position of the minor communities in Cyprus (*e.g.*, Maronites and Armenians). *M. Averoff* and *M. Zorlu* replied that they had discussed the problem and thought that the minor communities might be told to choose whether they wished to be regarded as members of the Greek or the Turkish Community for the purposes of such matters as voting and public service. *M. Averoff* pointed out that they were not numerous enough to merit any parliamentary representation. *M. Zorlu* said that small minorities did not normally have special protection in other countries. Following a suggestion of the Secretary of State, *M. Averoff* and *M. Zorlu* agreed that wording could be inserted in the constitution to guarantee the basic human rights of the minor communities and to make provision for their religious and educational affairs. The constitution could also provide that, by consent of the President and Vice-President, members of the minor communities could be employed within either the Greek or the Turkish percentage of the public services, including the Police and Armed Forces.

In answer to a question from the Secretary of State about the second section of paragraph 14 of the "Basic Structure," *M. Averoff* and *M. Zorlu* made clear that the Cypriot Army, like the Cypriot Security Forces, could be increased or decreased by agreement between the President and the Vice-President.

Lord Perth pointed out that it would be necessary to provide for compensation to be paid for the United Kingdom government officials and Police officers employed by the present Cyprus Government (other than those on direct secondment from the United Kingdom, who of course presented no problem). *M. Averoff* asked whether these persons could not be re-employed within the British bases, or whether the British Government could not pay their compensation out of the money which they would save as a result of the new settlement in Cyprus. *The Secretary of State* explained that Her Majesty's Government were anxious to avoid setting an undesirable precedent which could be quoted against them in other Colonial territories reaching independence; the normal pattern in such cases was for the newly independent Government either to retain the services of expatriates or to compensate them.

In answer to a question from the Secretary of State about paragraph 22 of the "Basic Structure," *M. Averoff* and *M. Zorlu* explained that by "separatist independence" was meant the possibility of Cyprus being partitioned into two independent States (in contrast to "partition" which implied the union of part of Cyprus with Turkey).

On paragraph 23 of the "Basic Structure," *Lord Perth* said that the most-favoured-nation provision as drafted might do economic harm to Cyprus.

*M. Averoff and M. Zorlu said that the maintenance of Commonwealth Prefer-
ence would not be excluded. The intention was to exclude more favourable bilateral agreements between Cyprus and countries other than the Three Powers,
and also to avoid the possibility of either Greece or Turkey securing a more favourable economic position in Cyprus than the other—of Greece, for example,
establishing a kind of economic enosis.**

The Secretary of State said that the Governor would have to be consulted
about the provision, in paragraph 26 of the "Basic Structure," for the Treaty to
enter into force within three months from signature. This period might well
need to be longer. *M. Averoff* agreed, and *M. Zorlu* suggested six months as a
possibility. It was agreed that this problem would be considered further. *Lord
Perth* stressed the advantages of naming a particular date for the achieving of
independence, rather than specifying a lapse of time.

In answer to a question from the Secretary of State, *M. Averoff* and
M. Zorlu said that they did not exclude the possibility of altering the "Basic
Structure" before it was finally published. For example, changes might be
made to take account of Commonwealth Preference and of the minor
communities.

The Secretary of State drew attention to a number of points which were
not covered by the Zürich documents and which would need to be considered:

(a) Nationality; it would be difficult to settle this finally until it was known
     whether Cyprus was to be a member of the Commonwealth.

(b) A legal definition would be required for the Republic of Cyprus; *i.e.*,
     the exact extent of its territory would have to be laid down.

(c) External financial aid would be required by the new Cypriot State at
     least initially; the United Kingdom would probably be willing to help
     and it is expected that Greece and Turkey would also be willing.

M/ Averoff expressed some doubts about (*b*), and both he and *M. Zorlu*
were evasive on the subject of Greek and Turkish financial aid. *M. Averoff* appeared to be genuinely astonished to learn that apart from the cost of the
emergency Her Majesty's Government was at present giving Cyprus an annual
subsidy of some millions sterling.

After agreement had been reached on the attached Press communiqué*
the meeting adjourned at 6:10 p.m.

---

* Author's emphasis.

* Not printed.

APPENDIX 21(1)

Summary Record of the First Plenary Session of the Conference on Cyprus Held at Lancaster House at 11 a.m. on Tuesday, February 17, 1959

SECRET

Present:

Secretary of State (*in the Chair*)	M. Averoff	M. Zorlu
	M. Seferiades	M. Birgi
Colonial Secretary Sir Hugh Foot (and advisers)	M. Palamas (and advisers)	M. Kuneralp (and advisers)

Archbishop Makarios	Dr. Kutchuk
Mr. Z. Rossides	Mr. Denktash
Mr. Chryssafinis	Mr. Orek

The Secretary of State said that he proposed to open the Conference with a statement of the position of Her Majesty's Government. Before doing so, however, he hoped it was agreed that the proceedings of the Conference would be confidential.

Her Majesty's Government welcomed the fact that the Conference was taking place. After all the difficulties of the Cyprus problem and the bitterness which it had caused, this was a moment of destiny for Cyprus and the countries associated with Cyprus. The Conference had become possible because of the Zurich Agreements which were the outcome of negotiations begun towards the end of 1958. Her Majesty's Government had supported these negotiations as a means of reaching agreement at any rate between Greece and Turkey, having in mind the basic requirements of any plan for Cyprus; that Her Majesty's Government's strategic needs should be made unchallengeable, that the two main communities in Cyprus should be reconciled, that Greco-Turkish friendship should be restored and that the Cypriots should be given the opportunity to develop their institutions. At the outset of the negotiations, Her Majesty's Government had explained that, provided British military requirements were met, they would approve the establishment of a new sovereign State of Cyprus. Against this background, the Zurich Agreements were reached.

After summarising the main provisions of the Zurich Agreements (the Basic Structure for Cyprus, the Treaty of Guarantee and the Treaty of Alliance), the Secretary of State then made on behalf of Her Majesty's Government in the United Kingdom a formal Declaration to the effect that, in the light of the Zurich Agreements and subject to certain conditions, Her Majesty's Government were willing to transfer sovereignty over Cyprus, with the exception of two areas, to the new Republic of Cyprus [Document III of Cmnd. 679]. The time-table of events leading to the transfer of sovereignty would have to be discussed. Her Majesty's Government also wished to see inserted in the Treaty of Guarantee an article to the effect that Greece, Turkey and the Republic of Cyprus would respect the integrity of the British sovereign areas and guarantee the necessary British rights and facilities. There were also numerous financial and other problems to be dealt with. The Cyprus Government was at present subsidised from the British Exchequer. The constitution of the army and security forces, the protection of the small communities and the question of nationality would have to be tabled, as well as a mass of administrative detail. But Her Majesty's Government intended, if their Declaration was accepted, to push ahead with the utmost goodwill towards the creation of the new State.

M. Averoff thanked the Secretary of State for convening the Conference and for the Declaration which he had made. Greece had supported the claim of the Greek Cypriots for nearly five years on the Cyprus question, and during that time many political and psychological difficulties had been revealed. Mistakes had been made by all sides and it had become clear that in view of the dangerous effects of the dispute it was necessary to seek a compromise. In that spirit he and M. Zorlu had sought a solution which if it did not satisfy the full demands of either party, at least secured the fundamental interests of all as fully as possible. After long and difficult negotiations, agreement was reached at Zurich in the presence of the heads of the Greek and Turkish Governments. The settlement brought freedom to the people of Cyprus. It gave the majority a larger share in the administration, but the minority was provided with appropriate rights. The Turkish Cypriots would not need to feel at the mercy of the majority. Provision was also made for the security needs of Turkey. It had not been necessary to discuss British security needs, since it was unthinkable that they should not be covered as the British Government wanted. The Government of Greece signed the Zurich Agreements because they were in the interest of both Greece and Turkey in view of the dangerous world situation; because they were in the interests of the people of Cyprus as a whole; and because the head of the Greek Cypriot Community said that he accepted them. The Greek Government signed because they themselves believed the agreement represented the best possible solution. But the favourable attitude of the Archbishop also weighed with them, because it was not their policy to impose their decisions upon the Greek Cypriots. For the same reason the Greek Government would not take any decision on the question whether the Republic of Cyprus would remain in the British Commonwealth: This was up to the Cypriots to decide. But their reluctance to impose decisions on the Cypriots did not mean that Greece would not stand by the Zurich Agreements, which represented the foreign policy of her Government in regard to Cyprus. The Greek Government would tell the Greek Cypriots that they believed the Agreements to be the best possible in the circumstances. Turning to the United Kingdom Declaration, M. Averoff said that he formally accepted it on behalf of the Greek Government as providing, together with the Zurich Agreements, the agreed foundation for the final settlement of the Cyprus problem. The time before the transfer of sovereignty should be short; this question had been discussed with M. Zorlu and with the Cypriots, and the Greek Government believed firmly that the date for the transfer should if possible be before the end of 1959. The Agreement was equally satisfactory for the Turkish Cypriots, who would be enabled to collaborate peaceably with the Greek Cypriots.

The moment for compromise had arrived and the people of Cyprus should now start to prepare a new constitution within the framework of the Zurich Agreements. The Cypriots would thereby be helping not only themselves but also the two countries most closely connected with their island. With the pressure of Communism increasing, Greece and Turkey could not afford the animosity created by the Cyprus question. They must come together in order to survive.

M. Zorlu thanked Her Majesty's Government for convening the Conference and for accepting the Zurich Agreements. The Turkish Government were in full agreement with the United Kingdom Declaration. He was grateful to M. Averoff for his exposition of the Zurich Agreements, which were the result of tough discussions. They came at the end of a long dispute which had cast more than a shadow over the relations between Turkey and Greece and between the Turkish and Greek Cypriots. The two Governments had, however, been inspired by the spirit of Ataturk and Venezelos and had reached a settlement which represented a binding and final solution and required only the acceptance of Her Majesty's Government in order to be put into effect. Now that that acceptance had been forthcoming, the Zurich Agreements were established as an unchangeable foundation and as the policy of the three Governments concerned. But the solution reached should not be imposed on the two Communities in Cyprus, and the opportunity for contact with their representatives during the negotiations had therefore been most welcome.

The Agreements were a compromise constituting a whole from which no simple part could be removed without danger. They marked the end of a long dispute between Greece and Turkey and the starting point of new friendship. This was the most striking feature of the talks at Zurich, and gave the greatest proof that peace and welfare on Cyprus would be preserved. It was to be hoped that the representatives of the two communities in Cyprus would find the same spirit of co-operation between themselves as had been achieved between himself and M. Averoff and between the Greek and Turkish Prime Ministers.

The Secretary of State suggested that in view of the important Declarations which had been made the Cypriot representatives might prefer to delay their comments until a later session. In answer to a question from M. Averoff, he confirmed that the text of the United Kingdom Declaration would be circulated as a Conference Document during the day. The Annex to the Declaration, which he had not read out, would be circulated at the same time.

Archbishop Makarios expressed appreciation for the spirit which had prevailed at Zurich and for the response which Her Majesty's Government had made. The agreement at Zurich and the intention of Her Majesty's Government to transfer sovereignty were a good basis for the solution of the Cyprus problem. He had some reservations on certain points in the draft Constitution which seemed to be unworkable. But he was sure that by close co-operation between the Greek and Turkish Cypriot representatives a detailed Constitution could be prepared satisfactorily. He also wished to raise several points about the two Treaties. He hoped that the Conference would mark the end of the unpleasant situation in Cyprus.

Mr. Denktash, speaking on behalf of Dr. Kutchuk, said that the Turkish Cypriot Delegation had noted what the three Governments and the representative of the Greek Cypriot Community had said. The Turkish Cypriot Community had always wanted peace and co-operation in Cyprus, and agreed with M. Zorlu that now was the time to accept the Zurich Agreements. He hoped to be able to make a further statement the next day after studying the documents to be circulated.

The Secretary of State then proposed that the Conference should be adjourned until the next day. He suggested that the three Foreign Ministers should have a meeting between themselves during the afternoon to clear up some outstanding points.

M. Averoff welcomed the spirit of understanding which had been shown by the representatives of the Cypriot Communities. At the suggestion of *Archbishop Makarios* it was agreed that a meeting should also be held that afternoon between the representatives of the Greek and Turkish Cypriots.

After discussion of the communiqué to be made to the Press, the Conference adjourned at 12.45 p.m.

SECRET

APPENDIX 21(2)

Summary Record of the Second Plenary Session of the Cyprus Conference Held at Lancaster House at 7 p.m. on Wednesday, February 18, 1959

SECRET

Present:

Secretary of State (in the Chair)	M. Averoff	M. Zorlu
Colonial Secretary Sir Hugh Foot (and advisers)	M. Seferiades	M. Birgi
	M. Palamas	M. Kuneralp
	(and advisers)	(and advisers)

Archbishop Makarios
Mr. Z. Rossides
Mr. Chryssafinis

Dr. Kutchuk
Mr. Denktash
Mr. Orek

The Secretary of State expressed his deep sympathy with the Turkish Delegation over the loss of life in the Turkish air disaster on the previous day. He then explained that the present Session had been called in order to hear the views of the representatives of the Greek Cypriot Community and the Turkish Cypriot Community on the Declaration made by the United Kingdom at the First Session the previous day. The Greek and Turkish Foreign Ministers had accepted that Declaration in declarations of their own which they had subsequently reaffirmed.

Archbishop Makarios, who also expressed his sympathy for the Turkish air disaster, said that the Greek Cypriots were grateful for the Greek and Turkish Governments' achievement at Zurich in creating a new and happy atmosphere in Greco-Turkish relations. Her Majesty's Government's prompt response, and their readiness to transfer sovereignty over Cyprus, had been most constructive. As he had mentioned at the First Session, however, he had reservations on certain points in the Zurich Documents. In the draft Constitution, the provisions of Article 7 about the levying of taxes might lead to difficulties in the mechanics of government. It was not clear whether the presidential and vice-presidential veto in Article 8 was intended to cover all ordinary administrative decisions on foreign affairs. Finally, the proportion of 30 per cent. Turks in the Civil Service was not justifiable. The Treaty of Alliance was not objectionable in itself, but it should be entered into on a basis of equality and should not be made fundamental to the Constitution. In the Treaty of Guarantee, Article 3 was unsatisfactory in giving each guarantor a right of intervention in the internal affairs of Cyprus. He hoped that the Three Governments would give serious consideration to these reservations. The Conference had presumably not been summoned on a take-it-or-leave-it basis. The Greek Cypriots accepted the Three Governments' proposals as a good basis towards the final solution.

Mr. Denktash, speaking on behalf of *Dr. Kutchuk*, said that the Cyprus dispute, which had caused so much misery and bloodshed during the last four years, originated in the differing views of the Greek and Turkish Cypriots. The Turkish attitude had been reasonable throughout, but the Greeks had always insisted on 100 per cent. of their demands. In the end, the conflict had become so violent that compromise had been imperative. Greece and Turkey had accordingly negotiated a settlement, in the confidence that it would not be rejected by the Greeks and Turks of Cyprus. The Turkish Cypriots were grateful to Greece and Turkey for producing the Zurich Agreements and to the United Kingdom for endorsing them. They were ready and willing to discuss the details and working arrangements of the Zurich plan, and in that spirit they had met Archbishop Makarios the previous afternoon. As they had informed the Archbishop, however, they regarded the Zurich Agreements as a final framework about which it was impossible to open negotiations. They could not accept the criticisms of the Zurich Documents which Archbishop Makarios had mentioned. If a Cypriot nation was to be born, sacrifices would be necessary from all sides. A compromise had been produced which the Turkish Cypriots were willing to accept and which they called on the Greek Cypriots to accept likewise.

M. Averoff said that the Greek Government proposed to stand by the Agreements which they had signed at Zurich and by their acceptance of the United Kingdom Declaration. It was his duty to make this clear, both to vindicate the good name of Greece and also to demonstrate to the people of Cyprus the Greek Government's confidence that the proposed arrangements created the conditions for a happy Island. He well understood the reservations of Archbishop Makarios, who of course had every right to change his views. He himself had reservations too, but neither these nor the Archbishop's reservations would in practice impede the proper working of the new State provided only that there was the necessary collaboration among the people of the Island. He did not wish to discuss the Archbishop's reservations in detail; but on the question of the percentage of Turks in the Civil Service, he wished to make clear that in the Greek Government's view it was necessary to give the Turkish Cypriots a larger proportion than the ethnic statistics warranted in order to rebuild their confidence. The Greeks and Turks of Cyprus had in the past lived together for centuries in a spirit of brotherhood. The people of Greece and Turkey were determined to work hand in hand in the face of the world dangers which surrounded them. Given this spirit of collaboration, there would be no need for any reservations over details of the settlement in Cyprus. The Turkish Foreign Minister had assured him privately that Turkey did not intend to use her right of intervention under the Treaty of Guarantee in anything but the gravest circumstances. Similarly the Greek Government would only use their right of intervention if the Turkish Cypriots attempted to bring about partition or to overthrow the legal Government of Cyprus. It was no insult to the Cypriots' pride that their independence should be guaranteed. Greece was a proud country, which had prospered during the 130 years of her independence; yet she also had originally been established under the guarantee of outside Powers.

M. Zorlu endorsed what had been said by M. Averoff. The Zurich Conference had created an atmosphere of friendship. The Agreements reached there were the result of compromise; they would work if the atmosphere of friendship and co-operation persisted. The two Cypriot communities must learn to live together in peace; there was much in the Zurich Agreements which presupposed close co-operation and understanding between the President and the Vice-President of the future Republic. The Agreements provided the foundation for a settlement; they had been worked out with great care and minute thought and it would not be possible to find any alternative to them. Archbishop Makarios should abandon his attempts to postpone or alter the Zurich decisions and should enable co-operation between the Greek and Turkish Cypriots to begin. M. Averoff had correctly stated Turkey's intention with regard to the Treaty of Guarantee; Turkey would not intervene over small matters.

The Secretary of State said that this was a moment of destiny for the people of Cyprus. He had been profoundly moved to hear M. Averoff speaking as a Greek of the Turkish brothers of the Greek Cypriots, and M. Zorlu's endorsement of that theme. It was clear that collaboration between Greece and Turkey was the essential basis for a happy future for Cyprus. The present Conference had been called on the understanding that there was basic agreement between all five parties. In the light of what had now been said, however, it was his duty as Chairman to consider whether any useful purpose would be served by calling a further meeting. He concluded that in the circumstances it was right to break off the meeting and to declare it closed.

Archbishop Makarios (speaking in Greek and interpreted by Mr. Rossides) said that there appeared to be a misunderstanding. He was being represented as rejecting the Zurich Agreements. But the Conference had surely been called so that he could express his views, not so that he should be presented with a *fait accompli*. Was it forbidden to discuss detailed points in the Zurich Agreements? Must everything which had been agreed between the Three Governments be accepted word for word, without any discussion or amendments? When he had discussed certain points with the Turkish Cypriot leaders the previous day, they had themselves realised that there were certain difficulties. For example, it might be desirable to have a co-ordinating committee between the two separate municipalities in each town. There should be some provision in case there was disagreement about the appointment or election of a President. With regard to taxation, there was a danger that the machinery of government would be brought to a halt. So far as the Treaties were concerned, the essential thing was that Cyprus should appear to be an independent country and not under foreign occupation.

M. Zorlu, on a point of order, said that the Conference had been convened on the basis of the agreement reached at Zurich. It had been understood that all the parties were agreed in accepting the Zurich documents. Now Archbishop Makarios was criticising individual points in these documents. The Archbishop should not suppose that the Zurich Agreements were a beginning from which he could start negotiations.

The Secretary of State said that Archbishop Makarios' attitude had changed the whole basis of the situation. He wished to ask the Archbishop a very direct question: did he or did he not accept the Zurich Documents and the Governmental Declarations as the foundation of the final settlement? In answer to a question from the Archbishop, he explained that by a foundation was meant something upon which one could build but from which one could not take away without endangering the whole structure.

M. Averoff said that acceptance of the Zurich Documents would not preclude clarifications or additions where those were necessary. For example, the co-ordinating bodies mentioned by Archbishop Makarios could be added, and provision made for settlement by lot in case the President and Vice-President could not agree on the appointment of the Chairman of these bodies. Those details should be worked out by the proposed Constitutional Commission of Greeks and Turks in Cyprus. The Basic Constitution agreed at Zurich was no more than an outline. But so far as it went it could not be changed except with the agreement of all the parties.

Archbishop Makarios said that he was not sure whether the people of Cyprus would accept all the documents without the change of a single word. *The Secretary of State* said this was not what was being asked; it was rather a question whether the Archbishop accepted the documents in essence as the foundation of the final settlement. *Archbishop Makarios* said that he could not accept them at this stage; he must ask his advisers, and would give his answer tomorrow. If an answer was required at once, he would have to say "No."

On the suggestion of *M. Averoff*, the *Secretary of State* then declared a recess for 15 minutes.

On resumption, the *Secretary of State* said that he had discussed the matter further with Archbishop Makarios, who felt unable to give his answer then but would do so by 9.45 a.m. the next morning. He had accepted this, and had made clear to the Archbishop that if the answer was "Yes" then the Conference would be reconvened, but that if the answer was "No" there would be no useful purpose in further Sessions. *Archbishop Makarios* confirmed that the position was as the Secretary of State had stated it.

M. Zorlu said that he would like to assure Archbishop Makarios that the Greek Cypriots could rely on the goodwill of the Turkish Government. *M. Averoff* said that the Turkish community could similarly rely on the goodwill of the Greek Government.

In adjourning the meeting, the *Secretary of State* asked that great discretion should he shown in regard to the Press. He suggested that the Press should be told only that discussions were still proceeding.

SECRET

APPENDIX 21(3)

Summary Record of the Third Plenary Session of the Cyprus Conference Held at Lancaster House at 3.45 p.m. on Thursday, February 19, 1959

SECRET

Present:

Secretary of State	M. Karamanlis	M. Zorlu
(*in the Chair*)	M. Averoff	M. Birgi
Colonial Secretary	M. Seferiades	M. Kuneralp
Sir Hugh Foot	M. Palamas	(and advisers)
(and advisers)	(and advisers)	

Archbishop Makarios	Dr. Kutchuk
Mr. Z. Rossides	Mr. Denktash
Mr. Chryssafinis	Mr. Orek

The Prime Minister said that the intention had been for this final session of the Conference to be attended by the Prime Ministers of Greece, Turkey and the United Kingdom. Unfortunately, the Prime Minister of Turkey was still in hospital and unable to be present; his miraculous survival from his aeroplane crash was a matter for rejoicing, and the loss of so many of his comrades a matter for deep sympathy.

At the request of the Prime Minister, *the Secretary of State* then reported on the stage which the Conference had reached. He recalled that at the first meeting on February 17 he had made a formal Declaration of the position of the United Kingdom Government, indicating their acceptance of the Zurich Agreements, upon certain conditions, as the basis for the final settlement of the Cyprus problem. He had also stated the Additional Article which the United Kingdom required to be inserted in the Treaty of Guarantee. The Greek and Turkish Foreign Ministers had then made Declarations reaffirming the Zurich Agreements and accepting the United Kingdom Declaration. The Representatives of the Greek and Turkish Cypriot communities had made preliminary statements at the First Session, and further statements at a Second Session on the evening of February 18, when Dr. Kutchuk had accepted the Zurich Agreements and the Declarations of the Three Governments as the agreed foundation for the final settlement of the Cyprus problem. Archbishop Makarios, on behalf of the Greek Cypriot community, had said that he would not be in a position to give his answer until that morning, February 19, when he had sent a message to the effect that his answer was "Yes." The present third and final session of the Conference had been summoned accordingly.

The Prime Minister then proposed that the necessary formalities should be completed by the signing and initialling of the appropriate Documents. One of the Documents was intended for signing by the three Prime Ministers and he had agreed with the Prime Minister of Greece that after the session was over they should take this Document to M. Menderes in his hospital for signature there.

[The following Documents were then signed or initialled, as specified (the Document numbering is taken from the British White Paper subsequently published on February 23, Command 679):

The French texts as agreed at Zurich of the Basic Structure for Cyprus, the Treaty of Guarantee and the Treaty of Alliance (Document No. II) were initialled by the three Foreign Ministers, by Archbishop Makarios and by Dr. Kutchuk.

The Declaration by the Government of the United Kingdom (Document No. III) was signed by the Foreign Secretary and the Colonial Secretary and initialled by the Foreign Ministers of Greece and Turkey, by Archbishop Makarios and by Dr. Kutchuk.

The Additional Article for the Treaty of Guarantee (Document No. IV) was initialled by the three Foreign Ministers, by Archbishop Makarios and by Dr. Kutchuk.

The Declaration by the Greek and Turkish Foreign Ministers (Document No. V) was signed by the Foreign Ministers of Greece and Turkey and initialled by the Foreign Secretary, by Archbishop Makarios and by Dr. Kutchuk.

The Declaration by Archbishop Makarios (Document No. VI) was signed by the Archbishop and was initialled by the three Foreign Ministers and by Dr. Kutchuk.

The Declaration by Dr. Kutchuk (Document No. VII) was signed by Dr. Kutchuk and initialled by the three Foreign Ministers and by Archbishop Makarios.

The Agreed Measures to Prepare for the New Arrangements in Cyprus (Document No. VIII) was, as pre-arranged, initialled by the three Foreign Ministers only.]

The Prime Minister said that this was a memorable occasion. The Eastern Mediterranean had always been a region of decisive importance. Britain, Greece and Turkey were all vitally concerned, and over the years had stood in varying relationship with each other. Usually they had been friends, sometimes they had been divided. Over the last generation there had been a growing realisation that unless they stood together their interests might be overwhelmed in common catastrophe. It had always been clear that the problem of Cyprus could only be resolved by agreement between these three countries as well as with Cyprus itself. Nearly four years had passed since the Tripartite Conference of 1955 in Lancaster House. Blood had been shed and strong passions aroused. Yet it was always known that ultimately there would have to be a settlement and that each of the parties would have to make concessions to reach it. The settlement now achieved recognised the right of the people of Cyprus to independent status. It recognised the Hellenic character of the majority, but also protected the national character of the Turkish community. It preserved the United Kingdom's essential defence facilities. The Foreign Ministers of Greece and Turkey had made clear in discussion that for their part they would not object to Cyprus remaining in some form of association with the Commonwealth, although of course the people of Cyprus themselves would need to express their views on that subject, which would also be of concern to other Commonwealth Governments. If in due course the Government of Cyprus declared that they wished to remain associated with the Commonwealth, the United Kingdom Government, in consultation with other members of the Commonwealth, would be ready to consider sympathetically how that wish could most appropriately be met. The immediate task was to put into effect the agreements reached at the present Conference. Much detailed work would be necessary. The spirit of partnership and inter-dependence would be essential for success.

M. Karamanlis thanked the Prime Minister for his speech and expressed his regrets for the absence of his friend M. Menderes. He was very happy that the negotiations in Zurich and in London had reached a successful issue and had demonstrated what the spirit of co-operation between free peoples could achieve.

The parties to the present settlement were godfathers at the birth of the new Republic of Cyprus. He was convinced that the settlement met the aspirations of the whole population on Cyprus in the best possible way. There had been no victor, except the Cypriots themselves. The settlement was founded on co-operation between Greeks and Turks, both in Cyprus and in Greece and Turkey. It would enable the majority in Cyprus to develop its life in the manner it wished. So far as Commonwealth membership was concerned, that would be up to the Cypriots; Greece took no stand in the matter. The settlement restored the traditional friendship between Greece and Britain. It also restored the close friendship between Greece and Turkey which had been founded by Ataturk and Venizelos.

M. Zorlu expressed the regret of the Prime Minister of Turkey that he could not be present; he read out a message of gratitude from M. Menderes for the many tokens of sympathy he had received. The present Conference had been called to solve one of the most intricate problems of diplomacy which the modern world had recently experienced. The task had been full of difficulties, but success had been achieved thanks to that spirit of mutual understanding which represented the solid foundation for the solution of the Cyprus question. The Turkish Government fully accepted the conclusions of the Conference and would stand by them in all circumstances. They looked forward to a new period of close co-operation between Greece and Turkey. The Conference owed a special debt of thanks to the leaders of the two Cypriot communities for their understanding and sense of responsibility.

Archbishop Makarios, after expressing his sympathy for the Prime Minister of Turkey, said that this was a day for unity and co-operation. It marked the beginning of a new charter for Cyprus. In overcoming his recent reservations he had acted in a spirit of trust and goodwill towards the Turkish Cypriot community and its leaders. It was his firm belief that the two communities could work together in understanding and confidence. Their differences were already a thing of the past. He wished to thank the British Government and the Governments of Greece and Turkey for the spirit of co-operation which had animated their work for a settlement. The difficulties had been great, but the spirit of co-operation had prevailed.

Dr. Kutchuk added his tribute to the Prime Minister of Turkey and expressed his happiness at the success of the Conference. The Governments concerned had had many difficulties, but from now on it was to be hoped that co-operation and goodwill would prevail. The sacrifices and concessions of the Turkish community had been worth while, since in return they had gained the friendship of the Greek community. His Delegation were grateful for the hospitality which had been shown to them in London.

The Prime Minister said that in conclusion there was a number of other matters to be attended to. Some of these could be discussed privately after the meeting adjourned. With regard to publicity, it was agreed that the full Documents should be published at 5 p.m. G.M.T. on Monday, February 23. He himself would need to make a statement to the House of Commons that evening, but he would confine himself to saying generally that the Conference had been successful and he would avoid giving any details.

It was agreed that a short Press communiqué should be issued at about 6 o'clock announcing the successful conclusion of the Conference in a spirit of close co-operation and foreshadowing the publication of the Documents on February 23.

The Conference adjourned at 5 p.m.

(As proposed by the Prime Minister, he and M. Karamanlis then visited M. Menderes in hospital where the three Prime Ministers signed a Memorandum setting out the Agreed Foundation for the Final Settlement of the Problem of Cyprus (Document No. 1 of Command 679).)

SECRET

APPENDIX 22(1)

Opinion by Hans Kelsen Commissioned by the United Nations in Relation to the Eligibility of the Future Republic of Cyprus as a Member of the United Nations, 12 May 1959

SECRET

7. *Article 3 of the Treaty of Guarantee.* It is against the background of the above multifarious rights and guarantees that Article 3 of the Treaty must be assessed and analysed. Article 3 provides as follows:

> In the event of any breach of the provisions of the present Treaty, Greece, the U.K. and Turkey undertake to consult together with a view to making representations, or taking the necessary steps to ensure observance of those provisions.
>
> In so far as common or concerted action may prove impossible, each of the three guaranteeing Powers reserves the right to take action with the sole aim of re-establishing the state of affairs established by the present Treaty.

This article is, to some extent, obscure. For example, Article 2 of the Treaty, as already indicated, contains an undertaking by the guarantors relating to the prohibition of activity which was aimed at promoting the partition of Cyprus, or its union with any other State. At first sight, the failure of one of the guarantors to take measures within its power to prohibit activity of the above sort in own territory, might be considered to come within the limit of all of the measures contemplated in Article 3, as that Article refers to a breach of "any of the provisions" of the Treaty. However, from the way in which Article 3 is drafted, in referring first to possible common action by all the guarantors, and by failing to provide for the participation of the Republic of Cyprus in such action in certain circumstances it would appear that the drafters of the Treaty had primarily in mind events occurring in Cyprus, not elsewhere, when Article 3 was drafted, and therefore, the reference in paragraph 2 of Article 3 to the "State of Affairs established by the . . . Treaty" should probably be deemed to refer primarily to the state of affairs of Cyprus. It is within this context that Article 3 provides for both joint or several action on the part of the guarantors. Joint action is envisaged after consultations between the guarantors, and may take the form of representations or of "necessary steps" to ensure the observance of the provisions of the Treaty. Individual action is envisaged where common or concerted action is impossible and, in this respect, it is to be noted that the guarantors "reserve" a right to take such action. By use of the word "reserve" it would appear that paragraph 2 of Article 3 of the Treaty is not intended to grant any new rights to the guarantors, but is merely a confirmation of such rights as they might be deemed to possess under other provisions of the Treaty and general international law.

8. *Statement of certain of the questions arising out of Article 3.* Apart from the matters just mentioned, a variety of questions may be postulated on the basis of Article 3. This note is primarily concerned with the following:

(i) Is Article 3 valid?
(ii) Can Article 3 be interpreted as granting the guarantors both a joint and several rights to resort to measures of enforcement, including military measures, if a breach of the Treaty occurs? Namely, do the references to "necessary steps" and to taking "action" imply, in the light of the history of certain treaties of guarantee (see the annex to this note), a right to resort to measures, particularly those involving the use of force, or would such a right now be superseded by the Charter of the U.N. and in particular Articles 2(3), 2(4) and 53?

B. *Validity of Article 3.*

9. The view is stated in the Annex to this note that the conclusion of a treaty of guarantee remains a perfectly proper and valid exercise of treaty powers by a sovereign State. It is pointed out in that Annex and the Security Council has itself agreed to assume the responsibilities and rights of a guarantor. It is as proper and valid to accept guarantees as to offer them. In this sense they may be regarded as a sign of good faith. Article 2(I) of the Charter provides that the U.N. "is based on the principle of the sovereign equality of all its Members", and, therefore the Charter places no automatic limitation on the free offer and acceptance of guarantees which represent a commonly accepted feature of international law.

10. However, there can be no doubt, that the Charter imposes upon the Members certain obligations which effect legal rights previously existing under international law in relation to action permissible to enforce treaty rights and which also bear upon the obligations undertaken in treaties. The Charter takes precedence over all other treaties, Article 103 provides that:

> In the event of a conflict between the obligations or the Member of the UN under the present Charter and their obligations under any other international agreement, their obligations under the Charter shall prevail.

It appears to be the generally accepted view that this Article relates not only to treaties concluded prior to the Charter, but also to subsequent treaties, even those to which one party is not a Member of the U.N.[4]

11. If it is for the moment assumed that the Charter forbids armed intervention, pursuant to alleged treaty rights, by individual States in the internal affairs of another State, and it is further assumed that Article 3 of the Treaty of Guarantee purports to grant a right of armed intervention to the guarantors, it

---

[4] See, for example, Goodrich and Hambro, *Charter of the UN* (Second and Revised Edition, Boston 1949), pp. 517-519, Kelsen, *The law of the UN* (NY, 1950), pp. 111-118, Bentwich & Martin, *A Commentary on the Charter of the UN* (London, 1950), pp. 179-180.

would appear that Article 103 of the Charter would prevail over Article 3 of the Treaty of Guarantee. It would not render that Article invalid (which would probably have been the case under Article 20 of the Covenant of the League of Nations[5]) but would instead restrict the rights of the guarantors to measures, short of armed intervention, which are permissible under the Charter. Armed intervention is not the only means for enforcing a guarantee.

C. *Use of force and the Treaty of Guarantee.*

12. Article 3 of the Treaty of Guarantee does not explicitly confer on the guarantors any right to take armed action in the event of a breach of the provisions of the Treaty. However, as already pointed out, the references in that Article to "necessary steps" and "action" might be interpreted by some as implying that military measures are permissible by one or more of the guarantors in certain circumstances.

13. Now that the implications just stated can be regarded as legally permissible, it is necessary, first of all, to have an analysis of the circumstances in which consideration might be given to resort to armed force. Broadly speaking, there appear to be two sets of such circumstances. First, a situation might arise where the independence, territorial integrity or security of the Republic of Cyprus is threatened by invasion from a third power. Second, the independence and territorial integrity, and the basic articles of the constitution might be threatened by revolutionary activity, on the island of Cyprus, aimed at overthrowing the constitution, or establishing partition, or union with another State. These two sets of circumstances will be considered separately.

(a) *Attack by a third Power.*

14. Greece, the U.K. and Turkey have guaranteed the independence, territorial integrity and security of Cyprus. It would therefore appear to be their duty, primarily under article 2 of the Treaty, (although Article 3 may also be argued to be relevant in this context[6]) to come to the aid of Cyprus if it is attacked by another Power. The assumption of such a duty is not inconsistent with the

---

[5] Article 20 of the Covenant reads as follows:

> 1. The Members of the League severally agree that this Covenant is accepted as abrogating all obligations or understandings *inter se* which are inconsistent with the terms thereof, and solemnly undertake that they will not hereafter enter into any engagements inconsistent with the terms thereof.
>
> 2. In case any Member of the League shall, before becoming a Member of the League, have undertaken any obligations inconsistent with the terms of this Covenant, it shall be the duty of such Member to take immediate steps to procure its release from such obligations.

[6] Article 3 refers to a "breach of the provisions of the . . . Treaty". A third Power invading Cyprus would not "breach" a Treaty to which it was not a party. However, the circumstances resulting from such an invasion might be deemed to give rise to a breach of the Treaty (e.g. the inability of Cyprus to maintain its independence), Article 3 then becoming relevant.

Charter. In this respect reliance may be placed upon Article 51 which provides that:

> Nothing in the present Charter shall impair the inherent right of individual or collective self-dependence if an armed attack occurs against a Member of the U.N., until the Security Council has taken measures necessary to maintain international peace and security. Measures taken by Members in the exercise of this right of self-defence shall be immediately reported to the Security Council and shall not in any way effect the authority and responsibility of the Security Council under the present Charter to take at any time such action as it deems necessary, in order to maintain or restore international peace and security.

Even if a very narrow interpretation of Article 51 is taken, and an armed attack were to occur on Cyprus before its admission to the U.N. the presence of Greek, U.K. and Turkish troops stationed on the island, as envisaged under the London Agreement, would permit of the argument that an attack on Cyprus constituted an attack on these States.

15. In as far as the right of self-defence may be invoked, in the case of attack by a third Power, it should be pointed out that this right is derived from general international law and does not depend for its validity on the terms or status of the Treaty of Guarantee.

(b) *Revolution on Cyprus.*

16. Article 3 of the Treaty of Guarantee would seem, both in the light of its terms and of the circumstances in which it was drafted, to be intended to deal primarily with the situation which might arise if the constitution of Cyprus were overthrown by internal revolution aimed at either limiting minority rights or at union with another State, or at partition. If the guarantors were then to take action of a military character it might, in certain circumstances, be justifiable as self-defence. Those circumstances would arise, if, in the course of a revolution, an armed attack were made on the troops of any one or more of the guarantors stationed on Cyprus. As already pointed out, however, the right of self-defence does not depend on the Treaty of Guarantee, it arises from general international law as confirmed and to some extent limited by Article 51 of the Charter.

17. The legal situation is more complex if the disturbances on Cyprus, while tending to upset the state of affairs created by the Treaty, do not lead to an attack on the troops of any of the guaranteeing Powers. At this particular point paragraphs 3 and 4 of Article 2 of the Charter become the governing legal considerations. Article 53 of the Charter may also be relevant in this respect, and will be briefly examined before Article 2, paragraph 3 and 4.

18. Chapter VIII of the Charter, in which article 53 falls, deals with regional arrangements, Article 53 provides for the utilization of such arrangements for enforcement action by the Security Council. It provides, further that "no enforcement action shall be taken under regional arrangements or by regional agencies without the authorization of the Security Council. . . .", subject to certain exceptions not applicable in the case of Cyprus. It could be argued that the Treaty of Guarantee constitutes a regional arrangement although, in this respect, practice is till uncertain as the U.N. has never formally recognized any

arrangement as a regional arrangement. However, if it were assumed that the Treaty constituted such an arrangement, enforcement action under Article 3 would presumably require the consent of the Council, unless, perhaps, in certain limited instances of individual action by a guarantor it might be open for that guarantor to argue that action was taken pursuant to a right it possessed under general international law, independent of the treaty.

19. It should also be pointed out that enforcement action requiring the consent of the Council, in the sense of Article 53, while clearly covering the use of force, may extend even further to cover measures of the nature outlined in Article 41 of the Charter, such as "complete or partial interruption of economic relations and of rail, sea, air, postal, telegraphic, radio and other means of communication, and the severance of diplomatic relations". If the Treaty of Guarantee constitutes a regional arrangement, therefore, the rights of the guarantors to take enforcement action on their own initiative is probably severely limited. However, no other instance is known where it has been argued that a simple treaty of Guarantee constitutes a regional arrangement, the agencies most commonly referred to in this respect (such as the Organization of American States and the Arab League) being of a far more elaborate nature with permanent organs established for the pacific settlement of disputes.

20. Whether or not Article 53 applies, it is quite clear that paragraphs 3 and 4 of Article 2 of the Charter are relevant in the circumstances discussed in this section. Article 2(3) provides that:

> All Members shall settle their international disputes by peaceful means in such a manner that international peace and security, and justice are not endangered.

Article 2(4) provides:

> All Members shall refrain in their international relations from the threat or use of force against the territorial integrity or political independence of any state, or in any other manner inconsistent with the purposes of the U.N.

21. A great amount of legal discussion has centered around the interpretation of these Articles, particularly within the context of the definition of aggression. A review of all the various opinions of this subject is beyond the scope of the present note. However, a short summary is necessary of both a restrictive and wide interpretation of these two Articles.

22. Quincy Wright is an exponent of perhaps the most popular view. He has defined the concept of aggression, as flowing from Article 2(4), as follows.[7]

> The use of threat to use armed force across an internationally recognized frontier, for which a government, *de facto* or *de jure* is responsible because of act

---

[7] Quincy Wright, "The Prevention of Aggression," 50 *American Journal of International Law* (1956), p. 526 and "U.S. Intervention in Lebanon," 53 *American Journal of International Law* (1959), p. 115.

or negligence, unless justified by a necessity for individual or collective self-defence, by the authority of the U.N. to restore international peace and security, or by consent of the state within whose territory armed force is being used.

If this view is considered the correct one, and if the guarantors were to resort to armed force in Cyprus, the circumstances not involving self-defence or the authority of the U.N., could the Treaty of Guarantee be construed as consent by Cyprus to the use of armed force? The view taken by Quincy Wright would appear to be that consent, in such cases, should be a real consent, given at the time when the intervention takes place and by a government so firmly in control that it can be considered competent to speak for the State in question.[8] According to this construction it would probably be difficult to construe the Treaty of Guarantee as providing a real consent, and Article 3 of the Treaty, to accord with international law today, would have to be interpreted to confer only rights short of the use of armed force in the circumstances contemplated in this paragraph.

23. A less restricted view of the right to resort to the use of armed force is taken by Stone. He states that:[9] "Article 2(4) does *not* forbid 'the threat or use of force' *simpliciter*: it forbids it only when directed 'against the territorial integrity or political independence of any State, or in any other manner inconsistent with the purposes of the U.N.'" By the preceding paragraph 3 of Article 2, Members also undertook to "settle their international disputes by peaceful means in such a manner that international peace and security and justice are not endangered". But the suggestion that this positive injunction of Article 2(3) to settle disputes by peaceful means carried with it so revolutionary a negative implication as the absolute prohibition of the use of force for the vindication of rights, even when no other means exists, is also dubious.

Stone considers that, if the view of Quincy Wright is correct, States might be required to tolerate indefinitely persistent illegalities and injustice by other States.[10] He writes further that:[11]

> Even if the grand design of the U.N. *was* to substitute collective joint enforcement and peaceful change for the traditional role of war as a means (in part at least) of vindicating rights, and effecting adjustments of the *status quo* so as to secure a tolerable level of justice, are we to say that resort to force has been completely outlined, even when no substitute form of relief is available?

---

[8] Quincy Wright, "U.S. Intervention in Lebanon," op. cit., pp. 119-125.

[9] Stone, *Aggression and World Order* (London, 1958), p. 95. For, in the first place, if Article 2(3) really imported such a blanket prohibition of the use of force, why should the draftsmen have felt it necessary to follow it immediately with a very much more limited prohibition, in Article 2(4), of the use of force against the territorial integrity and political independence of any State, etc.? Moreover, in the second place it is not easy to reconcile the blanket prohibition with the words "and justice" in Article 2(3).

[10] Stone, op. cit., pp. 78-99.

[11] Stone, op. cit., pp. 100-101. Stone's views here quoted are given with the intervention in mind of Israel, the U.K. and France in Egypt, in 1956.

It is not believed that such a position makes either moral, political or even legal sense. . . . No international organization based on such principles could long possibly survive in the world as it is. . . . For such an organization could only become a protective shield for those States whose predatory and imperial interests could sufficiently realize themselves without the need for 'armed attack' upon other Members. . . .

If Stone's view is considered correct a resort to armed force by the guarantors, in the circumstances presently under discussion, might be deemed a lawful vindication of rights. However, to meet the requirements of his view, it would appear essential for the guarantors to demonstrate that they had exhausted all the means of pacific settlement available to them, including but not necessarily limited to recourse to the U.N., before a resort to armed force might be legally justified. In any event, it is doubtful whether Stone's view accords with the intentions of the founders of the U.N., or the practice of the Organization in which recourse to armed force by one Member against another has usually met with condemnation. Finally, that view has not received any wide support amongst jurists who appear, for the most part, to incline towards the position as defined by Quincy Wright.

24. Revolution has never been prohibited by international law, and the development of that law has been such that it may now be doubted whether a treaty, such as the Treaty of Guarantee, can legally be interpreted as permitting the use of armed force in circumstances not otherwise sanctioned by the Law. It has, furthermore, already been pointed out that Article 3 of the Treaty does not explicitly refer to the use of armed force, weakening even further any purported right or intervention in the circumstances under discussion. Finally, the International Court of Justice, in the Corfu Channel Case, has declared that:[12]

> The Court can only regard the alleged right of intervention as the manifestation of a policy of force, such as has, in the past, given rise to most serious abuses and such as cannot, whatever the present defects in international organization, find a place in international law.

III. *Conclusions.*

25. On the basis of the foregoing it is submitted that the Treaty of Guarantee will be a valid international instrument when it comes fully into effect. However, in the present state of the development of the international law, Article 3 of that Treaty cannot validly be interpreted as granting the guarantors an unqualified right to intervene by use of armed force in the event of a breach of the provisions of the Treaty. Such use of force is only justifiable on grounds of self-defence, or under the authority of the U.N., or on the invitation of the State of Cyprus at the relevant time. A right of armed intervention does not arise automatically from the terms of the Treaty and even if the extreme view were adopted that such a right did arise it would be limited by the need, first,

---

[12] Corfu Channel Case, Judgement of April 9th, 1949: I.C.J. Reports 1949, p. 4.

for recourse to the means of pacific settlement available to the States concerned.

APPENDIX 22(2)

Opinion by Sir Frank Soskice Requested by Glafkos Clerides, President of the Cyprus House of Representatives, in Relation to the Implementation of Certain Articles of the Cyprus Constitution, 1 November 1963

I will at the end of this Opinion set out in sequence what in my view are the appropriate answers to the questions asked in Mr. Clerides' letter dated October 5th 1963; but before doing so I will make some general observations with regard to the Treaty of Guarantee.

The basic question on which, as I understand it, my opinion is asked is as follows: Serious difficulties have arisen with reference to the implementation of Article 123 and 173 of the Constitution, and also of Article 73 in relation to the imposition of taxes. Article IV of the Treaty of Guarantee provides that each guaranteeing Power in the event of breach of the Treaty, if common or concerted action proves impossible "reserves the right to take action with the sole aim of re-establishing the state of affairs created by the" Treaty. In these circumstances has Turkey the right under Article IV of the Treaty as one of the guaranteeing powers, if Articles 123 and 173 of the Constitution are not in due course implemented, and should concerted action not prove possible, herself to embark upon unilateral military intervention without authority from the Security Council?

International treaties unavoidably in general embody provisions expressed in terms less precise and less exactly formulated than domestic legislation. They are the result in the majority of cases of hard bargaining between representatives of conflicting national interests, and it is in the nature of things in general impossible to achieve complete precision when the intentions of the parties are written into the letter of the treaties. It has therefore been accepted that somewhat greater latitude is permissible in the interpretation of international treaties than of domestic legislation, and the general circumstances in which the treaty was entered into may be taken into consideration, as well as the written word of the treaty, in determining what really were the intentions of the parties. In particular there has been much difference of opinion about the legal effect of the many Treaties of Guarantee which have been entered into over the last century and a half.

Furthermore, international law as a whole is subject to a process of constant evolution, as new international situations present themselves. It is, therefore, unwise to attempt to formulate principles in general terms applicable to hypothetical future situations. The views I express in this Opinion should therefore be regarded as applicable only to the actual situation envisaged in the previous paragraph and the precise question asked in that paragraph with reference to Turkey's right to embark unilaterally upon a course of military intervention, and not to other hypothetical situations that might arise in the future.

The Treaty of Guarantee itself contains as its last paragraph an undertaking by the High Contracting Parties as soon as possible to register it with the

Secretariat of the United Nations Charter. This, in my opinion, as well as the general background against which the Treaty was entered into is an indication that the parties intended the Treaty to be construed as containing only such obligations and conferring only such rights as would not conflict with the obligations and restrictions imposed by the United Nations Charter. Article 103 of the Charter must I think be considered together with the Treaty, and Article 103 provides as follows:

> "In the event of a conflict between the obligations of the members of the United Nations under the present Charter and their obligations under any other international agreement, their obligations under the present Charter shall prevail".

In this context a number of Articles of the Charter of the United Nations would be relevant notably those contained in Chapter VIII under the heading "Regional Arrangements", that is to say, Articles 52 to 54, and also Article 51 which deals with the inherent right of self-defence, as well, of course, as the general Articles in Chapter I setting out the purposes and principles of the United Nations, and those contained in Chapters VI and VII dealing with the pacific settlement of disputes and the general enforcement powers of the Security Council. It is a feature of these Articles that they prohibit the use of force by Member Nations except in the most limited range of circumstances such as actual self-defence, unless with the authority of the Security Council.

In my opinion, in these circumstances, the words in Article IV of the Treaty of Guarantee "each of the three guaranteeing Powers reserves the right to take action" should not be construed in any sense which would involve a conflict with the restrictions imposed by the Articles of the Charter to which I have made reference. I will assume the absence of any 'threat to' or 'breach of the peace' within Article 39 of the Charter such as might bring into operation Articles 43 and 44. These Articles are in any event irrelevant to the present question; since even if a Member Nation used force in pursuance of these Articles, such use of force would not be pursuant to any Treaty, but in fulfilment of the duty to assist the Security Council imposed by these Articles of the Charter itself.

Furthermore, I will assume that no situation has or could, in relation to the basic question put to me, arise such as might bring into operation what are in effect the emergency provisions as to self-defence contained in Article 51 of the Charter of the United Nations.

The words "reserves the right to take action" do not, as I understand them purport to create a new right to take some action which would otherwise, apart from those words, not be permissible. In my opinion, they are more appropriate to keep in being some right to take action which would have existed independently of the Treaty under international law, in case, in the absence of such a saving provisions, the right which a guaranteeing Power would under international law in any event have possessed might be extinguished by the Treaty. A situation is envisaged in Article IV of the Treaty in which a breach of the Treaty has taken place and concerted action by the guaranteeing Powers has proved impossible. The effect of the words, in my opinion, is to preserve in such a situation such powers as each guaranteeing Power might individually have exercised under the general principles of international law even if there had been no Treaty of Guarantee. The question, if this view is correct, then arises whether in the actual circumstances envisaged in what I have above described as the basic question asked by Mr. Clerides any right to embark upon unilateral military intervention would have ensured to Turkey apart from the Treaty. There has for example been a right generally recognised in international law in one nation to use force to rescue or protect its own nationals in the territory of another State if that State treats them contrary to basic international legal principles, for example, by using unlawful violence against them. Article IV of the Treaty however only preserves the right to take action "with the sole aim of re-establishing the state of affairs created by the Treaty".

It is open to question how wide is the scope of the words in Article IV of the Treaty of Guarantee "re-establishing the state of affairs created by the present Treaty". Clearly the "state of affairs" includes the independence, territorial integrity and security of the Republic of Cyprus. It may be asked, however, whether it includes the fulfilment of such Articles of the Constitution as Articles 123 am 173, both of which are under Article 182 declared (in the case of Article 173 subject to some limitations) to be Basic Articles. Article II of the Treaty includes within those things that the Treaty guarantees "the state of affairs established by the Basic Articles of its Constitution". It seems to me necessary to read the words "the state of affairs created by the present Treaty" in Article IV of the Treaty as including, besides the independence, territorial integrity and security of the Republic of Cyprus, also "the state of affairs established by the Basic Articles of the Treaty" referred to in Article II. On the other hand I do not think the words in Article IV "re-establishing the state of affairs" read with the words in Article II "established by the Basic Articles" are equivalent to words such as "secure exact compliance with the requirements of the Basic Articles". They are in my view quite inappropriate for that purpose. The expression "the state of affairs" is I think a general phrase, descriptive of a broad situation and in my view in its application to Articles 123 and 173 of the Constitution could only permit of action under Article IV of the Treaty if the substance of the protection for the Turkish minority created by Articles 123 and 173 were (unless by general agreement) overset or removed. What constitutes the "substance" of this protection must involve a question of degree and cannot I think be further defined. In order to answer what I have called the basic question put to me the words in Article IV of the Treaty of Guarantee "with the sole aim of re-establishing the state of affairs created by the present treaty" in effect have to be read as if they were "with the sole aim of re-establishing the substance of the position created by Articles 123 and 173 of the Constitution".

Apart from the right to use force which I have just mentioned I do not know of any other right relevant in this context of forceful intervention independently of treaty. It is not easy to conceive of a practical situation in which the right of a guaranteeing power to use force to rescue its own nationals from unlawful treatment could be in a real sense relevant to the "sole aim" of preserving the state of things set up by the two relevant Basic Articles of the

Constitution; and in my opinion this right to use force in the very limited circumstances I have described can be disregarded.

But in my view, in any case, even if the words in question could be construed as creating a right unilaterally to use force, (and as stated I think they are not appropriate for this purpose) if the Treaty of Guarantee is a "regional arrangement" falling within the scope of Article 52 of the Charter of the United Nations, it is in my view impossible to disregard Article 53 of the Charter which requires that any forceful intervention can only take place with the authority of the Security Council.

The question thus arises whether the Treaty of Guarantee whether considered separately or as forming part of a wider arrangement brought into being by the Treaty of Guarantee read together with the Treaty of Establishment and the Treaty of Alliance should be regarded as such a "regional arrangement". The answer to this question, in my opinion, depends on the nature and content of these Treaties and in particular the Treaty of Guarantee, the history of events which preceded their making, and the circumstances in which they are made. So considered, in my opinion, there is no reason why the Treaty of Guarantee should not be regarded as constituting or, forming part of a "regional arrangement". It followed after and was clearly designed to put an end to the unhappy events which had taken place in Cyprus and to reconcile and put an end to sharp conflicts of opinion both inside and outside Cyprus, which if unresolved could have led to situations of increasing danger. In order that it may fall within the description of a "regional arrangement" within paragraph 1 of Article 52 or the Charter, it must be an arrangement "for dealing with such matters relating to the maintenance or international peace and security as an appropriate for regional action provided that such arrangements . . . and their activities are consistent with the Purposes and Principles of the United Nations". It seems to me that the Treaty does comply with these requirements. It recognizes and is designed to perpetuate a state of affairs relating to Cyprus which had emerged as the agreed solution to differences negotiated after prolonged periods of acute tension and disturbance; and its obvious objective is to re-introduce and maintain stability and peaceful relationships in Cyprus itself and generally in that part of the Mediterranean area. It enjoins consultation in the event of a breach of the Treaty and records the desire of the High Contracting Parties to co-operate. These features seem to me to bear in every sense the hall-mark of such a regional arrangement as is contemplated in Article 52 of the Charter.

For the reasons I have given, in my opinion, the words in question in Article IV of the Treaty of Guarantee, even if they could be said in any relevant circumstances to permit of unilateral military intervention, would not, in the circumstances which have arisen, allow of such action by Turkey unless authorised by the Security Council.

It is to be observed that the rights to take action conferred by Article IV are in another sense limited. Such as they are they only arise if there has been a breach of the Treaty. If Turkey should claim the right to resort to such unilateral action as the Security Council may authorise she must in my opinion be able to demonstrate that she has made genuine and reasonable endeavours to deal with the situation by concerted action with the other High Contracting

Parties. She could not in my view lawfully maintain that a situation had arisen in which the Security Council might authorise unilateral action unless she had genuinely sought to bring the other guaranteeing Powers into consultation with a view to concerted action, and not even then if she had put forward only arbitrary or unreasonable proposals from which she refused to depart despite representations made in the course of such consultations by the other Powers.

Mr. Clerides in his letter dated September 14th 1963 asks whether, in my opinion, the terms of the Treaty of Alliance can be said in any sense to modify the Treaty of Guarantee or to assist in the interpretation of the words "take action" in Article IV of the Treaty of Guarantee. I do not think they do and they do not in my opinion, require a meaning to be attributed to those words different from that which earlier in this opinion I have said I think is the right meaning. The Treaty of Alliance itself has to be registered under Article 102 of the Charter of the United Nations, and must and can, I think be read as requiring and authorising only such action as is permissible in accordance with the Articles of the Charter of the United Nations to which I have earlier made reference, in particular Articles 51 and 53.

Mr. Clerides in his letter of September 14th 1963 asks whether upon the principle "conventio omnis intelligitur rebus sic stantibus" it could be successfully argued that circumstances have arisen which would justify Turkey in withdrawing from the Treaty of Guarantee unilaterally without the consent of the other Powers and would discharge her from any duty of further compliance with the Treaty. As is well-known there is the most acute difference of opinion amongst international jurists, in the first place, whether such a doctrine exists at all as part of international law, and secondly, if it does exist as to what is its scope. Those writers who propound the doctrine, however, do not, as I understand, envisage that it would justify unilateral repudiation of a treaty obligation by one party to it except upon the happening of some change in the circumstances which was basic to the situation in the light of which the treaty obligations were negotiated and undertaken. In the case of the Treaty of Guarantee it could not be argued that any such change has in present circumstances supervened, relevant to any provision of the Treaty, other than that relating to the maintenance of "the state of affairs established" by the Basic Articles of the Constitution in Article IV. There could be no question, therefore, of the repudiation of any provision of the Treaty than this provision. In my opinion, however, the serious difficulties that have arisen in the implementation of Articles 123 and 173 of the Constitution could not be regarded as constituting such a vital change of circumstance as would justify repudiation of the provision. The differences between the Greek and Turkish authorities in Cyprus though no doubt intractable and difficult of solution do not in my opinion represent a new element which can be fairly said to invalidate the basic assumptions upon which this provision of the Treaty was negotiated. On the contrary in my opinion they are difficulties inherent in the nature of the Constitution and the Treaty obligations themselves. I do not myself think that, at any rate so far, anything has taken place which would justify repudiation in terms of the doctrine "rebus sic stantibus" as that doctrine is propounded by those who assert that it is an established principle in the field of treaty interpretation. It is not easy to answer the further question asked by Mr. Clerides in his letter, what, within the sphere of practical possibility, might constitute such a new super-vening circumstance as might justify unilateral repudiation. Conceivably, as an example, the appearance and growth through immigration or otherwise of some other minority group which could not be assimilated either into the Greek or Turkish community and made wholly unreal1istic the existing balance of numbers of the population, might constitute such a supervening change; but this is no more than purely hypothetical and in the highest degree unlikely as a practical example.

In view of the considerations above indicated I will set out by way of summary the questions which I understand to be asked and the answers which I think should be given, as follows:

1. Does the Treaty of Guarantee give the right to intervene in the event of amendment of Articles 123 and 173 of the Constitution? Yes, if the amendments are made without general agreement; but only if the amendments in substance disturb the protection afforded to the Turkish minority. Failure literally to comply with these Articles would not give such a right.
2. Does the Treaty of Guarantee, considered alone, or read with the other Treaties, constitute or form part of such a regional arrangement as is envisaged in Article 52 of the Charter of the United Nations? Yes.
3. Do the words "take action" contained in Article IV of the Treaty of Guarantee in the circumstances which have arisen entitle Turkey to embark upon unilateral military intervention without the authorisation of the Security Council? No, and the Security Council could not authorise such intervention unless Turkey could demonstrate that she had made genuine endeavours to secure concerted action with the other Guaranteeing Parties to the Treaty.
4. Do the difficulties which have arisen in connection with implementation of the provisions in the Constitution which give protection to the Turkish minority and notably Articles 123 and 173, entitle Turkey under the "rebus sic stantibus" principle to withdraw from the Treaty unilaterally and repudiate the obligations it imposes? No.

(Signed) Frank Soskice

November 1st 1963
1 Harcourt Buildings,
TEMPLE E.C.4

APPENDIX 22(3)

Opinion by E. Lauterpacht Requested by the Government of Cyprus on the Treaty of Guarantee, 30 January 1964

THE GOVERNMENT OF CYPRUS

NOTE

I have thought it best in present conditions not to attempt a formal Opinion on the various problems of international law which arise. Instead I have set down in the attached document some notes and ideas on the principal questions of law which have been raised at the meetings which I have attended during the past week.

(Signed) E. LAUTERPACHT
January 30, 1964.

I. TREATY OF GUARANTEE

A. *Contents*
1. *Obligations of Cyprus.*
    1. The obligations of Cyprus are clearly set out in Art. I of the Treaty. For present purposes it is necessary only to note:
    (A) That the Republic undertakes to ensure, inter alia, its territorial integrity. This means that it is both bound and entitled (i) to resist partition and (ii) to resist invasion, even from a guarantor.
    (B) That the Republic undertakes to ensure, inter alia, "respect for its Constitution". Prima facie, this must mean that the Republic is bound to observe the terms of its Constitution and, in particular, to change it only in accordance with the procedures for amendment therein contained. However, it is strongly arguable that "respect for the Constitution" should not be read as requiring the Republic to adhere to the letter of an instrument which experience has shown to be unworkable; and that, in consequence, the spirit of the requirement of respect for the Constitution may require the Republic to take even extra-constitutional steps for the purpose of maintaining the government of the island.
2. *Obligations of the United Kingdom.*
    2. The U.K., as one of the three guarantor powers, is bound by Art. II to recognise and guarantee the independence, territorial integrity and security of the Republic. If the guarantee means anything, it must mean that the U.K. is bound, should the island be attacked, to come to the defence of the Republic. The Guarantee Treaty may, in this respect, be likened to a treaty of

collective self-defence concluded under Article 51 of the Charter, though one in which the obligation to render assistance moves in one direction only.

3. The obligation to render assistance to the Republic is, in the first instance, one which is to be borne collectively by the three guarantors, but the possibility that they may not agree is expressly contemplated in Art. IV of the Agreement. Accordingly, there can be no warrant for saying either that one of them cannot act without the other two or that one of them cannot act if the threat to the Republic comes from another of the guarantors. As is clear from the content of the Treaty as well as from the historical background to it, the external threats to the Island could be expected to come only from Turkey or Greece; and the instrument would have been quite pointless if the guarantee were not intended to allow two guarantors to react to a breach of the Treaty by a third.

3. *Absence of any Turkish right to use force under the Treaty.*

4. The suggestion has been made that Turkey is entitled, by reason of Art. IV of the Treaty, to use force in the exercise of her right to preserve the Cyprus settlement. The following arguments may be used in refuting this suggestion.

A. *The exercise of the right of guarantee is dependent UPON BREACH OF THE Treaty.*

5. The right of the guarantors to act, whether collectively or individually, is conditional upon the occurrence of a breach of the provisions of the Treaty. (See the first line of Art. IV: "In the event of breach of the provisions of the present Treaty . . ."). Therefore, even assuming that the guarantors individually possessed a right to use force under the Treaty by unilateral decision (which they do not—see (b) below), there would be no justification for doing so in the present case.

(i) There has been no breach of the Treaty by Cyprus.

6. Presumably the only breach of the Treaty on which Turkey would rely would be an allegation that the Republic is not respecting its constitution (unless there is some suggestion that the idea of *enosis* is being revived). However, there is no evidence yet of any failure by the Republic of Cyprus to respect its constitution. In international terms the Republic of Cyprus is represented by its Government, which consists of both Greek and Turkish Cypriot elements. To the extent that any action has been taken without the concurrence of the Turkish Cypriot element, this is not because the latter element has been excluded from the Government but because it has withdrawn from it and adopted an attitude of non-cooperation. But the Government as such has not done anything which is unconstitutional. In due course, perhaps, it may become necessary for the Government of Cyprus to seek amendment of the Constitution and it may be necessary to do this other than is strict accord with the terms of the present Constitution. But if this step is taken, it will be because it has been forced upon the Government by the failure of the Turkish Cypriot communities to cooperate in the implementation of the 1960 Constitution.

(ii) Turkey is in breach of the Treaty.

7. In any event, Turkey is itself in breach of the Treaty and these breaches have themselves constituted to the present difficulties in the Island.

Accordingly, Turkey in not entitled to invoke an alleged breach by the Republic as a ground for its own intervention.

8. Turkey has violated the Treaty in at least three respects:

9. (a) She has threatened the territorial integrity and political independence of the Republic by action which has become increasingly menacing during the past few weeks: massing of forces on the Turkish coast and movements of naval forces in adjoining waters.

10. (b) She has violated the territorial integrity of the Republic by using the troops which she is permitted to station in the Island under the Treaty of Alliance for purposes not connected with the implementation of that Treaty. It should be noted that under the Treaty of Guarantee Turkey has no right to station troops in the territory of the Republic; and the presence there of a contingent under the Treaty of Alliance gives Turkey no right to intervene with those troops—as it has in recent weeks—in the internal administration of the country.

11. (c) She has violated her undertaking to prohibit activity aimed at promoting partition of the Island by permitting and encouraging pursuit of this policy both in Turkey and among the Turkish Cypriots.

Conclusion on A.

12. In all those circumstances, the condition precedent for even the assertion by Turkey of a right of action under Article IV of the Treaty has not been satisfied.

B. *Turkey has no right to intervene by force.*

13. In any event, even assuming that a state of affairs has developed which might be regarded as constituting a breach of the Treaty, there is still nothing in the Treaty which warrants a forcible intervention by Turkey.

14. (i) It is true that the second paragraph of Art. IV of the Treaty provides that

> "In so far as common or concerted action may not prove possible, each of the three guaranteeing Powers reserves the right to take action with the sole aim of re-establishing the state of affairs created by the present Treaty".

But this paragraph (indeed, the Article and the Treaty as a whole) must be read subject to the provisions of Articles 3(4) and 103 of the Charter of the U.N. The latter provides that in the event of a conflict between the obligations of the Members of the U.N. under the present Charter and their obligations under any other international agreement, their obligations under the Charter shall prevail. The former prohibits the use or threat of force against the territorial integrity or political independence of a member. If, Art. IV of the Treaty implies the use of force, clearly it cannot stand with Art. 2(4) of the Charter; and by reason of Art. 103 of the Charter the latter must prevail.

15. Nor is it possible to construe Art. IV of the Treaty as a contractual exception to Art. 2(4) of the Charter. There is no room in the pattern of Charter prohibition of the use of force for treaty exceptions which can be invoked against a State without its consent in each specific case.

16. The only exception to this—which itself forms a necessary part of the pattern—lies in the provisions of Chapter VII of the Charter (particularly, Art. 42) which can be regarded as an advance contractual acceptance by members of the U.N. of the possibility of the use of force against themselves. There is, however, a fundamental difference between this licence to use force in Chapter VII of the Charter and the terms of Art. IV(2) of the Treaty—a difference which excludes the argument that if members of the U.N. can contract into the use of force under the Charter they ought equally to be able to do so in the Treaty of Guarantee. The terms of Chapter VII of the Charter are a necessary concomitant of the prohibities of the use of force in Article 2(4).

17. The Charter contains in this respect two fundamental ideas: the first is that the use of force is in general prohibited; but the second is that if the general prohibition is to make sense and be effective there must exist in reserve to be used under the authority of an appropriate organ of the international community a power to use force against an aggressor. This is a very different matter to a group of States combining to form a system which permits one or more of them, uncontrolled by the Security Council, to use force against another. Indeed, it is significant that in that part of the Charter dealing with regional organisations recourse to enforcement measures is specifically made subject to Security Council authorization. (See Article 53(1) of the Charter.)

18. (ii) A second consideration excluding the use of force by Turkey is that the unilateral measures which a guarantor Power is permitted to take under Art. IV(2) of the Treaty are expressly limited to action taken "with the *sole* aim of re-establishing the state of affairs created by the present Treaty". As regards this, two things may be said:

    (a) That the unilateral use of force by Turkey (or, indeed, any other power) cannot by itself re-establish the state of affairs created by the present Treaty; and since this is so obvious, there can be no merit in the pretence that the use of force has such re-establishment as its aim.

    (b) That, in any event, the re-establishment of the state of affairs created by the Treaty is not the aim of Turkey. There have been repeated public declarations by that State since 1960 to the effect that partition is the appropriate solution of the Cyprus problem; and there is evidence that that is the solution which the Turkish Government is now actively seeking.

19. (iii) A third consideration militating against the unilateral use of force by Turkey lies in the terms of Art. 53 of the Charter. This provides in part that "...no enforcement action shall be taken under regional arrangements or by regional agencies without the authorization of the Security Council..." Although the character of the Treaty of Guarantee as a "regional arrangement or agency" may not be obvious to the reader, the fact is that the Treaty appears to have been so classified by the United Kingdom. This appears from the terms of the Report of January 9, 1964 addressed by the Acting U.K. representative to the U.N. to the President of the Security Council, which refers in 2 to the efforts of the Governments of the U.K., Greece and Turkey to resolve the situation in accordance with Arts. 33 and 52 of the Charter. Art. 52 fails under Charter VIII of the Charter which is headed "Regional Arrangements" and Art. 52(1) itself provides as follows:

"Nothing in the present Charter precludes the existence of regional arrangements or agencies for dealing with such matters relating to the maintenance of international peace and security as are appropriate for regional action, provided that such arrangements or agencies and their activities are consistent with the Purposes and Principles of the Charter."

20. Clearly, the U.K. would not have referred to this Article if it had not regarded the Treaty of Guarantee as falling within its terms; and that thought could be based only on a classification of the Treaty arrangements as constituting a regional arrangement or agency. The position was re-stated by the Prime Minister in the House of Commons on January 14, 1964. (See *H.C. Deb:* Vol. 687, cols. 34 and 35). There does not appear to have been any dissent from this position by either the Greek or Turkish Governments.

B. *Duration.*

21. Is the Treaty of Guarantee still a valid and subsisting treaty?

22. The Treaty contains no duration or denunciation clause. In those circumstances its duration and the right of say party to withdraw from it must be deduced from the other terms of the Treaty and on the basis of what the intention of the parties may be presumed to have been. This is really largely a matter of deciding whether the parties had it in mind that the treaty should be of a permanent character or otherwise be not unilaterally terminable. There is little authority which is helpful, though the problem has been the subject of considerable academic discussion. For practical purposes, it would probably be most convenient to accept the statement of the rule as formulated by the International Law Commission at its 15th Session in 1963:

"A treaty which contains no provision regarding its termination and which does not provide for denunciation or withdrawal is not subject to denunciation or withdrawal unless it appears from the character of the treaty and from the circumstances of its conclusion or the statements of the parties that the parties intended to admit the possibility of denunciation or withdrawal. In the latter case a party may denounce or withdraw from the Treaty upon giving to the other parties or to the Depository not less than twelve months notice to that effect." (U.N. Doc. A/CN.3/163, p. 38).

23. On the whole, I would be inclined to think that a treaty of guarantee such as the one under consideration is not unilaterally terminable. In the absence of clear evidence to the contrary which could only be gathered, if at all, from the records of the discussions leading up to the Treaty, my view would be that the Treaty of Guarantee was intended to establish and preserve a state of affairs free of denunciation at will by any one party. Otherwise, there would have been little sense in the Treaty. Substantial confirmation for this view is, I believe, to be drawn from the fact that Article 21 of the Zurich Agreement provided that both the Treaties of Guarantee and of Alliance were to have constitutional force. Article 181 of the Constitution gives effect to this and is listed as a Basic Article which, under Article 182, cannot be amended.

24. However, this is not to say that the Government of Cyprus cannot advance arguments in favour of the contention that even though the Treaty

may not be denouncable at will it should, in all the circumstances, now be regarded as at an end; and the following appear to me to be three such arguments:

25. (i) The Treaty suffers from two fundamental defects which, in theory, affected its initial binding character, but of which the full force has not been revealed until the present crisis, so that it has not been possible until now to appreciate the destructive effect which they have upon the instrument:

26. (a) The treaty is effectively a fetter upon the independence of Cyprus. It is unique in current practice. Although Cyprus is recognised as an independent sovereign state, it is unable to modify its constitution without the consent of three other States. The effect of this is to thwart the will of the majority (82%) of the population. In itself, this feature may be said not to distinguish the position of Cyprus from that of other countries who have accepted by treaty heavy limitations upon their freedom of action. There are, however, two features which distinguish the Cyprus situation from these others. First, these limitations were imposed upon Cyprus at the time, and as a condition, of her independence. Accordingly, they are not obligations freely entered into or accepted. Secondly, unlike other treaties, the Treaty of Guarantee give the guarantor powers a right of intervention in the Island which at least one guarantor power goes so far as to regard and treat as a right of forcible intervention. All this is quite inconsistent with the position of Cyprus as a fully independent and sovereign State. While the position was acceptable, because the difficulties involved in it were not fully appreciated, so long as the Constitution worked well, now that internal and international tensions have developed, it is manifest that the Treaty must be regarded as of no further legal value.

27. (ii) Closely associated with the above argument is one to the effect that the circumstances surrounding the conclusion of the Treaty, and in which it was based, have changed. The effect of such changes of circumstance has been formulated by the International Law Commission in Article 44 of its Draft Articles on the Law of Treaties as follows:

" . . .

2. Where a fundamental change has occurred with regard to a fact or situation existing at the time when the treaty was entered into, it may be invoked as a ground for terminating or withdrawing from the treaty if:

(a) the existence of that fact or situation constituted an essential basis of the consent of the parties to the treaty; and

(b) the effect of the change is to transform in an essential respect the character of the obligations undertaken in the treaty ..."

28. The following are the relevant circumstances:

(1) The ability of the two communities in Cyprus to live and work together. Events have shown that the Turkish Cypriot communities will not and cannot cooperate.

(2) The willingness of the Government of Turkey to refrain from provocative and inflammatory action. As already stated, there is evidence of Turkish activity favouring partition of the island.

(3) The willingness and ability of the United Kingdom to implement its undertakings to protect the island from external attack. The Secre-

tary of State for Commonwealth Relations has stated orally that the U.K. will not fight another N.A.T.O. member. Moreover, as recent events have shown, the U.K. has been obliged to seek military assistance from other States, not parties to the Cyprus settlement. This is a development that was not at all contemplated in 1959/60.

29. (iii) Thirdly, Turkey, by using her forces stationed is Cyprus, other than in the manner permitted by the Treaty of Alliance and the agreement for application, has violated its undertakings under the Treaty of Guarantee. This and other Turkish violations of the Treaty, coupled with the special circumstance that Turkey is a guarantor of the Treaty, constitute breaches of the Treaty so material and essential that Cyprus is entitled to treat them as amounting to a repudiation of the Treaty. (See Article 42 of the Draft Articles on the Law of Treaties adopted by the International Law Commission at its 15th Session, 1963.

"1. ...

2. A material breach of a multilateral treaty by one of the parties entitles:

(a) any other party to invoke the breach as a ground for suspending the operation of the treaty in whole or in part in the relations between itself and the defaulting State; ...

3. .... a material breach ... consists in:

(a) ...

(b) the violation of a provision which is essential to the effective execution of any of the objects or purposes of the treaty.
    ...")

III. The TREATY OF ALLIANCE

A. *Content*

30. No comment need be made on Articles I and II.

31. Reference may be made to Articles III and IV to emphasize that it is in virtue of these Articles, and of them alone, that Turkish forces are present in Cyprus. Accordingly, these forces may only be used under and in accordance with this Treaty and the Special Convention (appearance of application) made thereunder. The terms of Arts. II and IV of the Application Agreement emphasize the limited role of the Greek and Turkish contingents by stating that the forces are in Cyprus for common defence purposes; subjecting the forces to the directions of the Committee of Ministers; and excluding, in effect, any unilateral increase in forces.

B. *Duration*

32. The Treaty contains no duration or denunciation clause. Much the same considerations as have been set out in relation to the duration of the Treaty of Guarantee apply to this Treaty, particularly the point about the incorporation of the Treaties into the Constitution of the Republic. This would seem to be a consideration weighing heavily against the assertion of the right, quite frequently asserted, that treaties of alliance may be denounced. However, in case it should be desired to make the point that the Treaty of Alliance

can be denounced, it may be pertinent to refer to Article 17 of the Second Report on the Law of Treaties prepared by Sir Humphrey Waldock for the International Law Commission (A/CH.4/156/Add. 1, April 10, 1963) where he formulates the following rule:

> " . . .
>
> 3. (a) . . . a party shall have the right to denounce or withdraw from a treaty by giving twelve months' notice to that effect . . . to the other parties, when the treaty is—
>
> (i) . . .
>
> (ii) a treaty of alliance or of military cooperation . . ."

IV. Recourse to THE UNITED NATIONS.

33. (i) Recourse to the U.N. must in the first place be to the Security Council. The General Assembly is not now sitting and could only be called back into session under the Uniting for Peace Resolution. The basis for the application of this resolution would only exist in the event of the application of the veto in the Security Council.

34. (ii) The Security Council undoubtedly has competence to consider the matter, whether it is brought to its attention by Cyprus, any other State, or even by the Secretary-General in the exercise of his powers under Art. 99. It does not appear to matter whether the question is referred to the Security Council initially under Articles 34, 35 or 37 of the Charter.

35. (iii) The following are some of the possibilities open to the Security Council in the present situation:

36. (1) Simply to hear the parties and take no further action;

37. (2) Investigate the matter, whether by way of commission of inquiry or of special representative;

38. (3) Actively to assist in the negotiation of a settlement by processes of mediation or conciliation carried out by a commission or an individual;

39. (4) Indicate provisional measures. If the Council were to consider that the situation amounted to a threat to the peace, a breach of the peace or an act of aggression, it could indicate provisional measures under Art. 40. This provides as follows:

> "In order to prevent the aggravation of the situation, the Security Council may, before making the recommendations or deciding upon the measures provided for in Art. 39, call upon the parties concerned to comply with such provisional measures as it deems necessary or desirable. Such provisional measures shall be without prejudice to the rights, claims, or position of the parties concerned. The Security Council shall duly take account of failure to comply with such provisional measures."

The fact that such provisional measures are *without prejudice* may perhaps make them particularly helpful in the present situation.

40. (5) Authorise the establishment of a U.N. force. It would not be necessary, or indeed in accordance with established practice, for the Security Council to indicate the particular articles of the Charter under which it is acting. Accordingly, there would be no need for the Council first to determine,

under Art. 39, the existence of a threat to the peace, a breach of the peace or an act of aggression.

41. The following are the principal matters which the Council would have to consider in connection with the establishment of a U.N. force:

(a) *Mandate*

42. The Council would have to lay down the basis or objective of the Force's action. In the case of the Congo operation the mandate was laid down in the following terms:

> "(a) To maintain the territorial integrity and political independence of the Republic of the Congo;
> (b) To assist the Central Government of the Congo in the restoration and maintenance of law and order;
> (c) To prevent the occurrence of civil war in the Congo;
> (d) To secure the immediate withdrawal and evacuation from the Congo of all foreign military, para-military and advisory personnel not under the U.N. command, and all mercenaries." (Nov. 24, 1961, S/3002).

This was amended from time to time in the light of developments, but it may serve as a helpful precedent in the present situation. No time limit was laid down for the operation.

(b) *Finance and composition*

43. These two matters are in the present situation very closely connected. In its present financial situation, the U.N. cannot assume the responsibility, as it has in the Congo, for the cost of an adequate force. Accordingly, it must either decline to send anything but a token force or it must rely on forces which will not require payment. In this connection it should be born in mind that in the Congo operation two principles were followed: (i) that the U.N. retained sole competence with respect to decisions concerning the composition of the military units sent to the Congo, though giving consideration to the opinion of the Government there as one of the most important factors to be borne in mind in connexion with recruitment; and (ii) that contributions of forces from the permanent members of the Security Council were excluded.

44. Subject to political factors, there would not appear to be any reason in law why the Security Council should not accept an offer from a number of States individually or from a group of States to provide a force for Cyprus at the cost of these States. Clearly, however, the Security Council would have to retain the ultimate control of the operation.

V. RELEVANCE OF CONSTITUTIONAL LIMITATIONS UPON THE FREEDOM OF ACTION OF THE CYPRUS GOVERNMENT

45. The Turkish Government has already shown its awareness of the difficulties arising from the grant of a right of veto to the Vice-President in certain circumstances. The relevant Articles of the Constitution, as I understand them, are as follows:

Art. 46 confers executive power on the Council of Ministers. Decisions to be taken by an absolute majority.

Art. 49 confers on the Vice-President a right of final veto on decisions of the Council of Ministers concerning foreign affairs, as in Art. 57 provided.

Art. 57 (3) provides that the veto shall be exercised within four days of the date when the decision is transmitted to the office of Vice-President. This paragraph also contains a reference to the definition of "foreign affairs" set out in Art. 50.

Art. 50 (1) (a) contains a list of matters falling under the head of "foreign affairs", which includes the conclusion of treaties.

46. There are three ways of approaching these difficulties in the U.N.

(a) The first is to say that this is not a matter which can affect the credentials of Mr. Rossides.

(b) The second is to assert that the U.N. has not shown itself concerned in earlier cases with the constitutional powers of those who appeared before it.

(c) The other is to meet the argument on its merits and suggest that the constitutional limitation is not so wide as the Turkish Government may suggest and is, therefore, not relevant.

47. (a) Mr. Rossides already possesses credentials in respect of the placing of the Cyprus matter before the Security Council. In any case, if the Foreign Minister of Cyprus were to attend, he would not need to present credentials.

48. (b) The question of constitutional powers arose in the Congo case, though not in the same manner as here. Although there was some disposition by a number of States to examine the *Loi Fondementale* of the Congo, there was much support for the view that the *Loi* was irrelevant. (See A/4576 and the discussion in the General Assembly, 917th–924th meetings.) The fact that the credentials were issued by persons who are the undoubted Head of State or Foreign Secretary will also carry weight.

49. (c) Possibly it may be argued as a matter of substantive constitutional law that, if regard is had to Art. 50 of the Constitution, the power of veto does not extend to the reference of matters to the U.N. As indicated in para. 45 above, the definition of "foreign affairs" is, by Art. 57(3) stated to be that set out in Art. 50. The introductory part of the definition of "foreign affairs" in Art. 50(1) reads as follows:

". . . (a) foreign affairs, except the participation of the Republic in international organisations and parts of alliance in which the Kingdom of Greece and the Republic of Turkey both participate".

"Participation" can mean two things: either the original act of joining or subsequent participation in the activities of the organisation. If it means the former only, then the argument cannot be advanced. But if it can be said to cover both meanings, or the latter only, then it can be contended that the reference of a matter to the U.N. (in which both Greece and Turkey participate) is an item falling within the exception and is, therefore, outside the veto.

50. There are certain evident counter-arguments to the above, but they need not be weighed here. The suggestion made above, unless there is some

special political or legal reason for rejecting it, would seem to make a prima facie case for the constitutionality of what is being proposed; and if it is advanced by the representative of Cyprus it is unlikely to be strongly opposed.

APPENDIX 23

Conference on Cyprus: Final Statements at the Closing Plenary Session at Lancaster House on February 19, 1959*

I

STATEMENT BY THE PRIME MINISTER OF THE UNITED KINGDOM

This is the full Conference representing the three countries concerned and the representatives of the Cypriot people.

It had been our intention that this should be the final Conference, attended by the Prime Ministers of Greece, Turkey and the United Kingdom. But for reasons which you, alas, know so well, it is not possible for our friend, Mr. Menderes, the Prime Minister of Turkey, to be with us to-day.

We rejoice at his almost miraculous survival and we mourn with him and his compatriots the loss of so many of their comrades.

This is a memorable occasion. The Eastern Mediterranean has always been a region of decisive importance. There lies the key to so many vital areas in the world. You, our Greek, and you, our Turkish friends, live there; but the problems of the region are of scarcely less vital concern to us in this country than they are to you. Over the years Britain, Greece and Turkey have stood in varying relationships to one another. Usually we have been friends, sometimes we have been divided. Yet over the last generation there has been a growing realisation among our Governments, and I am happy to say among our people, that unless we stand together our most cherished ideals and our deepest interests will be overwhelmed in a common catastrophe. We knew this, and yet one source of discord still remained between us—the problem that we hope is happily settled to-day, the problem of Cyprus.

It has always been clear to me, and more particularly since the Tripartite Conference in this very room in 1955, that Cyprus was a problem which could only be resolved by agreement between our three countries, as well as with Cyprus itself. After all, it is the Cypriots who live in Cyprus. For their happiness and progress we are all responsible. That is why I rejoice, if I may say so humbly, at the courage and imagination which has inspired their leaders to-day. I feel sure that they will have their reward.

Nearly four years have passed since the Tripartite Conference; much blood—British, Greek and Turkish—has been shed. Strong passions have been roused. This should not surprise us, for we are all proud and ancient nations, tenacious in defence of our ideals and tough in defence of our interests. Yet I think it is true to say that even in the hours of the greatest bitterness we always knew in our hearts that one day there would have to be a settlement, which each of us could accept as consonant with our honour and

---

* Cmnd. 680, Misc. No. 5 (London: HMSO, 1959).

our continuing friendship. That settlement has now come. To reach it, each of us, all of us in this room, have had to make concessions, and I am sure that it was right for us to make these mutual concessions.

This settlement is one which recognises the right of the people of Cyprus to an independent status in the world. It is one which recognises the Hellenic character of the majority of the Cypriot people. But it is also one which protects the national character and culture of the Cypriot Turkish community. It is one which preserves to the United Kingdom the defence facilities which are essential not only for our narrow national purposes but for the greater alliances of which we are members.

In the course of our discussion the Greek and Turkish Foreign Ministers have made it clear that they for their part would not object to Cyprus remaining in some form of association with the Commonwealth, though of course, the people of Cyprus themselves will need to be given an opportunity of expressing their views when they have the constitutional means of doing so. It is also a question which must concern other Commonwealth Governments. If in due course the Government of Cyprus declare that they desire to remain associated with the Commonwealth, then the United Kingdom Government, in consultation with other members of the Commonwealth, will certainly be ready to consider sympathetically how that desire can most appropriately be satisfied.

Gentlemen, the task now before us is to put into effect the agreements which we have reached and signed to-day. For this purpose of course we all know much detailed work will be necessary. There will be a lot to be done, but it will be approached from the firm line of our agreement, and in this spirit the work will surely be fruitful.

I would only like to add this: I myself have always believed that when the future of the world is so uncertain and fraught with so many dangers, we cannot hope to win through except in a spirit of partnership between people and nations of what I call interdependence. This agreement has been made in that spirit, and it is therefore an expression at once of our hope and of our faith.

II

STATEMENT BY THE PRIME MINISTER OF GREECE

Mr. Prime Minister, thank you very much for the kind words which you have just spoken. I would like first to express my sincere regrets for the absence of my friend, Mr. Menderes, and my most cordial wishes for a very swift recovery. It is with gratitude that we have met here at this Conference called by you and we have been very appreciative of the hospitality you have extended to us.

I share your happiness at the successful issue of our combined efforts both in Zurich and here in London.

In the present moment we have to rejoice as godfathers at the birth of a new State, the Republic of Cyprus. I am especially moved at the occasion because, in our present times in which such a tremendous struggle is being waged against the powers of oppression, we of the free world have given a tangible example of what the spirit of co-operation between free peoples can achieve. It is my deep conviction that the solution we have reached meets in the best possible way the aspirations of the whole population of Cyprus, which is now attaining freedom and can, I am sure, look forward to great prosperity.

From the very outset of these negotiations our main preoccupation was that there should be no victor in them, except the people of Cyprus themselves. I am certain we have achieved this. It is the best solution because its main foundation is co-operation between Greeks and Turks, both in the Island, and in our two countries. And it is the best solution because it leaves to the Island's majority the rights enabling it to develop in the most appropriate manner all aspects of its life, while it secures to the minority a splendid opportunity for maintaining its character and institutions, as well as for enjoying their generous share of common authority and responsibilities.

This is why I express my confidence in the future of Cyprus. As you yourself rightly pointed out, Mr. Chairman, it is up to the Cypriots to decide about their future association with the Commonwealth. Greece takes no stand on that matter.

Your Beatitude, you, the leader of our Greek-Cypriot brethren, you are taking on your shoulders the heavy, but exalting responsibility of leading the people of Cyprus towards happiness, prosperity and well-being, in exemplary unity.

Dr. Kutchuk, you also will be bearing responsibilities which I am sure you will face successfully with the collaboration of your worthy advisers. This is the beginning of a new chapter in the history of Cyprus. I am sure that you also will wish to help in the successful writing of it.

But, Mr. Prime Minister, this happy outcome has other equally important aspects. It restores the traditional friendship between our two countries which, long before their present bonds of alliance, were linked by the bonds of struggles and glories shared. It also restores the close links of friendship between Greece and Turkey, and reinforces the edifice whose foundations were laid by Kemal Ataturk and Eleftherios Venizelos. The new State must and will be a new expression and symbol of these ties of friendship and co-operation.

In this spirit I greet the birth of the Republic of Cyprus, and welcome it to the comity of the world's nations.

III

STATEMENT BY THE MINISTER FOR FOREIGN AFFAIRS
OF TURKEY

I want to express first the regret of my Prime Minister at not being able to come here at this very happy moment. I will first read a message that he sent to the Conference:

"Let me first tell you all my emotion and gratitude for the many expressions of deep sympathy and sincere interest which I received from you and from my friend, Mr. Karamanlis and the other members of this Conference in relation to the tragic accident of last Tuesday. It is quite by a miracle that there have been some survivors, and I praise the Almighty for His clemency.

But I would not like to hide at the same time the feeling of deep sadness which overcomes me when I think of those who are now missing, and especially of those of my colleagues who had such a great part in the preparation, as far as the Turkish Government is concerned, of the work which we are now about to seal.

Let me also express to you especially, Mr. Chairman, the gratitude and admiration which I feel towards the numerous British citizens and authorities who spared no efforts in helping to relieve the victims of the accident and offer assistance and consolation."

Mr. Chairman, we are meeting to-day in order to achieve the solution of the most intricate problems of diplomacy and foreign policy which the modern world has experienced in recent times. Everybody knows how arduous and full of difficulties and risks the task has been; but thanks to the spirit of mutual understanding and sincere friendship which has been inspiring all of us, these huge obstacles have all been overcome and a settlement has been found which represents the solid and unshakeable foundation for the solution of the Cyprus question. The Turkish Government accepts fully the conclusions of the present Conference and is determined to stick to them in all circumstances. Turkey believes that the agreed solution represents an equitable and fair settlement of the Cyprus question. She is convinced that, provided it is observed by all, this solution, which takes care of the legitimate interests of all concerned, will open an era of peace, friendship and sincere co-operation between the two communities of the Island for the benefit of all of our countries and the whole free world to which we are proud to belong.

It will also create I am sure the auspicious climate for a new period of sincere co-operation between Greece and Turkey which will bring these two countries even closer to one another than ever in the past.

Permit me now to conclude by emphasising that the work which we have achieved represents without any doubt the result of our common efforts. However allow me to address a special expression of thanks to the leaders of the two communities without whose comprehension, sense of responsibility and willingness to co-operate it would have been very difficult to achieve this work. I hope that they will be guided in the future by the same spirit of Ataturk and Venizelos, and that they will find themselves always in complete agreement and co-operation to guide the Island of Cyprus in the best atmosphere of welfare and happiness. I am sure that the Conference will join me when I say that they deserve especially our appreciation and gratitude.

IV

STATEMENT BY THE REPRESENTATIVE OF THE GREEK-CYPRIOT COMMUNITY

May I first say a word about the Prime Minister of Turkey. To-day I hope he is well on the way to recovery after his recent shock from his aeroplane accident. It is the work of providence that the Prime Minister has been saved and we are thankful for it.

This is a great day, Mr. Chairman, in that the positiveness of unity and co-operation has prevailed over the negativeness of division and strife. It marks the beginning of a new charter for Cyprus both in the relations of its people with the people of the United Kingdom as well as in those between the Greeks and Turks in Cyprus.

Yesterday I had certain reservations. In overcoming them I have done so in a spirit of trust and good-hearted good will towards the Turkish community and its leaders. It is my firm belief that with sincere understanding and mutual confidence we can work together in a way that will leave no room for dissension about any written provisions and guarantees. It is the spirit in the hearts of men that counts most. I am sure that all past differences will be completely forgotten. They are already a thing of the past. At this closing meeting of the Conference I wish to express my cordial thanks to Her Majesty's Government and to the Governments of Greece and Turkey for the spirit of co-operation that animated their work for the settlement of this problem. I can assure this Conference that the same spirit will animate our thoughts and actions. I do not underrate the great difficulties that had to be overcome. The essential outcome of the Conference is the new spirit of unity and co-operation that has so effectively replaced that of division and strife. A new era, I firmly believe, opens up to-day for the people of Cyprus, an era of peace, freedom and prosperity. The two communities working closely together with God's guidance will, I have no doubt, be able to develop the welfare of the Island to their common benefit.

V

STATEMENT BY THE REPRESENTATIVE OF THE TURKISH-CYPRIOT COMMUNITY

Mr. Chairman, this atmosphere of success and rejoicing to-day is marred unfortunately by the accident of the Turkish Prime Minister, and we as Turks of Cyprus have mourned for the dead, and have thanked God for the safety of the Prime Minister.

We join in this new atmosphere of good relations and happiness. We appreciate the difficulties which the Governments concerned have had to face in order to give this day to us. Let us hope that we shall have from now on continuous co-operation in a spirit of good will and of give and take, of brotherliness and understanding, and that we shall all strive for the good of Cyprus and of those who are so closely connected to it. Whatever we have sacrificed or conceded as Turks of Cyprus has been worth sacrificing or conceding, because we feel that in return we have gained the full co-operation and friendship of the Greek community. We sincerely hope that that will be their feeling and the way they will take their concessions and their sacrifices.

We thank you, Mr. Chairman, and your Government for the hospitality shown to us, and we hope that in this new spirit and new understanding Cyprus will be a firm friend of all the three Governments who are now present in this room.

APPENDIX 24

Last Proclamation of Dighenis, the Leader of EOKA, Ordering the Cessation of the Struggle, Issued 9 March 1959 (translation)

E.O.K.A.
TO THE GREEK CYPRIOT PEOPLE

When on the 1st April 1955 I raised the standard of the liberation movement, I set as my objective the liberation of Cyprus and I asked for the support of the Greek Cypriot People and the solidarity of the whole Nation, which were given to me fully during our four-year struggle.

Now, after the Zurich Agreement between the Governments of Greece and Turkey, which was endorsed in London by Ethnarch Makarios also, I am obliged
TO ORDER THE CESSATION OF THE STRUGGLE.

He who would not accept the Agreement and would continue the struggle would DIVIDE not only the Cypriot People but probably the whole Nation; and the consequences of national discord would be infinitely more ruinous than those which some think will result from the solution which has been given.

I consider that this solution is better, even though it is not the one we expected and which would have satisfied our aspirations, than national discord; because in such discord WE WOULD LOSE ALL.

Instead of the war bugle I will to-day sound CONCORD, UNITY, LOVE so that on the ruins and ashes of the Cypriot epos, resplendent in glory and national majesty, you may build the new edifice of the young Republic.

It depends on its masterbuilders to lead it to the road of prosperity and progress. As for me, I am determined not to involve myself in politics and public life, either in Cyprus or in Greece. But I will follow with agony from afar the steps of my greatly tormented Country which has shed so much blood, sharing your joys and sorrows.

My conscience is clear that I have done my duty; it was the work of the politicians to exploit the epic struggles of the Cypriot people. This they have done as they could or as they thought best.

NOW WE MUST SHOW DISCIPLINE

ALL, UNITED, rally round the ETHNARCH, who is today the symbol of UNITY and STRENGTH and help him in his difficult task.

This is my wish and I call on all to conform.

E.O.K.A
THE LEADER
DIGHENIS

APPENDIX 25

Record of a Meeting of the Prime Minister of Greece with Archbishop Makarios, Attended Also by Minister of Foreign Affairs of Greece Averoff-Tossizza, Bishop of Kitium Anthimos and the Director of the Greek Foreign Ministry, A. Vlachos, at the Residence of the Prime Minister, 29 January 1959 (translation)

The Prime Minister began by explaining to the two Cypriot Prelates that during a recent meeting between the Greek Foreign Minister and the Turkish Foreign Minister, sustained talks had taken place on the possibility of a solution of the Cyprus problem based on the independence of the Island, but that the Turkish side had strongly insisted on the establishment of a Turkish military base in Cyprus. This claim had been categorically rejected by the Prime Minister, who had conveyed to the Turkish side through the Foreign Minister that insistence by Turkey on this point would mean the suspension of the talks and that on no account would he accept a solution entailing the establishment of a Turkish military base in the Island. The Prime Minister further stated that, although the Turkish position on this basic issue had not undergone any change, the Turkish Foreign Minister had come up with the idea that in case of an alliance between Turkey, Greece and independent Cyprus, a common Grecoturcocypriot Headquarters could be set up in Cyprus. The Prime Minister added that on this proposal, also, the Greek reaction had been reserved, the view being expressed that such a suggestion might be examined. The Archbishop did not voice any objection. The Prime Minister observed that it was possible that Cyprus would become a member of NATO, in which case it would be immaterial which forces would be assigned to man the Bases of the Alliance. On this point, the Archbishop observed that it would be in the absolute interest of the Cypriots for independent Cyprus to participate in the NATO Defence Alliance.

The Prime Minister then said that the exchange of views between the Greek and the Turkish Foreign Ministers had dealt with the system of government which an independent Cyprus might have. He added, however, that he had taken the opportunity of the transit through the Ellinikon Airport of the Turkish Foreign Minister to convey to him through the Ambassador in Ankara, Mr. Pesmazoglou, who was in Athens for service reasons, that insistence on the question of a Turkish base in Cyprus would mean the definite wrecking of the efforts to bring the views of the two sides nearer. It was worthy of note, the Prime Minister said, that in spite of this double confirmation, the Turkish Foreign Minister had already asked for a new meeting with his Greek colleague which would probably take place in Switzerland.

With regard to the structure of an independent Cyprus, there was convergence of views that the state would be a Republic with a Presidential regime, on the American model, the President being a Greek and the Vice-President a Turk, elected by direct suffrage by the people (the Greeks electing the President and the Turks the Vice-President). There was also convergence of views on the following points: a unitary House of Representatives to deal with general matters, composed of 70% Greeks and 30% Turks, and two Communal Chambers, one Greek and one Turkish, with competence in matters of education, personal status and religion, and with the right to impose dues on the respective Community for the institutions under their competence. The Turkish side, however, wanted, in addition, that on the one hand the Communal Chambers should have control over purely Turkish bodies* which, in other respects, would operate in conformity with the laws of the new State, and on the other hand that they be concerned with the economic development of the communities. The Greek side expressed strong reservations on the last two competences (control over purely Turkish bodies and concern for economic development).

To ensure the impartiality of legislation, there was convergence of views that if the unitary House of Representatives or other organ passed a Law or an Order or took any decision considered by the Turkish Community as discriminatory, the latter would have the right of recourse in respect of such legislation or instrument to an Arbitration Court composed of one Greek, one Turk and one neutral member, who would preside over such Court. The Prime Minister then said that during the exchange of views between the Greek Foreign Minister and the Turkish Foreign Minister the latter had expressed the view that the Turkish Vice-President should have the right of veto on matters of foreign affairs and defence. No serious objection had been expressed by the Greek side on this point. The Turkish side had expressed the view that there should be three Cypriot Security Forces: the Police, the Gendarmerie and a small Army. Two of these Forces would be headed by a Greek whilst the third would be headed by a Turk; the Deputy Heads of these Forces would conversely be two Turks and one Greek. The composition of the Forces, however, would be 50% Greeks and 50% Turks. The last point was categorically rejected by the Greek side which counterproposed 70% Greeks and 30% Turks.

As regards Justice, the Turks were interested in securing a "safe" composition of the High Court, and proposed that its President be a neutral.

The Foreign Minister added that the Turkish side had asked that the Vice-President (a Turk) should have the right of return of a Law or an Order to the organ issuing it for a second vote thereon. He also said that the Turks wanted that the ratio of 70% Greeks and 30% Turks should apply to the Public Service and that in the higher grades of the hierarchy this ratio would apply so far as there were suitable Turks available. He said further that the Turkish side had agreed that any competence not specifically reserved to the Communal Chambers would automatically fall within the competence of the unitary House of Representatives. The Foreign Minister mentioned another Turkish claim, namely that there should be separate municipalities which, it was noted,

---

* Author's Note: Obviously, this should be either that "the Turkish Communal Chamber should have control over purely Turkish bodies" or that "the Greek Communal Chamber should have control over purely Greek bodies and the Turkish Communal Chamber over purely Turkish bodies."

have already begun operating in certain towns, and he added that he had persistently rejected this proposal because the creation of separate municipalities would constitute to a certain extent, and albeit in a circumscribed manner, a separatist element. The two Prelates observed in reply that ad hoc issues which could have a separatist character no longer had the same character, and that the reason why they had been vigorously rejected in the past was because the efforts then were directed towards partition. Since, however, the present efforts were not for partition but on the contrary for the creation of a unitary state, such ad hoc matters should be considered only from the point of view of their practical operation and the interests of the Greek Cypriots. The Minister reiterated his view, but the Cypriot side replied that because the Turkish quarters in the various towns were in a very bad state and had many problems, it would be necessary to spend a great deal of money to remedy the situation. This expense would be borne by the Greek Cypriot taxpayers, and no matter how much was spent, the Turkish Cypriots would not be satisfied, something which would be a constant source of friction and thus indefinitely detrimental to peaceful co-existence. If, on the other hand, there were separate municipalities the Turkish Cypriots would not be able to blame anybody but themselves for their unsatisfactory operation. The two Prelates added that the matter was not of capital importance and that, in any case, the Greek side could not bear responsibility since it was acting always as the agent of the Cypriots. The Prime Minister intervened at this point and confirmed that the Greek Government was in fact acting as the agent of the Cypriots and that the Cypriot views would be taken into consideration during the definitive negotiations on the issue of municipalities.

Archbishop Makarios then stated categorically that a Turkish base in Cyprus was unacceptable, and that the relative Turkish proposal had rightly been rejected. The Archbishop asked what would be the significance of the mixed Grecoturcocypriot Headquarters. To the clarification given by the Foreign Minister, the Archbishop expressed no objection, stating that, since a Greek contingent would also participate, the establishment of the Headquarters would present no major difficulties.

With regard to the structure of the State, the Archbishop expressed his agreement, and, together with the Bishop of Kitium, stressed that the initiation of free political life in Cyprus would be of immense importance, especially since the position of the Greeks would be dominant; this was certain, irrespective of whether privileges were accorded to the Turks to safeguard them fully, privileges without which it would not be possible to have a free political life in Cyprus.

On the competence of the Communal Chambers, the Archbishop observed that there was no objection either in respect of the matters in which the Chambers would have competence or in respect of the imposition of dues, but with the express proviso that they would burden the respective Community. With regard to the other competences, he observed that they would be specific and said that he would not mind if the Turkish Bank for instance were under the control of the Turkish Communal Chamber.

On the question of the neutral Presidents of the Arbitration Court and the High Court, the Foreign Minister asked the Archbishop whether he had reservations for reasons of prestige, adding that he himself considered the formula most useful, in view of the composition of the population of the Island. The Archbishop hastened to reply that he would not like to have foreigners if the organs in which they participated were a kind of para-government, which of course was not the case.

On the question of the veto, the Archbishop accepted this right for the Vice-President on matters of foreign affairs and defence, but he expressed the view that provision should be made to define the matters of security and/or other matters on which the Vice-President should have no right of veto.

With regard to the Judiciary, the Archbishop accepted the proposed composition of the High Court, as well as the composition of the Courts by Judges of the same religion as the litigants in cases between litigants of the same religion and the mixed composition of the Courts in cases between litigants of different religions. On this point, the Bishop of Kitium supported the view that such a solution was advantageous. The Foreign Minister observed that the aim should be to have a unitary judiciary and that the High Court, acting as a Council of Judicature, should appoint the members of the various Courts. This was considered by the Prelates as useful.

Regarding the composition of the Security Forces and the Army, the Archbishop said that the Turkish claim for a 50% Greek Cypriot and 50% Turkish Cypriot composition had rightly been rejected. The Minister said that by way of compromise it might be agreed that Turkish Cypriots already serving beyond the 70%-30% ratio, would not be dismissed. The two Prelates agreed, but with the exception of the Auxiliary Police. The two Prelates also agreed on the composition of the Headquarters of the Security Forces and of the Army, namely that the Heads would be two Greeks and one Turk and the Deputy Heads two Turks and one Greek, respectively.

Generally, the attitude of Archbishop Makarios to what the Prime Minister said and to the clarifications given by the Foreign Minister was positive and encouraging for the continuation of the contacts with the Turks in order to exploit in the best possible manner their intentions as to the conclusion of an agreement. The two Prelates expressed the fear that the British would probably try to prevent an agreement between Greece and Turkey. On this point, the Minister said that part of the British Government wanted an agreement between Greece and Turkey, while another part, according to available information, is trying to torpedo the envisaged Grecoturkish rapprochement. He added that the British Ambassador in Athens had told him that the implementation of the Macmillan Plan could not be postponed indefinitely and that the Turkish electoral rolls would soon be published in Cyprus. In response to the strong reaction of the Minister, who had declared that Britain would be denounced as guilty of sabotage, the British had given the assurance that the electoral rolls would not be published, but that it was not possible for their publication to be postponed indefinitely. The British retraction on this point, even if only temporary, was noted.

The Prime Minister, again going over the emerging probable solution as a whole, stressed that in an independent Cyprus both the numerical and the qualitative superiority of the Greek element would ensure full control by the Greeks of the life and activities of the free Island. All present agreed to this.

During the meeting, mention was repeatedly made that Britain would retain sovereign bases, to which no objection whatsoever was expressed."

———————

"It was I who asked for this record to be made", says Averoff, "when I refused to accept the separate Municipalities, and I was told that I could not refuse, since we were acting as agents of the Cypriots. The Archbishop found my request reasonable and suggested that Angelos Vlachos prepare the record of the whole meeting. The latter prepared the record the same evening, he initialled all the pages and read it to the Archbishop who confirmed that it reflected what had been said".

———————

The above is a translation of the Record as set out in Evangelos Averoff-Tossizza, *Story of Lost Opportunities (The Cyprus Problem 1950–1963)* (in Greek) (Athens: E. Averoff-Tositza, 1981), Vol. 2, pp. 168-176.

APPENDIX 26

Speech by Archbishop Makarios to the People on His Return to Cyprus at St. John's Cathedral, Nicosia, 1 March 1959 (translation)

We praise and thank you, Lord, for delivering us from the ordeal of fire and water and giving us respite.

Here I am again amongst you in our beloved country—a free country. The clouds of slavery have been dissolved and the sun of freedom illuminates the Cypriot skies. The night of centuries is already giving way to the sweet light of day. And the spirit of our ancestors rises immortal from the depths of our long history to proclaim far and wide the great message: *"Nenikikamen"*.*

Cyprus is to-day free. Celebrate, my brothers. Hold your head up in pride. The cloak of servitude has been lifted for good. The chains of slavery have been broken and our hands are free to move in praise of the Lord and also to produce works of peaceful creation, welfare and progress.

How much pain and suffering, blood and sacrifice have been the price of this moment! We reverently pay tribute to the many generations of our ancestors who have relayed to us, alight, the torch of freedom and the beacon of the spirit and have bequeathed to us the sacred legacy of moral obligation and duty. We pay tribute to all the martyrs of Cypriot freedom. We shower their graves with the flowers of our love and the tears of our gratitude. At this moment their souls are hovering over us and are celebrating with us the Liberation of Cyprus.

Because our great dead are not dead. They are alive and they will continue to live through the legend of their heroism and the tradition of their virtue. They are alive and they will live for ever through the renown of their sacred struggles and the noble splendour of their sacrifices. They live and will live always in the serenity of the free Cypriot skies as legendary demigods whom the gratitude of succeeding generations will preserve eternally young and immortal. They live and will live in the hearts of our youth who will never stop being inspired morally and spiritually by their heroic deeds and their splendid acts of valour.

Let the bugles of victory sound over their white graves.

Heroes of Cyprus! Your sacrifice has not been in vain. The glorious epos which you have written opens today a brilliant new period of our history. A period of freedom. A period of progress and welfare. The seed which you have sown has already produced a rich harvest. The tree of liberty which you have watered with your blood is today offering its luxuriant fruit. From your Calgary has sprung the resurrection of our country.

They were the martyrs. But our struggle for freedom is ennobled by a multitude of heroes headed by General George Grivas, the legendary Dighenis, whose name has filled the most glorious pages of Cyprus History.

---

* "We have won"—spoken by Phidippides before dying, having run to Athens with news of the battle of Marathon.

To this superb man and the brave fighters of EOKA we pay, on this solemn occasion, a tribute of supreme gratitude and honour. Let us turn our thoughts to them, and let us remember that, without their struggle, the day of victory would not have dawned; without their heroism the day of liberty would have been far-off.

But to you also, heroic people of Cyprus, I pay at this moment the deepest tribute of love and honour. Because it is on your virtue that their valour and bravery were founded. On your fortitude was the armour of their victory forged. On your patriotism was the work of Cypriot Freedom constructed. I am proud to be at the head of such a people; and I am happy to know that with your virtue and your faith the task that begins today will doubtless be brought to an auspicious conclusion. Because let us not think that this day constitutes the end. On the contrary it constitutes the beginning of new, long, now peaceful, struggles, for the consolidation of what has been achieved and for further development and advancement. It marks the starting point of new campaigns to secure general welfare and progress and to demonstrate that our country is a prosperous and law abiding state.

For this purpose, however, it is necessary to have unshakeable faith, granite consistency and unwavering unity. Without faith in what has been achieved, without enthusiasm for the freedom we have acquired, the task we are now undertaking is doomed to failure. Let us maintain, then, our enthusiasm and our faith. United, as in the past, let us undertake, together and steadfastly, the new struggle of peace and progress, the struggle for the happiness of our children, the struggle for the greatness of our country.

Let us not forget that freedom is not only a privilege and a right; it is also a most heavy responsibility and a supreme duty. This is the duty we are now called upon to perform. A duty, both worthy and noble, towards our compatriots, towards all our fellow men, towards the whole world. In the performance of this duty let us never allow the intrusion of passions or prejudices. Let us extend an honest hand of friendship and co-operation to all. In particular, let us co-operate cordially and sincerely with our friendly Turkish compatriots. Harmonious co-operation between us is a guarantee of strength, increasing the expectation of success.

In these circumstances, I am sure that a bright future opens before us. We live in a rich and beautiful Island which, with hard work and love, we can convert into a real land of milk and honey. In this Island the letters and the arts have flowered for many centuries and the most noble civilizations have converged. The inventiveness and wisdom of Asia merge on our soil with the spirit of European science and expertise. Around our shores lie the uneasy aspirations of three continents and the controversies of two worlds. In this turbulent environment we are called upon to play the role of co-ordinator and conciliator. We are called upon to convert our Island into a golden bridge which will unite and not separate the conflicting forces. We are called upon to convert our Island into the great artery which will join materially and spiritually the North and the South, the West and the East.

The venture is not an easy one. It requires great effort, colossal work, heavy strain. We are a small people whose only strength lies in its spiritual power, whose only influence stems from its moral greatness. The greatness of the small can only be defined in terms of moral and spiritual advancement in parallel with steady progress in all sectors of national life. It is only the spirit that cannot be bound by geographic limits. Its radiation can penetrate everywhere, dissolve the ice of distrust and hate, warm hearts and promote world harmony and unity. In this sense the role of the Republic of Cyprus will be huge and its mission important and sacred.

We shall undertake this mission with faith, enthusiasm and love, with the same love exactly with which we shall undertake the work of internal reconstitution and reform. We shall convert our Island into an enormous creative workshop. In this workshop there will be room for everyone. All will be invited to make their contribution equally in order to have the right to share in the fruit of the common endeavour.

I hold the firm conviction that brilliant days are opening before us. For the first time in our history of three thousand years the responsibility for our future is in our hands. For the first time, after long centuries of servitude, we are free. We shall use our freedom in the best possible way: internally as a weapon of morality and progress and externally as a means of strengthening international ties and as an organ for the promotion of international solidarity and co-operation.

Centuries of anticipation and expectation, centuries of patience and sacrifice are at this moment following our historic course. Let us exert every effort not to appear inferior to those who sacrificed themselves to give us a free country. Let us exert every effort to appear worthy of the high mission that divine providence has destined for us. Proud and dauntless in the struggles for freedom, prove yourselves now tireless and bighearted in the struggles for peace and welfare. Be conscious of the power that is to-day placed in your hands.

And visualise our now free country full of youthful drive and force, full of creativity and vigour, treading the glorious road of happiness and joy. Take this vision into your hearts and you can be sure that the state which is founded to-day, with your love and sacrifice, will truly become a state of welfare and progress, morality and justice, a state of God.

APPENDIX 27(1)

The Cyprus Act, 8 & 9 Eliz. 2, chap. 52, 29 July 1960

ARRANGEMENT OF SECTIONS

CHAPTER 52

An Act to make provision for, and in connection with, the establishment of an independent republic in Cyprus.

[29th July, 1960]

BE it enacted by the Queen's most Excellent Majesty, by and with the advice and consent of the Lords Spiritual and Temporal, and Commons, in this present Parliament assembled, and by the authority of the same, as follows:

[Establishment of the Republic of Cyprus as an independent sovereign country.]
1. Her Majesty may by Order in Council (to be laid before Parliament after being made) declare that the constitution designated in the Order as the Constitution of the Republic of Cyprus shall come into force on such day as may be specified in the Order ; and on that day there shall be established in the Island of Cyprus an independent sovereign Republic of Cyprus, and Her Majesty shall have no sovereignty or jurisdiction over the Republic of Cyprus.

[The Sovereign Base Areas.]
2.—(1) The Republic of Cyprus shall comprise the entirety of the Island of Cyprus with the exception of the two areas defined as mentioned in the following subsection, and—
    (a) nothing in the foregoing section shall affect Her Majesty's sovereignty or jurisdiction over those areas ;
    (b) the power of Her Majesty to make or provide for the making of laws for the said areas shall include power to make such laws (relating to

297

persons or things either within or outside the areas) and such provisions for the making of laws (relating as aforesaid) as appear to Her Majesty requisite for giving effect to arrangements with the authorities of the Republic of Cyprus.

(2) The boundaries of the said areas shall, subject to the provisions of this section, be those defined by the maps, photographs and descriptive matter, authenticated by the signature of the Secretary of State, which have been deposited at the Commonwealth Relations Office and presented to Parliament by the Secretary of State by Command of Her Majesty.

(3) If Her Majesty by Order in Council declares that arrangements have been made—

(a) for the demarcation of the said boundaries by two or more Commissioners appointed as specified in the arrangements ;

(b) for the determination, in default of agreement between the Commissioners, of any question as to the interpretation of the maps, photographs or descriptive matter ; and

(c) for the variation of the boundaries, as defined by the maps, photographs and descriptive matter, by agreement between the Commissioners where it appears to them expedient to do so on any grounds specified in the arrangements,

and that the Commissioners have made a report that the boundaries have been demarcated in accordance with the arrangements, then as from such date not earlier than the date of the report as may be specified in the Order in Council the boundaries of the said areas shall be the boundaries demarcated by the Commissioners.

[Operation of existing laws.]

3.—(1) On and after the appointed day any existing law which operates as law of, or of any part of, the United Kingdom, being a law applying in relation to Cyprus or persons or things in any way belonging thereto or connected therewith, shall, save as provided after the passing of this Act by the authority having power to amend or repeal that law or by the following provisions of this Act, continue to apply in like manner in relation to the Republic of Cyprus or persons or things in any way belonging thereto or connected therewith :

Provided that, save as aforesaid and subject to the provisions of the Schedule to this Act, any such law which contains different provision with respect to a Commonwealth country mentioned in subsection (3) of section one of the British Nationality Act, 1948, and with respect to parts of Her Majesty's dominions outside the United Kingdom not so mentioned, or expressly excludes any such Commonwealth country to any extent, shall apply in like manner and to the like extent (if any) with respect to the Republic of Cyprus as it applies with respect to the said Commonwealth country.

(2) As from the appointed day, the provisions of the Schedule to this Act shall have effect with respect to the enactments therein mentioned.

(3) Her Majesty may by Order in Council make such further adaptations (whether in relation to the Republic of Cyprus or in relation to the areas mentioned in subsection (1) of section two of this Act) in any Act of the Parliament of the United Kingdom passed before the appointed day, or in any instrument

having effect under any such Act, as appear to Her necessary or expedient in consequence of the establishment of the Republic of Cyprus.

(4) An Order in Council under this section may be varied or revoked by a subsequent such Order and may, though made after the appointed day, be made so as to have effect from that day.

(5) An Order in Council under this section shall be subject to annulment in pursuance of a resolution of either House of Parliament.

(6) In this section "existing law" means any Act of Parliament (other than this Act) or other enactment or instrument whatsoever, and any rule of law, which is in force on the appointed day or, having been passed or made before the appointed day, comes into force after that day ; and sub-section (1) of this section shall apply in relation to existing law which operates as law of, or of any part of, Southern Rhodesia or any colony, protectorate or United Kingdom trust territory as it applies in relation to existing law which operates as law of, or of any part of, the United Kingdom, except that that sub-section—

    (a) shall not apply in relation to any law passed by the Federal Legislature of Rhodesia and Nyasaland ;

    (b) shall apply in relation to other law of, or of any part of, Southern Rhodesia so far only as concerns law which can be amended neither by a law passed by the Legislature thereof nor by a law passed by the said Federal Legislature ; and

    (c) shall apply in relation to other law of, or of any part of, Northern Rhodesia or Nyasaland so far only as concerns law which cannot be amended by a law passed by the said Federal Legislature.

References in this subsection to a colony, a protectorate and a United Kingdom trust territory shall be construed as if they were references contained in the British Nationality Act, 1948.

(7) Nothing in this section shall be construed as continuing in force any enactment or rule of law limiting or restricting the legislative powers of the Republic of Cyprus.

(8) Nothing in this section shall be construed as requiring the application of any existing law to the Republic of Cyprus and the areas mentioned in subsection (1) of section two of this Act as one country.

4.—(1) For the purpose of giving effect to any agreement for the establishment of the Republic of Cyprus, Her Majesty may by Order in Council provide that persons of such descriptions as may be specified in the Order shall cease to be citizens of the United Kingdom and Colonies on such date as may be so specified, and different dates may be specified in relation to different descriptions of persons :

Provided that a married woman shall not cease by virtue of an Order under this section to be a citizen of the United Kingdom and Colonies if on the date on which she would do so her husband is a citizen of the United Kingdom and Colonies and does not cease to be such a citizen on that date.

(2) If any person who in consequence of anything done before he attained the age of sixteen years ceased by virtue of an Order under this section to be a citizen of the United Kingdom and Colonies makes a declaration in the prescribed manner, within one year after his attaining the age of twenty-one years or such

longer period as the Secretary of State may allow, of his intention to resume citizenship of the United Kingdom and Colonies, the Secretary of State shall cause the declaration to be registered ; and thereupon that person shall become a citizen of the United Kingdom and Colonies.

(3) Where by virtue of an Order under this section a person of a description to which this subsection is applied by the Order ceases to be a citizen of the United Kingdom and Colonies and either—

(a) is not, immediately after the time when he ceases to be such a citizen, a citizen of a country mentioned in subsection (1) of section six of the British Nationality Act, 1948 (which relates inter alia to the registration of Commonwealth citizens as citizens of the United Kingdom and Colonies) ; or

(b) having been immediately after the said time a citizen of a country so mentioned, subsequently ceases to be one in consequence of an Order under section six of this Act or otherwise,

section six of the said Act of 1948 shall, as respects any application thereunder made before the end of the period of two years and six months beginning with the appointed day, apply in relation to him as if he were, or were still, a citizen of a country so mentioned.

(4) Subsection (2) of section six of the said Act of 1948 (which provides for the registration as a citizen of the United Kingdom and Colonies of a woman who has been married to such a citizen) shall not apply to a woman by virtue of her marriage to a person who ceases, or but for his earlier death would have ceased, to be a citizen of the United Kingdom and Colonies by virtue of an Order under this section.

(5) An Order in Council under this section may be varied or revoked by a subsequent such Order.

(6) An Order in Council under this section shall be subject to annulment in pursuance of a resolution of either House of Parliament.

(7) This section shall be construed as one with the British Nationality Act, 1948.

[Abolition of appeals to Privy Council.]

5. On and after the appointed day no appeal shall lie to Her Majesty in Council from any court in the Republic of Cyprus ; and any appeal to Her Majesty in Council from any court in the Island of Cyprus which is pending on the appointed day shall abate on that day.

[Provision in event of change in relationship of Republic to the Commonwealth.]

6.—(1) For the purpose of giving effect to any decision that the Republic of Cyprus shall not be a country specified in subsection (3) of section one of the British Nationality Act, 1948, Her Majesty may by Order in Council direct that subsection (1) of section three of this Act, so far as it relates to the said subsection (3), and paragraph 1 of the Schedule to this Act, shall cease to have effect.

(2) An Order in Council under this section may provide either that all the provisions of section three of this Act and of the Schedule thereto (except in so far as they relate to the areas mentioned in subsection (1) of section two of this Act) shall cease to have effect or that those provisions shall continue in force to

such extent and subject to such modifications as may be specified in the Order, may make such adaptations or modifications of any Act (other than this Act) in force at the making of the Order or passed before then and coming into force thereafter, or any instrument having effect under any such Act, as appear to Her Majesty in Council expedient for the purposes or in consequence of the Order, and may contain incidental, consequential and supplemental provisions.

(3) An Order in Council under this section may be varied or revoked by a subsequent such Order, and any amending Order may be made so as to have effect from any date not earlier than the making of the Order amended.

(4) No recommendation shall be made to Her Majesty in Council to make an Order in Council under this section unless a draft of the Order has been laid before Parliament and approved by a resolution of each House of Parliament.

[Short title and interpretation.]

7.—(1) This Act may be cited as the Cyprus Act, 1960.

(2) In this Act "the appointed day" means the day specified by Order in Council under section one of this Act, "the Island of Cyprus" includes any islands included in Cyprus before the appointed day, and references to the Island of Cyprus or any part thereof include references to the territorial waters of the Island or part.

SCHEDULE
PROVISIONS AS TO ENACTMENTS

1.—(1) Subsection (3) of section one of the British Nationality Act, 1948 (which specifies the Commonwealth countries whose citizens are British subjects or Commonwealth citizens) shall have effect as if the word "and" in the last place where it occurs were omitted and at the end there were added the words "and the Republic of Cyprus".

(2) In relation to the Republic of Cyprus, any reference in the said Act of 1948 or in the British Nationality Act, 1958, to the High Commissioner for Her Majesty's government in the United Kingdom shall be construed as a reference to the chief representative in the Republic of Cyprus of Her Majesty's said government, whether he is known by the title of High Commissioner for that government or by any other title.

2. The proviso to subsection (1) of section three of this Act shall not apply to the Exchange Control Act, 1947.

3. In subsection (4) of section two of the Import Duties Act, 1958, after the word "Ceylon" there shall be inserted the words "the Republic of Cyprus".

4. In the definitions of "Commonwealth force" in subsection (1) of section two hundred and twenty-five of the Army Act, 1955, and in subsection (1) of section two hundred and twenty-three of the Air Force Act, 1955, and in the definition of "Commonwealth country" in subsection (1) of section one hundred and thirty-five of the Naval Discipline Act, 1957—

(a) the word "or" (being, in the said Acts of 1955, that word in the last place where it occurs in those definitions) shall be omitted ; and
(b) at the end there shall be added the words "or the Republic of Cyprus".

5. Section four of the Visiting Forces (British Commonwealth) Act, 1933 (which deals with attachment and mutual powers of command) shall apply in relation to forces raised in the Republic of Cyprus as it applies in relation to forces raised in Dominions within the meaning of the Statute of Westminster, 1931.

6. In paragraph (a) of subsection (1) of section one of the Visiting Forces Act, 1952 (which specifies the countries to which that Act applies) the word "or" in the first place where it occurs shall be omitted, and at the end there shall be added the words "the Republic of Cyprus or".

7. In section four hundred and sixty-one of the Income Tax Act, 1952 (which relates to exemption from income tax in the case of certain Commonwealth representatives and their staffs)—
    (a) in subsection (2), the word "or" (in the last place where it occurs before the words "for any state") shall be omitted, and immediately before the words "for any state" there shall be inserted the words "or the Republic of Cyprus" ;
    (b) in subsection (3), after the word "or" (in the last place where it occurs before the words "and 'Agent-General'") there shall be inserted the words "the representative of the Republic of Cyprus or the High Commissioner".

8. In subsection (6) of section one of the Diplomatic Immunities (Commonwealth Countries and Republic of Ireland) Act, 1952, immediately before the word "and" in the last place where it occurs there shall be inserted the words "the Republic of Cyprus".

9.—(1) Subject to the provisions of this paragraph, the Colonial Stock Acts, 1877 to 1948, shall apply in relation to the Republic of Cyprus as they apply in relation to a Dominion within the meaning of the Colonial Stock Act, 1934.
(2) In section twenty of the Colonial Stock Act, 1877 (which relates to the jurisdiction of courts in the United Kingdom as to colonial stock) for the second paragraph there shall be substituted the following subsections, that is to say—
    "(2) Any person claiming to be interested in colonial stock to which this Act applies, or in any dividend thereon, may institute civil proceedings in the United Kingdom against the registrar in relation to that stock or dividend.
    (3) Notwithstanding anything in the foregoing provisions of this section, the registrar shall not by virtue of an order made by any court in the United Kingdom in any such proceedings as are referred to in this section be liable to make any payment otherwise than out of moneys in his possession in the United Kingdom as registrar.".
(3) The Colonial Stock Act, 1934, shall apply in relation to stock of the Republic of Cyprus as if in paragraph (a) of subsection (1) of section one of

that Act for any reference to Her Majesty's Government in the Dominion or to the Parliament of the Dominion there were substituted a reference to the Government or the Legislature of the Republic of Cyprus, and for any reference to any legislation being submitted for the Royal Assent there were substituted a reference to that legislation becoming law.

(4) During any period on and after the appointed day during which there is in force as part of the law of the Republic of Cyprus any instrument passed or made before that day which makes provision corresponding to the undertaking required by paragraph (a) of subsection (1) of section one of the said Act of 1934, paragraphs (a) and (b) of that subsection shall be deemed to have been complied with in the case of the Republic of Cyprus.

10.—(1) In subsection (2) of section four hundred and twenty-seven of the Merchant Shipping Act, 1894, as substituted by section two of the Merchant Shipping (Safety Convention) Act, 1949, the word "or" (in the last place where it occurs before the words "or in any") shall be omitted, and immediately before the words "or in any" there shall be inserted the words "or the Republic of Cyprus".

(2) In the proviso to subsection (2) of section six of the Merchant Shipping Act, 1948, the word "or" (in the last place where it occurs) shall be omitted, and at the end there shall be added the words "or the Republic of Cyprus".

11. In the definition of "excepted ship or aircraft" in paragraph 3 of the Third Schedule to the Emergency Laws (Repeal) Act, 1959, the word "or" (in the last place where it occurs before the words "or in any") shall be omitted, and immediately before the words "or in any" there shall be inserted the words "or the Republic of Cyprus".

12. The power conferred by section five of the Seal Fisheries (North Pacific) Act, 1912, to extend certain provisions of that Act to Cyprus shall cease to be exerciseable, and the words "and to Cyprus" in subsection (1) of that section are hereby repealed.

13.—(1) The references in section thirty-one of the Copyright Act, 1956, to a colony shall not include the Republic of Cyprus.

(2) If the Copyright Act, 1911, so far as in force in the law of the Republic of Cyprus, is repealed or amended by that law at a time when sub-paragraph (2) of paragraph 39 of the Seventh Schedule to the Copyright Act, 1956 (which applies certain provisions of that Act in relation to countries to which the said Act of 1911 extended) is in force in relation to the Republic of Cyprus, the said sub-paragraph (2) shall thereupon cease to have effect in relation to the Republic of Cyprus.

14. In subsection (2) of section two of the Indian and Colonial Divorce Jurisdiction Act, 1926 (which enables section one of the Act to be extended to certain countries, but not to any of the countries named in the said subsection (2)) the word "and" shall be omitted in all places where it occurs except the first

such place and except in the expression "Rhodesia and Nyasaland", and at the end there shall be added the words "and the Republic of Cyprus".

8 & 9 ELIZ. 2 *Cyprus Act*, 1960 CH. 52

Table of Statutes referred to in this Act

Short Title	Session and Chapter
Colonial Stock Act, 1877	40 & 41 Vict. c. 59.
Merchant Shipping Act, 1894	57 & 58 Vict. c. 60.
Copyright Act, 1911	1 & 2 Geo. 5. c. 46.
Seal Fisheries (North Pacific) Act, 1912	2 & 3 Geo. 5. c. 10.
Indian and Colonial Divorce Jurisdiction Act, 1926.	16 & 17 Geo. 5. c. 40.
Statute of Westminster, 1931	22 & 23 Geo. 5. c. 4.
Visiting Forces (British Commonwealth) Act, 1933.	23 & 24 Geo. 5. c. 6.
Colonial Stock Act, 1934	24 & 25 Geo. 5. c. 47.
Exchange Control Act, 1947	10 & 11 Geo. 6. c. 14.
Merchant Shipping Act, 1948	11 & 12 Geo. 6. c. 44.
British Nationality Act, 1948	11 & 12 Geo. 6. c. 56.
Merchant Shipping (Safety Convention) Act, 1949.	12, 13 & 14 Geo. 6. c. 43.
Income Tax Act, 1952	15 & 16 Geo. 6. & 1 Eliz. 2. c. 10.
Diplomatic Immunities (Commonwealth Countries and Republic of Ireland) Act, 1952.	15 & 16 Geo. 6. & 1 Eliz. 2. c. 18.
Visiting Forces Act, 1952	15 & 16 Geo. 6. & 1 Eliz. 2. c. 67.
Army Act, 1955	3 & 4 Eliz. 2, c. 18.
Air Force Act, 1955	3 & 4 Eliz. 2. c. 19.
Copyright Act, 1956	4 & 5 Eliz. 2. c. 74.
Naval Discipline Act, 1957	5 & 6 Eliz. 2. c. 53.
Import Duties Act, 1958	6 & 7 Eliz. 2. c. 6.
British Nationality Act, 1958	6 & 7 Eliz. 2. c. 10.
Emergency Laws (Repeal) Act, 1959	7 & 8 Eliz. 2. c. 19.

APPENDIX 27(2)

The Republic of Cyprus Order in Council 1960, no. 1368, 3 August 1960*

STATUTORY INSTRUMENTS
1960 No. 1368

CYPRUS
The Republic of Cyprus Order in Council, 1960

Made	*3rd August, 1960*
Laid before Parliament	*9th August, 1960*
Coming into Operation	*10th August, 1960*

At the Court at Buckingham Palace, the 3rd day of August, 1960
Present,
The Queen's Most Excellent Majesty in Council

Her Majesty, by virtue and in exercise of the powers conferred on Her by section 1 of the Cyprus Act, 1960(a), or otherwise in Her vested, is pleased, by and with the advice of Her Privy Council, to order, and it is hereby ordered, as follows:

[Citation at commencement.]
1. This Order may be cited as the Republic of Cyprus Order in Council, 1960, and shall come into operation on the 10th day of August, 1960.

[Designation and commencement of the Constitution of the Republic of Cyprus.]
2. The constitution set out in the documents in the Greek and Turkish languages which were initialled at Ankara on the 28th day of July, 1960, by representatives of Her Majesty's Government in the United Kingdom, the Kingdom of Greece, the Republic of Turkey, the Greek-Cypriot community and the Turkish-Cypriot community as, respectively, the Greek and Turkish texts of the Constitution of the Republic of Cyprus shall be that Constitution and shall come into force on the 16th day of August, 1960.

W. G. Agnew.

EXPLANATORY NOTE
(This Note is not part of the Order, but is intended to indicate its general purport.)
The purpose of this Order is to designate the constitution which is to be the Constitution of the Republic of Cyprus and to specify the date on which it is to come into force.

---

* 8 & 9 Eliz. 2. c. 52.

APPENDIX 28

Photocopies of Signatures to the Treaties and Other Documents Signed on 16 August 1960, with the Exception of the Treaty of Guarantee and the Statements and Exchanges of Notes

In witness whereof the undersigned, being duly authorised thereto, have signed this Treaty.

Done at Nicosia, this sixteenth day of August, 1960, in four copies in the English language, of which one shall be deposited in the archives of each of the Governments of the Republic of Cyprus, the Kingdom of Greece, the Republic of Turkey and the United Kingdom of Great Britain and Northern Ireland.

For the Republic of Cyprus:

For the Kingdom of Greece:

For the Republic of Turkey:

For the United Kingdom of Great Britain and Northern Ireland:

APPENDIX 29

Agreement between the Kingdom of Greece, the Republic of Turkey and the Republic of Cyprus for the Application of the Treaty of Alliance Signed at Nicosia on August 16th, 1960

The Kingdom of Greece, the Republic of Turkey and the Republic of Cyprus,

Being parties to the Treaty of Alliance signed at Nicosia on the 16th day of August, 1960,

Have agreed as follows:

ARTICLE I

DEFINITIONS

In this Agreement and its Annexes:

(a) "Treaty of Alliance" means the Treaty of Alliance between the Republic of Cyprus, the Kingdom of Greece and the Republic of Turkey signed at Nicosia on August 16th, 1960.

(b) "Additional Protocol No. I" and "Additional Protocol No. II" refer to the Additional Protocols Nos. I and II to the Treaty of Alliance.

(c) "Committee of Ministers" means the Committee of Ministers of Foreign Affairs mentioned in Additional Protocol No. II.

(d) "Tripartite Headquarters" means the Tripartite Headquarters provided in Articles III and IV of the Treaty of Alliance, as a whole. However, the term "Tripartite Headquarters" for technical reasons is also used in certain cases in this Agreement and its Annexes to denote the Commander and the Staff.

(e) "Operational Command" means the authority granted to a Commander, under the provisions of this Agreement, to assign missions or tasks to subordinate Commanders, to deploy units and to assign or re-assign forces as may be deemed necessary. It does not of itself include administrative command or logistical responsibility, but does include authority to assign separate employment of components of the units concerned.

(f) "Cypriot" means a citizen of the Republic of Cyprus.

(g) "Appropriate Authorities of the Republic of Cyprus" means such authority of the Republic of Cyprus, which is competent under the Constitution to deal with relevant matters.

(h) "Greek and/or Turkish Contingents" means the Greek and/or Turkish Contingents provided by Article I of Additional Protocol No. I of the Treaty of Alliance.

(i) "Greek and/or Turkish Forces" means formations or part of the said Contingents. The term "Forces" has a special meaning for the purposes of Annex "C" (Status of Forces) of this Agreement.

ARTICLE II

COMMON DEFENCE

1. For the purpose of implementation of Article I of the Treaty of Alliance the Committee of Ministers shall assign to the Tripartite Headquarters the preparation of plans for the common defence of Cyprus. The Committee of Ministers shall lay down the general directives and strategic concepts for the preparation of these plans, taking into account the overall defence structure and requirements of the three countries concerned.

2. The Committee of Ministers shall control and ratify the plans prepared by the Tripartite Headquarters in accordance with paragraph 1 of this Article and shall outline the conditions of their implementation.

3. With the exception of the provisions of Article V, paragraph 1, of this Agreement, all Forces located in the territory of the Republic of Cyprus for the implementation of the plans referred to in paragraph 1 of this Article shall come under the Operational Command of the Tripartite Headquarters which shall be responsible for the implementation of the plans concerning the Republic of Cyprus.

ATTACK AGAINST THE REPUBLIC OF CYPRUS

ARTICLE III

For the implementation of Article II of the Treaty of Alliance:

1. "Attack" means any attack by land, sea or air.

2. "Direct or indirect attack" means not only an attack conducted by an external enemy, but also the internal subversive activities directed against the independence and the territorial integrity of the Republic of Cyprus.

ARTICLE IV

1. Plans for the facing of a direct or indirect attack, directed against the independence and the territorial integrity of the Republic of Cyprus, shall be prepared by the Tripartite Headquarters on the basis of:

(a) General directives issued by the Committee of Ministers on its own initiative or upon a request of the Tripartite Headquarters. These directives shall define the general framework and the specific aims as well as any limitations thereto.

(b) The Forces stationed in the territory of the Republic of Cyprus (Army of the Republic of Cyprus, Greek and Turkish Contingents provided in paragraph 1 of the Additional Protocol No. I).

2. In these plans, provisions shall be made for the case in which additional Hellenic and Turkish Forces will be sent to Cyprus, as referred to in Article XIV of this Agreement.

ARTICLE V

1. The Authorities of the Republic of Cyprus shall be primarily responsible for dealing with the subversive activities mentioned in Article III, paragraph 2, of this Agreement. For this purpose they shall use by preference their Security Forces and only in case of emergency the Army of the Republic of Cyprus, without the intervention of the Tripartite Headquarters. In this case the Army shall no longer come under the Operational Command of the Tripartite Headquarters.

2. Intervention, in the above case, of the Tripartite Headquarters with its Hellenic and Turkish Forces, stationed in Cyprus, shall take place only upon decision of the Committee of Ministers, which may set forth, in its decision, any limitations as to their use.

3. In case of such an intervention by the Tripartite Headquarters, mentioned in paragraph 2 of this Article, the Army of the Republic of Cyprus shall be put under the Operational Command of this Headquarters.

4. In case of a threat of an attack by an enemy acting from without, the Tripartite Headquarters shall be responsible for dealing with it acting on the instructions of the Committee of Ministers. Nevertheless, in the event of a surprise attack by an enemy acting from without, the Tripartite Headquarters shall proceed automatically with the implementation of the plans for repelling it. At the same time it shall report without delay to the Committee of Ministers for further instructions.

5. In all the cases of its intervention the Tripartite Headquarters shall have consultations with the Appropriate Authorities of the Republic of Cyprus, in order to determine the necessary co-operation of the Security Forces of the Republic of Cyprus and the conditions for the implementation of this co-operation, or, in exceptional cases, to put these Forces entirely or in part under the Operational Command of the Tripartite Headquarters.

6. The Republic of Cyprus shall assume the obligation, in accordance with its Constitution, of putting at the disposal of the Tripartite Headquarters, upon request, any additional means necessary such as safe use of civilian communications, transportation, etc., for the successful implementation of the plans mentioned in this Agreement.

7. Whenever the successful implementation of the plans mentioned in this Agreement requires the proclamation of Martial Law, in whole or in part, a request to that effect shall be made to the Appropriate Authorities of the Republic of Cyprus, by the Tripartite Headquarters upon approval by the Committee of Ministers.

ARTICLE VI

THE TRIPARTITE HEADQUARTERS

1. The Tripartite Headquarters provided by Articles III and IV of the Treaty of Alliance shall consist of:

(a) the Commander and the Staff of the Tripartite Headquarters, and

(b) the Units and Services of the Army of the Republic of Cyprus to be assigned by it, and all the Hellenic and Turkish Forces stationed in the territory of the Republic of Cyprus.

2.–(a) Nicosia shall be the seat of the Commander and Staff of the Tripartite Headquarters.

(b) The seat of the Units and Services of the Hellenic and Turkish Forces shall be within Nicosia town area.

(c) The seat of the Units and Services of the Army of the Republic of Cyprus shall be determined by the Republic of Cyprus, in accordance with the relevant provisions of its Constitution, following an advisory proposal of the Tripartite Headquarters.

(d) In any event of a direct or indirect attack which, under the provisions of this Agreement, necessitates the intervention of the Tripartite Headquarters, it may redeploy units and services under its Operational Command.

ARTICLE VII

1. *Commander of the Tripartite Headquarters*
(a) The General Officer who shall assume the command of the Tripartite Headquarters, in accordance with Article V of the Treaty of Alliance, shall have the rank of Brigadier or Major General and shall be other than the Commanders of the national Forces, subject to the exception provided in paragraph 4 of this Article.

(b) The term of duty of the Commanders of the Tripartite Headquarters shall be of one year on a rotation basis among Cypriots, Greeks and Turks. The nationality of the first Commander as well as the subsequent order of rotation shall be determined by lot.

(c) The term of command of the first Commander of the Tripartite Headquarters shall be effective as from the arrival in the Republic of Cyprus of the Greek and Turkish Contingents mentioned in paragraph 1 of the Additional Protocol No. I.

(d) If the Republic of Cyprus believes that a Cypriot Commander of the Tripartite Headquarters is not sufficiently experienced, the Commanders of the Hellenic and Turkish national Forces shall be required to act as his advisers for as long as is deemed necessary.

The above special duties of these Commanders shall be distinct from their normal duties as members of the Advisory Committee mentioned in Article IX, paragraph 2, of this Agreement.

2. *Deputy Commander of the Tripartite Headquarters*
(a) There shall be a Deputy Commander of the Tripartite Headquarters with the rank of Colonel or Brigadier General. Whenever practicable, he should be senior to the Commanders of the Hellenic and Turkish Forces.

(b) The provisions of paragraph 1, sub-paragraph (b), of this Article shall apply for the Deputy Commander who shall not, however, be of the same nationality or ethnic origin as the Commander.

(c) In the event of absence or impediment of the Commander of the Tripartite Headquarters or vacancy of his post, the Deputy Commander shall assume his command and have the same authority as the Commander for a period not exceeding thirty days. Beyond this period, and until the end of the term of duty of the formal Commander, a new Commander of the same nationality shall be appointed. The Committee of Ministers shall be informed of any such event.

(d) With the exception of the situation referred to in sub-paragraph (c) of this paragraph, the Deputy Commander shall act as assistant to the Commander of the Tripartite Headquarters, in accordance with the latter's instructions.

3. *Chief of Staff of the Tripartite Headquarters*

(a) There shall be a Chief of Staff of the Tripartite Headquarters with the rank of Lieutenant Colonel or Colonel.

(b) The Chief of Staff shall not be of the same nationality as the Commander or the Deputy Commander.

4. The Cypriot nominees to the posts of Commander, Deputy Commander and Chief of Staff of the Tripartite Headquarters shall be the Commander, the Deputy Commander and the Chief of Staff of the Army of the Republic of Cyprus, respectively. The Cypriot nominees to the posts of Commander, Deputy Commander and Chief of Staff of the Tripartite Headquarters shall also retain their respective posts in the Army of the Republic of Cyprus, as its Commander, Deputy Commander and Chief of Staff.

ARTICLE VIII

TASKS AND RESPONSIBILITIES OF THE TRIPARTITE HEADQUARTERS

1.–(a) The Tripartite Headquarters establishes the plans according to Articles II and IV of this Agreement, and implements them in accordance with their provisions.

(b) It exercises operational command of the Army of the Republic of Cyprus (within the limitations of Article V, paragraph 1 and Article VI, paragraph 1(b), of this Agreement), of the Greek and Turkish Contingents referred to in paragraph 1 of the Additional Protocol No. I, and of those Forces referred to in Article XIV of this Agreement.

(c) It makes recommendations concerning the construction of military installations and fortifications required for the implementation of the plans referred to in this Agreement. These recommendations shall be subject to the approval of the Committee of Ministers, and the final decision will rest with the Republic of Cyprus which will bear the cost of the construction. Such installations and fortifications shall be controlled by the Tripartite Headquarters.

(d) It is kept informed about the major war materiel available to the Army of the Republic of Cyprus and to the Greek and Turkish Contingents. This information shall include particulars of the storing, the movement and the allocation of this materiel in order that the Tripartite Headquarters may intervene whenever it deems it necessary, for the purpose of ensuring the better implementation of the plans referred to in this Agreement.

(e) It is responsible for the training of the Army of the Republic of Cyprus. The responsibility of the Tripartite Headquarters on basic training shall be delegated after three years to the chain of Command of the Army of the Republic of Cyprus.

(f) It sets up a programme of joint general exercises, in which the Army of the Republic of Cyprus and the Hellenic and Turkish Forces stationed in the Republic of Cyprus participate. These exercises shall be conducted under the direction, and according to the directives of the Tripartite Headquarters. One of the aims of these exercises will be to check the operational readiness of these Forces.

(g) It submits advice to the Committee of Ministers and to the Appropriate Authorities of the Republic of Cyprus on all matters provided for in this Agreement, as well as on any other matter within its competence about which such advice may be requested.

(h) In accordance with Article IV of the Additional Protocol No. II, it submits to the Committee of Ministers its annual report which shall refer, *inter alia*, to the present state of the Forces under its Operational Command (e.g. units, their stationing, their strength, materiel, training status, operational readiness).

2. The Appropriate Authorities of the Republic of Cyprus shall be responsible for the maintenance of internal order and the application of Martial Law. Nevertheless, in matters concerning the security of the Forces under the Operational Command of the Tripartite Headquarters as well as the conduct of operations, the Appropriate Authorities of the Republic of Cyprus may delegate some responsibilities to the Tripartite Headquarters upon the latter's recommendation approved and conveyed by the Committee of Ministers.

ARTICLE IX

RESPONSIBILITIES OF THE COMMANDER OF THE TRIPARTITE HEADQUARTERS

1. The Commander of the Tripartite Headquarters shall be entitled, after consultation on important matters with his Advisory Committee as defined below, to make decisions, to issue orders and to submit recommendations to the Committee of Ministers on matters within the competence of the Tripartite Headquarters.

2. The Advisory Committee mentioned in paragraph 1 of this Article shall consist of the Commanders of the other two national Forces. The Commander of the Tripartite Headquarters may request his Deputy and Chief of Staff to attend the meetings of this Committee.

3. Any member of the Advisory Committee may request it to consider any matter within the competence of the Tripartite Headquarters and to submit its recommendations to the Commander thereof. The Committee shall satisfy such a request.

4. Without prejudice to the cases in which the Committee of Ministers has exclusive authority, the provisions of this Article shall not be construed as pre-

venting the Commander of the Tripartite Headquarters from making a decision, issuing an order or taking action in cases of urgency, within the competence of the Tripartite Headquarters. In such an event consultation with the Advisory Committee shall take place without any undue delay.

5. On any question or difficulties of a technical and current nature, which may arise concerning the application and operation of the military requirements of the United Kingdom in Cyprus, under the Treaty concerning the Establishment of the Republic of Cyprus signed at Nicosia on this day's date, the Tripartite Headquarters, after consultation with the United Kingdom Military Authorities in Cyprus, shall advise directly or upon request the Appropriate Authorities of the Republic of Cyprus on the steps to be taken by the Republic of Cyprus.

ARTICLE X

1. The flag of the Republic of Cyprus, with the flags of Greece and Turkey on either side, shall be hoisted over the building of the Tripartite Headquarters. The Greek or Turkish national flag together with the flag of the Republic of Cyprus shall be hoisted only at the Headquarters of the Hellenic and Turkish Forces, respectively, as well as over the premises where these Forces shall be garrisoned.

2. The Hellenic and Turkish Forces may celebrate their national holidays only within the precincts of their garrison area and/or within their official buildings, and may stage parades and march past only within the precincts of their garrison area. They may, however, participate in the public parades and march past on the Independence Day of the Republic of Cyprus or on any other occasion upon the request of the Appropriate Authorities of the Republic of Cyprus.

3. The official languages used by the Tripartite Headquarters shall be both Greek and Turkish. All the documents shall be prepared and issued in both languages. Documents addressed to the Tripartite Headquarters shall be made available by it in both official languages without delay.

ARTICLE XI

1. All the expenses for the functioning of the Tripartite Headquarters shall be equally allocated between the Republic of Cyprus, Greece and Turkey.

2. For this purpose the Commander of Tripartite Headquarters shall prepare an annual budget and submit it for approval to the Committee of Ministers.

3. During the first year of operation of the Tripartite Headquarters no budget shall be prepared. Instead, the expenses shall be approved from time to time, according to the same procedure.

4. The Republic of Cyprus shall provide the necessary public building or buildings for the installation of the Tripartite Headquarters, free of cost. The cost of maintenance of these buildings shall be included in the budget drawn up as above.

ARTICLE XII

1.–(a) The table of Organization and Major Equipment of the Tripartite Headquarters is set out in Annex "A" to this Agreement.

(b) The personnel allocated to the Tripartite Headquarters shall come under the allowed personnel ceiling for each national Contingent.

2. In the event that the plans mentioned in this Agreement should have to be implemented, the Staff establishment of the Tripartite Headquarters shall be supplemented according to Part II of Annex "A" to this Agreement. The provisions of paragraph 1, sub-paragraph (b), of this Article shall be applicable in this case.

3. The civilian personnel required for the operation of the Tripartite Headquarters shall consist of Cypriots. Their total number, which temporarily is included in Annex "A" to this Agreement, shall be determined at the time of the approval of the budget (or the expenses) of the Tripartite Headquarters according to Article XI of this Agreement.

4. In the event that additional Hellenic and Turkish Forces should have to be sent to the Republic of Cyprus, as provided for in this Agreement, the necessary completion of the Tripartite Headquarters shall take place accordingly. For this purpose the Tripartite Headquarters shall prepare supplementary Tables of Organization and Major Equipment, in accordance with appropriate plans, to be approved by the Committee of Ministers.

ARTICLE XIII

GREEK AND TURKISH CONTINGENTS

1.–(a) The Tables of Organization and Major Equipment of the Greek and Turkish Contingents provided in paragraph 1 of the Additional Protocol No. I are set out in Annex "B" to this Agreement.

(b) In the event of an increase or reduction of these Contingents in accordance with paragraph II of the Additional Protocol No. I, a new Table of Organization and Major Equipment shall be prepared subject to the approval of the Committee of Ministers.

2.–(a) The ceiling of the Greek and Turkish Contingents, set out in paragraph I of the Additional Protocol No. I, shall be deemed to include all Greek and Turkish military personnel on duty within the territory of the Republic of Cyprus as well as those who belong to these Contingents and are temporarily abroad for service, on furlough, medical treatment, etc. In excess of the above mentioned ceiling, Greek or Turkish military missions or personnel may be sent on temporary duty to the Republic of Cyprus with the approval of the Appropriate Authorities of the Republic of Cyprus and the Committee of Ministers.

(b) In the event of replacements, the ceiling set out for the Greek and Turkish Contingents in paragraph 1 of the Additional Protocol No. I, as well as their agreed major equipment, may be exceeded in proportion to the replacing personnel and equipment. This exception may not last for more than two weeks. The number of replacements shall be fixed by the Tripartite Headquarters in accordance with the existing policies for replacements in the respective countries.

(c) Whenever the Greek and Turkish Contingents exceed their ceiling as above, the Commander of the Tripartite Headquarters shall be informed thereof in due course and he, in turn, shall inform the Committee of Ministers and the Appropriate Authorities of the Republic of Cyprus.

3. The Commanders of the Hellenic and Turkish Forces shall have full authority over all Greek and Turkish military personnel, respectively, normally stationed in the territory of the Republic of Cyprus and not senior to them. They shall be responsible for the discipline of all their respective national military personnel not senior to them.

4. Wherever personnel coming from different national Forces are working together, the chain of command shall be applied according to rank. In the case of equality of rank, seniority in acquiring that rank shall be taken into consideration. The Tripartite Headquarters shall keep an up to date roster of the officers and NCOs of the three Forces and shall furnish to the Appropriate Authorities of the Republic of Cyprus an information copy including dependents, enlisted men and employees.

5. The civilian personnel required for the Hellenic and Turkish Forces shall consist of Cypriots.

ARTICLE XIV

ADDITIONAL HELLENIC AND TURKISH FORCES

1. With reference to Articles II and III of this Agreement, the following procedure shall govern any increase in the Greek and Turkish Contingents stationed in the territory of the Republic of Cyprus in accordance with paragraph I of the Additional Protocol No. I:

(a) The President and the Vice-President of the Republic of Cyprus acting in agreement may request the Governments of Greece and Turkey to increase the strength of the above mentioned Contingents. The matter shall be referred to the Committee of Ministers which shall request the Tripartite Headquarters to submit its views as to the strength, organization and major equipment of the eventual additional Forces. The final decisions of the Greek and Turkish Governments shall be communicated in due course to the President and the Vice-President of the Republic of Cyprus. It is understood that the additional Forces may be land, naval or air Forces.

(b) If an increase in the strength of the Greek and Turkish Contingents mentioned in paragraph I of this Article is deemed necessary by the Committee of Ministers, or is requested by the Tripartite Headquarters and approved by this Committee, the latter shall communicate a request to that effect, together with recommendations by the Tripartite Headquarters as to the strength, organization and major equipment of the eventual additional forces, to the President and the Vice-President of the Republic of Cyprus who shall decide, acting in agreement, whether this request shall be referred to the Governments of Greece and Turkey for a final decision on the matter.

(c) The proportion between the Greek and Turkish Contingents established in paragraph I of the Additional Protocol No. I, concerning personnel, as well as the proportion established in Annex "B" to this Agreement concerning major equipment, shall also be observed with regard to the additional Forces.

(d) Upon their arrival in the Republic of Cyprus, the additional Forces with their equipment shall be placed under the Operational Command of the Tripartite Headquarters, on the conditions effective for the Greek and Turkish Contingents provided for in paragraph I of the Additional Protocol No. I.

2. The procedure and rules set forth in paragraph 1 of this Article shall apply to any importation into the Republic of Cyprus for the use of the Greek and Turkish Contingents, of war materiel in excess of that provided for in Annex "B" to this Agreement or in paragraph 1 in this Article.

ARTICLE XV

1. The legal status of the Hellenic and Turkish armed Forces is set out in Annex "C" to this Agreement.

2.–(a) All the expenses of the Hellenic and Turkish armed Forces, stationed in the Republic of Cyprus, shall be borne by their respective Government.

(b) The Republic of Cyprus undertakes to provide for the use, as required by the Hellenic and Turkish Forces, of public utilities (water, telegraph, electric power, etc.) upon payment.

(c) Accommodation and training areas for the Hellenic and Turkish Forces shall be provided by the Republic of Cyprus which shall make every effort to secure them free of cost. Their cost of maintenance shall be borne by the Forces using them. In the event of common use by the above mentioned forces the cost shall he borne proportionately.

3. The Republic of Cyprus shall provide for the free use of roads and ports in its territory by the Hellenic and Turkish Forces under the same conditions as will be the case with the Army of the Republic of Cyprus.

4. The Republic of Cyprus shall ensure the use of airfields in its territory by the civilian and military aircraft of Greece and Turkey to serve the military transportation needs of the Hellenic and Turkish Forces, stationed in Cyprus, from these countries to the Republic of Cyprus and *vice versa*, under the international regulations of air transportation.

5. The Hellenic and Turkish Forces shall be garrisoned in the same area as near each other as possible and within a radius of five miles and they shall share the same recreational and other facilities. The Republic of Cyprus shall do its utmost in this direction.

6. The total pay (including basic monthly payment and all overseas allowances) shall be the same within each rank for all personnel of the Hellenic and Turkish Forces normally stationed in the territory of the Republic of Cyprus and shall be agreed upon by the two Governments concerned.

ARTICLE XVI

TRAINING OF THE ARMY OF THE REPUBLIC OF CYPRUS

1. The training of the Army of the Republic of Cyprus is set out in Annex "D" to this Agreement ("Training of the Army of the Republic of Cyprus").

2. The training of the Army of the Republic of Cyprus shall be carried out by Greek and Turkish military personnel in accordance with Article IV of the Treaty of Alliance. It shall cover all phases of training (basic, advance and unit training) for Officers, NCOs and Enlisted men.

3. The Appropriate Authorities of the Republic of Cyprus, in consultation with the Tripartite Headquarters, shall determine the general aims of the training of the Army of the Republic of Cyprus within the framework of the provisions of this Agreement.

4.–(a) All training of the Army of the Republic of Cyprus (Officers, NCOs and ORs) shall be undertaken by the Greek and Turkish military personnel. This personnel shall come under the ceiling of the Contingents as provided for in paragraph 1 of Additional Protocol No. I.

(b) The general proportion between Greek and Turkish training personnel shall be the same as that applied to the ethnic composition of the Army of the Republic of Cyprus according to the latter's Constitution. The same proportion shall apply, as far as practicable, to all ranks of the training personnel.

5.–(a) The Tripartite Headquarters shall decide with the concurrent opinion of the Commanders of the Hellenic and Turkish Forces the number of personnel of each rank to be assigned by the Greek and Turkish Contingents, respectively, for the training of the Army of the Republic of Cyprus.

(b) The actual nomination of this personnel shall be made by the Commanders of the Hellenic and Turkish Forces, respectively.

6.–(a) The Greek and Turkish training personnel shall form a group under a single command. The Chief of this Training Group shall be responsible to the Commander of the Tripartite Headquarters with regard to the training of the Army of the Republic of Cyprus.

(b) The Chief of the Training Group shall be a Greek and a Turk by yearly rotation. The Deputy Chief of the Training Group shall not be of the same nationality as the Chief. For the first year the Chief shall be designated by lot, but he shall not be of the same nationality as the Commander of the Tripartite Headquarters.

7. The Greek and Turkish training personnel shall exercise no command authority within the Army of the Republic of Cyprus.

8. The principle of mixed organizational structure of the Army of the Republic of Cyprus shall be adhered to also in training.

FINAL PROVISIONS

ARTICLE XVII

1. The Committee of Ministers shall have competence for the authoritative interpretation of the provisions of this Agreement including the Annexes thereto.

2. The Committee of Ministers shall be empowered to make amendments and additions to this Agreement and the Annexes thereto provided that such amendments and additions do not affect the Treaty of Alliance.

ARTICLE XVIII

1. The Annexes to this Agreement shall come into force and effect as an integral part of it.

2. This Agreement, including Annexes "A", "B", "C" and "D" thereto, shall come into force on the same date as the Treaty of Alliance.

In witness whereof the undersigned, being duly authorized thereto, have signed the present Agreement.

Done at Nicosia, this 16th day of August, 1960, in three copies in the English language, of which one shall be deposited with each of the High Contracting Parties.

For the Kingdom of Greece:

For the Republic of Turkey:

For the Republic of Cyprus:

ANNEX "A"

TABLE OF ORGANIZATION AND EQUIPMENT
FOR THE TRIPARTITE HEADQUARTERS
(COMMAND AND STAFF)

PART I.—BASIC ORGANIZATION

A. STRUCTURE

See Table of Organization of Tripartite Headquarters (Command and Staff) in Appendix I.

B. PERSONNEL

See Table of Personnel in Appendix 2.

C. MAJOR EQUIPMENT

1. *General*

Individual Equipment and weapons for the Officers and Other Ranks shall be supplied by the Commanders of the respective National Forces. All military personnel, assigned to the Tripartite Headquarters and having a rank, shall carry revolvers; Enlisted men shall carry rifles, except drivers, who shall carry submachine guns.

2. *Office Equipment*

Expenses for office equipment, furniture, etc., shall be covered by the annual budget (or expenses for the first year) of the Tripartite Headquarters.

3. *Transportation*

Transportation shall be furnished by the Republic of Cyprus in the following manner:

1 Car	:	For CG, Tripartite Hqs.
1 Car	:	For Deputy Commander, Tripartite Hqs.
2 Staff Cars	:	For the Officers of the Tripartite Hqs.
1 1/4 tons Jeep	:	For Message Centre.
1 Motorcycle	:	For Message Centre.

PART II.—SUPPLEMENTARY COMPOSITION

A. PERSONNEL

1. Additional personnel listed in this part shall be furnished by the Appropriate National Forces located in Cyprus.

2. The following personnel is added to that authorized in the usual composition:

(a) Staff Secretariat:

(1) Main Registry	:	2 Junior Officers, ARC
		4 Clerk-Typists, ARC
		3 Messengers, ARC

(2) Translation Section   :   4 Interpreters Civilian Cypriots. (Two of them must have a working knowledge of Greek, Turkish and English).

(3) Communication and
      Message Centre   :   2 Sergeants (Signal Corps),
         HA and TA
      5 EM (Signal Corps), 3 HA and 2 TA

(b) Staff Group   :   2 Majors, HA and TA
      1 Junior Officer, ARC
      4 Junior Liaison Officers,
         2 ARC, 1 HA & 1 TA
      2 Clerks, ARC
      1 Orderly, ARC
      3 Drivers, ARC
      3 Officers, Security Forces RC

3. Personnel total of Supplementary Composition:

Nationality	Officers	NCOs	EM	Civilians	Total
Republic of Cyprus	8	–	13	4	25
Greece	2	1	3	–	6
Turkey	2	1	2	–	5
Total	12	2	18	4	36

B. MAJOR EQUIPMENT

1. *Transportation*

On the responsibility of the Republic of Cyprus, the following equipment shall be added to the Supplementary Composition:

3 Staff Cars   :   For the Officers of the Tripartite Headquarters
8 Motorcycles   :   Five for the Staff Group, three for the Message Centre

2. *Signal Equipment*

The necessary additional signal equipment shall be furnished by the Hellenic and Turkish Forces located in Cyprus.

PART III.—GENERAL PROVISIONS

The provisions mentioned in the following paragraphs are applicable to both parts, Basic Organization and Supplementary Composition of this Annex:

1. The proportion in allocating military personnel in the Tripartite Headquarters among the Cypriots, Greeks and Turks is based on the proportion taken from the established personnel ceiling for the Army of the Republic of Cyprus and the Greek and Turkish Contingents in accordance with the rele-

vant provision of the Constitution of the Republic of Cyprus and Article 1 of Additional Protocol No. 1. The appointment of members of the Army of the Republic of Cyprus to the places reserved for them at the Tripartite Headquarters shall be made by the President and Vice-President of the Republic of Cyprus, acting in agreement.

2. The established proportion in this Annex shall be observed as strictly as possible in any future revision, whatsoever, of the composition of the Tripartite Headquarters, or increase or reduction of the number of personnel.

3. The Commander, the Deputy Commander and all Staff Officers must have a working knowledge of English.

4. All personnel allocated to the Tripartite Headquarters shall be free from any duty connected with their national forces, subject to the provisions of Article VII, paragraph 4, of this Agreement.

5. All Field Grade Greek and Turkish Officers (Majors to Colonels) assigned to the Tripartite Headquarters shall be graduates of their respective Staff Colleges.

6. All Company Grade Officers (Lieutenant to Captain), except as specified in Appendix 2 to this Annex, shall be Infantry Officers.

TABLE OF ORGANIZATION OF THE TRIPARTITE HQS
(COMMANDER AND STAFF)

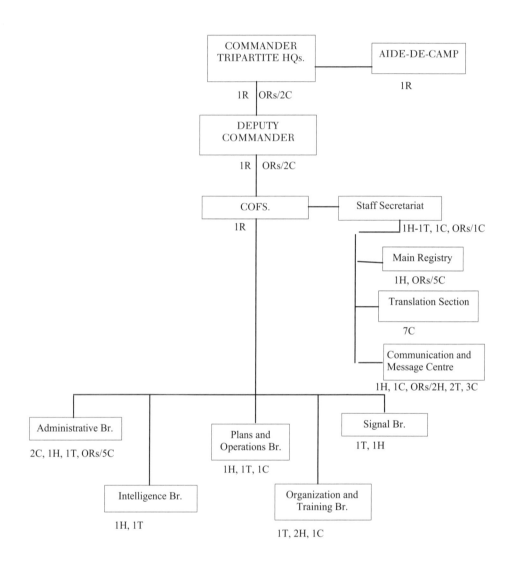

Abbreviations:

R = In rotation

C = Of the Republic of Cyprus

H = Hellenic Army

T = Turkish Army

ORs = Other Ranks

PERSONNEL

Serial No.	Allocation of Personnel	Officers							Other Ranks					Grand Total	Service	Nationality and Remarks
		Brig. Gen.	Colonels	Lt. Colonels	Majors	Captains	Junior	Total	First Sgts.	Sergeants	Corporals	Enlisted Men	Total			
1	Command:															
	Commander of Tr. Hqs.	1	–	–	–	–	–	1	–	–	–	–	–	1		Rot. (May be Major Gen.)
	Deputy Commander	–	1	–	–	–	–	1	–	–	–	–	–	1		Rot. (May be Brig. Gen.)
	Aide to the Commander	–	–	–	–	–	1	1	–	–	–	–	–	1		Rot.
	Orderlies	–	–	–	–	–	–	–	–	–	–	2	2	2		ARC
	Drivers	–	–	–	–	–	–	–	–	–	2	–	2	2		ARC
	TOTAL	1	1	–	–	–	1	3	–	–	2	2	4	7		
2	Staff Group:															
	(a) Chief of Staff	–	–	1	–	–	–	1	–	–	–	–	–	1		Rot. (May be Colonel)
	(b) Staff Secretariat															
	Secretary	–	–	–	1	–	–	1	–	–	–	–	–	1		⎫ Rot. (HA
	Asst. Secretary	–	–	–	–	1	–	1	–	–	–	–	–	1		⎭ and TA)
	Asst. Secretary	–	–	–	–	–	1	1	–	–	–	–	–	1		ARC
	Clerk	–	–	–	–	–	–	–	–	–	–	1	1	1		ARC
	(i) Main Registry:															
	Director	–	–	–	–	–	1	1	–	–	–	–	–	1		HA
	Clerks and typists	–	–	–	–	–	–	–	–	–	–	4	4	4		ARC
	Draftsman	–	–	–	–	–	–	–	–	1	–	–	1	1		ARC b
	(ii) Translation Section : a															
	Chief Interpreter	–	–	–	–	1	–	1	–	1	–	–	1	2		ARC
	Interpreters	–	–	–	–	–	6	6	–	–	–	–	–	6		ARC b
	(iii) Communication and Message Centre															
	Chief	–	–	–	–	1	–	1	–	–	–	–	–	1	SC	HA
	Assistant	–	–	–	–	–	1	1	–	–	–	–	–	1	SC	ARC
	Corporals	–	–	–	–	–	–	–	–	–	4	–	4	4	SC	2HA, 2TA
	Messengers	–	–	–	–	–	–	–	–	–	–	2	2	2		ARC
	Driver	–	–	–	–	–	–	–	–	–	–	1	1	1		ARC
	(c) Administrative Branch: c															
	Chief	–	–	–	1	–	–	1	–	–	–	–	–	1		ARC
	Assist. Personnel and Engineer	–	–	–	–	1	–	1	–	–	–	–	–	1	EC	HA
	Assist. Logistics	–	–	–	–	1	–	1	–	–	–	–	–	1	TC	TA
	Hqs. Commander	–	–	–	–	–	1	1	–	–	–	–	–	1		ARC
	Orderlies	–	–	–	–	–	–	–	–	–	–	3	3	3		ARC
	Drivers	–	–	–	–	–	–	–	–	–	–	2	2	2		ARC
	Carried forward	–	–	1	2	5	10	18	–	2	4	13	19	37	–	

a The Chief Interpreter and two of the Interpreters must have a working knowledge of Greek, Turkish and English.

b The Draftsman and the six Interpreters may be civilians.

c The Chiefs of the Branches shall not be senior to the Chief of Staff.

PERSONNEL—*continued*

Serial No.	Allocation of Personnel	Officers Brig. Gen.	Colonels	Lt. Colonels	Majors	Captains	Junior	Total	Other Ranks First Sgts.	Sergeants	Corporals	Enlisted Men	Total	Grand Total	Service	Nationality and Remarks
2	Staff Group–*contd.* Brought forward	–	–	1	2	5	10	18	–	2	4	13	19	37		
	(d) Intelligence Branch:															
	Chief	–	–	–	1	–	–	1	–	–	–	–	–	1		HA
	Assistant	–	–	–	–	–	1	1	–	–	–	–	–	1		TA (May be a Captain)
	(e) Plans and Operations Branch:															
	Chief	–	–	1	–	–	–	1	–	–	–	–	–	1		HA
	Assistant	–	–	–	1	–	–	1	–	–	–	–	–	1		TA
	Assistant	–	–	–	–	1	–	1	–	–	–	–	–	1		ARC
	(f) Organization and Training Branch:															
	Chief	–	–	1	–	–	–	1	–	–	–	–	–	1		TA
	Assistant	–	–	–	2	–	–	2	–	–	–	–	–	2		HA
	Assistant	–	–	–	–	1	–	1	–	–	–	–	–	1		ARC
	(g) Signal Branch:															
	Chief	–	–	–	1	–	–	1	–	–	–	–	–	1	SC	TA
	Assistant	–	–	–	–	1	–	1	–	–	–	–	–	1	SC	HA
	Total	–	–	3	7	8	11	29	–	2	4	13	19	48		
	Grand Total (1+2)	1	1	3	7	8	12	32	–	2	6	15	23	55		
	ALLOCATION BY NATIONALITY Rotation (ARC, HA & TA)	1	1	1	–	–	1	4	–	–	–	–	–	4		
	Rotation (HA & TA)	–	–	–	1	1	–	2	–	–	–	–	–	2		
	Army of the Republic of Cyprus	–	–	–	1	3	9	13	–	2	2	15	19	32		
	Hellenic Army	–	–	1	3	3	1	8	–	–	2	–	2	10		
	Turkish Army	–	–	1	2	1	1	5	–	–	2	–	2	7		
	Total	1	1	3	7	8	12	32	–	2	6	15	23	55		

Abbreviations:

ARC = Army of the Republic of Cyprus.
HA = Hellenic Army.
TA   = Turkish Army.
EC   = Engineer Corps.
SC   = Signal Corps.
TC   = Transportation Corps.
Rot. = In Rotation.

ANNEX "B"

TABLE OF ORGANIZATION AND MAJOR EQUIPMENT OF THE GREEK AND TURKISH CONTINGENTS IN CYPRUS

SECTION I.—GENERAL PROVISIONS

A. PERSONNEL

1. The breakdown of the established Greek and Turkish Contingents in accordance with Article I of the Additional Protocol No. 1 is shown below:

Armies and Ranks			Units							Allocation for Tripartite Hqs.	Training Group	Grand Total
			Command and Staff	H. and S. Company	Medical Detach.	Recon. Platoon	Heavy Weapons Co.	Infantry	Total			
HELLENIC ARMY	Officers	Col.	1	–	–	–	–	–	1	–	–	–
		Lt. Col.	1	–	–	–	–	–	1	1	–	–
		Maj.	3	–	–	–	–	2	5	3	–	–
		Capt.	6	2	3	–	1	10	22	3	–	–
		Junior	1	8	–	1	3	20	33	1	–	–
		Total	12	10	3	1	4	32	62	8+2°	–	–
	W.O.		–	1	–	–	–	–	1			
	Other Ranks	F. Serg.	–	5	–	–	1	8	14	–	–	–
		Serg.	–	21	2	4	4	90	121	–	–	–
		Corp	4	35	2	3	12	74	130	2	–	
		EM	6	74	5	13	41	396	535	–	–	–
		Total	10	136	9	20	58	568	801	2	–	–
	Grand Total		22	146	12	21	62	600	863	12	75	950
TURKISH ARMY	Officers	Col.	1	–	–	–	–	–	1	–	–	–
		Lt. Col.	1	–	–	–	–	–	1	1	–	–
		Maj.	3	–	–	–	–	–	3	2	–	–
		Capt.	6	1	2	–	1	4	14	1	–	–
		Junior	1	7	–	1	3	12	24	1	–	–
		Total	12	8	2	1	4	16	43	5+2°	–	–
	Other Ranks	NCOs	1	22	1	1	2	20	47	–	–	–
		Troop Serg.	–	9	–	2	6	36	53	–	–	–
		Corp.	2	19	2	2	8	44	77	2	–	–
		EM	8	68	4	11	28	252	371	–	–	–
		Total	11	118	7	16	44	352	548	2	–	–
	Grand Total		23	126	9	17	48	368	591	9	50	650

° + 2 Rotational
(a) These two spaces are the following:
 (i) One for the Commander or Deputy Commander or Chief of Staff of the Tripartite Head-
    quarters (in rotation).
 (ii) One for the Secretary or Assistant Secretary in the Staff Group of the Tripartite Headquar-
    ters (in rotation).
(b) The space for the Aide to the Commander of the Tripartite Headquarters, who shall be of the same nationality as the Commander, shall come under the strength of his national Contingent and shall be taken
temporarily from the relevant Training Group.

2.–(a) The personnel assigned to the Tripartite Headquarters is shown in
Annex "A".

(b) The personnel for the Training Group include Officers, NCOs and EM.
Their allocation by rank and service shall be determined in accordance
with the provisions indicated in Article XVI of this Agreement, in order
to meet the training requirements of the Army of the Republic of Cyprus. Any surplus shall be placed as riflemen in the rifle companies of
the respective Forces.

B. MAJOR EQUIPMENT

1. The major equipment is considered as follows:

(a) *Weapons:*
 (1) Revolvers
 (2) Submachine guns.
 (3) Rifles
 (4) Machine Guns
 (5) Recoilless Rifles (or Rocket-Launchers as substitutes)
 (6) Mortars

(b) *Vehicles:*
 (1) Motorcycles
 (2) Light Vehicles (1/4 to 2 1/2 tons)
 (3) Recovery Vehicles
 (4) Ambulances
 (5) Special Trailors (e.g. Water Trailors)

(c) *Signal Equipment:*
 (1) Radio sets
 (2) Switchboards

2. Major equipment of the Hellenic and Turkish Forces are shown separately in their sections of this Annex.

C. LOGISTICAL SUPPORT

1. The logistical support and financial management are national responsibilities and shall be dealt in accordance with the respective national regulations. Meanwhile, every effort shall be made to obtain goods locally by payment.

2. The quantity of ammunition per weapon is shown in the Appendix to
this section.

3. Concerning the carrying of weapons the following shall apply:

(a) Persons carrying Revolvers:
 (1) Officers (and Warrant Officers of Hellenic Forces)
 (2) MPs
 (3) Messenger in Military Post Office

      (4) Pointers and Loaders of Recoilless Rifles (or .3,5" Rocket-Launchers), Mortars and Machine Guns.

(b) Persons carrying Submachine guns:

      (1) NCOs

      (2) Drivers

      (3) MPs

      (4) Messengers

      (5) Troop Sergeants of Turkish Forces

      (6) Telemeter Operators

      (7) Switchboard Operators

      (8) Ciphers

      (9) Buglers

      (10) Leaders of Mortars and Machine guns.

(c) All the remaining shall carry rifles, except the light machine gun Pointers who shall not carry other weapon.

(d) All Hellenic and Turkish personnel assigned to the Tripartite Headquarters shall carry revolvers.

(e) 45 revolvers, 15 submachine guns and 15 rifles are provided for the Hellenic personnel in the Training Group and 30 revolvers, 10 submachine guns and 10 rifles for the Turkish personnel in the Training Group.

(f) The Detachments shall also keep 5% supplies for replacement of weapons except for machine guns, recoilless rifles (or rocket-launchers as substitutes) and mortars.

S/N	Details	Revolver	Sub-Machinegun	Rifle Normal	Rifle Tracer	Rifle Total	LMG B.A.R. Normal (Armor Piercing)	LMG B.A.R. Tracer	LMG B.A.R. Total	Machine Gun Armor Piercing	Machine Gun Tracer	Machine Gun Total	57 mm RR High Explosive	57 mm RR Armor Piercing	57 mm RR With Smoke	57 mm RR Total	75 mm RR / 3.5" RL High Explosive	75 mm RR / 3.5" RL Armor Piercing	75 mm RR / 3.5" RL With Smoke	75 mm RR / 3.5" RL Total	81 mm Mortar Explosive	81 mm Mortar Smoke	81 mm Mortar Illuminating	81 mm Mortar Total
1	1st Line ammo with the weapon	14	160	88	2	90	450	30	480	1400	300	1700	16	2	2	20	22	4	4	30	75	8	3	86
2	1st Line ammo at the unit	25	160	68	2	70	600	100	700	1400	300	1700	8	1	1	10	6	2	2	10	37	4	1	42
3	2nd Line ammo at the unit	25	160	68	2	70	250	70	320	1400	200	1600	16	2	2	20	16	2	2	20	56	6	2	64
	Total	64	480	224	6	230	1300	200	1500	4200	800	5000	40	5	5	50	44	8	8	60	168	18	6	192

S/N	Details	60 mm Mortar Explosive	60 mm Mortar Smoke	60 mm Mortar Illuminating	60 mm Mortar Total	Hand grenade per Rifle Company Defensive	Hand grenade per Rifle Company Fire	Hand grenade per Rifle Company Smoke	Hand grenade per Rifle Company Total	Signal Flares (One Star) White	Signal Flares (One Star) Red	Signal Flares (One Star) Green	Signal Flares (One Star) Total
1	1st Line ammo with the weapon	36	6	6	48	–	–	–	–	–	–	–	–
2	1st Line ammo at the unit	36	6	6	48	50	5	5	60	15	15	8	38
3	2nd Line ammo at the unit	36	6	6	48	120	10	10	140	10	14	6	30
	Total	108	18	18	144	170	15	15	200	25	29	14	68

SECTION II.—TABLE OF ORGANIZATION AND MAJOR EQUIPMENT OF THE HELLENIC FORCES IN CYPRUS

A. STRUCTURE
   See Table of Organization in Appendix 1.
B. PERSONNEL
   See Table of Personnel in Appendix 2.
C. MAJOR EQUIPMENT
   1. *Weapons. See* Table of Weapons in Appendix 3.
   2. *Vehicles. See* Table of Vehicles in Appendix 4.
   3. *Signal Equipment. See* Table of Signal Equipment in Appendix 5.

TABLE OF ORGANIZATION
HELLENIC FORCES

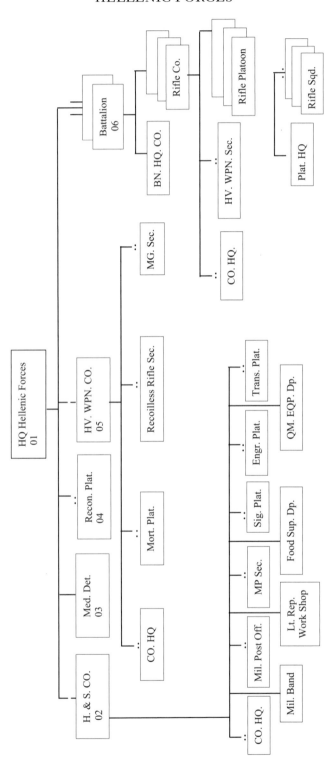

PERSONNEL—HELLENIC FORCES

Serial No.	Allocation of Personnel	Officers							Warrant Offrs.	Other Ranks					Grand Total	Service	Remarks
		Brig. Gen.	Colonels	Lt. Colonels	Majors	Captains	Junior	Total		First Sergeants	Sergeants	Corporals	Enlisted Men	Total			
1	*Command and Staff:*																
	Commander	–	1	–	–	–	–	1	–	–	–	–	–	–	1	Inf.	
	Executive Officer	–	–	1	–	–	–	1	–	–	–	–	–	–	1	"	
	Adjutant	–	–	–	–	1	–	1	–	–	–	–	–	–	1	"	
	Orderly-Clerk	–	–	–	–	–	–	–	–	–	–	1a	1	2	2	"	
	S—1 : S—4	–	–	–	1	–	–	1	–	–	–	–	–	–	1	"	
	Doctor	–	–	–	1	–	–	1	–	–	–	–	–	–	1	Med. C	
	Legal Serv. Officer	–	–	–	–	1	–	1	–	–	–	–	–	–	1	Leg. SC	
	Recruiting Officer	–	–	–	–	1	–	1	–	–	–	–	–	–	1	R.C.S.	
	Finance Officer	–	–	–	–	1	–	1	–	–	–	–	–	–	1	Fin. S.	
	Clerk-Typist	–	–	–	–	–	–	–	–	–	–	1	3	4	4	Inf.	
	S—2 : S—3	–	–	–	1	–	–	1	–	–	–	–	–	–	1	"	
	Assistants	–	–	–	–	2	–	2	–	–	–	–	–	–	2	"	
	Clerk-Typists	–	–	–	–	–	–	–	–	–	–	1b	1	2	2	"	
	Chief, Registry	–	–	–	–	–	1	1	–	–	–	–	–	–	1	"	
	Clerks	–	–	–	–	–	–	–	–	–	–	1	1	2	2	"	
	TOTAL	–	1	1	3	6	1	12	–	–	–	4	6	10	22		
2	*HQ and Service Company:* *(a) Co. Hq.* *(i) Hq. Group*																
	Commander	–	–	–	–	1	–	1	–	–	–	–	–	–	1	Inf.	
	Executive	–	–	–	–	–	1	1	–	–	–	–	–	–	1	"	
	First Sergeant	–	–	–	–	–	–	–	–	1	–	–	–	1	1	"	
	Clerk (QM)	–	–	–	–	–	–	–	–	–	1	–	–	1	1	"	
	Clerks	–	–	–	–	–	–	–	–	–	–	1	1	2	2	"	
	Mess. Stew./Cooks	–	–	–	–	–	–	–	–	–	–	1	3	4	4	"	
	Barbers	–	–	–	–	–	–	–	–	–	–	–	2	2	2	"	
		–	–	–	–	1	1	2	–	1	1	2	6	10	12		
	(ii) Command and Staff Group (As indicated above) *(b) Military Post Office*																
	Personnel	–	–	–	–	–	–	–	–	–	1	–	2	3	3	MPS	
		–	–	–	–	–	–	–	–	–	1	–	2	3	3		
	(c) Military Police Section																
	Commander	–	–	–	–	–	–	1	1	–	–	–	–	–	1	Inf	
	Personnel	–	–	–	–	–	–	–	–	–	1	10	–	11	11	" c	
								1	1		1	10		11	12		

a He must also have a working knowledge of Turkish.
b Also draftsman.
c Two of them drivers.

PERSONNEL—HELLENIC FORCES—*continued*

Serial No.	Allocation of Personnel	Officers							Warrant Offrs.	Other Ranks					Grand Total	Service	Remarks
		Brig. Gen.	Colonels	Lt. Cols.	Majors	Captains	Junior	Total		First Sergeants	Sergeants	Corporals	Enlisted Men	Total			
	(d) Signal Platoon.																
	Commander	–	–	–	–	–	1	1	–	–	–	–	–	–	1	Signal	
	Assistant NCO	–	–	–	–	–	–	–	–	–	1	–	–	1	1	"	
	Communication Centre																
	Chief	–	–	–	–	–	–	–	–	–	1	–	–	1	1	"	
	Ciphers	–	–	–	–	–	–	–	–	–	–	1	3	4	4	"	
	Tech. Store Keeper	–	–	–	–	–	–	–	–	–	–	1	1	1	1	"	
	H.P. Radio Repairman	–	–	–	–	–	–	–	–	–	–	1	1	1	1	"	
	Power-Battery Repairman	–	–	–	–	–	–	–	–	–	–	1	1	1	1	"	
	Radio Section																
	Chief	–	–	–	–	–	–	–	–	–	1	–	–	1	1	"	
	Operators	–	–	–	–	–	–	–	–	–	–	3	10	13	13	"	*a*
	Wire Section																
	Chief	–	–	–	–	–	–	–	–	–	1	–	–	1	1	"	
	Operators	–	–	–	–	–	–	–	–	–	–	2	5	7	7	"	
	Signal Men	–	–	–	–	–	–	–	–	–	–	2	4	6	6	"	*b*
		–	–	–	–	–	1	1	–	–	4	8	25	37	38		
	(e) Engineer Plat.																
	Commander	–	–	–	–	–	1	1	–	–	–	–	–	–	1	Engr.	
	Assistant NCO	–	–	–	–	–	–	–	–	–	1	–	–	1	1	"	
	Mine Sweepers	–	–	–	–	–	–	–	–	–	–	1	3	4	4	Inf.	
	Demolition Expert	–	–	–	–	–	–	–	–	–	1	1	–	2	2	Engr.	
	Water Supply Exp.	–	–	–	–	–	–	–	–	–	1	2	3	3	"	
	Construction Exp.	–	–	–	–	–	–	–	–	–	–	2	2	2	"	
	Electrician	–	–	–	–	–	–	–	–	–	1	–	1	1	"	
	Decorator	–	–	–	–	–	–	–	–	–	–	1	1	1	"	
	Carpenter	–	–	–	–	–	–	–	–	–	–	2	2	2	"	
	Driver	–	–	–	–	–	–	–	–	–	–	1	1	1	"	
		–	–	–	–	–	1	1	–	–	2	4	11	17	18		
	(f) Transportation Platoon.															S. & T. Corps	
	Commander	–	–	–	–	1	–	1	–	–	–	–	–	–	1	"	
	Assistant NCO	–	–	–	–	–	–	–	–	–	1	–	–	1	1	"	
	Drivers	–	–	–	–	–	–	–	–	–	–	3	14	17	17		*c*
		–	–	–	–	1	–	1	–	–	1	3	14	18	19		
	(g) Military Band.																
	Commander	–	–	–	–	–	1	1	–	–	–	–	–	–	1	MMS	
	Personnel	–	–	–	–	–	–	–	1	4	6	4	2	17	17	"	
		–	–	–	–	–	1	1	1	4	6	4	2	17	18		

a One of them driver of the Radio Set Vehicle.
b One of them messenger.
c Two Corporals are 1/4 Drivers for the Command and Staff.

PERSONNEL—HELLENIC FORCES—*continued*

Serial No.	Allocation of Personnel	Officers							Warrant Offrs.	Other Ranks					Grand Total	Service	Remarks
		Brig. Gen.	Colonels	Lt. Cols.	Majors	Captains	Junior	Total		First Sergeants	Sergeants	Corporals	Enlisted Men	Total			
	(h) Light Repair Workshop.																
	Commander	–	–	–	–	–	1	1	–	–	–	–	–	–	1	Tech. C.	
	Vehicle Technician	–	–	–	–	–	–	–	–	–	1	2	2	5	5	"	
	Vehicle Electrician	–	–	–	–	–	–	–	–	–	–	1	–	1	1	"	
	Blacksmith	–	–	–	–	–	–	–	–	–	–	–	1	1	1	"	
	Recovery Driver	–	–	–	–	–	–	–	–	–	–	–	1	1	1	"	
		–	–	–	–	–	1	1	–	–	1	3	4	8	9		
	(i) Food Supply Depot.																
	Food Supply Dep.	–	–	–	–	–	1	1	–	–	–	–	–	–	1	Trans. C.	
	Store Keeper	–	–	–	–	–	–	–	–	–	–	–	1	1	1	"	
	Clerk	–	–	–	–	–	–	–	–	–	–	–	1	1	1	"	
		–	–	–	–	–	1	1	–	–	–	–	2	2	3		
	(j) Equip. Depot.																
	Quartermaster	–	–	–	–	–	1	1	–	–	–	–	–	–	1	Ordn.	
	Technical Store-keeper	–	–	–	–	–	–	–	–	–	1	1	–	2	2	"	
	Pyrotechnician	–	–	–	–	–	–	–	–	–	1	–	–	1	1	Tech. C.	
	Armorers	–	–	–	–	–	–	–	–	–	2	–	–	2	2	"	
	Technical Clerk	–	–	–	–	–	–	–	–	–	–	–	1	1	1	"	
	Clerks	–	–	–	–	–	–	–	–	–	–	–	2	2	2	Inf.	
	Tailors	–	–	–	–	–	–	–	–	–	–	–	2	2	2	"	
	Shoemakers	–	–	–	–	–	–	–	–	–	–	–	3	3	3	"	
		–	–	–	–	–	1	1	–	–	4	1	8	13	14		
	TOTAL (02)	–	–	–	–	2	8	10	1	5	21	35	74	136	146		
3	*Medical Detach.* *Director (the doctor in Command & Staff)*																
	Dentist	–	–	–	–	1	–	1	–	–	–	–	–	–	1	Med.	
	Doctor	–	–	–	–	2	–	2	–	–	–	–	–	–	2	"	
	Medical NCO	–	–	–	–	–	–	–	–	–	1	–	–	1	1	"	
	Clerk	–	–	–	–	–	–	–	–	–	–	1	–	1	1	"	
	Aid men	–	–	–	–	–	–	–	–	–	1	1	4	6	6	"	
	Driver (ambulance)	–	–	–	–	–	–	–	–	–	–	–	1	1	1	"	
	TOTAL (03)	–	–	–	–	3	–	3	–	–	2	2	5	9	12		
4	*Reconnaissance Platoon.* *(a) Command Group*																
	Platoon Leader	–	–	–	–	–	1	1	–	–	–	–	–	–	1	Inf.	
	Asst. Platoon Ldr.	–	–	–	–	–	–	–	–	–	1	–	–	1	1	"	
	Driver-Messenger	–	–	–	–	–	–	–	–	–	–	–	1	1	1	"	
		–	–	–	–	–	1	1	–	–	1	–	1	2	3		

PERSONNEL—HELLENIC FORCES—*continued*

Serial No.	Allocation of Personnel	Officers							Warrant Offrs.	Other Ranks					Grand Total	Service	Remarks
		Brig. Gen.	Colonels	Lt. Cols.	Majors	Captains	Junior	Total		First Sergeants	Sergeants	Corporals	Enlisted Men	Total			
	(d) Recon & Intel. Squad.																
	Sqd. Leader	–	–	–	–	–	–	–	–	–	3	–	–	3	3	Inf.	
	Asst. Sqd. Leader	–	–	–	–	–	–	–	–	–	–	3	–	3	3	"	
	H.A.R. Pointers	–	–	–	–	–	–	–	–	–	–	–	3	3	3	"	
	H.A.R. Loaders	–	–	–	–	–	–	–	–	–	–	–	3	3	3	"	
	Rifle Men	–	–	–	–	–	–	–	–	–	–	–	3	3	3	"	
	Drivers 3/4 ton	–	–	–	–	–	–	–	–	–	–	–	3	3	3	"	
		–	–	–	–	–	–	–	–	–	3	3	12	18	18		
	TOTAL (04)	–	–	–	–	–	1	1	–	–	4	3	13	20	21		
5	*Heavy Weapons Co.* *(a) Command Grp.*																
	Commander	–	–	–	–	1	–	1	–	–	–	–	–	–	1	Inf.	
	First Sergeant	–	–	–	–	–	–	–	–	1	–	–	–	1	1	"	
	Telemeter Operator	–	–	–	–	–	–	–	–	–	–	–	1	1	1	"	
	Driver-Messenger	–	–	–	–	–	–	–	–	–	–	–	1	1	1	"	
		–	–	–	–	1	–	1	–	1	–	–	2	3	4		
	(b) 81 mm Platoon.																
	Platoon Leader	–	–	–	–	–	1	1	–	–	–	–	–	–	1	"	
	Asst. Platoon Ldr.	–	–	–	–	–	–	–	–	–	1	–	–	1	1	"	
	Sect. Commanders	–	–	–	–	–	–	–	–	–	3	–	–	3	3	"	
	Mortar Cmmdrs.	–	–	–	–	–	–	–	–	–	–	6	–	6	6	"	
	Pointers	–	–	–	–	–	–	–	–	–	–	–	6	6	6	"	
	Loaders	–	–	–	–	–	–	–	–	–	–	–	6	6	6	"	
	Ammunition Carriers Drivers	–	–	–	–	–	–	–	–	–	–	–	6	6	6	"	
		–	–	–	–	–	1	1	–	–	4	6	18	28	29		
	(c) Recoilless Rifle Section.																
	Commander	–	–	–	–	–	1	1	–	–	–	–	–	–	1	"	
	Rifle Commanders	–	–	–	–	–	–	–	–	–	–	3	–	3	3	"	
	Pointers	–	–	–	–	–	–	–	–	–	–	–	3	3	3	"	
	Loaders	–	–	–	–	–	–	–	–	–	–	–	3	3	3	"	
	Drivers	–	–	–	–	–	–	–	–	–	–	–	3	3	3	"	
		–	–	–	–	–	1	1	–	–	–	3	9	12	13		
	(d) Machine gun Section.																
	Commander	–	–	–	–	–	1	1	–	–	–	–	–	–	1	"	
	Machine gun Commanders	–	–	–	–	–	–	–	–	–	–	3	–	3	3	"	
	Pointers	–	–	–	–	–	–	–	–	–	–	–	3	3	3	"	
	Leaders	–	–	–	–	–	–	–	–	–	–	–	3	3	3	"	
	Ammun. Carriers	–	–	–	–	–	–	–	–	–	–	–	3	3	3	"	
	Drivers	–	–	–	–	–	–	–	–	–	–	–	3	3	3	"	
		–	–	–	–	–	1	1	–	–	–	3	12	15	16		
	Total (05)	–	–	–	–	1	3	4	–	1	4	12	41	58	62		

PERSONNEL—HELLENIC FORCES—*continued*

Serial No.	Allocation of Personnel	Officers							Warrant Offrs.	Other Ranks					Grand Total	Service	Remarks
		Brig. Gen.	Colonels	Lt. Cols.	Majors	Captains	Junior	Total		First Sergeants	Sergeants	Corporals	Enlisted Men	Total			
6	*Infantry.* *1st Infantry Battalion.* *(a) Command*	–	–	–	1	–	–	1	–	–	–	–	–	–	1	Inf. May be Lt. Col.	
	Adjutant-Intelligence	–	–	–	–	–	1	1	–	–	–	–	–	–	1	Inf.	
	Operations-Training	–	–	–	–	1	–	1	–	–	–	–	–	–	1	"	
		–	–	–	1	1	1	3	–	–	–	–	–	–	3		
	(b) Headquarters Company. *(i) Company Command Group.* Commander	–	–	–	–	1	–	1	–	–	–	–	–	–	1	"	
	First Sergeant	–	–	–	–	–	–	–	–	1	–	–	–	1	1	"	
	Clerk (Quartermaster)	–	–	–	–	–	–	–	–	–	1	–	–	1	1	"	
	Mess-Steward, Cook	–	–	–	–	–	–	–	–	–	–	1	1	2	2	"	
	Clerk	–	–	–	–	–	–	–	–	–	–	–	1	1	1	"	
	Barbers	–	–	–	–	–	–	–	–	–	–	–	2	2	2	"	
		–	–	–	–	1	–	1	–	1	1	1	4	7	8		
	(ii) Bn. Com. Group Clerk-Typist	–	–	–	–	–	–	–	–	–	–	1	–	1	1	"	
	Bugler	–	–	–	–	–	–	–	–	–	–	–	1	1	1	"	
	Intelligence Group	–	–	–	–	–	–	–	–	–	1	1	–	2	2	"	
	Driver	–	–	–	–	–	–	–	–	–	–	–	1	1	1	"	
		–	–	–	–	–	–	–	–	–	1	2	2	5	5		
	(iii) Communication Sqd. Sqd. Leader	–	–	–	–	–	–	–	–	–	1	–	–	1	1	"	
	Operators	–	–	–	–	–	–	–	–	–	1	1	6	7	7	"	
		–	–	–	–	–	–	–	–	–	1	1	6	8	8		

PERSONNEL—HELLENIC FORCES—*continued*

Serial No.	Allocation of Personnel	Brig. Gen.	Colonels	Lt. Cols.	Majors	Captains	Junior	Total	Warrant Offrs.	First Sergeants	Sergeants	Corporals	Enlisted Men	Total	Grand Total	Service	Remarks
	(c) 1ˢᵗ Rifle Co.																
	(i) Company Command Group.																
	Commander	–	–	–	–	1	–	1	–	–	–	–	–	–	1	Inf.	
	1ˢᵗ Sergeant	–	–	–	–	–	–	–	–	1	–	–	–	1	1	"	
	Clerk (QM)	–	–	–	–	–	–	–	–	–	1	–	–	1	1	"	
	Driver	–	–	–	–	–	–	–	–	–	–	–	1	1	1	"	
		–	–	–	–	1	–	1	–	1	1	–	1	3	4		
	(ii) Heavy Weapons Section.																
	Section Leader	–	–	–	–	–	–	–	–	–	1	–	–	1	1	"	
	57mm RR Commander (Pointer)	–	–	–	–	–	–	–	–	–	–	1	–	1	1	"	
	57 mm RR Loader	–	–	–	–	–	–	–	–	–	–	–	1	1	1	"	
	57 mm RR Driver	–	–	–	–	–	–	–	–	–	–	–	1	1	1	"	
	60 mm Mortar Commander (Pointer)	–	–	–	–	–	–	–	–	–	–	1	–	1	1	"	
	60 mm Mortar Loader	–	–	–	–	–	–	–	–	–	–	–	1	1	1	"	
	60 mm Mort. Driv.	–	–	–	–	–	–	–	–	–	–	–	1	1	1	"	
		–	–	–	–	–	–	–	–	–	1	2	4	7	7		
	(iii) 3.Rifle Platoons.																
	Platoon Leaders	–	–	–	–	–	3	3	–	–	–	–	–	–	3	"	
	Asst. Platoon Ldrs.	–	–	–	–	–	–	–	–	–	3	–	–	3	3	"	
	Messengers	–	–	–	–	–	–	–	–	–	–	–	3	3	3	"	
	Squad Leaders	–	–	–	–	–	–	–	–	–	9	–	–	9	9	"	
	Asst. Squad Leaders	–	–	–	–	–	–	–	–	–	–	9	–	9	9	"	
	B.A.R. Pointers	–	–	–	–	–	–	–	–	–	–	–	9	9	9	"	
	B.A.R. Loaders	–	–	–	–	–	–	–	–	–	–	–	9	9	9	
	B.A.R. Ammo Carriers	–	–	–	–	–	–	–	–	–	–	–	9	9	9	"	
	Rifle men	-	-	-	-	-	-	-	-	-	-	-	27	27	27	"	
		–	–	–	–	–	3	3	–	–	12	9	57	78	81		
	Total Rifle Co.	–	–	–	–	1	3	4	–	1	14	11	62	88	92		
	Total Inf. Battalion	–	–	–	1	5	10	16	–	4	45	37	198	284	300		
	Total (06) (For two Inf. Battalions)	–	–	–	2	10	20	32	–	8	90	74	396	568	600		
	Grand Total (01-06)	–	1	1	3	22	33	62	1	14	121	130	535	801	863		

WEAPONS—HELLENIC FORCES
(including the allotment of the Tripartite Headquarters and Training Group)

Units	Revolver	Sub–Machine Gun	Rifle	Light Machine Gun	Machine Gun	57 mm Recoilless Rifle	75 mm Recoilless Rifle	60 mm Mortar	81 mm Mortar	Signal Pistol
Command and Staff	12	–	10	–	–	–	–	–	–	–
Hq. and Service Company (a) Company Hq.	2	2	8	–	–	–	–	–	–	–
(b) Military Post Office	1	1	1	–	–	–	–	–	–	–
(c) Military Police Sec.	12	11	–	–	–	–	–	–	–	–
(d) Signal Platoon	1	17	20	–	–	–	–	–	–	2
(e) Engineer Platoon	1	3	14	–	–	–	–	–	–	–
(f) Transportation Platoon	1	18	–	–	–	–	–	–	–	–
(g) Military Band	2	10	6	–	–	–	–	–	–	–
(h) Light Repair Workshop	1	2	6	–	–	–	–	–	–	–
(i) Food Supply Depot	1	–	2	–	–	–	–	–	–	–
(j) Equipment Depot	1	4	9	–	–	–	–	–	–	–
Total for Hq. and Serv. Co.	35	68	76	–	–	–	–	–	–	2
Medical Detachment	3	3	6	–	–	–	–	–	–	–
Reconnaissance Platoon	1	8	9	3	–	–	–	–	–	1
Heavy Weapons Company (a) Company Hq.	1	3	–	–	–	–	–	–	–	2
(b) Mortar Platoon	13	16	–	–	–	–	–	–	6	–
(c) Recoilless Rifle Sec.	7	3	3	–	–	–	3	–	–	–
(d) Machine Guns Section	7	6	3	–	3	–	–	–	–	–
Total for Heavy Weapons Co.	28	28	6	–	3	–	3	–	6	2
Infantry Battalion (a) Command and Staff	3	–	–	–	–	–	–	–	–	–
(b) Hq. Company	1	6	14	–	–	–	–	–	–	1
(c) Rifle Company	8	18	57	9	–	1	–	1	–	1
(d) Total for Infantry Bn.	28	60	185	27	–	3	–	3	–	4
Total for 2 Infantry Bns.	56	120	370	54	–	6	–	6	–	8
Grand Total	123	227	467	57	3	6	3	6	6	13
Tripartite Hq.	12	–	–	–	–	–	–	–	–	–
Training Group	45	15	15	–	–	–	–	–	–	–
Plus 5%	9	12	24	3	–	–	–	–	–	–
Grand Total	189	254	506	60	3	6	3	6	6	13

VEHICLES—HELLENIC FORCES

Units		1/4 Ton	3/4 Ton	2-1/2 Ton	Recovery	Radio Set Vehicle	Ambulance	Total	Motorcycle	Water Trailers	Notes
Command and Staff		2	–	–	–	–	–	2	–	–	Shown in Transp Plat.
Hq. and Service Company	(a) Company Hq.	–	–	–	–	–	–	–	–	–	–
	(b) Military Post Office	–	–	–	–	–	–	–	1	–	–
	(c) Military Police Sec.	2	–	–	–	–	–	2	–	–	–
	(d) Signal Platoon	–	–	–	–	1	–	1	–	–	–
	(e) Engineer Platoon	–	1	–	–	–	–	1	1	–	–
	(f) Transportation Platoon	3	–	12	–	–	–	15	–	3	–
	(g) Military Band	–	–	–	–	–	–	–	–	–	–
	(h) Light Repair Workshop	–	–	–	1	–	–	1	–	–	–
	(i) Food Supply Depot	–	–	–	–	–	–	–	–	–	–
	(j) Equipment Depot	–	–	–	–	–	–	–	–	–	–
	Total for Hq. and Serv. Co.	5	1	12	1	1	–	20	2	3	–
Medical Detachment		–	–	–	–	–	1	1	–	–	–
Reconnaissance Platoon		1	3	–	–	–	–	4	–	–	–
Heavy Weapons Company	(a) Company Hq.	1	–	–	–	–	–	1	–	–	–
	(b) Mortar Platoon	–	6	–	–	–	–	6	–	–	–
	(c) Recoilless Rifle Section	3	–	–	–	–	–	3	–	–	–
	(d) Machine Guns Section	3	–	–	–	–	–	3	–	–	–
	Total for Heavy Weapons Co.	7	6	–	–	–	–	13	–	–	–
Infantry Battalion	(a) Command and Staff	1	–	–	–	–	–	1	–	–	–
	(c) Rifle Company	3	–	–	–	–	–	3	–	–	–
	(d) Total for Infantry Bn.	10	–	–	–	–	–	10	–	–	–
	Total for 2 Infantry Bns.	20	–	–	–	–	–	20	–	–	–
Grand Total		33	10	12	1	1	1	58	2	3	–

Note: Omnibusses for 90 seats allocated to Transportation Platoon.

SIGNAL EQUIPMENT—HELLENIC FORCES

Units	Radio Sets				Switchboards	
	SCR-399	AN/GRC-9	SCR-300	SCR-536	TC-12 (24 lines)	BD-72 (12 lines)
Signal Platoon	1	5	3	4	1	1
Recon. Platoon	–	1	4	–	–	–
Heavy Weapons Co.	–	1	4	13	–	–
2 Inf. Battalions	–	10	–	32	–	2
Total	1	17	11	49	1	3

Notes:

1. The SCR–399 with a 2KW AM–141 A/MRC is provided for communication with HGS, Athens.

2. AN/GRC–9's are provided for communication among:

(a) Hq. Hellenic Forces, Tripartite Hq. and Hq. Turkish Forces.

(b) Hq. Hellenic Forces, the two Inf. Battalions, the Recon. Platoon and the Heavy Weapons Company.

(c) Each Inf. Battalion and its Companies.

3. SCR 300's are provided for communication among:

(a) Heavy Weapons Company and its Platoons.

(b) Recon. Platoon and its sections.

4. SCR 536's are provided for communication within the components of Heavy Weapons Company and Rifle Companies.

5. One AN/GRC–9 and one BD–72 shall be allocated to the Tripartite Headquarters to meet its requirements.

6. One AN/GRC–9, three SCR–300 and four SCR–536 are included to the allocation of Signal Platoon as reserve radio sets.

SECTION III.—TABLE OF ORGANIZATION AND MAJOR EQUIPMENT OF THE TURKISH FORCES IN CYPRUS

A. STRUCTURE
　　See Table of Organization in Appendix 1.
B. PERSONNEL
　　See Table of Personnel in Appendix 2.
C. MAJOR EQUIPMENT
　　1. Weapons.　*See* Table of Weapons in Appendix 3.
　　2. Vehicles.　*See* Table of Vehicles in Appendix 4.
　　3. Signal Equipment.　*See* Table of Signal Equipment in Appendix 5.

TABLE OF ORGANIZATION
TURKISH FORCES

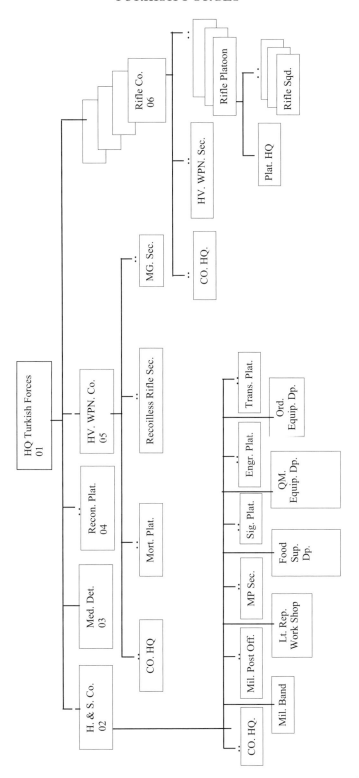

PERSONNEL—TURKISH FORCES

Serial No.	Allocation of Personnel	Officers							Other Ranks					Grand Total	Service
		Brig. Gen.	Colonels	Lt. Col.	Majors	Captains	Junior	Total	NCOs	Troop Sergeants	Corporals	Enlisted Men	Total		
1	*Command and Staff.*														
	Commander	–	1	–	–	–	–	1	–	–	–	–	–	1	Inf.
	Executive Officer	–	–	1	–	–	–	1	–	–	–	–	–	1	"
	Adjutant	–	–	–	–	1	–	1	–	–	–	–	–	1	"
	Orderly	–	–	–	–	–	–	–	–	–	–	1	1	1	"
	S--1 : S--4	–	–	–	1	–	–	1	–	–	–	–	–	1	" (may be QMC)
	Doctor	–	–	–	1	–	–	1	–	–	–	–	–	1	Med. O.
	Legal Serv. Offrs.	–	–	–	–	1	–	1	–	–	–	–	–	1	Leg. Sc.
	Recruiting Officer	–	–	–	–	1	–	1	–	–	–	–	–	1	Pers. C.
	QM. Officer	–	–	–	–	1	–	1	–	–	–	–	–	1	QM. C.
	Finance Officer	–	–	–	–	–	1	1	–	–	–	–	–	1	"
	Clerk-Typist	–	–	–	–	–	–	–	–	–	1	4	5	5	Inf.
	S--2 : S--3	–	–	–	1	–	–	1	–	–	–	–	–	1	"
	Asst Operations and Training Offr.	–	–	–	–	1	–	1	–	–	–	–	–	1	"
	Asst. Security Offr.	–	–	–	–	1	–	1	–	–	–	–	–	1	"
	Clerk-Typist	–	–	–	–	–	–	–	–	–	1a	1	2	2	"
	Chief, Registry	–	–	–	–	–	–	–	1	–	–	–	1	1	"
	Clerks *b*	–	–	–	–	–	–	–	–	–	–	2	2	2	"
	TOTAL (01)	–	1	1	3	6	1	12	1	–	2	8	11	23	
2	*HQ. and Service Company.* *(a) Co. Hq.* *(i) Hq. Group.*														
	Commander	–	–	–	–	1	–	1	–	–	–	–	–	1	Inf.
	CO NCO	–	–	–	–	–	–	–	1	–	–	–	1	1	"
	Clerk-Typists	–	–	–	–	–	–	–	–	–	1	1	2	2	"
	Mess Stews.-Cooks	–	–	–	–	–	–	–	–	–	–	3	3	3	"
	Barbers	–	–	–	–	–	–	–	–	–	–	1	1	1	"
	Bugler	–	–	–	–	–	–	–	–	–	–	1	1	1	"
		–	–	–	–	1	–	1	1	–	1	6	8	9	
	(ii) Command and Staff Group. (as indicated above) *(b) Military Post Office.*														
	Personnel	–	–	–	–	–	–	–	1	–	–	2	3	3	Inf.
		–	–	–	–	–	–	–	1	–	–	2	3	3	
	(c) Military Police Section.														
	Commander	–	–	–	–	–	1	1	–	–	–	–	–	1	Inf.
	MPs	–	–	–	–	–	–	–	–	1	2	6c	9	9	"
		–	–	–	–	–	1	1	–	1	2	6	9	10	

a Also Draftsman.
b One must have a working knowledge of Greek.
c Two also drivers.

PERSONNEL—TURKISH FORCES—*continued*

Serial No.	Allocation of Personnel	Officers							Other Ranks					Grand Total	Service
		Brig. Gen.	Colonels	Lt. Col.	Majors	Captains	Junior	Total	NCOs	Troop Sergeants	Corporals	Enlisted Men	Total		
	(d) Signal Platoon.														
	Commander	–	–	–	–	–	1	1	–	–	–	–	–	1	Sig. C.
	Assistant NCO	–	–	–	–	–	–	–	1	–	–	–	1	1	"
	Communication Centre.														
	Chief	–	–	–	–	–	–	–	1	–	–	–	1	1	"
	Cryptographers	–	–	–	–	–	–	–	–	–	1	3	4	4	"
	Radio Section.														
	Chief	–	–	–	–	–	–	–	1	–	–	–	1	1	"
	Radio Operators	–	–	–	–	–	–	–	–	3	2	8a	13	13	"
	Wire Section.														
	Chief	–	–	–	–	–	–	–	1	–	–	–	1	1	"
	Operators	–	–	–	–	–	–	–	–	–	2	5	7	7	"
	Signal men	–	–	–	–	–	–	–	–	1	–	3	4	4	"
		–	–	–	–	–	1	1	4	4	5	19	32	33	
	(e) Engineer Plat.														
	Commander	–	–	–	–	–	1	1	–	–	–	–	–	1	CEC.
	Asst. NCO	–	–	–	–	–	–	–	1	–	–	–	1	1	"
	Mine Sweepers	–	–	–	–	–	–	–	–	–	1	5	6	6	Inf.
	Demolition Experts	–	–	–	–	–	–	–	1	–	1	–	2	2	CEC.
	Water Supp. Exps.	–	–	–	–	–	–	–	–	–	1	2	3	3	"
	Construction Exps.	–	–	–	–	–	–	–	–	–	2	2	2	2	"
	Electrician	–	–	–	–	–	–	–	–	–	1	–	1	1	"
	Painter	–	–	–	–	–	–	–	–	–	–	1	1	1	"
	Driver	–	–	–	–	–	–	–	–	–	–	1	1	1	"
		–	–	–	–	–	1	1	2	–	4	11	17	18	
	(f) Transportation Platoon.														
	Commander	–	–	–	–	–	1	1	–	–	–	–	–	1	Trans. C.
	Asst. NCO	–	–	–	–	–	–	–	1	–	–	–	1	1	"
	Drivers	–	–	–	–	–	–	–	–	–	2	11	13	13	"
		–	–	–	–	–	1	1	1	–	2	11	14	15	
	(g) Military Band.														
	Conductor	–	–	–	–	–	1	1	–	–	–	–	–	1	Musician
	Personnel	–	–	–	–	–	–	–	6	3	3	3	15	15	"
		–	–	–	–	–	1	1	6	3	3	3	15	16	

a One also driver.

PERSONNEL—TURKISH FORCES—*continued*

Serial No.	Allocation of Personnel	Officers							Other Ranks					Grand Total	Service
		Brig. Gen.	Colonels	Lt. Col.	Majors	Captains	Junior	Total	NCOs	Troop Sergeants	Corporals	Enlisted Men	Total		
	(h) Light Repair Workshop.														
	Commander	–	–	–	–	–	1	1	–	–	–	–	–	1	Ord. C.
	Rifle Technician	–	–	–	–	–	–	–	1	–	–	–	1	1	Tec. C.
	H.P. Radio Tech.	–	–	–	–	–	–	–	1	–	–	–	1	1	Mec. C. (Sig.)
	Signal Equip. Tech.	–	–	–	–	–	–	–	1	–	–	–	1	1	"
	Electrician	–	–	–	–	–	–	–	1	–	–	–	1	1	Tec. C.
	Chief, Veh. Tech	–	–	–	–	–	–	–	1	–	–	–	1	1	Mec. (trans.)
	Wheeled Veh. Tech.	–	–	–	–	–	–	–	–	1	–	–	1	1	"
	Recovery Veh. Op.	–	–	–	–	–	–	–	–	–	1	–	1	1	"
	Asst. Vehicle Techs.	–	–	–	–	–	–	–	–	–	1	1	2	2	"
	Carpenter	–	–	–	–	–	–	–	–	–	–	1	1	1	Inf.
	Black Smith	–	–	–	–	–	–	–	–	–	–	1	1	1	"
	Shoemaker	–	–	–	–	–	–	–	–	–	–	1	1	1	"
	Tailor	–	–	–	–	–	–	–	–	–	–	1	1	1	"
		–	–	–	–	–	1	1	5	1	2	5	13	14	
	(i) Food Supply Depot.														
	Supply NCO	–	–	–	–	–	–	–	1	–	–	–	1	1	QMC
	Store Keepers	–	–	–	–	–	–	–	–	–	–	2	2	2	Inf.
		–	–	–	–	–	–	–	1	–	–	2	3	3	
	(j) QM Equipment Depot.														
	Supply NCO	–	–	–	–	–	–	–	1	–	–	–	1	1	QMC
	Store Keeper	–	–	–	–	–	–	–	–	–	–	1	1	1	Inf.
		–	–	–	–	–	–	–	1	–	–	1	2	2	
	(j) Ordnance Equipment Depot.														
	Supply Officer	–	–	–	–	–	1	1	–	–	–	–	–	1	Ord. C.
	Store Keeper and Clerk	–	–	–	–	–	–	–	–	–	–	2	2	2	Inf.
		–	–	–	–	–	1	1	–	–	–	2	2	3	
	TOTAL (02)	–	–	–	–	1	7	8	22	9	19	68	118	126	
3	*Medical Detachment.*														
	Director	–	–	–	–	1	–	1	–	–	–	–	–	1	Med. C.
	Dentist	–	–	–	–	1	–	1	–	–	–	–	–	1	"
	NCO	–	–	–	–	–	–	–	1	–	–	–	1	1	"
	Driver	–	–	–	–	–	–	–	–	–	–	1	1	1	"
	Aid men	–	–	–	–	–	–	–	–	–	2	3	5	5	"
	TOTAL (03)	–	–	–	–	2	–	2	1	–	2	4	7	9	

PERSONNEL—TURKISH FORCES—*continued*

Serial No.	Allocation of Personnel	Officers							Other Ranks					Grand Total	Service
		Brig. Gen.	Colonels	Lt. Col.	Majors	Captains	Junior	Total	NCOs	Troop Sergeants	Corporals	Enlisted Men	Total		
4	*Reconnaissance Platoon.*														
	(a) Command Group.														
	Platoon Leader	–	–	–	–	–	1	1	–	–	–	–	–	1	Inf.
	Platoon NCO	–	–	–	–	–	–	–	1	–	–	–	1	1	"
	Driver	–	–	–	–	–	–	–	–	–	–	1	1	1	"
	(d) Rec. and Int. Squads.														
	Squad Leaders	–	–	–	–	–	–	–	–	2	–	–	2	2	"
	Asst. Leaders	–	–	–	–	–	–	–	–	–	2	–	2	2	"
	B.A.R. Pointers	–	–	–	–	–	–	–	–	–	–	2	2	2	"
	B.A.R. Loaders	–	–	–	–	–	–	–	–	–	–	2	2	2	"
	Rifle men	–	–	–	–	–	–	–	–	–	–	4	4	4	"
	Drivers	–	–	–	–	–	–	–	–	–	–	2	2	2	"
	TOTAL (04)	–	–	–	–	–	1	1	1	2	2	11	16	17	
5	*Heavy Weapons Co.*														
	(a) Co. HQ.														
	Commander	–	–	–	–	1	–	1	–	–	–	–	–	1	Inf.
	Co. NCO	–	–	–	–	–	–	–	1	–	–	–	1	1	"
	Telemeter Operator	–	–	–	–	–	–	–	–	–	–	1	1	1	"
	Messenger-Driver	–	–	–	–	–	–	–	–	–	–	1	1	1	"
		–	–	–	–	1	–	1	1	–	–	2	3	4	
	(b) 81 mm Mortar Platoon.														
	Platoon Leader	–	–	–	–	–	1	1	–	–	–	–	–	1	Inf.
	Asst. Plat. Leader	–	–	–	–	–	–	–	1	–	–	–	1	1	"
	Sect. Commanders	–	–	–	–	–	–	–	–	2	–	–	2	2	"
	Mortar Commanders	–	–	–	–	–	–	–	–	–	4	–	4	4	"
	Pointers	–	–	–	–	–	–	–	–	–	–	4	4	4	"
	Loaders	–	–	–	–	–	–	–	–	–	–	4	4	4	"
	Ammunition Carriers	–	–	–	–	–	–	–	–	–	–	4	4	4	"
	Drivers	–	–	–	–	–	–	–	–	–	–	4	4	4	"
		–	–	–	–	–	1	1	1	2	4	16	23	24	
	(c) Recoilless Rifle Section.														
	Commander	–	–	–	–	–	1	1	–	–	–	–	–	1	Inf.
	Rifle Commanders	–	–	–	–	–	–	–	–	2	–	–	2	2	"
	Pointers	–	–	–	–	–	–	–	–	–	2	–	2	2	"
	Loaders	–	–	–	–	–	–	–	–	–	–	2	2	2	"
	Drivers	–	–	–	–	–	–	–	–	–	–	2	2	2	"
		–	–	–	–	–	1	1	–	2	2	4	8	9	

PERSONNEL—TURKISH FORCES—*continued*

Serial No.	Allocation of Personnel	Officers							Other Ranks					Grand Total	Service
		Brig. Gen.	Colonels	Lt. Col.	Majors	Captains	Junior	Total	NCOs	Troop Sergeants	Corporals	Enlisted Men	Total		
	(d) Machine gun Sect.														
	Commander	–	–	–	–	–	1	1	–	–	–	–	–	1	Inf.
	Machine gun Coms.	–	–	–	–	–	–	–	–	2	–	–	2	2	"
	Pointers	–	–	–	–	–	–	–	–	–	2	–	2	2	"
	Loaders	–	–	–	–	–	–	–	–	–	–	2	2	2	"
	Ammo Carriers	–	–	–	–	–	–	–	–	–	–	2	2	2	"
	Drivers	–	–	–	–	–	–	–	–	–	–	2	2	2	"
		–	–	–	–	–	1	1	–	2	2	6	10	11	
	TOTAL (05)	–	–	–	–	1	3	4	2	6	8	28	44	48	
6	*Rifle Company.*														
	(a) Company Hq.														
	Commander	–	–	–	–	1	–	1	–	–	–	–	–	1	Inf.
	Co. NCO	–	–	–	–	–	–	–	1	–	–	–	1	1	"
	Messenger	–	–	–	–	–	–	–	–	–	–	1	1	1	"
	Driver	–	–	–	–	–	–	–	–	–	–	1	1	1	"
		–	–	–	–	1	–	1	1	–	–	2	3	4	
	(b) Heavy Weapons Section.														
	Section Leader	–	–	–	–	–	–	–	1	–	–	–	1	1	Inf.
	57 mm RR Comm. (Pointer)	–	–	–	–	–	–	–	–	–	1	–	1	1	"
	57 mm RR Loader	–	–	–	–	–	–	–	–	–	–	1	1	1	"
	57 mm RR Driver	–	–	–	–	–	–	–	–	–	–	1	1	1	"
	60 mm Mort. Comm. (Pointer)	–	–	–	–	–	–	–	–	–	1	–	1	1	"
	60 mm Mort. Load.	–	–	–	–	–	–	–	–	–	–	1	1	1	"
	60 mm Mort. Driv.	–	–	–	–	–	–	–	–	–	–	1	1	1	"
		–	–	–	–	–	–	–	1	–	2	4	7	7	
	(c) 3 Rifle Platoons.														
	Platoon Leaders	–	–	–	–	–	3	3	–	–	–	–	–	3	Inf.
	Asst. Platoon Ldrs.	–	–	–	–	–	–	–	3	–	–	–	3	3	"
	Messengers	–	–	–	–	–	–	–	–	–	–	3	3	3	"
	Squad Leaders	–	–	–	–	–	–	–	–	9	–	–	9	9	"
	Asst. Squad Leaders	–	–	–	–	–	–	–	–	–	9	–	9	9	"
	B.A.R. Pointers	–	–	–	–	–	–	–	–	–	–	9	9	9	"
	B.A.R. Loaders	–	–	–	–	–	–	–	–	–	–	9	9	9	"
	B.A.R. Am. Carriers	–	–	–	–	–	–	–	–	–	–	9	9	9	"
	Rifle men	–	–	–	–	–	–	–	–	–	–	27	27	27	
		–	–	–	–	–	3	3	3	9	9	57	78	81	
	TOTAL (06)	–	–	–	–	1	3	4	5	9	11	63	88	92	
	Total 4 Rifle Co's.	–	–	–	–	4	12	16	20	36	44	252	352	368	
	GRAND TOTAL	–	1	1	3	14	24	43	47	53	77	371	548	591	

Notes.
1. In accordance with existing regulation, there are two types of Sergeant in Turkish Army which may be entitled as "NCO Sergeant" and "Troop Sergeant".
2. NCO's may be replaced by Troop Sergeant or *vice versa*.

WEAPONS—TURKISH FORCES
(including the allotment of the Tripartite Headquarters and Training Group)

Units	Revolver	Sub-Machine Gun	Rifle	Light Machine Gun	Machine Gun	57 mm Recoilless Rifle	75 mm Recoilless Rifle	60 mm Mortar	81 mm Mortar	Signal Pistol
Command and Staff	12	1	10	–	–	–	–	–	–	–
Hq. and Service Company — (a) Company Hq.	1	2	6	–	–	–	–	–	–	–
(b) Military Post Office	1	1	1	–	–	–	–	–	–	–
(c) Military Police Sec.	10	9	–	–	–	–	–	–	–	–
(d) Signal Platoon	1	18	14	–	–	–	–	–	–	2
(e) Engineer Platoon	1	3	14	–	–	–	–	–	–	–
(f) Transportation Platoon	1	14	–	–	–	–	–	–	–	–
(g) Military Band	1	9	6	–	–	–	–	–	–	–
(h) Light Repair Workshop	1	7	6	–	–	–	–	–	–	–
(i) Food Supply Depot	–	1	2	–	–	–	–	–	–	–
(j) QM Equipment Depot	–	1	1	–	–	–	–	–	–	–
(k) ORD Equipment Depot	1	–	2	–	–	–	–	–	–	–
Total for H. and S. Co.	18	65	52	–	–	–	–	–	–	2
Medical Detachment	2	2	5	–	–	–	–	–	–	–
Reconnaissance Platoon	1	6	8	2	–	–	–	–	–	1
Heavy Weapons Company — (a) Company Hq.	1	3	–	–	–	–	–	–	–	2
(b) Mortar Platoon	9	11	4	–	–	–	–	–	4	–
(c) Recoilless Rifle Sec.	5	4	–	–	–	–	2	–	–	–
(d) Machine Guns Section	5	4	2	–	2	–	–	–	–	–
Total for Heavy Weapons Co.	20	22	6	–	2	–	2	–	4	2
Rifle Co's. — Rifle Company	8	18	57	9	–	1	–	1	–	–
Total for 4 Rifle Co's.	32	72	228	36	–	4	–	4	–	4
Grand Total	85	168	309	58	2	4	2	4	4	9
Tripartite HQ.	9	–	–	–	–	–	–	–	–	–
Training Group	30	10	10	–	–	–	–	–	–	–
Plus 5%	6	9	16	2	–	–	–	–	–	–
Grand Total	130	187	335	40	2	4	2	4	4	9

VEHICLES—TURKISH FORCES

Units	1/4 Ton	3/4 Ton	2-1/2 Ton	Recovery	Radio Set Vehicle	Ambulance	Total	Motorcycle	Water Trailers	Notes
Command and Staff	2	–	–	–	–	–	2	–	–	Shown in Transp Plat.
(a) Company Hq.	–	–	–	–	–	–	–	–	–	–
(b) Military Post Office	–	–	–	–	–	–	–	1	–	–
(c) Military Police Section	2	–	–	–	–	–	2	–	–	–
(d) Signal Platoon	–	–	–	–	1	–	1	–	–	–
(e) Engineer Platoon	–	1	–	–	–	–	1	1	–	–
(f) Transportation Platoon	3	–	8	–	–	–	11	–	2	–
(g) Military Band	–	–	–	–	–	–	–	–	–	–
(h) Light Repair Workshop	–	–	–	1	–	–	1	–	–	–
(i) Food Supply Depot	–	–	–	–	–	–	–	–	–	–
(j) Equipment Depot	–	–	–	–	–	–	–	–	–	–
Total for . and S. Co.	5	1	8	1	1	–	16	2	2	–
Medical Detachment	–	–	–	–	–	1	1	–	–	–
Reconnaissance Platoon	1	2	–	–	–	–	3	–	–	–
(a) Company Hq.	1	–	–	–	–	–	1	–	–	–
(b) Mortar Platoon	–	4	–	–	–	–	4	–	–	–
(c) Recoilless Rifle Section	2	–	–	–	–	–	2	–	–	–
(d) Machine Guns Section	2	–	–	–	–	–	2	–	–	–
Total for Heavy Weapons Co.	5	4	–	–	–	–	9	–	–	–
Rifle Company	3	–	–	–	–	–	3	–	–	–
Total for 4 Rifle Co's.	12	–	–	–	–	–	12	–	–	–
Grand Total	23	7	8	1	1	1	41	2	2	–

Note: Omnibusses for 60 seats allocated to Transportation Platoon.

SIGNAL EQUIPMENT—TURKISH FORCES

Units	Radio Sets				Switchboards	
	SCR–399	AN-VRC/9	SCR–300	SCR–536	TC–12 (24 lines)	BD–72 (12 lines)
Signal Platoon	1	4	2	3	1	2
Recon. Platoon	–	1	3	–	–	–
Heavy Weapons Co.	–	1	4	10	–	–
4 Rifle Co's.	–	4	–	20	–	–
Total	1	10	9	33	1	2

Notes:

1. The SCR–399 with a 2KW AM–141 A/MRC is provided for Communication with TGS, ANKARA.

2. AN-VRC/9's are provided for Communication among:

(a) Hqs. Turkish Forces, Tripartite Hqs. and Hqs. Hellenic Forces.

(b) Hqs. Turkish Forces, Recon. Platoon, Heavy Weapons Co. and Rifle Co's.

3. SCR-300's are provided for Communication among:

(a) Recon. Platoon and its Sqds.

(b) Heavy Weapons Co. and its Platoon and Sections.

4. SCR-536's are provided for Communication within the components of Heavy Weapons Co. and Rifle Co's.

5. One AN-VRC/9 and one BD–72 shall be allocated to the Tripartite Hqs. to meet its requirement.

6. One AN-VRC/9, two SCR–300 and three SCR–536 are included to the allocation of Signal Platoon as reserve radio sets.

ANNEX "C"

STATUS OF GREEK AND TURKISH FORCES IN CYPRUS

ARTICLE I

1. In this Annex the expression:
(a) "Force" means the Greek and Turkish military personnel on the territory of Cyprus as referred to in Articles XIII and XIV of this Agreement.
(b) "Family" or "Dependents" means the spouse of a member of a Force, or a child of such member depending on him or her for support.
(c) "Sending State" means Greece or Turkey.
(d) "Military Authorities of the sending State" means those Authorities of a sending State who are empowered by its law to enforce the Military Law of that State with respect to members or its Forces.

ARTICLE II

1. It is the duty of a Force and of its members as well as of their dependents to respect the Constitution and the laws of the Republic of Cyprus and to abstain from any activity inconsistent with the spirit of this Agreement and of those Agreements which have been signed by the Governments of the United Kingdom, Greece and Turkey on 16th August, 1960, for the final settlement of the Cyprus problem. It is their particular duty to abstain from any political and communal activity.

2. The obligations of the above paragraph apply to the members of any other Military Mission of the sending States in the Republic of Cyprus, as well as to any member of the Armed Services of the sending States on mission in the territory of the Republic of Cyprus or in transit. They also apply to the families of the above while they are residing in the Republic of Cyprus.

3. It is the duty of the sending States to take the necessary measures to ensure the observance of the above paragraphs.

ARTICLE III

1. Members of the Force are exempted from passport and visa regulations on entering or leaving the territory of the Republic of Cyprus as well as from immigration inspection, but shall not be considered as acquiring any right to permanent residence or domicile in the territory of the Republic of Cyprus. The sending States shall inform the Appropriate Authorities of the Republic of Cyprus of the intended dates of arrival or withdrawal and replacement of Forces, at least one month in advance. This time limit shall not be strictly observed in cases where individuals or small groups are involved. In such cases the Appropriate Authorities of the Republic of Cyprus shall be accordingly informed at the earliest possible time.

2. The following documents only will be required in respect of members of the Force and must be presented on demand:

(a) Personal identity card issued by the sending State showing names, date of birth, rank, service and photograph.

(b) Movement order issued by the sending State and certifying to the Status of the individual as a member of a Force, to the unit that the individual belongs to and to the movement ordered. This movement order can also be collective.

(c) Both above documents are issued in both Greek and Turkish languages.

3. The dependents shall be so described in their passports.

4. If a member of the Force leaves the employ of the sending State and is not repatriated, the Authorities of the sending State shall immediately inform the Authorities of the Republic of Cyprus, giving such particulars as may be required. The authorities of the sending State shall similarly inform the authorities of the Republic of Cyprus of any member who has absented himself for more than twenty-one days.

5. If the Republic of Cyprus has requested the removal from its territory of a member of a Force or a dependent or has made an expulsion order against an ex-member of the Force or against a dependent, the Authorities of the sending State shall be responsible for receiving the person concerned within their own territory or otherwise disposing of him outside of the territory of the Republic of Cyprus.

ARTICLE IV

1. The Republic of Cyprus shall either:

(a) Accept as valid, without a driving test or fee, the military driving permit issued by the sending State or any Authority of the same State to a member of the Force, or

(b) issue its own driving permit or licence without a test to any member of the Force who holds a driving permit or military driving permit, issued by the sending State or any of its authorities.

ARTICLE V

1. Members of the Force shall normally wear uniform. Subject to any arrangement to the contrary between the Authorities of the sending State and the Appropriate Authorities of the Republic of Cyprus, the wearing of civilian dress shall be on the same conditions as for members of the Forces of the Republic of Cyprus. Regularly constituted units or formations of a force shall be in uniform when entering or leaving the territory of the Republic of Cyprus.

2. Service vehicles of a Force shall carry, in addition to their registration number, a distinctive nationality mark.

ARTICLE VI

Weapons, ammunition and other equipment possessed by the Force are shown in Annex "B" of this Agreement. Members of the Force carry arms according to their regulations. The Authorities of the sending State shall give sympathetic consideration to requests of the Republic of Cyprus concerning this matter.

ARTICLE VII

1. Subject to the provisions of this Article:
(a) The Military Authorities of the sending State shall have the right to exercise within the territory of the Republic of Cyprus, the criminal and disciplinary jurisdiction conferred on them by the law of the sending State over all persons subject to the Military Law of that State.
(b) The Authorities of the Republic of Cyprus shall have jurisdiction over the members of the Force and their dependents with respect to offences committed within the territory of the Republic of Cyprus punishable by the Law of the Republic of Cyprus.
2.–(a) The Military Authorities of the sending State shall have the right to exercise exclusive jurisdiction over persons subject to the Military Law of that State with respect to offences, including offences relating to its security, punishable by the Law of the sending State, but not punishable by the Law of the Republic of Cyprus.
(b) The Authorities of the Republic of Cyprus shall have the right to exercise exclusive jurisdiction over members of a Force and their dependents with respect to offences, including offences relating to its security punishable by the Law of the Republic of Cyprus but not punishable by the Law of the sending State.
(c) For the purpose of this paragraph and of paragraph 3 of this Article, as offences relating to the security of a State are considered:
  (i) treason against the State,
  (ii) sabotage, espionage or violation of any law relating to official secrets of the State, or secrets relating to the national defence of the State.
3. In cases where the right to exercise jurisdiction is concurrent the following rules shall apply:
(a) The Military Authorities of the sending State shall have the primary right to exercise jurisdiction over the member of its Force in relation to:
  (i) Offences solely against the security or property of that State or offences solely against the person or property of another member of the Force or dependent.
  (ii) Offences arising out of any act or omission done in the performance of official duty.
(b) In the case of any other offence the Authorities of the Republic of Cyprus shall have the primary right to exercise jurisdiction.
(c) If the State which has the primary right decides not to exercise jurisdiction, it shall notify the Authorities of the other State as soon as practicable. The Authorities of the State having the primary right to exercise jurisdiction shall give sympathetic consideration to a request from the Authorities of the other State for a waiver of its right in cases where that other State considers such waiver to be of particular importance.

4. The foregoing provisions of this Article shall not imply any right for the Military Authorities of the sending State to exercise jurisdiction over persons who are nationals or ordinarily residents of the Republic of Cyprus, unless they are members of the Force of the sending State, or over members of the Force of the other sending State or their dependents.

5.–(a) The Authorities of the Republic of Cyprus and those of the sending State shall assist each other in the arrest of members of a Force or their dependents in the territory of the Republic of Cyprus and in handing them over to the Authority which is to exercise jurisdiction in accordance with the above provisions.

(b) The Authorities of the Republic of Cyprus shall notify promptly the Military Authorities of the sending State of the arrest of any member of a Force or a dependent.

(c) The custody of an accused member of a Force over whom the Republic of Cyprus is to exercise jurisdiction shall, if he is in the hands of the sending State, remain with that State until he is charged by the Republic of Cyprus.

6.–(a) The Authorities of the Republic of Cyprus and those of the sending State shall assist each other in the carrying out of all necessary investigations into offences, and in the collection and production of evidence, including the seizure and, in proper cases, the handing over of objects connected with an offence. The handing over of such objects may, however, be made subject to their return within the time specified by the Authority delivering them.

(b) The Authorities of the Contracting Parties shall notify one another of the disposition of all cases in which there are concurrent rights to exercise jurisdiction.

7.–(a) A death sentence shall not be carried out in the territory of the Republic of Cyprus by the Authorities of the sending State if the legislation of the Republic of Cyprus does not provide for such punishment in a similar case.

(b) The Authorities of the Republic of Cyprus shall give sympathetic consideration to a request from the Authorities of the sending State for assistance in carrying out a sentence of imprisonment pronounced by the Authorities of the sending State under the provision of this Article within the territory of the Republic of Cyprus.

8. Where an accused has been tried in accordance with the provisions of this Article by the Authorities of one Contracting Party and has been acquitted, or has been convicted and is serving, or has served his sentence or has been pardoned, he may not be tried again for the same offence within the territory of the Republic of Cyprus by the Authorities of another Contracting party. However, nothing in this paragraph shall prevent the Military Authorities of the sending State from trying a member of its Forces for any violation of rules of discipline arising from an act or omission which constituted an offence for which he has been tried by the Authorities of the Contracting Party.

9. Whenever a member of a Force or a dependent is prosecuted under the jurisdiction of the Republic of Cyprus this member will be entitled:

(a) To a prompt and speedy trial.

(b) To be informed in advance of trial, of the charge or charges made against him.

(c) To be confronted with the witnesses against him.

(d) To have compulsory process for obtaining witnesses in his favour, if they are within the jurisdiction of the Republic of Cyprus.

(e) To have legal representation of his own choice for his defence or to have free or assisted legal representation under the conditions prevailing for the time being in the Republic of Cyprus.

(f) If he considers it necessary, to have the services of a competent interpreter, and

(g) To communicate with a representative of the Government of the sending State and, when the rules of the Court permit, to have such a representative present at his trial.

10.–(a) Regularly constituted Military Units or formations of a Force shall have the right to police any camps, establishments or other premises which they occupy as the result of an agreement with the Republic of Cyprus. The Military Police of the Force may take all appropriate measures to ensure the maintenance of order and security on such premises.

(b) Outside these premises, such Military Police shall he employed only subject to arrangements with the Authorities of the Republic of Cyprus and in liaison with those Authorities and in so far as such employment is necessary to maintain discipline and order among the members of the Force.

11. The Republic of Cyprus shall seek such legislation as it deems necessary to ensure the adequate security and protection within its territory of installations, equipment, property, records and official information of other Contracting Parties, and the punishment of persons who may contravene laws enacted for that purpose.

ARTICLE VIII

1. Each Contracting Party waives all its claims against any other Contracting Party for damage to any property owned by it and used by its land, sea or air armed services, if such damage:

(a) was caused by a member of the armed Forces of the other Contracting Party in the execution of his duties in connection with the operation of the Treaty of Alliance between the Republic of Cyprus, Greece and Turkey, or

(b) arose from the use of any vehicle, vessel or aircraft owned by the other Contracting Party and used by its armed services, provided either that the vehicle, vessel or aircraft causing the damage was being used in connection with the operation of the Treaty of Alliance between the Republic of Cyprus, Greece and Turkey or that the damage was caused to property being so used. Claims for maritime salvage by one Contracting Party against any other Contracting Party shall be waived, provided that the vessel or cargo salved was owned by a Contracting Party and being used by its armed services in connection with the operation of the Treaty of Alliance between the Republic of Cyprus, Greece and Turkey.

2.–(a) In the case of damage caused or arising as stated in paragraph 1 to other property owned by a Contracting Party and located in the territory of the Republic of Cyprus, the issue of the liability of the other Contracting Party shall be determined and the amount of damage shall he assessed, unless the Contracting Parties concerned agree otherwise, by a sole arbitrator selected in accordance with subparagraph (b) of this paragraph. The arbitrator shall also decide any counter-claims arising out of the same incident.

(b) The arbitrator referred to in subparagraph (a) above shall be selected by agreement between the Contracting Parties concerned from amongst the nationals of the Republic of Cyprus who hold or have held high judicial office. If the Contracting Parties concerned are unable, within two months, to agree upon the arbitrator either may request the Committee of Ministers to select a person with the aforesaid qualifications.

(c) Any decision taken by the arbitrator shall be binding and conclusive upon the Contracting Parties.

(d) The amount of any compensation awarded by the arbitrator shall be distributed in accordance with the provisions of paragraph 5(e)(i), (ii) and (iii) of this Article.

(e) The compensation of the arbitrator shall be fixed by agreement between the Contracting Parties concerned and shall, together with the necessary expenses incidental to the performance of his duties, be defrayed in equal proportions by them.

(f) Nevertheless, each Contracting Party waives its claim in any such case where the damage is less than £100. Any other Contracting Party whose property has been damaged in the same incident shall also waive its claim up to the above amount.

3. For the purpose of paragraph 1 and 2 of this Article the expression "owned by a Contracting Party" in the case of a vessel includes a vessel on bare boat charter to that Contracting Party or requisitioned by it on bare boat terms or seized by it in prize (except to the extent that the risk of loss or liability is borne by some person other than such Contracting Party).

4. Each Contracting Party waives all its claims against any other Contracting Party for injury or death suffered by any member of its armed services while such member was engaged in the performance of his official duties on the territory of the Republic of Cyprus.

5. Claims (other than contractual claims and those to which paragraphs 6 or 7 of this Article apply) arising out of acts or omissions of members of a Force on the territory of the Republic of Cyprus, done in the performance of official duty, or out of any other act, omission or occurrence for which a Force is legally responsible, and causing damage in the territory of the Republic of Cyprus to third parties, other than any of the Contracting Parties, shall be dealt with by the Republic of Cyprus in accordance with the following provisions:

(a) Claims shall be filed, considered and settled or adjudicated in accordance with the Laws and regulations of the Republic of Cyprus with respect to claims arising from the activities of its own armed Forces.

(b) The Republic of Cyprus may settle any such claims, and payment of the amount agreed upon or determined by adjudication shall be made by the Republic of Cyprus in its currency.

(c) Such payment whether made pursuant to a settlement or to adjudication of the case by a competent tribunal of the Republic of Cyprus, or the final adjudication by such a tribunal denying payment, shall be binding and conclusive upon the Contracting Parties.

(d) Every claim paid by the Republic of Cyprus shall be communicated to the sending States concerned together with full particulars and a proposed distribution in conformity with subparagraph (e)(i), (ii) and (iii) below. In default of a reply within two months, the proposed distribution shall be regarded as accepted.

(e) The cost incurred in satisfying claims pursuant to the preceding subparagraphs and paragraph 2 of this Article shall be distributed between the Contracting Parties, as follows:

  (i) Where one sending State alone is responsible the amount awarded or adjudged shall be distributed in the proportion of 25% chargeable to the Republic of Cyprus and 75% chargeable to the sending State.

  (ii) Where more than one State is responsible of the damage, the amount awarded or adjudged shall be distributed equally among them; however, if the Republic of Cyprus is not one of the States responsible, its contribution shall be half that of each of the sending States.

  (iii) Where the damage was caused by the armed services of the Contracting Parties and it is not possible to attribute it specifically to one or more of those armed services, the amount awarded or adjudged shall be distributed equally among the Contracting Parties concerned. However, if the Republic of Cyprus is not one of the States by whose armed services the damage was caused, its contribution shall be half that of each of the sending States concerned.

  (iv) Every half-year, a statement of the sums paid by the Republic of Cyprus in the course of the half-yearly period in respect of every case regarding which the proposed distribution on a percentage basis has been accepted, shall be sent to the sending States concerned together with a request for reimbursement. Such reimbursement shall be made within the shortest possible time in the currency of the Republic of Cyprus.

(f) In cases where the application of the provisions of subparagraphs (b) and (e) of this paragraph would cause a Contracting Party serious hardship, it may request the Committee of Ministers to arrange a settlement of a different nature.

(g) A member of a Force shall not be subject to any proceedings for the enforcement of any judgement given against him within the Republic of Cyprus, in a matter arising from the performance of his official duties.

(h) Except in so far as subparagraph (e) of this paragraph applies to claims covered by paragraph 2 of this Article, the provisions of this paragraph shall not apply to any claim arising out of or in connection with the navigation or operation of a ship or the loading, carriage, or discharge of a cargo, other than claims for death or personal injury to which paragraph 4 of this Article does not apply.

6. Claims against members of a Force arising out of tortious acts or omissions within the Republic of Cyprus not done in the performance of official duty shall be dealt with in the following manner:

(a) The Authorities of the Republic of Cyprus shall consider the claim and assess compensation to the claimant in a fair and just manner, taking into account all the circumstances of the case, including the conduct of the injured person and shall prepare a report on the matter.

(b) The report shall be delivered to the Authorities of the sending State, who then shall decide without delay whether they will offer an *ex gratia* payment, and if so, of what amount.

(c) If an offer of *ex gratia* payment is made, and accepted by the claimant in full satisfaction of his claim, the Authorities of the sending State shall make the payment themselves and inform the Authorities of the Republic of Cyprus of their decision and of the sum paid.

(d) Nothing in this paragraph shall effect the jurisdiction of the courts of the Republic of Cyprus to entertain an action against a member of a Force unless and until there has been payment in full satisfaction of the claim.

7. Claims arising out of the unauthorized use of a vehicle of the armed services of the sending State shall be dealt with in accordance with paragraph 6 of this Article, except in so far as a Force is legally responsible.

8. If a dispute arises as to whether a tortious act or omission of a member of a Force was done in the performance of official duty or as to whether the use of any vehicle of the armed services of a sending State was unauthorized, the question shall be submitted to an arbitrator appointed in accordance with paragraph 2(b) of this Article, whose decision on this point shall be final and conclusive.

9. The sending State shall not claim immunity from the jurisdiction of the courts of the Republic of Cyprus for members of a Force in respect of the civil jurisdiction of the courts of the Republic of Cyprus except to the extent provided in paragraph 5(g) of this Article.

10. The Authorities of the sending State and the Republic of Cyprus shall co-operate in the procurement of evidence for a fair hearing and disposal of claims in regard to which the Contracting Parties are concerned.

ARTICLE IX

1. Members of a Force and their dependents may purchase locally goods necessary for their own consumption, and such services as they need, under the same conditions as the nationals of the Republic of Cyprus.

2. Goods which are required from local sources for the subsistence of a Force shall normally be purchased through the Authorities which purchase such goods for the armed services of the Republic of Cyprus. In order to avoid such purchases having any adverse effect on the economy of the Republic of Cyprus, the competent Authorities of that State shall indicate, when necessary, any articles the purchase of which should be restricted or forbidden.

3. Subject to agreements already in force or which may hereafter be made between the authorized representatives of the sending State and the Republic of Cyprus, the Authorities of the Republic of Cyprus shall assume sole responsibility for making suitable arrangements to make available to a Force the buildings and grounds which it requires, as well as facilities and services connected therewith. These agreements and arrangements shall be, as far as possible, in accordance with the regulations governing the accommodation and billeting of similar personnel of the Republic of Cyprus. In the absence of a specific contract to the contrary, the laws of the Republic of Cyprus shall determine the rights and obligations arising out of the occupation or use of the buildings, grounds, facilities or services.

4. Local civilian labour requirements of a Force shall be satisfied in the same way as the comparable requirements of the Republic of Cyprus and with the assistance of the Authorities of the Republic of Cyprus through the employment exchanges. The conditions of employment and work, in particular wages, supplementary payments and conditions for the protection of workers, shall be those laid down by the legislation of the Republic of Cyprus. Such civilian workers employed by a Force shall not be regarded for any purpose as being members of that Force.

5. When a Force has at the place where it is stationed inadequate medical or dental facilities, its members and their dependents may receive medical and dental care, including hospitalization, under the same conditions as comparable personnel of the Republic of Cyprus.

6. The Republic of Cyprus shall give the most favourable consideration to requests for the grant to members of a Force of travelling facilities and concessions with regard to fares. These facilities and concessions will be the subject of special arrangements to be made between the Governments concerned.

7. Subject to any general or particular financial arrangements between the Contracting Parties, payment in local currency for goods, accommodation and services furnished under paragraphs 2, 3 and 4 and, if necessary, 5 and 6 of this Article shall be made promptly by the Authorities of the Force.

8. Neither a Force, nor its members, nor their dependents, shall by reason of this Article enjoy any exemption from taxes or duties relating to purchases and services chargeable under the fiscal regulations of the Republic of Cyprus.

ARTICLE X

1. Where the legal incidence of any form of taxation in the Republic of Cyprus depends upon residence or domicile, periods during which member of a Force is in the territory of the Republic of Cyprus by reason solely of his being a member of such Force shall not be considered as periods of residence therein, or as creating a change of residence or domicile, for the purposes of such taxation. Members of a Force shall be exempt from taxation in the Republic of Cyprus on the salary and emoluments paid to them as such members by the sending State or on any tangible movable property the presence of which in the Republic of Cyprus is due solely to their temporary presence there.

2. Nothing in this Article shall prevent taxation of a member of a Force with respect to any profitable enterprise, other than his employment as such member, in which he may engage in the Republic Of Cyprus, and, except as regards his salary, emoluments and the tangible movable property referred to in paragraph 1, nothing in this Article shall prevent taxation to which, even if regarded as having his residence or domicile outside the territory of the Republic of Cyprus, such a member is liable under the Law of the Republic of Cyprus.

3. Nothing in this Article shall apply to "duty" as defined in paragraph 12 of Article XI.

4. For the purpose of this Article the term "member of a Force" shall not include any person, who is a national of the Republic of Cyprus.

ARTICLE XI

1. Save as provided expressly to the contrary in this Agreement, members of a Force as well as their dependents shall be subject to the laws and regulations administered by the Customs Authorities of the Republic of Cyprus. In particular, the Customs Authorities of the Republic of Cyprus shall have the right, under the general conditions laid down by the laws and regulations of the Republic of Cyprus, to search members of a Force and their dependents and to examine their luggage and vehicles, and to seize articles pursuant to such laws and regulations.

2.–(a) The temporary importation and the re-exportation of service vehicles of a Force under their own power shall be authorized free of duty on presentation of a triptyque in the form shown in the Appendix to this Agreement.

(b) The temporary importation of such vehicles not under their own power shall be governed by paragraph 4 of this Article and re-exportation thereof by paragraph 8.

(c) Service vehicles of a Force shall be exempt from any tax payable in respect of the use of vehicles on the roads.

3. Official documents under official seal shall not be subject to customs inspection. Couriers, whatever their status, carrying these documents must be in possession of an individual movement order, issued its accordance with para-

graph 2(b) of Article III. This movement order shall show the number of dispatches carried and certify that they contain only official documents.

4. A Force may import free of duty the equipment for the Force and reasonable quantities of provisions, supplies and other goods for the exclusive use of the Force and, in cases where such use is permitted by the Republic of Cyprus, its dependents. This duty-free importation shall be subject to the deposit, at the customs office for the place of entry, together with such customs documents as shall be agreed, of a certificate in a form agreed between the Republic of Cyprus and the sending State signed by a person authorized by the sending State for that purpose. The designation of the person authorized to sign the certificates as well as specimens of the signatures and stamps to be used, shall be sent to the customs administration of the Republic of Cyprus.

5. A member of a Force may, at the time of his first arrival to take up service in the Republic of Cyprus or at the time of the first arrival of any dependent to join him, import his personal effects and furniture free of duty for the term of such service.

6. Members of a Force may import temporarily free of duty their private motor vehicles for the personal use of themselves and their dependents. There is no obligation under this Article to grant exemption from taxes payable in respect of the use of roads by private vehicles.

7. Imports made by the Authorities of a Force, other than for the exclusive use of that Force, and imports, other than those dealt with in paragraphs 5 and 6 of this Article, effected by members of a Force are not, by reason of this Article, entitled to any exemption from duty or other conditions.

8. Goods which have been imported duty-free under paragraphs 2(b), 4, 5 or 6 above:

(a) May be re-exported freely, provided that, in the case of goods imported under paragraph 4, a certificate, issued in accordance with that paragraph, is presented to the customs office; the Customs Authorities, however, may verify that the goods re-exported are as described in the certificate, if any, and have in fact been imported under the conditions of paragraph 2(b), 4, 5 or 6 as the case may be.

(b) Shall not normally be disposed of in the Republic of Cyprus by way of either sale or gift; however, in particular cases such disposal may be authorized on conditions imposed by the Authorities concerned of the Republic of Cyprus (for instance, on payment of duty and tax and compliance with the requirements of the controls of trade and exchange).

9. Goods purchased in the Republic of Cyprus shall be exported therefrom only in accordance with the regulations in force in the Republic of Cyprus.

10. Special arrangements for crossing frontiers shall be made by the Customs Authorities to regularly constituted units or formations, provided that the Customs Authorities concerned have been duly notified in advance.

11. Special arrangements shall be made by the Republic of Cyprus so that fuel, oil and lubricants for use in service vehicles, aircraft and vessels of a Force may be delivered free of all duties and taxes.

12. In paragraphs 1-10 of this Article:

"duty" means customs duties and all other duties and taxes payable on importation or exportation, as the case may be, except duties and taxes which are no more than charges for services rendered.

"importation" includes withdrawal from customs warehouses or continuous customs custody, provided that the goods concerned have not been grown, produced or manufactured in the Republic of Cyprus.

13. The provisions of this Article shall apply to the goods concerned, not only when they are imported into or exported from the Republic of Cyprus, but also when they are in transit through its territory.

ARTICLE XII

1. The customs or fiscal authorities may, as a condition of the grant of any customs or fiscal exemption of concession provided for in this Agreement, require such conditions to be observed as they may deem necessary to prevent abuse.

2. These Authorities may refuse any exemption provided for by this Agreement in respect of the importation into the Republic of Cyprus of articles grown, produced or manufactured in that State which have been exported therefrom without payment of, or upon repayment of, taxes or duties which would have been chargeable but for such exportation. Goods removed from a Custom Warehouse shall be deemed to be imported if they were regarded as having been exported by reason of being deposited in the warehouse.

ARTICLE XIII

1. In order to prevent offences against customs and fiscal laws and regulations, the Authorities of the Republic of Cyprus and of the sending States shall assist each other in the conduct of enquiries and the collection of evidence.

2. The Authorities of a Force shall render all assistance within their power to ensure that articles liable to seizure by, or on behalf of, the Customs or Fiscal Authorities of the Republic of Cyprus are handed to those Authorities.

3. The Authorities of a Force shall render all assistance within their power to assure the payment of duties, taxes and penalties payable by members of the Force or their dependents.

4. Service vehicles and articles belonging to a Force, and not to a member of such Force, seized by the Authorities of the Republic of Cyprus in connection with an offence against its customs or fiscal laws or regulations shall be handed over to the Appropriate Authorities of the Force concerned.

ARTICLE XIV

1. A Force, its members and their dependents, shall remain subject to the foreign exchange regulations of the sending State and shall also be subject to the regulations of the Republic of Cyprus.

2. The foreign exchange Authorities of the sending State and the Republic of Cyprus may issue special regulations applicable to a Force or its members as well as to their dependents.

ARTICLE XV

The present Annex shall remain in force in the event of hostilities to which the Treaty of Alliance between the Republic of Cyprus, Greece and Turkey, will apply. However, the provisions for settling claims in paragraphs 2 and 5 of Article VIII shall not apply to war damage. Also the provisions of Articles III and VII shall immediately be reviewed by the Contracting Parties, which may agree to such modifications as they may consider desirable regarding new Agreements.

ANNEX "D"

TRAINING OF THE ARMY OF THE REPUBLIC OF CYPRUS

GENERAL PRINCIPLES

ARTICLE I

1. The training of the Army of the Republic of Cyprus (Officers, NCOs and Enlisted men) shall be carried out by Greek and Turkish military personnel. The Tripartite Headquarters shall decide with the concurrent opinion of the Commanders of the Greek and Turkish Contingents the number of personnel of each rank to be assigned from the said Contingents. This assigned personnel shall form a single group under a single command.

2. The responsibility for basic military training in the General Training Centre and in the units shall be transferred to the chain of Command of the Army of the Republic of Cyprus at the end of a three year period. The starting date for this period shall begin from the date that Greek and Turkish training personnel actually report for duty.

ARTICLE II

The Appropriate Authorities of the Republic of Cyprus, in consultation with the Tripartite Headquarters, shall determine the general aims of the training of the Army of the Republic of Cyprus, within the framework of the provisions of this Agreement.

ARTICLE III

In preparing the training programmes the following basic principles shall strictly be observed:
  (a) Conformity with the aims of training determined by the Republic of Cyprus.
  (b) Conformity with the provisions of this Agreement.
  (c) Uniformity of method, spirit and rules.
  (d) Fulfilment of the requirements of the Army of the Republic of Cyprus in accordance with its Table of Organization.

ARTICLE IV

Unified principles and procedures of training shall be applied for the training of the Army of the Republic of Cyprus.

ARTICLE V

The training of personnel (Officers, NCOs and Enlisted men) of the units and support formations of the Army of the Republic of Cyprus shall be conducted by the Training Group within the territory of the Republic of Cyprus.

ARTICLE VI

The main categories of training applicable to the Army of the Republic of Cyprus to be conducted by the Training Group are the following:
  (a) Recruit basic military training.
  (b) Training for required specialties and technical training.
  (c) Officers and NCOs training.
  (d) Unit training.
  (e) Advanced training for Officers and NCOs.

TRAINING PHASES PARALLEL TO THE ORGANIZATION OF THE ARMY

ARTICLE VII

1. In order to establish a General Training Centre, a preparatory stage shall precede. The object of this stage shall be to carry out all preparations, both material and technical, necessary to start training. These preparations shall include camps, barracks, training areas, ranges, cooking facilities, necessary armament and other equipment, training aids, training programme, etc.

2. This preparatory stage shall be completed at the end of a three months period from the date a nucleus of the Training Group report for duty. It is not essential to cover, during this stage, all material requirements for the entire Army. Any remaining requirement shall be properly met parallel to the Time Phase Plan for the activation of the Army of the Republic of Cyprus.

ARTICLE VIII

1.–(a) A General Training Centre shall be established for the training of the army of the Republic of Cyprus.
  (b) The setting up of the General Training Centre shall be the responsibility of the Appropriate Authorities of the Republic of Cyprus, acting in consultation with the Tripartite Headquarters.
  (c) At the early stage the Tripartite Headquarters shall have the authority to provide out of the Training Group in a proportion of 60% Greek to 40% Turkish the necessary personnel for the functioning of the Centre but not for administrative purposes.
  (d) Special provisions shall be made for the early preparation of Cypriot military personnel, who shall progressively replace the Greek and Turkish personnel, with the exception of the instructors.

2. The Republic of Cyprus shall provide premises and installations, areas, weapons, equipment and training aids and all other facilities necessary for the functioning of the Centre, taking into account the recommendations of the Tripartite Headquarters.

ARTICLE IX

1. At the General Training Centre first priority shall be given to the training of the Cypriot military personnel required to cover immediate needs, such as:

(a) Military personnel for the Tripartite Headquarters and other related agencies of the Republic of Cyprus.

(b) Personnel who shall take over the functioning of the Training Centre from Greek and Turkish personnel.

(c) Key personnel for the Army of the Republic of Cyprus.

2. The training of the personnel referred to above should be concise, aiming at providing them with a general knowledge and a practical training in the duties they are to perform.

3. The normal training of those personnel, to whom this concise training period is applied, shall be resumed immediately after they are relieved by the first normally trained personnel of the Army of the Republic of Cyprus.

ARTICLE X

1. An increasing capability shall progressively be given to the General Training Centre to keep in pace with the Time Phase Plan for the activation of the Army of the Republic of Cyprus.

2. The Army of the Republic of Cyprus shall be trained in accordance with the Time Phase Plan for its activation which shall be determined by the Appropriate Authorities of the Republic of Cyprus in consultation with the Tripartite Headquarters.

3. From the duration aspect three types of training shall be conducted in the General Training Centre. These shall be the following:

(a) Concise training.

(b) Normal training.

(c) Training of Regular Officers and NCOs.

4. At the beginning a concise training course of eight weeks shall be conducted in the General Training Centre in order to train the personnel referred to in paragraph 1 of Article IX of this Annex. This type of training shall be applicable to all grades such as Officers, NCOs and Enlisted men. The personnel who have completed the concise training course shall man key administrative posts in the General Training Centre and other related agencies without delay.

5. Normal training shall apply to Candidates for Officer and NCO as well as the recruits and shall follow the concise training period and be repeated as many times as necessary. For planning purposes and as an indication, the duration of normal training shall last about six months for Officer Candidates, four months for NCO Candidates and three months for recruits. The application of normal training to military personnel of the various echelons shall be so co-ordinated that they complete their training in due time and be ready for assignment to the units according to the Time Phase Plan for the activation of the Army of the Republic of Cyprus.

6. The training of Regular (Career) Officers and NCOs shall be conducted in the General Training Centre by courses lasting over a year for Officers and

about eight months for NCOs. The actual commencement of these courses shall depend on the increasing capability of the General Training Centre and availability of Candidates for these courses.

7. Personnel selected for required specialties shall receive the necessary additional training in the General Training Centre after completion of their basic military training. This personnel shall be assigned to the units after the termination of their special training.

8. Efforts shall be made, to avoid major change, which may hinder the normal exercise of the training responsibility.

9. The training as a whole and throughout its several stages shall be governed by a practical spirit.

10. The principle of mixed organizational structure of the Army of the Republic of Cyprus shall be applied in training.

ARTICLE XI

After completion of training at the General Training Centre, a unified system of unit training, in accordance with the existing regulations of the Army of the Republic of Cyprus shall be applied to all units of the said Army. The unit training of the Army of the Republic of Cyprus shall normally be conducted in their garrison areas. To assist in unit training a portion of the Training Group shall be allocated to the units concerned.

ARTICLE XII

The Tripartite Headquarters:
(1) Shall be responsible for the preparation of the training programmes for the various categories of personnel as well as for the units. These programmes shall conform with the aims of training. The Appropriate Authorities of the Republic of Cyprus may object to these programmes as not being in accordance with the aims, whereupon the Tripartite Headquarters shall review the programmes. In case of disagreement between the Tripartite Headquarters and the Appropriate Authorities of the Republic of Cyprus as to whether the programmes conform with the aims of training, the Committee of Ministers shall finally decide.
(2) Shall be responsible for the proper application of the training programmes.
(3) Shall be entitled to carry out, from time to time, training inspections in order to ascertain that progress is being accomplished.
(4) Shall submit monthly training reports regularly and interim reports whenever it deems this necessary or, if requested to do so, to the Authorities of the Republic of Cyprus and the Committee of Ministers.

ACTIVITIES OF THE TRAINING GROUP

ARTICLE XIII

1. The Training Group, as provided in Article XVI of this Agreement, shall consist of a Chief, a Deputy Chief and Training Sections as required by the Organizational Structure of the Army of the Republic of Cyprus.

2. The Chief of the Training Group shall be a Greek or a Turk by yearly rotation. The Deputy Chief of the Training Group shall not be of the same nationality as the Chief. For the first year the Chief shall be designated by lot, but he shall not be of the same nationality as the Commander of the Tripartite Headquarters.

3. In the event of absence or impediment of the Chief of the Training Group, the Deputy Chief shall carry out the duties of the Chief for a period not exceeding thirty days. Beyond this period and up to the end of the term of duty of the Chief, a new Chief of the same nationality shall be appointed. The Appropriate Authorities of the Republic of Cyprus and the Tripartite Headquarters shall be duly informed.

ARTICLE XIV

1. The Training Group shall be responsible to the Tripartite Headquarters for the proper implementation of the training programme and prepare any training programme if asked to do so by the Tripartite Headquarters.

2.–(a) Shall continuously supervise, within its competence, the implementation of the programmes of training of the Army of the Republic of Cyprus.

(b) Shall report to the Tripartite Headquarters on any question of deficiency or irregularity that may occur to the course of the implementation of the training programmes.

3. Shall regularly submit monthly training reports to the Tripartite Headquarters and interim ones on its own initiative or on instructions by the Tripartite Headquarters.

ARTICLE XV

Both, Greek and Turkish training personnel, shall in principle be members of each training section. As soon as the organization of the Army of the Republic of Cyprus has been decided upon, the Table of Organization of the Training Group shall be determined in accordance with the provisions of Article XVI, paragraph 5, of this Agreement. However, in order to make the necessary preparations, a nucleus of the Training Group consisting of the Chief, the Deputy Chief and eight Instructor-Officers shall start operating at the time of the establishment of the Tripartite Headquarters from which it shall receive instructions as soon as possible. The training personnel shall arrive in the Republic of Cyprus in echelons. The last echelon shall arrive in time to be ready for the commencement of actual training.

ARTICLE XVI

The Appropriate Authorities of the Republic of Cyprus:
(1) Shall provide all means, equipment and other assistance required for the training of the Army of the Republic of Cyprus in consultation with the Tripartite Headquarters.
(2) Shall bear all expenses required for the training of the Army of the Republic of Cyprus.

ARTICLE XVII

The Appropriate Authorities of the Republic of Cyprus are requested to do their utmost for the speedy completion of the preparatory requirements, in time.

ARTICLE XVIII

The Tripartite Headquarters shall decide upon any details concerning the training, in conformity with the Organizational Structure of the Army of the Republic of Cyprus.

APPENDIX 30

Stella Soulioti, "Archbishop Makarios: A Personal Impression"

I met Archbishop Makarios for the first time on the day when he appointed me Minister of Justice in the first Cabinet of the Republic of Cyprus.

On the day of Independence, 16 August 1960, I was on holiday in Greece with my family. On 20 August, I received a telephone call from my brother, George Cacoyannis, who was in Cyprus. The Archbishop, he said, was looking for me; he had tried to reach me but could not find me, so he had asked George to do it for him and to offer me the portfolio of Minister of Foreign Affairs.* What is more, he wanted an answer immediately, by telephone. I said that this could not be done over the telephone, and I asked George to tell His Beatitude that I would return to Cyprus the next day and give him my answer.

I felt as if a calamity had befallen me. There were so many people who wanted to become Ministers; why did the Archbishop have to choose me. My immediate reaction was to refuse, and the more I thought about it the stronger I became in this conviction. It was not only that I did not want to be drawn into politics. I was unhappy about the terms of the Zurich and London Agreements. I also knew that a cabinet post meant that I would have little time for my family. As Foreign Minister I would have to travel abroad often. I would feel torn and constantly guilty. Dimitri, my husband, was unreservedly in favour. But would he, I asked myself and him, really accept the role of "husband of the Minister?"

By the next morning my mind was made up. I would return to Cyprus, thank the Archbishop for the great honour he had done me and continue my life and career as a lawyer in Limassol. It all seemed simple. I had not yet come up against Archbishop Makarios.

We arrived in Nicosia late in the evening of 21 August 1960. I was met at the airport by Glafkos Clerides, the President of the House of Representatives and an old friend. He told me that His Beatitude would see me at the Presidential Palace at eight the next morning.

I was at the Palace early. The building was the Colonial Governor's residence, known as "Government House." The British Coat of Arms was carved over the entrance. The Archbishop would have considered it a denial of

---

* Archbishop Makarios had all but appointed as Minister of Foreign Affairs a well respected leading lawyer and an erstwhile Member of the Cyprus Executive Council. However, the EOKA fighters, with Georkadjis in the lead, had reacted, not because they had anything against the person himself, but because they considered that the Council of Ministers should be composed of "fresh" personalities.

This was one of the unfortunate instances which would be quoted by those of Makarios's critics who wished to represent him as liable to change his mind or as being too much under the influence of the EOKA fighters.

history and an act of vandalism to have it removed. He was very proud of it and pointed it out to visitors as one shows off a prized possession. The Cyprus flag, which I was seeing for the first time, flew over the Palace. I was disappointed at the design: a yellow Cyprus on a white background—almost a flag of surrender.

This was my first visit to the House since 1955. I experienced a sense of pride that it was now the seat of government of an independent Cyprus. The interior was exactly as I remembered it. The same visitors' book lay open where it had always stood. Even some of the staff had been kept on. There was only one striking difference: the language spoken was now Greek instead of English. The terminology had changed overnight: Presidential Palace instead of Government House, Under-Secretary to the President instead of Private Secretary to the Governor. It all sounded new and strange.

Glafkos Clerides was already there, in the Archbishop's office. I waited in the ante-room for the summons to go in, with mounting nervousness. After all, I was about to meet, not only the President of the Republic and the Archbishop of Cyprus, but a legend in contemporary Cyprus history and a political figure that had already aroused much controversy in the world.

My nervousness vanished as soon as I saw the Archbishop. As I entered, he rose from behind his desk and came to meet me with a smile and an outstretched hand.

Archbishop Makarios was slim and of just over medium height. His habit made him appear taller than he actually was. His movements were spare and easy. The swing of his robe lent them a floating air. When he stood, he stood erect and absolutely still. Though of peasant stock, his bones were fine and his hands slender and expressive. There was a natural grace and dignity about him.

What struck me most at this first meeting was the complete lack of pretentiousness, making communication with him free, natural and open. I had seldom felt so much at ease at a first meeting with anyone. His irrepressible sense of humour became evident with the first words he spoke.

He wished me to be a member of the government, he said, and he had offered me the portfolio of Minister of Foreign Affairs, through my brother, as he did not know where to find me. Some people, he added with a smile, did not think it proper to have a woman Foreign Minister since the President and the Foreign Minister would have to travel abroad together. I replied as I had intended. I thanked him for the great honour he had done me in considering me for the office, but in any case I could not have undertaken something which was outside my field of knowledge and experience. I knew nothing about politics.

"None of us do," he said. "We shall all learn together. What we need are people with integrity, common sense and intelligence."

"But you do not know me, Your Beatitude. Besides, I would make a very bad politician. I hate public speaking; I very seldom appear in court. I prefer chamber work."

"You would be amazed at how much I know about you. Knowing people is my métier. I will give you two choices: the Ministry of Justice or the High Commission in London. Justice is within your field, and London you know well since you studied there. Nor do you need to make speeches if you don't want to."

I asked to be allowed to consult my husband. "No. You must decide here and now. You cannot leave that chair without telling me which of the two it is going to be. After all, you will not have to do it for life. You may have a change after two or three years."

There was a little more talk about the duty of all to help the young Republic. But I had the distinct impression that the real reason why the Archbishop was keen to have me in his government was twofold. The first was because I was a woman; it was then still something out of the ordinary to have a woman Minister or Ambassador and it would show the world that Archbishop Makarios was a modern Head of State, without prejudices. The Archbishop enjoyed creating a sensation, even a mild one like appointing a woman to a high office. The second reason was because he was intrigued by the fact that, at a time when he was besieged by so many people clamouring for official posts, here was somebody who needed persuasion to accept one.

My determination to resist broke down before the Archbishop's magnetic will. I chose the Ministry of Justice. The Archbishop smiled and, turning to Glafkos Clerides, said: "Spyros is lucky. He always wanted to be Foreign Minister." He was referring to Spyros Kyprianou who had actually been appointed Minister of Justice on 16 August 1960 and who would now become Minister of Foreign Affairs. He then asked the Under-Secretary to request Mr. Kyprianou to come to the Palace. In five minutes, Spyros was there. He entered the Archbishop's office, obviously puzzled at the urgent summons.

"I have called you because I want you to hand me your resignation, Spyros," the Archbishop said solemnly.

Spyros blanched. "Very well, Your Beatitude, but may I know why?"

"Because I have decided to appoint you Minister of Foreign Affairs."

The Archbishop picked up the phone at his elbow and asked to be connected to the Cyprus Broadcasting Corporation. He told them to put out on the next bulletin the announcement of the new appointments. Then, turning to me, he added: "And now, you may change your mind if you wish."

The interview had lasted about half an hour. Still bewildered, I went to meet my family at the hotel where we were staying. My husband was delighted; my daughter showed little emotion, but I sensed that she was not unhappy. I asked my husband to telephone my brother in Limassol and I went to a friend's house to sit quietly and absorb the fact. I felt as if I had done something terrible and irrevocable. I was not frightened so much as overawed. For about an hour I could not bring myself to tell my friend, but the time of the News was approaching and it did not seem right to let her hear it on the radio. I told her, rather as one confesses to some shameful act. She of course was thrilled.

A few minutes after the News, the telephone started ringing. The press had discovered me. The first journalist wanted to know something about me. "I am forty years old," I began. He roared with laughter. "And the Archbishop tried to hide your age. You don't ask a lady how old she is, he admonished us."

I returned to the hotel. The cameras were already there, and micro-phones were pushed under my nose. I had to answer their questions. The pa-pers appeared the next day with my photographs on the front pages—photographs taken on that day and photographs in my WAAF uniform, miraculously unearthed. I was mortified. I could not bring myself to look at them.

In the quiet of our room that night, I tried to understand how I had found myself in a situation which made me depressed and unhappy. There could be but one answer: the personality of Archbishop Makarios. It was of course too early for me to grasp this personality. Of one thing only I was im-mediately certain: the Archbishop possessed a magnetism, a charisma such as I had never come across before. In later years I was to have many clashes with him, disagreements on fundamental questions of principle, arguments of such a pitch as I have not had with anyone before or since. Yet, because our differ-ences of opinion were always out in the open, they never developed into un-dercurrents, shadows or resentments.

Archbishop Makarios has been called a Byzantine monk with a devious character whom one could not trust. This kind of disparaging remark ema-nated from the Archbishop's enemies who, finding fertile ground in the in-herent prejudice of the western world against prelates in politics, were quick to sow in it this image of the Archbishop. The device was first used by the British, then taken up by the Turks and perfected during the dictatorship in Greece, when the Archbishop's opponents, realising their impotence to meet him on the democratic arena of elections or the platform of open opposition, resorted to underhand and criminal means to oust him.

The prejudice against Archbishop Makarios's dual function—as head of state and head of the Church—stems from an insufficient knowledge of the history and tradition of the Autocephalous Church of Cyprus and the unique role of the Archbishop of Cyprus as ethnarch.[†] It was almost preordained that, on their awakening from centuries of foreign domination, the people should turn to their traditional leader for guidance; and he would have betrayed his destiny if he had denied them his leadership.

Archbishop Makarios had none of the attributes one commonly associ-ates with a monk. His background as a shepherd in the beautiful hills of his native village of Panayia in the heart of the Troodos mountain range gave him an ease of manner, an almost childlike impetuosity, an atmosphere of fresh air, which neither his religious nor his political life was able to dampen. He re-mained to the end a shepherd boy—a shepherd with the manners of a king.

It was not until the age of thirteen that the Archbishop became a nov-ice at the Kykkos Monastery situated a few miles from Panayia. This did not mean such a great change as one might suppose. The Monasteries of Cyprus are not places of seclusion where hermits dwell. They are rather places of work and instruction. The novices and monks are in no way cut off from their families or from the world. On the contrary, the public are encouraged to con-

---

[†] For a brief analysis of this aspect, see volume 1, introduction, 7-10.

gregate in the Monasteries and to attend church services there. Each Monastery has a "visitors' wing," a "ξενών," equipped as a modest boarding house, where anyone is welcome to stay. The reason for this is that Monasteries, being situated far from the main concentrations of population, were not easily accessible in the days before the advent of the motorcar. It was therefore necessary for worshippers to stay overnight if they wished to celebrate there the feast day of the particular saint to whom the Monastery is dedicated. Although modern means of communication have made this unnecessary, the tradition has remained and many families still spend a few days a year at a Monastery. The Kykkos Monastery, being the most isolated Monastery of Cyprus, which in the old days could only be reached by an arduous horse or mule ride, provided the best and most spacious accommodation for visitors.

The visitors are looked after by the young novices who mix with them freely. The Abbot is the father and mentor of the community and is very accessible. It is considered rude to visit a Monastery and not pay one's respects to the Abbot, be offered coffee and preserved fruit and sign the visitors book. In the winter months, the Abbots and some of the monks of the more isolated Monasteries move to the city, where the Monastery has an Annex, "μετόχιον." The novices can then attend the ordinary secondary schools together with the children of the city.

As the Annex of the Kykkos Monastery is situated in Nicosia, the Archbishop attended secondary school there. Being of a naturally sociable disposition, he made many friends among his classmates. These friendships he retained over the years, and it was a common joke that if you had been at school with the Archbishop he could deny you nothing. Loyalty to old friends was one of the Archbishop's most human traits.

The many facets of the Archbishop's personality combined complexity with utter simplicity—so much simplicity that it took me years to realise that some of his actions were really as simple as they appeared on the surface. The man who had such physical and spiritual courage that he despised any precautions to protect himself from known designs against his life could not bring himself to reprimand a subordinate, would not dismiss a clerk and had not the heart to refuse a favour. He might appear unyielding, but he was in fact eminently susceptible to reasonable argument. He could take a decision of the greatest political significance and carry it through resolutely, yet he might hesitate over a minor matter if he feared that it would cause hardship to an individual. His philosophy that nothing in this world is urgent, contrasted strangely with the speed with which he executed an idea once conceived. He was at the same time a visionary and a supreme realist.

Nevertheless, the Archbishop was the most predictable of persons, for there ran through his personality certain traits which were unfailingly constant.

The ruler who could command anybody to do anything never presumed on anyone's time. He was utterly unassuming, invariably courteous, always considerate. In my seventeen years of close collaboration with him, be never invited me to a working session, or even a formal meeting, through a secretary. He always telephoned himself, and he would be particularly careful that his request should not sound like an order. I remember the last time he asked me to work with him on a Saturday afternoon. The telephone conversation was something like this: "What are you doing this afternoon?" the Archbishop asked. "It seems that I shall be spending it at the Archbishopric, Your Beatitude," I replied. "Are you absolutely sure you have nothing better to do? Would five o'clock be convenient?" The Archbishop's natural breeding never ceased to amaze me.

The relationship between the Archbishop and his Ministers was one of respect and love. He was too human and too gentle to inspire fear or awe. We were not only his Ministers, we were his friends. He would worry about our personal difficulties and about our families. We did not hesitate to go and see him, even unannounced, on any subject, knowing that we could always count on his understanding and guidance. Almost bursting into his office early one morning, I said, "I have a weight on my soul, Your Beatitude, and I have come to unburden it on yours." "I must say, that is a true act of friendship, at this hour of the morning," he replied. After listening to the problem, he said: "Is that all? My soul does not feel any heavier; I only hope yours feels lighter."

The years of my association with the Archbishop were filled with crises. Not once did I see him lose his dignity, his *sang-froid* or his sense of humour, or betray the agony in his heart. He would preside over the Council of Ministers as if he had been born to the tradition of cabinet government—in the true spirit of *primus inter pares*. He would listen to all arguments carefully, never hurrying, never interrupting. His intelligence, his clarity of mind, his quickness in grasping all the aspects of a problem, enabled him to analyse a situation so logically and to sum it up in such a way that one felt there could be no other conclusion or avenue of action. And if the tension ever rose, he was prompt with a joke to lighten the atmosphere.

It has been said that Makarios preferred to be surrounded by "yes-men." Nothing could be further from the truth. The Archbishop had much more respect and affection for those of his co-workers who had the courage of their convictions and stood up to him. He placed more trust in them and took their view more into account.

Himself a true believer, Archbishop Makarios did not force religion on anyone. His faith was the source of the Archbishop's deep serenity. He was unafraid, even of death. He knew that he could have lived much longer had he heeded medical advice. He chose instead to face death squarely, to challenge him almost. He was fully aware of the consequences, for a few days after his first heart attack, he asked me whether we could complete, in eight months, a project we had long been planning. When I replied that we would need at least two years, he said; "Then you will have to finish it alone." In the last weeks of his life, the Archbishop gave the impression of somebody who had arrived at a grave decision and was somehow liberated.

If I were to choose the distinctive quality which secured for the Archbishop his unparalleled place in the hearts of his people, I would say it was his oneness with them. He was truly of the people, he shared his thoughts with them, he made them a party to his policies. "Listen to my speeches," he would say, "and you will know what I think." The people on their part knew that his actions were motivated by a single objective: their interest. They trusted him absolutely, even expecting him to perform miracles. This was brought home to me most forcibly one day in November 1974. An elderly woman who had lost home, husband and children, was comforting another, similarly bereaved woman, with the words: "Don't worry, the Archbishop will be back in a few days and all will be well."

The Archbishop's complete accessibility to his people was something that happened naturally: it could not be otherwise. He did not have to contrive it as is the fashion with modern heads of state nowadays. To me, brought up in the bureaucracy of "proper channels" and the theory that rulers must keep a little aloof, it was at first disconcerting that the Archbishop would see anybody at any time and on any matter, however trivial. His consideration for the people was paramount. He never spared himself. His attitude was: "It is my duty to listen to the people, to redress injustice."

I think I can best illustrate the Archbishop's identity with his people by relating two simple, but to those who knew him by no means surprising, incidents.

The Archbishop was returning from the Presidential Palace to the Archbishopric with one of his Ministers, Tassos Papadopoulos, for a working lunch. At the gate of the Palace an old village woman waved to the car to stop. His Beatitude gave the order to the driver and wound down the glass. "What is it, auntie?" he asked, using the traditional way of addressing elderly village women. She explained that she had been trying to gain access to the Palace since early morning to see him but the guards would not let her through. "Get into the car," said the Archbishop, "and tell me all about it." As they drove along the streets of Nicosia, the policemen on the route were saluting. The Archbishop turned to the old lady and said: "You see, auntie, the policemen are saluting you." "Do you think, my son, that it is me they are saluting?" she asked. "Well," replied the Archbishop, "we must be fair. Those on your side are saluting you; those on my side are saluting me." The Archbishop then drove her to her home at the other end of Nicosia before returning to the Archbishopric for lunch with his Minister.

Again: late one Saturday afternoon, a visitor called on the Archbishop unexpectedly. He was told that His Beatitude was in the Cathedral, next door to the Archbishopric. The visitor went to the Cathedral. The Archbishop was officiating at a funeral; there were no mourners. It was the funeral of a beggar who had no relatives or friends.

Archbishop Makarios grew in stature over the years and reached the apogee of statesmanship in the last months of his life. Never had I seen him take such historic and courageous decisions with so much assurance and conviction—a sense of destiny even.

To say that the Archbishop was infallible would do his memory a disservice. His greatness lay not in being infallible but in admitting to his mistakes. He was quick to apologise if he even suspected he had given offence. This same attitude was reflected in his political life. I well remember his sentiments towards Britain and the British immediately after Independence. He had fought the British for the cause of his people, but once the struggle was over, bygones were really bygones. He never harboured any resentment or bitterness, either towards Britain as a country or towards the politicians who had actively opposed him.

Some critics have wondered why Archbishop Makarios, who knew that the people would follow him to the death, did not assert his authority more strongly. The Archbishop did not believe in imposing his will on the people or shocking them into a policy which he felt they were not ready to accept. He rather believed in easing them into it, preparing them to accept it in their hearts before appealing to their intellect. The Archbishop achieved unity through love and respect. That was why the people followed him.

This event speaks better than any analysis of the Archbishop's relationship with his people.

On the 20th January 1975, there was a riot outside a foreign embassy in Nicosia, in protest against that Government's policies towards Cyprus. When the Archbishop heard that the rioters were getting out of hand, he went on the spot. He stood at the head of the crowd and tried to persuade the people to disperse. At one point, the masses chanted: "We are with you." The Archbishop immediately seized on this: "If you are with me, follow me." He turned and started walking away from the scene. The people forgot the riot and followed him silently, as if under a spell, to the steps of a building nearby.

A dialogue then took place between the ruler and the people, of which the only parallel is the dialogue between Oedipus and the citizens of Thebes, in the tragedy of Sophocles:

"I share your agony and your anguish," the Archbishop said, "but I appeal to you not to resort to acts of violence."

"But we have lost our homes, Your Beatitude."

"I assure you that, with your support, I shall do everything possible for the restoration of justice."

"Ask for the help of friendly countries," the people advised.

"I am ready to accept help from any source for the cause of my people," replied the Archbishop.

"Decisions are needed now, Your Beatitude."

"Decisions are taken by those who have the responsibility to take them," the Archbishop said. "Please go quietly."

"We trust you. We shall do as you say."

And the demonstrators dispersed.

The Archbishop's final contact with his people was the epitome of all that he meant to them. The whole of Cyprus lined the road from Nicosia to his last resting place in the hills where he was born. It was the only time that the crowds greeted Makarios in silence, but as the cortege passed they broke into spontaneous applause for the leader on his last appearance.

It will be many centuries before another Makarios is born to Cyprus. No doubt the historians of the future will evaluate Makarios in various ways. I can only feel blessed for having known him.

APPENDIX 31

Letter from Vice-President Fazil Kutchuk to Archbishop Makarios, 12 September 1961

KΥΠΡΙΑΚΗ ΔΗΜΟΚΡΑΤΙΑ   KIBRIS CUMHURIYETI
REPUBLIC OF CYPRUS

No. 59/60

12th September, 1961

Dear Archbishop,

Our Republic has just completed its first year during which I have watched the situation with patience and, in my sincere desire to afford a chance to the Republic to take its first steps without any hindrance, have on occasions suffered, without complaining, humiliation and insubordination. The purpose of this letter is to record the main incidents which have caused me great anxiety and concern, and to solicit Your Beatitude's assistance in order to avoid the recurrence of similar incidents.

In the first place, I have to mention the unnecessarily long discussions which usually take place at the meetings of the Council of Ministers between Greek and Turkish Ministers. It is indeed disappointing and discouraging to observe that whenever any matter affecting, however remotely and indirectly, one particular community comes up for discussion the Council is automatically splitted into two factions—Greek members on one side and Turkish members on the other. Furthermore, the antagonistic attitude adopted by certain Ministers during such discussions and the tone of their conversation leave much to be desired and indicate that some of us have not yet realised or appreciated the necessity of working in a spirit of understanding and co-operation. For example, during the consideration of the 1961 Estimates, I was very much disappointed that Greek Ministers objected to almost every Turkish project which it was proposed to include in the lists of works to be executed in 1961. They showed their reluctance and indeed their indignation at having to agree even on Your Beatitude's recommendation to the inclusion in the Estimates of any development project which would benefit Turkish villages or inhabitants. The minutes of the meetings of Council of Ministers are full of such examples.

Secondly, it has become apparent that matters referred to the Council of Ministers are first discussed at a meeting of Greek Ministers who come to the meeting already decided on the line of action that they, who constitute the majority, will adopt at the full meeting of the Council. In this way the Turkish Ministers have been given the impression that their presence at the meetings of the Council of Ministers is for the sake of formality only. In fact their presence serves only one purpose: that is, they are given an opportunity to express their points of view on controversial matters and to record their vote of dissension.

Thirdly, certain policy matters are dealt with without consulting and even informing the Vice-President and Turkish Ministers. On many occasions

I have come to know of decisions taken, even in respect of matters over which we have the right of veto, from the news columns of local press. The most recent example is the inclusion of Messrs. Rossides and Kranidiotis in the Cyprus Delegation at the Belgrade Conference.

Fourthly, the Public Service Commission has failed to discharge its duty. Now that we know the mentality of the members of this Commission it is futile to expect that the same Commission will be able to implement the 70:30 ratio in the public service. It is therefore a matter for serious consideration whether it would not be lawful for us to terminate the appointment of certain members of this Commission who have been impeding the work of the Commission rather than making any contribution to it.

Fifthly, it is indeed very discouraging and disappointing to see that—

(a) our Ministers, Ambassadors and other persons of high authority make statements every now and then to the following effect—

The Cyprus people "raises its voice in international organisations whose declared aim is to serve justice, freedom and self-determination. No justice is however done to its struggles and its voice remains unanswered".

"This struggle which was carried out by the entire (as one body) people of Cyprus under the leadership of Archbishop Makarios and General Grivas did not unfortunately lead to the predetermined object and the desired national goal. Adverse international conditions produced a new state of affairs".

"These achievements are not of course absolute, but the present reality does not completely close the circle of our pursuits".

"The realisation of our hopes and aspirations is not complete under the Zurich and London Agreements".

"We have acquired a bastion and starting point for peaceful campaigns".

"From these bastions we shall continue the struggle with a view to consummating victory".

"One of the reasons that I am a Minister is because I believe that from this position I can serve better the interests of the fighters". (The "Fighters" refer to an Association of ex-EOKA members who have reorganised themselves with the object of continuing with the struggle for union with Greece).

(b) the number of persons who openly condemn the Zurich and London Agreements and our Constitution is increasing from day to day; the activities of these persons are unconstitutional as they are not in the interests of the security of the Republic or the constitutional order, but yet they are not prosecuted;

(c) though it is known that in Cyprus the principle of "Self-determination" will create feelings of distrust and animosity between the two communities and will revive the old demands for "union" and "partition", yet it has been turned into a general topic for discussion. In other words, though "the integral or partial union of Cyprus with any other State or the separatist independence" is excluded by our Constitution, activities to the contrary are fostered by men in authority;

(d) there is a general tendency, especially amongst Government circles, to disregard certain provisions of our Constitution if experience showed that they are against the interest of the majority, and to find ways and means so as to render ineffective such decisions of the Supreme Constitutional Court as are against Government policy.

Lastly, it is a matter of deep regret for me to have to cite the following examples which indicate that some attempts have been made to foil our authority (especially that of the Vice-President of the Republic) during the year under review:

(a) The Minister of Foreign Affairs, for reasons of his own, has not yet implemented our agreement regarding the arrangements at Washington and New York. He has not complied with the Council's decision that he should submit to the Council reports on foreign affairs received from Mr. Rossides and other Ambassadors, nor has he complied with my request that he should supply to me copies of correspondence emanating from his office and having a bearing on foreign affairs. Despite my repeated requests to him he has refrained from allocating duties to Turkish officials posted to his Ministry. An impartial investigation into the affairs in this Ministry will reveal that discrimination against Turks and anything that is Turkish is, I regret to say, very prevalent. His activities in the Ministerial Committee of the Tripartite Agreement are not known to me and to the Turkish Ministers despite the fact that one of them is the Minister of Defence who should be kept fully informed of all the matters relating to the Tripartite Headquarters.

(b) The position in other Ministries headed by Greek Ministers is not very much different. Turkish officials, however well qualified and experienced they may be, have gradually been turned into dormant officials. The most recent example of this is the transfer of a Turkish Executive Engineer from the Office of the Divisional Engineer, Nicosia, to the office of the Senior Architect, Headquarters, P.W.D. Another glaring example is the nature of the duties assigned to the Economic Officer in the Ministry of Finance, the Assistant Director, Public Information Office, and the Administrative Officer in the Ministry of Labour and Social Insurance.

(c) Letters written on my behalf concerning complaints and representations made by Turkish citizens remain unanswered for an unduly long time and my requests for redress of injustice done to Turkish citizens are usually turned down with stereotyped replies.

(d) My requests to certain Ministers for the preparation of certain submissions to Council of Ministers are not complied with.

(e) The Director-General of the Cyprus Broadcasting Corporation has refused to give me an assurance that he will do his best to ensure that there will be no discrimination between Greek and Turkish programmes.

In view of all the above and other reasons which I need not mention here I have begun to doubt whether we have been acting correctly and constitutionally by allowing our Ministers, who hold office at our pleasure, to disregard our advice, wishes and directions and to take decisions contrary to them. I am afraid that the tendency on the part of the Ministers to disregard the President and the Vice-President of the Republic will wreck the very spirit of our Constitution. I think that the time has come for us to take a firm stand against those Ministers who will continue to disregard our advice and instructions. As you know executive power is to be ensured by us through the Ministers appointed by us. We have the power to terminate at any time the appointment of any Minister; there is no doubt, therefore, that we have the means with which to ensure that the executive power is exercised in accordance with our wishes and instructions. In my view the Ministers must realize that they are to act in accordance with the directions given to them by the President and Vice-President jointly. They are of course at liberty to consider the matters on the agenda of the meetings of the Council of Ministers and to take decisions thereon but when the President and Vice-President are agreed on any matter it is very improper on their part not to act in accordance with the wishes of the President and the Vice-President. I therefore take strong exception to certain Ministers, who are in the habit of defying the authority of the President and the Vice-President and referring to them at the meetings of the Council as persons without a vote.

As you know it is not my wish to be difficult, but I am afraid that if we want to run our Republic in accordance with the spirit of our Constitution we have to act very firmly and must not allow our own Ministers (i.e. our Agents) to act contrary to our directions. I would, therefore, suggest that from now on we must not let the Ministers waste time by discussing in vain controversial matters. When we come across such matters we two should first discuss them and, if we agree, we should issue directions to that effect to our respective Ministers in the Council asking them to decide and act accordingly. By this way we should only leave such matter to the vote of the Council on which we two, who are in a better position to judge the issues and who carry the political responsibility of the Government vis-à-vis the electorate, cannot agree despite all our sincere efforts to co-operate.

I should be grateful if you will afford me an opportunity to discuss the contents of this letter with you after you have studied and formed your opinion about them.

Yours sincerely,
(Dr. F. Kutchuk)

APPENDIX 32

Draft Letter from Archbishop Makarios to Vice-President Fazil
Kutchuk, September 1961

Dear Dr. Kutchuk,

Thank you for your letter No. 59/60 dated 12th September, 1961. I am
really sorry that you should have gone to the trouble of writing to me, as I am
sure that a discussion between us of the matters which cause you concern
would have been easier. However, since you have put your thoughts in a letter,
it might be helpful for you to have my reply in writing before we have a meeting. For your convenience, I shall take your points seriatim.

(1) *In the first place*: I cannot accept the implication that the long discussions
which sometimes take place at the meetings of the Council of Ministers are
due to the attitude of the Greek Ministers nor that it is the Greek Ministers
who adopt an antagonistic attitude. Such unnecessarily long discussions are, in
my view, due to the following factors:
   (a) The insufficient delegation of authority to Ministers, with the result
       that unimportant and immaterial questions, which could easily have
       been dealt with by a Minister alone or even by senior officials, are dis-
       cussed in Council. I have noticed that it is on such questions, rather
       than on matters of serious policy, that the longest and most heated ar-
       guments take place. This principle of concentration rather than dele-
       gation is most strongly advocated by Turkish Ministers who always op-
       pose most vehemently any proposal to delegate authority, although
       delegation is universally accepted as one of the essential principles of
       good government and no state can function efficiently without it.
       There is a volume of illustrations of this in the Minutes of Council, but
       I shall quote only a few which readily come to mind:
       (i)   Opposition to the delegation to the Minister of Finance of author-
             ity to issue Special Warrants;
       (ii) Opposition to the delegation to the Minister of Finance of author-
             ity to dedagger "daggered" items;
       (iii) Opposition to the delegation to the Minister of Finance of author-
             ity to control the "Emergency" Vote;
       (iv) Insistence that such routine questions as the payment of pensions
             and grant of study-leaves should be referred to Council;
       (v)   General opposition to the delegation of any Statutory authority to
             Ministers;
       (vi) Insistence on concentration was strongly apparent when the forma-
             tion of an Economic Planning Commission was discussed.
   (b) The reluctance on the part of certain Ministers to consult other
       relevant Ministries (such as the Ministry of Finance on questions in-
       volving finance) before making submissions to Council. This is amply

illustrated by many Submissions, especially those presented by the Minister of Agriculture, and by the Minutes of Council. The result of this is deferment, delay and discussion on insufficient data.

(c) The attempt of Turkish Ministers, especially during discussions concerning estimates, development and other projects, to introduce, in Council, new projects not included in the lists before Council even though such lists had been carefully prepared by Committees of experts and other appropriate officers and even though the Ministries concerned were fully represented on such Committees. In most cases no plans are ready in respect of such projects, no opportunity has been afforded to the technical experts to study them and no proper estimate of their cost is made. In spite of this, however, purely for the sake of showing goodwill and against all principles of good government, a number of such projects have on several occasions been included in such estimates and lists, as the Minutes of the Meetings of Council show. It is not to be wondered at that certain Ministers have shown their reluctance to agree to such a practice which would, if adopted, have the effect of nullifying any planning, study and preparation of projects and would inevitably lead to a waste of public money on non-essential or non-priority projects. It will easily be appreciated that chaos would soon result if every Minister insisted on including in every list of projects his own favourite projects presented at the twelfth hour during Council discussions without prior study. It is to projects sought to be included in circumstances such as the above that Greek Ministers have objected.

(d) The reluctance of certain Turkish Ministers to present Submissions to Council and their attempt to take Council by surprise and seek decisions on the spot, without due study and presentation of the subjects concerned. The Minister of Defence has hardly ever presented a Submission to Council on his own initiative even on matters of grave importance.

(2) *In the second place*: It has never been a secret that Greek Ministers have meetings with me, and it is equally not a secret that Turkish Ministers do the same with yourself. It is, however, incorrect to say that the Greek Ministers come to the Meetings of Council already decided on the line of action that they will adopt. In fact, the Minutes of Council are full of illustrations of Greek Ministers holding and advocating varying views amongst themselves and voting differently. On the other hand, there is hardly one illustration of the Turkish Ministers voicing different views amongst themselves or voting differently, all of them always voting the same way. There is, therefore, no factual support for the impression of the Turkish Ministers mentioned in your letter.

(3) *In the third place*: The presence of Messrs. Rossides and Kranidiotis at the Belgrade Conference is hardly an illustration of the statement that certain policy matters are dealt with, without consulting or informing the Vice-President and the Turkish Ministers. Surely the Head of State and President of the Republic, when attending a conference abroad, is free to choose his own assistants without prior decision or approval.

(4) *In the fourth place*: The statement that the Public Service Commission has failed to discharge its duty cannot be accepted. If it is meant by such statement that the Public Service Commission has failed to implement the 70:30 ratio in the Public Service, I would point out the following facts:

> Although on 16.8.1960, the ratio of Greeks and Turks in the Public Service was 78:22, it is now 76:24. This has been achieved against almost insuperable odds, and often in the face of hardship to the Greek members of the Public Service and to the detriment of the Service as a whole since the standard has in some cases been lowered to enable the admission of the required number of candidates. Let it be remembered that there is not always a sufficient number of Turkish candidates with appropriate qualifications to fill the posts allocated to them.

With regard to the suggestion that we should consider the termination of the appointment of certain members of the Commission, such appointments can, as you know, under the Constitution, only be terminated on account of misconduct, and I do not think that any member has been guilty of any behaviour justifying dismissal on such ground.

As you are aware, the task of the Commission is, intrinsically, a most difficult one, rendered even more difficult by the inherent cumbersomeness of a body consisting of ten men, and I do not think that they have, in their first year of service, acquitted themselves badly.

(5) *In the fifth place*:

(a) It would be most discouraging and indeed disquieting if a people were to declare itself content with its achievements and were to stop looking for improvement. This would surely mark the end of progress and the beginning of decline and would depict a most deplorable situation. I am unaware of the context of the quotations in paragraph (a) on page 3 of your letter; but such quotations seem to denote nothing more than a desire to struggle for better conditions, declaredly "by peaceful campaigns", and I do not see what is discouraging or disappointing in them.

(b) and (c) To prosecute persons who criticise the Zurich and London Agreements, as suggested in paragraph (b) on page 4 of your letter would, in my view, be not only against every principle of democracy and freedom of speech but would be a capital political error tending to intensify such criticism and render it more effective. And this, apart from the doubtful legality and constitutionality of such a course.

(d) I do not know to what the statement in paragraph (d) on page 5 of your letter alludes, but I, myself, have not ascertained any tendencies to "disregard provisions of our Constitution", as mentioned in your letter.

As opposed to the above, I should like to mention that Turkish persons in authority have on occasion declared that their policy in internal matters was aligned to the policy of Turkey (see, for instance, newspapers of 8.4.1961). This is an overt encouragement of "separatist independence" and, as such, much more to be condemned than the quotations mentioned in your letter.

Furthermore, certain statements by prominent members of the Turkish community which have been reported in the press, some of them even purporting to have been uttered by yourself, have caused the Greek community grave anxiety, as, for instance, the report of your talk at Louroudjina in June last.

(6) *Lastly*:

   (a) I take it that this matter refers to the arrangement regarding the Turkish Counsellor at Washington when the Ambassador is at the United Nations in New York. As you are aware, discussion of this matter in Council has shown that the decision of Council of 10th September, 1960, has, insofar as the Turkish side is concerned, been fully implemented, viz. the Turkish Counsellor is in charge of the Embassy in Washington when Mr. Rossides is at the U.N. But something further is claimed by the Turkish side, viz. that Mr. Rossides should be *precluded* from having any connection with the Washington Embassy while he is in New York and that the Turkish Counsellor should at such times be nominated "Charge d' Affaires". As has been amply demonstrated by legal authority and diplomatic practice, it is not possible for a "Charge d' Affaires" to be appointed unless the Ambassador is absent from the country to which he is accredited. If, therefore, we sought to satisfy the claim of the Turkish side which, as stated above, goes beyond the decision of Council, we would be considered ignorant of accepted international practice.

   I should like to mention in this connection that, as opposed to the attitude of the Turkish side, the Greek side has shown extreme patience and goodwill, on this same subject, namely: Although under the same decision of Council a Greek Counsellor should be appointed in the U.S.A., who should replace Mr. Rossides when he is absent from the country, no such Greek Counsellor has in fact yet been appointed, for the sake of economy, with the result that when Mr. Rossides is absent from the U.S.A., Turkish officers head both the Embassy in Washington and the U.N. Delegation.

   Yet the Greek side, acting not on a communal basis, but in the public interest of the Republic as a whole, has never complained regarding the non-implementation of the decision. It is rather strange to have the Turkish side complaining where the real grievance should be with the Greek side. It is occurrences such as these which render the work of Government unnecessarily complicated and impede progress.

   (b) I am certain that the assignment of duties complained of in paragraph (b) on pages 6-7 of your letter is commensurate with the rank of the officers concerned, but I will look into the matter.

   On the other hand, in Ministries headed by Turkish Ministers, every attempt is made to arrange the duties in such a manner that Turkish officers, even though in some cases not possessing the necessary qualifications, are placed in superior positions to their Greek colleagues, or means are found whereby responsibility is taken away from a Greek officer and given to a Turkish officer. Examples are:

(i) The posting of M. D. Shefki to the Veterinary Laboratory, although he possesses none of the qualifications and experience essential to research work;

(ii) The splitting of the medical district of Nicosia, hitherto a single district, into two sectors, one sector being given to a Turkish District Medical Officer;

(iii) The equalisation of all medical Specialists, thus putting old and experienced Specialists on the same level as newly appointed, inexperienced ones;

(iv) The attempt to reorganise the Agricultural Department in such a way as to curtail as far as possible the authority of Greek officers;

(v) The subjection of the Commander of the Army to humiliation in the eyes of junior officers of the Ministry of Defence.

(c) I am certain that any delay on the part of any Greek Minister to answer any letter written on your behalf, as mentioned in paragraph (d) on page 7 of your letter, must have been unintentional and due to the desire of such Minister to give full consideration to your query or request before replying to it.

(d) and (e) I am not aware of any outstanding requests made by you on the matters mentioned in paragraphs (d) and (e) on page 7 of your letter, and I shall be glad to look into this question if specific particulars are applied.

2. Having dealt with the specific matters over which you have expressed your concern, I shall now express my own concern over the following:

(1) The view adopted by the Turkish Ministers and other persons in authority leads to the conclusion that they do not consider the Republic as an integrated state and that they are not at all concerned with the Republic as a whole but only with what relates to the Turkish community. The following are some illustrations of the above statement:

(a) The attitude adopted by the Turkish Ministers during the recent discussion in Council regarding the Paphos Chiftliks case before the Supreme Constitutional Court. In this case, although the Republic is the respondent, the Turkish Ministers strongly argued in favour of the Applicants because they happen to be Turks;

(b) An attempt to increase the number of posts in the Public Service, irrespective of the extra burden on the Government and of the fact that such posts are not warranted by the volume of work;

(c) Insistence that all posts be filled, even though the Minister concerned states that there is no necessity to fill the posts in question;

(d) Recommendations that as high salaries as possible be fixed for those posts which are to be occupied by Turkish officers;

(e) The use of rights given to the Turkish community under the Constitution in such a way as to paralyse the State, e.g. the non-extension of the taxation legislation;

(f) The refusal of the Minister of Defence to participate in the discussion of the Agreement for technical assistance from the U.S. Government on the ground that the Ministry of Foreign Affairs was not run in accordance with the views of the Minister of Defence, based on communal considerations. (This is evidenced by letter of 28.3.61 of Minister of Defence to Minister of Foreign Affairs);

(g) The manning of the Turkish Outpatients Department with as many Medical Officers as the Nicosia General Hospital Outpatients Department, although the number of patients attending the former is much smaller and although a considerable number of Turkish patients still attend the latter;

(h) The constant attempt at division of the two Communities rather than co-operation and fusion, the most recent example being the structure of the Army, another example being the opposition of the Turkish side to integration of the Welfare Services;

(i) The delay of Turkish Ministers in presenting Submissions to Council when they wish to avoid the taking of a decision if they think that such decision may affect interests of individual members of the Turkish Community, e.g. delay of Minister of Agriculture in presenting Submissions re Government policy on Paphos Chiftliks;

(j) The presentation of Submissions to Council by yourself on personal matters affecting individual members of the Turkish Community, even when such matters fall within the domain of a Ministry.

3. You will have noticed that, for the sake of co- operation and the avoidance of conflict, I have myself refrained from raising such matters with the Ministers, who, I sincerely believe, are giving of their best and should not constantly be harassed; otherwise an unpleasant atmosphere of mistrust would be created, the Ministers' initiative curtailed and their task become impossible, to the detriment of the public interest.

4. I now come to your concluding suggestion which is to the effect that the Ministers must have no opinion or voice of their own, but must act as our "agents", according to directions issued to them by us. I can only say that your proposal would be contrary to the principles of democracy. I would like to add, in fairness to the Ministers, that I appreciate the way in which they put forward their views and have the courage of their convictions. I would have no esteem for any person who accepted to serve as a Minister under the conditions you suggest and I should mourn the day when the Council of Ministers was composed of robots. If there is any conflict between us and our Ministers on important matters of principle or policy, then, as you know, there is a proper remedy well in accord with accepted democratic principles.

5. I think it would help our young Republic to make progress if we looked at the public interest as a whole and did not allow grievances and discussions on minor issues to impede the formulation of greater policies and to cast a shadow on the relations between the two Communities. To this end, I would always be happy to discuss with you at any time any matter which causes you concern. I am sure that with sincerity and good will we can always find solutions.

Yours sincerely,
Archbishop Makarios

APPENDIX 33

Letter from Vice-President Fazil Kutchuk to Lyndon Johnson, Vice-President of the United States, 28 August 1962

VICE-PRESIDENCY
NICOSIA
28th August, 1962.

Dear Mr. Vice-President,

Since the establishment of the Republic of Cyprus we have tried whenever an opportunity presented itself to explain to Western Diplomats and particularly our American friends, the anxieties of the Turkish Community in Cyprus over the prevailing political and economic conditions in the Island. We have also submitted written reports for consideration.

On the occasion of your welcome visit, I have had prepared a brief memorandum in which our views, anxieties and recommendations are incorporated. I have great pleasure in handing this memorandum to you today and I feel confident that its contents will earn the consideration they deserve. A comprehensive detailed report containing also important documentary evidence is under preparation and will be submitted to you in due course.

The submission of this memorandum is, I think, particularly relevant in that I am informed that the subject of the Constitution and the relationship of the two communities in Cyprus came up for discussion during the recent Washington talks between President Kennedy and Archbishop Makarios.

Your very truly,
(Dr. M. F. KUTCHUK)
Vice-President of the Republic.

His Excellency Lyndon B. Johnson,
Vice-President of the United States of America.

MEMORANDUM

1. POLITICAL AGITATION

Although the Republic of Cyprus is now in its third year of existence as an independent state, the idea of ENOSIS (Union with Greece) is deliberately being kept in existence by the Greek Side: It is being aired and persistently kept alive by campaigns in the Greek Cypriot press, by Rightwing Cypriot Greek Leaders, and not least, by President Makarios himself. On the very eve of the second anniversary of Independence, on August 15th 1962, President Makarios said during a sermon delivered at Kykko Monastery, southwest of Cyprus:

"Greek Cypriots must continue to march forward to complete the work begun by the EOKA heroes of our liberation struggle . . . The struggle is continuing in a new form, and will go on until we achieve our goal."

Regrettably this is not the only instance in which President Makarios has uttered words of similar relevance. On another occasion he is reported to have made the following statement:

"We have acquired a hesitation and starting point for peaceful campaigns. From these bastions we shall continue the struggle with a view to consummating victory."

We believe that such public utterances on the part of Greek Cypriot leadership can only bring intrigue and confusion to Cyprus and are contrary to the spirit of partnership on which the Republic is founded. It can reasonably be argued that such utterances by Greek Cypriot leaders could provoke disturbances and intercommunal clashes of a kind which could quash all hopes for progress and co-operation.

The Zurich and London Agreements which were negotiated and agreed upon by all interested parties, was a compromise solution to the Cyprus question and was mainly based on balances and counter balances between the two Communities of the Island. Our Constitution was drafted on the basis of these Agreements after very long, arduous and protracted negotiations and indeed after some important concessions had been made especially on the part of the Turkish Community. Since then, unfortunately, the political situation within the new State has deteriorated on account of the persistent campaign by Greek Cypriot leaders for abrogation of these Agreements and for ENOSIS, despite repeated warnings by Turkish leaders that the survival and growth of the Republic depends upon the co-operation of the two Communities within the framework of the Constitution. This agitation is being conducted by the leaders of the Greek Community in spite of the solemn undertaking to abandon former aspirations which had been embodied as one of the basic articles of our Constitution.

2. CONSTITUTION

Greeks taking undue advantage of the privilege of majority vote and of the fact that they retained to themselves all key and executive posts have refused to implement several of the fundamental provisions in the Republic's Constitution and there is a persistent tendency on the part of the Greek press, Greek leaders and President Makarios himself to seek ways and means to nullify the Constitution. Turkish Cypriots on the other hand have accepted the Constitution in good faith and consistently uphold its full implementation. Never have they demanded anything which is not provided for in the Constitution.

Those provisions of the Constitution which recognised for Turkish citizens of the Republic certain safeguards and rights have been deliberately ignored or disregarded by the Greeks who have not only misrepresented and distorted facts but resorted to many intrigues and to the setting up of many artificial obstacles in order to make their implementation impracticable. Amongst these provisions are those articles concerning the 70/30 Greek/Turk ratio in the Civil Service, the separation of five main towns' municipalities, and the veto rights of the Vice-President on questions of Foreign Affairs and internal security.

Repeated representations by Turkish leaders requesting the settlement of these matters within a reasonable time have not only found no response from the Greeks but have been met by false accusations that Turks have been creating obstacles in the way of smooth functioning of the Republic. Whereas in actual fact non-implementation of the Constitutional provisions renders the position of the Government and their actions unconstitutional.

3. INTERNAL SECURITY

The Turkish Community is seriously perturbed by the failure of the Government to ensure security within the Republic. There have been dozens of unexplained and undetected murders since the Republic's birth and in each case guns of an unlawful nature and mysterious origin have been in evidence.

There have been instances of persecution of public figures, intimidation, threats and beatings; recently the Police Chief himself was threatened with death unless he quitted the Island within one month; there has been an armed attack upon the police; and on several occasions police patrols came across to gunmen who refused to surrender their weapons. The proprietor of a cinema has been threatened with death if he allowed his cinema to screen the film "Exodus". Mr. Lagoudontis, the Chief of the Intelligence Branch of the Police, was summarily deported from the Island on accusations—never denied officially—that he was conspiring against Government and public personalities and was responsible for certain actions which were committed with the object of creating disturbances between the two Communities. Moreover, information has leaked out that Lagoudontis was also responsible for certain actions which were committed in order to create conflict between members of the Turkish Community. It was stated that Lagoudontis was deported as a "matter of national necessity". It is significant that deaf ears have been turned to Turkish representations that full details of the case against Lagoudontis should also be made known to Turkish Leaders. The suggestion that the case of Lagoudontis should be inquired into by a neutral Commission has also been turned down.

4. COMMUNIST DANGER

It is our considered view that if the grievances of the Turkish Community are not removed and if it proves impossible to get the two sides to collaborate as provided for in the Constitution, a most important issue will have to be faced; i.e. the growth of Communism in Cyprus and a possible bid by Communists to assume power in future elections.

The Turkish Community has always been alive to this danger and vigorously opposed Communist expansion here. In the 1960 Presidential elections, AKEL (the Communist Party) was supported by about 35% of the Greek Cypriot Community. It is quite possible that the next elections, AKEL with outside help may attain authority and obtain a majority position in the House of Representatives and may dominate the Cabinet.

Repeatedly, the Turkish Community leaders have expressed their fears of Communist expansion to the Cyprus Government, as well as to Western diplomats in Cyprus. It is a regrettable fact that ever since he assumed power, President Makarios has made concessions to the Communists instead of taking measures to combat this movement on positive lines. He offered seats in the House of Representatives to AKEL members, and thus co-operated with AKEL to secure his own position. Moreover, he approved against Turkish opposition an agreement for the importation of sugar from Russia through AKEL and this he has been instrumental in securing for this Communist organisation a profit of more than $25,000 as well as internal moral stature and influence. Recently, the President went as far as to declare publicly that there was no Communist danger in Cyprus, but during his official visit to Washington earlier this year, he confided that if he is re-elected in 1965, he will combat Communism.

Never in its 21 year history, has AKEL been as powerful as to-day: Its membership exceeds 30,000 active party men and women, its satellite organisations work unfettered, and at the recent annual Congress the Secretary-General openly declared, for the first time, that the eventual aim of AKEL is to create a socialist Communist regime in Cyprus. It is significant that mainly because of the strong position of Communists that Archbishop Makarios felt impelled not to proceed with the election of village and urban authorities, but to retain the system of appointment which was introduced during the Emergency prior to Independence.

Communist penetration into the new State of Cyprus has also been revealed in the sphere of trade: Russia and satellite states have succeeded in obtaining against Turkish opposition bilateral trade agreements with Cyprus, in a bid to tie the Island's economy with that of Communist countries. This tactic, together with offers of technical and financial help, plus "cultural" propaganda, constitutes a familiar pattern of Soviet penetration into the State. Already, the construction of the enlarged Famagusta Harbour has been entrusted to a Polish Firm.

The Communist danger is the principal issue confronting the free world to-day, and the Turkish Community in Cyprus feels that a Communist bid to take over the Cyprus Administration is imminent.

5. POLICY OF "NON-ALIGNMENT"

The Turkish Community has always opposed the adherence of Cyprus to the "Non-Aligned" group of nations. We have often complained to President Makarios over this and suggested that our State should endeavour to establish closer relations with the Western Bloc. Indeed the Vice-President who under our Constitution must be a Turk and who has the same power and authority as the President on foreign affairs, announced publicly that he was against the Republic joining the "non-aligned" group of nations. Our efforts to get President Makarios to come to our viewpoint have failed, and he has continued to assert his intention to follow a "neutral" policy. It is noteworthy that President Makarios went to Belgrade Conference and repeatedly made statements that Cyprus would follow a non-aligned policy without a decisions to this effect being taken by the Council of Ministers. The reason for not taking such a decision was obviously to prevent the Vice-President from exercising his right of veto.

Whereas the Primary object of our foreign policy should be the consolidation of the independence of our State, the policy of non-alignment followed by President Makarios in complete disregard of the provisions of our Constitution, can only serve ulterior motives. It is evident that President Makarios has adopted this policy solely for the purpose of securing the votes of the other countries in this "group" in the event they succeed in raising the Cyprus question again in the U.N.O. or other international congresses.

It would not be out of place to mention here that the failure of the President to bring before the Council of Ministers the request of U.S.A. Government to establish a broadcasting station in Cyprus is again tied up with this absurd policy of non-alignment. The President has taken this attitude in order to please the so-called non-aligned group of nations (mainly U.A.R.) and in spite of the fact that the Vice-President and Turkish Ministers favoured all along the establishment of such a station in Cyprus.

It will be recalled that the President stated during his visit to U.S.A. that "Cyprus will not have an Army" for the reason that "Cyprus will remain neutral". This is no doubt one of the glaring examples of arbitrary action on the part of the Greek leaders because under our Constitution the establishment of a Cyprus Army is a mandatory provision.

6. SEPARATE COMMUNITIES

Racially, religiously, culturally, socially and politically the Greek and Turkish Communities in Cyprus have been two different entities. They speak different languages and adhere to different traditions. The two Communities have always lived together—harmoniously if Greeks did not press for political ends unacceptable to Turks such as ENOSIS and precariously when they did so. The fact that they are two different entities is acknowledged and realistically accepted in the Zurich settlement, and that consequently provision has been made in our Constitution for the establishment of Greek and Turkish Communal Chambers with legislative, executive and judicial powers, for the separation of municipalities, for separate education and co-operative development and for separate majority in voting system on certain vital matters.

It is the partnership of two separate Communities, rather than the fusion of both in one Community, that the Zurich Agreement recognised in the case of Cyprus.

There is good reason to argue that an economically strong and prosperous Turkish Community would make an active and influential partner of this Republic. Under the circumstances, we believe that it would be wrong to adopt a policy which assumed that the economic progress of both Communities was possible through aids to the Central Government. Experience has shown that the Central Government works mainly in the interests of the Greek Community. No matter what steps Turks take to see that development and other funds are evenly distributed, Greek authorities manage somehow that Turks get in actual fact even less than their numerical strength.

7. PROPORTIONAL SHARE OF AID

The Colonial Administration in its desire to please the majority, worked for the prosperity of the Greek Community and left Turkish land and villages in a comparatively undeveloped state. The Greeks are, therefore, now in a much better economic position than Turks in the new Republic, and unfortunately the present tendency is to favour the build-up of Greek prosperity and overlook the Turks, even in such vital aspects as communal education. While expenditure for Turkish education during the Colonial regime totalled £800,000 a year, to-day the amount earmarked from Government funds is only half of this amount and when the question of supplementary aid came up for consideration, President Makarios himself suggested and insisted that Turks should be given only £75,000 out of £500,000, i.e. only 12%.

We, therefore, stress the importance of the fair apportionment of all financial aid given to Cyprus. The application of such aid should be in the hands of a coordinating committee including representatives of both Communities to ensure its fair distribution, and it should be stipulated that the less developed Community should receive aid in a proportion greater than its numerical strength and according to its need for development.

We are no doubt very anxious that the Turkish Community should get its fair share in economic aid so that it has a chance to develop its resources and raise its financial strength to the same level of the Greek Community. Only thus can economic stability be secured, political stability promoted and Communism be checked. As otherwise if Turks are left in poverty Communism may eventually find its way among this Community also.

We feel it is essential that, just as in other countries where underdeveloped regions or zones are accorded special aid for development, the special position of the Turkish Community in Cyprus calls for special attention. We, therefore, earnestly ask the United States Authorities that, whenever projects of assistance to Cyprus are considered, the specialised apportionment should be stipulated to ensure meeting the needs of the Turkish Community as well and such aid should be chanelled to our Community through the Turkish Communal Chamber rather than through the Central Government.

8. SUMMARY OF RECOMMENDATIONS

(a) Political agitation for "ENOSIS" must cease and rule of law must prevail. ENOSIS is specifically ruled out in the Constitution and transgressions on this score shakes the very foundation of our young State.

(b) Stern measures should be taken against the organisation and spread of Communism; we feel that as a first step Communism should be outlawed.

(c) The foreign polity of Cyprus must be chanelled into the early aban-donment of the "non-aligned" status and must be firmly pro-Western.

(d) There must be strict observances of and adherence to all Constitutional provisions. The organs of the State must never be allowed to abuse power or act illegally or unconstitutionally under any pretext.

(e) The Government must take strong measures to restore security within the Republic as a Task of top priority.

(f) In view of the evident intention of Greek Cypriot leaders to abrogate the London and Zurich Agreements and to nullify the Constitution we feel it is appropriate for the Governments of the guaranteeing powers and of the United Sates of America as the leader of the Western World to exercise their influence in order to forestall a catastrophe which looms over this country.

APPENDIX 34

Record of Meeting of Minister of Justice Stella Soulioti with Douglas Heck, Counselor of the American Embassy, Nicosia, Saturday, 29 September 1962

SECRET

Mr. Heck said that the purpose for which he had requested this meeting was to clear up a misunderstanding concerning the recent visit to Cyprus of the Vice-President of the U.S.A. Mr. L. Johnson and that he wished to speak to me unofficially and as a friend.

Mr. Heck said that he was aware that a feeling of bitterness existed in the minds of the Greek population of Cyprus due mainly to Mr. Johnson's visit to Dr. Kutchuk's party and his acceptance of the key presented to him by the Turkish Mayor of Nicosia.

Mr. Heck wished to explain how the arrangements concerning Mr. Johnson's visit were made, particularly as regards Mr. Johnson's visit to Dr. Kutchuk. The programme had been drawn up by the Ministry of Foreign Affairs and Mr. Heck handed me a copy. On page 8 of the programme there is an item which reads as follows:

> "12.00 Noon   Arrive at Vice-President Kutchuk's Residence to call on Dr. Kutchuk. Drinks to meet other guests."

The idea was that the same thing would happen as on the occasion of Mr. Johnson's call on the President of the Republic, i.e. that Mr. Johnson would arrive before the time scheduled for the other guests and have an informal meeting with Dr. Kutchuk. But the programme had been thrown out of gear by the necessity for Mr. Johnson to have a rest after his address to the House of Representatives.

The American Embassy had been asked by Dr. Kutchuk's office whether Dr. Kutchuk could have one or two Ministers with him and the American Embassy had replied he could have whomever he wished. The American Embassy, however, had specifically arranged with Dr. Kutchuk's office that there were to be no speeches of any kind, a request which was repeated by Mr. Heck to Mr. Muftizade on arrival at Dr. Kutchuk's house. The American Embassy was not aware that the call on Dr. Kutchuk scheduled in the programme was going to be made an occasion for discussion of problems of the Turkish Community, nor were they aware of the persons who would be present. They were rather taken aback both when they saw who was present and when Dr. Kutchuk began talking about the Turkish Community's problems.

The American Embassy had avoided coming into any direct contact with the Office of the Vice-President regarding Mr. Johnson's visit, but had made all arrangements through our Ministry of Foreign Affairs. They had taken no part in the drawing up of the list of invitations to Dr. Kutchuk's party which, they understood, had been prepared in consultation with the Ministry of Foreign Affairs.

With particular reference to the presentation of the key and the address of the Turkish Mayor the American Embassy were taken completely by surprise especially as they had been assured more than once that there would be no speeches. The "ceremony of the key" and the Turkish Mayor's speech about "the sacred Turkish sail", Mr. Heck said, took place outside the "anteroom" where the private talk with Dr. Kutchuk had occurred.

Mr. Heck said that he would be grateful if I would see to it that the "record" was put right and he regretted that the occasion of Mr. Johnson's visit should have become the cause of a misunderstanding.

(Signed) STELLA SOULIOTI
Minister of Justice

SECRET

APPENDIX 35

Press Conference of Turkish Cypriot Members of the House of Representatives, 1 April 1961

Worthy members of the Press,

We have organised this press conference in order to inform you, the worthy members of the press, and the public opinion about the reason why the bill for the extension of laws imposing taxes and duties for another three months was not approved at the House of Representatives last night.

As you know, the Republic of Cyprus is a state established on the partnership of the Turkish and Greek Communities. In the Constitution rights were recognised separately for the two Communities and certain powers were given to them for the protection of such rights. Also the Constitution and the order created by this Constitution were guaranteed by the Governments of Turkey, Greece and the United Kingdom under the Treaty of Guarantee.

One of the powers given to the Turkish and Greek Communities for the protection of their rights is the requirement of separate majority of the representatives belonging to these Communities for passing of the laws imposing taxes and duties. Such power, it is not intended, as the Greeks allege, only for ensuring that such laws shall not be against either Community. Because other special rights and powers especially under articles 6, 28 and 137 of the Constitution, were given for the purpose of preventing any law to be discriminatory. Such provisions are enough for the prevention of discrimination. Therefore the real purpose of the rights and powers possessed by the two Communities in relation to the approval of the laws imposing taxes and duties is to ensure the compliance with the rights they possess under the Constitution and the Constitutional order.

Taxes and duties are imposed for the purpose of enabling the collection of money required to meet the expenses necessary for the carrying out of the state services. The income secured by the taxes and duties forms part of the budget. Expenditure under the budget must be incurred in compliance with the provisions of the Constitution. An approximate amount of six and a half million pounds which approximately forms one third of the provisions of the budgetary expenditure in intended for payment of salaries of the members of the public service. According to the article 123 of the Constitution the public service generally and at every grade of the hierarchy shall be composed at the proportion of thirty percent of the members of the Turkish Community. Therefore the thirty percent of the above mentioned amount should be paid to the Turkish Officers. But the authorities concerned by not filling the existing vacancies in the public service and thus not applying the thirty percent ratio in the relation to the Turkish Officers, although there is enough provision for the purpose in the budget, the thirty percent of this amount is not being paid to the Turks and surplus revenue is used for services beneficial to the Greek Community. Thus the income secured from taxes and duties in order to meet budgetary expenditure is being used in ways contrary to the provisions of the

Constitution. The Republic of Cyprus should function according to its Constitution and the Constitutional order. Income secured by taxes and duties secures the functioning of the Republic as a state. But the Republic is acting contrary to the provisions of the Constitution and is not implementing even the most important of the basic articles of the Constitution. It is obvious that the Republic shall not be allowed to act for ever in disregard to its Constitution.

Last night, the President of the House, on the complaint of some Turkish Representatives that the thirty percent ratio in relation to the Turkish Officers has not been applied, stated that this subject was not previously presented to the House by the Turkish Representatives and they did not request the discussion of it in the House. We regret such statement by the president of the House which is completely untrue. Because, Halit Ali Riza, a Turkish representative had, on 10th September, 1960, 21st September, 1960, 26 October, 1960, and 26th November, 1960, asked various questions of the authorities concerned about the thirty percent ratio in relation to the Turkish officers and workers and as he did not receive any answer to any of them requested the discussion of the subject in the House and in November, 1960 this subject was discussed in the House and Halit Ali Riza speaking on the subject expressed the importance of the subject and drew the attention of the authorities concerned and invited them to comply with the provisions of the Constitution.

Under article 188 of the Constitution, the Laws imposing taxes and duties expired on 31st December, 1960. This time given as from the establishment of the Republic was intended for giving the Executive an opportunity to prepare the required bills. During this period not only no bill was submitted to the House by the Executive but also agreement between the President and the Vice President of the Republic in connection with the subject of the application of this ratio between five months as from the establishment of the Republic which was a condition put forward by the Vice President in order to sign the agreements for the establishment of the Republic was not complied with. In spite of this a short time before 31st December, 1960, the Executive submitted a bill for the extension of the operation of the laws imposing taxes and duties until the end of 1961. Then, the danger of the non-implementation of the Constitution was explained both to the President of the Republic and the President of the House. On the promise given by the President of the Republic that the Constitutional provisions especially those relating to thirty percent ratio in relation to the Turkish Officers and in to order to show the good will of the Turkish Community once more the operation of these laws was extended for another three months. Although two months expired and the end of the third month was arrived at, the promise given by the President of the Republic was not kept and no noteworthy improvement was secured. The President of the Republic in a statement he gave to the press sufficed by putting all the responsibilities on the Public Service Commission. And the Executive submitted another bill for the extension of the operation of the laws imposing taxes and duties for another three months. Confronted with such a situation the Turkish group of the House realizing the heavy and high responsibility towards their Community decided not to allow such a bitter disregard of the rights of their community. However in order to make affective the votes of five of their friends who wanted to give another last chance to the Greek Community and to protect the Republic from any bad results the members of the group decided not to take part in the discussions of this bill. The five Representatives proposed an extension for two months and this reasonable proposal was refused by the Greek Representatives. When the Representatives out of the ten who were in the building of the House learned that the period of two months was not accepted by the Greek Members of the Finance Committee they decided to get into the House. Halit Ali Riza who spoke on behalf of the ten representatives stated that if the Greek Representatives accepted the period of two months although the representatives were determined not to approve this bill, they would not vote against the bill, that the two months were enough for doing a lot of works. Seeing what happened during this period, and if necessity arose, it was possible to extend this period again, the same principle being applied in approving of the period at an extraordinary session and the same procedure being followed as in the previous extension of the bill of same nature. He drew the attention of the Greek Representatives that if they did not accept this period all responsibility will be theirs. But unfortunately the Greek Representatives did not accept this reasonable proposal and thus prevented the approval of the bill. We regard the Greek Representatives responsible for the refusal of this bill and for any result which may come out of it.

In concluding we wish to stress the fact that we are determined to secure the full implementation of the Constitution and that we shall not be forced to any sacrifice.

APPENDIX 36

Statement by His Beatitude the President of the Republic Archbishop Makarios on the Situation Created by the Refusal of the Turkish Members of the House of Representatives to Vote the Income Tax Bill, 20 December 1961

I am profoundly sorry because the majority of the Turkish members of the House of Representatives, in abuse of the Constitutional provision requiring a separate majority for the passing of taxation Laws, refused to vote the Income Tax Bill. Flimsy pretexts, totally unconnected with the substance of the matter, that is, the scales of taxation, were advanced in an effort to justify this negative attitude. The Turkish members of the House of Representatives, exhibiting a manifest lack of a sense of responsibility, are undermining the very existence of the Republic of Cyprus, which I, as Head of State, have a duty to safeguard.

No State can subsist and function normally without financial resources. Income Tax constitutes a substantial part of the revenue of the State and is an instrument of economic and social policy.

In order to ensure the survival of the Republic of Cyprus, and in the interests of the Cypriot people as a whole, I consider it my duty to take all measures necessitated by the circumstances.

It is estimated that the revenue from Income Tax for 1961 will amount to £3,800,000. The estimated contribution of Turkish individuals and companies to this revenue will not exceed £82,000, whilst the estimated contribution of Greek individuals and companies will amount to £1,320,000. The remainder, amounting to £2,400,000, will be contributed by foreign companies and individuals.

From the above figures it is obvious that the contribution of the Greeks and the Turks to the Public Revenue in the form of Income Tax is, respectively, in the proportion of 16 to 1. In spite of this, the Greeks of Cyprus have never for a moment entertained the thought of depriving the Public Revenue of Income Tax, out of which the Turkish minority enjoys much more than its contribution and far in excess of the proportion of its population. Unfortunately this has not been realized or appreciated by the Turkish side.

As a temporary measure, to meet the inability of the Government, due to the depletion of the public revenue, to make additional grants to the Communal Chambers, beyond the amounts provided in the Constitution, I have to-day advised the Greek Communal Chamber to enact a law imposing, in respect of the Year 1961 in the form of personal tax on the Greeks, an amount equal to the income tax provided in the Bill not voted by the Turkish members of the House of Representatives and to revoke at the same time the Communal taxation already imposed. The income tax collected by the Government from Cypriot individuals and companies in respect of the year 1961 will be returned to the taxpayer after deduction of the tax payable by him under the Communal Chamber Tax Law.

As to the income tax payable by foreign companies and individuals, a new bill will be submitted to the House of Representatives to-morrow.

Despite the fact that the Greek taxpayers will feel considerable relief due to the situation created through the action of the Turks, the public revenue will be deprived of certain resources. As a result of such depletion of the revenue, the implementation of certain provisions of the Constitution, such as the filling of the vacancies in the Public Service in the ratio of 70:30 and the establishment of the Cyprus Army, will inevitably be delayed.

It is regrettable that the Turkish members of the House of Representatives, taking advantage and making improper use of the right of separate majority, have caused damage both to the Republic and to their community, which was benefitting disproportionately from the revenue derived from income tax.

I am compelled to state with regret that, taking into consideration the general interest of the people of Cyprus, I shall disregard any Constitutional provision which is abused by the Turkish side thus obstructing the smooth functioning of the State.

APPENDIX 37

Statement by Fazil Kutchuk, the Vice-President of the Republic, 21 December 1961

It is a matter of profound regret for me to have to be confronted with the present situation which has arisen as a result of the non-passing of the Income Tax Law by the House of Representatives.

Since the signing of the Zurich and London Agreements I have strived hard, indeed I have done all that was humanly possible, to prevent a deadlock such as the one we are now in. I seized every opportunity and tried to bring home to everyone, from the men in the street to the highest personalities of both Communities, that if it was our genuine desire to prosper together in this country we should show goodwill and understanding, readiness to co-operate in all spheres of life and respect of each others rights and feelings. As a matter of fact our Constitution is based on these principles. I therefore advocated at all times that in order to inspire confidence in all, our main task should be the implementation of the Constitution in full. Our Constitution recognized the existence of two Communities in Cyprus and the requirement that these two Communities should co-operate with goodwill and understanding, in running of certain vitally important affairs of the State, such as:

1–Foreign affairs, Defence and Internal Security, which are subject to veto of President and the Vice-President.
2–Ensurance of executive power generally.
3–Separate majority of Greek and Turkish Representatives in the House for the enactment of legislation on taxation and municipalities.

At the same time the Constitution recognised the majority system with certain safeguards against the oppression of the majority rule. Examples of these safeguards are:

(a) Establishment of separate municipalities in five main towns.
(b) Establishment of a Public Service with 70:30 ratio.
(c) Establishment of an Army with 60:40 ratio.
(d) Establishment of security forces with qualified ratio not below 70:30.
(e) Right of recourse to the Constitutional Court e.g. in cases of discrimination, etc.

Let us now take the above-mentioned examples seriatim and examine the position:

(a) *Separate Municipalities*: Though on my part I agreed to make the maximum possible concession it has not been possible to fix boundaries for two separate municipalities in the five towns. This in effect meant the strangulation of Turkish Municipalities which, unlike Greek

Municipalities which retained nearly all properties of the old municipalities, had to begin from the scratch. Unfortunately the Greek side
showed no understanding and whenever I raised the question the reply
I received has been "there are difficulties".

(b) *70:30 Ratio in the Public Service*: It has not been possible to make any
progress owing mainly to artificial obstacles created whenever the appointment or promotion of a Turk presented the slightest difficulty.
When no difficulty existed the filling of the particular vacancies has
been postponed for no good reason. It has been the tendency in all
Ministries and departments to strip Turkish officers holding any post f
some importance and seniority from all authority and responsibility. In
this way it has gradually become more difficult for Turkish Cypriots to
receive adequate service from the Public Service and to protect their
interests. My unceasing efforts to have this ratio implemented in accordance with agreements reached produced no response from the
Greek side.

(c) *Establishment of a Cyprus Army*: Insistence of the Greek side on the
establishment of the Army with mixed units all throughout despite the
advice of military experts (Greek and Turkish) that mixture in all units
at the initial stages was unworkable and might lead to undesirable consequences, and the refusal to vote adequate money for the purpose
have made it impossible to fulfil this constitutional obligation.

(d) *Establishment of Security Forces: i.e. Police and Gendarmerie*: Here
also care has been taken to remove Turks gradually from key positions.
Composition of all the Divisional Headquarters has been so made as to
eliminate Turks from important key positions. The recent incident at
Lapithos where a Turkish house has been searched by the Police without a warrant and in a most cruel manner is a glaring example of how
the security forces treat the ordinary Turkish Cypriot.

(e) *Right of recourse to the Supreme Constitutional Court*: Though it is encouraging that certain recourses made by me and other aggrieved
Turkish Cypriots to this Court have succeeded, in practice no effective
remedy has been secured. I have even noticed a tendency on the part
of the Greek side either to disobey directions of the Court or to act in
such a way as to render compliance with such directions as of no
significance.

I have stated above that the two Communities had an obligation under
the Constitution to co-operate. Let us now see whether the Greek side has left
the door open for such a co-operation:

1–*Foreign Affairs, Defence and Internal Security*: I have said that the
President and the Vice-President have a right of veto in these matters.
But the Greek side has been acting in such a way as to limit this power
to certain unimportant matters. It will be remembered that not very
long ago the Vice-President's right of vetoing the participation of
Cyprus in certain international conferences was questioned by the
Greek side. Certain statements made from time to time by

Mr. Rossides in the United Nations without first obtaining the approval of the Council of Ministers are other examples of the way in which the Vice-President's right of veto is not respected and is foiled.

2–*Ensurance of executive power.* While the President with his seven Ministers has been able to exercise this power the Vice-President has been denied almost any say. Nearly all my complaints, protests and requests (however justified and reasonable they may have been) either remained unanswered or have been refused. In certain important policy matters I have altogether been overlooked and though under the Constitution the Vice-President has almost identical powers, duties and responsibilities the tendency has always been not to recognise in me any privilege or authority.

3–*Separate majority of Greek and Turkish Representatives in the House for the enactment of legislation on taxation and municipalities*: I have always advocated that Turks should not be forced to exercise this constitutional right. To forestall such a situation I have exerted all human efforts. I implored that we must act quickly in the implementation in full of the provisions of the Constitution and thus inspire confidence in the Turkish Community which was gradually being pushed into depths of insecurity and into belief that all its rights were being usurped. I advocated that Greek leaders and press should be prevented from activities undermining the present constitutional order. It is most unfortunate that all my solicitations and implorations fell on deaf ears. The result has been that Turkish Representatives in the House, in the belief that their last chance to remind their Greek brethren of their constitutional obligations towards Turks would be lost to them for ever, have been forced to exercise a right which the Constitution gave to them. I do not wish at present to dwell on whether the Turkish Cypriots did well in exercising this constitutional right despite the fact that in the face of provocation and in the desperate position in which Turks have found themselves after 1 1/2 years working of the Republic their action may well be justified. What I would like to dwell on, is the attitude taken by the President of the Republic. This attitude has been explained in his statement which he issued on the 20th December, 1961. In this statement His Beatitude stated, inter alia—

(a) "The foundations of the Republic has been undermined by lack of a sense of responsibility on the part of the majority of the Turkish Members of the House."

    —For reasons explained above it is indeed questionable to lay the blame for the present deadlock on the Turkish Members of the House of Representatives. The real blame in my view lies in those authorities which have failed, obstructed or unduly delayed the implementation of the Constitution in full.

(b) "The contribution of the Greeks and Turks to the Public Revenue in the form of Income Tax is respectively in the proportion of 16 to 1."

—It is entirely wrong to argue that the Turkish Community is paying only 1/16th of the Income Tax paid by the Greek Community. It should be remembered that the correct taxation is not the race of the merchant or individual who pays the income tax but the racial composition of the market from which the Greek merchant derives his profits on which income tax is paid. It is not, therefore, correct to base oneself on the total sum paid by individuals without taking into account the above factor. Even if this were true then the contention of the Turks that they are being persistently prevented form improving their economic position is substantiated by figures.

(c) "The Turkish minority enjoys much more than the proportion of its population."

—It is regrettable that His Beatitude has deemed fit to use the term "Turkish Minority" in referring to the Turkish Community although he is well aware that the Constitution has recognised the existence of two Communities in Cyprus without reference to their numbers. As to the suggestion that the Turkish Community enjoys much more than the proportion of its population, this is not consistent with facts because is one takes into account the contribution made by the Turkish Community by direct and indirect taxation it will be seen that the Government expenditure in the Republic's budget directly affecting the Turkish Community are not disproportionate as argued by the President.

(d) "As a result of the depletion of the revenue the implementation of certain provisions of the Constitution such as the filling of the vacancies in the Public Service in the proportion of 70:30 and the constitution of the Cyprus Army will be delayed."

—According to the President there will be a depletion of about £1,400,000 as against a total revenue of about £19,000,000. This does not in my opinion constitute a justification for the drastic measures which the President has threatened to take, namely delaying the implementation of the 70:30 ratio and the constitution of the Cyprus Army. It appears, therefore, that the President's above threats have been prompted by some other motive.

(e) "Taking into consideration the general interest of the people of Cyprus I shall disregard any Constitutional provision which, if abused, may obstruct the regular functioning of the State."

—This, I regret to say, is very deplorable statement as it is an expression of an intention to violate the constitutional order and to disregard international agreements by the Head of a State. Our Constitution expressly states that any abuse of power by an organ is a matter for the Supreme Constitutional Court to decide upon. It is an unprecedented and indeed very unusual act for a Head of a State to take upon himself the jurisdiction vested in a Constitutional Court.

Furthermore, it is clearly laid down in our Constitution what powers our Head of State shall have. The above statement is obviously an expression of an intention to exceed these powers arbitrarily.

In my view it would have been more appropriate if His Beatitude had taken into account the reasons and circumstances which led to the deadlock before resorting to such actions as are not only unconstitutional but are of such a nature as to aggravate still more the position and hamper the relations between the two Communities.

On my part I would like to assure the public that, as hitherto, I shall continue to do my utmost to secure respect to our Constitution and the Order established there under and I shall not cease to exert all possible influence on all quarters to find a fair and reasonable solution to the present difficulties.

APPENDIX 38

Record of Meeting between Greek and Turkish Cypriots regarding the Income Tax Law, 9 January 1962

Presidential Palace, Tuesday, 9th January, 1962.

H.B. Archbishop Makarios,
The Minister of Finance,
The Minister of Justice,
The Attorney-General,
The Chief Revenue Officer,
Mr. Halit Ali Riza — Legal Adviser to the Turkish Communal Chamber.

1. A unified Income Tax Law should exist, such Law to be passed by the House of Representatives.
2. That 5% (five per centus) of the total Income Tax collected from all sources should be allocated to the Communal Chambers in the same proportion as the annual subvention under Article 88 of the Constitution, viz. 4:1. Provided that if such percentage falls below the sum of £250,000 it will be made up to that sum.
3. That a percentage varying between 70% and 90% of the Income Tax collected from members of the Greek and Turkish communities should be allocated to the Greek and Turkish Communal Chambers respectively, the exact percentage in each year to be decided by the Council of Ministers.

APPENDIX 39

Record of Meeting between Greek and Turkish Cypriots regarding Taxation and the Public Service, 26 September 1962

AIDE-MÉMOIRE

At the meeting held on 26/9/1962 between the Acting President of the Republic and His Excellency the Vice-President of the Republic with the Minister of Finance in attendance, the question of the saving of money from the Ordinary Budget for the purpose of transferring it to the Development Budget was discussed.

During the discussion the Vice-President pointed out that if the Council of Ministers would give a decision to freeze all vacant posts such a decision would be interpreted by the Turkish side as another maneuvre not to implement the 70:30 ratio. Such an interpretation would nip in the bud all efforts for ensuring Turkish co-operation for the enactment of the various Taxation Laws. Furthermore a decision to freeze all vacant posts would make the position of the Vice-President very difficult and would weaken the possibility of his mediation so as to bring an end to the misunderstanding between Greeks and Turks on the question of Taxation Laws. The Ag. President replied that while he was fed up with this question of maneuvres he appreciated the difficulties of the Vice-President. In the circumstances he agreed that it would not be good politics to take a decision at the Council of Ministers that all vacant posts would be frozen and announce such a decision. He explained, however, that the finances of Government were such that it would be most unwise to proceed with the filling of all vacant posts. After some further discussion it was agreed that only most essential posts should be filled and the others should temporarily be left vacant, The filling of these vacant posts would, however, be proceeded with within a few months' time when it was hoped that the revenue position of Government would improve as a result of the enactment of the Taxation Laws. In conclusion the following points were agreed upon:

(a) All Ministries and independent Departments of the Republic will bring about a minimum 7% out of all expenditure other than salaries and personal emoluments.

(b) An amount of £4 m. be transferred from the Consolidated Reserved Fund to the Development Budget.

(c) As a result of the above transfer there will be only a consolidated reserve fund of about £500,000. Since it will be unsafe to leave the Republic with such limited reserve, it was agreed that confidential and private instructions be given to the Chairman of the Public Service Commission not to proceed with the filling of any vacant posts, with the exception of such cases that the Council of Ministers would consider absolutely necessary, and thus create a reserve of about £350,000 from savings from the non-filling of such posts.

413

(d) All measures be taken for the taxation legislation of the Government to be enacted by the House and that as soon as the taxation legislation of the Government is enacted be the House and the revenue position improves, the filling of the vacant posts for which provision exists in the Budget to proceed in accordance with the rate of improvement of the revenue position.

APPENDIX 40

Record of Meeting Held at the Vice-Presidency between Greek and Turkish Cypriots regarding Taxation, 3 October 1962

Present:
Vice-President Dr. F. Kutchuk and his Under-Secretary,
Mr. R.R. Denktash, Chairman of the Executive Committee,
     Turkish Communal Chamber,
Mr. H.A. Riza, Member, House of Representatives.

Mr. G. Clerides, President, House of Representatives,
Mrs. S. Souliotou, Minister of Justice,
Mr. C. Tornaritis, Attorney-General of the Republic.

Mr. Clerides explained the purpose of the meeting and said that they had met in order to exchange views on the question of Taxation Laws with a view to finding a solution to the problem and thus secure for Government a dependable source of revenue. He added that because of the non-enactment of certain Taxation Laws the revenue of Government had dropped to such a level as to endanger the financial position of the Government. He requested Mr. H. A. Riza to explain the Turkish point of view on this matter.

Mr. H. A. Riza stated that the Taxation Laws were the concern not only of the Central Government but also of the two Communal Chambers which were rendering very important services to the peoples of Cyprus. In considering, therefore, the question of taxation the revenue sources of all these three organs of the Republic should be taken into account. He added that a subsidy of two million pounds to the Communal Chambers was not sufficient to meet the requirements of these Chambers and it was, therefore, necessary for these Chambers either to impose taxation on members of their respective communities or to ask for supplementary payments from the Central Government. In other words if the object was to bring about a unification of taxation, a mandatory provision to the effect that a certain proportion of the taxation will be paid over to the Communal Chambers will have to be made. Otherwise the Communal Chambers could not be expected to agree to forego their power of taxation.

Mr. Clerides replied by saying that though in principle he agreed with Mr. H. A. Riza, the fact that the Central Government had no financial control over Communal Chambers would make it impossible for the Central Government to agree to foot the Bill of the Communal Chambers, which were expanding at a rate which was out of proportion to the increase in taxation.

Mr. R. R. Denktash said that it was possible for Central Government to take for instance the expenditure on education during the British Regime as a basis and stipulate that additional increase would be at a fixed rate irrespective of the expansion or needs of the Communal Chambers.

Mr. Clerides stated that
(a) in his view the correct solution of the problem would be to find a for-
     mula whereby the financial expenditure of the Communal Chambers
     would be agreed upon by the Government;
(b) the Communal Chambers would cease to impose taxes; and
(c) the Government after agreeing on the ratio of the subsidy to the Greek
     and the Turkish Communal Chambers would undertake the financial
     expenditure of the services run by the Communal Chambers.

Finally Mr. Clerides explained that in his view the above could be
achieved by reaching an agreement and without any legislative act and that by
such agreement a convention could be created and thus put the matter on what
he believed to be the right basis.

Mr. Clerides and Mr. Tornarities stated that as men of reason and
having the interest of the country at heart, it was possible to come to a gentleman's agreement both with regard to imposition of taxes and to distribution of
revenue derived from such taxes. Both pointed out, however, that certain provisions of the Constitution prevented the enactment of Laws which would be
contrary to those provisions.

Mr. Clerides said that the Estate Duty Law was on the Agenda of the
House of Representatives and asked for the Turkish side to explain their difficulties.

Mr. H. A. Riza said that the question whether Vakf property was liable
to estate duty was very old matter. During his service in the Evkaf Office he
had raised the matter with the then Government and had advised the people
concerned not to pay estate duty on Vakf property. He was of the opinion that
no estate duty could be imposed on Vakf property and the proposed estate
duty should, therefore, exempt such property.

Mrs. S. Souliotou explained that the original Estate Duty Law made no
concession with regard to Vakf property, but in the year 1948 the Law was
amended and certain concessions were made to such property. Under the
amended Law while the corpus of Vakf and any revenue dedicated for religious
and charitable purposes were exempt from estate duty, the income of beneficiaries was liable to estate duty.

Mr. Clerides explained that to exempt the income of beneficiaries from
estate duty would give to them a discriminatory treatment and would open the
door to evasion of taxation.

Mr. H. A. Riza said that without an expert advice as to whether Vakf
property was liable to estate duty, his conscience would not allow him to vote
for such a Law. Mr. R. R. Denktash suggested that a provision should be made
in the proposed Law to the effect that the sections relating to Vakf properties
should remain inoperative until such time as the House of Representatives re-
considers the question after obtaining expert legal advice.

Mr. Clerides and Mrs. S. Souliotou stated that as far as they were
aware even in Turkey it was no longer possible to make deeds of dedication
and thus evade taxation.

After further discussion Mr. Clerides proposed that he would agree to
a provision being made in the proposed Law to the effect that all existing Vakf

properties would be exempt from Estate Duty Law, but such exemption would not cover property under any new deed of dedication. Mr. Tornaritis pointed out that the effect of such exemption would be in perpetuity as descendants of the beneficiaries of the existing Vakf would be exempted from estate duty for ages to come. Mr. Clerides explained that he would agree to this in view of his desire to prevent any evasion of tax in future.

Mr. Denktash said that the matter would be considered at a meeting to be held on the 4th October, and the decision to be taken at that meeting would be communicated to Mr. Clerides before the meeting of the House of Representatives on the 5th of October.

With regard to the question of Customs Tariff Law, Mr. Clerides undertook to have Mr. H. A. Riza's proposals to be reconsidered by the Special Committee of the House before the Bill is introduced to the House for voting.

On the general question of taxation it was agreed that a Committee, composed of Mr. Clerides, Mr. Tornaritis, Mrs. Souliotou and Mr. Solomides on the Greek side and of such persons from the Turkish side as Dr. Kutchuk, Messrs. Denktash and H. A. Riza would nominate, should meet and discuss the matter exhaustively in an attempt to find a satisfactory solution to the problem.

APPENDIX 41

Record of Meeting of Greek Cypriots regarding Taxation, 2 November 1962

SECRET

Points raised at the meeting at the Presidential Palace on the 2nd November, 1962, attended by the Acting President of the Republic, the Minister of Finance, the Minister of Justice and the Attorney-General of the Republic.

1. Both Chambers by a communal Law to provide, if they have not done so already, that no increase in any budgetary expenditure shall be proposed by any member thereof. Any such proposal shall emanate from their respective Executive Committee or Council.
2. Their respective Budget shall be subject to the control of the central government. For this purpose the Budget shall be submitted to the Minister of Finance. If the submissions of the Minister are not accepted by the respective Communal Chamber then the matter shall be referred to the Council of Ministers for decision.
3. The subvention to each Communal Chamber shall be increased. Each year the amount to be disposed for education purposes shall be fixed taking into consideration the respective needs of the Chambers as checked by central government, the financial position viewing the assets and liabilities in respect of that financial year and generally the surrounding circumstances. After determination of the total amount thus to be disposed of 82% thereof shall be made available for the Greek Communal Chamber and 18% thereof for the Turkish Communal Chamber.
4. The payment of the amount provided in paragraph 3 above shall be made on condition that the Communal Chambers shall abstain from the imposition of any personal tax on members of their respective Community provided that fees for services rendered (such as school fees and the like) they will be at liberty to impose and collect.

APPENDIX 42

Record of Meeting of Greek Cypriots regarding Taxation, 6 November 1962

SECRET

Points raised at the Meeting at the Presidential Palace on the 6.11.62
(Mr. Gl. Clerides, Ag. President of the Republic, Minister of Finance,
Minister of Justice, Attorney-General)

1. A sum not exceeding a percentage of X% of our ordinary revenue to go to the Communal Chambers.

2. The actual sum will be arrived at on the basis of their revenue, their fixed expenses plus a reasonable rate of development.

3. The X% to be earmarked for the Communal Chambers will be divided between the Communal Chambers in such ratio as may be decided.

4. The Communal Chambers will undertake not to drop their revenue from fees, etc.

5. The Minister of Finance will work out figures so that the matter may be further discussed on the basis of actuality.

APPENDIX 43

Record of Meeting between Greek and Turkish Cypriots regarding Taxation, 13 November 1962

CONFIDENTIAL

Brief minutes of the meeting held on the 13th November, 1962, at 5.30 p.m. at the Vice-Presidency.

Present:
> Dr. Kutchuk, Mr. Clerides, Mr. Denktash,
> Dr. Mudderisoglou, Mrs. Souliotou, Mr. Orek,
> Mr. Solomides, Mr. Tornaritis, Mr. Umit Suleyman,
> Mr. Muftizade.

At the request of Dr. Kutchuk, Mr. Clerides explained that they had met in order to find a way to increase the amount of Government subsidy to the two Communal Chambers so that they (the Chambers) may not have to impose taxation. The problem was, if Government were to take on the responsibility of financing Communal Chambers, how could it control their expenditure and their rate of expansion without in any way interfering with the type of education they provide and with other matters within their sphere of authority. He enquired if anyone had any suggestions to make.

Mr. Denktash asked what the Communal Chambers could expect from Government assuming the difficulties over taxation laws were settled and agreement was reached to enact these laws by the House of Representatives. He also asked what was the present position with regard to these laws.

Mr. Clerides explained that since the last meeting the Estate Duty Law had been enacted and an Immovable Property Tax Law was introduced to the House. But the Customs Tariff Bill was still pending before the House although a Committee meeting was fixed for hearing the views of Mr. Halit for the amendment of the schedule of the Law to include certain items which Mr. Halit on behalf of the Turkish Members wanted to be included. In fact Mr. Halit requested an adjournment of the Committee meeting stating that he was not yet ready to submit his proposals. Mr. Clerides requested him to inform him when he would be ready, but he stated that he would be leaving for England on business and requested that the matter be left until his return.

Mr. Orek said that the Customs Tariff Law did not present any difficulty. The revised rates were in force and he did not expect that Government would be led into the position of making refunds. He believed that the Minister of Finance would see his way to include in the Bill, or in the second Bill which was under preparation the items of goods which Turkish Members of the House wished to be included e.g. steel-wool. Discussion ensued and all agreed that the inclusion of the items recommended by the Turkish Members presented no serious difficulty. Hence there was no problem. Mr. Orek and

Mr. Suleiman suggested that the revenue to be derived from the Immovable Property Tax Law should continue to be paid over to the Communal Chambers and the Minister of Finance agreed with this suggestion for the reason that the revenue involved was very small.

As to financing the expenses of the Communal Chambers, Mr. Clerides said that he had in mind a proposal to the following effect:

(a) Both Communal Chambers to submit to the Minister of Finance their present level of expenditure. The Minister of Finance together with the Presidents of the Communal Chambers will then examine and determine the minimum level of expenditure of the respective Communal Chambers.

(b) An amount equal to the minimum level of expenditure determined as above to be made available each year to the Communal Chamber concerned. This amount shall be deemed to be the amount necessary to meet the annual requirements of the respective Communal Chamber and shall not be re-examined every year.

(c) Each year the Government shall make available a further sum of money for the promotion of the activities of the Communal Chambers, to be determined as follows:

(i) A fixed percentage of the Public Revenue appropriated to the Development Budget of the Republic to be agreed upon. For the purpose of calculating the Public Revenue appropriated to the Development Budget of the Republic no money resulting from foreign aid including loans will be taken into consideration.

(ii) The apportionment of this further sum will be made between the two Communal Chambers in a ratio agreed and fixed in advance and shall not vary from year to year.

(d) The Communal Chambers to agree not to exercise their right of imposing any taxation for which they have authority under the Constitution.

(e) The right of separate majorities in voting legislation imposing taxes and duties to be exercised as herein below provided.

Mr. Solomides explained in more detail the above proposal and pointed out that the additional sum would have to be commensurate with the amount of Government's annual revenue. Funds would, however, be made available for education in a way as if education was a Government service. Mr. Clerides explained further that since the provision for education in the Estimates would be voted as a bloc amount—without apportionment between Greek and Turkish Chambers—there was no possibility of making any discrimination. In what proportion would the bloc provision be apportioned between Greek and Turkish Chambers was a matter on which an agreement beforehand would have to be reached. In return all that the Chambers would be required to do would be to give an undertaking not to impose taxation.

Mr. Denktash and Mr. Orek said that the proposals appeared to be good provided agreement on certain objective criteria could be reached and legally sound methods for implementing them could be found. They enquired as to whether the ratio of apportionment would be based on population, on number of pupils or on number of schools. The former also asked whether the two Chambers would be at liberty to continue to accept subsidies from Turkish and Greek Governments for their needs, such as expansion and development expenses which Government subsidy would not cover. Mr. Tornaritis raised the point that besides education the Communal Chambers had other responsibilities. Mr. Orek stated that the subsidies of Turkish and Greek Governments must not in any case be taken into account.

Mr. Clerides replied that apportionment of the minimum subsidy would be based on the amounts of current expenditure of both communities; for the apportionment of the additional sum a certain ratio could be agreed upon by taking into consideration all relevant criteria. Subsidies from Greek and Turkish Governments would be the affair of the respective Chambers and would not in any way affect the amount of Government subsidy. Education included—for the purpose of convenience—all the responsibilities of Communal Chambers. Mr. Solomides agreed that the subsidy of Greek and Turkish Governments should not be taken into account but stated that such subsidy must not be utilised by the Communal Chambers in a way as to increase the Government's minimum contribution.

Mr. Muftizade enquired how it was proposed to give legal effect to the agreements that might be reached as a result of the discussions and make them binding on all concerned. Mr. Orek pointed out that in so far as the Turkish Community was concerned there was the danger of losing in matters of taxation the only safeguard at its disposal by agreeing to pass the Income Tax Law. If after passing that Law, it was found that the arrangements did not work or the agreements as to the amount of annual subsidy and the ratio of apportionment were not or could not be implemented, the Turkish Community would be unable to make use of that safeguard any more. Therefore, in his view, either the schedule of rates of income tax should be subject to annual voting or proposed arrangements should be incorporated in the Income Tax Law. He also pointed out that it would always be open for Greek members of the House of Representatives not to vote for a provision in excess of £2,000,000 for education purposes if they say that the need of the Greek Communal Chamber could be met by a subsidy from elsewhere plus the £1,600,000 provided by the Constitution.

Mr. Clerides stated that the safest way was to amend the Constitution but his understanding was that the Turkish Side was not prepared to consider such a proposition. The other alternative was to pass a law and thereunder make the amount of subsidy to be paid to the Communal Chambers a charge on the Consolidated Fund of the Republic. Mr. Tornaritis agreed that it was possible to do this and cited Article 166 of the Constitution. Mr. Solomides said that there was no end to taxation laws and the separate majority vote would always be there for the Turkish Community to make use of. He, on his turn, wished to be assured that future taxation laws would not be vetoed by Turkish members of the House. Replying to the first point Mr. Orek said that there was a difference between the Income Tax Law and any other taxation law. That difference lay in the fact that the resources of the Communal Chambers were limited almost only to revenue derived from income tax.

Mr. Denktash said that provided the agreements worked the Greek Side could rest assured that the Turkish members would not stand in the way unless it was obvious that a proposed tax was discriminatory against the Turkish Community.

After some further discussion and exchange of views Mr. Clerides suggested, and it was agreed, that the mechanism by which the various proposals (on which there seemed to be an agreement) could be implemented and made workable should, in the first instance, be formulated. It was, therefore, agreed that a Committee composed of Mr. Solomides, Mr. Denktash, Mrs. Souliotou, Mr. Orek and Mr. Tornaritis should draw up this mechanism and circulate to all the other members for study before a next meeting was convened.

APPENDIX 44

Note on Machinery for Implementation of Proposals regarding Taxation, 19 November 1962

SECRET

If, having made a gentleman's agreement and having paid to the Turkish Communal Chamber £ X for a number of years, the Turks then refuse to vote the Taxing Laws, there will continue to be an obligation to pay to the Turkish Communal Chamber a proportionate sum, if anything is paid to the Greek Communal Chamber, for the gentleman's agreement cannot be used against Article 88(2), which provides that any sum over the minimum must be apportioned between the two Chambers. Therefore, the Greek Communal Chamber will also have to suffer as a result of non-payment to the Turkish Communal Chamber.

2. On the basis of the sum paid to the Turkish Communal Chamber under the agreement, the Turkish Communal Chamber will regulate its expenditure accordingly. If the Turks then vote against a certain Taxing Law, and on account of that the subsidy to the Turkish Communal Chamber is cut, the Turks may apply to the Supreme Constitutional Court under Article 138 on the ground that the Budget is discriminatory and it may be no defence that the Greek Communal Chamber did not get any subsidy either. In the Supreme Constitutional Court the agreement cannot be invoked and, if it were, it might make matters worse because it would be argued that the subsidy was cut as a punishment for the Turks exercising a right given to them under the Constitution, allegedly without restrictions. It may also be argued that, once it is admitted that the needs of the Communal Chambers are more than the minimum £2,000,000 provided in the Budget, they cannot be cut down unless it can be proved that their needs have diminished, and not on any other ground.

3. Furthermore, the proviso to Article 88(2) may be interpreted as meaning that an increase in the sum of £2,000,000 amounts to an increase in the minimum, which should then be provided automatically in the Budget.

4. The argument of the Greek side throughout has been that the right of separate majority can only be exercised in cases of discrimination. If the agreement is made, it will mean acceptance of the interpretation of the Turks that the right of separate majority can be exercised for any reason or caprice and irrespective of discrimination, and that to restrict this right of "capricious" exercise is a concession on their part for which they will be rewarded with an increased subsidy.

CONCLUSION: Only by amending the Constitution can the agreement be implemented so as to avoid ambiguity and friction in the future, which may make things worse rather than better.

APPENDIX 45

Record of Meeting between Greek and Turkish Cypriots regarding
Taxation and Other Matters, 23 November 1962

TOP SECRET

Note on meeting on Friday, 23rd November, 1962, at the Presidential Palace
at 5 p.m. between Mr. Gl. Clerides, Ag. President of the Republic, Mr. R.
Denktash, President of the Turkish Communal Chamber, Mr. Osman Orek,
Minister of Defence, Mr. R. Solomides, Minister of Finance, and Mrs. Stella
Soulioti, Minister of Justice.

The Greek side said that careful consideration had been given to the
machinery for the implementation of the suggestions which had been made at
the meeting held on the 13th November, 1962, at the Vice-Presidency and had
arrived at the conclusion that the proper and, indeed, the only way to implement such suggestions was by amending the Constitution. These amendments
would be in three respects:

(a) Amendment of the Article (Article 88) providing for the subsidy to the
Communal Chambers so that it would be an obligation on the Government to make provision in the budget in accordance with the
agreement which would be reached;
(b) Amendment of the Article (Article 87) providing for the imposition of
taxation by the Communal Chambers so as to prevent Communal
Chambers from imposing taxes;
(c) Amendment or supplementing of the provision relating to the exercise
of separate majorities (Article 78) so that such right would be exercised
as follows:
(i) Where a law imposing duties or taxes is alleged, by the members of
the House of Representatives belonging to one Community, to be
discriminatory against that Community, this must be done at the
Standing Committee stage of consideration of the bill. A statement
giving full grounds for such alleged discrimination will then be presented by the members of the House belonging to such Community to the President of the House who will refer it to the Supreme
Constitutional Court for pronouncement as to whether the proposed Law is discriminatory or not.
(ii) If the Supreme Constitutional Count declares that the proposed
Law is discriminatory then the Bill will either be withdrawn or will
be amended so that discrimination may be eliminated. If the Supreme Constitutional Court declares that the law is not discriminatory then it will go forward and will be passed in the same way as
any other law, i.e. by simple majority.

2. Mr. Denktash said that he was under the impression that amendment of the Constitution was not possible, but Mr. Orek immediately said that he did not see why. Mr. Denktash then said that, as this was a new aspect, it would be necessary for them to make soundings as to the possibility of the Turkish side agreeing to it. Certain alternative suggestions, other than amendment of the Constitution, were made by the Turkish side but were found to be legally impossible of implementation. In particular, Mr. Orek suggested that it might be possible to refer a law for an opinion to the Supreme Constitutional Court at the Council of Ministers stage if the President or the Vice-President returned such bill on grounds of discrimination. It was, however, pointed out that this was not possible for two main reasons:

(a) there was no machinery for such reference in the Constitution; and
(b) in the absence of a constitutional provision, there would be no guarantee that the members of the House of Representatives would still not exercise their right of separate majority.

It was also pointed out that it would not be possible to amend the Constitution to ensure the grant of increased subsidies to the Communal Chambers without, at the same time, amending the provision which would give protection against abuse of the exercise of the right of separate majority.

3. Mr. Denktash said that, if it was finally decided to amend the Constitution, speeches in the House by Greek members to the effect that now that amendment of the Constitution had been embarked on, the Constitution would be totally amended, should be prevented. Mr. Clerides pointed out that it was equally necessary for the Turkish members to exercise discretion and not to say anything which would provoke the Greek side into an argument. Mr. Clerides said that if agreement were reached he would undertake to see to it that the proceedings in the House went off smoothly, e.g. one member speaking on either side, the texts having been agreed beforehand. The necessity for avoiding uncontrolled argument in the House in the event of an amendment to the Constitution being agreed was recognized by all.

4. General discussion then took place as to other questions requiring solution and, in particular, the following were mentioned:

(a) *The Municipalities*: The Greek side referred to the proposals that had been made by His Beatitude to Dr. Kutchuk some months ago.
(b) *The Army*: Mr. Orek said that the impression abroad was that the reason for the cessation of recruitment to the Army was the exercise of the Veto by the Vice-President rather than "finance". It was pointed out that the Veto was of course the reason; in addition, the annual expenditure of 1 1/2 million pounds on an Army of 2,000 men did not seem reasonable at a time when the resources of the Island were so limited, when the Island was trying to implement its development programme and when foreign aid was so slow in coming. Mr. Orek said that it might be possible to ask the Greek and Turkish Governments to con-

tribute to the expenditure for the formation of the Army, but this suggestion was considered impossible of realisation. In any case, such foreign aid as might be forthcoming would be much more productive and useful in other fields.

(c) *The 70:30 ratio*: Mr. Clerides said that the implementation of the 70:30 ratio was proceeding smoothly and the present composition of the public service was: Greeks 74.8%, Turks 25.2%.

(d) *The Public Service Commission*: There seemed to be agreement that the Public Service Commission was composed of too great a number of persons and could not work properly. A suggestion was made that the number of members should be reduced to 5 or even three and that it should be composed of persons commanding the highest respect and of the highest integrity and, if possible, possessing some knowledge of the public service.

5. It was agreed that the Turkish side would inform the Greek side when they were ready for further discussion. The Greek side made it clear that they were willing to discuss all problems and find a general solution.

MINISTRY OF JUSTICE, NICOSIA, 24th November, 1962

ADDENDUM 46

Joint Communiqué Issued at the End of the Official Visit of the President of the Republic of Cyprus to Turkey, 26 November 1962

Upon the invitation of His Excellency Cemal Gürsel, President of the Republic of Turkey, His Beatitude Archbishop Makarios, President of the Republic of Cyprus, paid a state visit to Turkey from November 22nd to November 16th, 1962.

His Beatitude Archbishop Makarios was accompanied by His Excellency Spyros Kyprianou, Minister of Foreign Affairs of Cyprus, as well as other Cypriot officials.

In the course of this visit the President of the Republic of Turkey and the President of the Republic of Cyprus had talks with the participation of His Excellency Ismet Inönü, Prime Minister of Turkey, His Excellency Feridun Cemal Erkin, Minister of Foreign Affairs of Turkey, and His Excellency Spyros Kyprianou, Minister of Foreign Affairs of Cyprus. Their Excellencies Ekram Alican, Hasan Dincer, Turhan Feyzioglu, Deputy Prime Ministers, were also present at the talks.

These talks took place in a cordial atmosphere of friendship and understanding and have been characterized by a spirit of sincerity and constructiveness.

The two Presidents and the Statesmen present reviewed questions of mutual interest and have observed that identity of views existed among them on the importance of maintaining close relations and cooperation between their two countries not only in their countries' interest but also as a contribution to international peace and security; and reiterated their resolution to deploy all efforts to have these relations further developed on the basis of equality and mutual respect.

Both parties were pleased to note improvement in the relations between Greeks and Turks in Cyprus since the signing of the existing agreements. They also expressed their sincere desire that this improvement in their relations should continue to develop so that they may live harmoniously together in fruitful cooperation.

APPENDIX 47

Extract from Minutes of Council of Ministers, 29 November 1962

State Visit of His Beatitude, Archbishop Makarios, President of the Republic, to India

1. The President said that his visit to India from the 31st October to the 15th November, 1962, accompanied by the Minister of Foreign Affairs, was a good-will visit and had no specific purpose except the strengthening of the relations between Cyprus and India. During his stay in India, the President had the opportunity of meeting the President and the Prime Minister of India, as well as other important personalities of both the Central Government and the Regional Government, with whom he had talks of a general character on subjects of common interest, such as foreign policy and ways and means of strengthening the trade and cultural relations between Cyprus and India. The President stated that during his meetings in India he had noticed a sincere desire on the part of the Indian leaders to maintain and strengthen the relations and cooperation between the two countries. The President had taken the opportunity to convey to the Indian people the moral support of Cyprus against the Chinese aggression. The President said that he believed that by expressing to the Indian people sympathy in their just cause and their struggle against the aggressor, he was conveying the feelings of the Members of the Council and generally of the people of Cyprus. His Beatitude further believed that the stand taken by Cyprus in this issue had been deeply appreciated by both the Government of India and its people and that it had contributed towards the promotion of friendship between the two peoples.

2. The Minister of Agriculture and Natural Resources enquired whether any statement had been made by the President regarding the non-aligned policy followed by the Republic. The President said that during his discussions with Mr. Nehru the latter had stated that, despite the Chinese aggression, his Government believed that it should continue following a non-aligned policy; this statement had been repeated by the Indian Prime Minister during his public speeches. The President added that the question of a non-aligned policy had, however, been discussed by him at length with the Turkish Government.

State Visit of His Beatitude, Archbishop Makarios, President of the Republic, to Turkey

3. The President stated that, at the invitation of the President of Turkey, he had paid an official visit to Turkey, accompanied by the Minister of Foreign Affairs, from the 22nd to the 26th November, 1962. His talks

with the Turkish Government had been conducted in a very warm and friendly atmosphere, despite the fact that the welcome accorded by some groups had not been very kind. The President said that he had discussed with the Turkish Government certain parts of the Cyprus Constitution which had created difficulties as regards the smooth running of the Government machinery. These concerned the establishment of separate municipalities, the creation of a Cyprus Army of 2,000 men, the separate majority of votes in the House of Representatives and the 70:30 ratio in the Public Service. The President said that he and the Cyprus Minister of Foreign Affairs had two meetings with the President, the Prime Minister and the Foreign Minister of Turkey, as well as with other Turkish officials, during which it was generally acknowledged that substantial progress had been made in connection with the above questions since the signing of the Agreements. The Turkish Government expressed the view that most of the difficulties encountered would be easily overcome with the passage of time and the strengthening of confidence and cooperation between the two communities in Cyprus. The President said that the Turkish Government had realised that the Cyprus Government's sincere intention was to make the two communities live together in friendship, cooperation and mutual respect within the framework of the Agreements to the interest of the people of Cyprus as a whole. The President believed that his State visit to Turkey had proved very beneficial in that it had given him the opportunity to reassure the Turkish Government of the wish for close cooperation, trust and mutual respect between the Greek and the Turkish communities in Cyprus and to dispel any misunderstandings as regards motives or intentions. The President added that the Turkish Government had realised that there were certain difficulties concerning the functioning of the Government machinery, especially if there was no good-will and mutual trust.

4.   The President said that he had explained to the Turkish Government the practical difficulties concerning the question of separate Municipalities, having added that, so long as there was a provision, rightly or wrongly, in the Constitution about this question, he respected it. The President stated that he had also told the Turkish Government that when the Greek and Turkish Governments were discussing the question of separate Municipalities at Zurich, they had, perhaps, in mind that the Greek and Turkish population in the towns lived in separate quarters; they had thus agreed with the establishment of separate Municipalities on account of the Turks' fear that the Turkish quarters in the five main towns might be neglected, if the Municipalities remained mixed in which case the Greeks would have a majority. The President added that he had further explained to the Turkish Government that there appeared to be no practical solution to the problem without affecting the Greeks and their properties. Only in the central Turkish quarters was the population 100% Turkish, but with the extension of the areas the population became mixed; in certain streets the Turks might form 80% or 90% of the population and in

some other cases the population might be 50% Greeks and 50% Turks; this is the practical difficulty for the separation of the Municipalities, which would be faced after the end of December when the Municipal Laws expire. We would then meet a situation in which no Municipal Laws would exist. The Turkish Government expressed the wish that, by that time, a solution might be found. The President said that during the discussion he had explained to the Turkish Government the proposals he had submitted to the Vice-President for the solution of this problem. The Turkish Government made no comments on the proposals but expressed the wish that a solution might be found by the end of December.

5. As regards the establishment of a Cyprus Army, the President said that he had informed the Turkish Government that, personally, he was not in favour of the creation of an Army of 2,000 men, purely for financial reasons. He had added, however, that, so long as there was a provision in the Constitution concerning this matter, he respected it. The President stated that he had explained to the Turkish Government that an army of 2,000 men had not been created because there was disagreement regarding its structure. He had referred to the point of disagreement having explained that the Vice-President had exercised his right of veto.

6. With regard to the question of separate majority in the House, the President said that he had told the Turkish Government that he understood that this provision had been included in the Constitution for the protection of the Turkish community, in case the Greek majority in the House or in the Government followed a discriminatory policy on taxation legislation. The said provision would, however, create many obstacles to the Government and to the progress of the Island if the Turkish members made abuse of this right and did not vote a Bill, not because they had different views on certain points of the Bill, but for their own reasons or when they exercised this right as a means of bargaining for other things which had no connection with the Bill under discussion.

7. Finally, regarding the implementation of the provision in the Constitution concerning the 70:30 ratio in the Public Service, the President said that he had informed the Turkish Government that progress had recently been made and that the Turkish proportion was now 25.2. The provision could not be applied at once, especially because it was for all grades in the Service. On the other hand the Constitution provided that the provision would be applied as far as practically possible. The Turkish Government realised all the difficulties and said that they hoped that mutual confidence and trust would be established and that practical means and ways would be found to overcome the difficulties.

8. The President said that he had also discussed the question of non-aligned policy and that the Turkish Government had informed him that they agreed that Cyprus could follow the policy it wished. They did not want to interfere and had given the President the impression that they approved of this policy because they considered that

it would not be bad for a country like Cyprus, which was rather under the influence of the West, were at the same time a member of the group of non-aligned countries. In other words, the President added, one might say that the Turkish Government had agreed with the non-aligned policy followed by Cyprus.

APPENDIX 48

Note on Conversation of Minister of Justice Stella Soulioti with British High Commissioner Sir Arthur Clark, 7 December 1962, 11.45 a.m.

The British High Commissioner accompanied Mr. Cleary, the new British Deputy High Commissioner, on his first courtesy visit to me. The High Commissioner mentioned His Beatitude's talks in Ankara on His Beatitude's recent visit to Turkey and said that the British Ambassador in Ankara had sent a report which indicated that the talks had been of great benefit, especially in bringing home to the Turkish Government the practical difficulties which are encountered as a result of certain provisions of the Constitution, something of which the Turkish Government had been unaware. So far, the British High Commissioner said, the Turkish Government had only heard one side of the story and had not realised that there were real technical and other difficulties in the working of the Constitution.

The High Commissioner said that, as a result of the talks, the Turkish Government had issued certain instructions to their Ambassador in Cyprus, and he thought that there would be no further abuse of the exercise of the right of separate majority, which would henceforth be exercised for the purpose for which it was meant, namely, to avoid discrimination against a certain community on matters of taxation, and not for any other purpose.

With regard to the Municipalities, the High Commissioner said that the Turkish Government now understood that it was not possible to effect physical geographic separation, but it was unlikely that they would accept anything short of separate municipal councils which would collect rates from their respective communities and would arrange, through the co-ordinating committee, to solve difficulties such as "who would clean the streets", possibly sharing a common service. This was a matter of political expediency for the Turkish side which they would find hard to relinquish.

With regard to the Army, the High Commissioner said that the Turkish Government now appreciated the difficulties of having separate Greek and Turkish Units and realised that the Army should be composed of Cypriot citizens and not of Greeks and Turks. They also appreciated the financial difficulties involved in setting up an Army of 2,000 men.

Generally, about the Ankara talks, the High Commissioner said that the Turkish Government appreciated His Beatitude's frank exposition of the problems created by certain constitutional provisions.

Stella Soulioti
Minister of Justice

APPENDIX 49

Letter from Glafkos Clerides to Rauf Denktash, 11 December 1962

CONFIDENTIAL

Dear Rauf,

I thought I would take the opportunity to write to you and explain certain ideas which occurred to me in connection with the subject of the unification of taxation on which we had a number of meetings.

You will recall that at our last meeting as a Sub-committee we had the task of finding means by which to make legally binding the matters which we had previously discussed. Certain views were expressed by myself regarding the best possible way to make legally binding any agreement we may reach on the subject of the increase subsidy to the Communal Chambers.

The main object of increasing the subsidies to the Communal Chambers is that the Communal Chambers will no longer have to fend for themselves in order to find sufficient funds to pay for the expenses of education and other matters falling within the jurisdiction of the Communal Chambers, but that Government would undertake the financial responsibility of the Communal Chambers. Government is considering to undertake the financial expenditure for the Communal Chambers because it realises that it is difficult for the Communal Chambers to cover the expenses of education if they were to rely only on the subsidy provided under Article 88(2) of the Constitution and thereafter to have to close the gap between the amount of money received by way of subsidy under the said Article and the amount of money which each Communal Chamber actually requires. Moreover unless Government undertook the financial expenditure of the Communal Chambers it would mean that each Communal Chamber acting under Article 86(f) and 88(1) would have to impose personal taxes and fees on members of their respective community to cover the difference between the amount of money given by the Government by way of subsidy and the actual requirements of such Communal Chamber. This would mean that there would be taxation both by Government and by the Communal Chambers with the result that the citizens of the Republic would be taxed twice.

It is further obvious that it would be an undue burden on both communities, if each one separately had to cover by taxation the gap which results from the subsidy provided by the Constitution and the actual requirements of the Chambers.

From what I have said above it is clear that we are interested in three things:

(a) Adequate subsidy provision to cover the agreed expenses of the Communal Chambers.

(b) Legal safeguard to the effect that if Government were to provide adequate subsidy, the Communal Chambers would not either for the purposes of future development or for any other purpose, exercise their right to impose taxation and thus the citizen be taxed twice again. It is obvious, of course, that if Government undertakes the entire financial burden of the Communal Chambers, it may have to increase Government taxation and under the circumstances Government would not like to see communal taxation imposed on people who are already heavily taxed by the Government.

(c) The third point which Government requires legally binding safeguards is that the right of separate majority in connection with taxation legislation would not be improperly exercised and thus leave the Government unable to fulfil its obligation.

I have looked carefully into the Constitution and as a lawyer I would like to put certain propositions to you for your consideration:

(a) Article 88(2) of the Constitution provides that the Government in respect of each financial year will make available £2 m. to be allocated to the Greek and Turkish Communal Chamber in the manner provided by the Constitution. The proviso to that Article gives to the House of Representatives the power of increasing the minimum of £2 m. and authorizes the House of Representatives to make the allocation of such increase of the minimum to the respective Communal Chambers in such a manner as the House of Representatives may decide.

You know that in the past an attempt was made to increase the minimum subsidy provided by the Constitution, but as no agreement between the Greek and the Turkish Members as to the ratio of the allocation between the respective Communal Chamber could be arrived at, the matter went before the Constitutional Court.

My belief is that we would be justified to amend the proviso to Article 88(2), once we reach an agreement on the amount and manner any additional subsidy is to be given to the Communal Chambers, and thus make sure that in future no arguments arise as to how any additional subsidy is to be given to the Communal Chambers.

The Constitution itself provides that certain articles which are not basic can be amended by separate Greek and Turkish majority and I see no reason why the Greeks and the Turks should not exercise a right given to them by the Constitution to amend certain non-basic articles for the purpose of regulating the manner in which Government will come to the financial assistance of the Communal Chambers. I may tell you that from the Greek point of view the proviso to article 88(2) as it stands now leaves greater freedom of movement to the community which has the majority in the House. My personal view, however, is that this is not a matter which ought to be considered either from a Greek or a Turkish point of view, since what we are interested is to find a way to take from the Communal Chambers the extreme financial burden under which they are labouring at present.

The advantages for Government of having the proviso amended can be summed up as follows:

(i) Government will know what provision it has to make for each year for the Communal Chambers and thus will be able to plan expenditure and development having regard to all commitments including the commitment to the Communal Chambers. If it is left for each year for the House of Representatives to decide what increase would be given by way of subsidy to the Communal Chambers, then Government will be unable to plan owing to the fact that it will not know how much the House would vote by way of increase.

(ii) Government will know the annual commitment to the Communal Chambers, which may amount to three or four million pounds, and thus be able to plan its taxation policy for the purpose of raising the necessary funds to cover the expenditure.

(iii) There will be no conflict between Government and Communal Chambers on the subject of increase of taxation since from the increase of any taxation both Communal Chambers will benefit having regard to the fact that the one part of the proposal made is based on the principle that the Government will divert for development purposes of the Communal Chambers a certain percentage to be agreed of the Development Budget.

(b) I have already expressed my view how the matter of the subsidies can be regulated in the Constitution by amending the proviso to Article 88(2). The question of restraining the Communal Chambers from exercising their right to impose personal taxes and fees under Article 87(f) and 88(1) can in my opinion be dealt in the following manner.

(i) If one examines the Constitution one would find that Article 87(f) gives authority to the Communal Chambers to impose personal taxes and fees on members of their respective communities to cover the needs of the bodies and institutions under the control of the Communal Chambers as provided in Article 88. This Article was a basic Article of the Zurich Agreement and it gave an unrestricted right to the Communal Chambers to impose personal taxes and fees on Members of their community. Although there was no restriction in the Zurich Agreement of that right, it was agreed at the time of the drafting of the Constitution that the right of the Communal Chambers to impose personal taxes and fees would be restricted and would only be exercised for the purpose of collecting sufficient money to cover the gap between the amount of £2 m. given by way of subsidy and the actual requirements of the respective Communal Chambers.

(ii) In my view there is no reason at all why we should touch or amend this Article at all. What need be done is that in amending the proviso to Article 88(2) to state that by the increased subsidy, the financial requirements of the Communal Chambers are deemed to have been met and, therefore, the Communal Chambers will abstain from exercising their right of imposing personal taxes and fees under 88(1). This would only be natural and it would be acting under the Constitution, since the Constitution in effect provides that any increase of the subsidy to the Communal Chambers results in a decrease in the amount of taxation which they are entitled to impose for the purpose of meeting their requirements. It follows, therefore, that if we agree that the full requirements of the Communal Chambers are met, then there will be no gap to be covered by the Communal Chambers by exercising their right to impose personal taxes and fees.

(c) The last point on which I would like to elaborate is the question of the right of separate majorities.

It is true that the right of separate majorities is one of the basic Articles of the Constitution. There is nothing, however, which could prevent us, if we agree, to regulate the manner in which that right is to be exercised. My suggestion is that we could devise a procedure whereby when a taxation Bill is at the Committee stage of the House, if either the Greek Members or the Turkish Members believe that there is discrimination then they could state so giving the reasons for their belief. The matter would then be referred to the Constitutional Court for its opinion and if the Constitutional Court gives a written opinion that the Bill contains discriminatory provisions or has a discriminatory effect on one of the two communities, then the Executive to be requested to withdraw the Bill or amend it and if the Executive refuses, the Members will use their right of separate majority to defeat the Bill. If, however, the Constitutional Court does not find that there is any discrimination, then neither community would use their right of separate majority to defeat the Bill.

I fully appreciate that whatever agreement we reach we have to take the necessary steps on both sides not to make a political issue of the question of any amendment and I am ready to tell you in advance that I am prepared to take full responsibility and give full guarantees that no Greek Member in the House whether he be of the Patriotic Front, Independent or of the A.K.E.L. will make any statement which will be beyond the scope of the matters we may agree upon.

I have written to you this confidential letter for no other purpose than to give you in a concise form a true picture of what is in my mind and I would like the opportunity for further discussion with you by personal contact for the purpose of hearing any difficulties, doubts etc. which you may have and may wish me to clarify.

Yours Sincerely,
(Signed) Gl. Clerides
President of the House of Representatives

Comparative Statement

Expenditure on Greek Education
Revised Estimate, 1962

(A) Administration
    (i) Personal Emoluments   £22,500
    (ii) Cost-of-living allowance   6,225
    (iii) Other Charges   140,044   £168,769

(B) Elementary Education
    (i) Personal Emoluments i.e.   1,038,500
    salaries, bonuses and allowances
    (ii) Cost-of-living allowance   275,874
    (iii) Other Charges   384,800   £1,699,174

(C) Secondary Education
    (i) Personal Emoluments i.e.   772,782
    salaries, bonuses and allowances
    (ii) Cost-of-living allowance   213,481
    (iii) Other Charges   148,680   £1,134,943
                                        Grand total   £3,102,886

Expenditure on Turkish Education
Estimate, 1962

(A) Administration   £22,179
(B) Elementary Education – salaries   217,479
(C) Secondary Education – salaries   226,583
(D) Cost-of-living allowance   113,063
(E) Other allowances   23,126
(F) Other Charges   90,624
                                                             £693,054

Total expenditure on Education
Greek   £3,102,886
Turkish   693,054
Grand total   £3,795,940

           Greek Education   0.817 of the total
           Turkish Education 0.183 of the total
                             1.000

APPENDIX 50

Letter from Rauf Denktash to Glafkos Clerides, 21 December 1962

CONFIDENTIAL

Dear Glafcos,

Thank you for your letter of 11th December, 1962, the contents of which I have carefully considered. I feel that at this early stage of our Republic your proposals are a little too revolutionary involving as they do changes in the Constitution. I sincerely believe that all of the objectives aimed at in your letter can be easily achieved without necessitating any drastic measures such as amending the Constitution or enacting ad hoc legislation, albeit of a procedural character.

The increase of subsidies to the Communal Chambers is the main problem and the intention to meet the deficiencies of the budgets of the two Chambers is most welcome. This can easily be done under the Constitution by the House voting for an increase. I was glad to read in your letter that you are in a position (and indeed I have always believed that you and the President were in the position) to control the situation in the House, and I have no doubt that a full and sincere explanation to the Members by you explaining the reasons and necessity for an increase will be well received by them all. This main hurdle can, therefore, be overcome by a mutual effort in the House. Indeed when we first met no change of the Constitution was contemplated by either side and it may be convenient to quote here the following passages from the minutes of our meeting on the 13th November, 1962:

(a) Both Communal Chambers to submit to the Minister of Finance their present level of expenditure. The Minister of Finance together with the Presidents of the Communal Chambers will then examine and determine the minimum level of expenditure of the respective Communal Chambers.

(b) An amount equal to the minimum level of expenditure determined as above to be made available each year to the Communal Chamber concerned. This amount shall be deemed to be the amount necessary to meet the annual requirement of the respective Communal Chamber and shall not be re-examined every year.

(c) Each year the Government shall make available a further sum of money for the promotion of the activities of the Communal Chambers, to be determined as follows:

(i) A fixed percentage of the Public Revenue appropriated to the Development Budget of the Republic to be agreed upon. For the purpose of calculating the Public Revenue appropriated to the Development Budget of the Republic no money resulting from foreign aid including loans will be taken into consideration.

(ii) The apportionment of this further sum will be made between the two Communal Chambers in a ratio agreed and fixed in advance and shall not vary from year to year.

(d) The Communal Chambers to agree not to exercise their right of imposing any taxation for which they have authority under the Constitution.

(e) The right of separate majorities in voting legislation imposing taxes and duties to be exercised as herein below provided.

It is my belief that by signing a mutual agreed protocol between the leaders of the two Communities on the one hand and Presidents of the Communal Chambers and the President and Vice-President of the House of Representatives on the other hand, we can ensure implementation of your original proposals. In this way we shall be able to provide specifically in the protocol what will be the proportion of yearly increase and at what proportion this increase will be apportioned between the two Communities.

The next problem is to prevent the Communal Chambers from imposing taxation on their own once the Government undertakes the entire financial burden of the Communal Chambers. This can be achieved (a) by a declaration of policy (the wording of which can be agreed upon between ourselves) in the two Chambers to the effect that the Communal Chambers will abstain from imposing *any* taxation as long as the Government fulfils its above-referred undertaking; or (b) by legislation to be passed by the two Chambers to this effect. The fear that the Chambers may, despite of such undertaking, by legislation proceed to impose additional taxation cannot be real as no individual (Greek or Turk) can be imagined to bow to such an action and concede to be taxed twice once the Central Government has agreed to meet all expenses. Politically it will be impossible for the Chambers to proceed to taxation under these circumstances and from a legal point of view any taxation law so passed by the Chambers may well be declared to be null and void in view of the fact that there is no deficiency for the meeting of which such taxation would be called for. Further, if any of the Communal Chambers, went back on its aforesaid declared policy or legislation by being completely blind to the realities of shortage of hard cash, Government could stop the increased subsidy either immediately (if the increase is made subject to the undertakings) or at the next budgetary year.

The third point on which Government requires legally binding safeguards is the question of separate majority vote in connection with taxation legislation. Government wants, quite rightly, to be assured that this power will not be improperly used. Your suggestions as to how we should go about it, are premature and in my view not necessary. I have no doubt in my mind that the executive authority, both on the Greek and Turkish side, by using its influence and good will on the members of the House by keeping them fully informed of what is going on and why certain taxation legislation is necessary and by letting the Turkish side know the reasons necessitating such legislation, is in a position to see that this power of the House is not used in the negative. The public opinion here as well as in Greece and Turkey is also a strong factor which will keep this power in good harness. I think that the past can give all of us a good lesson on this point and I sincerely believe that once we start running the Government machine on the basis of mutual trust and understanding (and the few meetings we have had have given all of us very high hopes that this can be easily achieved) this power will never be used in the negative. In fact my opinion is that all these powers were given in order that parties may invite each other to a round table conference and discuss the problem anew, and not for any side to consider the matter closed and leave the other side to use its power under the Constitution for reasons best known to itself at that initial stage. If such problems are discussed at the highest level they can certainly be solved provided there is mutual goodwill. This is the crux of the whole matter. It may be argued that individual members may wish to resort to this power every now and then, but I can assure you that unless a matter of high policy is involved affecting the very existence of the Turkish Community Turkish Members of the House will not use their power of separate majority in the negative.

Let us, therefore, avoid touching the Constitution in any manner whatsoever. Let us see whether by a courageous gesture of goodwill on all sides we cannot be the man of our words and thus solve these immediate matters in the way enumerated above. I believe that we can achieve the objectives aimed at without making any changes in our Constitution and the fact that we shall be able to solve our problems within the present frame of our Constitution will give all of us and the people as a whole real good hope for the future. This will be a test of sincerity and goodwill, of our intention to co-operate as good citizens of this young Republic and of our ability to keep our words as men of honour both on the Government side as well as on the Communal Chamber side. Let us try this (which does not necessitate any changes in the Constitution) and see how it will work; if it does not we can look where it has failed and then remedy the fault. I am afraid that if we start with changes *now* and even then we come to a standstill then we will have nowhere else to go. Let us keep any drastic solution to the very last, until goodwill, sincerity and mutual trust is fully established—and it can be established, as I said above, by giving ourselves the chance to prove our words by deeds.

Hoping to hear from you and looking forward to meeting you again,

Yours sincerely,
(R. R. Denktash)

APPENDIX 51

Glafkos Clerides, "Outline of Negotiations Relating to the Subject of the Unification of Taxation," December 1962

Under the provisions of the Constitution taxation Legislation is enacted by the House of Representatives. It, requires, however, separate majority of the Greek and Turkish Members of the House. This provision has given in the past considerable difficulty and has caused substantial loss of revenue to the Government. There are two main reasons which make this provision unworkable.

The first reason is that the Turkish Members of the House made use of it, not in the manner it was intended i.e. for the purpose of defeating any legislation on taxation which would be discriminatory to their community, but for the purpose of using it as a weapon to force the Government to agree to demands made by them. The anomaly of the situation which arose over the income tax legislation can be shortly described as follows:

The Council of Ministers unanimously approved the Bill which was submitted to the House imposing income tax upon the citizens of the Republic. In other words the three Turkish Ministers and the Vice-President agreed with the Bill. As a result the Vice-President did not exercise his right of returning the Bill to the Council of Ministers for reconsideration, nor did he apply to the Constitutional Court to challenge the Bill as being in any way discriminatory. The bill, therefore, was submitted to the House of Representatives in the normal way. Out of the 15 Turkish Members of the House of Representatives 12 formed a group called the Independent Group, which by its name and its action showed that it did not follow the policy of the Vice-President or the Turkish Ministers. When the Bill was debated at the House the Independent Turkish Group took the view that the Bill ought not to be enacted because, as they alleged, the Government did not proceed with sufficient speed to implement the provisions of the Constitution regarding the proportion of Greeks and Turks to be employed in the Civil Service of the Republic and because the Government did not proceed with the full recruitment of the Army of 2,000 men provided by the Constitution nor did the Government bring about the geographical partition of the Municipalities into Greek and Turkish municipal areas.

For the above reasons, publicly stated in the House, the Turkish Members of the Group voted against the Bill and, therefore, it failed to get the separate Turkish majority. As a result the country remained without income tax. It will be observed that there was no difference of opinion between the Greek and the Turkish Members on the substance of the Bill nor was it alleged that the Bill in itself discriminated against the Turkish community. In other words, in the view of the Turkish Members, the Constitution gave a right to the minority Group in the House to defeat a taxation Bill because the majority of the minority group were not satisfied with the policy of the Vice-President or the Turkish Ministers or of the entire Government. If this interpretation is true then it is obvious that this provision of the Constitution is unworkable. In effect it provides that if the 35 Greek Members plus seven Turkish Members vote in favour of a Taxation Bill, eight Turkish Members may defeat it because they have the majority of the minority group.

In addition, however, to the difficulty which arises with the question of separate majorities on taxation Bills and the improper use made of that right by the majority of the Turkish minority group in the House, there are other instances where Taxation Bills pending before the House could not be enacted and remained pending for a considerable time resulting to a substantial loss of revenue to the Government, because there were conflicting interests between the Greek and Turkish Members of the House who have to consider what sources of taxation will have to be left open for their respective Communal Chambers, which under the Constitution, have the right to impose personal taxes and fees to cover their respective needs of Education. The Greek side had realized for some time that the second difficulty was one that could have been remedied provided agreement was reached between the two communities regarding the matter of financing the Communal Chambers.

Under the Constitution the Government is obliged to give a subsidy to the two Communal Chambers of £2 m. out of which an amount of not less than £1.600.000 is given to the Greek Communal Chamber and an amount of not less than £400.000 is given to the Turkish Communal Chamber. The House of Representatives has the right to increase the minimum total amount payable to both Communal Chambers and decide the allocation to the respective Communal Chambers of the increased amount. An attempt was made in the past for an increased subsidy to be given to the Communal Chambers, but as no agreement could be arrived at as to how the increased amount would be given to the respective Communal Chambers, the attempt failed.

The fact that a real difficulty exists in enacting taxation legislation is accepted by the Turkish community as it will be seen from the second paragraph of page 1 of Appendix A. Mr. Riza who was present at the meeting held at the Vice-Presidency on the third October, 1962, the object of which was to find the causes which created difficulties in enacting taxation legislation puts the matter as follows:

"Mr. H. A. Riza stated that the taxation Laws were the concern not only of the central Government, but also of the two Communal Chambers which were rendering very important services to the people of Cyprus. In considering, therefore, the question of taxation the revenue sources of all these three organs of the Republic should be taken into account. He added that a subsidy of £2 m. to the Communal Chambers was not sufficient to meet the requirements of these Chambers and it was therefore, necessary for these Chambers either to impose taxation on members of their respective communities or to ask for supplementary payments from the central Government. *In other words if the object was to bring about a unification of taxation, a mandatory provision to the effect that a certain proportion of the taxation will be paid over to the Communal Chambers will have to be made.* Otherwise the Communal Chambers could not be expected to agree to forego their powers of taxation."

Mr. Clerides replied to the above statement of Mr. Riza by saying that although in principle he agreed with what Mr. Riza stated he had to observe that the Government had no financial control over the two Communal Chambers and thus it would make it impossible for the Government to agree to foot the Bill of the Communal Chambers, which were expanding at a rate which was out of proportion to the increase in taxation.

At a subsequent meeting held on the 13th November, 1962, at which meeting the Vice-President, Dr. Kutchuk, the President of the House of Representatives, Mr. Clerides, the President of the Turkish Communal Chamber, Mr. Denktash, the Vice-President of the House of Representatives, Dr. Muterisoglou, the Minister of Finance, Mr. Solomides, the Minister of Justice, Mrs. Soulioti, the Minister of Defence, Mr. Orek, Mr. Umit Souleiman, a Turkish Member of the House, Mr. Tornaritis, the Attorney-General, and Mr. Muftizade, Under-Secretary to the Vice-President, were present, Mr. Clerides made the following proposal regarding the manner of financing the Communal Chambers by the Government.

As to financing the expenses of the Communal Chambers, Mr. Clerides said that he had in mind a proposal to the following effect:

(a) Both Communal Chambers to submit to the Minister of Finance their present level of expenditure. The Minister of Finance together with the Presidents of the Communal Chambers will then examine and determine the minimum level of expenditure of the respective Communal Chambers.

(b) An amount equal to the minimum level of expenditure determined as above to be made available each year to the Communal Chamber concerned. This amount shall be deemed to be the amount necessary to meet the annual requirements of the respective Communal Chamber and shall not be re-examined every year.

(c) Each year the Government shall make available a further sum of money for the promotion of the activities of the Communal Chambers, to be determined as follows:

(i) A fixed percentage of the Public Revenue appropriated to the Development Budget of the Republic to be agreed upon. For the purpose of calculating the Public Revenue appropriated to the Development Budget of the Republic no money resulting from foreign aid including loans will be taken into consideration.

(ii) The apportionment of this further sum will be made between the two Communal Chambers in a ratio agreed and fixed in advance and shall not vary from year to year.

(d) The Communal Chambers to agree not to exercise their right of imposing any taxation for which they have authority under the Constitution.

(e) The right of separate majorities in voting legislation imposing taxes and duties to be exercised as herein below provided.

(i) Where a law imposing duties or taxes is alleged, by the Members of the House of Representatives belonging to one community, to be discriminatory against that community, such allegation must be made at the stage where the Bill is before the Finance Committee of the House. It must be accompanied by a statement giving full grounds for the alleged discrimination. The President of the House shall refer to the Supreme Constitutional Court the statement containing the allegations that the Bill is discriminatory or that any part thereof is discriminatory together with any statement made to the contrary and shall require the Constitutional Court to give an opinion as to whether the proposed Bill is discriminatory or not.

(ii) If the Supreme Constitutional Court is of opinion that the proposed Bill or any part thereof is discriminatory then the President of the House will inform the Executive, which may either withdraw the Bill or amend it so that any discrimination may be eliminated.

(iii) If the Constitutional Court is of opinion that the Bill or any part thereof does not discriminate against either community, then the right of separate majority will not be exercised by members of either community in such a way as to defeat the Bill.

(iv) If after the Constitutional Court pronounces that the Bill or any part thereof are discriminatory and either the Executive or the majority of the Members of the House persist with the enactment of the Bill into law, then the members of either community to be at liberty to use their right of separate majority to defeat the Bill.

At the same meeting of the 13th November both the Under-Secretary to the Vice-President Mr. Muftizade and the Minister of Defence, Mr. Orek, raised the question of how it was proposed to give to the above points legal effect and make them binding on all concerned. Mr. Orek, (see Annex "B", page 3, 4th paragraph) pointed out that insofar as the Turkish community was concerned there was a danger of losing in matters of taxation, the only safeguard at its disposal by agreeing to pass the Income Tax Law. If after passing that Law, it was found that the arrangements did not work or the agreements as to the amount of annual subsidy and the ratio of apportionment were not or could not be implemented, the Turkish community would be unable to make use of that safeguard any more i.e. to re-enact an Income Tax Law on the members of the Turkish community.

Mr. Clerides replied to Mr. Orek that the safest way was to amend the Constitution, but his understanding was that the Turkish side was not prepared to consider such a proposition. He, therefore, proposed and it was agreed that the mechanism by which the various proposals (on which there seemed to be an agreement) could be implemented and made workable should, in the first instance, be formulated. As a result it was agreed that a Committee composed of the Minister of Finance Mr. Solomides, of Mr. Denktash President of the Turkish Communal Chamber, of the Minister of Justice, Mrs. Soulioti, of the Minister of Defence, Mr. Orek and the Attorney-General, Mr. Tornaritis, should draw up proposals and circulate them to all the other members for study before a next meeting was convened (see Annex "B", page 4, last paragraph).

On the 23rd November, 1962, a meeting of the Committee set up to consider ways of making the proposals legally binding was held under the chairmanship of Mr. Clerides who, in view of the absence of His Beatitude Archbishop Makarios on an official visit to Turkey, presided over the meeting. The meeting was attended by Mr. Rauf Denktash, President of the Turkish Communal Chamber, Mr. Solomides, Minister of Finance, Mrs. Stella Soulioti, Minister of Justice and Mr. Orek, Minister of Defence. What took place at that meeting can be seen from Appendix "C" and need not be repeated here. The Greek side said that after careful consideration was given to the manner of making legally binding the implementation of the suggestions which had been made at the meeting held on the 13th November, 1962, at the Vice-Presidency reached the conclusion that the proper and, indeed, the only way to make the proposals legally binding on all, was by amending the Constitution.

The short reasons for this view was that any legislation enacted by the House of Representatives first would not be binding on the Communal Chambers and, therefore, there would be no guarantee that the Communal Chambers in return for the increased subsidy would not proceed to impose taxation. Secondly, any legislation enacted by the House of Representatives with regard to increased subsidies could be amended by simple majority and, therefore, would not provide a safeguard for the Turkish community. Thirdly, an amendment of the Constitution would be required in order to give the Supreme Constitutional Court jurisdiction to hear a case stated, i.e. whether a Bill contained discriminatory provisions or not, prior to the enactment of the Bill into Law.

Mr. Denktash stated that he was under the impression that amendment of the Constitution was not possible but Mr. Orek said that he did not see why an amendment could not be made. Mr. Denktash then replied that, as this was a new aspect, it would be necessary for him to make soundings as to the possibility of the Turkish side agreeing. Certain alternative suggestions, other than amendment of the Constitution were made by the Turkish side, but were found to be legally impossible. Mr. Denktash said that, if it was finally decided to amend the Constitution, speeches in the House by the Greek Members to the effect that now that amendment of the Constitution had been embarked on, the Constitution should be totally amended, should be prevented. Mr. Clerides pointed out that it was equally necessary for the Turkish Members to exercise discretion and not to say anything which would provoke the Greek side into an argument. He further stated that if agreement were reached, he would undertake to see to it that the proceedings in the House went off smoothly, e.g. one Member speaking on the subject on either side, the text of such speeches having been agreed beforehand. This necessity of avoiding uncontrolled argument in the House in the event of an amendment of the Constitution was recognized by all present.

In view of the fact that after the meeting of the 23rd November, 1962, Mr. Denktash had not informed Mr. Clerides of the results of the soundings which he undertook to make to discover the views of the Turkish community on the issue of amending the Constitution, Mr. Clerides on the 11th December, 1962, wrote a letter to Mr. Denktash (Appendix "D") in which he explained the whole position and pointed out that the amendments required are not amendments of basic Articles of the Constitution, but of those Articles for which the Constitution provided the mechanism for amendment i.e. that such Articles could be amended by a separate Greek and Turkish majority. He further pointed out that, since it was agreed that the amendments proposed were beneficial to both communities and that they would greatly relieve the financial pressure on the Communal Chambers as well as facilitate the enactment of taxation legislation, full use should be made of the mechanism for amending the Constitution in the manner provided by the Constitution.

On the 21st December, 1962, Mr. Denktash replied to Mr. Clerides (Appendix "E") that in his view the objectives aimed at could be achieved without making any changes in the Constitution by signing a protocol containing the proposals of Mr. Clerides. He proposed that the protocol should be signed by the President and the Vice-President of the Republic, the President and the Vice-President of the House of Representatives and the Presidents of the two Communal Chambers.

It is clear from what has transpired that although the Turkish side were in agreement that the proposals made by Mr. Clerides were acceptable, provided that a legal way of making the proposals binding could be found, when it was discovered that there would be no other legal way of making the proposals legally binding on all concerned, other than by amending the Constitution, they abandoned the position of wanting the proposals to be legally binding and proposed that a protocol should be signed between the leaders of the two communities, which in fact would be of no legal effect.

The stage which has been reached in these negotiations is such that it is difficult to see how the Government could accept the responsibility of financing the two Communal Chambers without having any legal safeguard to the effect that the two Communal Chambers will not, in planning their own programmes of development, create financial obligations which, if the Government is not prepared to accept, the Communal Chambers will proceed to implement by imposing taxation, thus defeating the whole object of the increased subsidies to the Communal Chambers. Further it is obvious that the Government may become unable to fulfil its financial obligations, not only to the Communal Chambers but generally if no legally binding agreement is reached as to the manner the right of separate majorities will be exercised in the future. It seems, therefore, that there is very little room for the negotiations to succeed.

APPENDIX "A": For the text, see appendix 40.

APPENDIX "B": For the text, see appendix 43.

APPENDIX "C": For the text, see appendix 45.

APPENDIX "D": For the text, see appendix 49.

APPENDIX "E": For the text, see appendix 50.

APPENDIX 52

Report of Committee Appointed to Make Recommendations for the Implementation of the 70:30 Ratio in the Civil Service, September 1960

RECOMMENDATIONS FOR THE IMPLEMENTATION OF THE 70:30 RATIO IN THE CIVIL SERVICE

In pursuance of an agreement reached between the President-Elect and the Vice-President-Elect, the Joint Consultative Committee was entrusted with the duty of making recommendations for the implementation of the 70:30 ratio in the Civil Service. The Committee held several meetings and submit the following unanimous recommendations:

POINTS OF PRINCIPLE

2.   The Committee proceeded with their assignment bearing in mind the following points of principle upon which agreement had been reached between the President-Elect and the Vice-President-Elect:

(i)   That the Joint Consultative Committee should meet and prepare a report within 10 days (from 4th July) setting out recommendations for implementation of the 70:30 ratio. If no final report could be produced by that time, the Under-Secretaries to furnish an interim report to the Leaders.

(ii)   That the compromise scheme whereby the Service was divided into six Grades should be used as a basis.

(iii)   That the ratio of 70:30 should be implemented, as far as possible, in all grades.

(iv)   That in applying this ratio there would be no objection to the proportion of 70:30 being observed in the division of the total salaries drawn by the respective members of the two communities, but that preference should be given to the numerical proportion.

(v)   That full implementation of the ratio should take place within 5 months from the date of the establishment of the Cyprus Republic.

(vi)   That care should be taken not to prejudice, as far as possible, the right of promotion of the existing members of the Civil Service.

(vii)   That the Committee might make recommendations, if necessary, for the creation of supernumerary posts in order not to prejudice the right of promotion of officers or in order to enable the implementation of the ratio.

(viii)   That existing vacancies should be utilised for the implementation of the ratio.

(ix)   That the Committee should take into consideration the present
          Schemes of Service and that if divergence therefrom was necessary
          that would only be done with the consent of the Leaders.
(x)   That in case of disagreement the Leaders should be informed.
(xi)   That recommendations as to names should not be made but that
          only posts should be considered.

It was, however, agreed that the Committee could make any other recommendations for the implementation of the ratio outside the above points of
principle, provided that such recommendations were not contrary to those
points.

REMEDIES FOR OFFICERS AFFECTED
THROUGH THE APPLICATION OF THE RATIO

3.   The Committee recommend that any officer who proves to the
satisfaction of the appropriate authority for making promotions and appointments that his prospects of promotion to a "promotion" post or to a "first entry
and promotion" post have been prejudicially affected by the application of the
70:30 ratio should be compensated by:

(a) the creation for him of a supernumerary post; or
(b) by his being allowed, at his own option, to retire prematurely on aboli-
      tion of office terms. The officer should, however, be allowed to com-
      mute up to £350 of his pension or one quarter of it whichever is the
      greater.

The Committee also recommend that this safeguard should be available for a
period of 7 years from the date of Independence, to officers on the permanent
establishment who were in the Service before the 19th February, 1959.

SUPERNUMERARY POSTS

4.   The Committee agreed that supernumerary posts created in
order not to prejudice the rights of promotion of officers should be against vacancies in the lowest grades of the relevant posts. It was also agreed that these
supernumerary posts:

(a) should not be taken into consideration for the 70:30 ratio; and
(b) should in all respects be of the same status as the substantive posts and
      that the officers promoted to them should be treated in exactly the
      same way as the holders of the substantive posts to which they had not
      been promoted in all matters e.g. seniority, promotion, superannuation
      and other benefits.

5.   It was further agreed that if after making appointments and
promotions as recommended by the Committee, it is found that either community is short of its due share in a particular Grade, and this shortage cannot

be made good by normal process within a reasonable time, supernumerary posts should be created in those posts and departments within that Grade where that community is not adequately represented. Such supernumerary posts should not be taken into consideration for the 70:30 ratio and should not necessarily be subject to the condition that a corresponding number of posts in lower grades should be frozen.

      6.   As regards officers who at present hold supernumerary posts against vacancies in other posts, the Committee recommend that the posts of such officers who may not be absorbed in the approved establishment when vacancies are filled, should be subject to allocation on the 70:30 ratio. A list of such posts is attached as Appendix I.

BENEFITS TO OFFICERS WHO ELECT TO RETIRE

      7.   It is suggested that the recommendation made at paragraph 3(b) above should be given the force of law in the form of a legal instrument.

      8.   The Committee recommend that the holders of Provident Fund posts who, having proved that their promotion prospects have been prejudicially affected by the application of the 70:30 ratio, elect to retire should be given the following retiring benefits:

(i)   Those officers whose prospects of promotion to *pensionable* post have been prejudicially affected, should receive benefits as if they were retiring from a pensionable post on abolition of office terms, on condition that they forfeit the Government bonus standing to their credit in the Provident Fund;

(ii)   Those officers whose prospects of promotion to a *Provident Fund* post have been prejudicially affected, should be paid, in addition to their normal entitlement under the Provident Fund Law, an *ex-gratia* lump sum equal to one half of the total amount standing to their credit in the Fund.

SIX GRADES

      9.   The compromise scheme which divided all public service posts into six Grades was accepted subject to the condition laid down in the decision reached by the President-Elect and the Vice-President-Elect at their meeting of the 21st July,1960. The decision in question reads as follows:

> "The President and Vice-President have agreed that Scale 14 shall be transferred from Grade IV to Grade III but that it shall be the duty of the appropriate body to ensure that, in implementing the 70:30 ratio during the five months from the date of Independence, all vacancies that now exist and those which will occur during the period in question in all promotion posts for Scale 14, shall be filled by members of that community which is short of its due allocation in each of such posts.

The President and Vice-President have asked the Greek and Turkish representatives to convey to Greek and Turkish Civil Servants, that any individual officer who will prove that his prospects of promotion have been prejudicially and directly affected by the implementation of the 70:30 ratio will be fully compensated by the State".

In connection with the words "directly affected" appearing in the second paragraph of the above decision the Committee recommend that, it should be interpreted as if the words "whether immediately or not" existed after the word "affected". The scheme amended as above is attached (Appendix II).

Detailed tables showing all posts as appearing in the current Estimates, together with their establishments and their present distribution between the two communities are attached as Appendix III.

10. The Committee recommend that promotion from one Grade to another should be on a racial basis, in accordance with the 70:30 ratio. Promotions from one post to another within a Grade, however, to be on the usual basis of official qualifications, experience and merit.

ALLOCATION OF VACANCIES

11. Lists showing the existing vacancies in each Grade and the allocation recommended are attached as Appendix IV. As will be seen from these lists the Committee has not attempted to make allocations in cases where there are vacancies in more than one post in the same Department. It is considered that this is a task which should be undertaken by the Public Service Commission. These allocations are subject to the condition that promotions within the same Grade must precede the implementation of the recommended allocation. It is of course understood that the Commission in making the allocation will observe the principles that promotions within a particular Grade will be by merit, and promotions from one Grade to another on a racial basis, in accordance with the 70:30 ratio. The Commission shall, however, ensure that, in implementing the 70:30 ratio during the 5 months from the date of Independence, all vacancies that now exist and those which will occur during the period in question in all promotion posts for Scale 14, shall be filled by members of that community which is short of its due allocation in each of such posts. Promotion posts for officers on Scale 14 are shown in Appendix III by an asterisk.

12. The resulting position in each of the six Grades after the allocations recommended in paragraph 9 above is as follows:

(i)   Supergrade:
       Total No. of posts =   17
       Proportion under 70:30 ratio = 12 Greeks : 5 Turks
       Present position = 11 Greeks and 4 Turks
       Recommended allocation of 2 vacancies = 1 Greek and 1 Turk

(ii)   <u>Grade I</u>:

Total No. of posts =   94

<u>Less</u>:

Overseas officers   :   <u> 3</u>

                    91

Proportion under 70:30 ratio = 64 Greeks : 27 Turks

Present position: 48 Greeks and 11 Turks

Recommended allocation of 32 vacancies =

                 18 Greeks and 14 Turks

      Total   :   66 Greeks and 25 Turks

      Greeks :   + 2

      Turks :   − 2

(iii)   <u>Grade II</u>:

Total No. of posts =   216

<u>Less</u>:

Overseas officers   :   <u>11</u>

                  205

Proportion under 70:30 ratio = 144 Greeks and 61 Turks

Present position: 124 Greeks and 32 Turks

Recommended allocation of 49 vacancies =

                 24 Greeks and 25 Turks

      Total   :   148 Greeks   :   57 Turks

      Greeks :   + 4

      Turks :   − 4

(iv)   <u>Grade III</u>:

Total No. of posts =   1396

<u>Less</u>:

Overseas officers   :   <u> 4</u>

                 1392

Proportion under 70:30 ratio = 974 Greeks and 418 Turks

Present position: 956 Greeks and 217 Turks

Recommended allocation of 219 vacancies =

                 65 Greeks and 154 Turks

      Total   :   1021 Greeks   :   371 Turks

      Greeks :   + 47

      Turks :   − 47

(v)   <u>Grade IV</u>:

Total No. of posts =   425

<u>Less</u>:

Overseas officers   :   <u> 6</u>

                 419

Proportion under 70:30 ratio = 293 Greeks : 126 Turks

Present position: 296 Greeks and 61 Turks

Recommended allocation of 64 vacancies =

                 10 Greeks and 54 Turks

<pre>
         Total   :   306 Greeks   :   115 Turks
         Greeks :   + 13
         Turks   :   − 11
</pre>

(vi)   <u>Grade V</u>:
      Total No. of posts =   2518
      <u>Less</u>:
      Overseas offrs.   :   <u>1</u>
                               2517
      Proportion under 70:30 ratio = 1762 Greeks : 755 Turks
      Present position: 1817 Greeks and 621 Turks
      Recommended allocation of 189 vacancies =
                       50 Greeks and 139 Turks

<pre>
         Total   :   1867 Greeks   :   760 Turks
         Greeks :   + 105
         Turks   :   +   5
</pre>

13.   The Committee further recommend that the Public Service Commission should be forthwith entrusted with the duty of making promotions and appointments in accordance with the allocation shown in Appendix IV subject to the conditions laid down in paragraph 11; the shortage of any particular community being adjusted thereafter but within five months from the date of Independence.

TEMPORARY OFFICERS

14.   The Committee unanimously recommend that no temporary officer fully qualified either under the present schemes of service or under the revised schemes, should be dismissed to facilitate the application of the 70:30 ratio. As regards the remaining temporary officers the Committee consider that it is not within their terms of reference to make any recommendations but they feel that the matter is one to be taken up separately by the Associations with the two Leaders.

15.   The minutes of the meetings held by the Committee should be made available to the members of the Public Service Commission.

<pre>
         Staff Side   Official Side
(Signed) G. Coutas   (Signed)   A. C. Contos
          Ph. Kypris   Dj. Muftizade
          A. Panaretou   H. Artemis
          M. Salahiddin   N. P. Josephides
          M. A. Behdjet
</pre>

List of supernumerary appointments
against vacancies in other posts

Supernumerary appointments		Posts against which supernumerary appointments have been made	
2	Customs and Excise Officers, 2nd Grade (F.6)	2	Customs and Excise Officers, 1st Grade (F.6)
1	Computer (D.11)	1	Senior Computer (D.11)
1	Land Clerk, 2nd Grade (D.11)	1	Land Clerk, 1st Grade (D.11)
2	Senior Warders (J.9)	2	Inspectors (J.8)
1	Lab. Technician, 2nd Grade (M.4)	1	Lab. Technician, 1st Grade (M.3)
1	Radiographer (M.4)	1	Senior Radiographer (M.3)
16	Postmen (Temp) (C.W.19)	3	Postmen (Temp) (C.W.19)
		8	Postal Officers, 3rd Grade (Temp) (C.W.19)
		4	Postal Officers, 3rd Grade (Temp) (C.W.19)
		1	Postal Officer, 2nd Grade (C.W.18)
5	Customs Boatmen (C.W.24)	5	Customs Coxswains (C.W.24)
7	Customs Guards (F.7)	7	Senior Customs Guards (F.7)
1	Storeman (Temp) (F.20)	1	Storeman (F.20)
7	Foremen, 2nd Grade (I.5)	7	Foremen, 1st Grade (I.5)
1	Prison Warder (J.10)	1	Senior Warder (J.9)
110	Clerical Assistants (D.26)	6	Principal Clerks (D.24)
		13	Clerks, 1st Grade (D.24)
		30	Clerks, 2nd Grade (D.24)
		25	Stenographers (D.25)
		25	Accounting Offrs., 3rd Gr. (F.2)
		11	Clerks seconded to other duties or on leave without pay
155		**155**	

COMPROMISE SCHEME

Proposed Grades for the application of the 70:30
proportion to the Civil Service

Grade	No. of posts	Description
Supergrade	17	Posts on fixed salaries of £1,900 p.a. or more, or a salary scale rising to £1,900 or more
Grade I	96	Posts on the following salary scales: A : £1,460 – 1,800 B : £1,380 – 1,700 1A : £1,452 – 1,644 2 : £1,236 – 1,548 2+1 : £1,236 – 1,596 (combined) or fixed salaries between £1,548 and £1,800
Grade II	219	Posts on the following salary scales: 3 : £1,128 – 1,362 4 : £1,020 – 1,200 5 : £ 900 – 1,200 5+2 : £ 900 – 1,548 (combined) 5+3 : £ 900 – 1,362 (combined) or fixed salaries above £1,056 but below £1,548
Grade III	1398	Posts on the following salary scales: 6 : £900 – 1,056 7 : £720 – 990 8 : £720 – 900 9 : £642 – 810 10 : £570 – 720 13+9: £426 – 810 (combined) 14 : £300 – 594 (combined) or fixed salaries between £642 and £1,056 (inclusive)
Grade IV	426	Posts on the following salary scales: 11 : £498 – 642 12 : £426 – 642 13 : £426 – 594 15+11: £354 – 642 (combined) 15+13: £354 – 594 (combined) or fixed salaries between £426 and £642 (inclusive)
Grade V	2519	Officers on the following salary scales: 15 : £354 – 522 16 : £264 – 426 17 : £264 – 372 18 : £234 – 336 19 : £144 – 204 15+16: £264 – 522 (combined) or fixed salaries below £426

SUMMARY

GRADES	Approved Establishment	Greeks	Turks	Vacancies	Overseas	Supernumerary
Supergrade	17	11	4	2	–	–
Grade I	94	48	11	32	3	–
Grade II	216	124	32	49	11	–
Grade III	1396	956	217	223	4 (1 Italian)	4
Grade IV	425	296	61	66	6	4
Grade V	2517	1817	621	225	1	147
	4665	3253	946	597	25	155
Supernumerary	155					
	4820			4820		

Proportions:	Greeks	=	3248
	Turks	=	1392
			4640
	Overseas		25
	Total		4665

SUPERGRADE

Proportions:	Greeks	=	12
	Turks	=	5
	Total	=	17

Post	A.E.	G.	T.	V.	Remarks
Under-Secretaries to President & Vice-President	2	1	1	–	
Joint Secretaries	2	1	–	1	Reserved a Turk
Chief Engineer, P.W.D.	1	1	–	–	
Chief Medical Officer	1	1	–	–	
Administrative Officers to Ministries	10	6	3	1	Reserved a Greek
Chief Establishment Officer	1	1	–	–	
	17	11	4	2	

GRADE I

	A.E.	G.	T.	V.		Remarks
A.1	4	2	1	1		
A.5	3	1	1	–		(one overseas)
A.10	3	–	–	3		
A.15	1	–	–	1		
CI.1	4	2	1	1		
CI.5	1	1	–	–		
CW.1	6	1	–	5		
CW.6	2	1	–	1		
CW.11	2	1	–	–		(one overseas)
CW.16	1	1	–	–		
CW.20	1	1	–	–		
F.4	2	1	1	–		
F.8	2	2	–	–		
F.13	1	1	–	–		
F.17	1	1	–	–		
M.1	22	12	–	10		
I.1	5	–	–	5		
I.6	(5)3	1	–	2	(4)	Two posts blocked in view of two supernumerary appointments in Asst. Town Planning Officers.
I.9	1	–	1	–		
I.11	1	1	–	–		
J.1	16	10	4	2		
J.6	1	–	–	1		
L.1	4	3	1	–		
D.4	3	2	1	–		
D.5	1	–	–	–		(one overseas)
D.9	1	1	–	–		
D.13	1	1	–	–		
D.16	1	1	–	–		
	(96)94	48	11	32	(34)	

Proportions: Greeks   =   64
              Turks   =   27
                           91
              Overseas   3
              Total   94

GRADE II

	A.E.	G.	T.	V.		Remarks
A.2	(27)26	15	4	7		No provision for one post
A.6	7	4	1	2		
A.11	10	3	2	4		(one overseas)
CI.2	(2)1	–	–	1	(2)	No provision for one post
CI.6	1	1	–	–		
CW.2	12	10	2	–		
CW.7	4	2	–	2	(3)	1 vacancy blocked against S.N. appointment
CW.12	9	–	–	1		(8 overseas)
CW.17	1	1	–	–		
CW.21	(2)1	–	–	1	(2)	1 post blocked against supernumerary appointment in Apprentice Pilot
F.1	3	–	–	3		
F.5	4	–	–	4		
F.9	4	2	–	2		
F.14	(1)–	–	–	–	(1)	No financial provision
M.2	75	57	16	2		
I.2	15	8	1	5		(one overseas)
I.7	(2)4	3	1	–		(2 supernumerary against Town Planning Officers)
J.2	11	7	4	–		
J.7	1	–	–	1		
D.1	1	–	–	1		
D.6	9	1	–	8		
D.10	12	7	1	4		
D.14	1	–	–	1		
D.17	1	1	–	–		
D.21	(4)3	2	–	–	(1)	(one overseas) No provision for one post
	(219)216	124	32	49	(55)	(11 overseas)

Proportions: Greeks   =   144
              Turks   =   61
                            205
              Overseas   11
              Total   216

GRADE III

	A.E.	G.	T.	V.		Remarks
A.3	(153)152	102	33	17	(18)	1 post to be abolished
A.7	21	14	1	6		
A.12	35	25	1	8		(one overseas)
A.16	2	–	–	2		
CI.3	34	24	6	4		
CI.7	5	5	–	–		
CW.3	(75)74	63	3	8	(9)	No provision for one post
CW.8	4	3	–	1		
CW.13	15	6	–	9		
CW.18	43	24	13	6		
CW.22	12	6	2	2		(one overseas & 1 Italian)
F.2	102	59	8	35		
F.6	87	71	12	6		(2 supernumerary)
F.10	24	18	4	2		
F.15	16	10	4	2		
F.18	2	1	–	1		
M.3	69	31	13	24		(one overseas)
I.3	57	39	13	5		
I.8	29	20	5	4		
I.10	1	1	–	–		
I.12	1	–	–	1		
J.3	14	8	5	1		
J.8	8	3	–	5		
L.2	19	12	4	3		
D.2	20	12	5	3		
D.7	12	9	2	1		
D.11	242	190	38	16		(2 supernumerary)
D.15	5	5	–	–		
D.18	16	13	1	2		
D.22	13	8	5	–		
D.24	254	168	37	49		
J.E.8.1	8	6	2	–		
	(1398)1396	956	217	223	(225)	(3 overseas & 1 Italian) (4 supernumerary)

Proportions:	Greeks	=	974
	Turks	=	418
			1392
	Overseas		4
	Total		1396

GRADE IV

	A.E.	G.	T.	V.		Remarks
A.8	26	22	–	4		
A.13	3	2	–	1		
CI.8	5	3	2	–		
CW.4	13	11	2	–		
CW.9	7	7	–	–		
CW.14	1	1	–	–		
CW.23	1	1	–	–		
F.11	49	36	11	2		
F.19	11	7	2	2		
M.4	139	99	19	23		(2 supernumerary)
I.4	1	1	–	–		
J.4	7	5	–	2		
J.9	21	14	9	–		(2 supernumerary)
L.3	(40)39	28	8	3	(4)	
D.19	30	24	6	–		
D.25	63	30	1	26		(6 overseas)
J.E.S.2	9	5	1	3		
	(426)425	956	217	66		(4 supernumerary)

Proportions: Greeks   =   293
              Turks   =   126
                                       419
              Overseas   6
              Total   425

GRADE V

	A.E.	G.	T.	V.		Remarks
A.4	78	54	16	8		
A.9	228	193	21	14		
A.14	40	40	–	–		
CI.4	8	5	1	2		
CW.5	98	73	8	17		
CW.10	(40)39	32	6	1	(2)	One post blocked.
CW.15	38	26	7	5		
CW.19	107	80	28	15		(16 supernumerary)
CW.24	58	22	28	13		(5 supernumerary)
F.3	37	28	8	1		
F.7	239	146	78	22		(7 supernumerary)
F.12	1	1	–	–		
F.16	10	8	–	2		
F.20	15	13	1	2		(1 supernumerary)
M.5	556	398	92	65		(1 overseas) (1 supernumerary deducted from No. of vacancies).
I.5	(73)74	52	13	14	(15)	(7 supernumerary) One post to be abolished.
J.5	32	19	10	3		
J.10	141	61	77	4		(1 supernumerary)
L.4	47	31	7	9		
D.8	3	1	1	1		
D.12	74	39	13	22		
D.20	22	17	3	2		
D.23	7	5	2	–		
D.26	395	384	121	–		(110 supernumerary)
D.27	160	79	78	3		
D.28	3	2	1	–		
J.E.8.3	9	8	1	–		
	(2519)2517	1817	621	225		(147 supernumerary)

Proportions: Greeks   =   1761
             Turks   =   755
                          ‾‾‾‾
                          2516
             Overseas   1
                          ‾‾‾‾
             Total   2517

AGRICULTURE

	A.1	A.E.	G.	T.	V.		
Grade I	Chief Agric. Officer, Crops etc.	1	1	–	–		(G=3) (T=1)
	Chief Agr. Officer, Animal Husbandry	1	1	–	–		
	Chief Veterinary Offr.	1	–	1	–		
	Land Development Offr.	1	–	–	1		
		4	2	1	1		
	A.2						
Grade II	Agr. Offrs., Class I & II	(16)15	10	2	3	(4)	Provision for 15 posts only
	Vet Offrs., Class I & II	7	4	1	2		
	Soil Conser. Engineers Class I & II	2	1	–	1		(G=18) (T=8)
	Vet Offr. (temp)	1	–	1	–		
	Horticulturalist	1	–	–	1		
		(27)26	15	4	7	(8)	
	A.3						
Grade III	Agr. Supts., 1st Gr.	24	20	3	1		
	Vet. Inspectors, 1st Gr.	2	2	–	–		(G=106) (T=46)
■	Agr. Supts., 2nd Gr.	30	20	9	1		
■	Vet. Inspectors, 2nd Gr.	6	4	1	1		
■	Mechanical Supt.	1	–	–	1		
■	Agr. Supts., 2nd Gr. (temp)	(2)1	1	–	–	(1)	Post to be abolished when vacancy in Gr. is filled.
■	Sen. Poultry Instructress	3	2	1	–		
	Poultry Instructresses	6	2	1	3		
	Agr. Assistants	57	38	14	5		
	Soil Cons. Assts.	8	4	1	3		
	Asst. Mech. Supts.	2	2	–	–		
	Vet. Assistants	8	4	3	1		
	Draughtsmen	2	2	–	–		
	Vet. Assts. (temp)	2	1		1		
		(153)152	102	33	17	(18)	
	A.4						
Grade V	Storekeeper	1	1	–	–		(G=55) (T=23)
	Agr. Foremen	52	38	9	5		
	Storemen	4	3	–	–	(1)	1 post blocked against supernumerary appointment in Laboratory Attendant.
	Laboratory Assts.	2	1	–	1		
	Veterinary Foremen	11	5	5	1		
	Laboratory Attendants	4	3	2	–		1 supernumerary against vacancy in Storeman.
	Storekeeper (temp)	1	1	–	–		
	Agr. Foremen (temp)	1	–	–	1		
	Lab. Attendants (temp)	2	2	–	–		
		78	54	16	8	(9)	(1 supernumerary)

■ Promotion posts for officers on scale 14.

FORESTS

A.5	A.E.	G.	T.	V.	
Grade I Chief Forest Officer	1	–	1	–	
Senior Asst. Chief Forest Officer	1	1	–	–	
Principal For. College	1	–	–	–	(one overseas officer)
	3	1	1	–	
A.6					
Grade II Asst. C. of Forests	7	4	1	2	(G=5) (T=2)
A.7					
Grade III Forest Engineer	1	1	–	–	(G=15) (T=6)
Forest Officers	3	2	–	1	
Asst. Forest Offrs.	10	7	1	2	
Prosecution Offrs.	3	2	–	1	
Telephone Supt.	1	–	–	1	
Forest Surveyor	1	–	–	1	
Mechanical Supt.	1	1	–	–	
Asst. Forest Surveyor (temp)	1	1	–	–	
	21	14	1	6	
A.8					
Grade IV Forest Rangers	26	22	–	4	(G=18) (T=8)
A.9					
Grade V Foresters and Forest Guards	222	187	21	14	(G=160) (T=68)
Storekeeper	1	1	–	–	
Mechanical Assts.	4	4	–	–	
Storeman (temp)	1	1	–	–	
	228	193	21	14	

WATER DEVELOPMENT

	A.10	A.E.	G.	T.	V.	
Grade I	Chief Water Dev. Officer	1	–	–	1	(G=2)
						(T=1)
	Asst. Chief Water Dev. Officer	1	–	–	1	
	Engineer/Hydrologist	1	–	–	1	
		3	–	–	3	
	A.11					
Grade II	Supt. Of Works	1	1	–	–	(G=7)
						(T=3)
	Geologist, Class II (temp)	1	1	–	–	
	Senior Water Engineers	2	–	–	1	(one overseas officer)
	Executive Engineers	6	1	2	3	(Reserved for 3 Govt. Scholars 2 G., 1 T.)
		10	3	2	4	(one overseas officer)
	A.12					
Grade III	Senior Inspectors	2	1	–	–	(one overseas officer)
■	Inspectors	10	6	–	4	
	Chief Foremen	2	2	–	–	(G=24)
						(T=10)
	Technical Assts.	21	16	1	4	(O=1)
		35	25	1	8	
	A.13					
Grade IV	Asst. Chief Foremen	3	2	–	1	(G=2)
						(T=1)
	A.14					
Grade V	Foremen, 1st & 2nd Grades	39	39	–	–	(G=28)
						(T=12)
	Storekeeper	1	1	–	–	
		40	40	–	–	

■ Promotion post for officers on scale 14.

METEOROLOGICAL

	A.15.	A.E.	G.	T.	V.	
Grade I	Meteorologist	1	–	–	1	
	A.16.					
Grade II	Met. Asst. 1st Grade	1	–	–	1	(G=1)
						(T=1)
	Met Asst. 2nd Grade	1	–	–	1	
		2	–	–	2	

COMMERCE & INDUSTRY

	Cl.1	A.E.	G.	T.	V.		
Grade I	Senior Officer Co-ordination etc.	1	1	–	–		(G=3) (T=1)
	Senior Offr., Imports, etc.	1	1	–	–		
	Senior Offr., Exports, etc.	1	–	1	–		
	Senior Offr., Tourism	1	–	–	1		(Reserved for a Greek)
		4	2	1	1		
	Cl.2						
Grade II	Senior Tourist Offr.	(1)–	–	–	–	(1)	No provision in 1960 Estimates
	Scientific Officer, Entomologist	1	–	–	1		
		(2)1	–	–	1	(2)	
	Cl.3						
Grade III	Senior Comm. & Ind. Assistant	1	–	–	1		(G=24) (T=10)
	Comm. & Ind. Assts., 1st Grade	3	2	–	1		
	Tourist Officer	1	1	–	–		
■	Commr. & Ind. Assts., 2nd Grade	7	5	1	1		
	Economic Assistant	1	–	1	–		
	Hotel Inspector	1	–	–	1		
	Produce Inspector	1	1	–	–		
	Comm. & Ind. Assts., 3rd Grade	18	15	4	–		(1 supernumerary)
	Comm. & Ind. Asst. 3rd Grade (temp)	1	–	–	–	(1)	(To remain vacant in view of super. post)
		34	24	6	4	(5)	(1 supernumerary)
	Cl.4						
Grade V	Managers, Info. Bureaux	3	2	–	1		(G=6) (T=2)
	Receptionists	3	2	–	1		
	Receptionists (temp)	1	1	–	–		
	Telephone Operator (temp)	1	–	1	–		
		8	5	1	2		

■ Promotion post for officers in scale 14.

OFFICE OF OFFICIAL RECEIVER AND REGISTRAR

	Cl.5	A.E.	G.	T.	V.
Grade I	Official Receiver & Registrar	1	1	–	–
Grade II	Cl.6 Assistant Official Receiver & Registrar	1	1	–	–
Grade III	Cl.7 Examiners	5	5	–	–
Grade IV	Cl.8 Asst. Examiners	5	3	2	–

PUBLIC WORKS

		A.E.	G.	T.	V.		
Supergrade	Chief Engineer	1	1	–	–		
	C.W.1						
Grade I	Deputy Chief Engineer	1	–	–	1		
	Asst. Chief Engineers	2	–	–	2	(G=4)	
						(T=2)	
	Senior Architect	1	–	–	1		
	Architect/Quantity Surveyor	1	1	–	–		
	Architect	1	–	–	1		
		6	1	–	5		
	C.W.2						
Grade II	Asst. Architects	2	2	–	–	(G=8)	
						(T=4)	
	Workshop Manager	1	1	–	–		
	Electrical Engineer	1	1	–	–		
	Executive Engineers	7	6	1	–		
	Asst. Electr. Engineer (temp)	1	–	1	–		
		12	10	2	–		
	C.W.3						
Grade III	Secretary	1	1	–	–	(G=52)	
						(T=22)	
	Building Supt.	1	1	–	–		
	Chief Foremen	8	6	1	1		
	Senior Technical Assts.	3	3	–	–		
	—do— (temp)	1	1	–	–		
■	Technical Assts., 1st Grade	14	13	–	1		
■	Technical Assts., 1st Gr. (temp)	3	3	–	–		
	Electrical Supt.	(1)–	–	–	–	(1)	No provision in view of post of Asst. El. Engineer
	Techn. Asst., 2nd Gr.	34	28	–	6		
	—do— (temp)	6	5	1	–		
	Draughtsmen	2	1	1	–		
	Boiler Maker	1	1	–	–		
		(75)74	63	3	8	(9)	
	C.W.4						
Grade IV	Asst. Chief Foremen	11	9	2	–	(G=9)	
						(T=4)	
	Head Fitter	1	1	–	–		
	Asst. Storekeeper	1	1	–	–		
		13	11	2	–		
	C.W.5						
Grade V	Foremen, 1st and 2nd Gr.	95	72	6	17	(G=69)	
						(T=29)	
	Instrument Mechanic	1	1	–	–		
	Telephone Operator	1	–	1	–		
	Storeman (temp)	1	–	1	–		
		98	73	8	17		

■ Promotion posts for officers in scale 14.

ANTIQUITIES

	C.W.6	A.E.	G.	T.	V.		
Grade I	Chief Antiquities Offr.	1	1	–	–		
	Curator of Museum	1	–	–	1		
		2	1	–	1		
	C.W.7						(G=3)
							(T=1)
Grade II	Curator of Ancient Monuments	1	–	–	–	(1)	Blocked in view of S. N. appointment in Asst. Curator of Museum
	Asst. Curator of Museum	1	2	–	–		
	Asst. Curator of Ancient Monuments	1	–	–	1		
	Archaeological Survey Officer (temp)	1	–	–	1		
		4	2	–	2	(3)	
	C.W.8						
Grade III	Asst. Archaeol. Survey Officer (temp)	1	1	–	–		(G=3)
							(T=1)
	Asst. Curator (Records)	1	1	–	–		
	Technical Assts.	2	1	–	1		
		4	3	–	1		
	C.W.9						
Grade IV	Surveyor	1	1	–	–		(G=5)
							(T=2)
	Librarian	1	1	–	–		
	Senior Museum Assts.	2	2	–	–		
	Chief Foreman	1	1	–	–		
	Senior Foremen	2	2	–	–		
		7	7	–	–		
	C.W.10						
Grade V	Asst. Record Keeper	1	1	–	–		(G=27)
							(T=12)
	Museum Assistants	8	4	3	1		
	Museum Attendants	4	4	–	–		
	Museum " (temp)	2	1	1	–		
	Foremen	4	4	–	–		
	Custodians, 1st Gr.	5	5	–	–		
	Custodians, 2nd Gr.	13	10	2	–	(1)	(Blocked in view of one temp. post of Museum Attendant)
	Archaeol. Survey Asst. 1st Gr. (temp)	1	1	–	–		
	Archaeol. Survey Assts. 2nd Gr. (temp)	2	2	–	–		
		(40)39	32	6	1	(2)	

CIVIL AVIATION

	C.W.11	A.E.	G.	T.	V.	
Grade I	Chief Civil Aviation Officer	1	1	–	–	
	Chief Operations Officer	1	–	–	–	(overseas officer)
		2	1	–	–	(one overseas officer) (G=6) (T=3)
	C.W.12					
Grade II	Airport Manager	1	–	–	1	Reserved for a Turk
	Senior Air Traffic Control Officer	1	–	–	–	Overseas officer
	Air Traffic Control Officer	7	–	–	–	Overseas officers
		9	–	–	1	(8 overseas)
	C.W.13					
Grade III	Operations Officer, 1st Grade	1	1	–	–	(G=10.5) (T=4.5)
■	Operations Officer, 2nd Grade	9	–	–	9	
	Operations Officer, 3rd Grade	5	5	–	–	
		15	6	–	9	
	C.W.14					
Grade IV	Airport Assistant, 1st Grade	1	1	–	–	
	C.W.15					
Grade V	Airport Asst. 2nd Gr.	4	4	–	–	
	Firemen/Marshals	9	7	2	–	(G=27) (T=11)
	Operations Assts.	5	5	–	–	
	Airport Guards (temp)	20	10	5	5	
		38	26	7	5	

■ Promotion post for officers on scale 14.

POST OFFICE

	C.W.16	A.E.	G.	T.	V.	
Grade I	Postmaster-General	1	1	–	–	
	C.W.17					
Grade II	Asst. Postmaster-General	1	1	–	–	
	C.W.18					
Grade III	Supt. 1st Grade	1	–	–	1	
	" 2nd Grade	2	1	–	1	(G=30) (T=13)
■	Postal Officers, 1st Grade	10	5	3	2	
	Postal Officers, 2nd Grade	30	18	10	2	
		43	24	13	6	
	C.W.19					
Grade V	Postal Officers 3rd Grade	54	36	14	4	(G=75) (T=32)
	Postal Officers, 3rd Grade (temp)	11	2	1	8	
	Postmen	32	23	6	3	
	" (Temp)	10	19	7	–	16 supernumerary against vacancies in higher posts
		107	80	28	15	(16 supernumerary)

■ Promotion posts for officers serving on scale 14.

		PORTS					
	C.W.20	A.E.	G.	T.	V.		
Grade I	Chief Port Officer	1	1	–	–		
	C.W.21						
Grade II	Harbour Master and Senior Pilot	(1)–	–	–	–	(1)	To be kept vacant because of creation of post of Apprentice Pilot.
	Port Supt. & Pilot	1	–	–	1		
		(2)1	–	–	1	(2)	
	C.W.22						
Grade III	Port Officers & Pilots	4	2	–	–		One overseas Officer and 1 Italian
	Tug Master	1	–	1	–		(G=8)
■	Quay Inspectors & Piermasters	2	1	1	–		(T=4)
	Customs & Excise Offr. 2nd Grade	2	1	–	1		
	Asst. Quay Inspectors	3	2	–	1		
		12	6	2	2		
	C.W.23						
Grade IV	Engineer-Tugboat	1	1	–	–		
	C.W.24						
Grade V	Senior Cust. Guards	2	–	–	2		
	Customs Guards	16	8	8	–		(G=41)
	" " (temp)	4	–	–	4		(T=17)
	Customs Coxswains	5	–	–	5		
	Customs Boatmen	19	4	20	–		(5 supernumerary against vacancies in Customs Coxswains)
	Mates, Tugboat	2	2	–	–		
	Firemen, Tugboat	3	3	–	–		
	Lightkeepers	5	5	–	–		
	Customs & Excise Officers, 3rd Gr.	2	–	–	2		
		58	22	28	13		(5 supernumerary)

● In addition there are 40 temporary Customs Guards (16 G. and 24 T.) and 23 temporary Customs Boatmen (4 G. & 19 T.) holding Emergency posts and kept by direction of Governor up to 31.8.60.

■ Promotion post for officers serving on scale 14.

TREASURY

	F.1	A.E.	G.	T.	V.	
Grade II	Accountants	3	–	–	3	(G=2)
						(T=1)

	F.2	A.E.	G.	T.	V.	
Grade III	Supervisors of Accts.	9	7	1	1	(G=71)
						(T=31)
	Accounting Officers, 1st Grade	18	13	2	3	
	Pay Officers & Asst. Pay Officers	10	9	1	–	
	Technician	1	–	–	1	
	Acct. Officers, 2nd Gr.	35	30	4	1	
	Acct. Officers, 2nd Gr. (temp)	4	–	–	4	
	Acct. Officers, 3rd Gr.	25	–	–	25	There are 25 supernumerary Clerical Assts. against these vacancies
		102	59	8	35	

	F.3	A.E.	G.	T.	V.	
Grade V	Machine Operators	17	14	3	–	
	Machine Operators (temp.)	7	5	1	1	(G=26)
						(T=11)
	Currency Clerks	13	9	4	–	
		37	28	8	1	

CUSTOMS

		A.E.	G.	T.	V.	
Supergrade	———					
	F.4					
Grade I	Chief Customs Officer	1	1	–	–	
	Asst. Chief Customs Offr.	1	–	1	–	
		2	1	1	–	
	F.5					
Grade II	Collectors of Customs	4	–	–	4	
	F.6					
Grade III	Asst. Collectors of Customs	6	5	–	1	(G=61)
						(T=26)
■	Customs & Excise Offrs., 1st Grade	20	12	4	4	
	Chief Inspector Preventive Service	1	1	–	–	
	Inspectors, Preventive Service	6	5	–	1	
	Customs & Excise Offrs., 2nd Grade	53	47	8	–	(2 supernumerary against vacancies in Grade I)
	Tobacco Surveyor	1	1	–	–	
		87	71	12	6	(2 supernumerary)
	F.7					
Grade V	Customs & Excise Officers, 3rd Grade	79	52	20	7	(G=167) (T=72)
	Senior Customs Guards	12	–	–	12	
	Customs Guards	98	62	43	–	(7 supernumerary against vacancies in Senior Customs Guards)
	Asst. Inspectors Prev. Service	7	5	2	–	
	Preventivemen	43	27	13	3	
		239	146	78	22	(7 supernumerary)

■ Promotion post for officers serving on scale 14.

INLAND REVENUE

F.8	A.E.	G.	T.	V.	
Grade I Chief Revenue Officer	1	1	–	–	
Assistant Chief Revenue Officer	1	1	–	–	
	2	2	–	–	
F.9					
Grade II Senior Investigation Officer	1	–	–	1	(G=3) (T=1)
Principal Assessors	3	2	–	1	
	4	2	–	2	
F.10					
Grade III Assessors	7	6	1	–	(G=17) (T=7)
Asst. Assessors	12	10	2	–	
Principal Collection Officer	1	–	–	1	
Assistant Principal Collection Officer	1	–	–	1	(Post to be abolished)
District Col. Officers	3	2	1	–	
	24	18	4	2	
F.11					
Grade IV Junior Asst. Assessors	3	2	1	–	(G=34) (T=15)
Assistant District Collection Officers	4	3	1	–	
Tax Collectors	40	29	9	2	
Tax Collectors (Temp.)	2	2	–	–	
	49	36	11	2	
F.12					
Grade V Telephone Operator	1	1	–	–	

STATISTICS AND RESEARCH

F.13	A.E.	G.	T.	V.	
Grade I Chief Statistics Offr.	1	1	–	–	
F.14					
Grade II Asst. Statistics Offr.	(1)–	–	–	–	(1) (No financial Provision for 1960)
F.15					
Grade III Senior Statistics Asst.	1	1	–	–	(G=11) (T=5)
Statistics Assts. 1st Gr.	3	2	–	1	
■ Statistics Assts. 2nd Gr.	3	2	1	–	
Statistics Clerks	9	5	3	1	
	16	10	4	2	
F.16					
Grade V Machine Operators	6	6	–	–	(G=7) (T=3)
Machine Operators (Temp.)	4	2	–	2	
	10	8	–	2	

■ Promotion post for officers serving on scale 14.

STORES

	F.17	A.E.	G.	T.	V.	
Grade I	Senior Stores Officer	1	1	–	–	
	F.18					
Grade III	Asst. Senior Stores Officer	1	–	–	1	(Reserved for a Turk)
	Stores Office Supervisor (temp)	1	1	–	–	
		2	1	–	1	
	F.19					
Grade IV	Asst. Storekeepers	6	3	1	2	(G=8)
						(T=3)
	Asst. Storekeepers (temp)	5	4	1	–	
		11	7	2	2	
	F.20					
Grade V	Storemen	10	8	–	2	(G=10.5)
						(T=4.5)
	Storemen (temp)	5	5	1	–	supernumerary against vacancy in permanent post
		15	13	1	2	(1 supernumerary)

MEDICAL

		A.E.	G.	T.	V.	
Supergrade	Chief Medical Officer	1	1	–	–	
	M.1					(G=15)
						(T=7)
Grade I	Asst. Chief Med. Offrs.	2	1	–	1	1 reserved for a Turk
	Specialists	13	6	–	7	
	District Med. Offrs.	5	3	–	2	
	Senior Dental Offr.	1	1	–	–	
	Analyst	1	1	–	–	
		22	12	–	10	
	M.2					
Grade II	Dental Officers	8	7	1	–	(G=53)
						(T=22)
	Asst. Analyst	2	1	–	1	
	Med. Officers, Cl. I and II	64	48	15	1	
	Med. Officers (temp)	1	1	–	–	
		75	57	16	2	
	M.3					
Grade III	Med. Lab. Superintendent	1	1	–	–	(G=48)
						(T=21)
	Senior Med. Lab. Technologists	3	2	1	–	
	Inspector of Pharmacies	1	–	–	1	
	Chief Pharmacist	1	1	–	–	
	Senior Pharmacists	7	6	1	–	
	Chief Health Inspector	1	–	1	–	
	Health Insp. 1st Gr.	7	6	2	1	
	Superv. Med. Stores	1	–	–	–	
	Hospital Steward	1	–	–	1	
	Senior Matron	1	–	1	–	
	Lab. Technician, 1st Gr.	1	–	–	1	
	Med. Lab. Technologist, 1st Gr.	3	1	2	–	
	Matrons	4	3	–	1	
	Sister Tutors	2	1	1	–	
	Midwifery Supervisor and Tutor	1	–	–	1	
	Senior Health Visitors	2	–	–	2	
	Mental Nursing Supt.	1	–	–	1	
	Senior Physiotherapist	1	–	–	–	(one overseas)
	Senior Radiographer	1	–	–	1	
	Lay Worker	1	–	–	1	
	St. Haralambos Home (temp)					
	Staff Nurses (Female)	20	9	2	9	
	Staff Nurses (temp)	2	–	–	2	
	Tuberculosis Nurses	5	1	2	2	
	Supt. Nurses Home (temp)	1	1	–	–	
		69	31	13	24	(one overseas)
	M.4					
Grade IV	Dental Mechanic	1	1	–	–	
	Lab. Technician, 2nd Gr.	1	2	–	–	1 supernumerary against vacancy in 1st Gr.
	Med. Lab. Technologists 2nd Grade	6	1	–	5	
	Pharmacists	29	25	3	1	
	Student Pharmacists	3	1	–	2	
	Health Inspectors, 2nd and 3rd Grades	44	35	9	–	
	Housekeeper & Home Sister	1	1	–	–	

Nursing Sisters	35	19	4	12	(G=97) (T=42)
Charge Nurses	3	1	1	1	
Mental Nurses	10	6	2	2	
Mental Hosp. Steward	1	1	–	–	
Occupational Therapist	1	1	–	–	
Physiotherapist	1	1	–	–	
Radiographers	3	4	–	–	1 supernumerary against Senior Radiographer
	139	99	19	23	(1 supernumerary)

	M.5					
Grade V	Dental Assistants	2	1	–	1	
	Dental Attendants	8	6	2	–	(G=389) (T=167)
	Student Lab. Technician	1	1	–	–	
	Lab. Attendant	1	1	–	–	
	Student Med. Lab. Technician	3	3	–	–	
	Mortuary Attendant	1	1	–	–	
	Med. Lab. Attendants	2	1	1	–	
	Storekeeper, Nicosia GH.	1	1	–	–	
	Storemen	4	4	–	–	
	Laundry Supervisor	1	1	–	–	
	Asst. Housekeeper	1	–	–	–	Overseas officer
	Junior Nursing Sisters	4	–	2	2	
	Staff Nurses, Male	4	3	1	–	
	" " " (Temp.)	2	2	–	–	
	Asst. Nurses, Male	16	15	1	–	
	" " " (Temp.)	5	4	–	1	
	" " Female	42	22	7	13	
	" " " (Temp.)	5	–	–	5	
	Tuberculosis Health Visitors	3	3	–	–	
	Tuberculosis Health Visitors (temp)	1	1	–	–	
	Asst. Tub. Visitors	2	2	–	–	
	Community Health Visitors	12	9	–	3	
	Midwives	32	23	9	–	
	Midwives (Temp.)	5	–	2	3	
	Male Orderlies	42	30	12	–	
	Female Attendants	4	3	1	–	
	Student Nurses, Male	75	67	6	2	
	" " Female	168	131	36	1	
	" " F. (Temp.)	20	–	–	20	(Advertised)
	Asst. Occupational Therapists, Male	4	3	–	1	
	Asst. Occup. Therapist, Female	3	2	–	1	
	Female Attendants	34	20	5	9	
	Asst. Physiotherapist	1	1	–	–	
	Student Physiotherapist	1	–	1	–	
	Asst. Radiographers	9	5	–	4	
	Welfare Assistants	4	3	1	–	
	Foreman Cabinet Maker	1	1	–	–	
	Head Cook	1	1	–	–	
	Cooks	13	13	–	–	
	Telephone Operators	4	4	–	–	
	Hospital Porters	13	10	4	–	1 supernumerary
	Dispensary Attendant (Temp.)	1	–	1	–	
		556	398	92	66	(1 overseas) (1 supernumerary)

ADMINISTRATION

		A.E.	G.	T.	V.		
Grade I	**I.1** District Officers	5	–	–	5		(G=3.5) (T=1.5)
Grade II	**I.2** Administrative Offrs.	4	3	–	–		(G=10.5) (T=4.5) One overseas post will be abolished
	Administrative Assts., 1st Grade	6	5	1	–		Posts will be abolished
	Asst. District Offrs.	5	–	–	5		
		15	8	1	5		(one overseas)
Grade III	**I.3** Adm. Assts., 2nd Gr.	24	13	6	5		(G=40) (T=17)
	—do— 3rd Gr.	27	20	7	–		
	Chief Foremen	6	6	–	–		
		57	39	13	5		
Grade IV	**I.4** Ranger, Minor Forests	1	1	–	–		
Grade V	**I.5** Foremen, 1st Grade	11	–	–	11		(G=51) (T=22)
	Foremen, 2nd Grade	29	31	5	–		7 supernumerary against Gr. I.
	Bailiff	1	–	1	–		
	Foreman, E.M.I. Works	1	–	–	1		
	Irrigation Guard, E. M. I. Works	1	1	–	–		
	Guards, Minor Forests	(30)29	20	7	2	(3)	(One vacancy for Larnaca to be abolished)
		(73)72	52	13	14	(15)	(7 supernumerary)

PLANNING & HOUSING

		A.E.	G.	T.	V.		
Grade I	**I.6** Chief Planning Officer	1	1	–	–		(G=2) (T=1)
	Town Planning Officers	(3)1	–	–	1	(2)	Two vacancies to be kept unfilled.
	Housing Architect	1	–	–	1		
		(5)3	1	–	2	(4)	
Grade II	**I.7** Housing Manager	1	1	–	–		
	Assistant Town Planning Officers	(1)3	2	1	–		Two supernumerary against vacancies in Town Planning Officers.
		(2)4	3	1	–		(2 supernumerary)
Grade III■	**I.8** Technical Assistants	10	8	–	2		(G=20) (T=9)
	Building Inspectors	19	12	5	2		
		29	20	5	4		

■ Promotion post for officers serving on Scale 14.

REGISTRATION

	I.9	A.E.	G.	T.	V.
Grade I	Registration Officer	1	–	1	–
Grade III	I.10 Assistant Registration Officer	1	1	–	–

MIGRATION

	I.11	A.E.	G.	T.	V.
Grade I	Migration Officer	1	1	–	–
Grade III	I.12 Assistant Migration Officer	1	–	–	1

JUDICIAL

	J.1	A.E.	G.	T.	V.	
Grade I	Chief Registrar Supreme Court	1	–	–	1	
Grade II	J.2 Assistant Chief Registrar	1	1	–	–	
Grade III	J.3 Registrars, 1st & 2nd Grades	8	5	2	1	(G=8)
	Assistant Registrars	4	3	1	–	(T=4)
		12	8	3	1	
Grade IV	J.4 Court Stenographers	6				(G=5)
	1st and 2nd Grades		5	–	2	(T=2)
	" " (temp)	1				
		7	5	–	2	
Grade V	J.5 Court Usher	1	1	–	–	(G=22)
	Bailiffs, 1st and 2nd Grades	31	18	10	3	(T=10)
		32	19	10	3	

PRISONS

	J.6	A.E.	G.	T.	V.		
Grade I	Senior Superintendent	1	–	–	1		
	J.7						
Grade II	Superintendent	1	–	–	1		
	J.8						
Grade III	Asst. Superintendent of Prisons	3	–	–	3		
	Chief Inspectors	2	2	–	–		(G=6) (T=2)
	Inspectors	3	1	–	2		
		8	3	–	5		
	J.9						
Grade IV	Senior Warders	10	7	6	–		(2 supernumerary)
	Senior Warders (temp)	9	5	3	–	(1)	
	Storekeeper	1	1	–	–		(G=15) (T=6)
	Tailor Instructor	1	1	–	–		
		21	14	9	1		
	J.10						
Grade V	Warders	134	59	76	–		(1 supernumerary)
	Wardresses	2	–	–	2		
	Wardresses (temp)	2	1	1	–		(G=99) (T=42)
	Instructors	3	1	–	2		
		141	61	77	4		

LABOUR & SOCIAL INSURANCE

	L.1	A.E.	G.	T.	V.		
Grade I	Senior Inspector of Factories	1	1	–	–		(G=3) (T=1)
	Senior Employment Offr.	1	–	1	–		
	Senior Industrial Relations Officer	1	1	–	–		
	Senior Social Insurance Offr.	1	1	–	–		
		4	3	1	–		
	L.2						
Grade III	Labour Officers, 1st Gr.	5	4	1	–		(G=13) (T=6)
	Boiler Inspector	1	1	–	–		
	Labour Officers, 2nd Gr.	11	7	3	1		
	Supt. Rehab. Centre	1	–	–	1		
	Insurance Officer	1	–	–	1		
		19	12	4	3		
	L.3						
Grade IV	Asst. Labour Officers	(38)37	26	8	3	(4)	(G=27) (T=12)
	Asst. Labour Officer (temp)	1	1	–	–		Provision for 37 posts only in view of temp. post.
	Mechanical Inspector	1	1	–	–		
		(40)39	28	8	3	(4)	
	L.4						
Grade V	Labour Assistants	25	18	4	3		(G=33) (T=14)
	Insurance Clerks	16	9	1	6		
	Office Juniors	6	4	2	–		
		47	31	7	9		

AUDIT

D.1	A.E.	G.	T.	V.	
Grade I Senior Auditor	1	–	–	1	

D.2	A.E.	G.	T.	V.	
Grade III Auditors	3	2	–	1	(G=14) (T=6)
Examiners, 1st Gr.	6	4	2	–	
Examiners, 2nd Gr.	11	6	3	2	
	20	12	5	3	

ATTORNEY-GENERAL

D.4	A.E.	G.	T.	V.
Grade I Crown Counsel	3	2	1	–

GEOLOGICAL SURVEY

D.5	A.E.	G.	T.	V.	
Grade I Chief Geological Survey Officer	1	–	–	–	Overseas officer

D.6	A.E.	G.	T.	V.	
Grade II Geologists	7	–	–	7	(G=6) (T=3)
Chemist	1	1	–	–	
Palaeontologist (temp)	1	–	–	1	
	9	1	–	8	

D.7	A.E.	G.	T.	V.	
Grade III Draughtsman, 1st Grade	1	1	–	–	(G=8) (T=4)
Surveyors/Draughtsmen	4	3	1	–	
Field and Laboratory Assistants	7	5	1	1	
	12	9	2	1	

D.8	A.E.	G.	T.	V.
Grade V Foremen	3	1	1	1

LANDS AND SURVEYS

	D.9	A.E.	G.	T.	V.	
Grade I	Chief Lands & Surveys Officer	1	1	–	–	
	D.10					
Grade II	Senior Land Officer	1	–	–	1	(G=8)
						(T=4)
	Chief Survey Officer	1	1	–	–	
	Land Officers	9	6	1	2	
	Land Officers (Temp.)	1	–	–	1	
		12	7	1	4	
	D.11					
Grade III	Senior Surveyors	2	1	–	1	(G=169)
						(T=73)
	Senior Draughtsman	1	1	–	–	
■	Land Clerks, 1st Grade	33	19	6	8	
■	Surveyors, 1st Grade	6	5	–	1	
	Surveyor, 2nd Grade	20	16	3	1	
■	Draughtsmen, 1st Grade	8	3	2	3	
	Draughtsmen, 2nd Grade	48	39	8	1	
	Senior Computer	1	–	–	1	
	Computers	2	3	–	–	1 super-numerary against senior computer.
	Senior Photolithographer	1	1	–	–	
	Land Clerks, 2nd Grade	120	102	19	–	1 supernumerary
		242	190	38	16	(2 supernumerary)
	D.12					
Grade V	Photolithographer	1	1	–	–	(G=52)
						(T=22)
	Land Clerical Assts.	73	38	13	22	
		74	39	13	22	

■ Promotion post for officers serving on scale 14.

MINES

	D.13	A.E.	G.	T.	V.	
Grade I	Senior Mines Officer	1	1	–	–	
	D.14					
Grade II	Asst. Senior Mines Officer	1	–	–	1	Reserved for a Turk
	D.15					
Grade III	Sub-Inspector, 1st Gr.	1	1	–	–	
	Sub-Inspector of explosives	1	1	–	–	(G=3.5)
						(T=1.5)
	Sub-Inspectors, 2nd G.	3	3	–	–	
		5	5	–	–	

PRINTING OFFICE

	D.16	A.E.	G.	T.	V.	
Grade I	Government Printer	1	1	–	–	
	D.17					
Grade III	Overseer of Works	1	1	–	–	
	D.18					
Grade III	Senior Printers	16	13	1	2	(G=11) (T=5)
	D.19					
Grade IV	Printers, 1st & 2nd Grades	30	24	6	–	(G=21) (T=9)
	D.20					
Grade V	Printers' Assistants	22	17	3	2	(G=15) (T=7)

PUBLIC INFORMATION

	D.21	A.E.	G.	T.	V.		
Grade II	Senior Information Officer	(1)–	–	–	–	(1)	(G=3) (T=1) No financial provision Overseas Officer.
	Features Officer	1	–	–	–		
	Press Officer	1	1	–	–		
	Publications Officer	1	1	–	–		
		(4)3	2	–	–	(1)	
	D.22						
Grade III	Assistant Press Officers	2	1	1	–		(G=9) (T=4)
	Assistant Publications Officers	2	1	1	–		
	Photographer	1	1	–	–		
	Press Assistants	5	3	2	–		
	Publications Assistants	3	2	1	–		
		13	8	5	–		
	D.23						
Grade V	Assistant Photographers	3	2	1	–		(G=5) (T=2)
	Mobile Cinema Operators	3	2	1	–		
	Dark Room Operator	1	1	–	–		
		7	5	2	–		

GENERAL CLERICAL STAFF

	D.24	A.E.	G.	T.	V.	
Grade III	Principal Clerks	15	9	–	6	(G=178) (T=76)
■	Clerks, 1st Grade	54	35	6	13	
	Clerks, 2nd Grade	185	124	31	30	
		254	168	37	49	
	D.25					
Grade IV	Stenographers, 1st and 2nd Grade	62	30	1	25	(G=44) (T=19) Six overseas officers in London Office
	Stenographer, 2nd Gr. (temp)	1	–	–	1	
		63	30	1	26	(six overseas)
	D.26					
Grade V	Clerical Assistants	393	384	121	–	(G=276.5) (T=118.5) 110 supernumerary against vacancies (see X below)
	Clerical Assistants (Temp.)	2	–	–	–	
		395	384	121	–	

■ Promotion post for officers serving on Scale 14.

X	Principal Clerk	6
	Clerk, 1st Grade	13
	Clerk, 2nd Grade	30
	Stenographers	25
	Accounting Offr. 3rd Gr.	25
		99
	Clerks seconded to other duties or on leave without pay	11
		110

MESSENGERS

	D.27	A.E.	G.	T.	V.	
Grade V	Messengers	157	78	77	2	(G=112) (T=48)
	—do— (Temp.)	3	1	1	1	
		160	79	78	3	

GOVERNMENT HOUSE

	D.28	A.E.	G.	T.	V.
Grade V	Head Gardener	1	–	1	–
	Telephone Operators	2	2	–	–
		3	2	1	–

JOINT EDUCATIONAL SERVICES

	J.E.S.1	A.E.	G.	T.	V.	
Grade III	Headmaster, Reform School	1	1	–	–	(G=6)
						(T=2)
	Asst. Headmaster, Reform School	2	1	1	–	
	Asst. Masters, Reform School	3	2	1	–	
	Headmaster, Deaf School	1	1	–	–	
	Headmaster, Blind School	1	1	–	–	
		8	6	2	–	
	J.E.S.2					
Grade IV	Teachers, Deaf School	6	3	1	2	Filled by Elementary school teachers.
	Teachers, Blind School	3	2	–	1	
		9	5	1	3	(G=6)
						(T=3)
	J.E.S.3					
Grade V	Matron, Reform School	1	1	–	–	(G=6)
						(T=3)
	Asst. Matron, Reform School	1	1	–	–	
	Instructors, Reform School	5	4	1	–	
	Matron, Deaf School	1	1	–	–	
	Office Junior, Blind Sch.	1	1	–	–	
		9	8	1	–	

APPENDIX IV

Index No.	Vacant Posts	Recommended allocation of vacancies	
		Greeks	Turks
	SUPERGRADE		
	1 Joint Secretary	–	1
	1 Administrative Officer to Ministry	1	–
		1	1
	GRADE I		
A.1	Land Development Officer	1	–
A.10	Chief Water Development Officer		
	Asst. Chief Water Development Officer	2	1
	Engineer-Hydrologist		
A.15	Meteorologist	–	1
CI.1	Senior Officer, Tourism	1	–
CW.1	Deputy Chief Engineer		
	2 Asst. Chief Engineers	3	2
	Senior Architect		
	Architect		
CW.6	Curator of Museum	1	–
M.1	1 Asst. Chief Medical Officer		
	7 Specialists	3	7
	2 District Medical Officers		
I.1	5 District Officers	4	1
I.6	1 Town Planning Officer	1	1
	1 Housing Architect		
J.1	1 President District Court	1	1
	1 Chief Registrar, Supreme Court		
J.6	1 Senior Supt. Of Prisons	1	–
		18	14

GRADE I

	Present Position					Recommended Allocation		Remarks
	A.E	G.	T.	V.		G.	T.	
A.1	4	2	1	1		1	–	
A.5	3	1	1	–				
			(one overseas)					
A.10	3	–	–	3		2	1	
A.15	1	–	–	1		–	1	
CI.1	4	2	1	1		1	–	
CI.5	1	1	–	–				
CW.1	6	1	–	5		3		
CW.6	2	1	–	1		1		
CW.11	2	1	–	–				
			(one overseas)					
CW.16	1	1	–	–				
CW.20	1	1	–	–				
F.4	2	1	1	–				
F.8	2	2	–	–				
F.13	1	1	–	–				
F.17	1	1	–	–				
M.1	22	12	–	10		3	7	
I.1	5	–	–	5		4	1	
I.6	(5)3	1	–	2	(4)	1	1	2 posts blocked
I.9	1	–	1	–				
I.11	1	1	–	–				
J.1	16	10	4	2		1	1	
J.6	1	–	–	1		1	–	
L.1	4	3	1	–				
D.4	3	2	1	–				
D.5	1	–	–	–				
			(one overseas)					
D.9	1	1	–	–				
D.13	1	1	–	–				
D.16	1	1	–	–				
	(96)94	48	11	32	(34)	18	14	

Proportions: Greeks   =   64
             Turks   =   27
                     91
           +   3   overseas
                     94

Recommended allocation:

Greeks:	48	+	18	=	66
Turks:	11	+	14	=	25
					91
Greeks	=		+	2	
Turks	=		–	2	

GRADE II

Index No.	Vacant Posts	Recommended allocation of vacancies	
		Greeks	Turks
A.2	3 Agr. Officers, Class I & II 2 Veter. Officers, Class I & II 1 Soil Conservation Engineer, Class I & II 1 Horticulturalist	3	4
A.6	2 Asst. Conservator of Forests	1	1
A.11	1 Senior Water Engineer 3 Executive Engineers	3	1
CI.2	Scientific Officer, Entomologist	–	1
CW.7	1 Asst. Curator of Ancient Monuments 1 Archaeological Survey Officer (Temp.)	1	1
CW.12	Airport Manager	–	1
CW.21	Port Superintendent and Pilot	–	1
F.1	3 Accountants	2	1
F.5	4 Collectors of Customs	3	1
F.9	1 Senior Investigation Officer 1 Principal Assessor	1	1
M.2	1 Assistant Analyst 1 Medical Officer, Class I & II	–	2
I.2	5 Assistant District Officers	3	2
I.7	1 Supt. Of Prisons	–	1
D.1	Senior Auditor	1	–
D.6	7 Geologists 1 Palaeontologist (Temp.)	5	3
D.10	1 Senior Land Officer 2 Land Officers 1 Land Officer (Temp.)	1	3
D.14	Asst. Senior Mines Officer	–	1
		24	25

GRADE II

	Present Position					Recommended Allocation		Remarks
	A.E	G.	T.	V.		G.	T.	
A.2	(27)26	15	4	7	(8)	3	4	One post blocked
A.6	7	4	1	2		1	1	
A.11	10	3	2	4		3	1	
				(one overseas)				
CI.2	(2)1	–	–	1	(2)	–	1	–do–
CI.6	1	1	–	–				
CW.2	12	10	2	–				
CW.7	4	2	–	2	(3)	1	1	
CW.12	9	–	–	1		–	1	
				(8 overseas)				
CW.17	1	1	–	–				
CW.21	(2)1	–	–	1	(2)	–	1	–do–
F.1	3	–	–	3		2	1	
F.5	4	–	–	4		3	1	
F.9	4	2	–	2		1	1	
F.14	(1)–	–	–	–	(1)			–do–
M.2	75	57	16	2		–	2	
I.2	15	8	1	5		3	2	
				(one overseas)				
I.7	(2)4	3	1	–				
				(2 supernumerary)				
J.2	11	7	4	–				
J.7	1	–	–	1		–	1	
D.1	1	–	–	1		1	–	
D.6	9	1	–	8		5	3	
D.10	12	7	1	4		1	3	
D.14	1	–	–	1		–	1	
D.17	1	1	–	–				
D.21	(4)3	2	–	–	(1)			–do–
				(one overseas)				
	(219)216	124	32	49	(55)	24	25	

Proportions: Greeks = 144
               Turks   =   61
                         205
                    +   11
                         216

Recommended allocation:

Greeks:	124	+	24	=	148
Turks:	32	+	25	=	57
Greeks	=	+	4		
Turks	=	–	4		

GRADE III

Index No.	Vacant Posts	Recommended Allocation of vacancies	
		Greeks	Turks
A.3	1 Agr. Superintendent, 1st Gr.		
	1 Agr. Superintendent, 2nd Gr.		
	1 Vet. Inspector, 2nd Gr.		
	1 Mechanical Supt.		
	3 Poultry Instructresses	4	13
	5 Agr. Assistants		
	3 Soil Conservation Assts.		
	1 Veterinary Assistant		
	1 Veterinary Assistant (Temp.)		
A.7	1 Forest Officer		
	2 Asst. Forest Officers		
	1 Prosecution Officer	1	5
	1 Telephone Superintendent		
	1 Forest Surveyor		
A.12	4 Inspectors (Water Development)	–	8
	4 Technical Assistants		
A.16	1 Meteorological Asst. 1st Gr.	1	1
	1 –do– 2nd Gr.		
CI.3	1 Senior Commerce and Ind. Asst.		
	1 Commerce and Ind. Asst. 1st Gr.		
	1 –do– 2nd Gr.	–	4
	1 Hotel Inspector		
CW.3	1 Chief Foreman		
	1 Technical Asst. 1st Gr.	–	8
	6 Technical Assts. 2nd Gr.		
CW.8	1 Technical Asst. (Antiquities)	–	1
CW.13	9 Operations Officers, 2nd Gr.	5	4
CW.18 (Postal)	1 Supt. 1st Grade		
	1 Supt. 2nd Grade	6	–
	2 Postal Officers, 1st Grade		
	2 Postal Officers, 2nd Grade		
CW.22	1 Customs & Excise Officer, 2nd Grade	1	1
	1 Asst. Quay Inspector		
F.2	1 Supervisor of Accounts		
	3 Accounting Officers, 1st Gr.		
	1 Technician		
	1 Accounting Officer, 2nd Gr.	12	23
	4 –do– (Temp.)		
	25 –do– 3rd Gr.		
F.6	1 Asst. Collectors of Customs		
	4 Customs & Excise Officers, 1st Grade	–	6
	1 Inspector, Preventive Service		
F.10	1 Principal Collection Officer	–	2
	1 Asst. Principal Collection Officer		
F.15	1 Statistics Asst. 1st Gr.	1	1
	1 Statistics Clerk		
F.18	1 Asst. Senior Stores Officer	–	1

M.3	1 Inspector of Pharmacies		
	1 Health Inspector, 1st Gr.		
	1 Hospital Steward		
	1 Laboratory Technician, 1st Gr.		
	1 Matron		
	1 Midwifery Supervisor & Tutor		
	2 Senior Health Visitors	16	8
	1 Mental Nursing Supt.		
	1 Senior Radiographer		
	1 Law Worker, St. Haralambos Home		
	9 Staff Nurses (Female)		
	2 –do– (Temp.)		
	2 Tuberculosis Nurses		
I.3	5 Administrative Assistants 2nd Gr.	1	4
I.8	2 Technical Assistants		
(Planning & Housing)	2 Building Inspectors	–	4
I.12	1 Asst. Migration Officer	–	1
J.3	1 Registrar, 1st & 2nd Gr.	1	–
J.8	3 Asst. Supt. Of Prisons	3	2
	2 Inspectors		
L.2	1 Labour Officer, 2nd Grade		
	1 Supt. Rehabilitation Centre	1	2
	1 Insurance Officer		
D.2	1 Auditor	2	1
	2 Examiners, 2nd Gr.		
D.7	1 Field & Laboratory Asst.	–	1
	(Geological Survey)		
D.11	1 Senior Surveyor		
	8 Land Clerks, 1st Grade		
	1 Surveyor, 1st Gr.		
	1 Surveyor, 2nd Gr.	–	16
	3 Draughtsmen, 1st Gr.		
	1 Draughtsman, 2nd Gr.		
	1 Senior Computer		
D.18	2 Senior Printers	–	2
D.24	6 Principal Clerks		
	13 Clerks, 1st Gr.	10	39
	30 Clerks, 2nd Gr.		
		65	158

GRADE III

	Present Position					Recommended Allocation		Remarks
	A.E	G.	T.	V.		G.	T.	
A.3	(153)152	102	33	17	(18)	4	13	One post blocked
A.7	21	14	1	6		1	5	
A.12	35	25	1	8		–	8	
			(one overseas)					
A.16	2	–	–	2		1	1	
CI.3	34	24	6	4		–	4	
CI.7	5	5	–	–				
CW.3	(75)74	63	3	8	(9)	–	8	–do–
CW.8	4	3	–	1		–	1	
CW.13	15	6	–	9		5	4	
CW.18	43	24	13	6		6	–	
CW.22	12	6	2	2		1	1	
		(one overseas & 1 Italian)						
F.2	102	59	8	35		12	23	
F.6	87	71	12	6		–	4	(6)≠two super-numerary
F.10	24	18	4	2		–	2	
F.15	16	10	4	2		1	1	–do–
F.18	2	1	–	1		–	1	
M.3	69	31	13	24		16	8	
			(one overseas)					
I.3	57	39	13	5		1	4	
I.8	29	20	5	4		–	4	
I.10	1	1	–	–				
I.12	1	–	–	1		–	1	
J.3	14	8	5	1		1	–	
J.8	8	3	–	5		3	2	
L.2	19	12	4	3		1	2	
D.2	20	12	5	3		2	1	
D.7	12	9	2	1		–	1	
D.11	242	190	38	16		–	14	(16) two super-numerary
D.15	5	5	–	–				
D.18	16	13	1	2		–	2	
D.22	13	8	5	–				
D.24	254	168	37	49		10	39	
J.E.S.1	8	6	2	–				
	(1398)1396	956	217	223	(225)	65	154	(158)

(3 overseas & 1 Italian)
(1 supernumerary)

Proportions: Greeks   =   974
    Turks   =   418
    1392
    +   4
    1396

Recommended Allocation:

Greeks: 956   +   65   =   1021
Turks: 217   +   154   =   371

Greeks   =   +   47
Turks   =   –   47

≠   The allocation of vacancies shown in brackets is based on the assumption that the officers holding the supernumerary appointments are of both communities and of sufficient number to permit of the allocation; if not, the figures outside the bracket show the posts which can be filled after deduction of supernumerary appointments.

GRADE IV

Index No.	Vacant Posts	Recommended Allocation of vacancies	
		Greeks	Turks
A.8	4 Forest Rangers	–	4
A.13	1 Asst. Chief Foreman (Water Dev.)	–	1
F.11	2 Tax Collectors	–	2
F.19	2 Asst. Storekeepers	1	1
M.4	5 Medical Lab. Technologists, 2nd Grade 1 Pharmacist 2 Student Pharmacists 12 Nursing Sisters 1 Charge Nurse 2 Mental Nurses	–	23
J.4	2 Court Stenographers 1st and 2nd Grades	–	2
L.3	3 Asst. Labour Officers	–	3
D.25	25 Stenographers 1st and 2nd Grade 1 Stenographer, 2nd Gr. (Temp.)	8	18
J.E.S.2	2 Teachers, Deaf School 1 Teacher, Blind School	1	2
		10	56

GRADE IV

	Present Position					Recommended Allocation		Remarks
	A.E	G.	G.	V.		G.	T.	
A.8	26	22	–	4		–	4	
A.13	3	2	–	1		–	1	
CI.8	5	3	2	–				
CW.4	13	11	2	–				
CW.9	7	7	–	–				
CW.14	1	1	–	–				
CW.23	1	1	–	–				
F.11	49	36	11	2		–	2	
F.19	11	7	2	2		1	1	
M.4	139	99	19	23		–	21	(23)≠2 supernumerary
I.4	1	1	–	–				
				–				
J.4	7	5	–	2		–	2	
J.9	21	14	9	–				2 supernumerary
L.3	(40)39	28	8	3	(4)	–	3	
D.19	30	24	6	–				
D.25	63	30	1	26		8	18	
				(6 overseas)				
J.E.S.2	9	5	1	3		1	2	
	(426)425	296	61	66		10	54	(56)≠(4 supernumerary)

(6 overseas)

Proportions:	Greeks	=	293		Recommended Allocation:					
	Turks	=	126							
			419		Greeks:	296	+	10	=	306
		+	6		Turks:	61	+	54	=	115
			425							
					Greeks	=	+	13		
					Turks	=	–	11		

≠   The allocation of vacancies shown in brackets is based on the assumption that the officers holding the supernumerary appointments are of both communities and of sufficient number to permit of the allocation; if not, the figures outside the bracket show the posts which can be filled after deduction of supernumerary appointments.

GRADE V

Index No.	Vacant Posts	Recommended Allocation of vacancies	
		Greeks	Turks
A.4	5 Agr. Foremen		
	1 Laboratory Assistant		
	1 Vet. Foreman	1	7
	1 Agric. Foreman (Temp.)		
A.9	14 Foresters & Forest Guards	–	14
CI.4	1 Manager, Information Bureau		
	1 Receptionist	1	1
CW.5	17 Foremen, 1st and 2nd Grades	–	17
CW.10	1 Museum Assistant	–	1
CW.15	5 Airport Guards	1	4
CW.19	4 Postal Officers, 3rd Grade		
	8 " " (Temp.)	11	4
	3 Postmen		
CW.24	2 Senior Customs Guards		
	4 Customs Guards (Temp.)		
	5 Customs coxwains	13	–
	2 Customs & Excise Officer, 3rd Grade		
F.3	1 Machine Operator (Temp.)	–	1
F.7	7 Customs & Excise Officers, 3rd Grade		
	12 Senior Customs Guards	22	–
	3 Preventivemen		
F.16	2 Machine Operators (Temp.)	–	2
F.20	2 Storemen	–	2
M.5	1 Dental Assistant		
	2 Junior Nursing Sisters		
	1 Assistant Nurse (Male) (Temp.)		
	13 Asst. Nurses (Female)		
	5 Assts. Nurses (Female) (Temp.)		
	3 Community Health Visitors		
	3 Midwives (Temp.)		
	2 Student Nurses (Male)	–	65
	1 Student Nurse (Female)		
	20 –do– –do– (Temp.)		
	1 Asst. Occupational Therapist (M)		
	1 –do– (Female)		
	9 Female Attendants		
	4 Assts. Radiographers (less 1 S.N.)		
I.5	11 Foremen, 1st Grade		
(Administration)	1 Foreman, E.M.I. Works	5	9
	2 Guards, Minor Forests		
J.5	3 Bailiffs, 1st and 2nd Grades	3	–
J.10	2 Wardresses		
	2 Instructors	4	–
L.4	3 Labour Assistants		
	6 Insurance Clerks	2	7
D.8	1 Foreman (Geological Survey)	–	1
D.12	22 Land Clerical Assistants	13	9
D.20	2 Printers Assistant	–	2
D.27	2 Messengers		
	1 –do– (Temp.)	3	–
		79	146

GRADE V

	Present Position					Recommended Allocation		Remarks
	A.E	G.	T.	V.		G.	T.	
A.4	78	54	16	8		1	7	
A.9	228	193	21	14		–	14	
A.14	40	40	–	–				
CI.4	8	5	1	2		1	1	
CW.5	98	73	8	17		–	17	
CW.10	(40)39	32	6	1	(2)	–	1	One post blocked.
CW.15	38	26	7	5		1	4	
CW.19	107	80	28	15		–(11)≠	–	(4)≠16 supernumerary
CW.24	58	22	28	13		8(13)≠	–	5 supernumerary
F.3	37	28	8	1		–	1	
F.7	239	146	78	22		15(22)≠	–	7 supernumerary
F.12	1	1	–	–				
F.16	10	8	–	2		–	2	
F.20	15	13	1	2		–	1	(2)≠1 supernumerary
M.5	556	398	92	65		–	65	
		(one overseas)						
I.5	(73)72	52	13	14	(15)	–(5)≠	7	(9)≠7 supernumerary
J.5	32	19	10	3		3	–	
J.10	141	61	77	4		3(4)≠	–	1 supernumerary
L.4	47	31	7	9		2	7	
D.8	3	1	1	1		–	1	
D.12	74	39	13	22		13	9	
D.20	22	17	3	2		–	2	
D.23	7	5	2	–				
D.26	396	384	121	–				110 supernumerary
D.27	160	79	78	3		3		
D.28	3	2	1	–		–	–	
J.F.S.3	9	8	1	–				
	(2519)2518	1817	621	225	(227)	50 (79)≠	139 (145)≠	

(one overseas)
(147 supernumerary)

Proportions:	Greeks	=	1762		Recommended Allocation					
	Turks	=	755							
			2517		Greeks:	1817	+	50	=	1867
		+	1		Turks:	621	+	139	=	760
			2518							
					Greeks	=		+	105	
					Turks	=		–	5	

≠   The allocation of vacancies shown in brackets is based on the assumption that the officers holding the supernumerary appointments are of both communities and of sufficient number to permit of the allocation; if not, the figures outside the bracket show the posts which can be filled after deduction of supernumerary appointments.

APPENDIX 53

Glafkos Clerides, "Municipalities: Outline of Negotiations Regarding the Question of Municipalities in the Five Towns," January 1963

The object of this paper is to present in a nutshell the intricate problem of finding a form of local Government for the five main towns of Cyprus.

Normally such a problem would have been the easiest to solve because forms of local Government for Municipal areas have been in existence in this country and in various other countries for many centuries and precedents could be found which would have been acceptable so long as they were based on the principle of elected Municipal Council with defined duties and responsibilities exercising the normal functions of local Government. The problem, however, although a simple one in its nature it has been complicated by certain constitutional provisions which in effect require the creation of separate Municipalities in the five largest towns of the Republic, that is to say Nicosia, Limassol, Famagusta, Larnaca and Paphos, for the Turkish inhabitants of those towns.

At the time of the drafting of the Constitution it was found impossible to agree to the demarcation of boundaries of the regions of each town over which the Greek and the Turkish Municipality would exercise their respective jurisdiction. Despite the fact that the work of drafting the Constitution occupied a mixed Constitutional Commission for nearly a year in which Greece, Turkey, the Greek Cypriots and the Turkish Cypriots were represented, the Commission found it impossible to define any areas or regions for the Greek or the Turkish Municipalities in each of the main towns already referred to and for this purpose the Constitutional Commission agreed to insert Article 177, transferring the responsibility of fixing the boundaries of the regions in the five main towns to the President and the Vice-President of the Republic.

If one were to examine Article 173 of the Constitution in isolation from the true facts, one should have thought that its application is simple enough since it speaks clearly that separate Municipalities should be created to serve the Turkish inhabitants. The difficulty arises, however, from the fact that in none of the towns concerned the population lives exclusively in areas inhabited by Greeks or Turks and that there are areas in which the population is mixed.

The President and the Vice-President acting under Article 177 appointed Committees in each town consisting of Greeks and Turks which Committees met and tried to reach agreement in defining the areas of the respective jurisdiction of each Municipal Council. In other words what the Constitutional Commission had been unable to solve in the course of a discussion lasting nearly a year and found it necessary to use the device of passing the problem to the President and the Vice-President, continues today, despite the Committees set up by the President and the Vice-President to examine and define regions of jurisdiction for the respective councils in each of the five main towns, to remain an unsolved problem.

On the Turkish insistence of the members of the Constitutional Commission an Article was inserted in the Constitution providing that the Municipal Laws which existed prior to Independence and which provided for one mixed Municipal Council with a Mayor and a Deputy Mayor in each of the aforesaid towns were to expire. The Turkish point of view was that a solution to the problem could have been found within six months of the day of Independence. The President and the Vice-President with the Committees appointed by them to discuss and define areas of the respective Municipal Councils in each town had a number of meetings, but failed to reach agreement within six months. The House of Representatives, therefore, was asked to enact legislation by which—

(a) The Turkish Municipal Councils, which were set up *de facto* by the Turkish inhabitants during the period of Emergency and which the British despite their being contrary to the Law allowed to exist, were recognized *de jure*.

(b) Extending the Municipal Law which existed prior to Independence and making it at the same time applicable to the Turkish Municipal Councils which were recognized *de jure* by the same law.

The House of Representatives in all extended the Municipal Laws eight times giving thus the President and the Vice-President a credit of time of two years within which to reach an agreement.

With the progress of time it became abundantly evident that the geographical division of the Municipalities into defined areas over which the Greek and Turkish Municipalities would exercise their respective jurisdictions, was an impossible task and in any event, even if it were possible, it would be against the financial and other interests of both communities. It was further obvious that further prolongation of the existence of two Municipalities established *de jure*, but having no areas within which to exercise their jurisdiction defined by Law created considerable complications.

The President, therefore, of the Republic on the 19th March, 1962, made certain proposals to the Vice-President which were designed to by-pass the difficulty of defining regions for the separate Greek and Turkish Municipal Councils, which as already stated has been proved an impossible task, and at the same time were designed to fully safeguard the Turkish interests. The said proposals were in a general form and the Vice-President on hearing them intimated to the President that he would like the President's proposals to be made publicly known so as to see Turkish reaction.

On the 19th of March, 1962, the President of the Republic Archbishop Makarios issued to the press the following communiqué outlining the proposal made by him to the Vice-President.

> "His Beatitude at today's meeting with the Vice-President of the Republic Dr. Kutchuk stated his views regarding the separation of municipalities in the five main towns, as is provided for in the relevant Constitutional provision.

In His Beatitude's view, the geographical separation of the municipalities, irrespective of its financial repercussions, is difficult to materialize without affecting the interests of the Greek and Turkish citizens. His Beatitude suggested the maintenance of a united municipal authority and the proportional representation of Greeks and Turks thereon in accordance with the proportion of the population in each town.

With a view to safeguarding the rights of the Turkish citizens, His Beatitude suggested that—

1. The staff to be engaged and employed with the municipal authorities be in proportion to the Greek and Turkish population in each town.
2. A percentage of the annual budget of each municipality, to be fixed in advance, be made available for the needs of the Turkish citizens in a way to be suggested by the Turkish members of the Municipal Council.
3. In each of the five towns where the Mayor is a Greek the Deputy Mayor shall be a Turk, if this is justified by the proportion of the Turkish Population."

On the 20th March, 1962, the President of the Turkish Communal Chamber, Mr. Rauf Denktash, commenting on the Archbishop's proposals described President's Makarios statement as an "unrealistic approach" to the question. He went on to say that since 1958 there have been separate Turkish Municipalities in the major towns and all that remained was to make administrative arrangements for the drawing of boundaries. He claimed that Municipal separation was in existence *de facto* and *de jure* and pointed out that the provision for separate Municipalities was a basic article of the Cyprus Constitution, incorporated into it from the Zurich Agreement and as such it could not in any way be amended, altered or repealed.

The statement of Mr. Denktash has the merit, of course, of simplicity because he told the public that "all that remained to be done" was the drawing of boundaries which, in fact, was the stumbling block which prevented the Constitutional Commission from reaching an agreement and which also prevented the President and the Vice-President and the Committees set up by them in each town from finding a solution to the problem. His contention, however, that any amendment of the Constitution regarding the question of separate Municipalities could not take place because it was a basic article of the Constitution and that no amendment, alteration or repeal of such an Article could be made, is equally a simplification of the legal position.

The fact that it may be difficult or impracticable to maintain separate Municipalities in the main towns of Cyprus was recognized both by Greece and Turkey at Zurich as well as by the Joint Constitutional Commission which has its meetings in Nicosia.

Both the Zurich agreement and the Constitution of the Republic found it necessary to incorporate under Article 173 of the Constitution, i.e. the Article which provides for the creation of separate Municipalities for the Turkish inhabitants, a proviso imposing upon the President and the Vice-President of the Republic the duty to examine within a period of four years of the coming into operation of the Constitution the question whether or not the separation of the Municipalities in the main towns shall continue. The Constitution came into operation on the 16th of August, 1960, i.e. on the day of Independence, the President and the Vice-President have therefore a duty imposed on them by the Constitution to consider whether the separation of the Municipalities should continue. Nor could it be argued that the separation had not taken place. Mr. Denktash, in the first part of his statement, is perfectly right in alleging that the separation of the Municipalities did in fact take place both *de jure* and *de facto*. As already pointed out in this paper the House of Representatives enacted legislation which recognized the existence of the Turkish Municipalities in the main towns and, therefore, two Municipalities existed in each of the aforesaid towns i.e. a Greek and a Turkish Municipality. Since, therefore, it was found impossible and impracticable to delineate the territorial regions over which these two Municipalities would exercise their jurisdiction, it is obvious that the President and the Vice-President acting under the proviso of Article 173 of the Constitution could have concluded that it was no longer desirable to continue with the existence of separate Municipalities.

It will be remembered that the object of issuing to the press the communiqué containing the proposals of the President was to facilitate the Vice-President to assess the reaction of Turkish opinion to the said proposals. It will also be observed that by the statements of the President of the Turkish Communal Chamber, Mr. Rauf Denktash, which appeared in the press on the same day as the President's proposals, no time was allowed to elapse for Turkish opinion to manifest itself because the comments of Mr. Denktash on the President's proposals were designed to forestall Turkish public opinion.

The Vice-President of the Republic, Dr. Kutchuk, following the statement of Mr. Denktash made a statement on March the 21st, that is to say 48 hours after the proposals of Archbishop Makarios, President of the Republic, were given to the press, stating that he had rejected the President's suggestion for joint Greek Turkish Municipal Councils in the five main towns and that the Vice-President insisted on the Turkish view point that geographical partition of the Municipalities could be brought about. He also declared that the Turks had no trust in "safeguards".

It is clear from what is stated above that the Vice-President of the Republic, who received the proposals of His Beatitude Archbishop Makarios on the 19th March, and who requested their publication for the purpose of assessing Turkish public reaction to them remained silent on the proposals until the 21st of March, 1962, probably because he desired to know what position publicly the President of the Turkish Communal Chamber would take on the proposals.

The unfortunate result of all this was that the attempt, which was made on the 21st March, 1962, by the President of the Republic to find a solution of the deadlock regarding the Municipalities, failed to produce results because of the Turkish insistence on geographical separation of the Municipalities. Again the House of Representatives was asked to extend the Municipalities Law and give further credit of time and again the House extended the Laws expressing at the same time, as it did on each occasion when an extension was asked for, the wish that a solution be found in the near future.

The President of the Republic made a further attempt to solve the problem on the 17th December, 1962. He invited the Vice-President of the Republic again to discuss the problem of the separate Municipalities and a meeting was held at the Presidential Palace for that purpose. At that meeting the Vice-President of the Republic submitted proposed principles to be applied in fixing the geographical limits of the Greek and Turkish Municipalities in the five main towns. For the sake of accuracy the proposals of the Vice-President are set out in full.

"The frontage of all property abutting on a street will be measured and if the total length of the frontage of the property belonging to the members of the Greek Community in that street is greater, then that street will be included in the sector of the Greek municipality.

Provided, however, that if there is no access to such a street other than through streets falling within the sector of the Turkish municipality such a street will not be included in the region of the Greek municipality but will be deemed to have fallen within the sector of the Turkish municipality.

Provided that for the purpose of the above proviso a street will not be deemed to have no access if there is access to it through a ring or trunk road (and, in the case of Nicosia, also through encircling streets just above the moats) irrespective of whether such a road is within the Greek or Turkish sector.

Provided also that the areas within the ports and customs compounds in Famagusta, Limassol, Larnaca and Paphos will not be included in the regions of any of the two municipalities. The municipal services in these compounds will be carried out jointly under the direction of the co-ordinating body envisaged in para. 3 of Article 173 of the Constitution.

Note: 1. The same principles will apply in the case of a street where the total length of the frontage of the property belonging to members of the Turkish community is greater.

2. In taking the measurements of the frontage, the properties belonging to Government, semi-Government institutions and non-Cypriot persons or institutions will be disregarded.

3. The situation with regard to streets where the difference in the length of the frontage of the properties belonging to persons of each community is very small, will be subject to review by the President and the Vice-President once every two years: Provided that the President and the Vice-President may at their discretion allocate the streets in question partly to the Greek and partly to the Turkish municipality."

One need not comment at length on the above proposals of the Vice-President of the Republic. It suffices to say that they are extremely impracticable and unworkable. It will be observed, however, that although the Constitution provides for separate Municipalities for the Turkish inhabitants, the Vice-President in his proposed principles has not been able to find criteria fixing the boundaries of the respective Municipalities on the basis of inhabitants i.e. Greek and Turkish Cypriots, but has tried to find a solution on the basis of ownership. Even on the basis of ownership the Vice-President is not suggesting to take into account all factors relating to properties i.e. value, nature of property etc., but simply takes one fact i.e. the length of the frontage of each property. It is further obvious that there may be many instances and in fact there are where Greek Cypriots are tenants of properties belonging to Turkish Cypriots and vice versa.

The fact that the Vice-President has been unable to suggest any sound criteria for the separation of the Municipal areas constitutes further proof of the impracticability and unworkability of the entire conception of separate Municipalities based on communal division. Apart, however, from the question of finding sound criteria for the separation, a further problem arises, i.e. the problem of day to day administration of the separate Municipal areas. If one were to accept the proposals of the Vice-President it is clear that many streets next to each other or one leading into the other may belong to one or the other Municipality and the areas of the jurisdiction of the two Municipalities will be so intermixed that it will become impracticable and extremely expensive to maintain Municipal services.

The President of the Republic, Archbishop Makarios, after considering the principles proposed by the Vice-President for the fixing of boundaries of the Greek and Turkish Municipal Councils came to the conclusion that they provided no solution to the problem. The question of separating the Municipal areas either on the basis of community plus property, ownership or tenancy or ownership or tenancy alone, had all been carefully considered during the course of the past two years and various proposals were studied by the Committees set up to define the regions of the respective Municipal Councils without, however, resulting to any agreement.

During the course of the above referred meeting between the President and the Vice-President it was agreed to call in the President of the House of Representatives, Mr. Clerides, and the President of the Turkish Communal Chamber, Mr. Rauf Denktash, to express their views on the subject. The Attorney-General was already present acting as Legal Adviser of the Government. The President of the House of Representatives, Mr. Clerides, explained that in his view there was a duty on the President and the Vice-President acting under the proviso of Article 173 of the Constitution to consider whether separate Municipalities should exist or not. He advised that it might be an opportune moment for both sides to solve the problem by first carrying an experiment for a limited period and if the results of the experiment were satisfactory to proceed to re-examine the whole question. In his view the right approach to the problem was to set up mixed Councils to administer the Municipal affairs of each of the five towns with proportionate representation on such Councils based on the Communal population of each of the said towns, giving at the same time all the necessary legal safeguards to assure the Turkish side, which would be numerically smaller, that no discrimination whatsoever could be practiced by the majority against them, and leaving entirely for the Turkish members of each Municipal Board to decide the manner in which a certain percentage of the estimates of the Joint Committee, fixed by law, would be disposed of for the Turkish inhabitants of each of the said towns.

The President of the Communal Chamber, Mr. Rauf Denktash, on hearing the proposal of Mr. Clerides replied that it was an interesting proposition, but before the Vice-President of the Republic, Dr. Kutchuk, and himself would express an opinion on it would like to see it more fully developed on paper and asked whether it would be possible for Mr. Clerides and the Attorney-General, Mr. Tornaritis, to prepare a paper setting out the main points of the proposal so that it could be studied by them. The President of the Republic stated that he was in favour of the proposal and that he thought that an experimental period of one year would not be an unreasonable step bearing in mind the difficulties which the problem had presented.

On Saturday the 22nd December, 1962, the President of the House of Representatives and the Attorney-General drafted a document containing the main principles of the proposal made by the President of the House of Representatives and handed it over as requested to the office of the Vice-President. A meeting was also fixed between the President and the Vice-President of the Republic for the 24th of December at 10.00 a.m. in the morning for the purpose of hearing the Turkish views on the subject. The proposals drafted by the President of the House of Representatives and the Attorney-General were as follows:

"1. The Municipal Corporation Law (Cap.240) will be re-enacted subject to the necessary drafting amendments.

Provided that such Law in its application to the towns of Nicosia, Limassol, Famagusta, Larnaca and Paphos shall be subject to the following modification, that is to say instead of the existing municipal councils in each such town there will be a Joint Committee composed as in paragraph 2 hereof provided to perform all the functions performed by a council of a municipal corporation under the provisions of the aforecited Law subject to the modification provided in paragraph 3 hereof.

2. (1) The members of the Joint Committee will be appointed by the President and the Vice-President of the Republic.

(2) Each Joint Committee shall consist of Greek and Turkish members proportionately to the Greek and Turkish population of each town;

Provided that the number of the Turkish members shall not be less than two and not more than five;

Provided further that the total number of the Committee in respect of each town shall be fixed by the President and the Vice-President of the Republic.

(3) There shall be a Chairman of the Joint Committee who will be a Greek and Vice-Chairman of the Committee who will be a Turk to be appointed by the President and the Vice-President of the Republic. Such Chairman and Vice-Chairman shall perform the functions performed by the Mayor and Deputy Mayor, respectively, under the provisions of the aforecited Law:

Provided that the Vice-Chairman shall be the Controlling Officer with regard to the disposal of the funds appropriated in the estimates for projects approved by the Committee on the recommendation of its Turkish members.

3. The Joint Committee in performing its functions under the afore-cited Law shall—

    (a) in the estimates prepared by the Joint Committee of each town an appropriate percentage (fixed by Law) of the revenue of such town shall be disposed of in the manner recommended by the Turkish members of the Joint Committee;

    (b) if in disposing such part of the estimates as provided in the immediately preceding sub-paragraph it will become necessary to interfere with property belonging to, or held by, a Greek the Greek members of the Committee shall not exercise their voting rights in such a way as to prevent the implementation of the proposed scheme;

    (c) the assets and liabilities of such municipal council in each of the aforesaid towns as on the 1st day of December, 1962, shall devolve on, and be undertaken by, the Joint Committee of the town concerned:

        Provided that disposing such assets or in satisfying such liabilities a separate account shall be kept by the Joint Committee;

    (d) the regular personnel of each council in each of the aforecited towns serving on the 1st December, 1962, will be retained for services under the Joint Committee.

4. The modifications set out in paragraphs 2 and 3 hereof shall continue to be in force until the 31st December, 1963, whereupon the whole situation shall be reviewed by the President and the Vice-President of the Republic."

Prior to the meeting of the 24th December, 1962, the Vice-President of the Republic forwarded in writing the Turkish views on the proposals made by the President of the House of Representatives, Mr. Clerides. The document was in the form of a letter addressed to the President of the Republic and dated 22nd December, 1962, i.e. it was drafted on the same day as the date on which the proposals of the President of the House of Representatives were received. The document reads as follows:

VICE-PRESIDENCY.

22nd December, 1962.

Your Beatitude,

Municipalities

The proposals drafted by Messrs. Clerides and Tornaritis have been very carefully and exhaustively considered to-day at a general meeting attended by the Turkish Ministers, the Turkish members of the House of Representatives, the President and members of the Executive Committee of the Turkish Communal Chamber and certain other Turkish leaders.

2. Before arriving at a conclusion I asked everybody present to bear in mind that at our meeting on Thursday last I was given to understand—

(a) that you were determined not to agree to any geographical separation of the municipalities;

(b) that you would not allow any Greek inhabitant or any Greek property, however few and small, to come under the jurisdiction of a Turkish municipality or vice versa;

(c) that you were not prepared to agree to the extension of the Municipal Laws beyond the 31st December, 1962, nor would you accept separation along the limits of the areas where Greek and Turkish municipalities now function; and

(d) that you were contemplating to direct the Council of Ministers to fix new boundary lines for each town area and to make arrangements for the performance of municipal services by Government Departments or by ad hoc bodies.

3. Bearing in mind—

(a) the above assertions made by the President of the Republic;

(b) the fact that certain vital provisions of the Constitution with regard to municipalities and other matters affecting the interests of the Turkish Community have not yet been implemented;

(c) the constitutionality and/or legality of the proposals drafted by Messrs. Clerides and Tornaritis;

(d) the shortness of time which did not allow Turkish leaders to assess the repercussions of the new proposals on the public opinion; and

(e) the fact that, mainly because of the existence of a group in the Greek community persistently striving for the abrogation of the Agreements and the Constitution and the treatment accorded to Turks in certain affairs, such as foreign affairs, internal security and defence matters, the full confidence of Turks has not yet been won,

those present at the meeting came to the following unanimous conclusions:

(1) that the time was yet premature either for examining the question whether or not the separation of municipalities should continue, or for considering any change in our Constitution;

(2) that the proposals drafted by Messrs. Clerides and Tornaritis envisaged departure from, or alteration of, the Constitutional provisions;

(3) that once joined it would be unconstitutional and illegal to separate again the municipalities should the proposed experiment fail;

(4) that counter proposals to the following effect should be made—

(i) that separate Greek and Turkish municipalities should continue to function for services prescribed in the Constitution;

(ii) that the Municipal Law should be so amended as to be consistent with the Constitutional provisions and the amended Law should be extended for a period of at least one year.

(iii) that mixed Coordinating Bodies as prescribed in Article 173(3) of the Constitution should be set up forthwith, these Bodies should be vested (by agreement between us) with as much necessary power and authority as were possible, and, should experience show that these Bodies were working in a satisfactory manner, their power and authority should gradually be increased;

(iv) that the safeguards in the proposals of Messrs. Clerides and Tornaritis should be made applicable after necessary adaptations to the Coordinating Bodies.

4. It will be observed that there is not much difference between the proposals drafted by Messrs. Clerides and Tornaritis and the recommendations in (i) – (iv) above. In making these recommendations scrupulous care has been taken to see that no departure is made from the letter and the spirit of our Constitution. I hope, therefore, that Your Beatitude will see your way to accept these recommendations which I believe will be a progressive step towards the solution of one of our problems.

(Dr. F. Kutchuk)
Vice-President of the
Republic.

An extended meeting was held on Monday the 24th December at 10.00 a.m. in the morning at which in addition to the President of the Republic, the Vice-President of the Republic, the President of the House of Representatives and the President of the Turkish Communal Chamber, the Minister of Labour, Mr. Papadopoulos, the Minister of Commerce and Industry, Mr. Araouzos, and the Minister of Defence, Mr. Orek, were present. The Attorney-General was also present and the Under-Secretaries to the President and the Vice-President.

At that meeting the differences were examined between the proposals made by the President of the House of Representatives and the proposals contained in the letter addressed by the Vice-President of the Republic to the President of the 22nd December, 1962.

The Vice-President and his advisers first made the point that the proposals of the President of the House of Representatives could not be accepted. They pointed out, inter alia, that if accepted, by virtue of paragraph 4 of those proposals, it would not be possible to return to the status quo i.e. separate Municipalities, if at the end of the year the experiment failed. It was explained to the Vice-President and his advisers that the intention was that at the expiration of one year, if the experiment failed, both sides would be able to return to the position existing to-day and that, therefore, if paragraph 4 required redrafting there would be no objection of doing so. The Vice-President and his advisers maintain that in substance there was no great difference between the proposals of the President of the House of Representatives and the counter proposals of the Vice-President of the Republic. They stated that they had no objection to a Joint Committee being established with increased powers and subject to safeguards for the Turkish community, but that in their view the separate Municipalities existing to-day should not be abolished, but continue to operate.

The President of the Republic Archbishop Makarios pointed out that this would lead to more complications. If the proposal of the Vice-President was accepted i.e. to maintain a Greek Municipal Council, a Turkish Municipal Council and a Joint Committee, there would be complications of jurisdiction between all the three bodies and it would become more imperative to define areas of jurisdiction and thus geographical division of Municipalities would have to be considered again.

Finally the President of the Turkish Communal Chamber requested, by way of information, to know what fixed percentage of the revenue of the Joint Municipal Council would be set aside by Law to be spent in accordance with the wishes of the Turkish Members of the Council for the Turkish inhabitants.

In reply the President of the Republic made the following suggestion:

25% of the estimates of the Joint Committee would be set aside in Nicosia to be spent in the manner recommended by the Turkish members. 25% of the estimates of the Paphos Joint Committee would be reserved to be spent in accordance with the wishes of the Turkish members of that Committee. 16% for Famagusta, 14% for Limassol and 20% for Larnaca.

It was then agreed that the meeting would be adjourned until the afternoon in order to consider the proposal of the President of the House of Representatives in the light of the new information, particularly bearing in mind the declaration made by the President of the Republic that paragraph 4 of the said proposals could be amended so as not to preclude the possibility of returning to the position existing at that time should the experiment fail.

The next meeting took place on the same day at 4.30 in the afternoon and was attended by the same persons which attended the morning meeting. At that meeting the Attorney-General reduced to writing point by point the matters which were agreed upon and it will be observed that a further safeguard was requested by the Turkish side and granted, i.e. that the Controlling Officer for the amounts reserved in each town to be spent according to the wishes of the Turkish members of the respective Joint Councils, should be the Deputy Chairman of the Council who in accordance with the proposals would be Turkish.

The final draft of the matters agreed upon are set out herein below:

Present:
President of the Republic,
Vice-President of the Republic,
President of the House of Representatives,
President of the Turkish Communal Chamber,
Minister of Labour,
Minister of Commerce and Industry,
Minister of Defence,
Attorney-General,
Under-Secretaries to President and Vice-President.

1. The Municipal Corporation Law (Cap.240) will be re-enacted subject to the necessary drafting amendments.

Provided that such Law in its application to the towns of Nicosia, Limassol, Famagusta, Larnaca and Paphos shall be subject to the following modification, that is to say instead of the existing municipal councils in each such towns there will be a Joint Committee composed as in paragraph 2 hereof provided to perform all the functions performed by a council of a municipal corporation under the provisions of the aforecited Law subject to the modification provided in paragraph 3 hereof.

2. (1) The members of the Joint Committee will be appointed by the President and the Vice-President of the Republic.

(2) Each Joint Committee shall consist of Greek and Turkish members proportionately to the Greek and Turkish population of each town:

Provided that the number of the Turkish members shall not be less than two and not more than five:

Provided further that the total number of the Committee in respect of each town shall be fixed by the President and the Vice-President of the Republic.

(3) There shall be a Chairman of the Joint Committee who will be a Greek and Vice-Chairman of the Committee who will be a Turk to be appointed by the President and the Vice-President of the Republic. Such Chairman and Vice-Chairman shall perform the functions performed by the Mayor and Deputy Mayor, respectively, under the provisions of the aforecited Law:

Provided that the Vice-Chairman shall be the Controlling Officer with regard to the disposal of the funds appropriated in the estimates for projects approved by the Committee on the recommendation of its Turkish members.

3. The Joint Committee in performing its functions under the aforecited Law shall—

(a) in the estimates prepared by the Joint Committee of each town an appropriate percentage (fixed by Law) of the revenue of such town shall be disposed of in the manner recommended by the Turkish members of the Joint Committee;

(b) if in disposing such part of the estimates as provided in the immediately preceding sub-paragraph it will become necessary to interfere with property belonging to, or held by, a Greek the Greek members of the Committee shall not exercise their voting rights in such a way as to prevent the implementation of the proposed scheme;

(c) the assets and liabilities of such municipal council in each of the aforesaid towns as on the 1st day of December, 1962, shall devolve on, and be undertaken by, the Joint Committee of the town concerned:

Provided that disposing such assets or in satisfying such liabilities a separate account shall be kept by the Joint Committee;

(d) the regular personnel of each council in each of the aforecited towns serving on the 1st December, 1962, will be retained for services under the Joint Committee.

4. The modifications set out in paragraphs 2 and 3 hereof shall continue to be in force until the 31st December, 1963.''

Several details remained to be worked out and in view of the fact that the meeting had lasted for a considerable time it was agreed to adjourn and meet again on the 26th December at 10.00 a.m. in the morning. A joint communiqué was drafted in the presence of all, was agreed upon and issued to the press which was as follows:

Present:
President of the Republic,
Vice-President of the Republic,
President of the House of Representatives,
President of the Turkish Communal Chamber,
Minister of Labour,
Minister of Commerce and Industry,
Minister of Defence,
Attorney-General,
Under-Secretaries to President and Vice-President.

"Common ground was found for eventual agreement on the subject.
As it will be necessary to work out several details, a new meeting has been arranged for Wednesday next."

On Wednesday the 26th December, 1962, the meeting took place and at the commencement of that meeting the Vice-President of the Republic informed the President Archbishop Makarios that he wished to make a statement. He then read the following statement:

"Since we met to discuss the question of municipalities I have been very seriously considering the effect on the Turkish public opinion of the proposal to establish a Joint Committee with power to run municipal affairs in the 5 largest towns. During the course of our lengthy discussions I noted that Your Beatitude's intention is to do away with *completely* the present Greek and Turkish Municipal Councils. I and my advisers, on the other hand, have tried hard to reconcile as far as possible your proposals with those embodied in my letter of the 22nd December, 1962, which made it abundantly clear that I would agree to the establishment of a Joint Committee with increased powers if necessary provided the present Turkish Municipal Councils were to remain in existence in one form or another.

During the preparation of the communiqué which was issued after our last meeting, it became evident that there was still an unbridged gap in the minds of both sides as to the nature of the Joint Committee, the powers to be conferred upon such a Committee and as to the future of the present Greek and Turkish Municipal Councils. In order that we may not waste more time I thought it advisable to clarify our respective positions in respect of this issue at the outset of to-day's meeting. Though it is my ardent wish to try and find a solution satisfactory to both sides on this issue, I feel that I must state frankly that it is impossible for me to agree at this stage to the establishment of a Joint Committee which would absorb or replace *completely* the existing Greek and Turkish Municipal Councils. However, I am prepared to agree, for a trial period, to the establishment of such a Joint Committee as *would not affect* the corporate nature of the existing Municipal Councils.

(Dr. F. Kutchuk)"

It will be seen from the statement of the Vice-President that at the meeting of Wednesday the 26th December, 1962, he reverted to the position contained in his letter of the 22nd December, 1962, addressed to the President and that, therefore, all the items which were agreed upon at the meeting of Monday the 24th December in the afternoon no longer were acceptable to the Turkish side. The President of the Republic maintained at that meeting the position that the matters which were agreed upon at the meeting of Monday the 24th December, 1962, could provide the basis of a solution and that since it was agreed that this period should be for a year, it would be to the interest of all concerned if further efforts were made towards that direction. He stated that if the Turkish side was prepared to accept the agreed principles an extension of the Municipality Law could be given in order to give time for a Committee to draft a law incorporating the provisions agreed upon and filling in other necessary details.

The Vice-President, however, stressed the point that responsibility on this matter under the Constitution in so far as the Turkish community was concerned was placed on him and not on his advisers and that he could not agree to a Joint Committee being set up to administer the Municipalities, unless the existing Greek and Turkish Municipal Councils were also maintained and their functions and jurisdictions defined. Thus ended the negotiations without agreement being reached.

The Turkish Members of the House of Representatives introduced a bill into the House providing for the prolongation of the existing Municipalities for a period of one year as from the 1st January, 1963. Under the Constitution a Law relating to Municipalities requires, in order to be enacted into Law, to be passed by a separate majority of the Greek and Turkish Members. The Bill submitted to the House of Representatives by the Turkish Members failed to be enacted into Law owing to the fact that although it obtained the separate majority of the Turkish Members (all the 15 Turkish Members voted for it) it did not obtain the separate majority of the Greek Members. (All the Greek Members voted against it). The Greek views and Turkish views on the Bill appear from the report of the Parliamentary Committee of Interior to which the Bill was referred and which is as follows:

"Mr. Halit Ali Riza's statement on behalf of the Turkish Representatives who submitted the Bill:
"We have submitted this bill for the following reasons:
(1) We are determined to uphold the Constitutional order with all lawful means at our disposal;
(2) The Constitution provides and envisages the existence of municipalities in the towns of the Republic including the five largest mentioned in the Constitution;
(3) Although we believe that, law or no law, the Turkish municipalities are established and exist in the five largest towns of the Republic i.e., Nicosia, Famagusta, Larnaca, Limassol, and Paphos, under para. 1 of Article 173 of the Constitution, we take into consideration the interests of both of the peoples of the Republic and wish to prevent the threat-

ened destruction even partly of the local government which is so essential for a democratic regime;

(4) At every extension of the Municipal Corporations Laws we expressed our desire and hope that the new Municipal Corporations Laws envisaged by the Constitution should be prepared and submitted to the House with no more delay. We note with appreciation that the Committee of Interior and the House also had expressed such desire and hope. We believe that for the preparation of such laws there was no absolute need for H.E. the President and H.E. the Vice-President of the Republic to come to an agreement in fixing the limits of the Turkish and Greek Municipalities in each of the such five towns under Article 177 of the Constitution, although such agreement would have been most welcome. This time, we find to our great disappointment for sake of so much needed good relations between the two Communities and the so much respect for the Constitutional order that not only the said required new legislation was not submitted to the House but also no bill has been submitted by the Minister of Interior for the extension of the existing Municipal Corporations Laws.

(5) We noted with pleasure and satisfaction that at long last H.E. the President and H.E. the Vice-President of the Republic had recently come together to find a solution to the municipalities issue. Although it has been a disappointment to learn from their respective statements that they could not reach an agreement, and we don't want to make any comment on the matter, as the reasons of their disagreement are clearly seen from such statements, yet no reasonable person would, under the circumstances, expect a satisfactory solution or agreement between the two in the very short period of time given to the discussions between them which started only about ten days before the date on which the existing Municipal Corporations Laws were due to expire. We believe that, taking into consideration the complexity of the question not only politically but also technically, much more time should be allowed for such discussions to continue, which we hope and expect would be with an open mind and elasticity within the framework and provisions of the Constitution and not based on fixed, unchangeable ideas and assumptions;

(6) Therefore in short with every good will and intention, in order to—

    (a) prevent further deterioration of the relations between the two Communities to be caused by any attempted action due to non-existence of any law on municipalities passed by the House;

    (b) uphold the Constitutional order which is the only hope of survival of the Republic; and

    (c) protect the interests of all concerned in the Republic,

we have submitted this bill of which the effect, if approved, by the House, would be to prolong the operation of the existing Municipal Corporations Laws for a certain period of time; we suggest a year but will accept any reasonable period.

We hope that, in spite of the adverse statement by H.E. the President of the Republic on 29th December, 1962, upon which we don't here wish to make any comment, good will and good sense would prevail and our colleagues, the Greek Representatives will support this bill.

The Greek Members, having carefully heard the statement of Mr. Halit Ali Riza, state:
(1) They fully agree with the views of the President of the Republic, Archbishop Makarios, that geographical partition is inapplicable in practice.
(2) They reject as legally untenable the allegation that, law or no law by the House, it would be possible to have legal Greek and Turkish municipalities.

    The legislative power for the purpose of setting up of municipalities is vested solely in the House of Representatives.
(3) Events have shown that despite the eight extensions of the municipal laws and despite the repeatedly expressed desire of the Home Affairs Committee and of the House itself for a satisfactory solution on the matter serving the interests of the Cypriot people as a whole, it has become clear from the recent statements of the President and the Vice-President that there is no common basis for understanding on account of the insistence of the Turkish leadership upon geographical partition which, as already stated, is inapplicable in practice. The suggestions made by the Vice-President are tantamount to virtual geographical partition.
(4) We believe that further extension of the Municipal Laws would serve no useful purpose but, on the contrary, would lead to perpetuation of a dangerous suspense which would in the end prove a permanent obstacle to finding a reasonable solution.
(5) Therefore, in a spirit of good will and in order to prevent deterioration of relations between the two communities, we consider the suggestions made by the President of the Republic for joint committees to administer municipal affairs, with full legal safeguards for the interests of the Turkish community, as a right course, leading to unification of the municipalities and the adoption of genuine institutions of local government."

FINAL NOTE:

It is to be regretted that the Vice-President of the Republic did not accept the proposals made which had several advantages.
(a) The creation of Joint Committees consisting of Greeks and Turks for a period of one year provided an experiment which would have clearly shown that it was practicable and possible for the existence of unified Municipalities in the five main towns of Cyprus.

(b) It would have reduced financial expenditure on both communities with regard to the financial burden of maintaining separate Municipalities.

(c) It avoided the thorny problem of geographical division which has been, as already stated, the stumbling block in finding a solution to the question of the Municipal administration of the five main towns.

(d) It offered the Turkish side full guarantees and safeguards.

(e) It had considerable financial advantages.

With regard to the financial advantages the position is as follows:

NICOSIA: The population of the town of Nicosia is as follows:

Greeks	30,943
Turks	14,686
Revenue from the Greek population excluding grants in aid or loans	£200,840
Revenue from the Turkish population excluding grants in aid or loans	£ 37,733
Joint revenue from Greeks and Turks	£238,573
Contribution to the joint revenue by the Greeks	84%
Contribution to the joint revenue by the Turks	16%

If the proposals for joint administration of the Municipal affairs of the town of Nicosia were accepted by the Turkish side they have been offered 25% of the total revenue to be spent in accordance with the recommendations of the Turkish Members of the Joint Committee for the Turkish inhabitants despite the fact that their contribution is 16%.

FAMAGUSTA:

Greek population	28,654
Turkish population	6,120
Revenue from Greek population	£166,080
Revenue from Turkish population	£ 11,428
Joint revenue	£177,508
Greek contribution to the joint revenue	93 1/2 %
Turkish contribution to the joint revenue	6 1/2 %

The Turks were offered under joint administration 16% of the joint revenue of the town of Famagusta despite the fact that their contribution is only 6 1/2 %.

LARNACA:

Greek population	21,874
Turkish population	4,058
Revenue from Greek population	£67,934
Revenue from Turkish population	£ 4,687
Joint revenue	£72,621
Greek contribution to the joint revenue	93 1/2 %
Turkish contribution to the joint revenue	6 1/2 %

The Turks under the proposals for joint administration were offered 20% of the joint revenue despite the fact that their contribution is only 6 1/2%.

LIMASSOL:

Greek population	37,725
Turkish population	6,115
Revenue from Greek population	£194,401
Revenue from Turkish population	£ 8,660
Joint revenue	£205,461
i.e. Greek contribution to the joint revenue	94 1/2 %
Turkish contribution to the joint revenue	5 1/2 %

The Turks under the proposals for joint administration were offered 14% of the joint revenue despite the fact that their contribution is 5 1/2 %.

PAPHOS:

Greek population	6,232
Turkish population	2,851
Revenue from Greek population	£36,652
Revenue from Turkish population	£ 7,360
Joint revenue	£46,012
Greek contribution to the joint revenue	80%
Turkish contribution to the joint revenue	20%

The Turks under the proposals for the joint administration were offered 25% of the joint revenue despite the fact that their contribution to the joint revenue was only 20%.

Detailed analysis of the above figures is shown in Appendices "I" and "J" inclusive.

APPENDIX "A"

Communiqué Issued by the President of the Republic, Archbishop Makarios, on the 19th March, 1962, Containing the Outline of His Proposals to the Vice-President Regarding the Solution of the Municipal Problem

"His Beatitude at today's meeting with the Vice-President of the Republic Dr. Kutchuk stated his views regarding the separation of municipalities in the five main towns, as is provided for in the relevant Constitutional provision.

In His Beatitude's view, the geographical separation of the municipalities, irrespective of its financial repercussions, is difficult to materialize without affecting the interests of the Greek and Turkish citizens. His Beatitude suggested the maintenance of a united municipal authority and the proportional representation of Greeks and Turks thereon in accordance with the proportion of the population in each town.

With a view to safeguarding the rights of the Turkish citizens, His Beatitude suggested that—

1. The staff to be engaged and employed with the municipal authorities be in proportion to the Greek and Turkish population in each town.
2. A percentage of the annual budget of each municipality, to be fixed in advance, be made available for the needs of the Turkish citizens in a way to be suggested by the Turkish members of the Municipal Council.
3. In each of the five towns where the Mayor is a Greek the Deputy Mayor shall be a Turk, if this is justified by the proportion of the Turkish population."

APPENDIX "B"

Proposed Principles Which Will Be Used In Fixing the Limits of the Greek
and Turkish Municipalities in the Five Largest Towns

The frontage of all property abutting on a street will be measured and
if the total length of the frontage of the property belonging to the members of
the Greek Community in that street is greater, then that street will be included
in the sector of the Greek municipality.

Provided, however, that if there is no access to such a street other than
through streets falling within the sector of the Turkish municipality such a
street will not be included in the region of the Greek municipality but will be
deemed to have fallen within the sector of the Turkish municipality.

Provided that for the purpose of the above proviso a street will not be
deemed to have no access if there is access to it through a ring or trunk road
(and, in the case of Nicosia, also through encircling streets just above the
moats) irrespective of whether such a road is within the Greek or Turkish sector.

Provided also that the areas within the ports and customs compounds
in Famagusta, Limassol, Larnaca and Paphos will not be included in the regions of any of the two municipalities. The municipal services in these compounds will be carried out jointly under the direction of the co-ordinating body
envisaged in para.3 of Article 173 of the Constitution.

Note: 1. The same principles will apply in the case of a street where the
total length of the frontage of the property belonging to members of the Turkish community is greater.

2. In taking the measurements of the frontage, the properties belonging to Government, semi-Government institutions and non-
Cypriot persons or institutions will be disregarded.

3. The situation with regard to streets where the difference in the
length of the frontage of the properties belonging to persons of
each community is very small, will be subject to review by the
President and the Vice-President once every two years: Provided that the President and the Vice-President may at their
discretion allocate the streets in question partly to the Greek
and partly to the Turkish municipality.

APPENDIX "C"

Draft Prepared by the President of the House of Representatives and the Attorney-General Containing the Proposals of the President of the House of Representatives Regarding the Solution of the Problem of the Municipalities

1. The Municipal Corporation Law (Cap.240) will be re-enacted subject to the necessary drafting amendments.

Provided that such Law in its application to the towns of Nicosia, Limassol, Famagusta, Larnaca and Paphos shall be subject to the following modification, that is to say instead of the existing municipal councils in each such town there will be a Joint Committee composed as in paragraph 2 hereof provided to perform all the functions performed by a council of a municipal corporation under the provisions of the aforecited Law subject to the modification provided in paragraph 3 hereof.

2. (1) The members of the Joint Committee will be appointed by the President and the Vice-President of the Republic.

(2) Each Joint Committee shall consist of Greek and Turkish members proportionately to the Greek and Turkish population of each town:

Provided that the number of the Turkish members shall not be less than two and not more than five;

Provided further that the total number of the Committee in respect of each town shall be fixed by the President and the Vice-President of the Republic.

(3) There shall be a Chairman of the Joint Committee who will be a Greek and Vice-Chairman of the Committee who will be a Turk to be appointed by the President and the Vice-President of the Republic. Such Chairman and Vice-Chairman shall perform the functions performed by the Mayor and Deputy Mayor, respectively, under the provisions of the aforecited Law:

Provided that the Vice-Chairman shall be the Controlling Officer with regard to the disposal of the funds appropriated in the estimates for projects approved by the Committee on the recommendation of its Turkish members.

3. The Joint Committee in performing its functions under the aforecited Law shall—

    (a) in the estimates prepared by the Joint Committee of each town an appropriate percentage (fixed by Law) of the revenue of such town shall be disposed of in the manner recommended by the Turkish members of the Joint Committee;

    (b) if in disposing such part of the estimates as provided in the immediately preceding sub-paragraph it will become necessary to interfere with property belonging to, or held by, a Greek the Greek members of the Committee shall not exercise their voting rights in such a way as to prevent the implementation of the proposed scheme;

    (c) the assets and liabilities of such municipal council in each of the aforesaid towns as on the 1st day of December, 1962, shall devolve on, and be undertaken by, the Joint Committee of the town concerned:

Provided that disposing such assets or in satisfying such liabilities a separate account shall be kept by the Joint Committee;
(d) the regular personnel of each council in each of the aforecited towns serving on the 1st December, 1962, will be retained for services under the Joint Committee.

4. The modifications set out in paragraphs 2 and 3 hereof shall continue to be in force until the 31st December, 1963, whereupon the whole situation shall be reviewed by the President and the Vice-President of the Republic.

22nd December, 1962.

APPENDIX "D"

Reply of the Vice-President of the Republic Containing Turkish Comments on
the Proposal of the President of the House of Representatives for the Solution
of the Problem of Municipalities

5/59

VICE-PRESIDENCY.
22nd December, 1962.

Your Beatitude,

Municipalities

The proposals drafted by Messrs. Clerides and Tornaritis have been
very carefully and exhaustively considered to-day at a general meeting attended
by the Turkish Ministers, the Turkish members of the House of Representatives, the President and members of the Executive Committee of the Turkish
Communal Chamber and certain other Turkish leaders.

2. Before arriving at a conclusion I asked everybody present to bear in
mind that at our meeting on Thursday last I was given to understand—

(a) that you were determined not to agree to any geographical separation of the municipalities;

(b) that you would not allow any Greek inhabitant or any Greek property, however few and small, to come under the jurisdiction of a
Turkish municipality or vice versa;

(c) that you were not prepared to agree to the extension of the Municipal Laws beyond the 31st December, 1962, nor would you accept separation along the limits of the areas where Greek and
Turkish municipalities now function; and

(d) that you were contemplating to direct the Council of Ministers to
fix new boundary lines for each town area and to make arrangements for the performance of municipal services by Government
Departments or by ad hoc bodies.

3. Bearing in mind—

(a) the above assertions made by the President of the Republic;

(b) the fact that certain vital provisions of the Constitution with regard
to municipalities and other matters affecting the interests of the
Turkish Community have not yet been implemented;

(c) the constitutionality and/or legality of the proposals drafted by
Messrs. Clerides and Tornaritis;

(d) the shortness of time which did not allow Turkish leaders to assess
the repercussions of the new proposals on the public opinion; and

(e) the fact that, mainly because of the existence of a group in the
Greek community persistently striving for the abrogation of the
Agreements and the Constitution and the treatment accorded to

Turks in certain affairs, such as foreign affairs, internal security and defence matters, the full confidence of Turks has not yet been won, those present at the meeting came to the following unanimous conclusions:

(1) that the time was yet premature either for examining the question whether or not the separation of municipalities should continue, or for considering any change in our Constitution;

(2) that the proposals drafted by Messrs. Clerides and Tornaritis envisaged departure from, or alteration of, the Constitutional provisions;

(3) that once joined it would be unconstitutional and illegal to separate again the municipalities should the proposed experiment fail;

(4) that counter proposals to the following effect should be made—

(i) that separate Greek and Turkish municipalities should continue to function for services prescribed in the Constitution;

(ii) that the Municipal Law should be so amended as to be consistent with the Constitutional provisions and the amended Law should be extended for a period of at least one year.

(iii) that mixed Coordinating Bodies as prescribed in Article 173(3) of the Constitution should be set up forthwith, these Bodies should be vested (by agreement between us) with as much necessary power and authority as were possible, and, should experience show that these Bodies were working in a satisfactory manner, their power and authority should gradually be increased;

(iv) that the safeguards in the proposals of Messrs. Clerides and Tornaritis should be made applicable after necessary adaptations to the Coordinating Bodies.

4. It will be observed that there is not much difference between the proposals drafted by Messrs. Clerides and Tornaritis and the recommendations in (i) – (iv) above. In making these recommendations scrupulous care has been taken to see that no departure is made from the letter and the spirit of our Constitution. I hope, therefore, that Your Beatitude will see your way to accept these recommendations which I believe will be a progressive step towards the solution of one of our problems.

(Dr. F. Kutchuk)
Vice-President of the
Republic.

Copy to: G. Clerides Esq., President of the House of Representatives,
C. Tornaritis, Esq., Attorney-General of the Republic.

APPENDIX "E"

Points Agreed Upon at the Meeting of Monday the
24th December 1962 at 3 p.m.

Present:
President of the Republic,
Vice-President of the Republic,
President of the House of Representatives,
President of the Turkish Communal Chamber,
Minister of Labour,
Minister of Defence,
Attorney-General,
Under-Secretaries to President and Vice-President.

1. The Municipal Corporation Law (Cap.240) will be re-enacted subject to the necessary drafting amendments.

Provided that such Law in its application to the towns of Nicosia, Limassol, Famagusta, Larnaca and Paphos shall be subject to the following modification, that is to say instead of the existing municipal councils in each such towns there will be a Joint Committee composed as in paragraph 2 hereof provided to perform all the functions performed by a council of a municipal corporation under the provisions of the aforecited Law subject to the modification provided in paragraph 3 hereof.

2. (1) The members of the Joint Committee will be appointed by the President and the Vice-President of the Republic.

(2) Each Joint Committee shall consist of Greek and Turkish members proportionately to the Greek and Turkish population of each town:

Provided that the number of the Turkish members shall not be less than two and not more than five:

Provided further that the total number of the Committee in respect of each town shall be fixed by the President and the Vice-President of the Republic.

(3) There shall be a Chairman of the Joint Committee who will be a Greek and Vice-Chairman of the Committee who will be a Turk to be appointed by the President and the Vice-President of the Republic. Such Chairman and Vice-Chairman shall perform the functions performed by the Mayor and Deputy Mayor, respectively, under the provisions of the aforecited Law:

Provided that the Vice-Chairman shall be the Controlling Officer with regard to the disposal of the funds appropriated in the estimates for projects approved by the Committee on the recommendation of its Turkish members.

3. The Joint Committee in performing its functions under the aforecited Law shall—

(a) in the estimates prepared by the Joint Committee of each town an appropriate percentage (fixed by Law) of the revenue of such town shall be disposed of in the manner recommended by the Turkish members of the Joint Committee;

(b) if in disposing such part of the estimates as provided in the immediately preceding sub-paragraph it will become necessary to interfere with property belonging to, or held by, a Greek the Greek
members of the Committee shall not exercise their voting rights in
such a way as to prevent the implementation of the proposed
scheme;

(c) the assets and liabilities of such municipal council in each of the
aforesaid towns as on the 1st day of December, 1962, shall devolve
on, and be undertaken by, the Joint Committee of the town concerned:

    Provided that disposing such assets or in satisfying such li-
abilities a separate account shall be kept by the Joint Committee;

(d) the regular personnel of each council in each of the aforecited
towns serving on the 1st December, 1962, will be retained for
services under the Joint Committee.

4. The modifications set out in paragraphs 2 and 3 hereof shall continue to be in force until the 31st December, 1963.

APPENDIX "F"

Joint Communiqué Issued by the President and the Vice-President of the Republic at the Afternoon Meeting of Monday the 24th December, 1962

Present:
President: President of the Republic,
Vice-President of the Republic,
President of the House of Representatives,
President of the Turkish Communal Chamber,
Minister of Labour,
Minister of Defence,
Attorney-General,
Under-Secretaries to President and Vice President.

"Common ground was found for eventual agreement on the subject.
As it will be necessary to work out several details, a new meeting has been arranged for Wednesday next."

APPENDIX "G"

Statement of the Vice-President of the Republic Made at the Meeting of
Wednesday, the 26th of December, 1962

Since we met to discuss the question of municipalities I have been very
seriously considering the effect on the Turkish public opinion of the proposal
to establish a Joint Committee with power to run municipal affairs in the five
largest towns. During the course of our lengthy discussions I noticed that Your
Beatitude's intention is to do away with *completely* the present Greek and
Turkish Municipal Councils. I and my advisers, on the other hand, have tried
hard to reconcile as far as possible your proposals with those embodied in my
letter of the 22nd December, 1962, which made it abundantly clear that I
would agree to the establishment of a Joint Committee with increased powers
if necessary provided the present Turkish Municipal Councils were to remain
in existence in one form or another.

During the preparation of the communiqué which was issued after our
last meeting, it became evident that there was still an unbridged gap in the
minds of both sides as to the nature of the Joint Committee, the powers to be
conferred upon such a Committee and as to the future of the present Greek
and Turkish Municipal Councils. In order that we may not waste more time I
thought it advisable to clarify our respective positions in respect of this issue at
the outset of to-day's meeting. Though it is my ardent wish to try and find a
solution satisfactory to both sides on this issue, I feel that I must state frankly
that it is impossible for me to agree at this stage to the establishment of a Joint
Committee which would absorb or replace *completely* the existing Greek and
Turkish Municipal Councils. However, I am prepared to agree, for a trial period, to the establishment of such a Joint Committee as *would not affect* the
corporate nature of the existing Municipal Councils.

(Dr. F. Kutchuk)

Nicosia,
26th December, 1962.

Report of the Committee of Interior on the Bill Submitted by the Turkish
Members for Further Extension of the Municipal Laws

Mr. Halit Ali Riza's statement on behalf of the Turkish Representatives
who submitted the Bill:
"We have submitted this bill for the following reasons:
  (1) We are determined to uphold the Constitutional order with all lawful
      means at our disposal;
  (2) The Constitution provides and envisages the existence of municipalities
      in the towns of the Republic including the five largest mentioned in the
      Constitution;
  (3) Although we believe that, law or no law, the Turkish municipalities are
      established and exist in the five largest towns of the Republic i.e.,
      Nicosia, Famagusta, Larnaca, Limassol, and Paphos, under para. 1 of
      Article 173 of the Constitution, we take into consideration the interests
      of both of the peoples of the Republic and wish to prevent the threat-
      ened destruction even partly of the local government which is so essen-
      tial for a democratic regime;
  (4) At every extension of the Municipal Corporations Laws we expressed
      our desire and hope that the new Municipal Corporations Laws envis-
      aged by the Constitution should be prepared and submitted to the
      House with no more delay. We note with appreciation that the Com-
      mittee of Interior and the House also had expressed such desire and
      hope. We believe that for the preparation of such laws there was no
      absolute need for H.E. the President and H.E. the Vice-President of
      the Republic to come to an agreement in fixing the limits of the
      Turkish and Greek Municipalities in each of the such five towns under
      Article 177 of the Constitution, although such agreement would have
      been most welcome. This time, we find to our great disappointment
      for sake of so much needed good relations between the two Com-
      munities and the so much respect for the Constitutional order that not
      only the said required new legislation was not submitted to the House
      but also no bill has been submitted by the Minister of Interior for the
      extension of the existing Municipal Corporations Laws.
  (5) We noted with pleasure and satisfaction that at long last H.E. the
      President and H.E. the Vice-President of the Republic had recently
      come together to find a solution to the municipalities issue. Although
      it has been a disappointment to learn from their respective statements
      that they could not reach an agreement, and we don't want to make any
      comment on the matter, as the reasons of their disagreement are
      clearly seen from such statements, yet no reasonable person would,
      under the circumstances, expect a satisfactory solution or agreement
      between the two in the very short period of time given to the
      discussions between them which started only about ten days before the
      date on which the existing Municipal Corporations Laws were due to
      expire. We believe that, taking into consideration the complexity of the

question not only politically but also technically, much more time should be allowed for such discussions to continue, which we hope and expect would be with an open mind and elasticity within the framework and provisions of the Constitution and not based on fixed, unchangeable ideas and assumptions;

(6) Therefore in short with every good will and intention, in order to—

   (a) prevent further deterioration of the relations between the two Communities to be caused by any attempted action due to non-existence of any law on municipalities passed by the House;

   (b) uphold the Constitutional order which is the only hope of survival of the Republic; and

   (c) protect the interests of all concerned in the Republic,

we have submitted this bill of which the effect, if approved, by the House, would be to prolong the operation of the existing Municipal Corporations Laws for a certain period of time; we suggest a year but will accept any reasonable period.

We hope that, in spite of the adverse statement by H.E. the President of the Republic on 29th December, 1962, upon which we don't here wish to make any comment, good will and good sense would prevail and our colleagues, the Greek Representatives will support this bill.

The Greek Members, having carefully heard the statement of Mr. Halit Ali Riza, state:

(1) They fully agree with the views of the President of the Republic, Archbishop Makarios, that geographical partition is inapplicable in practice.

(2) They reject as legally untenable the allegation that, law or no law by the House, it would be possible to have legal Greek and Turkish municipalities.

   The legislative power for the purpose of setting up of municipalities is vested solely in the House of Representatives.

(3) Events have shown that despite the eight extensions of the municipal laws and despite the repeatedly expressed desire of the Home Affairs Committee and of the House itself for a satisfactory solution on the matter serving the interests of the Cypriot people as a whole, it has become clear from the recent statements of the President and the Vice-President that there is no common basis for understanding on account of the insistence of the Turkish leadership upon geographical partition which, as already stated, is inapplicable in practice. The suggestions made by the Vice-President are tantamount to virtual geographical partition.

(4) We believe that further extension of the Municipal Laws would serve no useful purpose but, on the contrary, would lead to perpetuation of a dangerous suspense which would in the end prove a permanent obstacle to finding a reasonable solution.

(5) Therefore, in a spirit of good will and in order to prevent deterioration of relations between the two communities, we consider the suggestions made by the President of the Republic for joint committees to administer municipal affairs, with full legal safeguards for the interests of the Turkish community, as a right course, leading to unification of the municipalities and the adoption of genuine institutions of local government.

1962 Municipalities Budgets

	Greek Municipalities			Turkish Municipalities			
Town	Greek population	Revenue, 1962 excluding grants-in-aid or loans	Expenditure, 1962 excluding expenditure from loans	Turkish population	Revenue, 1962 excluding grants-in-aid or loans	Expenditure, 1962 excluding expenditure from loans	Remarks
Nicosia	30,943	£ 200,840	£ 198,371	14,686	£ 37,733	£ 54,510	The revenue of the Turkish Municipality of Nicosia includes the town rates of £10,000 for 1962.
Famagusta	28,654	166,080	165,923	6,120	11,428	11,428	The revenue of this Turkish Municipality includes the town rates for 1962 amounting to £3,000.
Larnaca	21,874	67,934	65,419	4,058	4,687	10,169	The revenue of this Turkish Municipality includes the town rates for 1962 estimated at £1,500.
Limassol	37,725	194,401	185,604	6,115	8,660	12,182	The revenue of the Turkish Municipality of Limassol does *not* include the town rates of about £2,400 for 1962.
Paphos	6,232	36,652	36,300	2,851	7,360	7,070	The revenue of the Turkish Municipality of Paphos does *not* include the town rates of about £2,000 for 1962.

Notes:

(1) The Greek population includes the population of other Christian Denominations, e.g. Armenians, Roman Catholics, etc..

(2) The revenues in the case of both the Greek and Turkish Municipalities do not include credit balances brought forward from 1961.

Grants made by the Turkish Communal Chamber in 1962 to Turkish Municipalities to enable them to balance their budgets:

Nicosia Turkish Municipality £16,777
Limassol   "   "   £ 3,600
Larnaca   "   "   £ 2,730
Famagusta and Paphos: No grants made.

Contribution and Expenditure Statement (in %)

Town	Total revenue of Greek and Turkish Municipalities in 1962	Percentage contribution by each Municipality		Total expenditure of Greek and Turkish Municipalities in 1962	Percentage of expenditure by each Municipality	
		Greek	Turkish		Greek	Turkish
Nicosia	£238,573	84 %	16 %	£252,881	78 1/2 %	21 1/2 %
Famagusta	£177,508	93 1/2 %	6 1/2 %	£177,351	93 1/2 %	6 1/2 %
Larnaca	£ 72,621	93 1/2 %	6 1/2 %	£ 75,588	86 1/2 %	13 1/2 %
Limassol	£205,461	94 1/2 %	5 1/2 %	£197,786	93 1/3 %	6 2/3 %
Paphos	£ 46,012	80 %	20 %	£ 43,370	83 2/3 %	16 1/3 %

Note: In computing the revenues of the Turkish Municipalities of Limassol and Paphos account has been
taken of their income from town rates which in
respect of 1962 was estimated to be as follows:

Limassol	£2,400
Paphos	£2,000

The town rates of the other Turkish Municipalities
had already been included in their revenues.
These were as follows:

Nicosia	£10,000
Famagusta	£ 3,000
Larnaca	£ 1,500

APPENDIX 54

Record of Meeting in London between Sir Arthur Clark, Director of Information Services and Cultural Relations, and Stella Soulioti, Cyprus Minister of Justice, 6 July 1964

The meeting had been arranged at the request of Sir Arthur Clark.

2. Sir Arthur explained the general arrangements for the Commonwealth Prime Ministers' Conference. He said that, as far as he knew, nobody was going to raise the Cyprus question at the Conference. The Turks had apparently approached the Pakistani Delegation with a view to their raising the Cyprus question; it appeared, however, that the Pakistanis were not keen to take the initiative, but had promised to support the "Moslem" view if the matter did arise. Sir Arthur said that if the Cyprus question were raised, the position of the United Kingdom Government would be that the matter was before the United Nations and it was hoped that it would be settled satisfactorily.

3. Sir Arthur thought that Canada wished to discuss the peace-keeping force in Cyprus, and he considered it might be a good idea if Mr. Kyprianou, on meeting the Canadian Prime Minister, might say that he was at the latter's disposal if there were anything he wished to discuss.

4. With regard to the question of Southern Rhodesia, Sir Arthur said that Britain was keen that the question should not be brought up before the week-end, as it was hoped that talks at Chequers might help to soften the various attitudes. On the substance of the problem, the United Kingdom Government would probably give some sort of undertaking that it would not support independence unless there was fair African representation.

5. The conversation then turned on the Cyprus problem generally. The following points emerged:
   (a) That the United Kingdom Government is still worried about the anti-British feeling on Cyprus. The reasons which had led to this feeling were repeated by Mrs. Soulioti as they had been previously stated to Mr. Duncan Sandys (record of meeting between Mr. Sandys and Mrs. Soulioti on 30th May, 1964).
   (b) The British still favour the solution of an independent Cyprus with a democratic constitution, the British Bases being possibly converted into NATO Bases. Britain would certainly not oppose ENOSIS if such a solution were agreed. The question of "consideration" to Turkey was an element to be borne in mind; some territorial grant would possibly be necessary. Alternatively, if the Bases were turned into NATO Bases, this might give a feeling of security to Turkey and the Turkish Cypriots and might be sufficient "consideration."

(c) Sir Arthur said that those who now advocated Enosis, mentioning specifically the Americans, were in favour of Cyprus becoming just a province of Greece, not a "self-governing" party of Greece, as they (the Americans) considered that only thus would the Greek security forces be able to deal with communistic activity effectively.

(d) The British wonder what the attitude of President Makarios and the Cyprus Government would be if the question of Enosis were put now. Since the position taken by the Cyprus Government was the achievement of full independence with a democratic constitution, would the President and the Government support a movement for Enosis *prior* to the achievement of such full independence. It was pointed out to Sir Arthur that it was an essential element in the Government's position that the people of Cyprus should be able to exercise their will freely and determine their own future.

(e) A resettlement scheme under the United Nations auspices for those Turks who wished to leave Cyprus would probably be an essential ingredient to any solution. Sir Arthur did not think that there would be any considerable movement of Turks to Turkey, as only the political and T.M.T. leaders would wish to go.

(f) Sir Arthur thought that if the present Turkish leadership resigned, things would be made easier as the more moderate elements might then come to the fore. He did not think the more extremist elements would, on the contrary, then assert themselves, as there was dissatisfaction amongst the Turks with the policies so far followed. Nor would Ankara be able to do very much about such a turn of events, even if it did not like it. He thought that there were some elements amongst the Turks, apart from Dr. Ihsan Ali, who still desired co-existence and were dissatisfied with the Turkish leadership, and that such moderates had manifested themselves before he had left Cyprus.

(g) In answer to a question as to why Britain had let Cyprus down by not carrying through its promise of support to the establishment of a fully independent State with majority rule, Sir Arthur just said that a peaceful solution had then been contemplated. He could not explain why the December events should have changed Britain's attitude, beyond saying that the magnitude of the bloodshed had been a shock.

It appears that the British are convinced that it had been the intention of some Greeks (not the Cyprus Government as such) to impose their will on the Turks by force of arms. They are also convinced that the Turkish plans were only defensive contingency-plans arising out of many fears, one of which was Enosis and another that Communism would gain ascendancy in Cyprus.

6. Discussing, generally, the events of December 1963 and subsequent developments, the following points emerged:

(a) Although the danger that armed clashes might take place had been thought possible, and Sir Arthur had himself alerted the Commander of the Base Areas to this possibility with a view to arrangements being made for the evacuation of British families in such eventuality as far back as May, 1963, yet it had been the hope of the British Government that our difficulties could be solved by negotiation, bloodshed thus being averted. Sir Arthur said it had genuinely been thought that the President's proposals would bring about talks with a view to an amicable amendment of the Constitution. In fact, Sir Arthur had been urging the Turks to consider the proposals seriously and to agree to discuss them. The rejection of the proposals by Turkey had come as a complete surprise.

(b) Sir Arthur did not consider that this rejection and the events of December, 1963, were part of a Turkish plan to create partition. The rejection was due, he thought, to the obstinate and narrow-minded attitude taken by the Turks that not one iota of the Constitution should be changed. The same attitude had prevailed during the talks on the municipalities question, when Ankara, at the instigation of Ozkol, instructed Dr. Kutchuk to change course. Dr. Kutchuk's excuses that he had not understood the discussions were, of course, utter lies.

(c) Sir Arthur said it was true the Turks had been preparing an underground force for some time; in fact, they had carried on the T.M.T. from since before Independence, and Sunalp had taken the Turkish underground organisation in hand as soon as he arrived in Cyprus. Sir Arthur was, however, convinced that the Turks had been preparing for a defensive operation and not to put a plan of partition into effect. The British estimate of the arms possessed by the Turks had been higher than the actual, whereas their estimate of arms in the hands of the Greeks had been lower than the actual.

(d) Sir Arthur is convinced that the events of December, 1963, did not start as part of a pre-arranged plan, either by the Greeks or by the Turks, but were accidental, though the Greeks, and particularly the Police, appeared to encourage their continuance once the spark had gone off.

(e) The events at Omorphita had greatly shocked everyone and the Turks were really desperate at that time, and a Turkish invasion was imminent, though Turkey was not so well prepared for it.

Tourdyk had moved on Christmas Day in anticipation of such an invasion so as to cover the invading forces.

(f) Sir Arthur thought that, immediately after bringing in the truce force, Britain should have referred the matter to the United Nations instead of arranging the London Conference. That would have avoided much of the criticism and bad feeling.

(g) Sir Arthur said that it was true that the British troops were on the whole pro-Turkish, possibly due to the fact that they considered the Turks to be the weaker party, and also because they were sorry for them for what had happened in places like Omorphita. Sir Arthur said that Marley's case had alerted the British Commanders and had made them screen the soldiers carefully in order to avoid similar incidents. It appears that approaches similar to that made to Marley had been made by the Turks to other British soldiers. Instructions as to strict impartiality had also been given.

7. Mrs. Soulioti took the opportunity to explain to Sir Arthur the situation regarding the Courts and the administration of justice. Sir Arthur exhibited no reaction.

MINISTER OF JUSTICE

London
6th July, 1964

APPENDIX 55

Statement by the President of the Republic, Archbishop Makarios, 29 December 1962

    The constitutional provision regarding separate Municipalities in the five main towns of the Island is not workable in practice. The relevant article of the Constitution provides for the creation of separate Municipalities for the Turkish inhabitants of the five largest towns of the Island, but does not give to such Municipalities any right to include within their territorial areas any Greeks or any Greek properties or, generally, any inhabitants other than Turks. The delimitation of territorial areas is impossible, due to the fact that the populations are more or less inter-mixed. For this reason, the relevant provision of the Constitution is unworkable in practice.

    Irrespective of the soundness or not of the said Constitutional provision, I have tried to understand the real reasons why the Turks wanted the creation of separate Municipalities. Perhaps the only justification is that the mixed Municipal Council of a unified Municipality might fix the budgetary expenditure for various municipal works without taking into consideration the recommendations of the numerically fewer Turkish members of such Council and in a manner not serving the best interests of the Turkish townsmen. For the purpose of removing any possible anxiety or fears of the Turks on this point I proposed that there should be legislative provision to the effect that a percentage of the Municipal revenue in each town, to be agreed upon and fixed in advance, should be used in such manner as the Turkish members of the Council would recommend. I also made certain proposals for further safeguarding Turkish interests against any possibility or probability of discrimination against the Turkish townsmen by the Greek majority in the Municipal Council.

    At a recent meeting with the Turkish leadership, I experienced particular pleasure because my proposals, after discussion and certain modifications suggested by the Turkish side, formed the common basis for the solution of the problem of the Municipalities. On this agreed basis a joint communiqué was issued and it was decided to discuss and work out certain details at a further meeting. I was surprised and disappointed, however, when at the next meeting the Turkish leadership changed their minds and reverted to their original position for separate Municipalities.

    During the past two years the Municipalities Law was extended eight times in the hope of finding a workable solution. At the last meeting, however, with the Turkish leadership I realised that no such hope exists and I therefore see no reason or purpose for extending once again the Municipalities Law. To postpone facing up to a problem does not constitute a solution. Nor does the provision of the Constitution for partitioning the Municipalities provide us with a solution, since it is unworkable in practice.

    No question of the territorial partition of the Municipalities arises either now or in the future. Furthermore, so long as the Turkish side rejects the notion of unified Municipalities, despite legal safeguards of the interests of the

Turkish townsmen, I am unable to visualise any other solution than the non-extension of the Law and the inevitable cessation of the existence of the Municipalities.

I deeply regret that we have been led to this. As from the first of January the institution of Municipalities will no longer exist. Because of the cessation of the existence of the Municipalities the Government will take all necessary legislative measures for the due performance of all the functions hitherto performed by the Municipal Councils. Furthermore, the property of the Municipalities will devolve on the Government which will undertake to provide for the townsmen services in all spheres in which the Municipalities were hitherto offering such services.

APPENDIX 56

Report to Archbishop Makarios on a Conversation Held between Glafkos Clerides and Sir Arthur Clark at the Request of the Latter, 1 February 1963

SECRET

To-day, 1st February, at 3.00 o'clock in the afternoon Sir Arthur Clark telephoned and asked to see me urgently. After giving him an appointment he called at 4.00 o'clock at my office. It must be noted that this is the first time Sir Arthur Clark has asked to see me since the question of the Municipalities has arisen. At the meeting he began by saying "I am sure you know my Government's position on the question of the Municipalities" he then went on to make the following points:

(a) My Government considers that the question of the Municipalities should be solved by internal negotiations in Cyprus because any interference from outside at this stage on this issue would be a step back and not indicative of progress in the Cyprus situation.

(b) He pointed out, however, that reports which have appeared in the press that his Government considers the issue as purely internal and not a matter for intervention, were not accurate. His Government's position was that the matter should be solved by negotiations between Greeks and Turks and that intervention should only be considered as a last resort if the situation deteriorated and in fact became ugly.

(c) He further said that his Government had been pressed very strongly by the Turkish Government to consider the question of intervention now, but that in his Government's opinion intervention could only be used as a last resort if a state of affairs arose which would justify it.

(d) On the question of the validity of the Law enacted by the Turkish Communal Chamber setting up Municipalities, he said that the legal advice he had was that the Turkish Communal Chamber had no competence to enact such a law and that also the Boards set up by the Government are not valid, because the Law under which the Government acted was obviously and clearly intended for rural areas and not for municipal areas. He said, however, that this legal advice was asked by him from London unofficially and was given to him just for his own information.

(e) He then referred to the possibility of the situation deteriorating by the Government implementing the decision to assign the property of the Municipalities to the Boards and tried to find out from me the following:

(i) Whether the Government would postpone the implementation of the decision pending the determination of the Constitutional Court of the recourses which have been filed by both sides.

545

(ii) Whether the Constitutional Court had power and was likely to order the suspension of the operation of the decision of the Council of Ministers pending the examination of the issues by the Constitutional Court.

(iii) Whether the Government would immediately after the return of the decision by the Vice-President (which he informed me the Vice-President will be making) will immediately proceed with the implementation of that decision.

On questions (i) and (iii) I replied that I had not discussed the matter with His Beatitude of the Greek Ministers and I could not, therefore, say what steps the Government would take. On the question of (ii) I told him that the Constitutional Court could only order a stay of the Council's decision, if the decision regarding the property of the Municipalities was attacked before the Constitutional Court and an application was made for a stay pending the determination of the matter by the Court.

He then asked whether, as a matter of policy and in view of the challenge of the legality both of the Turkish Municipalities and of the Boards, it would not be better for the Government to wait the decisions of the Court, rather than to proceed to apply the decision while the legality of both bodies was still in doubt.

My reply to that was that as a matter of law there would be nothing preventing the Government from proceeding with the implementation of this decision, unless that specific decision was attacked but, as I already told him, I had not discussed the policy on this issue with the President or with the Greek Ministers.

He then told me that he had seen the Vice-President on Thursday morning before the meeting of the Council of Ministers and that the Vice-President had promised that he would ask to see the Archbishop before going to the meeting of the Council of Ministers and ask for talks. Sir Arthur went on to say that shortly before the Vice-President left for the Presidential Palace for the Council meeting, Mr. Muftizade telephoned and informed him that the Vice-President had been advised not to see the Archbishop prior to going to the Council of Ministers. Sir Arthur *believes that this advice was given to the Vice-President by the Turkish Ambassador*. However, Mr. Muftizade told   Sir Arthur that in the Council, when the item referring to the properties of the Municipalities came up for discussion, the Vice-President would ask to postpone taking a decision and instead have talks on the main issue of the Municipalities. It appears, however, that when the Turkish members asked for a break in the meeting of the Council of Ministers they had consultations and that again they were advised not to mention negotiations on the Municipalities.

Sir Arthur told me that he has seen Dr. Kutchuk to-day and that he has gathered the impression that the Turkish attitude has stiffened considerably due to the decision to give the properties of the Municipalities to the Improvement Boards. He also feels that the position of the Turkish Government has stiffened as a result of the said decision.

Sir Arthur said that Dr. Kutchuk had expressed the wish that I should unofficially call on him in order to see if we could find a way of re-opening talks. I replied that I felt that I could not call on Dr. Kutchuk because this would create the impression that the Archbishop or the Greek side had sent me there to ask for negotiations. Sir Arthur then asked whether unofficially some Turkish Members of the House and perhaps Mr. Denktash could meet with me either alone or together with some other persons nominated by the Greek side to consider the question of negotiations.

I replied that this is a matter which requires careful consideration and that I would require time to consider it. He asked whether I could give him my reply either by this evening or by to-morrow morning. He said that he felt that the sooner a way was found to open negotiations the better for everybody. I said that I would not be ready to give him a reply before Monday. He asked whether he could call and see me at 12.30 on Monday. An appointment has been made for Sir Arthur to see me on Monday at 12.30.

He then went on to say that considerable confidence had been created abroad in the stability of Cyprus and that it was a pity to destroy that confidence by failing to solve the question of the Municipalities and allow the situation to deteriorate to such an extent that this confidence would be shaken. People would say that the Cypriots are not even capable of solving their Municipal problem. How then can Cyprus be considered as a stable place in which to invest capital? He himself, since the question of the Municipalities had arisen, had to reply to a number of queries from firms in England.

I gathered the impression that Sir Arthur is of the opinion that both sides want talks, but that as a matter of prestige neither side will ask for talks and that, therefore, some way must be found to open negotiations without either side losing face. I then put to him this question. "From your talks with the Turkish side did you gather the impression that when they speak about talks they mean talks along the lines on which we were negotiating or do they make it a condition that the talks would be to find a way of establishing Municipalities in accordance with Article 173 of the Constitution i.e. separate Municipalities with geographical boundaries?"

The substance of his reply is as follows:

From talks he had with Dr. Kutchuk, Orek, Muftizade and Denktash was convinced that up to the 29th of December they had abandoned the question of geographical partition of the Municipalities, but that they are now reverting to it possibly because they require it as a bargaining position. If talks were to begin it would be better not to make it a condition precedent to the commencement of negotiations that the separate Greek and Turkish Municipal Councils shall be abolished right away.

During the course of the talks he said that he felt that the Turkish Ambassador here in Cyprus was very inflexible particularly on anything that might remotely be considered as an amendment of the Constitution and that this no doubt has a considerable effect on the Turks here.

APPENDIX 57

Proposals Made in April and May 1963 by the President and Vice-President of Cyprus for an Interim Solution, following the Decisions of the Supreme Constitutional Court Relating to the Municipalities

A. PROPOSALS BY HIS BEATITUDE ARCHBISHOP MAKARIOS TO DR. KUTCHUK 29/4/1963
B. LETTER BY THE UNDER-SECRETARY TO THE VICE-PRESIDENT TO THE UNDER-SECRETARY OF THE PRESIDENT REJECTING THE SAID PROPOSALS 29/4/1963
C. COUNTER-PROPOSALS BY THE VICE-PRESIDENT OF THE REPUBLIC TO THE PRESIDENT OF THE REPUBLIC 29/4/1963
D. NEW PROPOSALS BY HIS BEATITUDE ARCHBISHOP MAKARIOS 1/5/1963
E. NEW PROPOSAL BY DR. KUTCHUK 8/5/1963

"A"

PROPOSALS BY HIS BEATITUDE ARCHBISHOP
MAKARIOS TO DR. KUTCHUK

1. In each former municipal area there shall be set up a Board to exercise the former municipal administration and administer the municipal property.
2. Each Board shall consist of not more than fifteen and not less than five members, appointed by the President and the Vice-President of the Republic, due regard being had to the proportional representation on the Board of the two Communities.
3. There shall be a Chairman and Vice-Chairman of the Board to be designated from amongst its members by the President and the Vice-President of the Republic.
4. The powers and duties of a former council of a municipality, as provided in, and subject to the conditions laid down by, the Municipal Corporations Law (Cap.240), shall be vested in the Board as if the force of that Law had not come, for this purpose, to an end.
5. There shall be set up by the Board in each of the five largest towns a Greek Care Taking Committee and a Turkish Care Taking Committee.
6. The Greek Care Taking Committee shall consist of such number of the Greek members of the board and the Turkish Care Taking Committee shall consist of such number of the Turkish members of the Board as the Board may determine and nominate for the purpose.
7. Each Committee shall be presided by a member nominated for the purpose by the Committee.
8. Each Care Taking Committee shall deal with any of the following matters when they affect solely a member of its respective Community:

(a) the collection of taxes, rates or fees;

(b) certain sanitary services;

(c) the issue of certain licences, such as professional licences, etc.

9. Each Care Taking Committee shall have in connection with the matter falling within its competence all the powers of the Board.

10. This arrangement shall remain in force for six months.

"B"

COPY

No. 5/59/8

Nicosia, 29th April, 1963

Dear Under-Secretary,

I have laid before His Excellency the Vice-President the draft which you have to-day sent me about the question of municipalities.

The Vice-President, after consultation with his advisers, has asked me to request you to inform His Beatitude the President that the draft contains such provisions as are completely unacceptable by the Turkish Side. That such provisions as are incorporated in the draft were unacceptable by the Turkish Side was clearly stated at the two meetings held last week. The Vice-President was therefore surprised to see that such a draft with such provisions was prepared, particularly in view of the discussions put forth at the last of the two meetings.

On the direction of the Vice-President I enclose draft proposals for a Bill which is considered to be in accordance with the Constitution and the decisions of the Supreme Constitutional Court.

(Signed) Dj. Muftizade
Under-Secretary

"C"

PROPOSALS OF DR. KUTCHUK TO MAKE TEMPORARY PROVISION FOR THE ADMINISTRATION OF TOWNS

1. In each of the five largest town of the Republic, that is to say, Nicosia, Limassol, Famagusta, Larnaca and Paphos, there shall be established two Committees one for the Greek and the other by the Turkish inhabitants thereof.

2. Each Committee shall consist of not more than 10 and not less than 5 members, nominated by the President and the Vice-President of the Republic and such nominations shall be published in the Official Gazette of the Republic and, if not less than .... in the case of a Turkish candidate and not less than .... in the case of a Greek candidate, ob-

jections in writing are made to the President or the Vice-President in writing the nominees thereof shall be deemed to have been elected.

The wishes of the president or the Vice-President shall be accepted in respect of the nominees of his own community.

3. The powers and duties of a former Council of a municipality, as provided in, and subject to the conditions laid down by, the Municipal Corporations Law and Law No.10 of 1961, shall be vested in the respective Committees, as if the force of the said Laws had not come, for this purpose, to an end.

4. In their functions the Committees shall adhere to the provisions of the Constitution embodied in Articles 174, 175 and 176 in respect of the property of the members of their respective Communities.

5. In each such town as in para.1 mentioned, there shall be established co-ordinating bodies as provided by paragraph 3 of Article 173 of the Constitution.

6. Such co-ordinating bodies shall be responsible for the arrangements for the supply of water and electricity to the said towns and for such other functions as may be agreed upon from time to time.

7. (a) The Communal Chambers shall be entitled to make such rules and regulations as they deem fit for the better carrying out of municipal services as provided by Article 87(g) of the Constitution.

   (b) In such regulations the Communal Chamber may provide for supervision of the accounts, approval of estimates etc. of such Committees as provided by Article 89 1(b) of the Constitution.

8. The Law to be made in accordance with those proposals shall remain in force until such time as the House of Representatives passes an appropriate legislation for municipalities as envisaged by the Constitution. Provided that if no such legislation is enacted within a period of one year from the date of the coming into operation of such Law, such Law shall be deemed to be the Municipalities Law construed and applied subject to the provisions of the Constitution, and the Committees established by such Law shall be the Municipal Councils respectively of the Greek and the Turkish Municipalities in the said five largest towns.

"D"

NEW PROPOSALS OF HIS BEATITUDE ARCHBISHOP MAKARIOS

(1) As an interim measure the House of Representatives shall enact a Law authorizing the Council of Ministers to carry out the normal administration within the former municipal areas.

(2) The Council of Ministers shall appoint Greek and Turkish public officers for the purpose of carrying out the decisions of the Council of Ministers relating to the said administration as well as to supervise and be responsible to the Council of Ministers for the day-to-day administration.

(3) In the five largest towns the following provisions shall apply:

  (a) The Greek officers appointed as above shall be responsible for carrying out the decisions of the Council of Ministers and the day-to-day administration so far as they relate to Greek townsmen and the Turkish officers so appointed shall be responsible for carrying out the decisions of the Council of Ministers and the day-to-day administration so far as they relate to Turkish townsmen.

  (b) The Greek municipal employees shall come directly under the control of the Greek officers appointed as above and the Turkish municipal employees shall come directly under the control of the Turkish officers appointed as above.

  (c) The Greek officers appointed as above shall be responsible for preparing and submitting to the Council of Ministers draft estimates of revenue and expenditure relating to the Greek townsmen and the Turkish officers appointed as above shall be responsible for preparing and submitting to the Council of Ministers draft estimates relating to the Turkish townsmen.

       The Council of Ministers upon receipt of the draft estimates shall cause a comprehensive budget of revenue and expenditure to be prepared which on its approval by the Council of Ministers shall become the yearly budget.

  (d) All revenues collected from the Greek townsmen shall go to the approved estimates for the Greek townsmen and all revenues collected from the Turkish townsmen shall go to the approved estimates for the Turkish townsmen.

(4) The former municipal property assets and liabilities shall be vested in the Council of Ministers for administration purposes the Council acting as trustee in this respect for and on behalf of the townsmen.

(5) This temporary arrangement shall remain in force until appropriate legislation is enacted in this respect by the House of Representatives or not later than one year whichever is the earlier.

"E"

NEW PROPOSALS BY DR. KUTCHUK
VICE-PRESIDENT OF THE REPUBLIC

(1) As an interim measure the House of Representatives shall enact a Law authorizing the Council of Ministers to carry out the normal administration (i.e. "such administrative functions as are traditionally regarded as pertaining to, and as are required by the special nature and necessities of the administration of towns") within the former municipal areas except in the five largest towns.

       In the five largest towns the following provisions shall apply:

  (a) The Greek Ministers shall be responsible for carrying out the administration so far as they relate to Greek townsmen and the Turkish Ministers shall be responsible for carrying out the administration so far as they relate to Turkish townsmen. The Greek and Turkish Ministers may delegate their powers to such person or persons as they may respectively approve in order to ensure that municipal services in such towns are rendered to the Greek and Turkish townsmen respectively.

(b) The Greek municipal employees shall come directly under the control of the Greek Ministers and the Turkish municipal employees shall come directly under the control of the Turkish Ministers.

(c) The Greek Ministers shall be responsible for preparing draft estimates of revenue and expenditure relating to the Greek townsmen and the Turkish Ministers shall be responsible for preparing draft estimates relating to the Turkish townsmen for each calendar year.

Estimates so prepared shall be submitted to the President and the Vice-President for approval.

(d) All revenues collected from the Greek townsmen shall go to the approved estimates for the Greek townsmen and all revenues collected from the Turkish townsmen shall go to the approved estimates for the Turkish townsmen.

(e) The President and the Vice-President of the Republic shall jointly be responsible for the carrying out of the joint services and for matters which require a degree of co-operation.

(f) The Communal Chambers shall have the power respectively to exercise supervision over the aforesaid municipal functions of Greek and Turkish Municipal Officers and may regulate by subsidiary legislation better carrying out of these services and functions.

(2) In other municipal areas the Council of Ministers shall appoint Greek and Turkish public officers for the purpose of carrying out the decisions of the Council of Ministers relating to the said administration as well as to supervise and be responsible to the Council of Ministers for the day-to-day administration.

(3) The former municipal property, assets and liabilities shall be vested in the Council of Ministers for administration purposes the Council acting as trustee in this respect for and on behalf of the townsmen. In the five largest towns however the former municipal properties, assets and liabilities of the Greek and Turkish townsmen shall be vested respectively in the Greek and Turkish Ministers who will continue utilizing these properties in the same manner and for the same purpose as they were used up to the 31st December, 1962.

(4) This temporary arrangement shall remain in force until appropriate legislation is enacted in this respect by the House of Representatives or not later than one year whichever is the earlier. Provided that if at the expiration of one year no appropriate legislation has been enacted, the temporary law shall be deemed to be the Municipalities Law of the Republic and thereupon the Greek and Turkish members of the Council of Ministers shall, in respect of the Municipalities of the 5 largest towns, be replaced by elected Greek and Turkish Councillors respectively. Such elections to be held within 30 days of the expiration of the above-referred period of one year and the Councils so created to be

the separate Greek and Turkish Municipalities envisaged by the Constitution with such powers as the Municipalities had prior to the establishment of the Republic.

APPENDIX 58

Letter from Greek Foreign Minister Evangelos Averoff to Archbishop Makarios, 19 April 1963 (translation)*

The reaction of the Greek Government of Karamanlis to the idea of proposing constitutional amendments and its effect on Makarios

Mr Evangelos Averoff in his book *A Story of Lost Opportunities* writes that the Greek Government had positive information that Makarios had decided to seek constitutional amendments of a far-reaching nature and that to the Greek Government's representations calling for caution he replied reassuring them that he would not attempt anything spectacular and that, in any case, before attempting anything he would give the Greek Government notice in advance. In view, however, of the fact that information continued to reach the Greek Government that Makarios intended to seek amendments beyond the issue of the separate majorities and the municipalities, with which the Greek Government agreed, and that in substance he intended to abolish basic provisions of the agreements, Averoff felt it necessary to write to him and warn him of the dangers that might result from such a course, both for Cyprus and Greece. The translation of the letter into English reads as follows:

TOP SECRET

Your Beatitude,

I thank you warmly for your kind letter, which I received through a friend, Ambassador Kranidhiotis. We have had real difficulties both as to substance and form in responding to your request, but we have overcome them because we feel sincere affection towards you and because we recollected that the burdens resulted from the bloody liberation struggle of Cyprus.

Your letter, Archbishop, I read with care and I have listened with great attention to all that was transmitted to me on your behalf by Mr Kranidhiotis.

The issues are so serious that I felt I should tell you all my thoughts.

I would have liked very much to share your optimism as to all that you have communicated to me about the non-existence of a risk of disrupting Greco-Turkish relations as a result of your policies.

Unfortunately, though I am by nature an optimist, I cannot agree with you. Greco-Turkish relations have already been disturbed most seriously. The Cyprus concerns which in the past were developing normally have already started to poison all other Greco-Turkish problems, and they risk, if they develop sharply, shaking the very foundation of Greek-Turkish relations.

This has the greatest importance for the Nation.

---

* Excerpted from Glafkos Clerides, *Cyprus: My Deposition* (Nicosia, Cyprus: Alithia Publishing, 1989), vol. 1, pp. 151-54.

Firstly, in the terribly exposed—and for that reason dangerous—geographical area occupied by Greece, she is not surrounded by many friends. Certainly the security of Greece is not in any way served by the breaking off of her political relations with Turkey, the only neighbour who is also an ally in NATO.

Secondly, the Holy Ecumenical Throne, for which both we and all foreign churches feel deep respect, and the valued and important Greek Community of Istanbul will face great and serious dangers, which, as events have proved, are not fully averted by the existence of satisfactory texts of international agreements or by any political measures.

Thirdly, other matters which arise as a result of the proximity of the two countries, matters which in their totality assume vital importance for Greece, become unavoidably difficult.

Certainly, when Greek national dignity or the basic interests of Hellenism are threatened, Greece, despite the absolutely essential but difficult task of reconstruction, knows how to disregard any dangerous consequences and to follow the line which she considers her duty dictates.

This, as you well know, we have done during the Cyprus struggle. Unquestionably we would have done so now, if the Cyprus problem had still been developing or if the difficulties resulting from the implementation of the agreements were of primary importance.

If we leave aside for the moment the fact that we also have signed the treaties which established the Cyprus Republic and the fact that Greece always honours her signature, we would show the same disregard to the dangers involved, if by intransigent and bold tactics the liberated Cyprus Republic could secure a substantially better regime.

Today, however, for several reasons, it is obvious that bold tactics, apart from the fact that they raise questions as to possible developments and for this reason suspend economic progress, cannot lead to positive results, but create serious dangers for the Cyprus Republic, the free life of which, as you yourself have observed, started in a very encouraging manner, while its future appeared hopeful.

If the agreements contain provisions which are difficult to implement in practice, certainly they should be amended by mutual accord, and this would be possible, in fact we have reasons to believe even easy, if it is attempted in an atmosphere of friendship, trust and good Greek-Turkish relations.

The Government, as you know, has done a lot to assist you in that direction.

Unfortunately, for reasons which I understand, a different approach has been followed; and I believe for Cyprus, which is so dear to us, for other cherished sections of Hellenism and for the wider interests of the country many dangers are evident.

In the face of these dangers, I would like you, as a valued and prudent prelate, the person directly responsible for a section of Hellenism, but indirectly bearing responsibility for Hellenism as a whole, to know the position of the Greek Government.

In the situation which has been created, the Government has had to toughen her relations with Turkey. It had done this already in an emphatic but responsible manner, avoiding publicity and easy but harmful applause. No one knows where the resulting serious tension will lead and for this reason we are taking the necessary precautions. In any event and despite this, without prejudice to the safeguarding of the national dignity and our most substantive interests, our basic intention continues to be improved and, if possible, closer Greek-Turkish relations.

More specifically, in what concerns the Cyprus issues, we shall continue to help you in the same way as we have done so far, but we will publicly dissociate our policy if it is proved that you have attempted a unilateral abolition of the agreements or part of them. This course is imperative for Greece particularly, independently of the practice followed by civilised countries in respecting their signature. Greece can in no way accept the creation of a precedent by which one of the contracting parties can unilaterally abrogate or ignore troublesome provisions of international treaties which it has undertaken to respect.

Certainly, I do not rule out the possibility that such a different position between us will be exploited internally, and because of this wrong impressions will be created in Cyprus as to the possibility of implementing in practice such divergent policies. On an issue so serious, which, recurring so often, can constantly dangerously destabilise the vulnerable Greek ship, I believe strongly that there is no room for irresponsible petty policies or mistakes in evaluating what is the will of the Nation. As a result, I am determined in this case to recommend to the Government and insist that the people of Greece should be called to express their view specially on this subject. I believe that my view will be accepted. In this way we shall all know where we stand and whether the Greek people wish to undertake a very dangerous venture with a wealth of patriotic feelings but poor means or to remain on the road of a self respecting and prudent march towards steady progress and a fine future for our Nation.

We have co-operated, Archbishop, with sincerity and affection at tragic and difficult times for Cyprus and for all the Nation. I consider that, at this moment of threatening danger, I had a duty to brief you with the same sincerity and the same affection which I always had and still have for you. In times when I see grave dangers looming for cherished sections of Hellenism (Cyprus and Constantinople) and the weakening of the more general position of Greece, I must not permit myself to think, knowing your principles, stature and position, that you are interested only in the fate of Cyprus and not that of the entire Nation.

I do not ask you to do anything in particular. We have worked for your independence and we wish to respect it absolutely. You will do what you think is for the best. I simply wanted you to know our thoughts and on their basis, we, completely undistracted by political controversies, shall do our duty towards the Nation.

With deep respect and affection,
EVANGELOS AVEROFF-TOSITSAS
Foreign Minister

Certainly, the letter of the Greek Foreign Minister explained, with great tact, but also with clarity, the point of view of the Greek Government. It outlined the dangers involved and in plain language warned Makarios against any unilateral abrogation of the agreements or of part of the agreements. The letter, although it did not take up any position against the idea of proposing amendments, as distinct from unilateral abrogation, prescribed certain conditions the existence of which were considered necessary before such a course could be followed. It stated that amendments could be proposed if absolutely necessary and of a very limited scope, i.e., municipalities and separate majorities, if an atmosphere of friendship and trust existed and during a period when Greek-Turkish relations were good. When Makarios finally decided to move and propose amendments, none of the above conditions was fulfilled and certainly the amendments he proposed were of a much wider scope than the Greek Government had indicated. Further, it could not be argued that it was absolutely necessary, at that particular time, to make a move for constitutional amendments.

APPENDIX 59

Letter from Sir Arthur Clark to Air Chief Marshal Sir Denis Barnett, Commander, British Forces Cyprus, 5 March 1963

TOP SECRET AND PERSONAL

5th March, 1963

Municipalities, etc.

Although at our last meeting I was still hopeful of a peaceful solution over the local municipal dispute, I now begin to have some doubts because of the rigid attitude of Ankara. The dispute has now dragged on for two months, tempers are becoming frayed and they are, all of them, emotional people, as *we* know to our cost.

2. Therefore we should, I feel, now be prepared for a breakdown and have our plans ready accordingly.

3. This is not to be taken as alarmist. There is still hope and negotiations continue after a fashion. It is therefore *vital* that not a word should get out about any contingency planning we are doing. So for the present I hope this can be kept at top staff level and on paper only. I have promised to let you know, as soon as I see any signs of the situation becoming critical. If we come to this point, we can then widen the circle of knowledge.

4. You already have certain planning in hand. But I feel that it would be wise for us now to prepare, as I have said *on paper*, for breakdown and the possibility of inter-communal trouble.

5. As I see it, the sequence of events might be as follows:

(1) a clash between Greeks and Turks in one of the main towns, most probably Nicosia (e.g., over the Nicosia Municipal Market, if Greek policemen on Government orders tried conclusions with the Turkish butchers, or between rival demonstrations, egged on by extremists): this would lead to disturbances and rioting, mainly in the central areas or old town where the two communities are cheek by jowl;

(2) wherever it first arose, this might soon be followed by similar disturbances in the other main towns;

(3) there would be nothing anti-British in it; although any of our people stupid enough to be caught up in it might suffer hurt;

(4) the Greek side of the Government would try to restore order by use of its security forces, but these, the Police and Gendarmerie would be split, since the Turkish elements would be most unlikely to use force or arms against Turks;

(5) with luck, however, any initial disturbances might flicker out and each side retire to lick it wounds;

(6) but such rioting and violence could very easily get out of hand; at this point the Turkish Army Contingent would probably intervene in defence of the Turks and Turkish areas; at which no doubt the Greek Contingent would feel compelled to take similar action;

(7) then we would be faced with a complete mess, because the underground organisations, i.e., ex-EOKA and T.M.T., would simultaneously go into action, having armed themselves from their secret stocks of weapons.

6.   If my forecast is anywhere near the mark, what is our part in all this and what should we be planning to do? I enclose as an appendix to this letter my current thoughts on the problems that *could* face us.

7.   I hope that this, without being in any way alarmist, gives you enough to work on for present purposes. Den Dalton and Reg Carr (Consular Officer) are available for any detailed discussions your chaps may want to hold.

(Arthur Clark)

APPENDIX

Cyprus Contingencies Today, i.e., as at 1.3.63.

I.   Communications (e.g., in event of telephone lines being cut or C.I.T.A. employees absenting themselves from work)
   (a) *Yours*, with Dhekelia and retained sites.
         You are already planning emergency arrangements.
   (b) *Mine*, with London, with you and other Service authorities.
         My links with London and with you, by cypher and radio, are good and safe. But I would welcome improved radio-telephone with you and a radio-telephone link with R.A.F. Nicosia.
   (c) *Helicopter Service*
         As long as present tension lasts, I hope that plans to discontinue the service may be held in suspense. It may prove invaluable for liaison between us, and as an urgent and safe courier means.
   (d) *Courier service*
         This works reasonably well at present, but escorts would have to be stepped up.

II.   Safety of Service Families Living Outside S.B.A.s

   (a) In the initial stages, it would probably be enough to do as you have planned, i.e., to warn them to keep away from trouble or trouble-spots, to stay at home as much as possible, and to avoid becoming involved.
   (b) But it might be advisable to have on paper plans for a certain amount of concentration, i.e., of outlying families in fringe or danger areas: there may be some so placed.
   (c) In the last resort, but this is a most remote contingency, I suppose you would pull them all back into the Base Areas.

III.   Protection of British Lives and Property in the Republic

         Fortunately the British community in the Republic are a fairly robust lot, who, having survived the Emergency, know the drill. Oddly enough, the Cypriots respect even the "last pillars of the British Empire" who adorn Kyrenia. They can be relied on to take quite good care of themselves, either by force of personality or by being so naively obtuse that even a rioting mob would laugh, I hope!
         Nevertheless, I would like to be reassured that, if I had to call on R.A.F. Nicosia or the S.B.A.s to succour any British citizens in the more isolated spots, this could be done, despite Service pre-occupations. This could involve several excursions in different directions by armed parties of about a section or so, leaving at a moment's notice and travelling fast.

IV.   Security of British High Commission, and its staff.

I reckon we can take care of ourselves. But, if our Security staff or transport is over-stretched at any time, I would hope that R.A.F. Nicosia could help out, perhaps to the tune of several vehicles and taking over the normal security of the Office, i.e., a twenty-four hour guard system, with a few in reserve on the premises. This would free our Security Officers for other duties.

V.   Intervention By Us To Restore Law and Order

This is tricky. Under the Treaties, it is for the Cyprus Government to decide (their own security forces having failed) when to call in the Greek and Turkish Army Contingents. As I have said in my covering letter, the Turkish Contingent is quite likely to anticipate this, with consequences one cannot forecast.

We come into the picture only if Article IV of the Treaty of Guarantee is invoked or becomes operative. This would call for tripartite consultation between the three Governments—Britain, Greece and Turkey. I hate to think that this should ever become necessary. It would mean using British troops again in an independent country of the Commonwealth to restore law and order (rather like the suspension of the Constitution in Newfoundland—goodness knows how many years ago!). And I doubt whether you have the forces here now to do it. I would, however, welcome your own personal estimation of our capability in terms of what you could spare *after* the obligations in I-IV of this memorandum have been met and alongside the major task of keeping Akrotiri operational.

The aspect that worries me most is that, if we had to face simultaneously domestic troubles in Cyprus and the undertaking of an unpopular military excursion in the Near East, could you cope with Items I-IV of this memorandum and simultaneously withdrawal or abstention of S.B.A.s labour force (13,000 or so), interruption at the ports, denial of electricity, cutting of water pipe-lines, etc. In such circumstances items II(c) and III would be making really heavy demands on us at the same time.

APPENDIX 60

Statements by the President and Vice-President of Cyprus Regarding the Resignation of Ernst Forsthoff, President of the Supreme Constitutional Court, 25–29 May 1963

In answer to questions put by correspondents of the Turkish press to the Vice-President Dr. F. Kutchuk, on the resignation of the President of the Supreme Constitutional Court, he made the following statement:

The resignation of Professor Forsthoff, the President of the Supreme Constitutional Court, is a matter of great regret and of grave importance, and I feel that it is my duty to shed as much light on this question as will put it in its proper perspective and make the public know the true facts.

Unfortunately for Cyprus and for the cause of justice, Professor Forsthoff has had to resign because of the fact that attempts have been made by some Greek circles to subject him to undue pressure. These pressures assumed an unbearable intensity particularly during the time the Constitutional Court began deliberating its judgment in the municipalities cases. As a result of these pressures Professor Forsthoff came to see me late at night on the 21st April, 1963, and lodged a complaint against the behaviour of certain members of the Greek community who, amongst other malicious tactics, had openly accused his Assistant of pro-Turkish activities and hinted that his (the Assistant's) life was in danger, but that for the time being he was being protected by them. It became evident that it was their intention to make life as an independent and free judge impossible and unbearable for Professor Forsthoff. The Professor made the same complaint to the President of the Republic and brought to his and my notice that certain members of the Greek community had so behaved and had brought about such conditions that it was no longer possible for him to carry out his duties in Cyprus. No doubt, the object was, either to influence Professor's judgments in the municipal cases or make him leave the Island before delivering these judgments. At a meeting held at the Presidential Palace on the 22nd April, 1963, it was found possible to convince the Professor, after great difficulty, to continue to work and give his judgments in the municipal cases before to left Cyprus on leave of absence.

The haste with which Professor's resignation was given publicity by the Greek side without first considering its implications which may cause grave consequences by having to leave vacant a very vital post for an indefinite and uncertain long period and without considering the advisability to request the Professor to withdraw his resignation is very significant indeed. The fact that in the Court there are many pending recourses in which very important constitutional principles are involved and in which judgments were reserved after full hearing, has not even been taken into account and I regret that my offer to invite Professor to withdraw his resignation has not found any support on the part of the Greek side.

In his letter of resignation the Professor stated that certain matters which came to his knowledge after his return to Germany had compelled him to resign. These, according to the Professor, were to the effect that his Assistant, Dr. Heinze, had been shadowed by detectives everywhere he went and that it was maintained, amongst other malicious insinuations, that he (Dr. Heinze) was pro-Turkish. I hesitate to give details of those malicious insinuations as I do not wish to assist the fabricators of lies by giving publicity to their lies. The Professor further stated in his letter of resignation that he was shocked by the baseness of the actions meted out against Dr. Heinze and that after mature consideration he had decided to resign. He expressed his deep regret at having to take such a decision but that, in the circumstances, he had no other alternative.

It is clear from the Professor's oral complaints and letter of resignation that he and his Assistant were subjected to pressure by means of most indecent and malicious tactics. Their integrity and honesty were put at stake by fabricating horrible lies and by indirect threats on their lives. In the circumstances they either had to submit to the Greek pressure and sacrifice the principle of justice or stick by their conscience and the principles of justice and take the consequences. Professor Forsthoff and his assistant have preferred to I resign rather than yield to these unbearable pressures. There can be no doubt that Cyprus stands to lose by this episode which will stand as a black mark in the young history of our Republic.

It is significant that while this pressure was being exercised on the Professor and his Assistant, the Greek press was advising the Greek leaders to abolish the Supreme Constitutional Court as a first step to the abrogation of the Agreements and the Constitution. The malicious tactics and the accusations levelled against the Professor and his Assistant which brought about their resignation are no doubt closely connected with the Greek master-plan to undermine the Constitution. Be that as it may, its effect on the reputation of Cyprus as a State under the rule of Law is very grave and its consequences on the confidence of our two peoples in law and order are most disastrous. By creating a situation which led to the resignation of Professor Forsthoff, just because, in a case concerning a serious constitutional principle, he chose to act without fear or favour, these Greek circles who are responsible for this situation will carry a very heavy burden on their shoulders.

I think that the information which I have given above is sufficient to enlighten the public as to the true facts which brought about the resignation of the Professor. In the interests of the Republic I would prefer not to give further details about this resignation. I hope that I shall not find myself in the unhappy position of making public all details, as the President of the Republic and circles close to him are well aware of the details and of the reasons which have artificially been created from time to time and have recently accumulated to such a proportion as to leave no alternative to the Professor but to resign.

Nicosia,
25th May, 1963

STATEMENT MADE BY THE PRESIDENT OF THE REPUBLIC ARCHBISHOP MAKARIOS

The resignation of Professor Forsthoff from the office of President of the Supreme Constitutional Court and, particularly, the reasons for such resignation given in his letter, have caused me great regret.

In the letter addressed to me and the Vice-President submitting his resignation, Professor Forsthoff states that after his return to Germany he learned that his assistant, Dr. Heinze, had for weeks been shadowed, that it was maintained that he (the assistant) was bribed by the Turkish side and led a luxurious life beyond his means. These allegations, Professor Forsthoff states in his letter, he considers as also reflecting on him, and for this reason he submits his resignation.

It is a fact that at a meeting with me and the Vice-President, before his departure from Germany, Professor Forsthoff said that certain rumours about his assistant had been communicated to him, namely that his assistant was pro-Turkish and was being bribed by the Turks. I said that I never paid attention to rumours, and the matter was then considered as closed.

When I received Professor Forsthoff's letter of resignation, I contacted the Vice-President and we agreed on the issue of a communiqué and also on the course to be followed in the matter.

It was with the greatest surprise and the deepest regret that I read the statement by Dr. Kutchuk to-day, interpreting the reasons for Professor Forsthoff's resignation in a completely arbitrary manner, leading to the conclusion that the resignation of the President of the Supreme Constitutional Court was due to pressure applied by the Greek side on the basis of a plan, and even that the lives of the Professor and his assistant had been put in danger.

Moreover, the Vice-President in his statement mentions that there are other details which, in the interest of the Republic, he would prefer not to disclose. I do not know whether Dr. Kutchuk had private information of such a serious nature from Professor Forsthoff, which has not been communicated to me. If Dr. Kutchuk did, in fact, have such information from any source, he was duty bound to communicate it in the first place to me and not, lightly, to make a public statement of such an objectionable nature which exposes the reputation of the Republic.

25th May, 1963

STATEMENT MADE BY DR. KUTCHUK, THE VICE-PRESIDENT OF THE REPUBLIC, ON THE 28th MAY, 1963

I have read with surprise the statement of Archbishop Makarios, the President of the Republic, in reply to my earlier statement in which I informed the public of the truth about Professor Forsthoff's resignation. It is noteworthy that the Archbishop has not been able to disagree with the facts contained in my statement but he has tried to avoid the main issues and gloss over the true facts lightly. The Archbishop tried to represent that Professor Forsthoff's resignation was due to the existence of rumours against his Assistant. This is not true. The Professor resigned not because a few persons of ill-will fabricated rumours against his Assistant but because persons in high authority thought fit for ulterior political reasons to communicate these rumours to him and to his Assistant *with the purpose of intimidating or influencing them while the Court judgments were being deliberated in the municipal cases* and because these persons brought about such an atmosphere which made it impossible for the Professor to continue his work in Cyprus. Full details of these complaints had been given to me and to the Archbishop both orally and in writing. Unfortunately no serious step was taken to tackle these complaints and the mere dismissal of the charges brought against the Professor's Assistant as 'rumours' (as indeed they were) did not help the Professor. The suggestions as to how the matter should be put right then and my suggestions as to what to do were not heeded by the Archbishop.

It is significant that after the Professor was so compelled to send us his letter of resignation the Archbishop maintained that the Professor could no longer carry on with his work in Cyprus and refused to consider the possibility of requesting him to withdraw his resignation on the understanding that matters would be put right for him to carry on with his duties without interference. The hurried way in which the resignation was made public, the choice of the Archbishop to repeat in detail the malicious rumours and thus republish them (for no reason at all) and his omission (having gone into all these unnecessary details) to mention the fact that it was by *detectives* that the Professor's Assistant had complained of being shadowed, with all its implications, indicate the spirit in which the Archbishop has approached this problem.

I regret to have to state, that no agreement was reached between me and the Archbishop on the issue of a communiqué and on the course to be followed in the matter as alleged in Archbishop's statement. In fact I told the Archbishop that having in mind the serious accusations levelled against my community and the Professor and his Assistant I felt it my duty to come out with a full declaration as to the facts and the Archbishop told me that I was free to act as I wished. Further the Archbishop's allegation that I interpreted the reasons for Professor Forsthoff's resignation arbitrarily is not correct. The reasons for resignation are quite clear and need no interpretation. As to the impression created that I have information on this matter which I have not passed on to the Archbishop I should refer him to my previous statement in which I categorically stated that all the details of the Professor's complaints were known to the Archbishop and the circles close to him. The attitude of the Archbishop trying to ignore all these facts as non-existent is most regrettable.

It is a matter of grave regret that here in Cyprus, one of our most senior judicial officers should be treated the way Professor Forsthoff and his Assistant have been treated by named responsible persons and yet the President of the Republic should take no action to put matters right except by a mere declaration to the effect that in his view rumours should not be heeded. Under these circumstances the choice of the judiciary seems to be either to decide according to the wishes of the Greek side or else circumstances would be created by rumours and accusation (such as that they are pro-Turkish, or bribed by Turks), by threats and insolence (such as that their lives are in danger because of their being pro-Turkish), and by having detectives to shadow them, so as to make it impossible for them to continue to administer justice according to the dictates of their conscience without fear or favour. Furthermore, in a country where these circumstances have been allowed to be brought about, the fact that the President of the Republic himself on many occasions publicly stated that he would not apply the Constitution or abide by the decisions of the Supreme Constitutional Court must also have weighed heavily with the decision to resign of a man of honour and dignity such as Professor Forsthoff. Indeed the cumulative effect of all these left the Professor with no alternative but to resign.

This is a deplorable state of affairs unbecoming a civilized society, and incompatible with they dignity of a State under the rule of law and clearly indicates where the root of all evil and the causes of inter-communal suspicion, mistrust and unrest lie in Cyprus to-day.

Needless to say that when all these occur at the level of the Supreme Constitutional Court with the full knowledge and connivance of some persons occupying the highest responsible positions in the Republic the issue assumes extreme importance and becomes a matter of grave concern. These should have been faced with courage and determination. It is most regrettable that the Archbishop, having all the information at his disposal as I have, has chosen not to take any action and when I was compelled to expose the ills confronting us he has chosen to avoid the issues by making ambiguous statements and raising matters completely irrelevant to these main issues.

In a matter like this I could not remain inactive and choose the silence of the President nor could I fail to make public the complaints of an eminent jurist while his resignation was being used, by the persons who forced the same upon him, as a new ground for attacking the Constitution and the very roots of the Republic. My feeling is that this matter should have been faced fairly and squarely and investigated so as to prevent for ever a repetition of such conduct. It may not be too late even now to do so.

STATEMENT MADE BY HIS BEATITUDE THE PRESIDENT OF THE REPUBLIC ARCHBISHOP MAKARIOS

The reasons for Professor Forsthoff's resignation have been clearly stated by himself and have already been set out in my previous statement. I do not believe that a professor of Dr. Forsthoff's calibre has asked Dr. Kutchuk to undertake to interpret these reasons and, adding reasons of his own, to arrive at unwarranted conclusions.

I do not wish to assist the Vice-President in his efforts to render the subject of the resignation of Dr. Forsthoff a political issue between the two communities, and I do not therefore propose to continue this discussion with him in public.

28th May, 1963

STATEMENT MADE BY DR. KUTCHUK, THE VICE-PRESIDENT OF THE REPUBLIC, ISSUED ON THE 29th MAY, 1963

I can well understand why the Archbishop chose to back out of the discussion he himself started publicly over the question of the resignation of Professor Forsthoff. As I have already stated in my previous statements, after the short and hasty announcement from the Presidential Palace of Professor Forsthoff's resignation and the false interpretations given by the Greek press to the reasons which led to it, I found it necessary to enlighten the public by giving them the true facts on a matter of vital importance for all Cypriots.

The mere fact of resignation and the circumstances in which it took place are in themselves clear evidence of a grave situation in Cyprus. I am sorry to observe that in an important situation like this where not only the fundamental rights of the Turkish community but also those of every individual living in Cyprus are involved, the Archbishop has failed to take the necessary measures to remedy the situation. The Archbishop's backing out of public discussion does not of course relieve him of the obligation to take all appropriate measures. I hope that he will not evade this responsibility as he has evaded discussion.

APPENDIX 61

Letter from Archbishop Makarios to Ernst Forsthoff, 27 May 1963

Nicosia, 27th May, 1963

Dear Professor Forsthoff,

Your letter of the 21st May, 1963, informing me of your resignation from the office of President of the Supreme Constitutional Court of the Republic of Cyprus, with de facto effect as from the 21st May, 1963, and de jure effect as from the 15th July, 1963, has been received by me with the deepest regret.

The great efforts made by you towards the solution of the constitutional problems of our young Republic have always been appreciated by me most warmly, and I fully realize how difficult your task has been and how hard you have tried to help Cyprus. The able and impartial way in which you have dealt with the many complicated constitutional issues, your profound knowledge and wide experience were extremely valuable to the Republic. Your resignation, therefore, which deprives Cyprus of your services, is all the more regretted.

Quite apart, however, from my regret that Cyprus is losing an eminent jurist, I was extremely disturbed about the reasons for your resignation, stated in your letter. I recollect that at the meeting we had a few days prior to your departure from Cyprus, at which the Vice-President of the Republic was also present, you mentioned some of the rumours contained in your letter and, as I then told you, I did not pay any attention to such rumours. From your letter, however, I understand that after your return from Germany you got further information concerning your assistant. I would be very grateful if you might wish to give me the details of such information which will assist me in this respect.

I wish once more to assure you of my highest regard and appreciation.

With my best wishes

Archbishop Makarios

Professor Dr. Ernst Forsthoff
Wolfbrunnesteige 13
Heidelberg-Schlierbach
W. Germany

APPENDIX 62

Report of the Commission of Inquiry into the Explosions at the Bairaktar and Omeriye Mosques on 25 March and Fire at Ay. Kassianos School in Nicosia on 29 March 1962 Submitted to the Council of Ministers, October 1962

To: COUNCIL OF MINISTERS,
Nicosia,
CYPRUS.

> From: COMMISSION OF INQUIRY, under Notification No. 140 (Explosions at the Bairaktar and Omeriye Mosques) Order 1962, and Notification No. 144 (Fire at Ay. Kassianos School) Order 1962.

PART I

Sirs,

1.　　We have the honour to submit the report of the Commissions of Inquiry which were constituted by Orders published as Appendix III of the Official Gazette of the Republic of Cyprus No. 141 of the 30th March, 1962, and No. 142 of the 5th April, 1962, respectively. In the exercise of the powers vested in the Governor under Articles 2 and 3 of the Commissions of Inquiry Law, Cap. 44, which by virtue of Article 188 of the Constitution are now vested in the Council of Ministers, you ordered—

3. "The Commission of Inquiry shall forthwith make a full investigation into the circumstances of the explosions which took place on or about the 25th March, 1962, at the Bairaktar and Omeriye Mosques in Nicosia, including all facts connected with the explosions in question"

and

3. "The Commission of Inquiry shall forthwith make a full investigation into the circumstances of the fire which took place on or about the 29th March, 1962, at the School of Ayios Kassianos in Nicosia, including all facts connected with the said arson."

2.　　The Commission consisted of the President of the High Court of Justice as Chairman and Mr. Justice Zekia and Mr. Justice Triantafillides as members.

3.　　On April 10th at the office of the Minister of Justice the oaths prescribed by law were administered to the members of the Commission.

4.　　On April 10th, 17th and 24th the Commissioners after first meeting with the Minister of Justice, met for the purpose of conferring with Counsel for the Commission, appointed by the Attorney-General, to arrange for a proper representation at the Inquiries of all persons interested and the marshalling of material for presentation as well as the consideration of other matters relevant to the public sittings. These last named were advertised in the newspapers, to give the public and persons interested full information concerning the place and time of the public sittings, the first of which was held in the Assize Courtroom Nicosia, at 3.30 p.m. on May 3rd, 1962.

  5. The following advertisements were placed in the press and due publication was announced by the Cyprus Broadcasting Corporation.

> "Commissions of Inquiry (Explosions in Bairaktar and Omerie Mosques) and (setting fire to Ayios Kassianos School),
>   ORDER, 1962
> "Public Notice is hereby given that the Commissions will hold their first sitting on May 3, at 3 p.m. in the District Court of Nicosia, to be continued from the 7th May onwards.
>   All persons who have information to be placed before the Commissions or who desire to be represented in the proceedings before the Commissions are hereby requested to communicate on or before May 1st, either personally or through their Counsel with either
>   Mr. Chris C. Fissentzides,
>   Registrar,
>   Supreme Constitutional Court,
>   OR
>   Mr. Naim Hami,
>   Registrar, High Court of Justice,
> Secretaries of the Commissions,
> or appear personally before the Commissions on the 3rd May, 1962."

  6. The Commission sat on the following dates:—May 3, 7, 8, 9, 10, 11, 17, 18, 21, 24, 25, 1962.

  7. Counsel for the interested parties appeared as follows:

> The Attorney-General Mr. C. Tornaritis addressed the opening sitting. He was accompanied by
>
> Mr. A. Franges, Counsel for the Republic, who appeared throughout as Counsel for the Commission.
>
> Mr. A. Indianos for the Greek Education Office and the Greek Communal Chamber;
>
> Mr. R. R. Denktash for the Evcaf Department and the Turkish Communal Chamber, until he took the witness stand to give evidence, and
>
> Mr. Ali Dana for the Evcaf Department, and the Turkish Communal Chamber, after Mr. Denktash became witness before the Commission.
>
> Mr. George Cacoyannis appeared on and after May 24th, as Counsel for the Minister of the Interior in his official and personal capacity.
>
> Mr. L. Clerides appeared for Mr. Nicos Sampson.

8.   During the course of the hearing 54 witnesses were brought by Counsel before the Commission and were examined on oath, cross-examined and re-examined. Included in this number is one person who gave evidence on his own behalf. A list of witnesses is attached as an Appendix to this report.

9.   On the opening day of the sittings, namely May, 3rd, 1962, the Commissioners in company with the Attorney-General and Counsel for the Commission, visited the two Mosques and the School. The last sitting of the Commission was on May 25th, 1962.

10.   In the narrative which follows, the word Greek and Turk have for convenience been used to mean respectively Greek-Cypriot and Turkish-Cypriot.

11.   The Commissioners encountered some difficulty in interpreting the instructions contained in the paragraphs numbered 3 above, namely, defining the scope of the investigations. Finally and after much consideration, they endeavoured to ascertain who actually caused the explosions and fire, and secondly the circumstances under which they took place. It was in relation to the motive that the Commissioners experienced the greatest difficulty. Towards the end of the hearings and after conference with Counsel for all parties appearing before the Commission, there was unanimous agreement among Counsel on the following statement concerning motive which the Commissioners have accepted:

> "The motive of the persons responsible for the explosions in the Mosques and the setting of the fire to the Gymnasium was to create a distrust and bad feeling between Greek and Turkish Communities and to wreck the atmosphere of good-will and understanding which the President and Vice-President of the Republic were trying hard to establish. This is the statement that has been agreed to by all Counsel appearing in this Commission."

12.   There was no evidence upon which the Commission could properly ascertain the identity of the persons who arranged the equipment and set off the explosions in the Mosques; nor the identity of the person or persons who set fire in the school. It is a fair conclusion that the outrageous acts in question were certainly non-representative of either community but were those of vicious people with complete lack of civic responsibility who wished to prevent friendly relations between the two communities.

PART II
FINDING OF FACTS

The explosions at Omeriye and Bairaktar Mosques occurred about 1.30 a.m. on March 25, 1962. Although the noises they created were heard by many people the places where they came from were not learned until 06.30 hours, in the case of Omeriye and about 07.00 hours in the case of Bairaktar.

Neither the investigations of the Police nor any one else resulted in facts being placed before the Commission from which it could properly identify any person or persons as being the perpetrators of or being responsible for the explosions.

OMERIYE MOSQUE

This Mosque, quite an old one in the walled portion of the city in the Greek sector and not far from the Turkish sector, is situated in a "square" bounded by Omeriye St., Tricoupi St., Ares St., Hiltiades St., Hadji Yoorgakki St., and Patriarch Gregorious Street. It is now used only by women and is entered by two gates one on Tricoupi Street, the other on Omeriye Street. It is open Monday to Thursday, both inclusive, from 15.30 to 16.30 hours, and on Friday from 8.00 to 13.00 hours. On Saturday it is closed.

The Mosque proper is connected to the minaret by a shed containing benches, old furniture and the muezzim's cleaning tools. Access to the shed from the Mosque is through a large wooden double door at one side of the main hall, which was fastened closed by a bolt. A stone was placed against the foot of one of the two halves on the inner (hall) side.

On Friday, March 23rd, the muezzin locked the door referred to and also the 2 doors which lead into the Mosque from the outside and left shortly after 13.00 hours. Everything was in good order. So far as the evidence discloses, except for some boys playing in the grounds on Saturday, March 24th, no one was seen to enter or leave the premises, until 05.45 hours on March 25. Then P.S. N. Malekos, who was on his way after having been on duty at the Archbishopric all night and had heard the explosions, noticed damage to the minaret. He stopped to investigate and remained at the Mosque until relieved by Det. Sergt. Economides, C.I., and Acting Chief Inspector C.I.D. Violaris, who took charge of the investigation about 06.15 hours. They were joined by Supt. Kiazim Nami and Det. Inspector B. Dilaver, who arrived about 06.45 hours. Police enquiries revealed the street lights on Omeriye, Tricoupi Streets and Galip St., near Tricoupi, had been broken apparently by unidentified youths a night or two before the explosion.

The damage to the minaret was small, consisting of a chip off its bottom step, and a tearing away of part of the first ventilation opening above the ground.

The damage to the shed—which appears not to have been caused by the explosion—is difficult to ascertain. In any event, if any damage was done it appears to have been caused to the tiles of the roof which was not in very good repair. It should be said that until an explosives expert, Capt. Tyrrell, at the request of the Commission, examined the Mosques on the day he gave his evidence, May 5th, there had been no sufficient expert examination of the explosions. His evidence disclosed there was one explosion at Omeriye Mosque, and that at the ventilation aperture, ignited by a long fuse which in turn had been ignited by a detonator placed on the bottom step of the minaret. Until he made his examination it had been thought there was one explosion at the bottom step which had blown many tiles off the shed roof and forced inwards the door to the hall of the Mosque throwing a stone behind such door across the floor of the Mosque. In Captain Tyrrell's opinion the damage to the shed roof and the Mosque doors and the removal of the stone could not have been caused by the explosion, but was caused by some other means at which he was not prepared to guess.

The damage to the Mosque proper appeared to be confined to the breaking inwards of the door leading to the shed. The two leaves were detached from their hinges.

The total cost of all repairs was estimated at £115.

The explosion in the minaret was caused by an explosive substance which was totally consumed. It was not caused by a bomb in the usually accepted meaning of the word—that is to say an explosive substance contained in a hard case, often metal.

It was set off by a detonator placed on the bottom step of the minaret as already stated. From the detonator two wires led to a battery connected to a clock, which had been altered so that its mechanism at the expiration of 15 minutes more or less from the time of its setting would close two metal points together. This in turn permitted the electric current to flow from the battery to cause the detonator to ignite the fuse which burned until it reached the explosive material, setting fire to it. The clock and the battery were found on the ground outside the shed.

BAIRAKTAR MOSQUE

The Mosque is a National Shrine of the Turks, it lies in the Greek sector. In the Mosque is the Tomb of Bairaktar, the Turkish warrior and standard bearer, who fell during the time of the Turkish occupation of Nicosia. It is situated on the Constanza Bastion of the walled city and faces Constantinos Paleologou Street.

In front and almost around the Mosque there is a big flower garden which is surrounded in front and all along Constantinou Paleologou Street by a low wall with iron railings on top.

There is an entrance gate to this garden on Constantinou Paleologou Street which is locked by means of a padlock.

The main entrance to the Mosque through this garden consists of a two leaf door secured from outside by a padlock fastened on two iron rings on each leaf and from inside by means of wooden flaps (mandalia on top).

On entering the Mosque on the left hand side there is a room with a communicating door which is always left open. It is in that room the tomb of Bairaktar is to be found.

On the right hand side there is a staircase leading to the attic where there is a door, secured from inside by a bolt, opening on a small terrace through which one can have access to the minaret. Straight on is the main hall of the Mosque with the pulpit at its extreme opposite and the women's compound on the left hand side. The women's compound has a door opening onto the yard which is secured from inside by means of a bolt.

There are in all thirteen windows in the Mosque which have iron railings embedded within the frame of the window and glass panes from inside.

The Mosque has been supplied with electricity since 1948.

It is open every day from 07.00 to 08.00 to 18.15 hours. On March 24th (Saturday) the muezzim closed the doors and the gate at the street at the usual time.

The evidence does not disclose the suspicious actions of any persons between that time and 01.30 hours on March 25th when the explosions were heard by many people, none of whom realized where they took place. It was not until the muezzim, Jemal Ibrahim, arrived about 07.00 hours that the damage was discovered. He found the padlock on the gate at the street was missing, the two front doors of the Mosque had been forced open and the interior injury to the Mosque and its minaret hereinafter described.

The two doors forming the main or front entrance were forced open with one iron ring on the outside of the right door extracted from its place and hanging on the padlock, locked and hung from the left door. The extracted iron ring bore signs of filing.

In the main hall there was a lot of debris and dust. The pulpit will have to be rebuilt, a number of electric light bulbs were broken, the gallery above the entrance will have to be rebuilt and the various broken pieces of furniture and other articles and furnishings destroyed will have to be replaced. There was small damage at the base of an arch.

In the most sacred room of the Mosque, the wooden super structure resting upon the Tomb of Bairaktar, suitably draped with cloth drapes and a Turkish flag, was completely destroyed. The force of the explosion knocked off a small section of the edge of the top of the tomb near the floor.

In the women's compound there was no damage except a slight hole in a pillar where some drilling had been done in preparation for the placing of a charge of explosive mixture. The compound escaped because the wires leading from a charge of explosive mixture in a cupboard to the electric current, later described, were not connected to it.

The minaret was severely damaged by an explosion which took place just above the level of the Mosque roof and blew a large hole in the minaret wall. It will have to be rebuilt. Fragments of a pipe bomb, such as those used in the Emergency, were found in the debris of the minaret and on the roof of the Mosque, but such fragments, according to the opinion of Captain Tyrrell, could not have been connected with the explosion in the minaret that night and they bore traces of an explosive substance different from that used in the explosions on the night in question.

The estimated total cost of repairs as given by Mr. Oguz Bashak, Civil Engineer and a member of the Turkish Communal Chamber, is £1,220. In his opinion the explosions were placed so as to wreck the Mosque completely. On the other hand Captain Tyrrell was of the opinion that the perpetrators were not out to cause serious damage to the building. On the whole it is not safe to conclude they intended to cause more damage than they did.

The explosions, five in number, were all set off at the same time by electricity, according to the evidence. The explosive charges were connected to a clock which had been altered in the same manner as the clock used at Omeriye Mosque, but in this case the electric current was supplied from the electric cables which came into the building. The explosions were planned to occur 15 minutes after the clock was connected up. It is evident the workmen had considerable knowledge of electricity, of the building and of its wiring but for some reason did not connect up the wiring in the women's compound. It may be a co-incidence, but the wall clock in the main hall, found undamaged on the floor after being taken off the wall before the explosions, had stopped at 11.30 hours. The explosion occurred at 01.30 hours—2 hours later, exactly the time the experts estimated it would take 2 electricians to complete the preparation for the explosions.

AYIOS KASSIANOS GYMNASIUM

This school is situated on Athenas Avenue opposite the Flatro Bastian in the Greek sector, near the Turkish sector. It consists of 10 rooms, of which one, situated at the southern part of the building, is used to store school desks. Two windows open on to the school yard. A door leads to a hall inside the building. The floor is tiled, the walls are of tile and concrete construction. The ceiling is of wooden construction covered with tile. In the room desks were stored when a fire occurred on the night of March 28/29, 1962. The fire burned itself out and was discovered after this had occurred when a canteen operator came to work about 05.30 hours on March 29. Access to the windows of the room in question can be obtained through a narrow passage between the school building and the canteen and such passage and the area immediately below the windows is, thus, protected against observation from the street.

Investigation by the Police disclosed some window panes in the room had been broken; a tin of petrol had been poured over the desks and set on fire by the use of matches. Due to lack of oxygen in the air the fire smothered itself out after partly burning some of the desks. Some finger prints were found on the three cans which had contained a liquid smelling petrol, but police were unable to identify them. Inquiries have also failed to disclose who set the fire.

GENERAL

It is our opinion that no definite conclusions can be safely drawn from the names of the newspapers found, nor the material and equipment used in the explosions and fire.

Taken altogether and after careful consideration of all of it, the evidence may create some suspicions, but they are only suspicions.

Separate representations of two Commissioners are attached.

All of which is respectfully submitted.

(Signed) J. L. WILSON
Chairman
(Signed) M. Zekia
Commissioner
(Signed) M. Triantafyllides
Commissioner

EXPLANATORY NOTE AND OBSERVATIONS
MADE BY JUDGE M. ZEKIA, A MEMBER
OF THE COMMISSION

I propose to give very briefly my reasons subscribing to a joint report and to the conclusion arrived therein.

The outrages committed in both Mosques have been described by all parties taking part in the Inquiry in a most condemnatory language. The Attorney-General in his opening address referred to these sacrilegious acts as "unprecedented and atrocious acts of violence against sacred places of worship".

The Bairaktar mosque is a singularly prominent place of worship for all Turks all over the world both from religious and national point of view. Bairaktar was the Standard bearer who scaled the wall of the town and lost his life during the conquest of the town by Turks. The mosque has a symbolic significance due to the national hero who has been buried within its precincts. Its tomb is regarded as a national shrine which is situated in a special compartment of the mosque and it is visited in full veneration by all Turks and Moslems as a sanctum sanctorum. Non-Moslem visitors also occasionally visit the place.

The perpetrators of this hideous crime, as far as the evidence goes might not have intended to bring down the whole building of the Mosque or that the time at their disposal was not sufficient to plant the bombs in such a way as to blow up the whole building. But the perpetrators succeeded to destroy completely the superstructure of Bairaktar Tomb covered with drapery and the Turkish flag and the pulpit of the mosque from where the Imam renders his prayers and delivers his sermons and also to cause extensive damage to the furniture and other articles and fixtures inside the mosque as well as to opening a big hole in the minaret to render it beyond repair.

The motive of these outrages, as commonly accepted, was to disrupt the normal relations of the two communities and the acts perpetrated were no doubt designed to bring about such unfortunate results. Happily, however, due to the prompt action taken by the responsible quarters of both communities and the wise handling of the situation the object of these criminals was frustrated.

The all-important issue in the matter, however is the question as to who had designed the outrages and planted the bombs in both these mosques. The answer to this was a very difficult one and having given to it our anxious consideration we have come to the conclusion recorded in the concluding part of the joint report.

There is no doubt that the outrages described were not committed or instigated by any responsible authority of either community. These are acts of a group of persons who were either victims of fanaticism or paid for this despicable job.

It is a natural presumption, and indeed a very strong one, that a Turk or Turks, unless utterly devoid of any religious and national sentiment and with a strong motive behind it, would not have committed such acts. It is highly improbable for a person to commit sacrilege at his own sacred place of worship. Strong evidences indeed is required to rebut such a presumption.

On the other hand it constitutes a serious charge and accusation to state that a section of another community has committed such outrages and unless one has concrete evidence, as distinct from circumstances, giving rise to weak or strong suspicions should refrain from doing so. The evidence tending to rebut the natural presumption in the case of Turks and the evidence implicating a section of the Greek community, to my mind, is so inadequate and inconclusive that it makes it utterly unsafe to come to the conclusion as to which community or section thereof the perpetrators belong.

I do not think it will serve any purpose to go in detail to the evidence adduced for the purpose of ascertaining the identity of the criminals. With a view to demonstrating the inconclusiveness of such evidence I refer to it in a few words:

The material found on the scene of the crime, (such as in the case of the mosques the Greek papers in which the explosive substances were, apparently, wrapped in and in the case of the school the packet of Turkish made cigarettes found outside the school store) for obvious reasons carry no weight. Again what the old man over-heard when the two Turkish young men (aged 16 and 18) spoke while in the public garden of the mosque, one saying that he was going to Bairaktar Square and the other to Omeriye), and also the two ladies one of whom saw a car which passed repeatedly from the street near Omeriye Mosque and the other who saw, two or three days before the explosions, two Turkish youngsters one of whom uttered the words "aha bounda", even if we believe these witnesses, would help nothing, in my mind, in the investigations of this case.

With regard to the movements of the dog handlers on the night of the 24th March such movements, not being located in the proximity of either of the two mosques or connected otherwise with the explosions it is difficult to regard such movements with any degree of suspicion.

I would like to refer to the statement of Gurkan over which a great deal of fuss was made. The tape-recorded statement of late Ahmed Gurkan contributed, in my mind, nothing in shedding any light as to the identity of the criminals who participated in these outrages. That statement may partially explain the reason why the Minister of the Interior made his public statement as to the identity of the perpetrators a day or two after the explosions in the mosques. In the first place the inherent weakness of Gurkan's statement is apparent; it is hearsay upon hearsay. He said that he had heard from an official of the Turkish Embassy that he (that official) had some information to the effect that Turks were involved in the bombing of the mosques.

The Commission, having exercised their power under section 7(f) of the Commission of Inquiry Law, admitted, contrary to the Rules of Evidence, this tape-recorded statement but this does not mean that the probative value of that statement is in any way to be considered on a different footing than the weight attached to evidence of a similar nature. However, part of his statement is admittedly untrue, i.e. the part referring to Mr. Denktash's visit to London. His allegations in his statement that he frequented the Turkish

Embassy and had close relations with some officials of that Embassy have been contradicted by an official statement issued by the Embassy of the Turkish Republic.

As to the veracity of late Gurkan one cannot forget that not long prior to his death he was convicted of forgery for which he was heavily fined and suspended from the Bar for a period of five months.

Accessibility to the mosques and school premises, familiarity with the electric installation in Bairaktar Mosque were all of very little help since members of both communities could gain access, forcibly or otherwise, to such places and the electric system in the Bairaktar Mosque—originally installed by Greek technicians—could easily be ascertained by anybody by merely paying a visit to the said mosque.

The fact that both mosques are in the Greek sector of the town and the outrages occurred on the Greek Independence Day, taking into account the historical background of the day, it might create suspicions against a fanatical group of Greek extremists but there is nothing more to go further in order to arrive at a finding in this direction.

In short the evidence made available to the Commission neither taken in isolation nor put together could provide us with an answer to the question as to who has caused the outrage under inquiry. The Inquiry in this respect ended leaving us practically at the point we have started.

Although it is not within the scope of the terms of reference, yet, relying on the indulgence of the Hon. Members of the Council, I should like to make some observations:

It is to my mind of paramount importance for the Government to take special measures to protect places of worship and other sacred places and monuments which are of religious or national character and happen to be situated within areas inhabited by members of the community to which such buildings and monuments do not belong. While the freedom of the press has to be protected and maintained at all costs, to my mind, steps should be taken that distorted facts and unfounded reports tending to disturb seriously the normal relations between the two communities should not be published in the local press in utter disregard of the law of the country. As soon as the Authorities ascertain the falsity of such reports it is desirable by radio announcements to contradict them and let the public have the truth of the matters involved. This practice, I believe, will discourage a lot the publication of inaccurate reports. In addition strong appeals to the press from influential quarters should be made, as frequently as possible, with a view to moderating their tone in leveling accusations and making recriminations against the one or the other of the communities or sections thereof. Exaggerated amounts of insignificant incidents touching inter-communal relations occupy, unfortunately considerable space in some papers. All such publications are bound to render a lot of harm to such relations and should be avoided as far as possible. An appeal to the common and good sense of the press with a view to minimizing such exaggerations and unfair comments should constantly be made by Government.

No doubt there is and there will be problems of inter-communal character for the authorities to solve or to endeavour to solve. As an ardent supporter of sincere co-operation and good will between the two communities, I take the opportunity to suggest that a top-level committee representative of the leadership of both communities should be set up to go into these problems periodically. Such committee in the first place should take the necessary measures to prevent the deterioration of inter-communal relations. Later, when the time is ripe and circumstances permit, the committee should face the situation with courage and determination and consider ways and means of removing the existing mistrust and improve inter-communal relations to a desired degree. If it is conceded by both sides that, in the light of the realities of the day, it is to the national interest of both communities to establish closer relations, then there is no reason why they should not do so. It is, however, a prerequisite for the implementation of any positive and concerted action that the rule of law should prevail. If the law-abiding members of both communities pull together, I have no doubt that the law of the country will take complete command of the situation in this Island.

In case all efforts, including the machinery provided under the Constitution, bear no fruit in solving our problems, the good offices of the motherlands—Turkey and Greece—might be resorted to. I have no doubt that both countries are genuinely interested in the solution of our problems and, having in their heart the welfare and prosperity of the Island as a whole, they will do their best to help us in settling matters. It goes without saying that I do not consider it an act of interference on the part of the said two countries if they are called to help us in the formative and infancy stage of the Republic.

(Signed) M. Zekia
Member of the Commission

To: Council of Ministers
Nicosia

From: M. A. Triantafyllides,
member of the Commission of Inquiry,
set up under Notification No. 140,
Explosions at the Bairaktar and Omeriye
        Mosques Order,
1962, and Notification No. 144,
Fire at Ay. Kassianos School Order, 1962.

Sirs,

As indicated at the conclusion of the Report of the Commission of Inquiry, two of its members have decided to submit also separate representations. Such a course has been adopted by the undersigned with the object of assisting, as far as possible, the Council of Ministers in placing things in their proper perspective.

As stated in the Report of the Commission there was no evidence upon which the Commission could properly ascertain the identity of the persons responsible for the explosions in the Mosques and the arson at the Gymnasium.

There have been established, however, many other factual aspects of the events under examination and some conclusions and observations in relation thereto are to be found hereinunder.

I. Regarding the explosions in the Mosques
(1) The sites and timing of the explosions
in relation to the motive of the perpetrators.

It is common ground that the motive of, inter alia, the perpetrators of the explosions was to create distrust and bad feeling between the Greeks and Turks and wreck the atmosphere of good-will and understanding which the President and Vice-President of the Republic were trying hard to establish. This is stated to be so in the Report of the Commission at page 3.

There remains now to examine the relationship of such motive to the current situation in the Republic at the time.

There can be no doubt that there have been from time to time stresses and difficulties between Greeks and Turks in Cyprus and all the time efforts are being made by the President and Vice-President of the Republic and by other right-thinking people to ease the tensions that are thus created.

In the search for the proximate cause which motivated the culprits of the explosions in the Mosques to choose the night of the 24th to the 25th March, 1962, for the timing of such explosions it is very useful to examine whether shortly before the said night the President and the Vice-President of the Republic were trying hard in any particular field with a view to resolving difficulties and, thus, promoting goodwill and understanding.

As it is common knowledge, and it also appears in the record of the evidence at page 279 et seq., shortly before the night in question the President and Vice-President of the Republic were meeting in an effort to resolve the municipalities' problem, which has caused quite some stresses among Greeks and Turks till now. Such efforts had not, for the time being culminated in agreement. The President, after a meeting with the Vice-President on the 19th of March, 1962, issued a statement making public his proposals for unified municipalities and the Vice-President issued a statement in reply not accepting such proposals but indicating also, in a way, that one of the obstacles to agreement was the lack of the proper atmosphere between Greeks and Turks. It is clear that the efforts towards agreement were not to be given up, the wish to find a solution was there on both sides, and for any progress to be made mutual trust and goodwill were essential more than ever.

It is not, therefore, unreasonable to think that the perpetrators of the explosions were out to wreck finally any chances for an eventual solution of the municipalities' problem by creating resentment and mistrust among the Turkish community towards the Greek community.

With this object in view they could not have chosen more suitable targets or more appropriate timing.

Bairaktar Mosque is much venerated by Turks in Cyprus and has never been molested or interfered with by Greeks, even in the worst days of intercommunal strife. So an attack on Bairaktar Mosque was bound to hurt the feelings of the Turks in the extreme.

It appears, moreover, that in order to make matters worse and ensure that the Turks would at once be led to assume that the explosions were set off by Greeks, the perpetrators, not only chose Mosques which were in the Greek sector, but also committed the outrages in question on the night of the 24th to the 25th March, 1962, the 25th March being a National Day on which the Greeks celebrate the anniversary of the Greek rising for Independence against the then Ottoman Empire.

As a matter of fact the said perpetrators succeeded in creating quite some tension for a time but fortunately due to the action taken by responsible people all round the ultimate object of promoting Greek-Turkish strife was frustrated.

(2) Certain conclusions concerning the perpetrators and their actions.

The employment of electrical detonation coupled to locally adapted time-devices, activated by means of a battery at Omeriye Mosque and by making no less than 11 connections with the electricity installation at Bairaktar Mosque, show clearly that the perpetrators were quite proficient saboteurs and not mere amateurs. Also the identical methods of detonation and the simultaneous of the explosions leave no doubt that the explosions at both Mosques formed part of the carrying out of one and the same conspiracy.

The perpetrators must have been familiar with their targets and especially the inside thereof. They knew that the electricity installation at Omeriye Mosque was out of order and so they took along a special battery for the purpose.

They also had, as is stated also at page 9 of the Report of the Commission, considerable knowledge of electricity, of the building and the wiring at Bairaktar Mosques otherwise it would have been impossible to have performed such a perfect job of electrical connections, as that performed in such Mosque, for the purpose of detonating the explosive charges; It is a job which must have taken two electricians, working together, two hours to complete. In order to really appreciate the full significance of these said 11 connections with the electricity installation at Bairaktar it must be borne in mind that the perpetrators were working all the time in the dark with only torchlight, probably, to help them, because the electricity supply must have been switched off before the electricity installation could be interfered with at so many points.

At Bairaktar Mosque an explosive charge was found in a cupboard in the room known as the women's compound. The wires lending to such charge were not connected and thus no detonation took place. It is not reasonable to assume that such connection was due to faulty craftsmanship as this would not be consistent with the quality of the rest of the work of the culprits. Probably the connection was not effected due to lack of time in view of the need to synchronize the explosions at Bairaktar Mosque with those at Omeriye Mosque or may be the perpetrators at the last moment decided not to effect such connection in order not to cause greater damage or for some other reason.

Concerning the actual intentions of the perpetrators it is stated at page 9 of the Report of the Commission that it is not safe to conclude that they intended to cause more damage than they did. Actually on this point there was some considerable difference of opinion between Mr. O. Bashak, a civil engineer (see page 93 of the record of the evidence) and Captain Tyrrel (see pages 146-149 of the record of the evidence). The fact remains that, apart from rather extensive damage done to the minaret at Bairaktar Mosque, no other serious damage was caused to the main structure of either of the two Mosques in question and the efforts of the culprits appear to have been directed towards causing such damage, which though superficial in many respects, it could still be relied upon to cause deep resentment among the Turks e.g. the destruction, together with its drapes and flag, of the wooden superstructure of the tomb of Bairaktar and the destruction of the pulpit at Bairaktar Mosque. There was clearly no effort or intent to demolish the two Mosques in question to such an extent as to put an end to their existence or their historical significance.

On the other hand it appears that some care was also taken to avoid damaging things unnecessarily. A pendulum clock that was hanging from the wall of the Bairaktar Mosque was taken down and placed on its back on the floor so that it actually escaped damage. According to the muezzin of the Mosque that clock was hanging at its place and working on the previous evening (see page 83 of the record of the evidence) and according to the evidence of Sub-Inspector Dilaver this clock stops when laid flat on the floor and restarts on being put up again in a perpendicular position (see page 41 of the record of the evidence). So it appears that it was taken down by the culprits at about 11:30 p.m. of the 24th March, 1962, i.e. two hours before the explosions and when placed on the floor it stopped.

(3) Conclusions and observations on the basis
of certain findings at the Mosques after the
explosions.

The findings at the Mosque after the explosions were not subjected to
examination by an explosions expert immediately after such explosions because
no such expert exists yet in the ranks of the Republic's security forces and the
expert requested from and made available by the Sovereign Base Areas turned
out to be a bomb-disposal expert only. During, however, the hearings before
the Commission arrangements were made for the services of an explosions expert, Captain R. H. Tyrrel, R.A.O.C., to be secured.

A simple perusal of the evidence of Captain Tyrrel, (see pages 145-158
of the record of the evidence), shows him to be a man of great experience and
knowledge in his field, and a witness who put forward only such opinions as he
could justify. In view of his unquestionable impartiality the weight of his evidence is very considerable. Nor is such weight to be affected to any substantial
extent by the fact that he first visited the Mosques some weeks after the explosions, because it is easily apparent from his evidence that he based his opinions
on findings which either did not perish with the passage of time or were preserved by the police, in the meantime, as exhibits or through photographs.
Had he been there on the spot immediately after the explosions he might have
been able to unearth more clues, but that should not otherwise detract from
the validity of his conclusions.

The result of Captain Tyrrel's examination of Omeriye Mosque is set
out at page 6 of the Report of the Commission and need not be repeated in
extenso. It suffices to mention that it establishes that the most obvious damage
caused at the material time to such Mosque i.e. the throwing off of the tiles of
the roof of the shed connecting the Mosque proper with the minaret (see exhibit 7(J)), the breaking open of the door leading from such shed to the interior
of the Mosque (see exhibit 7(H)) and the throwing of a heavy stone across the
floor of the Mosque for about 15 feet, were not caused at all by an explosion in
the shed and could not have been caused by the explosion in a ventilation aperture of the minaret (see pages 149-150, 152-153, 155-158 of the record of the
evidence).

There can be no doubt, however, that the said damage to the tiles of
the shed and to the door leading into the Mosque proper and the removal of
the stone across the floor of the Mosque took place on the night in question
and it would be utterly unrealistic to suppose that they were caused by a second set of intruders unconnected with the perpetrators of the only explosion at
such Mosque, in the ventilation aperture of the minaret. It is significant to
note in this respect that though such perpetrators apparently gained access to
the minaret through the roof of the shed, such entry cannot account for all the
full extent of the considerable displacement and destruction of the tiles of the
roof of the shed; such entry cannot also, reasonably, account for the kind of the
damage caused to the door connecting the shed with the Mosque proper, and
in any case no sign of breaking in or out of the Mosque proper or any other
interference with the interior of such Mosque was discovered, and it cannot,
under any stretch of the imagination, account for the removal of the aforesaid

stone all the way from the said door to about the middle of the Mosque proper. According to Captain Tyrrel such stone did not leave any marks across the floor; a factor which tends to show that it did not skid across the floor but it was carried from one point to the other.

In view of the above, one is made to conclude that the culprits who, with a view to wrecking good relations between the Greeks and Turks, perpetrated the outrage at Omeriye Mosque, chose, rather than cause greater damage to the Mosque by actual explosions, to stage matters in such a way viz. by the apparent displacement of the tiles, the breaking in of the door and the removal of the stone, so as to give the desired impression that rather more damage due to an explosion had been caused.

A similar disturbing feature is to be found among the findings at Bairaktar Mosque. It concerns the pipe-bomb fragments, to which reference is made at page 9 of the Report of the Commission. Such fragments were found on the roof of Bairaktar Mosque next to the minaret and outside the Mosque in the yard, again next to the minaret, and as a matter of fact some of them were mixed with the debris of the minaret which had fallen in the said yard.

In view of such fragments it had been naturally assumed that a pipe-bomb had exploded in the minaret, causing severe damage to it (see exhibit 8(K)). There was no suggestion or even possibility that such fragments could have been connected with any of the other explosions at Bairaktar Mosque that night; they all took place inside the mosque and none of them were caused by a pipe-bomb.

According to the evidence of Captain Tyrrel (see pages 145-146, 150-152 of the record of the evidence) the fact that no pieces of metal at all were found embedded in the inside walls of the minaret establishes that no pipe-bomb exploded in the minaret and the damage to the minaret was caused by an explosive charge, not encased in a pipe, which was placed under one of the steps. Some pieces of pipe which were subsequently discovered in the minaret were shown by Captain Tyrrel to be unconnected with even the pipe-bomb fragments (see pages 145-146 of the record of the evidence).

It is also significant that the pipe-bomb fragments in question were found to bear traces of an explosive substance different from that used in the other explosions on the night in question. This was ascertained by the Government Analyst (see page 121 et seq. of the record of the evidence).

The same Analyst also ascertained that pieces of a fez of the imam of the Mosque which were found scattered all over the inside of the Mosque, thus leading to the assumption that one of the bombs was exploded in such fez, did not in fact bear any signs of explosive substance on them.

One is thus again made to conclude that the perpetrators of the outrage of Bairaktar Mosque, with a view to furthering their known sinister motives, staged matters so as to give the impression that a pipe-bomb had exploded in the minaret and they scattered about fragments of a pipe-bomb which had apparently exploded elsewhere or on some other occasions, in order to aggravate the whole picture, especially as it is common knowledge that such pipe-bombs were used in great numbers by KCKA during the recent liberation struggle. They also appear to have scattered around the Mosque pieces of the imam's fez in a further effort to incite resentment among the Turks.

II. Regarding the arson at the Gymnasium.

Such outrage appears to be a sequence of follow-up of the explosions.

As found by the Commission in its Report the arson of the Gymnasium was caused by perpetrators with the same motive as that of the perpetrators of the explosions in the Mosques.

It should not, however, be necessarily concluded that the perpetrators of the explosions and the arson were the same persons or belonging to the same conspiracy. The explosions bore the hallmark of expert execution whereas the arson was a more amateurish affair.

As a matter of fact the whole set-up and the findings at the Gymnasium after the arson such as to indicate that the whole operation was carried out in a hurry, without much planning and its real significance lies in the fact that in the space of a few days another incident occurred which could have made to flare up dangerously an already tense situation.

III. In general

It should be mentioned, by way of completing the overall picture, that the Commission has also examined many other collateral matters which appear from the record of the evidence and need not be enumerated, including the question of a tape-recorded statement of the late advocate A. M. Gurkhan. Some of the said matters appear to have been the indications warranting the making by the Minister of Interior of a relevant statement on the 26th March, 1962—and the Commission by its terms of reference was not called upon to decide thereon one way or the other—but as they did not amount to proof of the identities of the individual persons responsible for the outrages under examination, they need not be elaborated upon any further; it was thought, however, fit to refer to them at this stage in order to explain why they were not dealt with at any length or at all.

Some useful lessons may be drawn from the results of the work of the Commission of Inquiry, though, as stated, unfortunately the identities of individual culprits could not be established.

The first thing to be noted, with some relief and hope for the future, is that, according to the Report of the Commission at page 4, the culprits of the events under examination were non-representative of either community. So no question of collective or communal responsibility arises. For this reason the question of the community or communities to which the culprits belonged did not need to be specifically determined; of course, certain conclusions may be drawn in this respect, and the undersigned is always at the disposal of the Council to put forward his own views on such issue, as well as on any other issue, should the Council so require.

What matters most now is the positive action to be taken in the light of the Report of the Commission. Since vicious non-representative elements are prone to callously take such unconscientious advantage of the occasional stresses and difficulties among the Greeks and Turks, it becomes imperative for representative Greeks and Turks to face up to this danger by guarding not only against such outrages as the explosions and the arson but also by taking positive steps in easing and resolving in time the aforesaid stresses and difficulties. The leadership of Greeks and Turks in Government is doing a great lot indeed towards that direction but it is high time for other people in responsible positions in both communities to get organized for such an effort on a permanent basis.

(Signed) M. A. Triantafyllides
Commissioner

Nicosia, the 3rd October, 1962.

POSTSCRIPT

It is only proper to state that all the responsible authorities involved have done their best in assisting the Commission in its task. In this respect just praise is due also to the administrative and secretarial staff of the Commission for their conscientious efforts; the voluminous record of the hearings before the Commission, which has been forwarded to the Council of Ministers, bears witness to the great amount of work done by the staff of the Commission in the space of very few days and after office hours and it is hoped that the Council of Ministers will, in the circumstances, make due allowance for any faulty passages in such record.

APPENDIX A

List of Witnesses

1. Orhan Mevlut
2. Christakis Nicolaides
3. Sgt. N. Malekos
4. Y. Ktorides
5. Insp. Aziz Ahmet
6. Insp. Behitch Dilaver
7. Sgt. R. Bagrie
8. Ft. Lt. Spommer
9. C. H. Griggs
10. P.C. A. I. Hassan
11. Ahmet Ogfi
12. Artemou Leonidha
13. Theod. Constantinou
14. St. M. Savvides
15. Pan. Michael
16. Pan Ioannou
17. Leand Cacoyiannis
18. Polyd. Arghyrou
19. Djemal Ibrahim
20. Ahmet Niazi
21. Sot. Anastassiades
22. G. Pierides
23. Ach. Djabouras
24. Pan N. Panayides
25. N. M. Aloupas
26. Chr. Decatris
27. O. Bashak
28. Ph. Ktorides
29. Ioannis Economides
30. Milt. Violaris
31. Renos Symeou
32. A. Christofides
33. Sub. Insp. I. A. Gurkel
34. P.C. Vedat Mehmet
35. Mustafa Ali
36. Mehmet Hassan
37. Assim Adil (tendered)
38. Hassan Houssein Yagmour (tendered)
39. Captain R. H. Tyrrell
40. Chief Supt. M. Pantelides
41. Chief Supt. C.I.D. Salih Hassan
42. Ahmet Niazi, Commander Gendarmerie
43. Ioannis Myrianthous
44. Marianna Phokaidou
45. Philippos Theodorou
46. Eraclis Frangos
47. Insp. Daniel Socratous
48. Andreas Seimenis
49. Remzi Houssein
50. Mr. Polycarpos Georghadjis, Minister of the Interior
51. Mrs. Ismet Gurkan
52. Mr. Nicos Sampson
53. Supt. Kiazim Nami
54. Mr. Raouf R. Denktash

APPENDIX 63

Transcript of Tape-Recorded Statement Made by Ahmet Musafer Gurkan Produced by the Minister of Interior on 21 May 1962 before the Commission of Inquiry into the Explosions at the Bairaktar and Omeriye Mosques in Nicosia, 25 March 1962

(Note: The original language of the statement is mixed Greek and English. The Greek parts have been translated into English.)

". . . He came to my neighbourhood, opposite; it is behind Neapolis, do you understand? There is a school, etc.. Next to us there are Christians but a next door neighbour of mine is a local quarter commander of T.M.T.. He is in charge of that quarter, also of my quarter.

Q.   Who is in charge of that quarter?

A.   At first I did not believe it but on Monday night I saw Colonel Remzi Tirpan, the assistant of Torgut Sunalp, enter into the house of that man, his name is Kemal Ahiz Kal. My number is 12, after that either 10 or . . . Remzi Tirpan.

Q.   That is the assistant of Sunalp?

A.   Yes.

Q.   Yes, so?

A.   I saw Remzi Tirpan come to the house of this man Monday and on Tuesday night I went with my wife to his house.

Q.   To that of Keman Ahiz Kal?

A.   Yes.

Q.   You mean on Monday night?

A.   On Monday night, after the incident.

Q.   After it had happened?

A.   Yes, after. On Tuesday night I went with my wife and we sat together and he told me that we have rejoicing news, he said. I said, 'What', he said, 'Did you not see the car of Remzi Tirpan together with his lieutenants?' 'Yes, yes, I saw'. He said that he gave order to us for alertness, to be alert, to stand by, to be alert, because, he said, there is emergency now' and I said 'Are you ready against the Greek people because I said, you see, I think they are armed'. 'Yes', he said to me 'if they are armed, we are armed too'. He told me that he has given others under his command in that quarter just near the boundary and everywhere in every quarter which has a boundary with Greeks there are such units of T.M.T. and Tirpan told them that they must make their arms ready and also he must order his men to be on the alert and that they must keep watch on the Greeks every night by turn. To-night somebody, the other night B, the other night C, the other night D, that's it. Because Tirpan said he has great doubts that the Greeks will attack.

These words come from Sunalp because Sunalp is Denktash's man and Denktash is a man of the British, Denktash says to Sunalp that the Greeks will attack and that he must be on the alert. These things mean flames, these are flames and people are cotton wool; if you touch cotton wool with a flame, there is a . . .

Q.   A conflagration?

A.   A conflagration, that's it.

Q.   You say, you told me that they have issued an order. What is it?

A.   They have issued.

Q.   T.M.T.?

A.   Tirpan has ordered these T.M.T. people that they should be on the alert, that they must stand by, always at the ready, and the organisation to be watchful, to watch every night for any Greek movements if there are any attacks and everybody, somebody, must be awake, they must not sleep, they must stay awake all night on the watch. And I, on Tuesday morning on the day that I was going early before I went to the house of that man, early, I got up at 6 to go to work and at 7 I saw Turkish vehicles, Turkish Contingent weapon carriers, about ten of them. They were passing in convoy towards Famagusta Gate, from Kyrenia Gate towards Famagusta Gate and the guns . . .

Q.   Were for the alert position?

A.   Alert position and there are soldiers near the guns, I do not know what. And they saw some people because there were some workers going to work and they clapped.

Q.   And in this way they saluted?

A.   Yes.

Q.   And now, about these explosions, what is happening?

A.   Dirvana was very angry today because there were no watchmen. I was going at about 11.30 to the Embassy, the Turkish Embassy, to express my anxiety about the events and also to express my thankfulness to Dirvana for his stopping the incidents because he himself personally stopped the incidents, but Dirvana was not there, and his assistant, I mean to say, the Counsellor of the Embassy, was having a conversation with Dr. Kutchuk; Dr. Kutchuk was there, and I could converse only with Mr. Pamir who is our man, you see, at the Embassy. He told me that the first confidential reports indicate that these bombs were planted by Turks.

Q.   Who said that?

A.   Pamir.

Q.   Pamir said that . . .

A.   Those bombs were planted by Turks.

Q.   Oh, yes.

A.   Because, he told me, in order to plant these bombs and to attach them to the . . . one must be aware . . . and secondly he must be very acquainted with the details of the electricity installation. This is how they were going on. I asked, the statements . . .

Q.   Pamir? Pamir? Who is this Pamir?

A.   He is the Press Attache of the Turkish Embassy and at the same time the Director of the Turkish Information Service in Cyprus.

Q.   Ah, ah, so?

A.   He is in charge of the Morse system with which they send messages.

Q.   I understand, I got it; yes, so?

A.   And I said to him, "What are you going to do now?" He said to me "These things", he says, "we cannot disclose because they are a disgrace for the Turkish Cypriots. We", he says, "will reply to Georkadjis that the Turks are innocent, etc., etc.. But", he says, "unfortunately, we are aware of this and because of this", he says, "we shall make every effort, we should calm down the Turks because the Turks in the street are innocent people. Those are to blame who . . ."

Q.   They are innocent.

A.   Yes, Yes. And he told me that Dirvana, he says, was very angry, he says, and he told him, yes I also saw last night and, he said, there are no watchmen here etc., and so he was very nervous, very angry. He even said that he was angry because the Police let the people in and they destroyed the evidence. Yes. "And now", he says, "we must make every effort to stop inter-communal conflict", and Dirvana, as you know, yesterday he did his best to control the mob from parading in the Greek quarters.

Q.   To send them away. They intended to parade in . . .

A.   In Ledra Street.

Q.   They had such an intention?

A.   Certainly, certainly, they all gathered early in the morning.

Q.   Oh, my!

A.   But unfortunately Dirvana is on his own.

Q.   Now, Sunalp . . .

A.   Sunalp is Denktash's man and I have information that Denktash, 3-4 weeks ago, went to Beirut; he pretended that he went to Beirut, and he stayed 3-4 days, but Denktash did not go to Beirut, he went to London. He received information from the British Government, instead of going to Beirut, he went to London.

Q.   But Denktash?

A.   Denktash. There are people who saw him, Denktash, in London.

Q.   You don't say.

A.   Yes. I also received information 3 weeks ago and to-day I got a news-paper from London, a Turkish newspaper which comes out in London, a weekly; it is published by our own people. It writes that, it does not give a name, but it writes that a Turkish leader, instead of going to Beirut, he came to London and this man is a spy of the British.

Q.   Bring me the paper to read, make a translation for me.

A.   Yes, I will.

Q.   Now, what do they say about this matter, that you say it is Denktash who placed the bombs, that is, under his leadership, he did not place them himself.

A.   Yes.

Q.   How is it, do you have information or is it your suspicion?

A.   Pamir has told me this: we know that it is the Turks who placed this thing, and that of the Turks the fanatic Turk who wants intercommunal relations to be strained is Denktash. "And we are sure", he says, "that Denktash ordered his own people to do this thing." Pamir told me this but he said we cannot disclose these things and we shall try to say that Georkadjis is lying. The Turks are innocent, it is not the Turks who placed them. Because this is how politics are, it is very insulting for the Turks. This is what Pamir says, Pamir who is the head of the Turkish Information Service here.

Q.   So it is 100% certain?

A.   Certainly, this is what it means. Because about 2-3 weeks ago I went and saw Pamir on this matter, that Denktash went to London instead of Beirut, and Pamir immediately sent a Cypher Code, Morse, to Turkey that Denktash went to London instead of Beirut. Because Dirvana does not like Denktash, Dirvana hates Denktash, because Denktash went to Turkey with Kutchuk and requested the Turkish Government to replace Dirvana because Dirvana is "tangalakis" and is a philhellene etc., etc., shows that . . . Mr. Pamir told me that the Greek-Turkish relations are so strong, became so strong, that in order to damage it, the Bairaktar Mosque ought to have been damaged. That is, if the bomb explosion had been elsewhere, it would not have been so serious as in the case of Bairaktar.

Q.   Did the Turkish Government believe that it is not the Greeks who have done these things?

A.   It believed.

Q.   That it is the Turks who have done this?

A.   Yes, because Dirvana's speech to the students was that "until the perpetrators of these acts are detected you must not resort to any move", he said. This means that the perpetrators of these crimes, of these acts, may be Turks. He hints at this.

Q.   With the speech he made it is as if he were saying that . . .

A.   Yes, yes, certainly, this is what it means. It is clear, it may be Turks, why hasten to go to the Greek quarter and create a disturbance. This is what it means.

APPENDIX 64

Interview with Glafkos Clerides, *Cyprus Today*, May–June 1963

CULTURAL TRENDS IN CYPRUS

The cultural face of Cyprus is naturally determined by its geographical position, heritage, contemporary developments and its dealings with foreign cultures.

The island, situated as it is in the Eastern Mediterranean, has stood since the dawn of history at the crossroads of the main civilizations from the East and West. Its inhabitants, always conscious of their Greek heritage, which dates back to the second millennium B.C., have always shown themselves able to absorb foreign influences and mould them into a conservative and solid culture within the wider bounds of the Greek creative spirit. Students of the cultural tradition of Cyprus find Greek thought and the Christian faith have played the most important roles in its development, as elsewhere in Europe with which at the height of the Renaissance Cyprus was politically and culturally united. This spiritual communion of Greek thought and Christian faith has always maintained Cyprus as an integral part of the Greek world and the sole European bastion in the East. At the same time, the consciousness of spiritual unity with the West has formed the basis of the island's education which has always been concerned with the maintenance of human dignity and freedom.

Cyprus' cultural relations with other foreign countries, based as they are, on a conscious effort to preserve absolute unity with the rest of the Greek world, endeavour to broaden the island's horizons concerning the whole of contemporary free society which is striving to renew and consolidate the principles of the fundamental human values. We welcome new ideas for discussion and opportunities for cultural exchanges with all countries of the free world. To the international cultural forum we bring our Greek individuality and the European character of our civilization and ideals.

Cyprus, the cradle of many European ideals, will uphold its position in complete awareness of its cultural responsibilities.

The Editor

AN INTERVIEW WITH THE PRESIDENT
OF THE HOUSE OF REPRESENTATIVES
MR GLAFKOS CLERIDES
His Views on the Council of Europe, the Common Market, the Island's
Constitutional difficulties and Municipal deadlock.

Question 1.   What are your impressions, Mr President, from your recent
visit to Strasbourg and what do you envisage as the role of Cyprus in the
Council of Europe?

Answer 1:   I have recently attended the 15th Ordinary Session of the Consultative Assembly of the Council of Europe which commenced its work on the
28th of March, 1963. This, of course, was not the first time I have attended
meetings of the Consultative Assembly of the Council of Europe. My general
impressions are that the Council of Europe is passing through a new period of
reactivation and is again assuming its old important role in European affairs.
This reactivation of the Council of Europe may be due to two important factors. Firstly, the origin of the Council of Europe and the purpose for which it
was created was to provide a Body which would discuss European problems
and would have as its paramount object the unification of Europe thus eliminating the possibility of wars between European states. During the latter part
of its life, because of the creation of the Common Market and the desire of a
large number of States in Europe either to become members of the Common
Market or to associate with it, it became evident that as more and more European countries joined the six of the Common Market, the interest in the Council of Europe correspondingly would dwindle. The situation now, however, is
rapidly changing because of the deadlock in the negotiations between Great
Britain and the Common Market and of the fact that the EFTA countries are
still outside the Common Market. It has, therefore, been realized that at least
for the next few years there is no foreseeable possibility of any substantial increase of the number of the countries making up the Common Market and
consequently the Council of Europe still has an important role to fulfil in
bringing about the unification of Europe. In fact if the membership of the
Common Market does not substantially increase, the Council of Europe will be
the only forum at which countries of the Common Market and those outside
the Common Market will be able to meet and freely discuss European problems and, in particular, those problems appertaining to the efforts being made
for the unification of Europe.

The second fact which has substantially strengthened the revival of the
importance of the Council of Europe is that a number of European countries
which either by tradition or because of certain Treaty obligations maintain a
neutral policy have come to the conclusion that membership to the Council of
Europe is not inconsistent with their policy of neutrality and have joined the
Council of Europe. Thus in the last fifteen years Sweden and Austria became
members and on the 29th of March, 1963, Switzerland, the last European neutral country, became a member of the Council of Europe.

Before answering the second part of your question i.e. "What the Role
of Cyprus should be in the Council of Europe", I would like to make certain

introductory remarks. To begin with I would like to point out that Cyprus has three Representatives at the Council of Europe. Each representative, in accordance with the Constitution of the Consultative Assembly of the Council of Europe, has a separate vote which he exercises freely in accordance with his personal beliefs and in accordance with the policies of the political party to which he belongs without binding the Republic in any way. The difference, which is often not realized, between representation at the Council of Europe and the United Nations lies in the fact that in the United Nations each delegation has one vote and votes in accordance with the policy of its Government and, therefore, binds its Government, whereas in the Council of Europe each delegate has one vote which he exercises, as I already stated, in accordance with his own personal beliefs or in accordance with the policy of the political party to which he belongs. Thus it is not uncommon in the Council of Europe to find delegates from a country voting differently from the rest of their delegation and agreeing with some delegates from other countries, who happen to belong to parties holding the same political beliefs. Therefore, when I answer the question what I consider the role of Cyprus at the Council of Europe, I am merely expressing my own personal views as a delegate to that Assembly and in no way do I commit the Government of the Republic of Cyprus nor do I speak for the other two delegates who are entitled to have their own views and vote in accordance with their own political convictions. So far as Cyprus is concerned, however, I must say that in the past on every issue that has arisen the Cyprus delegates, having discussed the issues amongst themselves, found it possible to vote unanimously.

Although as I have already stated I am not bound to exercise my vote in accordance with any policy decision of the Government, nevertheless because I believe and support the policy of non-alignment of the Government, I consider that the role of Cyprus at the Council of Europe should be:

(a) To assist in every effort which tends to help the unification of Europe.

(b) To judge every issue and take a position strictly on the principles of non-alignment.

It is, perhaps, necessary for me to explain what I consider to be true non-alignment. In this respect I think I can do no better than to quote verbatim certain passages from the speech of the President of the Republic, Archbishop Makarios, made at the Belgrade Conference of non-aligned countries in September 1961, from which the principles of true non-alignment clearly emerge:

(a) "The conference has been described as the conference of neutrals. But our neutrality is not conceived in the sense of remaining indifferent and passive to world problems, nor is our role seen as that of seeking a point of compromise between the two sides without relating such compromise to the merits of the case and to basic principles. Our posture on world problems is, and should be, primarily guided by the principles of justice and freedom consistent with the spirit of the United Nations and its Charter. . . ."

(b) "It is not the purpose of this conference to create a third bloc. The concept of a bloc would involve limitations in objectivity, the very thing to be avoided in any constructive dealing with world problems. . . . our essential position and our common ground is that of non-alignment. Such non-alignment is the source of our freedom of judgement and independent approach to world problems, allowing our stand to be determined by what is right and just in each case. Our non-commitment to any bloc becomes our commitment—and a strong commitment—to moral principle."

(c) "The right of self-determination of all peoples is the corner stone of the Charter of the United Nations. Any solution which ignores the will of the people concerned cannot be a sound and lasting solution nor can it preserve peace."

(d) "The collective voice of humanity has already made its decisive pronouncement against colonialism, by the resolution adopted in the last general Assembly of the United Nations, which Cyprus had the honour to cosponsor. Colonialism which in the past was an established and avowed system of domination of one people over another, has been definitely and irrevocably condemned. The age of domination by force, in whatever form, can no longer be tolerated. It is incompatible with the spirit of our age. The sooner this is realized by the colonial powers the better it is for themselves and world peace. For there can be no real stability of peace where people are kept in any form of subjection against their will. Freedom is a man's birth right, and every suppression of freedom is a violation of that right and a threat to peace."

(e) "Equality of rights must be secured for all peoples irrespective of colour, creed or race."

I believe that Cyprus may, within the above principles, play a constructive role at the Council of Europe by supporting everything which leads to the unification of Europe, by taking at the same time a stand on issues appertaining to the freedom of peoples still under the colonial rule of some of the member countries of the Council and by opposing every violation of human rights, whether such violation is carried out by the countries belonging to one bloc or the other, whether it is against their own citizens or against their colonial subjects. I believe that Cyprus, though a small country, may achieve true greatness if without fear or favour, without commitment to East and West, but by using as the only measuring rod the justice and merits of each case takes its stand on each issue.

Question 2.   What subjects debated at the Consultative Assembly of the Council of Europe are of particular interest to Cyprus?

Answer 2:   During the 15th session of the Consultative Assembly of the Council of Europe a number of subjects of interest to Cyprus were debated. Perhaps the most important one, from our point of view, was the debate which followed the report of the Political Committee of the Council of Europe prepared by Mgr Pier Pflimlin on the general policy of the Council. During this debate the Assembly heard an exposé by the Lord Privy Seal Mr Heath on the reasons which led to the deadlock in the negotiations for the admission of Great Britain to the Common Market as well as an analysis of the French point of view given by the Deputy Foreign Minister of France. It is of particular importance to Cyprus to follow these debates, to establish contact with the delegations from the various countries which, in accordance with the Constitution of the Council of Europe, are made up not only of Representatives of the parties in power, but also of Representatives of the parties in opposition. By such contacts we are able to keep a close watch on the trend of political thought in Europe and to consider in advance the possibility of changes in Europe which may have a direct bearing on the economy of Cyprus. Of particular importance to us are the debates of the Consultative Assembly on the question of economic aid to underdeveloped countries. Equally we are interested in such subjects as the European economic relations, the uniform interpretation of European Treaties, the International Institute for the unification of private Law, the Charter and Rules of Procedure of the European Conference on local authorities and other questions relating to social and cultural matters.

In conclusion one may say that attending the Council of Europe provides for Cyprus a means of keeping a finger on the pulse of Europe and, therefore, being well informed of all trends of thought on European economic and political possible developments. This is of particular importance to a country such as Cyprus which, by virtue of its size, cannot find it possible to have Embassies or legations in all European capitals.

Question 3.   What are your views on the question of Cyprus joining the Common Market?

Answer 3:   It is my personal conviction that Cyprus should not apply to join the Common Market as a full member. If Cyprus was offered and accepted full membership of the Common Market, in view of the nature of its economy and of the fact that its industries are not in a position to compete with European industries, such membership would prove detrimental to its economy. Cyprus, however, has to consider seriously the question whether or not to seek some form of association with the Common Market. In this respect an application by the Government of the Republic has already been made. Whether in the final analysis Cyprus should associate itself with the Common Market or not, it must be examined with a realistic approach and must certainly depend on the question of the nature of association and the advantages offered to Cyprus with regard to such association. Cyprus cannot ignore the question whether Great Britain in the last analysis will be admitted in the Common Market. We, as a Commonwealth country, enjoy certain preferential tariffs in the United Kingdom which is by far the largest market for our agricultural products. It is, therefore, essential in considering whether to accept any form of association with the Common Market to weigh and compare the final terms offered to us with the advantages which we enjoy as a member of the Commonwealth.

Question 4.   There is a great deal of discussion both in Cyprus and abroad about the political, administrative and other difficulties which result from the Constitution of the Republic of Cyprus. Could you, Mr President, give your views on the basic problems which the sui generis Constitution of the Republic creates?

Answer 4:   In answering this question I do not propose to single out those provisions of the Constitution of Cyprus which create political and administrative difficulties except in so far as it is necessary, by way of illustration, to refer to such provisions. In my view it would not be a constructive approach to single out certain provisions of the Constitution and attempt to base an analysis of the situation on them. One has to go to the root of the matter and examine the basic concept of the Constitution of the Republic of Cyprus. It must be stated at the outset that the Constitution of Cyprus is the product of an anomalous situation which existed at the time of the Zurich conference and as such reflects the anomalies of the time. It is a well-known fact that prior to Cyprus achieving its independence, we have passed through a stage of artificially created, but nevertheless serious inter-communal conflict. The Zurich and London Agreements were accepted as a necessary step to bring about the Independence of Cyprus and thus to give an opportunity to the people of Cyprus to begin a new life. To look, therefore, on those Agreements and on the Constitution as something which is unalterable is to decide that the constitutional and political growth of Cyprus has been arrested in its infancy. Such an approach is unrealistic and amounts to an attempt to place Cyprus politically and constitutionally into a straight jacket.

I am, of course, aware of the fact that the Constitution of the Republic of Cyprus is guaranteed by Great Britain, Greece and Turkey. I will not concern myself here with examining the legal issues arising out of the said guarantees nor do I think anything constructive would result from arguing on their legal effect. I am, however, as a Cypriot greatly interested in and concerned about the political implication behind such guarantees.

Although there are three guaranteeing powers, this part of my observations relates only to two of the guarantors i.e. Greece and Turkey and in no way refers to the third guarantor i.e. the United Kingdom.

It has become abundantly clear during the course of the last two years that on a number of occasions questions which should primarily be the concern of the people of Cyprus have become the subject of debates in the National Assemblies of Greece and Turkey. In Greece the opposition has used the Cyprus question on more than one occasion as a weapon to attack the Government and in Turkey the Government itself has used the Cyprus question in internal politics. It is, therefore, undesirable and detrimental to the true interest of the people of Cyprus to have as guarantors countries which use the question whether the Cyprus Constitution should be amended or not either as an issue which the opposition uses to attack the Government or as a means for a Government to maintain its weak position at home.

It is my personal view that the people of Cyprus whether they are Greeks or Turks or whether they belong to any other group, while at this stage carrying on under the present Constitution, should sit round a conference table and consider the basic principles of the Constitution of their country. I am fully aware that there are questions on which a minority may require certain safeguards. This, however, is a problem which could be solved with goodwill and for which precedent may be found from other countries which have faced similar problems. The best guarantee of adherence to any Constitution lies in the fact that the people of the country to which it applies accept it. It is certainly an unhealthy principle that the viability of the Constitution of any given country should depend on foreign guarantors.

The answer to the constitutional difficulties which Cyprus is facing can only be found if the leaders of both communities, with statesman-like vision and courage, agree to call a conference to examine the Constitution of Cyprus and make recommendations for its amendments. It goes without saying that it should be made abundantly clear that all safeguards as internationally understood and accepted and based on precedent from other countries will be given for the protection of minorities.

It is, perhaps, necessary for me at this point to state what are the fundamental underlying concepts of the Constitution with which I disagree. Before, however, proceeding any further on the subject I would like to clarify one particular point. Objections have been raised from time to time by the Turkish leadership to statements made by Greek leaders advocating necessary amendments to our Constitution. In one particular instance it has been suggested by Turkish leaders that if the President of the House of Representatives disagrees with the provisions of the Constitution he should resign. Firstly I want to point out that I consider it my inherent and inalienable right as a citizen of a free and democratic Republic to express my views on all issues including the Constitution of the Republic, to criticise its defects and to make, what I believe to be, constructive suggestions for its amendment. Secondly I wish to state that in my opinion to resign a public office because one sees certain defects in the Constitution would be the easy way out. It would not be the way of any person who wishes to serve his country.

I will now revert to the examination of the underlying concepts of our Constitution which I believe to be fundamentally wrong. Briefly they may be formulated as follows:

Though the Constitution of the Republic rightly, in my opinion, takes cognizance of the fact that there are two communities in Cyprus, it wrongly proceeds on the assumption that the only way for the two communities to co-exist is by ensuring constitutional and political communal segregation.

For the sake of complete accuracy, however, it must be pointed out that the Constitution in taking cognizance of the existence of two communities ignores the fact that the Greek community constitutes 82% of the population of the island while the Turkish community represents only 18% and fixes Turkish representation in the Council of Ministers and the House of Representatives as well as participation in the Civil Service at 30%.

The increased political representation given by the Constitution to the Turkish community would not have created political and administrative difficulties had it not been coupled, at the level of the legislature, with separatist provisions. It could be argued that it was a necessary psychological step to give a minority representation beyond its numerical strength and its contribution to the economy of the country, but no justification exists for giving the minority, on taxation legislation and certain other matters, the right of separate majority, particularly since other provisions exist protecting the minority from any attempt to be discriminated against.

Our Constitution due to the underlying basic concept of communal segregation, in many respects is completely *sui generis*. Thus election to all political offices is based on communal vote alone. The segregational concept is carried to extremes even when the election is to an office which by its very nature carries responsibility to both communities. Thus for example the President of the House of Representatives is elected by the vote of the Greek Members of the House, instead of being elected by the House as a whole, while the Vice President is elected by the vote of the Turkish Members with the result that he cannot, in the absence of the President, substitute or act for him.

However, the most obnoxious example of the principle of Communal segregation is to be found in the provisions of the Constitution relating to the administration of justice. Thus a Greek must be tried by a Greek Judge, a Turk by a Turkish Judge and if the case involves a Greek and a Turk, however trivial, it must be tried by a Court composed of one Greek and one Turkish Judge. Cypriot Judges, whether Greeks or Turks, have in the past administered justice honourably and to the best of their ability. Why then, for the sake of the concept of communal segregation, impose restrictions in their jurisdiction based on communal considerations and thus bring about an impracticable system of administering justice and at the same time cast a doubt on the integrity of our Judges?

The concept of political and constitutional communal segregation reaches its final climax when we come to the field of education.

The Constitution by its provisions leaves each community, through the means of two elected Communal Chambers, responsible for the education of its members. The Government, though it gives to the two Communal Chambers an annual subsidy of £2,000,000, has no say in the education of the people of Cyprus. The subsidy, however, given by the Government does not cover the financial needs of the two Communal Chambers which are given power under the Constitution to impose personal taxes and fees on members of their respective communities for the purposes of covering the deficit between the subsidy given by the Government and the amount actually required. Thus the Turkish education and other communal services cost approximately £800,000 per annum. The Turkish Communal Chamber receives an annual subsidy of £400,000, leaving a deficit of £400,000 which it has to find by imposing taxes and fees on its members or obtaining financial aid from Turkey. It is absolutely impossible for the Turkish community, however severely it taxes its members to provide £400,000 per annum. This is obvious from the fact that Turkish income tax paid to the Turkish Communal Chamber yields only £80,000 per annum. Similarly the Greek Communal Chamber receives an annual subsidy of £1 1/2 m. from the Government while the cost of Greek education and other Communal services is approximately £3,000,000. The Greek Communal Chamber has, therefore, either by communal taxation, or by obtaining help from the mainland of Greece, to cover a substantial part of the cost of the education of its members.

It is clear to my mind that the Constitution deals with educational services in an unrealistic and unworkable manner. It imposes separately on the communities, and in particular on the Turkish community, financial burdens which are far beyond their capacity to meet. It is true that the Constitution provides that the subsidies given by the Government may be increased and thus the deficit of the two Communal Chambers decreased but even this provision is unrealistic. No Government will accept to finance the two Communal Chambers, without having financial control over their budgets. To do otherwise would amount to say, you spend and I will pay the bills. Another difficulty of the system is that the development of education in both communities will proceed at different rates and will depend on the financial strength of each community. In any event the rate of development of education for both communities, since there is no control between the two Communal Chambers and Government, will always be out of step with the general plans of the Government for the overall development of the country.

It is my honest opinion that the Constitution should be amended so as to impose on the Government the financial responsibility for the education of the country giving at the same time the Government the necessary control over communal expenditure. Finally I believe that the principle of communal taxation should be abolished.

In dealing with the effect of the concept of political and constitutional communal segregation on the provisions of the Constitution, one has to consider that part of it which deals with the local Government of the five main towns. The creation of separate municipalities based on communal criteria has come to be known, during the last two years, as the problem of separate Municipalities. I will not at this point express my views on this aspect of the Constitution because it forms the subject of a separate question.

In addition to those provisions of the Constitution which create political, constitutional and administrative difficulties and which, as we have already seen, are based on the separatist concept explained above, there are certain other provisions which render the Constitution totally unworkable and cannot be justified under any principle. Thus the Constitution provides that any Law imposing taxation and any law relating to Municipalities and the electoral Law require separate majorities of the Greek and Turkish Members of the House of Representatives. The net result is that though a taxation Bill may be unanimously approved by the Council of Ministers, including the Turkish Vice-President and the three Turkish Ministers, and though it may receive the overwhelming majority of Greek and Turkish votes in the House of Representatives, nevertheless it can be defeated, if it does not receive the separate majority of the Greek or Turkish votes. The House of Representatives consists of 35 Greek Members and 15 Turkish Members. If, for example, 35 Greek Members and 7 Turkish Members vote in favour of a Taxation Bill i.e. the Bill receives a total of 42 votes in favour, it can be defeated by eight Turkish votes.

There is no justification at all for such provision which is obviously contrary to every democratic principle. If this provision of the Constitution was intended as a safeguard for the minority from any attempt by the majority to impose taxation legislation of a discriminatory nature, then it is completely unnecessary because the Constitution gives the right to the Vice-President, who must always be a Turk, to challenge such legislation before the Constitution Court on the ground that it discriminates against either of the two communities.

The provision of the Constitution which imposes the procedure of separate majorities has already caused the Republic to remain without an Income Tax Law, despite the fact that the provisions of the Income Tax Bill, which was defeated by the exercise of the right of separate majorities, were agreed upon by the Turkish Members of the House. Thus the Turkish Members used their right of separate majority against the Bill neither because they disagreed with its provisions nor because it was discriminatory against their community, but simply as a weapon to force the Government to yield to Turkish demands unconnected with matters of taxation.

Even if one assumes that in future a more prudent use will be made of the right of separate majorities and even if one closes his eyes to the undemocratic principle involved, the application of the procedure of separate majorities will always cause serious difficulties and may well make it impossible for the Government to carry out vital taxation policy. One must remember that election to all political offices, including the office of "Representative" is based on communal vote alone and that as long as the Communal Chambers have the right to impose communal taxation there will always be a conflict of interest between Government and communal taxation.

Finally I wish to deal very briefly with the provisions of the Constitution which regulate the participation of the two communities in the Civil Service of the Republic. Under the Constitution the Civil Service must be composed of 70% Greeks and 30% Turks. This provision, of course, ignores the fact that the population proportion between the two communities is 80% Greeks and 18% Turks. To my mind this provision could be justified if looked upon as a means of procuring employment for the Turkish community which is not only smaller in population, but also poorer in financial resources. Certainly no one should resent any constitutional provision the effect of which would be to give financial strength to the minority and thus create a better standard of living. The insistence, however, that the ratio of 70% to 30% in the participation in the Civil Service should be applied in all grades, creates serious problems and difficulties for the efficient working of the Government Civil Service on which the proper administration of the country depends. Further, if strictly applied, it discriminates against Greek or Turkish Civil Servants whose promotion to higher grades may be prevented, not because they do not posses the necessary qualifications for such promotion, but simply because the vacant posts in the higher grades must be allocated in accordance with an artificial communal ratio fixed by the Constitution.

Thus, if a Greek Civil Servant possesses all the qualifications to be promoted to a vacancy in a higher post, his promotion may be denied to him because the Greek Community may have its 70% in that grade. The same, of course, can apply to a Turkish Civil Servant, though this is less likely in view of the fact that there were, prior to Independence during the colonial administration, only 18% Turks in the Civil Service.

Question 5:   How do you think, the difficulties arising out of the Constitution can be faced?

Answer 5:   I believe that the only way to face the difficulties arising out of the nature of our Constitution is for the leaders of the two Communities to agree to the principle of setting up a Committee to examine the Constitution and make recommendations for its amendment. It must be clear in the terms of reference of such Committee that the interests of minorities will be protected by reasonable safeguards. The Committee should have the right to use the services of experts of international repute to advise them on all issues. The findings of the Committee should be made publicly known within a specified time. Finally it must be made abundantly clear that the Constitution of the Republic of Cyprus is an internal matter for the people of Cyprus and that no outside interference will be tolerated.

Question 6:   What are the reasons which led to the political deadlock in the problem of Municipalities and along what direction do you see a possibility of finding a solution?

Answer 6:   Shortly the reasons which led to the political deadlock over the issue of the Municipalities may be stated as follows:
   (a) The impossibility of applying the provision of the Constitution for the geographical partition of the five main towns into separate Municipalities based on communal criteria.
   (b) The insistence of the Turkish leadership on the creation of separate Municipalities.
   (c) The constitutional provision which makes it necessary that any law relating to Municipalities requires separate Greek and separate Turkish majority in order to be enacted into Law.
   (d) Adverse outside interference on a purely domestic issue.
   The Constitution of the Republic of Cyprus provides that separate Municipalities shall be created in the five main towns of the Republic. The jurisdiction for legislating and thus creating the separate Municipalities is exclusively given to the House of Representatives which in enacting such legislation has to adhere to the provision of separate majorities. It is, however, constitutionally necessary that before such a law is enacted that the President and the Vice-President of the Republic must agree on the boundaries of the separate municipal areas in each town. Therefore, it is a condition precedent that before Municipalities can be created and in fact operate that there shall be agreement on the boundaries of the separate Municipal areas. The impossibility of defining the areas can be clearly demonstrated from the following facts:
      (i) The Constitutional Commission during the period of a whole year found it impossible to define such areas and for the purpose of not delaying further the Independence of the Republic, passed on this responsibility to the President and the Vice-President.

(ii) The President and the Vice-President immediately after Independence set up Committees to prepare maps showing their recommendations as to the demarcation of the Municipal areas in each town, but these Committees again failed to produce any agreed recommendations.

The impossibility of finding a way to define geographical areas and create separate Municipalities based on the criteria of community is due to the fact that never in the history of Cyprus the two communities ever dreamt of living in separate areas. Thus the Zurich Agreement decided to apply, for the first time in history, the principle of communal segregation. A factual examination will show that there are many areas in which Greeks and Turks live side by side and that the ownership of property by the two communities does not follow the pattern of communal areas. This fact is clearly apparent from the proposed principles formulated by the Vice-President of the Republic for determining what streets will fall within the Greek Municipality and those which will fall within the Turkish Municipality. His Excellency made the following proposal.

"The frontage of all property abutting on any street will be measured and if the total length of the frontage of the property belonging to the members of the Greek community in that street is greater, then that street will be included in the sector of the Greek Municipality. The same principle will apply in the case of a street where the total length of the frontage of the property belonging to the members of the Turkish community is greater".

One need not comment at length on the above proposals of the Vice-President of the Republic. It suffices to say that they are extremely impracticable and unworkable. It will be observed, however, that the Vice-President has tried to find a solution by distinguishing ownership of property on the basis of Communal criteria without taking into consideration the nature of the property and what is more important, without being able to suggest a principle which also takes into consideration the occupants of such property. It is an undisputed fact that there are many properties belonging to Turks which have Greek tenants and vice versa. It is equally clear that if the principles suggested by the Vice-President were accepted, many streets abutting to or leading into each other will fall in the area of one or the other community and thus the resulting two municipal areas will not have any territorial cohesion. This fact alone demonstrates how impractical the division of the towns into separate areas, based on communal criteria, is and how expensive it will become to run such Municipalities.

Apart, however, from the difficulty of defining areas, there is a further and basic reason why there should be in each of the five main towns only one Municipal authority. The five towns of the Island are not large enough to justify the economic running of more than one Municipality. This is particularly true when one considers such towns as Larnaca and Paphos. Thus Larnaca, for example, has a total population of 26,000 people out of which 21,874 are Greeks and 4,058 are Turks. The revenue derived from the Greeks is £67,934 and that derived from the Turks is £4,687. Even if we accept the Turkish allegation that the annual revenue of a Turkish Municipality in Larnaca is £7,000, it must be obvious, even to the man with the most limited intelligence, that it is uneconomical to run a Municipality for 4,687 people and that it is impossible to give proper municipal services including the maintance and lighting of streets on a revenue of £7,000.

The insistence of the Turkish leadership on the creation of separate Municipalities, despite the fact that it has been clearly demonstrated that it is not possible to bring about the geographical division of the main towns into communal Municipal areas and that such division even if possible would be financially detrimental to the true interests of the townsmen of those towns, is based on the contention that the Constitution provides for separate Municipalities and that there must be strict adherence to the Constitution.

Proposals were made to the Turkish leadership for unified Municipalities with full safeguards for the interests of the Turkish townsmen and with additional financial advantages for them. These proposals which are well known and need not be repeated here, were rejected by the Turkish leadership on the ground that, under the Constitution, we must begin with separate Municipalities, and that until such separate municipalities are created the question of unification does not arise. It has been pointed out to the Turkish side that even if their above contentions are accepted as correct, there is a way of solving the problem without going outside the provisions of the Constitution.

A law could be enacted creating two separate Municipal Corporations, i.e. a Greek and a Turkish one, in each of the five main towns as well as a Co-ordination Committee as provided by the Constitution.

In view, however, of the fact that the Constitution imposes the duty on the President and the Vice-President within four years from the date of Independence to consider whether we should continue with separate or unified Municipalities the President and the Vice-President, who have for the last two years examined this matter, could now agree that it would be to the advantage of all concerned to unify the Municipalities and thus a provision could be inserted in the same law creating the separate Municipalities that on a certain date the separate bodies created by it will be unified. The Law should go further and provide that within a short period after the unification elections for Municipal Councillors will be held and that the communal representation on the Municipal Councils will be in proportion to the Greek and Turkish inhabitants of each town.

Finally the Law should contain provisions that upon the unification of the Municipalities a certain percentage of the revenue of each Municipality will be used for the Turkish townsmen in a manner decided by the Turkish Councillors and out of a vote under their control. Already the Turkish side is aware of the percentages suggested by the President of the Republic which are well above the contribution to the joint revenue by the Turkish townsmen.

I believe that along this line a solution of the municipal problem can be found which will be to the interest of both communities. It is, therefore, more constructive to put an end to recriminations and sit round a conference table to produce a solution on the lines indicated above. This, however, may be an impossible task if the Turkish Government, through its Foreign Minister, makes statements which do great damage to the relations between the two communities and encourage the support of solutions which are by their very nature unworkable and contrary to the true interest of the people of Cyprus.

APPENDIX 65

Statement by Rauf Denktash, 11 June 1963

*After conferring with Dr. Kutchuk and other Turkish leaders the following
statement was issued by Mr. Rauf Denktash, the President of the Turkish
Communal Chamber*

Mr. G. Clerides, the President of the House of Representatives, has
come forward with a most outspoken statement which has confirmed beyond
any doubt that the policy of the Greek leaders in Cyprus is to abrogate the
Agreements which have an international force and to amend the Constitution
in such a way as to take away the rights of the Turkish Community and place
them in the position of a simply minority group with minor ordinary safeguards. It has now become apparent how justified the Turkish Community
were when on many occasions they expressed their anxiety and mistrust of the
Greek leaders who as from the very date of the establishment of our Republic
have persistently refused to implement those parts of the Constitution which
gave Turks certain rights.

Mr. Clerides suggested that Committees should be set up to examine
our Constitution and make recommendations for its amendment. I do not
propose to deal in this statement with all the points raised by Mr. Clerides in
support of his unacceptable proposals the full text of which I have not yet seen.
His proposals tend to create a new situation in Cyprus which is tantamount to
setting aside all the Agreements and the principles under which our Constitution was accepted and drafted. Mr. Clerides is well aware that the Constitution
is the outcome of a round table conference which lasted for over 18 months.
In this conference he himself (as representative of his Community) as well as
many experts of international fame (such as Professor Bridell, Professor Tsatsos
and Professor Erim) participated and contributed. As a result of long and arduous discussions and deliberations it became possible to agree on a form of
Constitution, which everybody endorsed as being the only means by which the
various conflicting interests could be brought together and balanced to the satisfaction of the two Communities in Cyprus. Before taking any serious and
genuine steps to implement this Constitution in its entirety and before experi-
menting its actual application in practice for at least a sufficient number of
years, to come out, soon after its introduction, with a suggestion to set it aside,
is indeed very surprising and at the same time very distressing. Since
Mr. Clerides was of the view that our Constitution and the Agreements are
unworkable (as he now alleges) it would have been more statesmanlike and
courageous of him, and in fact more honest, not to participate in the drafting of
such a Constitution and not to solemnly affirm "faith to and respect for" it as a
member of the House of Representatives under this Constitution.

I am sure that Mr. Clerides is well familiar with the spirit in which the
Zurich and London Agreements were agreed upon and our Constitution was
drafted. This spirit was to reconcile the conflicting interests of the two

communities which manifested themselves in the desire to join their respective motherlands and to establish a balanced and harmonious relationship between them and at the same time affording to both a chance to work in a spirit of equality and partnership for the future development, politically and economically, of our country. To allege now that the Agreements and the Constitution were accepted as a necessary step to bring about the independence of Cyprus and thus to give an opportunity to the people of Cyprus to begin a new life, is, I regret to say, a distortion of facts.

In his statement Mr. Clerides stated that Greece and Turkey cannot be accepted as guarantors of the Agreements and our Constitution. This is very strange as time and again Greek leaders and in particular the President himself stated that the independence of Cyprus did not create a nation but a State, and that Greeks living in Cyprus shall always remain Greek and Turks as Turk. This being the case it is not difficult to understand the motive behind Mr. Clerides' unacceptable and contradictory remarks about the guaranteeing powers.

In conclusion I would like to state once more that the difficulties which we are experiencing in Cyprus do not emanate from the nature of the Constitution or the Agreements as alleged by Mr. Clerides, but from the artificial obstacles purposely created by Greek leaders who have not been straightforward enough to honour the undertakings they have given, the Agreements they have made and solemn affirmations they have taken. This state of affairs has contributed to a great extent to inflate the already existing mistrust on the part of the Turkish Community towards Greek leaders because of their known ulterior aims. Instead of fostering, by making unrealistic proposals, this mistrust which has been created as a result of the conduct of Greek leaders who frequently and systematically indulged in pro-Enosis campaigns and flagrantly disregarded the Constitution and the Agreements, I would have expected Mr. Clerides, as a person occupying a very responsible post, to work for the implementation of the Constitution in its entirety and thus help to remove the mistrust. This is the only solution to our problems.

Nicosia,
11th June, 1963

APPENDIX 66

Record of Meeting between Minister of Foreign Affairs Spyros Kyprianou and the Lord Privy Seal Edward Heath, Strasbourg, 6 May 1963

TOP-SECRET

Mr. Heath enquired about the situation in Cyprus and added that, as he was informed, there was some anxiety and uneasiness. After explaining the present position with regard to the question of the Municipalities, of which Mr. Heath seemed to be fully informed, Mr. Kyprianou stressed the following:

a) Various difficulties arising from the Constitution, unless solved in a satisfactory manner, shall become causes of frequent friction between the Greek majority and the Turkish minority in the island. Such issues are the Municipalities, the right of separate majority in regard to certain legislation, etc.

b) The most dangerous, however, element in the whole situation is the purported right of the three so-called guaranteeing powers to intervene or interfere in Cyprus. This question may be examined from two aspects, the legal aspect and the realistic. The legal position of the Treaty of Guarantee is a matter to be seriously considered because whatever the interpretation given to certain of its provisions, it is extremely doubtful whether this Treaty should be regarded as a valid document in the light of a number of other conflicting commitments of the parties to it, as well as other relevant considerations. (Mr. Kyprianou spoke in some detail on this). Irrespective, however, of the legal aspect of this Treaty, any intervention would automatically result in a conflict with much wider repercussions. If any country would wish to create such a situation, it would not require any legal cover in order to pursue this extremely dangerous course of action.

c) Any discussion or argument on the Treaty of Guarantee has, until recently, been rather academic in the sense that neither the Cypriot side nor the Turkish side, which has been the only one to mention often the purported rights of Turkey under the said Treaty, seriously held the view that any intervention might be considered possible. Recently, however, the repeated statements by the Turkish Foreign Minister and other Turkish leaders, both in Ankara and Cyprus, about possible Turkish intervention in the island, by virtue of the said Treaty, has created a great amount of anxiety and has increased the sense of uncertainty about the future. It is not possible to tell the public of Cyprus that they should forget altogether their original legitimate demand, which has been an ideal fervently cherished by generations and at the same time to accept the idea that the independence of their country should be curtailed and its sovereignty limited. The situation must be cleared up, and the sooner the better. There is no third choice. It has to be one of the two: *Either* all concerned accept the fact that Cyprus is a fully independent and sovereign State and all rights of other countries in regard to Cyprus are abolished, if they do exist at all, *or* it would be impossible for anyone to convince the people to be patient for long, hoping for the best.

d) In view of the whole situation and in an effort to be constructive, it might perhaps be advisable to consider some alternative arrangements, in a realistic approach, which might help to remove most of the anxieties and minimise the dangers for the future of the country. It should not be out of the question to convince all concerned of the necessity, in the light of the present circumstances, to replace the two Treaties, namely the Treaty of Guarantee and the Treaty of Alliance, with a bilateral Treaty of Alliance between the United Kingdom and Cyprus. This would be quite appropriate not only in view of the fact that the United Kingdom maintains military bases on the island, but also because both countries belong to the Commonwealth. Cyprus cannot, for long, survive as an independent country if through various treaty arrangements, the internal situation prevailing in either Greece or Turkey, at any particular moment, may create problems for Cyprus. It is simply unacceptable that peace and tranquility in Cyprus should continue to depend to a large extent on the internal politics in either Greece or Turkey, and it is an undeniable fact that the present difficulties in the island are mainly due to the internal situation in Turkey.

Mr. Heath said that he realised all these difficulties and that the British Government, if it were to consider the suggestion explained above, would have to examine it mainly from two aspects, the one being what further commitments, in addition to the existing ones, would have meant for the British Government if a bilateral Treaty were to replace the two existing Treaties; and secondly the degree of the Turkish reaction to such a proposition. Mr. Kyprianou said that, in his view, no additional commitments would on the whole have to be undertaken by the British Government. As to the second consideration raised by Mr. Heath, it might be expected that there had to be unfavourable Turkish reaction, but such reaction might be minimised to a large extent if the Americans were to be convinced of the idea that such a solution would have to be sought sooner or later—and the sooner the better—so that further anomalies may be avoided. Furthermore, the Minister added, one should always bear in mind that the Government of the Republic could not for long remain silent on this matter in view of the great dangers involved. It way have to resort to either the United Nations or to other courses of action in order to protect the integrity and sovereignty of the country. If, therefore, a solution to this question is not found on the basis of the proposal for a bilateral Treaty, as explained above, the Cyprus Government would find itself compelled, at a certain point, to raise the question in another form and on another basis.

After some further discussion, it was agreed, at Mr. Heath's suggestion, that a further meeting should be held between Mr. Heath and the Minister, in London, early next week, and that the whole question should be also discussed with Mr. Duncan Sandys, Secretary of State for Commonwealth Relations. (A meeting between Mr. Sandys and Mr. Kyprianou has been arranged for Wednesday, 15 May, 1963, at Mr. Sandys' house in London).

APPENDIX 67

Letter from Foreign Office to British Ambassadors in Ankara, Athens and Washington and British High Commissioner in Nicosia, 21 May 1963

CONFIDENTIAL

C 1015/88
(No. 54, Confidential)

Foreign Office,
May 21, 1963

Sir,

Mr. Kyprianou called on the Lord Privy Seal on the 15th of May at his own request.

2. After referring briefly to the problems facing the export of Cyprus wines to the European Economic Community, *Mr. Kyprianou* went on to discuss the internal situation in Cyprus. He said that the new proposals put forward by Archbishop Makarios for a 6 to 8 months' interim period during which the Council of Ministers would take over the municipalities had been rejected. The Turks had suggested that the Ministerial Council itself should be divided into two; this proposal was quite clearly impossible. By a majority decision the Council had decided to nominate officers to carry out certain duties in connexion with the municipalities. Mr. Kyprianou did not think that the Turks would accept this. Indeed he thought there was little chance of either an interim or permanent solution emerging in the near future. He thought there was danger ahead unless a general solution to all the problems facing the Cyprus Government emerged. His own solution was briefly that Greece and Turkey should withdraw from the Treaty of Guarantee, leaving Cyprus, as a Member of the Commonwealth, connected solely with the United Kingdom.

3. When *the Lord Privy Seal* said this did not seem to him to be a starter, *Mr. Kyprianou* said that if Her Majesty's Government did not exclude this idea, then at least they could begin to think about it. *Mr. Heath* pointed out that few people were very likely to want to upset the treaty and there did not seem to be much point in antagonising others. *Mr. Kyprianou* said that some decision was needed, possibly even involving the United Nations; his idea was quite realistic. The United Kingdom was quite near to Cyprus in its Commonwealth capacity.

4. *The Lord Privy Seal* asked whether Archbishop Makarios had any new ideas on the municipalities problem. *Mr. Kyprianou* said that he did not think so. The truth was that Ankara did not want an agreement, possibly because of other disputes with Greece. There was a psychological aspect to the dispute. It was clearly absurd to envisage physical intervention, but the sheer mention of the possibility tended to create the feeling that Cyprus was not independent. The threat of the Treaty of Guarantee hung over Cyprus' head. There was a clear need for contingency planning, since any day some-

body might start something, perhaps even claiming he did it by virtue of the treaty. Too many things came under the treaty; why, for instance, did the municipalities problem? The Cyprus Government found they could do nothing without the consent of Turkey and Greece. The Greeks were not interfering at present, but one could never tell what would happen in the future.

5. *The Lord Privy Seal* asked if there had been any progress in building up an effective political party in Cyprus. *Mr. Kyprianou* said that the so-called Patriotic Front was all there was at the moment except for the Communist Party. Some thought had been given to the need for creating a new political party and in some ways this would be advantageous, but an the other hand it would probably mean a split in the Patriotic Front. There was a clear need that Makarios should be accepted as the leader. In any case, fewer non-Communists were now co-operating in any way with AKEL.

6. *Mr. Kyprianou* said that one of the main questions worrying him was the question of what to do about the activities of the Turkish Ambassador. There seemed little hope of conciliatory advice coming to the Ambassador from Ankara and he was becoming intolerable. He had himself tried reminding the Turkish Ambassador of the position of Dr. Kutchuk as Vice-President of Cyprus. The Turkish Government did not "occupy" the position of Vice-President. But this had little effect on the Ambassador. Mr. Kyprianou, however, as he had told the Commonwealth Secretary, appreciated the efforts of the High Commissioner in Cyprus.

7. Mr. Kyprianou's chief worry was that the hand of the Cyprus Government would be forced by events. The idea was gaining ground that as a Commonwealth country Cyprus might outgrow the tutelage of Greece and Turkey. It would not be difficult to convince the Greek Government of the need to abandon Cyprus. It was just the Turkish Government who would be difficult. *Mr. Heath* said that he thought that most people were proud of the Zurich and London Settlement. *Mr. Kyprianou* replied that Greece and Turkey were proud, but Cyprus was not. She felt the limitations on her independence.

8. *Mr. Kyprianou* said that he had proof that the Turkish military contingent in Cyprus was helping to organise and train the underground Turkish movement. What would happen tomorrow or the day after tomorrow was his great worry. He was perfectly willing to envisage safeguards of all kinds for the Turkish community, but the continual treaty restrictions upon the Government of Cyprus were intolerable. It was all very well to tell people they had independence but this was difficult to believe when they found they could not even exercise the elementary right of self-determination. He recognised that the separate majorities provision had helped somewhat in the running of Cyprus, but it could also prove a hindrance. Even now there was no income tax law because of this provision.

9. Finally, *Mr. Kyprianou* said that he could come to London any time privately for talks. It was perhaps a good omen that the United States had started to realise that changes in the Cypriot Constitution were necessary. *The Lord Privy Seal* pointed out that the Turks were certain to resist such changes. *Mr. Kyprianou* agreed but said that not many changes were envisaged, only about five or six in fact, such as reform of the separate majorities provision over

taxation, a solution of the municipality problem and, in his opinion the most important, a reform of the role of Greece and Turkey in the affairs of Cyprus. These reforms, he added, were necessary for the efficient government of Cyprus.

10. I am sending copies of this despatch to Her Majesty's Ambassadors at Athens and Washington, and to the United Kingdom High Commissioner at Nicosia.

I am, with great truth and respect,
Sir,
Your Excellency's obedient Servant,
(For the Secretary of State)

His Excellency
Sir Denis Allen, K.C.M.G.,
&c., &c., &c.,
Ankara.

CONFIDENTIAL

APPENDIX 68

Opinion, Sir Frank Soskice, 1 November 1963

I will at the end of this Opinion set out in sequence what in my view are the appropriate answers to the questions asked in Mr. Clerides' letter dated October 5th 1963; but before doing so I will make some general observations with regard to the Treaty of Guarantee.

The basic question on which, as I understand it, my opinion is asked is as follows: Serious difficulties have arisen with reference to the implementation of Article 123 and 173 of the Constitution, and also of Article 78 in relation to the imposition of taxes. Article IV of the Treaty of Guarantee provides that each guaranteeing Power in the event of breach of the Treaty, if common or concerted action proves impossible "reserves the right to take action with the sole aim of re-establishing the state of affairs created by the" Treaty. In these circumstances has Turkey the right under Article IV of the Treaty as one of the guaranteeing powers, if Articles 123 and 173 of the Constitution are not in due course implemented, and should concerted action not prove possible, herself to embark upon unilateral military intervention without authority from the Security Council?

International treaties unavoidably in general embody provisions expressed in terms less precise and less exactly formulated than domestic legislation. They are the result in the majority of cases of hard bargaining between representatives of conflicting national interests, and it is in the nature of things in general impossible to achieve complete precision when the intentions of the parties are written into the letter of the treaties. It has therefore been accepted that somewhat greater latitude is permissible in the interpretation of international treaties than of domestic legislation, and the general circumstances in which the treaty was entered into may be taken into consideration, as well as the written word of the treaty, in determining what really were the intentions of the parties. In particular there has been much difference of opinion about the legal effect of the many Treaties of Guarantee which have been entered into over the last century and a half.

Furthermore, international law as a whole is subject to a process of constant evolution, as new international situations present themselves. It is, therefore, unwise to attempt to formulate principles in general terms applicable to hypothetical future situations. The views I express in this Opinion should therefore be regarded as applicable only to the actual situation envisaged in the previous paragraph and the precise question asked in that paragraph with reference to Turkey's right to embark unilaterally upon a course of military intervention, and not to other hypothetical situations that might arise in the future.

The Treaty of Guarantee itself contains as its last paragraph an undertaking by the High Contracting Parties as soon as possible to register it with the Secretariat of the United Nations Charter. This, in my opinion, as well as the general background against which the Treaty was entered into is an indication that the parties intended the Treaty to be construed as containing only such obligations and conferring only such rights as would not conflict with the obligations and restrictions imposed by the United Nations Charter. Article 103 of the Charter must I think be considered together with the Treaty, and Article 103 provides as follows:

> "In the event of a conflict between the obligations of the Members of the United Nations under the present Charter and their obligations under any other international agreement, their obligations under the present Charter shall prevail".

In this context a number of Articles of the Charter of the United Nations would be relevant notably those contained in Chapter VIII under the heading "Regional Arrangements", that is to say, Articles 52 to 54, and also Article 51 which deals with the inherent right of self-defence, as well, of course, as the general Articles in Chapter I setting out the purposes and principles of the United Nations, and those contained in Chapters VI and VII dealing with the pacific settlement of disputes and the general enforcement powers of the Security Council. It is a feature of these Articles that they prohibit the use of force by Member Nations except in the most limited range of circumstances such as actual self-defence, unless with the authority of the Security Council.

In my opinion, in these circumstances, the words in Article IV of the Treaty of Guarantee "each of the three guaranteeing Powers reserves the right to take action" should not be construed in any sense which would involve a conflict with the restrictions imposed by the Articles of the Charter to which I have made reference. I will assume the absence of any 'threat to' or 'breach of the peace' within Article 39 of the Charter such as might bring into operation Articles 43 and 44. These Articles are in any event irrelevant to the present question; since even if a Member Nation used force in pursuance of these Articles, such use of force would not be pursuant to any Treaty, but in fulfilment of the duty to assist the Security Council imposed by these Articles of the Charter itself.

Furthermore, I will assume that no situation has or could, in relation to the basic question put to me, arise such as might bring into operation what are in effect the emergency provisions as to self-defence contained in Article 51 of the Charter of the United Nations.

The words "reserves the right to take action" do not, as I understand them purport to create a new right to take some action which would otherwise, apart from those words, not be permissible. In my opinion, they are more appropriate to keep in being some right to take action which would have existed independently of the Treaty under international law, in case, in the absence of such a saving provisions, the right which a guaranteeing Power would under international law in any event have possessed might be extinguished by the Treaty. A situation is envisaged in Article IV of the Treaty in which a breach of the Treaty has taken place and concerted action by the guaranteeing Powers has proved impossible. The effect of the words, in my opinion, is to preserve in such a situation such powers as each guaranteeing Power might individually have exercised under the general principles of international law even if there had been no Treaty of Guarantee. The question, if this view is correct, then arises whether in the actual circumstances envisaged in what I have above described as the basic question asked by Mr. Clerides any right to embark upon unilateral military intervention would have ensured to Turkey apart from the Treaty. There has for example been a right generally recognised in international law in one nation to use force to rescue or protect its own nationals in the territory of another State if that State treats them contrary to basic international legal principles, for example, by using unlawful violence against them. Article IV of the Treaty however only preserves the right to take action "with the sole aim of re-establishing the state of affairs created by the Treaty".

It is open to question how wide is the scope of the words in Article IV of the Treaty of Guarantee "re-establishing the state of affairs created by the present Treaty". Clearly the "state of affairs" includes the independence, territorial integrity and security of the Republic of Cyprus. It may be asked, however, whether it includes the fulfilment of such Articles of the Constitution as Articles 123 and 173, both of which are under Article 182 declared (in the case of Article 173 subject to some limitations) to be Basic Articles. Article II of the Treaty includes within those things that the Treaty guarantees "the state of affairs established by the Basic Articles of The Constitution". It seems to me necessary to read the words "the state of affairs created by the present Treaty" in Article IV of the Treaty as including, besides the independence, territorial integrity and security of the Republic of Cyprus, also "the state of affairs established by the Basic Articles of the Treaty" referred to in Article II. On the other hand I do not think the words in Article IV "re-establishing the state of affairs" read with the words in Article II "established by the Basic Articles" are equivalent to words such as "secure exact compliance with the requirements of the Basic Articles". They are in my view quite inappropriate for that purpose. The expression "the state of affairs" is I think a general phrase, descriptive of a broad situation and in my view in its application to Articles 123 and 173 of the Constitution could only permit of action under Article IV of the Treaty if the substance of the protection for the Turkish minority created by Articles 123 and 173 were (unless by general agreement) overset or removed. What constitutes the "substance" of this protection must involve a question of degree and cannot I think be further defined. In order to answer what I have called the basic question put to me the words in Article IV of the Treaty of Guarantee "with the sole aim of re-establishing the state of affairs created by the present treaty" in effect have to be read as if they were "with the sole aim of re-establishing the substance of the position created by Articles 123 and 173 of the Constitution".

Apart from the right to use force which I have just mentioned I do not know of any other right relevant in this context of forceful intervention independently of treaty. It is not easy to conceive of a practical situation in which the right of a guaranteeing power to use force to rescue its own nationals from unlawful treatment could be in a real sense relevant to the "sole aim" of preserving the state of things set up by the two relevant Basic Articles of the Constitution, and in my opinion this right to use force in the very limited circumstances I have described can be disregarded.

But in my view, in any case, even if the words in question could be construed as creating a right unilaterally to use force, (and as stated I think they are not appropriate for this purpose) if the Treaty of Guarantee is a "regional arrangement" falling within the scope of Article 52 of the Charter of the United Nations, it is in my view impossible to disregard Article 53 of the Charter which requires that any forceful intervention can only take place with the authority of the Security Council.

The question thus arises whether the Treaty of Guarantee whether considered separately or as forming part of a wider arrangement brought into being by the Treaty of Guarantee read together with the Treaty of Establishment and the Treaty of Alliance should be regarded as such a "regional arrangement". The answer to this question, in my opinion, depends on the nature and content of these Treaties and in particular the Treaty of Guarantee, the history of events which proceeded their making, and the circumstances in which they are made. So considered, in my opinion, there is no reason why the Treaty of Guarantee should not be regarded as constituting or, forming part of a "regional arrangement". It followed after and was clearly designed to put an end to the unhappy events which had taken place in Cyprus and to reconcile and put an end to sharp conflicts of opinion both inside and outside Cyprus, which if unresolved could have led to situations of increasing danger. In order that it may fall within the description of a "regional arrangement" within paragraph 1 of Article 52 of the Charter, it must be an arrangement "for dealing with such matters relating to the maintenance of international peace and security as appropriate for regional action provided that such arrangements . . . and their activities are consistent with the Purposes and Principles of the United Nations.". It seems to me that the Treaty does comply with these requirements. It recognizes and is designed to perpetuate a state of affairs relating to Cyprus which had emerged as the agreed solution to differences negotiated after prolonged periods of acute tension and disturbance; and its obvious objective is to re-introduce and maintain stability and peaceful relationships in Cyprus itself and generally in that part of the Mediterranean area. It enjoins consultation in the event of a breach of the Treaty and records the desire of the High Contracting Parties to co-operate. These features seem to me to bear in every sense the hall-mark of such a regional arrangement as is contemplated in Article 52 of the Charter.

For the reasons I have given, in my opinion, the words in question in Article IV of the Treaty of Guarantee, even if they could be said in any relevant circumstances to permit of unilateral military intervention, would not, in the circumstances which have arisen, allow of such action by Turkey unless authorised by the Security Council.

It is to be observed that the rights to take action conferred by Article IV are in another sense limited. Such as they are they only arise if there has been a breach of the Treaty. If Turkey should claim the right to resort to such unilateral action as the Security Council may authorise she must in my opinion be able to demonstrate that she has made genuine and reasonable endeavours to deal with the situation by concerted action with the other High Contracting Parties. She could not in my view lawfully maintain that a situation had arisen in which the Security Council might authorise unilateral action unless she had genuinely sought to bring the other guaranteeing Powers into consultation with a view to concerted action, and not even then if she had put forward only arbitrary or unreasonable proposals from which she refused to depart despite representations made in the course of such consultations by the other Powers.

Mr. Clerides in his letter dated September 14th 1963 asks whether, in my opinion, the terms of the Treaty of Alliance can be said in any sense to modify the Treaty of Guarantee or to assist in the interpretation of the words "take action" in Article IV of the Treaty of Guarantee. I do not think they do and they do not in my opinion, require a meaning to be attributed to those words different from that which earlier in this opinion I have said I think is the right meaning. The Treaty of Alliance itself has to be registered under Article 102 of the Charter of the United Nations, and must and can, I think be read as requiring and authorising only such action as is permissible in accordance with the Articles of the Charter of the United Nations to which I have earlier made reference, in particular Articles 51 and 53.

Mr. Clerides in his letter of September 14th 1963 asks whether upon the principle "conventio omnis intelligitur rebus sic stantibus" it could be successfully argued that circumstances have arisen which would justify Turkey in withdrawing from the Treaty of Guarantee unilaterally without the consent of the other Powers and would discharge her from any duty of further compliance with the Treaty. As is well-known there is the most acute difference of opinion amongst international jurists, in the first place, whether such a doctrine exists at all as part of international law, and secondly, if it does exist as to what is its scope. Those writers who propound the doctrine, however, do not, as I understand, envisage that it would justify unilateral repudiation of a treaty obligation by one party to it except upon the happening of some change in the circumstances which was basic to the situation in the light of which the treaty obligations were negotiated and undertaken. In the case of the Treaty of Guarantee it could not be argued that any such change has in present circumstances supervened, relevant to any provision of the Treaty, other than that relating to the maintenance of "the state of affairs established" by the Basic Articles of the Constitution in Article IV. There could be no question, therefore, of the repudiation of any provision of the Treaty than this provision. In my opinion, however, the serious difficulties that have arisen in the implementation of Articles 123 and 173 of the Constitution could not be regarded as constituting such a vital change of circumstance as would justify repudiation of the provision. The differences between the Greek and Turkish authorities in Cyprus though no doubt intractable and difficult of solution do not in my opinion represent a new element which can be fairly said to invalidate the basic assumptions upon which this provision of the Treaty was negotiated. On the contrary in my opinion they are difficulties inherent in the nature of the Constitution and the Treaty obligations themselves. I do not myself think that, at any rate so far, anything has taken place which would justify repudiation in terms of the doctrine "rebus sic stantibus" as that doctrine is propounded by those who assert that it is an established principle in the field of treaty interpretation. It is not easy to answer the further question asked by Mr. Clerides in his letters what, within the sphere of practical possibility, might constitute such a new supervening circumstance as might justify unilateral repudiation. Conceivably, as an example, the appearance and growth through immigration or otherwise of some other minority group which could not be assimilated either into the Greek or Turkish community and made wholly unrealistic the existing balance of numbers of the population, might constitute such a supervening change; but this is no more than purely hypothetical and in the highest degree unlikely as a practical example.

In view of the considerations above indicted I will set out by way of summary the questions which I understand to be asked and the answers which I think should be given, as follows:

1. Does the Treaty of Guarantee give the right to intervene in the event of amendment of Articles 123 and 173 of the Constitution? Yes, if the amendments are made without general agreement; but only if the amendments in substance disturb the protection afforded to the Turkish minority. Failure literally to comply with these Articles would not give such a right.

2. Does the Treaty of Guarantee, considered alone, or read with the other Treaties, constitute or form part of such a regional arrangement as is envisaged in Article 52 of the Charter of the United Nations? Yes.

3. Do the words "take action" contained in Article IV of the Treaty of Guarantee in the circumstances which have arisen entitle Turkey to embark upon unilateral military intervention without the authorisation of the Security Council? No, and the Security Council could not authorise such intervention unless Turkey could demonstrate that she had made genuine endeavours to secure concerted action with the other Guaranteeing Parties to the Treaty.

4. Do the difficulties which have arisen in connection with implementation of the provisions in the Constitution which give protection to the Turkish minority and notably Articles 123 and 173, entitle Turkey under the "rebus sic stantibus" principle to withdraw from the Treaty unilaterally and repudiate the obligations it imposes? No.

(Signed) Frank Soskice

November 1st 1963
1 Harcourt Buildings,
TEMPLE E.C.4

APPENDIX 69

First Document Setting Out Turkish Plans, October/November 1960 (translation)

1.   We accepted the Zurich and London Agreements as "a transitory phase" and it was for this reason that we signed them.

If it had been said they are not "a transitory phase" but a "final solution" we would not have accepted but would have prolonged the intercommunal dispute for a further period and would have left the UN face to face with Taksim which they stated to be "impossible and impracticable".

As regards the administration of the Republic created by the Zurich agreements which we accepted as a "transitory phase":

(a) Turkey's rights on Cyprus would have gained international recognition.

(b) During the time gained by preparing better we would have profited by the blunder and mistakes of the Greek Cypriots and in time by accusing them of violating the agreements we would attain our total independence.

During the course of the "transitory phase" all our behaviour and actions would have been directed towards the situation as shown in (a) and (b) paragraphs and accepted by us as the "final aim".

2.   The reasons for us in not being able to accept the Zurich agreements and the Republic created by these agreements as a "final solution" are these:

(a) This administration which is based on the seven:three ratio, despite existing guarantees, is a Greek Cypriot administration. Under the administration, the Turkish structure which is in any case weak, is sentenced to be eroded in time.

(b) Because the Turkish Cypriots will not be left with a national cause in the face of the "unification" process started to "Cypriotify" the Turks; that is maximum cooperation with the Greek Cypriots, the non-opposition to the Greek Cypriots, getting on well and viewing with understanding every caprice of the Greek Cypriots in order not to make difficulties; the result of this process means the elimination of the Turkish Cypriots as a separate community.

(c) Lack of financial possibilities, material difficulties are of a nature to bring down to naught our "separate community" status in a very short time.

(d) The agreements have come about based on the principles of mistrust of the communities towards each other, enmities and on the fact that they could live together only as "separate and equal communities". Considered from the viewpoint of a final solution, the principle of separate and equal community is destined to collapse unless we maintain it fastidiously or create an atmosphere of mistrust and enmity.

(e) The aim of the community administrators who did not allow the people to lift their heads for 25 years during the British rule was to rear a community "which was always obedient, faithful and bowed down to everything so as not to give cause to the British Government to trample on the community. And now, those who consider these agreements as a final solution are inviting the community "to bow down to the Greek Cypriots forever and at whatever cost not to create difficulties" and thus a community cause is existent no longer. If the Republic is a final solution, in the face of these suggestions firstly the trust of the Turkish Cypriots towards their own community and later its confidence in Turkey will be shaken. Due to such agents as unemployment and lack of credits, everything will fall into the lap of the Greek Cypriots.

Under these conditions our acceptance of the Zurich Agreements as a "final solution" would have meant us placing with our own hands the sentence of annihilation on the Turkish Cypriots.

It was for this reason that before the agreements "a compact had been reached with the Turkish Government of the time to the effect that these agreements were a transitory phase; during this period maximum economic and other assistance would be made to us and that in order to realise our final aim we would continue our 'separate community' cause as a national cause".

Also it is gratifying to state that during our first contacts with the honourable head of state of our Revolutionary Government. (Government formed soon after the coup d'etat against Menderes' Government trans. Note.), Gursel Pasa "an agreement on the same principles had been reached and it was made very clear in the most categorical fashion that the agreements were nothing but a phase for us and for Turkey".

4.   There is a major reason for the Turkish Cypriots' acceptance of the agreements and the establishment of the Republic as a phase and to keep their eyes open in order not to fall into a neglectful sleep: This major reason is that the Greek Cypriots have in their totality accepted the Republic administration as a transitional phase. From the first day all their actions have been directed towards the destruction of these agreements.

(a) With their newspapers, their official and non official little words they are disseminating that the agreements are transitional that these agreements could not be accepted by any free person and that they were imposed on them. The foreign journalists who visit the island are swallowing up this propaganda and thus the idea that "the Turks should give up the artificial rights obtained artificially" has been taking root.

(b) The Greek Cypriots (rightist or leftist) are arming themselves up at an unprecedented speed.

(c) The Police Organisation, Customs and the administrative mechanism are being organised in a way to suffocate the Turks.

(d) Practically none of the rights given to the Turks under the Zurich agreements have been handed over. The Greek Cypriots through a policy of delay are busy with wearing out, making weary, splitting the Turks and creating Turkish leaders who accept that these rights are truly superfluous.

(i) The municipalities have not been separated. The re-determination of the borders can continue for years; important obstacles and irregularities and injustices which might necessitate our rebellion as a community are expected. As a result of the "wearing away practice" for the last one and a half years the spirit of struggle of the Turkish Cypriots is being extinguished.

The issue of separate municipalities represents a basis of our "separate community status". Even if this separation is of material inconvenience to the Turks, it is necessary to continue this separation at whatever cost and to maintain the issue of "separate municipalities" as a cause.

Today those few persons who have suffered personal damages due to the separation of the municipalities and those "opponents who blindly follow the claim that at whatever cost to get on well" with the Greek Cypriots, have started exerting great energy to do away with this separation and to unite the municipalities. Messers Ahmed Muzaffer Gurkan and Ayhan Hikmet who pass as "opponents" are making statements to foreign journalists that the unification of the municipalities is a necessity and that the reason for Denktash and Doctor Kuchuk wanting separate municipalities was the continuation of the "Taksim" thesis.

We request clear cut directives as to whether or not the separate municipalities issue should be upheld as a cause. We are of the opinion that if the unification of municipalities path is followed based on material reasons this would be the collapse of the sound ground on which our "separate community status" is based on.

(ii) The difficulties which we have encountered on the issue of 70:30% are known to you. Two and a half months of the five-month period set for the application of this ratio have passed. The Greek Cypriots have no intention of finishing this work within five months. The "method of application and the application schedule agreed upon between Makarios and Dr. Kuchuk is on the verge of being thrown into the waste paper basket by the Greek Cypriot members of the Civil Service Commission. Makarios also has gone as far as saying that "this agreement has no binding value."

If at the end of the 5 month period the 70:30% ratio is not adopted what will the Turkish side do? Will it apply to the Constitutional Court and struggle for another five years? Or will we be able to choose the path of obtaining our rights as a community?

We should not forget that the 70:30 ratio should have been applied within the period between the London agreement and the birth of the Republic. We have been sacrificed to Greek Cypriot caprices, and by adhering to the "for goodness sake let there be no difficulties" directives, we were not able to wrest an obtainable right at the right time. The result has been that the community's right in itself has been shaken. If this issue is not finished at the end of 5 months "Dr. Kuchuk and his friends who have promised that this was to be applied within 5 months, will be left in a very difficult position!"

(iii) In the Ministries with the incitement and control of the Greek
Cypriot clerks the Turkish affairs are being stalled. The Greek
Cypriot police and clerks are doing everything they can in order to
give the impression that we are living under a Greek Cypriot administration. The principle that "the Turkish clerks will serve the
Turkish villages" which is one of the conditions of the "separate
community" status is not being applied anywhere.

Should we insist on its application? The Turks of Chatoz
(Serdarli) had not given their taxes to the Greek Cypriot collector
of taxes who had gone to the village to collect taxes. Now they are
to be sent to court. Our demand that "we want Turkish clerks" is a
demand which will offend and instigate anew the Greek Cypriots.

According to us we should insist on this claim and should not
give as concession one more of our separate community rights.

(iv) The cooperation amongst the Greek Cypriots in the Council of
Representatives in order not to carry out a single performance in
favour of the Turks has reached its zenith.

Everything is being done in order not to form the Cyprus army.
The Army Commander and his Assistant is being offered less salaries than the Police Commander and his Assistant; it is being said
that the soldiers will be given an amount which can be said to be
ludicrous.

They don't have the intention of adding even a penny to the
£400,000 minimum assistance guaranteed by the constitution of
the central government in respect of our £800,000 Educational and
Communal Budget. On the other hand up to now the amount of
six million British pounds assistance has been made by various
"private channels" to the Greek Cypriot Communal Assembly.

We believe that in the face of the path taken by the Greek
Cypriots in order to extinguish the Communal Chambers which are
the sole symbol of our "Separate Community Status", the government of our motherland will make the supreme sacrifice and will
materially support us.

If we fall into a situation whereby we cannot continue the offices of the communal assembly due to material impossibilities we
would destroy the existing agreements in line with Greek Cypriot
desires.

(v) Development investments from the budget are being secretly diverted to the Greek Cypriot villages. Not one Turkish deputy can
obtain money for an investment he deems necessary. Maximum
effort is being exerted in order to make the Turkish deputies into
puppets.

(vi) The Police appointments have been made in such a way as to make
the Turkish commanders ineffective. The Turks of the island are
toys in the hands of the Greek Cypriot commanders.

5. The way out according to us is this:

(i) The reality that the agreements are a transitory phase and the belief that our separate community status is vital in realising this objective will be told to every Turk and this belief will be disseminated throughout the island in such a way that it can be passed from generation to generation.

(ii) To show maximum reaction to every action and endeavour of the Greek Cypriots to destroy out "Separate Community" status. (We believe that it is our right to react in order to protect our Constitutional rights).

(iii) The main lines of the "national cause" should be imposed on those who love to play the opposition within the community. They should be prevented from engaging in publications and propaganda that might harm the national cause.

Dr. Ihsan Ali who is an admirer and adorer of the Greek Cypriots and has been confirmed to have connections with the British Intelligence and the extremist Greek Cypriot ENOSIS leaders and his accomplice a sex pervert (Muzafer Gurkan) and Ayhan Hikmet who has been confirmed to have relations with the communists should be made to abandon their actions and writings which serve the Greek Cypriot aims. If they don't believe in the existence of a national cause they must be silenced.

Today the Turkish Cypriots are in an impasse. The Community does not know what to do due to their daily problems of unemployment, lack of credits and lack of employment fields and the failure to obtain jobs from the Greek Cypriots creates question marks within the community and creates extreme doubt as regards the existence or non-existence of a national cause. In the face of this situation the path of not believing those who speak of "separate community rights" will be chosen. It will be said: "What separate community? There is no employment institution, only those who trust the Greek Cypriots can live, life lines of those who draw away from the Greek Cypriots are cut". We are face to face with the need to wipe away this belief and to create a society which believes in itself and in the 1955-58 years.

In short a national plan should be presented to the administrators and we should adjust our words and actions in accordance to this national plan. If the basic lines of this national plan is the continuation and consolidation of the separate community status, if it is the domination of Turkism over Cyprus someday", then we could continue the struggle and we could win over the public. However if this plan will be in the shape of "we have come to the end of everything, get on well with the Greek Cypriots, don't be spoilt, don't offend your Greek Cypriot friends whom you are obliged to open your hand by creating an uproar because some of your small rights have been swallowed"; then it will be necessary for us to renew our situation and to think whether or not we will shoulder this responsibility under these conditions.

SH/MP

True translation.
Translated by Sureya Hami,
Director, Press and Information Office
(K. Psyllides)

24.2.1987

Note: Although this document is not dated, its approximate date has been determined to begin the last week of October or the first week of November, 1960. This is estimated as follows: Para 4(ii) of the document states that "two and a half months of the five-month period set for the application of this (70:30) ratio have passed". As the decision of the President and Vice-President was to implement this ratio within five months from the date of the establishment of the Republic, this means the document was written half way through the 5-month period between 16 August 1960 and February 1960 i.e. the last week of October or the first week of November 1960.

It should be noted that the document together with the document dated 14.9.63 (Annex 8) were found in the safe of the Turkish Cypriot Minister of Agriculture Mr. Plumer. As confirmed by Mr. Tassos Papadopoulos on 22.2.87 in a personal communication, the safe was opened in the presence of Mr. T. Papadopoulos then acting Minister of Agriculture, Mr. Mouskos, Director-General of the same Ministry, a technician from the Accountant-General's Department and two members of the Intelligence Service.

[Similar documents were, according to the Intelligence Service, also found in the safe of the Turkish Cypriot Defence Minister Mr. Orek.]

APPENDIX 70

Second Document Setting Out Turkish Plans Signed by Fazil Kutchuk
and Rauf Denktash, 14 September 1963 (translation)

*A cursory glance at the general policy of the Turkish Community as regards the
future of the Republic on the occasion of the completion of three years since the
establishment of the Republic*

Three years have now elapsed since the establishment of the Cyprus
Republic. By the signing of the Zurich and London Agreements, which are the
foundation of the Constitution, while the Turkish Community abandoned its
basic aim of being united with its motherland and agreed to the establishment
of this Republic, the Greek Cypriots also in their turn gave up their basic aim
of Enosis and agreed to become partners with the Turks in the Administration
of the Republic. It was agreed that the Republic to be set up under the Zurich
agreements would be of a peculiar character (sui generis) and it was accepted
from the first days that the viability of this Republic is based on the good-willed
and understanding cooperation between the two communities which constitute
this Republic by showing loyalty to the promises made and to the agreements
undertaken.

Unfortunately from the first days the Greeks have indicated that they
had not signed these agreements in good-will and attacked the Zurich Agreements through the press and other media. Even Makarios, who personally
signed the Zurich Agreements did not refrain from admitting on the occasion
of the EOKA anniversary on 1 April 1960 (when the Constitution had not yet
cone into force officially), that the Zurich Agreement was a spring-board for
future victories.

Since the proclamation of the Republic the Turkish Community has
made it known in various ways that the Greek Cypriots had no intention to accept and implement with sincerity and integrity these Agreements and they
have made statements, published articles and prepared reports showing that in
the application of these Agreements they have resorted to every trick to render
inoperative the articles which recognise even the most insignificant rights to
the Turks.

It has become explicit beyond doubt that at present the Greek Cypriots
have no intention at all to set up the separate Municipalities and the Cyprus
army, that they will never implement the requirement of the employment of
Turkish civil servants comprising of 30% and that they will not take into account the Turks' existing right of say through veto concerning such vital aspects
for the Turkish Cypriot Community as foreign policy, defence and domestic
security. The most serious aspect of the issue for the Turkish Community is
that the Greek Cypriots have started disputing even the guarantee agreement
which is the sole basis for the implementation of the Constitution and the fact
that Makarios without even feeling the necessity to get the views of the Turkish
Community in this regard has assumed the status of head of state and has had

the insolence and boldness in stating that they will not recognise the guarantee agreement. For this reason for us it is superfluous to explain in this report the injustices, pressures, threats and blackmail made by the Greek Cypriots in this deceitful manner against the Turks since the Constitution went into force. (We already have prepared reports on this score).

The real aim of this report is to formulate the counter policy to be followed by the Turkish Community in the face of the de facto situation created by the Greek Cypriot side through a systematic policy.

Undoubtedly in dwelling upon the principles of any policy to be followed it is necessary to indicate the real objectives of such a policy. Up until now the basis of the policy conducted by the Turkish Community was based on the necessity of the full implementation of the Constitution of the Republic. This policy was catering to the needs of the Turkish Community as long as the Greek Cypriots insistently evaded the de facto implementation of the Constitution, however this policy has become very ineffective in the face of the Greek Cypriot policy to completely amend or to abolish the Constitution.

In our opinion in particular after Makarios' statement to the effect that 'the year 1964 will be a decisive year for the amendment of the Constitution', the Turkish Community faces the necessity of following a more active policy. What should the basic target of such active policy be? The answer to this question must be given separately depending on each of two possible alternatives the Greek Cypriots may follow:

1.   The Greeks may finally abrogate or try to annul the Zurich and London Agreements and the Constitution.
2.   They may continue with their 3 year old policy of the de-facto 'amendments' by not allowing the implementation of the Constitution and to de-facto reduce the Turks into a minority by enlarging the compass of the Constitution.

In the event of the Greeks officially abrogating the constitution or trying to amend it, in our view there is only one thing the Turkish Community will do; take its destinies in its own hands and establish a Cyprus Republic outside the Zurich Agreements in accordance with the axiom 'when the obstacle is removed one reverts to the forbidden.' The success of such a move will necessitate a very hard struggle on the part of the Turkish Community and conditioned on many internal and external factors. No doubt the most important of the external factors will be the material and moral help of the motherland. Practically there is no possibility of the Turkish Community being able to fight under the present conditions without obtaining in advance the consent and subsequent support of the motherland. Therefore, it is essential that we should agree in advance with our motherland on the line of action based absolutely on a detailed plan. Makarios has not yet made a serious effort to abrogate or amend the Agreements. There is ample time to prepare such a plan and we must make the most of it.

As a matter of fact under the Treaty of Guarantee the motherland can intervene alone if the Constitution is abolished officially. But the only result of this intervention would be to return to the legal status established under the

Zurich Agreements. As the Greeks are determined despite the intervention not to allow this legal status to survive, and, taking into consideration the negative effect which intervention would create at UNO and amongst world opinion, it is a matter of dispute whether it would be worthwhile taking the risks which will be created for the motherland from a unilateral intervention. Therefore, in the event of the Greeks abolishing the Constitution officially, the Turkish Community, taking its destinies in its own hands, should go ahead with the establishment of a Turkish Republic and so, if nothing else, the dangers from an actual intervention would, at the beginning, be averted.

We can sum up the main points of such a plan as follows:

1. The Turkish Vice-President of the Republic will be accepted as President of the Republic by the Turkish Community, and a Government consisting entirely of Turks will be set up in accordance with the provisions of the existing Constitution.

2. Our motherland will recognise immediately the government to be formed which will ask our motherland for help.

3. The intervention of the motherland will follow the request for this help and if need be Turkish Republic rights will be recognised to the Turkish Cypriots settled in Turkey (in principle this right exists under the present Constitution in the form of quota), they will be given passports prepared in the name of the Turkish Republic and thus their infiltration into Cyprus will be secured.

4. The Turkish members of the House of Representatives and the Turkish members of the Communal Chamber will form the House of the Republic and proclaim the provisions of the existing Constitution for the establishment of a Republic composed entirely of Turks or as another alternative a provisional constitution should be drawn up and proclaimed.

5. After recognition by the motherland the Turkish Republic will immediately sign with the motherland trade agreements as a result of which the Turkish Community will meet its material requirements in the ensuing conditions. No doubt the object of such an agreement will be to give legality to the help from the point of view of international law.

6. There is no doubt that this move of the Turkish community will meet with Greek Cypriot opposition and counter moves and probably the Greeks will undertake de facto aggression against the Turks.

As a result of these aggressive acts of theirs a struggle will start between the two Communities and this struggle will decide the outcome.

7. When the struggle begins, the Turkish Community, interspersed throughout the island, will forcibly concentrate in an area and will be compelled to defend it. The selection of the area will depend on the strategic plan which will be prepared by experts. Before the struggle starts it will be necessary to prepare detailed plans to increase the (military) mobility of the Turkish Community and concerning the equipment, stocks and the shipment of supplies and reinforcements from the motherland.

8. Detailed projects should be prepared from now and the necessary financial plans should be made and the necessary nucleus must be set up from now within the Turkish Communal Assembly so that the civil servants existing

in the present administrative mechanism could continue their work uninterrupted from the very first days of their transfer to the new administration.

The above is an outline of the plan, and before a complete and detailed plan is prepared in respect of all fields it will be necessary and advisable to reach a definite and final decision concerning the basic idea. We are sure that the Turkish Community will make every possible sacrifice in this question.

Now as regards the policy to be followed in the face of the Greek Cypriots' maintaining the present situation, that is the continuation of the de facto amendment of the Constitution: In our view if the Greeks continue this policy the target of the Turkish Community should again be the establishment of a separate Republic. The Turkish Community can no longer tolerate continuation of this state of affairs. However since the Constitution will not be openly violated by the Turkish Community, the Turkish Community is again obliged to advance to the final goal at a slower tempo. For this reason the following plan comes to mind in response to the second possibility.

1. The plan which is designed to be implemented in respect of the first option should be prepared as soon as possible.

2. A violent pressure movement should be initiated in every field in order to force the Greek Cypriots to implement the Constitution. The most natural result of such an action will be that the members of the Turkish civil service in general will have to oppose the Greek Cypriots during the course of their duties basing their actions on the Constitution. As a result it will be inevitable to appoint such elements in the Turkish Communal Assembly in accordance with the 8th article of the first plan.

3. From the economic point of view, in order to render the Turkish Community self-supporting and to ensure the success of the first plan we must establish useful industries. As these industries will be boycotted by the Greek Cypriots, we will secure markets in Turkey to enable these enterprises to survive.

4. With a view to invigorating the Turkish Community financially and making preparations for the implementation of the first plan, it is necessary that speedy and frequent links should be established between Cyprus and the motherland particularly by sea (ferry-boat, etc) and that the population of the Turks in the Island should be increased to the maximum through the entry of people from Turkey as tourists.

5. The Turkish Community, after it has completely prepared itself financially, militarily and morally should put its first plan into operation by taking advantage in the event that the Greek Cypriots create a Constitutional crisis.

Until now the Greek Cypriots have given us many opportunities on this matter and from now on it is obvious that they will provide more opportunities on account of their behaviour.

Nicosia, 14.9.1963

(Dr. Fazil Kuchuk)
Vice-President of the Republic

(Rauf Denktash)
President of the Turkish
Communal Chamber

True translation.
Translated by Sureya Hami,
Director, Press and Information Office
(K. Psyllides)

24.2.1987

Note: It should be noted that this document together with the undated document appended as Annex 9 were found in the safe of the Turkish Cypriot Minister of Agriculture Mr. Plumer. As confirmed by Mr. Tassos Papadopoulos on 22.2.87 in a personal communication, the safe was opened in the presence of Mr. T. Papadopoulos then acting Minister of Agriculture, Mr. Mouskos, Director-General of the same Ministry, a technician from the Accountant-General's Department, and two members of the Intelligence Service.

[Similar documents were, according to the Intelligence Service, also found in the safe of the Turkish Cypriot Defence Minister Mr. Orek.]

APPENDIX 71

The So-Called "Akritas Plan" Drawn Up toward the End of 1963 (translation)*

Document of Akritas (P. Georkadjis) as to the Objectives of the Greek Cypriot Side and the Prospects as they appeared towards the end of 1963

TOP SECRET
HEADQUARTERS

RECENT POLITICAL DEVELOPMENTS

The recent public statements of the Archbishop have outlined the course which our national issue will follow in the immediate future. As we have stressed in the past, national struggles are neither assessed nor solved from one day to the next, nor is it always possible to fix definite time limits for the achievement of the various stages of their development. Our national cause must be examined in the light of the developments and circumstances obtaining at the time, and the measures to be taken, the tactics and the time of implementation of each measure must be determined by the circumstances existing then, both internationally and internally. The entire effort is difficult and must pass through various stages because the factors which influence the final result are many and varied. It is sufficient that all should understand that each measure taken is the result and consequence of study and of previous studies and at the same time constitutes the basis of the next measure. It is sufficient to recognize that the measures which are prescribed today constitute only the first step, one simple stage towards the final and unalterable national objective, to the full and unfettered exercise of the right of self-determination of the people.

Since the purpose remains unalterable, what is left to be examined is the question of tactics. This must of necessity be divided into internal tactics and external (international), because both the manner of handling and of presentation of the issue will differ in each case.

A.   First, external tactics (international).

In the final stages of the struggle, the Cyprus problem was presented to international public opinion and diplomatic circles as a demand for the exercise of the right of self-determination of the people of Cyprus. To the exercise of this right the question of the Turkish minority was insinuated, in circumstances which are well-known, and the intercommunal violent clashes were used as a pretext in an attempt to show that co-existence of the two

---

* As published in Spyros Papageorgiou, *Crucial Documents on the Cyprus Problem (1959–1967)* (in Greek) (Nicosia, Cyprus: Ekdoseis K. Epifaniou, 2000), vol. 1, 250-57.

communities under a unitary government was impossible. Finally, in the eyes of many international circles, the problem was solved by the London-Zurich Agreements, a solution which was presented as the result of negotiations and agreement between the two sides.

(a) Consequently, our first target has been to cultivate internationally the impression that the Cyprus problem has not really been solved and that the solution requires revision.

(b) Our first objective has been our endeavour to be vindicated as the Greek majority and to create the impression that:
 (i)   The solution given is neither satisfactory nor just;
 (ii) The agreement reached was not the result of the free and voluntary acceptance of a compromise of the conflicting views;
 (iii) That revision constitutes a compelling necessity for survival, and not an attempt on the part of the Greeks to repudiate their signature;
 (iv) That the co-existence of the two communities is possible, and
 (v)   That the strong element on which foreigners ought to rely is the Greek majority and not the Turks.

(c) All the above, which constituted a most difficult operation, have been achieved to a satisfactory degree. Most diplomatic missions have already come to believe that the solution given is neither just nor satisfactory, that it was signed under pressure and without real negotiations, and was imposed under various threats. It is a significant argument that the solution reached has not been ratified by the people because our leadership, acting wisely, avoided calling the people, by plebiscite or otherwise, to give its formal approval, something which the people, in the spirit prevailing in 1959, would certainly have done. Generally, it has been established that the administration of Cyprus so far has been carried on by the Greeks, the Turks confining themselves to a role of negation and obstructionism.

(d) Second objective. The first stage having been completed, we must programme the second stage of our activities and objectives on the international level. These objectives in general can be outlined as follows:
 (i)   The aim of the Greeks is to remove unreasonable and unfair provisions of administration and not to oppress the Turks;
 (ii) The removal of these provisions must take place today because tomorrow it will be too late;
 (iii) The removal of these provisions, although reasonable and imperative, is not possible because, due to the unreasonable attitude of the Turks, concerted and agreed action with the Turks is ipso facto impossible. Consequently, unilateral action is justified;
 (iv) The question of revision is an internal affair of the Cypriots, not giving to anyone the right of intervention by force or otherwise;
 (v)   The proposed amendments are reasonable, just and safe-guard the reasonable rights of the minority.

(e) It is generally acknowledged that today the international climate is against any form of oppression and, more specifically, against the oppression of minorities. The Turks have already succeeded in persuading international public opinion that Union of Cyprus with Greece amounts to an attempt to enslave them. Furthermore, it is considered that we have good chances of success in our efforts to influence international public opinion in our favour if we base our demand, as we did during the struggle, on the right to exercise our own free will for self-determination rather than Union with Greece (Enosis). However, in order to be able to exercise the right of full and free self-determination, we must first free ourselves of all those provisions of the Constitution and of the Agreements (Treaty of Guarantee, Treaty of Alliance etc.) which prevent the free and unfettered expression and implementation of the wishes of the people and which hold dangers of external intervention. It is for this reason that the first target of attack has been the Treaty of Guarantee, which was the first to be cited as no longer recognised by the Greek Cypriots.

When this is achieved no legal or moral power can prevent us from deciding our future ourselves freely and exercising the right of self-determination by a plebiscite.

It is evident from the above, that for the success of our plan a chain of actions and developments is imperative, each of which is necessary, otherwise future actions will remain legally unjustified and politically unattainable, while at the same time we would expose the people and the country to serious consequences. The actions to be taken can be summed up as follows:

(a) Amendment of the negative elements of the agreements and parallel lapse of the Treaties of Guarantee and Alliance. This is necessary because the need for amendments of the negative aspects of the Treaties is generally accepted internationally and is considered justified (we can even justify unilateral action), while at the same time outside intervention to prevent us amending them is unjustified and inapplicable;

(b) As a result of the above actions, the Treaty of Guarantee (right of intervention) would become legally and substantively inapplicable;

(c) Once Cyprus is relieved (of the Treaties of Guarantee and Alliance) of the restrictions on the exercise of the right of self-determination, the people will be able freely to give expression to and implement their desire;

(d) Lawful response by the forces of the State (Police or even friendly military forces) to any internal or external intervention, because we will then be completely independent.

Thus, actions (a)-(d) are absolutely necessary and in the chronological order indicated.

It is therefore obvious that if we hope to have any chance of success internationally in respect of our above actions, we cannot and must not reveal or declare the various stages of the struggle before the previous one is completed.

For instance, if it is accepted that the above four stages are necessary, then it is unthinkable to speak of amendments (stage (a)) if stage (d) is revealed. For how would it then be possible to argue that the revision of negative aspects is necessary for the functioning of the State and the Agreements?

The above as regards targets, aims and tactics in the international field. And now as to the internal front.

B.   Internal Front.

Activities in the internal field must be considered in the light of the manner in which they will be interpreted internationally and of their repercussions on the national cause.

1.   The only danger which could be described as insurmountable is the possibility of external intervention by force, not so much because of the material damage, nor because of the danger itself (which, in the last analysis, could be met by us partly or wholly by force), but mainly because of the possible political consequences. If intervention is threatened or takes place before stage (c), then the legality of such intervention would be debatable, and even possibly justifiable. This fact has a lot of weight both internationally and in the United Nations. The history of many recent instances teaches us that in not a single case of intervention, whether legally justified or not, has either the United Nations or any other power succeeded in evicting the invader without serious concessions detrimental to the victim. Even in the case of the Israeli attack against Suez, which was condemned by almost all member states of the United Nations, and in respect of which Soviet intervention was even threatened, though Israel withdrew, yet it received (kept) as a concession the port of Eilat on the Red Sea. Naturally, much graver dangers exist for Cyprus.

If, on the contrary, we consider and justify our action under (a) above well, then, on the one hand, intervention will not be justified and, on the other, it cannot be carried out before consultations between the Guarantor Powers, Britain, Greece and Turkey. It is at this stage of consultations (before intervention) that we need international support. We shall have it if the amendments proposed by us appear reasonable and justifiable.

Hence, the first objective is to avoid intervention by careful selection of the amendments we will propose at the first stage.

Tactics: Reasonable constitutional amendments after efforts for common agreement with the Turks have been exhausted. Because common agreement is not possible, we shall attempt to justify unilateral action. In parallel, the actions at (ii) and (iii) will be implemented at this stage.

2.   It is obvious that in order that intervention may be justified a more serious reason must exist and a more immediate danger than simple constitutional amendment.

Such a reason could be: (a) the immediate declaration of Enosis before the completion of actions at (a)-(c)above; or (b) serious intercommunal conflict which would be presented as a massacre of the Turks.

Reason (a) has already been dealt with in the first part and, consequently, it remains only to consider the danger of intercommunal conflict. Since we do not intend, without provocation, to attack or kill Turks, the possibility remains that the Turkish Cypriots, as soon as we proceed to the unilateral amendment of any article of the Constitution, will react spontaneously, creating incidents and clashes, or intentionally stage, under orders, killings, atrocities or bomb attacks on Turks, in order to create the impression that the Greeks have indeed attacked the Turks, in which case intervention would be necessary for their protection.

Tactics: Our actions for constitutional amendments will be in the open and we will always show ourselves ready for peaceful negotiations. Our activities will not be provocative or violent in any way. Should incidents occur, they will at first be dealt with lawfully by the lawful security forces, in accordance with a plan. All actions will be of a lawful nature.

3.   Until the right of unilateral amendment of the Constitution is established and accepted, actions and decisions which require positive dynamic action on our part, such as the unification of Municipalities, must be avoided. Any such decision would require the Government to intervene dynamically in order to bring about the unification and to take over municipal property by force, which would probably compel the Turks to react dynamically. On the contrary, it is easier for us, by legal means, to amend, for instance, the provision relating to the 70:30 ratio in the public service, in which case it is the Turks who would have to take positive dynamic action, while for us this procedure would not constitute action, but "non-action". The same applies to the issue of separate majorities with regard to taxation legislation. These measures have already been considered and a series of similar measures have been chosen for implementation. Once our right of unilateral amendment of the Constitution is established de facto by such actions, we shall be able to advance, at our discretion and depending on our strength, more decidedly.

4.   It would, however, be naive to believe that it is possible for us to proceed to substantive acts of amendment of the Constitution, as a first step of our general plan as outlined above, without the Turks attempting to create or to stage violent clashes. For this reason, the existence and strengthening of our Organisation is an imperative necessity because:

(a) In the event of spontaneous Turkish reaction, if our counter-attack is not immediate, we run the risk of facing panic among the Greeks, particularly in the towns, thus irretrievably losing substantial vital areas; whereas an immediate and decisive show of our strength may bring the Turks to their senses and confine their actions to sporadic insignificant acts;

(b) In the event of a planned or staged Turkish attack, it is imperative to suppress it by force in the shortest possible time, because if we succeed in gaining command of the situation in one or two days, no outside intervention would be possible, probable or justified;

(c) In either of the above cases, dynamic and effective response to the Turks would very greatly facilitate our subsequent action for further amendments. It would then be possible for such amendments to be implemented without any reaction because the Turks would know that any reaction on their part would be either impossible or seriously damaging to their Community; and

(d) In the event of more generalised or generalised conflict, we must be ready to proceed immediately to the actions at (a) to (d), including the immediate declaration of Enosis, because then there would be no reason to wait or to engage in diplomatic activity.

5.   At no stage should we neglect the factor of enlightenment and response to the propaganda and the reactions of those who do not and cannot know our plans, as well as the reactionaries. It has been shown that our struggle must pass through at least four stages and that we must not reveal our plans and intentions publicly or prematurely. Complete confidentiality is more than a national duty. IT IS A VITAL NECESSITY FOR SURVIVAL AND SUCCESS.

This however will not prevent the reactionaries and the irresponsible demagogues from indulging in an orgy of exploitation of patriotism and provocations. The plan provides them with fertile ground, because it gives them the opportunity to allege that the efforts of our leadership are confined to the objective of constitutional amendment and not to pure national objectives. Our task becomes more difficult because, by necessity and depending on the prevailing circumstances, even the constitutional amendments must be made in stages. All this must not, however, draw us into irresponsible demagogy, street politics or to a race as to who bids higher in the stakes of nationalism. Our acts will be our most truthful defenders. In any event, because the above task must have made substantial progress and have yielded fruit long before the next elections, it is necessary for obvious reasons that in the relatively short time in between we must show exemplary self-restraint and sang-froid. At the same time, however, we must not only maintain the present unity and discipline of the patriotic forces, but intensify it. This can only be achieved by appropriate briefing of our members and through them of our people.

In the first instance, we must expose the reactionaries in their true light. They are petty and irresponsible opportunists, as their recent past has shown. They are negative reactionaries who rabidly oppose our leadership, but without at the same time offering a substantive and practical solution. We need a steady and strong government in order to promote our plans up to the last moment. These opponents are verbalists and sloganists with beautiful words and slogans, but incapable and unwilling to proceed to concrete acts or to suffer sacrifices. For example, even at the present stage, they offer nothing more concrete than recourse to the United Nations, that is, words again and without cost to themselves. They must, therefore, be kept at a distance and isolated.

In parallel and at the same time we shall brief our members about our above plan and intentions, BUT ONLY ORALLY. Our sub-headquarters must, in gatherings of leaders and members, analyse and explain the above, fully and continuously, until each one of our members understands them fully and is in a position to brief others. NO WRITTEN REPORT IS PERMITTED. THE LOSS OR LEAKAGE OF ANY DOCUMENT RELATING TO THE ABOVE AMOUNTS TO HIGH TREASON. No act can damage our struggle as vitally and decisively as the revealing of the present document or its publication by our opponents.

With the exception of word-of-mouth briefing, all our actions and especially publications in the press, resolutions, etc., must be very restrained and no mention of the above should be made. Similarly, in public speeches and functions, only responsible persons may make, under the personal responsibility of the Leader of the Sub-Headquarters, references in general terms to the plan outlined above and this only after the express approval of the Leader of the Sub-Headquarters who must check the text. ON NO ACCOUNT ARE REFERENCES TO SUCH A SPEECH IN THE PRESS OR ANY OTHER PUBLICATION PERMITTED.

Tactics: Full briefing of our people and of the public BY WORD OF MOUTH. Publicly we shall endeavour to appear as moderates. Projection of our plans in writing or references to them in the press or in writing are strictly prohibited. Officials and other responsible persons will continue the enlightenment of the people and the task of raising their morale and fighting spirit, but such enlightenment excludes making our plans public through the press or otherwise.

Note: This document will be destroyed by fire on the personal responsibility of the Leader of the Sub-Headquarters in the presence of all the members of its General Staff within 10 days of its receipt. Copies in whole or in part are prohibited. Members of the staff of the Sub-Headquarters may have a copy only on the personal responsibility of the Leader of the Sub-Headquarters but may not remove it from the seat of the sub-Headquarters.

The Leader AKRITAS

APPENDIX 72

Recommendations for Amendment of the Constitution of the Republic of Cyprus Prepared in Early November 1963

PAPER 1

RECOMMENDED AMENDMENTS IN THE FOLLOWING PARTS OF THE CONSTITUTION

PART III.   PRESIDENT OF THE REPUBLIC, VICE-PRESIDENT OF THE
                   REPUBLIC, COUNCIL OF MINISTERS.

PART VIII.   THE FORCES OF THE REPUBLIC i.e. ARMY, POLICE,
                   GENDARMERIE.

PART VI.   THE INDEPENDENT OFFICERS OF THE REPUBLIC i.e.
                   ATTORNEY-GENERAL AND DEPUTY ATTORNEY-GENERAL.
                   AUDITOR-GENTRAL AND DEPUTY AUDITOR-GENERAL.
                   THE GOVERNOR AND THE DEPUTY GOVERNOR OF THE
                   ISSUING BANK OF THE REPUBLIC.
                   ACCOUNTANT-GENERAL AND DEPUTY
                   ACCOUNTANT-GENERAL.

PART VII.   THE PUBLIC SERVICE.

PART XII.   MUNICIPALITIES. ARTICLES 173-178.

PART III

PRESIDENT OF THE REPUBLIC, VICE-PRESIDENT OF THE REPUBLIC AND THE COUNCIL OF MINISTERS

In beginning the consideration of what amendments are necessary, in this chapter one should begin with Article 46 which is the key to the whole situation created by the present Constitution. Article 46 provides that the Executive power is ensured by the President and the Vice-President of the Republic and it further sets out the manner of appointment of Ministers, the allocation of Ministries and the existence of three specifically named Ministries (i.e. Finance, Foreign Affairs and Defence) one of which must be held by a Turkish Minister. The following amendments are, therefore, necessary in order to correct the situation:

(a) The Executive power is ensured by the President of the Republic.
(b) The Vice-President of the Republic, acting in his capacity of leader of the minority, ensures the exercise of such executive power as strictly necessary for the protection of the rights of the minority defined in the Constitution.
(c) The Executive Power is exercised by the President of the Republic acting through the Council of Ministers.

It follows from what is stated above that it is the responsibility of the President to have a Council of Ministers and that, therefore, the appointment of Ministers and the signing of the instrument of appointment of Ministers is a matter for the President as Head of the State. At present the instrument of appointment of Ministers is signed both by the President and the Vice-President of the Republic. Equally the allocation of the Ministers chosen by the President to the various Ministries is a matter for the President. It is recognized, however, that so far as the three Turkish Ministers are concerned, the President will appoint them out of a list of candidates submitted by the Vice-President. The provision contained in this article that out of the three Ministries i.e. Finance, Foreign Affairs and Defence, one must be given to a Turkish Minister, must be abolished.

Finally it is recommended that provisions should be made in this Article about the procedure of dismissing Ministers. The dismissal of Ministers should be made by the President of the Republic. In the case of Turkish Ministers the dismissal will be carried out by the President acting on the recommendation of the Vice-President. At present the right of dismissing Greek Ministers is given to the President and the right of dismissing Turkish Ministers is given to the Vice-President.

We may now consider the amendments necessary in Article 36. The provision contained in Article 36(1) i.e. that the Vice-President is the Vice-Head of the Republic must be deleted and instead it must state that the Vice-President of the Republic takes precedence over all persons in the Republic next after the President of the Republic. The third paragraph of the same Article should be deleted and replaced by a provision to the effect that the Vice-President of the Republic acts as President of the Republic in the absence of the President or in case of his temporary capacity. Similarly Article 44(2) should be amended to provide that in the event of a vacancy in the Office of the President of the Republic, the Vice-President will act as President during such vacancy and that in the event of a vacancy in the Office of the Vice-President, the President of the House of Representatives will act as Vice-President of the Republic.

In Article 36, Sub-section (2), which provides that the President of the House of Representatives and the Vice-President of the House of Representatives deputize for the President and the Vice-President should be deleted and amended according to the above suggestions.

In Article 38(b) the right of the Vice-President to be present at the presentation of credentials of foreign diplomatic envoys should be abolished. This right exists in no other country and if the amendments are carried out to the effect that the Vice-President acts as President of the Republic in the absence of the President or in the case of his temporary capacity the role of the Vice-President is no longer that of the Head of the Turkish community, but of the Vice-President of the country. There is, therefore, no need for his presence at the presentation of credentials. Consequential amendments will be necessary in other Articles.

Articles 51, 52 and 57 dealing with the issues of the right of return and the promulgation of laws and decisions require to be amended to ensure the following:

(a) The right of return of laws and decisions is a prerogative which should be exercised only by the Head of the State.
(b) It is recognized, however, that there may be decisions or laws which viewed from the point of the minority may be considered as affecting particularly the minority and in such case the Vice-President will have the right to request the President of the Republic to return the law or decision for re-consideration.
(c) Upon such request the President will be bound, without examining the contention that the law or decision particularly affects Turkish rights, to return the law or decision for reconsideration transmitting at the same time the views and grounds on which the Vice-President requests the reconsiderations of the law or decision.

Coming now to the right of promulgation, (Articles 52 & 57) it is submitted that this right should be exercised by the President alone. In every country the act of formal promulgation is prerogative of the Head of the State. Even under the present Constitution the act of promulgation is purely formal and it is clear from the relevant Constitutional Court decisions that neither the President nor the Vice-President have the right to refuse to promulgate a law or decision properly enacted or taken. Where constitutional provisions are made enabling either the President or the Vice-President to challenge a law or decision before a Court as unconstitutional prior to promulgation, then the President will be bound not to proceed and promulgate such law or decision until the matter is resolved.

Article 50 giving the President and the Vice-President a right of veto on foreign policy and security must be abolished and consequential amendments will have to be made in other Articles and in particular to Articles 47, 48 and 49.

Article 53 of the Constitution which provides for the exercise of the prerogative of mercy should be amended along the following principles:

(a) The President as the Head of State exercises the right of mercy or clemency.
(b) The President appoints a Board consisting of the Minister of Justice, the Minister of Interior, the Attorney-General, the Deputy Attorney-General to consider all applications for clemency and make recommendation to him. The President acts on their unanimous recommendation.
(c) If there is no unanimity the view in favour of clemency will always prevail.
(d) Death warrants, after the procedure outlined above, will be signed by the Minister of Interior.

Note: In Cyprus in view of the fact that the Prisons are under the Ministry of Justice and executions must take place by Prison Officers within the Prisons, it may be considered necessary that the death warrant should be signed by the Minister of Justice.

Article 54 of the Constitution dealing with the Executive functions of the Council of Ministers requires consequent amendments in view of the suggestions made in this paper.

Article 58(3) which provides the manner of terminating the appointments of Ministers should be amended so that the President of the Republic terminates all appointments of Ministers by signing the instrument of termination. In the case, however, of the Turkish Ministers the President will act on the recommendation of the Vice-President.

Article 60 of the Constitution which provides for a joint Secretariat of the Council of Ministers headed by two Secretaries one belonging to the Greek and the other belonging to the Turkish community should be amended so as to provide for one Secretary, who will hold the office on criteria of qualifications and ability irrespective of the community to which he belongs.

The above recommendations cover in general all the Articles contained in Part III of the Constitution. There are, however, certain other Articles which are closely connected with this Part and to which reference is made in this Part. It would, therefore, be convenient to deal with them before beginning with Part IV which deals with the House of Representatives.

PART VIII

THE FORCES OF THE REPUBLIC

Articles 129-132 require amendments.

Article 121 provides that the Republic shall have an Army of 2,000 men of whom 60% shall be Greeks and 40% Turks. It is recommended that this Article should be amended merely to state:

(a) That the Republic may have such forces for the defence of its territory as may be provided by a Law.
(b) The ratio of participation of the two communities in such forces shall be a fair one and in no event below the ratio of their numerical strength.

Section (2) of the same Article which provides that in order to have compulsory service the agreement of the President and the Vice-President of the Republic is required should be amended and compulsory service should be a matter provided by legislation. This is the normal practice in all countries of the world.

Article 130 which provides that the Security Forces of the Republic i.e. Police and Gendarmerie shall consist of 2,000 men which may be increased or reduced by agreement between the President and the Vice-President should be amended to provide:

(a) That the numerical strength of these forces shall be provided by a law.
(b) That any increase or decrease of the force is a matter of legislation. This is the normal practice in all countries. The situation as envisaged to-day in the Constitution is that the President and the Vice-President

may agree to increase the force. Their agreement, however, will be ineffectual if the legislative body does not approve the increase in the Budget. If on the other hand it is maintained that the agreement of the President and the Vice-President to increase the Security Forces creates an obligation and a charge on the Consolidated Fund, then the position is that money can be spent without the approval of the House of Representatives. This is clearly not the right approach. It is doubtful whether a legal interpretation could be given to the effect that the President's and the Vice-President's agreement creates a charge on the Consolidated Fund.

Article 130(2) which provides for the ratio of the participation of the communities in the Police and the Gendarmerie should be amended to the effect that there will be a fair participation of the two communities and in no event such participation will be below the ratio of their numerical strength.

It is recommended that the division of the Security Forces into Police and Gendarmerie should be abolished.

Article 131(1) which provides the manner of the appointment of the Heads and Deputy Heads of the Army, the Police and the Gendarmerie of the Republic should be amended so as to provide that the appointment of the above-mentioned officers shall be made by the Head of the State i.e. the President.

Article 131(2) which provides that one of the Heads of the Army, the Police and the Gendarmerie shall be a Turk and that where the Head of the Army, the Police and the Gendarmerie belong to one community the Deputy Head shall belong to the other community should be amended to the effect that the Heads and the Deputy Heads of the aforesaid forces should belong to different communities. Where the President of the Republic under the above provisions appoints a Turk he will do so out of a list of Candidates submitted to him by the Vice-President.

Article 132 which provides that forces stationed in parts of the territory of the Republic inhabited in proportion approaching 100% by members of one community shall belong to that community should be abolished.

PART VI

THE INDEPENDENT OPFICERS OF THE REPUBLIC

Article 112(1) requires amendment to the effect that the President of the Republic will appoint two persons to act as Attorney-General and Deputy Attorney-General of the Republic. The provision that the Attorney-General and the Deputy Attorney-General of the Republic shall not belong to the same community should be retained. The appointment, however, of the Attorney-General or the Deputy Attorney-General, if the appointee is decided to be a Turk, should be made by the President of the Republic out of a list of candidates submitted to him by the Vice-President. The proviso to Article 112(5) which entrusts the conduct of criminal cases to the Attorney-General or the Deputy Attorney-General on community criteria should be abolished.

THE AUDITOR-GENERAL AND THE DEPUTY AUDITOR-GENERAL

Article 115 should be amended to the effect that the President of the Republic appoints the Auditor-General and the Deputy Auditor-General. The proviso that the Auditor-General and the Deputy Auditor-General shall belong to different communities should be retained. Where it is decided to appoint a Turk as Auditor-General or as Deputy Auditor-General, the appointment should be made by the President of the Republic out of a list of candidates submitted by the Vice-President of the Republic.

THE GOVERNOR AND THE DEPUTY GOVERNOR OF THE ISSUING BANK OF THE REPUBLIC

Article 118 should be amended to the effect that the President of the Republic appoints the Governor and the Deputy Governor of the Issuing Bank of the Republic. The proviso that the Governor and the Deputy Governor should belong to different communities should be retained. If, pursuant to the above provisions, it is decided to appoint a Turk as Governor or Deputy Governor of the Bank, the appointment should be made by the Head of State, i.e. the President, from a list of candidates submitted by the Vice-President.

THE ACCOUNTANT-GENERAL AND THE DEPUTY ACCOUNTANT-GENERAL

The same amendments should be carried out in Article 126 regarding the appointment of an Accountant-General and a Deputy Accountant-General.

PART VII

THE PUBLIC SERVICE

Article 123 which provides that the Public Service shall be composed of 70% Greeks and of 30% Turks should be deleted. Instead it should be provided that the Public Service shall be composed of citizens of the Republic and that in appointing civil servants a fair distribution of posts between the two communities will be applied. It is recommended that it should be stated that the ratio of participation of the two communities to the Public Service shall not be below that which exists at the present date.

Note: It would be difficult to suggest that Turkish officers appointed at present will be dismissed in order to bring their ratio in true proportion with that of their population.

Article 123(2) which provides that the quantitative distribution (i.e. a fair distribution) shall be applied so far as this will be practically possible in all grades of the hierarchy in the Public Service should be retained in view of the fact that the operative words in this Section are "as far as practically possible".

Article 124(1) and (2) should be amended to reduce the number of the members of the Public Service Commission to five i.e. three Greeks and two Turks.

Article 125(3) sub-paragraph (2) should be deleted. Similarly sub-paragraph (3) and (4) should also be deleted. Instead it should be provided that if the Commission acted in a manner which is discriminatory to either of the two communities, the Chairman of the Commission will be bound on a unanimous request of the Greek members, if the alleged discrimination relates to the appointment of a Greek, to refer the matter to the High Court for a decision. Similarly the Chairman of the Committee will be bound to refer the matter to the High Court, on a unanimous request by the Turkish members of the Committee, on the ground that the appointment related to a Turk and that there was discrimination in failing to appoint him.

MUNICIPALITIES

Articles 173, 174, 176, 177 and 178 should be deleted and instead it should be provided that Municipalities should be created in the five largest towns and such other places as by law provided and that in towns or other places where the population consists of members of both communities the representation of the communities on the municipal authorities shall be in accordance with the ratio of the communal population of such towns or places.

It is recommended that as a safeguard to the Turkish community it should be provided that that part of the Budget of the municipal authorities which deals with expenditure for maintenance or improvement of municipal services should be so arranged as not to discriminate against either community and that either community will have a recourse to the High Court if there is a case of discrimination.

PAPER 2

AMENDMENTS RECOMMENDED IN THE FOLLOWING PARTS
OF THE CONSTITUTION

PART IV.   THE HOUSE OF REPRESENTATIVES.

PART V.   THE COMMUNAL CHAMBERS.

PART IV

THE HOUSE OF REPRESENTATIVES

Article 61 of the Constitution should be amended by deleting the words "except those expressly reserved to the Communal Chambers under this Constitution". The necessity of this amendment will appear when reading that part of the paper which deals with the Communal Chambers. It is recommended that the Communal Chambers should be abolished.

In Article 62 the proviso that the number of Representatives may be increased by a resolution of the House carried by a majority comprising 2/3 of the Greek Representatives and 2/3 of the Turkish Representatives should be amended so as to remove the necessity for separate majorities. It will be necessary to provide instead of the separate majorities required for such a resolution that any increase in the number of Representatives shall bear the same ratio for the two communities and that no increase of the Representatives of one community shall be made without increasing the number of Representatives of the other community in the same ratio.

Article 67 of the Constitution which provides for the dissolution of the House by its own decision carried by an absolute majority including at least 1/3 of the Representatives elected by the Turkish community should be amended so as to avoid the necessity of specifically mentioning that such a resolution would include at least 1/3 of the Representatives elected by the Turkish community. It is suggested that it would be sufficient for the protection of Turkish interests if a 3/4 absolute majority is required. In such a case the resolution cannot be passed relying entirely on Greek votes.

Article 72 of the Constitution which provides that the President of the House of Representatives shall be a Greek and shall be elected by the Greek Representatives should be amended. It should be provided that the President of the House of Representatives shall be elected from amongst the Representatives of the House by the Representatives of the House. In other words there should be no communal criteria in the person to be selected as President nor of the persons electing him. The responsibility of the President of the House must be to the whole House as such and not to communities. It is, therefore, improper that there should be a provision that he should be Greek or Turkish and that he should be elected by members of one or the other community.

Provision must be made that there shall be two Vice-Presidents of the House elected by the whole House. One of whom should be Greek and the other Turkish. The offices of the Vice-Presidents should not be considered as offices which require remuneration for a full time job. In other Parliaments there are as many as five or six Vice-Presidents, their duty being to relieve the President for sitting for long hours during the deliberations in the Assembly. Vice-Presidents receive a small allowance above that of Members of the House for the extra responsibility. The Vice-Presidents will act for the President in his absence by rotation.

Article 72(4) which provides that the President of the House and the Vice-President appoint respectively two Representatives to act as Greek Clerks of the House and one Representative to act as Turkish Clerk of the House and are attached to their respective offices should be amended so that the election of two Greek Clerks and one Turkish Clerk will be made by the whole House. Similar provision must be made for the two Administrative Clerks (one Greek and one Turkish). All Clerks and Administrative Clerks elected by the House as a whole will be under the direction of the President of the House. Two Clerks of the House i.e. a Greek and a Turk should be receiving additional remuneration to that of the Representatives on the basis of a full time scale.

In Article 74 after paragraph (3) provision should be made for calling the House to an extraordinary sitting if it proves necessary due to urgency. The Constitution in its present form provides for an extraordinary session, but not for an extraordinary sitting.

In Article 76 provision should be made that the President of the House, may if he considers it necessary, call a meeting of the House and circulate the agenda for such a meeting even if at the end of the last sitting he did not inform the House of that fact. Detailed provisions will have to be made as to the time to be allowed between giving notice of such meeting and circulating the agenda and the date on which the meeting is fixed.

Article 78(2) which provides for separate majorities with regard to laws imposing taxations, electoral law and municipalities should be deleted.

In Article 85 a consequential amendment will have to be made to the effect that election petitions shall be finally adjudicated by the High Court instead of the Constitutional Court.

Finally it is recommended that the period of 45 days within which by-elections must be declared by the House should be extended to at least a period of three months and that in the case of a vacancy occurring as a result of a person having been convicted of an offence involving dishonesty or moral turpitude the date of the occurrence of such a vacancy shall be counted as from the date of the final determination of any appeal.

It is also recommended that provision should be made in the Constitution whereby Ministers will have to at attend the House on specified dates to answer questions put to them by Members. Questions, of course, will have to be submitted in advance. This practice is followed in most countries. In America where the Presidential system exists, Ministers are bound to appear before Committees and answer questions. The Committee meetings of the American Senate are held in public.

PART V

COMMUNAL CHAMBERS

It is recommended that the institution of Communal Chambers be abolished and instead the following arrangements be made:

(a) The Government will undertake the financial responsibility for the costs of education.
(b) In order to enable the Government to carry out this responsibility a Ministry of Education should be established with two Ministers, one responsible for Greek education and Greek communal affairs and the other responsible for Turkish education and Turkish communal affairs.
(c) Both Ministers of Education will submit to the Minister of Finance the present level of expenditure for the education of the two communities. After determining the present minimum level of expenditure the amount of such expenditure will be made available each year to the respective Ministers of Education. This amount shall be deemed to be the amount necessary to meet the annual requirements of the respective education of the two communities.
(d) Each year the Government shall make available a further sum of money for expansion of the education and other communal services to be determined as follows:
   (i) A fixed percentage of the public revenue appropriate to the Development Budget of the Republic to be agreed upon. For the purposes of calculating the public revenue appropriated to the Development Budget of the Republic money resulting from foreign aid including loans will be taken into consideration.
   (ii) The apportionment of this further sum will be made between the two Communal Chambers in a ratio agreed and fixed in advance by the Constitution and shall not vary from year to year.

The services other than education which will be in the domain of the Greek and Turkish Ministers respectively will be as follows:

(a) All religious matters.
(b) Personal status.
(c) The composition and distances of Courts dealing with civil disputes relating to personal status and to religious matters.
(d) Matters which where the interests and institutions are purely of a communal nature such as charitable and sporting foundations, bodies and associations created for the purpose of promoting the well being of the respective communities.

With regard to any legislation that will be required to carry out the above functions, it is recommended that the Greek or Turkish Ministers, as the case my be, will submit to the House of Representatives the appropriate Bill. The Bill will then be referred by the President of the House, if it is introduced by the Greek Minister, to the Greek Members of the House who will sit under the chairmanship of the Greek Vice-President for enactment. If the Bill is introduced by the Turkish Minister of Education, the President of the House will refer it to the Turkish Members of the House who will then sit under the chairmanship of the Turkish Vice-President to enact the Bill.

Bills thus enacted will be referred to the President of the Republic for promulgation who will be bound to promulgate them subject to the general provisions made under Article 57, relating to promulgation.

It is recommended that all teachers should cease to be communal officers and should become public officers of the Republic. Detailed provisions will have to be made as to the manner of appointment, promotion, dismissal etc. of Greek and Turkish teachers by the creation of special bodies under the two Ministers of Education. It is not recommended that the Public Service Commission will make appointments, promotions, retirement and dismissal of teachers.

Finally it is recommended that co-operative movements should not be within the scope of communal advancement or welfare.

Note 1: In connection with the amount of money to be made available to the two Ministers of Education, it is intended that normal financial procedure which applies in respect of other Ministries or services of the Republic will also apply to the Ministry of Education. Equally the amount made available for educational purposes will be included in the annual Budget of the Republic for approval by the whole House.

Note 2: With regard to ecclesiastical Courts, it is recommended that they should be abolished and that their jurisdiction should be transferred to the Civil Courts of the Republic with a direction that in cases of Greeks the Cannon Law or Ecclesiastical Law shall be applied and in case of Turks the Turkish Marriage Law will be applied. Cases relating to Greeks will be tried by a Greek Judge of the Civil Courts, cases relating to Turks will be tried by a Turkish Judge of the Civil Courts.

PAPER 3

INTRODUCTORY NOTES ON THE CHAPTERS OF THE CONSTITUTION DEALING WITH THE JUDICIARY i.e. PARTS IX (ARTICLES 133-151) AND X (ARTICLE 172-164)

The object of the amendments of Parts IX and X (Supreme Constitutional Court and the High Court and Subordinate Courts) is to bring about the unification of the judicial system of the Republic.

The term "unification of the judicial system of the Republic" is used in this paper to denote two things.

(a) The abolition of the Constitutional Court as a separate Court and the consequent transfer of its jurisdiction to the Civil and Criminal Courts of the Republic.

(b) The abolition of those provisions of the Constitution which compel the Republic to establish and maintain Courts composed of Greek-Cypriot Judges to try Greek-Cypriot litigants, Turkish Courts composed of Turkish-Cypriot Judges to try Turkish-Cypriot litigants and mixed Courts composed of Judges belonging to both communities for the purpose of trying cases in which the litigants belong to both communities.

The amendments proposed are contained in an Appendix to this paper and relate to the following matters:

(a) Composition of the High Court.
(b) Manner of appointment of the Judges of the High Court.
(c) Manner of appointment of the President of the High Court.
(d) Jurisdiction of the High Court.
(e) Appeal from the High Court.

For the purpose of enabling the reader to understand the amendments without reading through the legal drafts contained in the Appendix, the principles on which the amendments are based are set out herein below. It has also been thought that no drafting should take place before the principles are examined (by the Greek side) and agreed upon so that the draftsmen will have positive instructions what to draft.

(a) *Composition of the High Court;* (b) *Appointment of Judges of the High Court;* (c) *Manner of appointment of the President and Judges of the High Court.*

It is recommended that the Supreme Constitutional Court should be abolished and that the High Court, which now consists of four Judges including a neutral President, should in future be composed of six Judges all of them citizens of the Republic. It is recommended to increase the number of Judges from four to six in order to enable the High Court to cope with the increased volume of work which is bound to result from the abolition of the Constitutional Court and the consequent transfer of its jurisdiction to the normal Courts of the Republic.

The High Court at present consists of four Judges. There is, therefore, in existence a validly constituted High Court and promotions to the High Court to fill vacancies should be made in the following manner:

(i) The High Court shall make recommendations to the President of the Republic for the filling of vacancies and or appointment of Judges to the High Court.

(ii) The President of the Republic, as the Head of State, will sign the instrument of appointment of the Judges recommended by the High Court to be appointed as Judges of that Court.

(iii) The President of the Republic will be bound to appoint as President of the High Court the senior Judge from amongst the Judges of the High Court. (For the purpose of determining seniority service as a Judge prior to independence is taken into consideration).

Note: At present appointment of Judges of the High Court is done by agreement of the President and the Vice-President. The function of appointing Judges to the High Court in all civilized states is a function which is exercised by the Head of the State. In democratic states, however, for the purposes of securing the independence of the Judiciary the Head of the State merely confines himself to signing the instrument of appointment and is bound to act on the recommendations of an appointing authority. The present system whereby the President and the Vice-President appoint Judges of the High Court by agreement is unsatisfactory for two main reasons:

(i) The President and the Vice-President are political persons and the appointment of Judges to the High Court should have no connection with politics.

(ii) The Vice-President exercises a function which should only be exercised by the Head of the State subject, of course, to the limitation stated above i.e. that the President signs the formal instrument of appointment accepting the recommendations of the High Court.

In order to secure minority rights, it is suggested that out of the six Judges of the High Court two will be Turkish Cypriots.

Three Judges i.e. two Greeks and one Turk will form a quorum. It is, therefore, envisaged that the High Court will be composed of two Courts each one consisting of three Judges as described above. The President of the High Court will be presiding over one Court and the next Judge in seniority will be presiding over the other Court.

The full High Court i.e. six Judges will have the power to sit together in the exercise of their appellate jurisdiction if, in the opinion of the High Court, a case involves the consideration of legal issues requiring the attention of the full Appellate Court. Such decision may be taken before the hearing of an appeal or during the hearing at any time prior to the delivery of judgement. It is not the intention that the full Court shall act as a Court of Appeal from the High Court. Where, however, the High Court exercises original jurisdiction such jurisdiction will be exercised by a Court composed of three of its Judges (i.e. two Greeks and one Turk) and appeal will lie to the High Court sitting in full. Where the High Court sits as a full Court, the necessary quorum will be five Judges.

(d) *Jurisdiction of the High Court.*

The amendments recommended are those necessary to transfer the jurisdiction of the Constitutional Court to the High Court. Certain Articles have to be completely deleted or amended in consequence of amendments recommended in earlier chapters. It must be noted that the jurisdiction of the High Court on constitutional matters will be that of an Appellate Court. In other words constitutional matters will be raised by the citizens before the Ordinary Courts of the Republic and appeals from their decision will be made in the normal way to the High Court. The High Court will also have original jurisdiction in constitutional matters under certain Articles which give the right to the President and the Vice-President of the Republic to refer certain matters to the present Constitutional Court for its decision.

The matters on which the High Court will have original jurisdiction in constitutional matters are as follows:

(i) Under Article 137 of the Constitution recourse made by the President and the Vice-President of the Republic either separately or conjointly on the ground that any Law or decision of the House of Representatives or any provision thereof discriminates against either of the two communities.

(ii) Under Article 138 recourse made by the President and the Vice-President of the Republic either separately or conjointly on the ground that the Budget approved by the House of Representatives discriminates.

(iii) Under Article 139 of the Constitution recourse by any organ or authority of the Republic on the ground that there is any conflict or contest of power or competence arising between organs of the Republic.

(iv) Under Article 140 recourse by the President and the Vice-President of the Republic acting jointly, prior to the promulgation of any law or decision of the House of Representatives, requesting the opinion of the Court whether any Law or decision enacted by the House of Representatives is contrary to the Constitution.

(v) Under Article 141 request by the President or the Vice-President for the opinion of the Court whether any law or decision imposing formalities, conditions or restrictions is not to the public interest.

(vi) Under Article 142 request by the President for the opinion of the Court that any Law or decision relating to communal matters is contrary to the Constitution.

(vii)   Under Article 143 recourse to the High Court on the question whether there exists such urgent and exceptional unforeseen circumstances as to justify a House of Representatives which continues to be in office until the assumption of office of a newly elected House to make any laws or to take any decisions under Article 68 of the Constitution.

(viii)   Under Article 147 recourse by the Attorney-General of the Republic with regard to the question of the existence of such permanent or temporary capacity, or absence otherwise than temporary of the President or the Vice-President of the Republic as would prevent him to perform effectively his duties.

(e) *Appeals from the High Court.*

Finally it is recommended that the right of appeal from decisions of the High Court to the Privy Council should be restored. Canada, Australia and other Commonwealth countries have retained the right of appeal to the Privy Council. Retention of the right of appeal to the Privy Council will constitute an answer to the argument for the existence of neutral Presidents or equality in the numbers of the Greek and Turkish Judges of the Court since appeal from its decisions will lie to the Privy Council.

PAPER 4

AMENDMENTS RECOMMENDED IN THE FOLLOWING PARTS OF THE CONSTITUTION

PART I.　　　　GENERAL PROVISIONS.

PART II.　　　　FUNDAMENTAL RIGHTS AND LIBERTIES.

PART I

GENERAL PROVISIONS

Article 1. This Article provides that the state of Cyprus is an independent and sovereign Republic with a presidential regime, the President being Greek and the Vice-President being Turk elected by the Greek and Turkish communities in Cyprus respectively.

Note No.1: It has not been recommended that the presidential regime should be replaced by a Parliamentary regime i.e. a type of Government where there is a Prime Minister and a Cabinet all of whom are members of Parliament. In such a case there will be a President, but the functions of the President will be entirely different from those exercised to-day by the President.

The reason why no suggestion is made for amending this Article, is because any alteration of this Article would require a new Constitution and not amendments to the present Constitution.

Note No.2: In this note two points are raised for consideration without making any recommendations.

(a) Whether it should be provided in the Constitution that the President should be Greek and the Vice-President should be Turk.
(b) Whether the President should be elected by the Greeks and the Vice-President by the Turks or whether both should be elected by the whole country.

Article 3 provides that the official languages of the Republic are Greek and Turkish. The question is raised for consideration whether for a definite period to be provided for in the Constitution English should also be made an official language. This was done in India and other countries for the reason that in those countries where are more than one official languages and it is impossible to be certain of the identity of the texts of laws and decisions unless a language which can be used as a common denominator is made also an official language.

Article 4(1) provides that the Republic shall have its own flag of neutral design and colour chosen jointly by the President and the Vice-President of the

Republic. The flag of a country is not a matter which is left to the President or the Vice-President, but it is a matter regulated by law.

It is, therefore, recommended that the Article should be amended by deleting the words "chosen jointly by the President and the Vice-President of the Republic," and substituted by a provision that the matter will be regulated by legislation.

Section (2) of Article 4 which provides that the authorities of the Republic and any public corporation or public utility body shall fly the flag of the Republic and shall have the right to fly on holidays together with the flag of the Republic both the Greek and the Turkish flags at the same time should be amended so as to make it compulsory for the aforementioned bodies to fly the flag of the Republic only.

Articles 3 and 4 which give the right to the communal authorities and to the citizens of the Republic to fly the Greek and Turkish flags should be deleted. This will not mean that they will not be able to fly the flags of Greece and Turkey since there will be no prohibition in the Constitution from doing so. There is no other Constitution in the world where permission is given to fly flags. The only provision usually contained in a constitution is that the official flag of the Republic is the one which is made the national flag by a law of the country concerned.

Finally Article 5 gives the right to the Greek and Turkish communities to celebrate respectively the Greek and Turkish national holidays. This Article should also be deleted since every one is free to celebrate any holidays he wishes and there is no restriction of celebrating the aforesaid holidays in the Constitution.

PART II

FUNDAMENTAL RIGHTS AND LIBERTIES

It is recommended that Section 5 of Article 11 be amended so as to give the Police authority to hold a person in order to conduct enquiries for longer than 24 hours before bringing him before a Judge.

It is recommended that the maximum period should be 48 hours.

Article 22 should be amended so as to permit civil marriage between persons of different religion or community.

Section (4) of Article 23 which gives authority to the Communal Chambers to compulsorily acquired property for educational purposes should, in view of the recommendation made for the abolition of Communal Chambers, be amended.

Sub-section (c) of the same Article which provides that the compulsory acquisition takes effect upon the payment in cash and in advance of the equitable compensation awarded by a Civil Court, should be amended to the effect that the compulsory acquisition becomes completed from the moment the acquisition order is published and that the owner of the property will receive either agreed compensation or compensation determined by a Civil Court.

Section (6) of Article 23 which provides that in the event of agricultural reform, lands shall be distributed only to persons belonging to the same community as the owner from whom such land has been compulsorily acquired, should be deleted in view of the fact that if applied it would prevent any agricultural reform from becoming feasible.

Section (8) of Article 23 should be amended by deleting the words "Communal Chambers" wherever it appears in that Article.

Article 25, Section (2) should be amended by adding after the words "in the interest of the security of the Republic or the constitutional order or the public safety or the public order or the public health" the words "or the economic development of the country".

The proviso in the same Section to the effect that the conditions or restrictions imposed in the public interest shall not be contrary to the interest of either community, should be deleted.

Paper 5

RECOMMENDED AMENDMENTS IN THE FOLLOWING PARTS
OF THE CONSTITUTION

PART XI.   FINANCIAL PROVISIONS.

PART XII.   MISCELLANEOUS PROVISIONS.

PART XIII.   FINAL PROVISIONS.

PART XI

FINANCIAL PROVISIONS

Only one minor amendment is recommended in this Section. Article 167(6) provides that the House of Representatives may approve or refuse its approval to any expenditure contained in a Supplementary Budget, but may not vote an increase amount or an alteration in its destination. Although provision is made that the House may not increase a Supplementary Budget, no provision is made that the House may not increase the Budget or alter the destination of sums included in the Budget. Mr. Clerides as President of the House of Representatives ruled on a number of occasions that in his opinion the House could not increase the Budget or alter the destination of amounts included in the Budget. He supported, however, this opinion, on inferences and not because there was any express provision of the Constitution to that effect. Mr. Clerides deduced that since the House has no power either to introduce a Bill which increases the Budget or a Supplementary Budget, the House could not increase the Budget of the Republic. It could be argued with equal force that on the basis of the doctrine of construction *"expressio unius exclusio ulterius"*, the House has such a power. The Constitution specifically prohibits the increase of a Supplementary Budget while saying nothing about the increase of the Budget.

It is, therefore, recommended that this defect should be remedied by an express provision to the effect that the House of Representatives cannot increase the Budget or alter the destination of the sums included therein.

No other amendments are recommended in this Section unless, of course, the Minister of Finance, from a technical point of view, has any recommendations to make.

PART XII

MISCELLANEOUS PROVISIONS

The relevant Articles of this Part i.e. Articles 173 to 178 which deal with the questions of the Municipalities have been dealt with in Paper No.1 under the heading "Miscellaneous" page 8.

PART XIII

FINAL PROVISIONS

It is recommended that Sections (2) and (3) of Article 180 should be amended. These two sections deal with the question of interpreting the Constitution and provide that any conflict between the two texts of the Constitution shall be determined by the Supreme Constitutional Court by reference to the draft Constitution signed at Nicosia on the 6th April, 1960, (i.e. English text), due regard being had to the letter and spirit of Zurich Agreements.

It is recommended that so far as Section (2) of Article 180 the words "shall be determined by the Constitutional Court" be substituted "shall be determined by the High Court" and that the words "due regard being had to the letter and spirit of the Zurich Agreement dated 11th February 1959, and of the London Agreement dated 19th February, 1959" be deleted. This will obviously be necessary if the amendments recommended in this document are accepted.

Section (3) of Article 180 should be deleted for the same reasons as given above.

Article 181 which provides that the Treaty guaranteeing the independence, territorial integrity and Constitution of the Republic concluded between the Republic, the Kingdom of Greece, the Republic of Turkey and the United Kingdom and the Treaty of Military Alliance shall have constitutional force, should be deleted.

This recommendation is made independently of any question whether there should be guaranteeing powers. If it is necessary to have guaranteeing powers, what the guaranteeing powers are entitled to guarantee is the independence and territorial integrity of the Republic. They are not, entitled to guarantee the Constitution of the Republic, which is an internal matter for the Republic. Similarly it is unthinkable that a Treaty of Military Alliance between the Republic, Greece and Turkey will be made, by virtue of the provisions of this Article, to have constitutional force.

Article 182(1) which provides that the basic Articles of the Constitution incorporated from the Zurich Agreement dated 11th February, 1959, are basic Articles of the Constitution and cannot in any way be amended, whether by way of variation, addition or repeal, should be deleted.

It is recommended that constitutional amendments should be made possible and that the following procedure should be adopted:

(a) Suggestions for constitutional amendments may be made either by the President of the Republic acting through the Council of Ministers, in which case the recommendation before it is allowed to reach the House must be approved by the Council of Ministers.

(b) If the recommendation emanates from the House of Representatives, it must be in the form of a resolution stating the specific amendments recommended and approved by a 2/3 majority.

   (c) Where the recommendations emanate from the President of the Republic with the approval of the Council of Ministers they must be sent to the House in the form of a resolution specifying the amendments required and the reasons thereof.

      The resolution of the Council of Ministers will then be published in the Gazette and a period of two months will be allowed to lapse before the House of Representatives debates the resolution.

   (d) If the House approves the resolution by a 2/3 majority, the President of the House will inform the Executive that on principle the House agrees with the necessity of the amendments proposed and the Council will proceed to draft and submit a Bill to the House incorporating the proposed amendments. The Bill will then be published in the Gazette and will be enacted following the normal procedure.

Where the initiative for the amendment of the Constitution originates from the House of Representatives, the resolution of the House recommending amendments will be transmitted to the Executive. If the Executive agrees to the amendments contained in the resolution of the House the proposed amendments will be published in the Gazette and after allowing a period of two months will be incorporated in a Bill and submitted to the House for enactment following the normal procedure of the House.

No amendment of the Constitution will be possible which diminishes any of the Human Rights guaranteed by the Constitution without a general referendum. In such case the normal procedure of dissolving the House should be followed, the issues placed before the electorate, a new House should be elected with authorization from the electorate to proceed to the amendments.

It is recommended that a table be annexed at the end of the Constitution showing the Sections of the Constitution which are intended as safeguards for the minority. No amendment of those sections should take place unless the resolution recommending the amendments is carried by a 2/3 majority of the Turkish Representatives.

Article 183. The proviso to Article 183(1) giving the President and the Vice-President a right of veto against any decision of the Council of Ministers for the declaration of emergency should be abolished. Similarly Section (3) of Article 183 should be deleted and any further reference to the right of veto of the President and the Vice-President in the ensuing Articles should be deleted.

No recommendation is made with regard to Article 185(1) and (2) which provides that the territory of the Republic is one and indivisible and that the integral or partial union of Cyprus with any other state or the separatist independence is excluded.

APPENDIX 73

Proposals Entitled "Suggested Measures for Facilitating the Smooth Functioning of the State and for the Removal of Certain Causes of Intercommunal Friction," Presented 30 November 1963

SECRET

The Constitution of the Republic of Cyprus, in its present form, creates many difficulties in the smooth government of the State and impedes the development and progress of the country. It contains many *sui generis* provisions conflicting with internationally accepted democratic principles and creates sources of friction between Greek and Turkish Cypriots.

At the Conference at Lancaster House in February, 1959, which I was invited to attend as leader of the Greek Cypriots, I raised a number of objections and expressed strong misgivings regarding certain provisions of the Agreement arrived at in Zurich between the Greek and the Turkish Governments and adopted by the British Government. I tried very hard to bring about the change of at least some provisions of that Agreement. I failed, however, in that effort and I was faced with the dilemma either of signing the Agreement as it stood or of rejecting it with all the grave consequences which would have ensued. In the circumstances I had no alternative but to sign the Agreement. This was the course dictated to me by necessity.

The three years' experience since the coming into operation of the Constitution, which was based on the Zurich and London Agreements, has made clear the necessity for revision of at least some of those provisions which impede the smooth functioning and development of the State.

I believe that the intention of those who drew up the Agreement at Zurich was to create an independent State, in which the interests of the Turkish Community were safeguarded, but it could not have been their intention that the smooth functioning and development of the country should be prejudiced or thwarted, as has in fact been the case.

One of the consequences of the difficulties created by certain constitutional provisions is to prevent the Greeks and Turks of Cyprus from co-operating in a spirit of understanding and friendship, to undermine the relations between them and cause them to draw further apart instead of closer together, to the detriment of the well-being of the people of Cyprus as a whole.

This situation causes me, as President of the State, great concern. It is necessary to resolve certain of the difficulties by the removal of some at least of the obstacles to the smooth functioning and development of the State.

With this end in view I have outlined below the immediate measures which I propose to be taken.

1.   *The right of veto of the President and the Vice-President of the Republic to be abandoned.*

The right of veto given under the Constitution of the Republic to the President and the Vice-President can be exercised separately by each one of them against:

(a) laws or decisions of the House of Representatives concerning foreign affairs, defence and security; and
(b) decisions of the Council of Ministers concerning foreign affairs, defence and security.

It is a right of final veto and, therefore, different from any other measure provided in certain Constitutions whereby the President of the country has a right of limited veto in the sense that he is entitled not to promulgate a law immediately, but to return it for reconsideration. Provisions for the return of laws and decisions for reconsideration exist in the Cyprus Constitution independently from the provision of final veto.

The Constitution of Cyprus has been based on the doctrine of separation of powers between the Executive and the Legislature. The balance between them must be carefully maintained and friction avoided, if it is to work. The right of veto cuts right across the principles involved and could bring the President and Vice-President into direct conflict with the Legislature.

The exercise of the right of veto is a negative power in the sense that it does not enable the President or the Vice-President to take decisions, but it gives them the power to prevent a decision of the Council of Ministers or of the House of Representatives, on matters of foreign policy, defence or security, from taking effect. It is obvious that it cannot be considered as a power which affords the President or the Vice-President the opportunity to deal with an existing situation in a constructive manner.

More difficulties are encountered because of the fact that the right of veto is not vested only in one person but in two persons, the President and the Vice-President of the Republic, thus increasing the occasions when a deadlock may occur. An example in point is the use of the veto by the Vice-President on the subject of the composition of the units of the Army of the Republic.

Under the Constitution the Army of the Republic must consist of 60% Greeks and 40% Turks. The Council of Ministers, by majority, decided that the organizational structure of the Army should be based throughout on mixed units comprising both Greeks and Turks. The Vice-President, who wanted the structure to be based on separate units of Greeks and Turks, exercised his right of veto against the above decision of the Council, with the result that there is no decision on this matter and the Army has remained ineffective.

In the case of the Army, no great harm has resulted, since it is doubtful whether the Republic can really afford its expansion to 2,000 men at present and cope simultaneously with the heavy financial burdens of economic development and expansion of educational and social services. But it is easy to envisage situations where exercise of the veto could result in more far-reaching and damaging repercussions.

Therefore, the right of veto should be abandoned and reliance placed instead on the provisions for the return of laws and decisions for reconsideration, and the various other relevant safeguards.

2.   *The Vice-President of the Republic to deputise for the President of the Republic in case of his temporary absence or incapacity to perform his duties.*

Under the provisions of the Constitution, the Vice-President of the Republic does not deputise for the President in the event of his absence or incapacity to act, but the President of the House of Representatives does so instead.

This provision creates the impression that a person belonging to the Turkish community and elected by it cannot deputise in a post the nature of which bears responsibility to Cyprus as a whole. It produces a situation whereby, in the absence of the President of the Republic, the Vice-President is overlooked and the President of the House of Representatives steps above him.

The practical effect of this is that it hinders the continuity of the smooth functioning of the executive power. The Vice-President of the Republic is a member of the Executive, he participates in the deliberations of the Council of Ministers, he knows the reasons and background of decisions taken and is, therefore, in a much better position to continue with the implementation of such decisions than the President of the House of Representatives, who is not a member of the Executive, and on whom the burden of acting as Head of the Executive is suddenly thrust.

It is for the above reasons that the Vice-President should deputise for the President of the Republic during his temporary absence or incapacity to perform his duties.

As a result of the new status of the Vice-President certain consequential or relative amendments have to be made.

3.   *The Greek President of the House of Representatives to deputise for the President as a whole and notes as at present the President by the Greek Members of the House and the Vice-President by the Turkish Members of the House.*

Under the provisions of the Constitution the President of the House of Representatives, who must be a Greek, is elected by the Greek Members of the House and the Vice-President, who must be a Turk, is elected by the Turkish Members. Further, the Turkish Vice-President cannot deputise for the President in case of his temporary absence or incapacity.

The function of the President of the House, who presides over the entire Assembly, is one which bears responsibility to the House as a whole and not to a particular section of it. It is, therefore, improper that the election of the President of the House should be carried out by the Greek Members only. As far as can be ascertained there is no other Constitution where the President of the Legislative Assembly is elected by one section of the Assembly.

The participation of Representatives of both communities in electing the President of the House will also create conditions which will gradually train the two communities to co-operate in electing persons to political officers. It will lead both Greek and Turkish Representatives to closer contact with the office of the President of the House and will facilitate the solution of problems which arise in considering legislative measures.

For the same reasons the Vice-President of the House should be elected by the House as a whole and not by the Turkish Members only.

4.   *The Vice-President of the House of Representatives to deputise for the President of the House in case of his temporary absence or incapacity to perform his duties.*

Under the provisions of the Constitution the Vice-President of the House cannot deputise for the President of the House of Representatives. In case of temporary absence or incapacity of the President of the House his duties are entrusted to the eldest Greek Representative or to such Greek Member of the House as the Greek Members may decide. In the case of the Vice-President his duties are performed by the eldest Turkish Representative or by such other Turkish Member as the Turkish Members may decide.

The fact that the Vice-President never presides over the House and never deputises for the President creates a situation whereby neither does he feel that he owes responsibility to the whole House nor do the Greek Members feel that they owe any duty or responsibility towards the Vice-President.

Apart from the fact that this provision of the Constitution tends to show that the Vice-President is a figure Vice-Head it also affects the smooth functioning of the House. It may occur that the eldest Greek or Turkish Member is not the right person to perform the duties of President or Vice-President of the House. If, on the other hand, the Greek or the Turkish Members of the House nominate other Greek and Turkish Representatives to act as President and Vice-President, respectively, by decisions taken on each occasion, there will be no experienced Acting President or Vice-President to take over at a given time.

Finally, in view of the non-existence of a permanent Vice-President of the House entitled to deputise for the President, there is no one familiar with the work involved either in regard to the political aspect of the functions of the President or to the duties connected with the administration of the House.

5.   *The constitutional provisions regarding separate majorities for enactment of certain laws by the House of Representatives to be abolished.*

The Constitution provides that any law imposing taxation and any law relating to Municipalities and any modification of the Electoral Law requires separate majorities of the Greek and Turkish members of the House of Representatives taking part in the vote.

This provision is obviously contrary to all democratic principles. Its effect is that, though a Bill may be unanimously approved by the Council of Ministers and though it may receive the overwhelming majority of votes in the House of Representatives, nevertheless it is defeated if it does not receive the separate majority of the Greek or Turkish Representatives taking part in the vote.

The House of Representatives consists of 35 Greek Members and 15 Turkish Members. If, for example, 35 Greek Members and 7 Turkish Members vote in favour of a Bill, i.e. the Bill receives a total of 42 votes in favour, it can be defeated by 8 Turkish votes. Even 2 Turkish Representatives can defeat a Bill if only 3 Turkish Representatives take part in the vote.

This provision obstructs the enactment of vital legislation, generally, and impedes the development of the country. In particular, it has already caused serious adverse effects on the State by preventing or delaying the enactment of taxation legislation. Thus, on one occasion, by the exercise of the right of separate majorities, the State remained completely without taxation legislation for several months.

When, subsequently, an Income Tax Bill was introduced to the House the Turkish Representatives again used their right of separate majority to defeat the Bill, with the result that the State remained without an Income Tax Law.

In an attempt to minimize the grave consequences of the situation thus created, an unorthodox system has been devised whereby one Income Tax Law was enacted by the House imposing taxation on non-citizens of the Republic and two separate Income Tax Laws were enacted by the Greek and Turkish Communal Chambers imposing a form of income tax on Greeks and Turks respectively. Thus, the Republic has three income tax systems, which cause administrative dislocation and rise to a multitude of legal contentions. Further, in view of the fact that the Government has no control over the Communal Chambers, any amendment may at any time be made by the respective Communal Chamber in its income tax legislation, thereby creating incalculable difficulties for assessment purposes. The existence of three separately controlled tax systems requires separate accounting; the consequent slow rate of assessment and collection of the income taxes encourages tax evasion to a level unknown before in Cyprus.

Past experience has shown that the right of separate majorities was not exercised by the Turkish Representatives because of disagreement with provisions of the taxation legislation before the House. The Turkish Members used this right against taxation Bills neither because they disagreed with their provisions nor because such Bills were discriminatory against their community, but for matters unconnected with taxation legislation.

A further difficulty in the enactment of taxation legislation, arising out of the separate majorities provisions, is demonstrated by the fact that such legislation submitted to the House requires months of frustrating negotiations.

Even if one assumes that in the future a more prudent use will be made of the right of separate majorities, the application of this procedure will always cause serious difficulties. It may well make it impossible for the Government to effect proper development of the direct taxes as revenue procedure and also as unified instruments of social and economic policy. No Government is able to carry out a programme of development unless it can also plan and control its resources.

There is no justification at all for the provision of separate majorities. If such provision were intended as a safeguard against discriminatory legislation, then it is completely unnecessary because there are other provisions in the Constitution affording adequate safeguards and remedies. Any legislation which is discriminatory can be challenged before the Constitutional Court by the Vice-President of the Republic. Furthermore, Article 6 of the Constitution provides that no law or decision of the House of Representatives shall discriminate against any of the two communities or any person as a person or as a member of a community. Any citizen has a right given to him by the Constitution to challenge any law or decision which discriminates in such a manner as to affect his interests directly.

6.　　　*Unified Municipalities to be established.*

The Constitution provides that separate Municipalities shall be created in the five main towns of the Republic.

Not only does this provision not serve any useful purpose but it has also proved to be unworkable.

The impossibility of finding a way to define geographical areas and create separate Municipalities, based on communal criteria, is due to the fact that never before did the Greek and Turkish Cypriots contemplate living in separate areas.

A factual examination will show that there are many areas in which Greeks and Turks live side by side and that the ownership of property by the two communities does not follow the pattern of communal areas. This fact is clearly apparent from the proposed principles formulated by the Vice-President of the Republic for determining which streets will fall within the Greek Municipality and which will fall within the Turkish Municipality. The Vice-President proposed that:

> "The frontage of all property abutting on any street will be measured and if the total length of the frontage of the property belonging to the members of the Greek community in that street is greater, then that street will be included in the sector of the Greek Municipality. The same principle will apply in the case of a street where the total length of the frontage of the property belonging to the members of the Turkish community is greater".

It should be observed that by this proposal, the Vice-President has tried to find a solution by distinguishing ownership of property on the basis of communal criteria without taking into consideration the occupants of such property. It is an undisputed fact that there are many properties belonging to Turks which have Greek tenants and vice versa. Many streets abutting on or leading into each other will fall in the area of one or the other Municipality and thus the resulting two municipal areas will not have any territorial cohesion. This fact alone demonstrates the impracticability of the division of the town into separate areas on the basis of communal criteria.

Apart, however, from the fact that geographical separation is not feasible, the separation of Municipalities will be financially detrimental to the townsmen. There would be duplication of municipal services and the cost of their running might become so prohibitive as to render their proper functioning almost impossible.

The impossibility of agreeing on the separate areas became apparent during the year-long deliberations of the Constitutional Commission. In view of the inability of the Constitutional Commission to reach agreement on this point, the responsibility was transferred to the President and the Vice-President of the Republic by the insertion of Article 177 of the Constitution, whereby the President and the Vice-President were empowered to define boundaries of the areas of each Municipality. Owing to the above difficulties, however, they failed to reach an agreement on the determination of the boundaries.

Under the proviso to Article 173.1 of the Constitution the President and the Vice-President of the Republic have a duty, within a period of four years from the date of the coming into operation of the Constitution, to examine the question whether or not the separation of the Municipalities in the five main towns shall continue.

It is obvious that the reason why this provision was inserted was that, even at the time when the Zurich Agreement was drafted, doubts were entertained as to the desirability or practicability of such an arrangement and it was, therefore, thought necessary to give the President and the Vice-President power to reconsider the position within a specified period from the date of Independence.

If it were put forward that the separation of the Municipalities in the five main towns was provided for in order to protect the Turkish inhabitants of such towns against any discrimination, other safeguards may be provided in this respect, such as:

(a) the municipal council in each of the five main towns should consist of Greek and Turkish councillors in proportion to the number of the Greek and Turkish inhabitants of such town by whom they shall be elected respectively;

(b) there should be earmarked in the annual budget of each such town, after deducting any expenditure for common services, a sum proportionate to the ratio of the Turkish population of such town. This sum should be disposed of for municipal purposes recommended by the Turkish councillors.

7. *The administration of Justice to be unified.*

The Constitution separates the administration of Justice on the basis of communal criteria by providing that in all cases, civil and criminal, a Greek must be tried by a Greek Judge, a Turk by a Turkish Judge and that cases, however trivial, involving both Greeks and Turks, must be tried by a mixed Court composed of Greek and Turkish Judges.

This division is not only entirely unnecessary but, what is more important, is detrimental to the cause of Justice. The very concept of Justice defies separation.

The mere fact that a Greek must be tried by a Greek and a Turk by a Turk is in itself a slur on the impartiality and integrity of the Judges. It is inevitable that when a Judge assumes jurisdiction on the basis of communal criteria he begins to think that the interests of his community stand in danger of being jeopardized and that he is there to protect such interests. The Judge will, therefore, gradually lose the sense of being a judge above communal criteria. This is particularly so in mixed cases, where each Judge will eventually come to feel that his presence is necessary in order to protect the party belonging to his community from possible injustice by his brother Judge. As a consequence of this, Judges will lose their respect for each other, will begin to regard each other with suspicion and may develop the mentality, not of a judge, but of an arbitrator appointed by one of the parties to a dispute. This mentality will inevitably seep into the minds of the people as a whole, who will consider Judges as advocates in the cause of their community and expect them to act as such.

It is another consequence of the dichotomy of Justice that the public is bound to compare sentences imposed by Greek Judges on Greeks and by Turkish Judges on Turks and to draw conclusions from such comparisons. In view of the fact that the jurisdiction of Judges is based on communal criteria, the result of such comparisons will be to foster the belief that there exists separate Justice for Greeks and Turks. This will diminish the respect of the people for the administration of Justice.

Thus Justice will not only cease to be done but will also cease to be seen to be done. Nothing is more certain to undermine Justice and to bring it into disrepute than the situation described above.

Apart from the aforesaid most important considerations, the system which has had to be devised in order to implement these provisions of the Constitution is also unnecessarily costly.

In view of the fact that Greek cases are more numerous than Turkish cases, the Greek Judges are burdened with a much larger volume of work than the Turkish Judges. Due to the separation imposed by the Constitution, Turkish Judges, even if not fully occupied and although willing, cannot relieve their Greek colleagues by taking cases in which the parties involved are Greek. There must, therefore, be maintained a greater number of Judges than would be warranted by the number of cases if they could be evenly distributed. The fact that even a trivial case, as well as a preliminary enquiry, must be heard by two Judges if the parties belong to different communities results in unnecessary waste of time and money, delay and hardship to the litigant, and is yet another reason for having a greater number of Judges than would otherwise be necessary.

A further result of the separation of the administration of Justice is the duplication of registry work and therefore of court personnel, thus creating an additional financial burden.

The measure of civilization of a country and its stability greatly depend on the fair administration of Justice and on the confidence enjoyed by its judiciary. If the principle of Justice is undermined the consequences to the State cannot but be serious and, in Cyprus, if the present system continues, Justice is certain to suffer.

Before the Constitution came into force, the court system prevailing in Cyprus had been operating extremely well for many years, Justice being administered by Greek and Turkish Judges, honourably and impartially, irrespective of community. There can be no greater proof of this than the fact that even at the height of intercommunal strife, when Justice was still unified, never was a shadow of doubt cast on the integrity of the Judges or any complaint made about their impartiality.

There is, therefore, no reason for the imposition of restrictions on the jurisdiction of the Judges of the Republic, on communal criteria, thus establishing a system which is bound to undermine justice and is most impracticable in its application.

8.　　*The division of the Security Forces into Police and Gendarmerie to be abolished.*

Since the establishment of Independence the Security Forces of the Republic have been divided into Police and Gendarmerie and operate as two separate and distinct Forces in defined areas and under separate command.

This division of the Security Forces is entirely unnecessary and should be abolished for the following reasons:

(a) with the existence of two Forces under separate command, separate Headquarters for each Force had to be established. This has led to unnecessary financial expenditure;

(b) the creation of separate commands necessitates concentration of many officers at Headquarters and causes a waste of manpower, especially in the higher ranks. At least 200 officers are engaged in additional administrative posts due to the division and duplication of the administration. There now also exists a greater ratio of officers vis-à-vis men without a corresponding increase in the total numerical strength. This increase in personnel costs the State an additional expenditure of at least £150,000 per annum;

(c) due to the division of the Security Forces and their command into two, both at Headquarters level and at Divisional level, the cohesion and strength of the Security Forces is adversely affected and results, inter alia, in lack of uniformity of discipline and in friction between the two separate Forces;

(d) in case of an emergency or other grave situation neither Force will have readily available for immediate use the full strength of the Security Forces and their reserves.

Finally, the experience gained in having only one Force, the Police Force, which worked efficiently and effectively for so many years proves that there is no valid reason for the division of the Security Forces into Police and Gendarmerie, a course not even warranted by the size of the Island.

9.   *The numerical strength of the Security Forces and of the Defence Forces to be determined by a Law.*

The Constitution provides that the Security Forces of the Republic shall consist of the Police and the Gendarmerie and shall have a contingent of 2,000 men which may be reduced or increased by agreement of the President and the Vice-President of the Republic.

This is an unworkable provision because, even if the President and the Vice-President agree to increase the numerical strength of the Security Forces, such agreement will be completely ineffectual unless the House of Representatives approves the resulting increase in budgetary expenditure. Under the Constitution the President and the Vice-President cannot, by agreeing to increase the Security Forces, create a charge on the Consolidated Fund.

The question of increasing or decreasing the numerical strength of the Security Forces should, in the first instance, be decided by the Council of Ministers in the normal way and legislation be introduced to the House for enactment.

The Constitution also provides that the Republic shall have an Army of 2,000 men. This provision is impracticable as no implementation of the numerical strength of the Army can take place unless the House of Representatives approves the financial expenditure required. Furthermore, no provision exists for the increase or decrease, depending on ordinary requirements, of the numerical strength of the Army. Constitutional provision should, therefore, be made that the Republic shall have such Defence Forces as may be regulated by Law.

10.   *The proportion of the participation of Greek and Turkish Cypriots in the composition of the Public Service and the Forces of the Republic to be modified in proportion to the ratio of the population of Greek and Turkish Cypriots.*

The Constitution provides that 70% of the Public Service shall be composed of Greek Cypriots and that 30% shall be composed of Turkish Cypriots. It further provides that this ratio shall be applied, as far as practicable, in all grades of the Public Service.

The Constitution also provides that the Security Forces shall be composed of 70% Greek Cypriots and 30% Turkish Cypriots and that the Army shall be composed of 60% Greek Cypriots and 40% Turkish Cypriots.

It is an accepted fact that the proper administration of a country depends on the efficiency of its Public Service. This is of particular importance in Cyprus owing to the fact that, as a result of Independence, new institutions have been created adding further complexities to the normal problems of administering the country. Furthermore, the Government, by undertaking a five-year development plan which provides for Government expenditure of approximately £10 million per year, is casting an additional burden on the Public Service.

The percentages of participation of the two communities in the Public Service as fixed by the Constitution bear no relation to the true ratio of the

Greek and Turkish inhabitants of the Island which is 81.14% Greeks and 18.86% Turks.

Generally speaking any provision the effect of which is that certain posts in the Public Service or certain percentage of such posts are reserved for persons belonging to a community, religious group or ethnic minority is contrary to the internationally accepted principles of Human Rights. Thus under Article 21(2) of the Universal Declaration of Human Rights of the United Nations it is provided that "Everyone has the right of equal access to the Public Service of his country".

It can, of course, be argued that the fixing of a percentage of participation of a community in the Public Service of a country is for the purpose of securing to the citizens constituting such community a right of equal access to the Public Service of the country.

The best way of securing the right of equal participation in the Public Service is not by fixing a percentage, but by provisions in the Constitution giving the right to citizens, who applied and were not appointed to the Public Service, to challenge the decision of the appointing authority before the competent court on the ground that they were discriminated against.

If, however, the method to be followed for securing equality of access is by fixing the ratio of participation of a community in the Public Service, then, in order to minimize discrimination, such ratio must be a fair one so as to afford an equal opportunity to the community constituting the minority to participate in the Public Service, without at the same time preventing the majority of the population from having an equal opportunity of participation in the Public Service of the country.

The present constitutional provision, by specifying that 70% of the Public Service shall be composed of Greek Cypriots, when in fact the Greek Cypriots constitute more than 81% of the population, and that 30% of the Public Service shall be composed of Turkish Cypriots, when in fact the Turkish Cypriots constitute less than 19% of the population, does not afford an equal opportunity to the majority of the citizens of the Republic to participate in the Public Service. It is, therefore, clearly discriminatory.

The implementation of the above provision of the Constitution creates serious problems for the State.

It makes it necessary, in considering appointments and promotions, to use criteria other than those universally accepted, such as qualifications, efficiency and suitability of the candidate, because the appointing authority has to take into consideration the community to which the candidate belongs. As a result the best candidates cannot always be selected. Further, particular hardship is created in the case of promotions. Public servants who possess all the required qualifications and experience for promotion to higher grades may have to be overlooked in favour of less qualified or efficient public servants, solely in order to give effect to an artificially fixed communal ratio of participation in the Public Service. The result of the situation thus created is that the efficiency of the Public Service is adversely affected.

If the provision is to be implemented without affecting the promotion of public servants, the alternative is to create unnecessary posts and impose a further financial burden on the State. The Government now spends 31% of its

Ordinary Budget for salaries and other allowances to public servants, not including pensions. It is clear, therefore, that any increase of unnecessary expenditure in expanding the Public Service would be highly detrimental to the economy of the country.

In addition to what is stated above this provision cannot be implemented for the following reasons:

In many cases in which the Public Service Commission decided to allocate posts to the Turkish community, it was found that no qualified Turks were available for appointment, with the result that a number of posts remained vacant and in some cases the Commission had to appoint Greeks on a temporary basis until qualified Turkish candidates might become available.

In some instances the minimum qualifications specified in the schemes of service were lowered in order to enable Turkish candidates to enter the Public Service, but even with such lower standards no Turkish qualified candidate could be found.

The fact that the Commission had to draw from a population forming less than 19% of the population of the Island in order to fill the 30% of the posts in the Public Service made it very difficult to find qualified Turks for many posts.

Further, the exigencies of public business and the pattern of business and professional activity in the Island require that the Public Service should contain an adequate proportion of Greek officers. The language problem of itself demands this.

It can be seen from what is stated above that not only is the provision that the Public Service shall be composed of 30% Turks unjust and discriminatory against the Greeks, but it is also impracticable, it creates serious difficulties and impedes the efficient functioning of the Public Service.

The reasons given above regarding the ratio of participation of the two communities in the Public Service apply to a great extent to the ratio fixed for the participation of the two communities in the Security Forces. It must be stated that the 60:40 ratio of participation of Greeks and Turks in the Army discriminates to an even greater extent against the Greeks.

Nevertheless, in so far as the present ratio of Greeks and Turks in the Public Service, the Security Forces and the Army exceeds the population ratio, no abrupt steps should be taken to reduce it. The proper balance can be achieved over a period of time through normal appointments, thus avoiding hardship or unfairness to existing members of the Services of the Republic.

11. *The number of the Members of the Public Service Commission to be reduced from ten to five.*

The Constitution provides that there shall be a Public Service Commission consisting of a Chairman and nine other Members appointed jointly by the President and Vice-President of the Republic and that seven Members of the Commission shall be Greeks and three Members shall be Turks.

Practical experience has shown that, for the purposes for which the Public Service Commission is intended and bearing in mind the nature of the duties it has to perform, it is too large a body to work efficiently.

A smaller body will have a better chance of securing closer co-operation and understanding amongst its Members, and valuable time, wasted in lengthy arguments resulting from the divergence of opinion of its many Members, will be saved. Generally, a more constructive approach to the problems facing the Commission will result.

12.   *All decisions of the Public Service Commission to be taken by simple majority.*

The Constitution provides that any decision of the Public Service Commission shall be taken by an absolute majority vote of its Members.

This general provision, however, is qualified by other provisions making it necessary that in matters of appointments, promotions, transfers and discipline such majority must include a certain minimum number of Greek and Turkish votes depending on whether the decision relates to a Greek or a Turk. In short, a power of veto is given to a section of the Greek or Turkish Members to negative majority decisions.

It is obvious that this procedure for taking decisions by the Public Service Commission creates a situation whereby the Greek and Turkish Members feel that their paramount purpose, as Members of the Commission, is to protect Greek and Turkish interests and not to serve the true interests of the Public Service. Thus, even in the mode of deciding an issue communal criteria are superimposed on the universally accepted criteria adopted by similar bodies elsewhere. This is of particular significance in view of the fact that the Public Service Commission, in addition to being the appointing authority, is also the disciplinary body for the Public Service.

Furthermore, the procedure laid down in the Constitution creates situations leading to deadlock resulting in a state of uncertainty amongst the public servants and often preventing the speedy appointment of officers to vital posts.

If this situation is allowed to continue, it will result in undermining the efficiency of the Public Service.

It may be argued that, in taking decisions, the Public Service Commission may act in a discriminatory manner. In such a case there is adequate remedy provided by Articles 6 and 146 of the Constitution. The former Article prohibits discrimination against any of the two communities or any person as a person or by virtue of being a member of a community, while the latter Article provides that any person may make a recourse to the Constitutional Court against any decision, act or emission contrary to any of the provisions of the Constitution, one of which is Article 6, if any legitimate interest, which he has either as a person or by virtue of being a member of a community, is adversely affected.

13.   *The Greek Communal Chamber to be abolished.*

The Constitution provides that there shall be two Communal Chambers, one Greek and one Turkish, each having jurisdiction in matters of religion, education, cultural affairs and personal status over members of its respective community, as well as control over communal co-operative societies.

This provision appears to have its origin in the concept that the Republic ought not to interfere with religious, educational, cultural and other cognate matters the administration of which should be regarded as a safeguarded right in the case of the minority.

When this concept was extended to the Greek majority the result was to place the entire education of the country outside the sphere of Government economic and social policies and to create financial problems and other difficulties for the Communal Chambers, reflecting adversely on the State. With a view to minimizing these difficulties the Communal Chambers should be abolished and a new system should be devised providing for their substitution by appropriate authorities and institutions.

Should the Turkish community, however, desire to retain its Chamber, in the new system, such a course is open to it.

I have dealt with certain of the difficulties created by our Constitution.

In conclusion I would stress that it is not my intention by any of these proposals to deprive the Turkish community of their just rights and interests or proper safeguards. The purpose is to remove certain causes of friction and obstacles to the smooth working of the State.

The main object of a Constitution should be to secure, within its framework, the proper functioning of the State and not to create sources of anomaly and conflict. Experience has proved that our Constitution falls short of this object, and certain of its provisions have created great difficulties in practice. In the interests of our people we must remedy this. I earnestly believe that the proposed settlement of the various points of difficulty will be to the benefit of the people of Cyprus as a whole. I hope that the Turkish Cypriots will share this view.

Archbishop Makarios
President of the Republic of Cyprus

Nicosia,
30th November, 1963

APPENDIX 74

Proposed Turkish Cypriot "Reply to President's Memorandum," Undated

REPLY TO PRESIDENT'S MEMORANDUM

The President's memorandum entitled "suggested measures for facilitating the smooth functioning of the State and for the removal of certain causes of inter-communal friction" was handed to me by the President himself on the 30th November, 1963. Before handing it to me he outlined its contents and said, inter alia:—"Many people do not want a Constitution for Cyprus; what they want is ENOSIS, but despite this I have prepared this Memorandum to which I request you to give your reply within a week from to-day". It was obvious to me from the outset that the "suggested measures" were of a sweeping nature attacking the very roots which gave life to our Republic and that the ulterior intention was to leave the Turks at the absolute mercy of the Greeks. It was clear, therefore, that they were completely unacceptable to the Turkish side but nevertheless I told the President that I would give very careful consideration to his Memorandum but that I required much more time than a week. As I was leaving the Presidential Palace I could not help summarizing my views to the Minister of Foreign Affairs there and then. I told him that what the President had said appeared to me to be worse than ENOSIS. Since that day I have had several long consultations with my colleagues, the representatives of the Turkish Community, and advisers and we tried to find whether any ground whatsoever existed for us to consider the possibility of negotiations on these suggestions. We failed to find any such ground and found nothing which would in any way modify my original estimation of these "suggestions" as expressed to the Foreign Minister. We could not help noticing that detailed agreement was reached on all the points which are now being presented to us as provisions in the Constitution which prevent the smooth functioning of the State and that since the establishment of the Republic, the Greek side has followed the stern policy of not making any genuine effort to implement them in spite of our repeated representations and demands. We were surprised, therefore, to see that the so-called suggestions for "facilitating the smooth functioning of the State and for the removal of certain causes of intercommunal friction" contained nothing but a call for the complete abrogation of the very parts which for the last three years the Turkish side has been asking the Greek side to honour and implement.

BACKGROUND TO THE FINAL SETTLEMENT OF
THE CYPRUS PROBLEM

(i) Historical

The Independent Republic of Cyprus came into being soon after an armed strife between the two communities in Cyprus, in consequence of an agreed settlement between the leaders of the two communities and the Foreign Ministers of the immediately and directly concerned countries, viz: Great Britain, Turkey and Greece. In order to be able to understand the significance of the President's "suggestions" it is necessary to understand—(a) the causes of strife between the two communities in the pre-republic days; (b) the political settlement which each party originally sought to achieve and (c) the manner in which a final compromise settlement was reached after a long and painful period of agitation and violence.

Cyprus, an offshore island of Turkish mainland, was part of Turkey from 1571 until 1914 when Great Britain by a unilateral action annexed the Island to the Crown as a Crown Colony. Neither Turkey nor the Turkish Community in Cyprus and the Cypriots living in Turkey gave their consent to this annexation. The unilateral British action was subsequently ratified by the Turkish and Greek Governments in 1923 at the Treaty of Lausanne. As a result of this undemocratic treatment of the Turkish Community, a great number of Turks were forced to emigrate to Turkey leaving behind in Cyprus members of their family.

(ii) Separate Communities

The Greek Community which lived and flourished as a separate community under the Turkish rule continued to enjoy the same semi autonomous community status under the British rule. Thus, the two communities, which were in truth and in fact completely separate from each other because of religion, language, culture, custom, belief and political aspirations, continued to remain and lived as two separate communities. This separation became more and more accentuated as the Greek Community started identifying itself with "mother Greece" and claimed the annexation of Cyprus to Greece (ENOSIS). The Turks in return never ceased to identify themselves with Turkey and expressed their will (in the face of Greek demands) and their consciousness to remain part and parcel of Turkey. The separate and conflicting political consciousness and identity of the two communities reached its climax when the Greek Community organized themselves and started to force their way towards ENOSIS in complete disregard of the existence of the Turkish community. The Greeks, in their attempt to overpower and silence the Turkish Community started a campaign of insults, injustice, discrimination and hostility against the Turks all of which acts, and the bitter experience of co-existence over a long period of time, embedded the deep rooted idea in the mind and psychology of the Turks that if the Greeks found the chance they would not treat Turks fairly and squarely. And indeed as this campaign for ENOSIS grew in tempo under the leadership of the Church the attack on Turks and Turkish rights, the insults to and humiliation of Turks at every sphere of life, discrimination at Government services and at municipal functions increased in proportion thereby forcing Turks to rely more and more on their community's resources for self-support and protection.

(iii) Last Phase

The last phase of ENOSIS campaign started in 1954–55. All offers by the British Government for limited self-government with promises to proceed to full self-government over a period of years by a process of experience and evolution as has been the case in other countries of the commonwealth were turned down by the Church which declared that anyone who collaborated with the British Government for a Constitution was a traitor to the ENOSIS cause. Finally in 1955 terrorist activity was commenced by the Greeks against the British and the Turks, not with a view to achieving independence but with a view to unifying Cyprus with Greece. Here it would not be out of place to quote from a statement by EOKA issued during the Emergency prior to Independence: "We have two enemies before us. The first is the English and the second the Turks. We will first deal with the English and throw them out of the Island; then we shall annihilate the Turks. Our aim is Enosis. It is our duty to see that this aim is materialized whatever the cost may be." The Turks' position in such a struggle was very difficult. They would not consent to the unification of Cyprus with Greece, but they were resolved to fight for their cause which was—"If any change was to be made in the status of Cyprus the Island should go back to Turkey, its rightful owner". The communist Greeks on the other hand wanted at some stage of this struggle to accept self-government—on a majority-rule basis. Turks' answer to that was that under the majority-rule system, self-government was worse than ENOSIS.

As the 1954–58 struggle became more bitter and Greece started to back up the ENOSIS campaign openly by taking the Cyprus case to the United Nations, the intercommunal strife became deeper and deeper and it became obvious to all concerned that the Cyprus issue could only be settled if the interests of all parties were taken care of in a compromise settlement. In 1955 Britain called a Tripartite Conference in London between Britain, Turkey and Greece—the two motherlands of the Greek and Turkish communities in Cyprus, but no settlement could be reached as Greece insisted on ENOSIS, Turkey refused to accept such a solution and Great Britain would not yield to such demands. Turkey insisted on equal rights for both communities in any solution as she was fully aware of the behavior of the Greeks towards the Turks and of Turkish anxieties. Later the solution of "partition" was advanced and accepted by the Turks on the principle of self-determination for both communities on basis of equal treatment. The catastrophic events which followed need no mentioning. For every Greek who died in Cyprus for ENOSIS, a Turk died for preventing it until the Cyprus case was debated several times at the United Nations when finally in 1958 a resolution was passed to the effect that the interested parties should try and find a just solution by private negotiation between themselves.

(iv) Zurich and London Agreements

It is as a result of that resolution that negotiations started between the Greek and Turkish Foreign Ministers after due notice of the fact was given to the lenders of the Turkish and Greek communities and their approval taken. Great Britain blessed these negotiations by agreeing to accept any just settlement which the two motherlands of the two communities in Cyprus would reach. It is under these circumstances and with the full knowledge and consent of the leaders of both communities that the conference at Zurich was convened and concluded. Proposals and counter proposals were made by the two Foreign Ministers after constant contact and consultation with the leaders of the two communities. The Conference at Lancaster House in London on 11th February, 1959 was called after we signified that we were ready to accept the settlement as a fair settlement and the London Agreement at Lancaster House was signed in the belief that it finally solved the Cyprus problem against this background. The then Foreign Minister of Greece summarized these circumstances to the Conference at Lancaster House as follows:

> During the political struggle over the Cyprus question it was revealed that there were a lot of difficulties, objective political difficulties, internal political difficulties, and psychological and emotional difficulties in many countries and in many people. These three kinds of difficulties, objective internal political and psychological, revealed that after a while it was necessary to arrive at a *compromise*.

As to the intention of those who drew up the agreement at Zurich the Greek Foreign Minister stated and we all agreed that:

> We think that in this task of finding the solution we shall cover relatively the interest of every party. And we have been successful. After long talks, after long negotiations, which many times were not very easy, because the problem was complicated, I think we have arrived at a solution, an agreement in which the principles of democracy and of modern humanity are upheld and also the fundamental principles of every one.

and he continued:

> We signed these agreements because this is in the common interest of our countries in the middle of a world which is full of dangers and dangers which do not allow us to ignore them. We signed these agreements because we felt that they cover relatively and absolutely satisfactorily the interests of the people of Cyprus as a whole. We also signed these agreements because the respected man (referring by hand to the President) at the head of the Greek Community in Cyprus and whom we considered in all our deliberations as representing the will of the Greeks of Cyprus, having been informed by us, said that he was in agreement with these agreements. I do not think that we signed only because we had his agreement. We signed I think because it was our conviction that we have reached the relatively best possible solution.

But I want to add that we took into consideration his opinion for the fundamental reason that we had declared during our discussions that we will not impose these decisions by force or by other ways on the Greek Cypriots.

The U.K. Foreign Minister explained that London Conference was "called as I understand it on a basis of agreement between the representatives of the two communities here present and the three Governments".

MY VIEWS ON THE PRESIDENT'S SUGGESTIONS

I have had to go into the background of the Zurich and London settlement in some detail because the president in his suggestions has, unfortunately, tried to ignore all the facts leading to the settlement.

INTERCOMMUNAL CO-OPERATION.
No Winner—No Loser—No Dilemma—No ENOSIS

It is impossible to reconcile the president's statement that at Lancaster House in February 1959 he was "faced with a dilemma either of signing the agreement as it stood or of rejecting it with all the grave consequences which would have ensued" with the above-quoted official statements made in his presence by the representatives of the Turkish, British and Greek Governments taking part in the said Conference. Nor is it possible to accept as correct the President's categorical statement that "the intention of those who drew up the agreement at Zurich was to create an independent state in which the interests of the Turkish Community were safeguarded". That the intention was to create an independent State there is no doubt—but this would be a State in which, in the words of the Foreign Minister of Greece, "no one would be the winner and no one would be defeated but every one would be relatively satisfied. It was obvious that no one would have one hundred percent of what he wanted, but clearly should have his fundamental interests ensured in the best way". It was to be a State where the fear by the Turks of ENOSIS or complete Greek domination would be eliminated; a State in which the Greek and Turk would work in full co-operation as partners in a joint venture.

It was only on this basis that the British Government agreed to transfer the sovereignty over Cyprus which she had taken from Turkey, by virtue of the Treaty of Lausanne, "to a new independent state of Cyprus, a new state created on the basis of friendship, on the basis of agreement between Greece and Turkey, and between the communities in Cyprus" as explained by the British Foreign Minister at London Conference. In short, the agreements leading up to the independence of Cyprus were set against a complicated background and circumstances completely peculiar to Cyprus. It goes without saying that these peculiar and special circumstances had to be taken into account while considering a plan for the solution of the Cyprus problem. As it was summarized by the British Foreign Minister in London Conference these basic requirements were (and still are) "firstly that the strategic needs of the British Government should be met in a manner which was impossible to challenge, which was absolutely clear for all to see; secondly, that there should be conciliation of the two main communities in Cyprus; thirdly that there should be a recreation of the Greco-Turkish friendship which is so important for security and stability in the Eastern Mediterranean, that after all must be a requirement in any solution of the Cyprus problems; and finally, the fourth basic requirement was that the Cypriots themselves should be given the opportunity to develop their institutions".

Sui Generis Provisions

The President seems to have forgotten all these when he complains of the sui generis provisions in our Constitution.

It is because of these basic requirements and special conditions (which remain completely unaltered, if not more emphasized, by the attitude of the Greek leadership during the last three years), that we had to have some sui generic provisions in the "final settlement of the problem of Cyprus" and in the Constitution which was drafted on the basis of the said settlement. None of these sui generic provisions are contrary, as is now alleged after three years, to any democratic principle. It was clearly stated by the Greek Foreign Minister and accepted by all of us that "we have arrived at a solution where the principles of democracy and modern humanity are upheld". All constitutions may have sui generic provisions, because constitutions are made to fit the basic requirements of a country which they are meant to serve. This is obvious from the fact that each country has its own constitution dealing with its local conditions and no country attempts to adopt the constitution of the other without making such amendments as would make it applicable in that particular country. The American constitution also has many sui generis provisions but one does not hear the President of U.S.A. challenging the validity or application of his country's constitution on the meager excuse that it contains sui generis provisions.

"I Tried to Change . . ."

The President says in his "suggestions": "I tried very hard to bring about the change of at least some provisions of the Zurich agreement". I think it may be useful to quote from the verbatim report of the said Conference, as to what the President actually said:

"I have some reservations on certain points over the draft resolutions which seem not to be workable. I am fully convinced, however, that by close co-operation between the representatives of the Greek and Turkish Communities in a spirit of goodwill a detailed constitution will be prepared satisfactorily". In fact subsequent to the signing of the "Agreed foundations for the final settlement of the Cyprus problem" at the London Conference Greeks and Turks co-operated in a spirit of "goodwill and understanding" through the Constitutional Commission and Transitional Committee for about eighteen months before a "satisfactory" Constitution was "drafted", accepted and signed by the President on behalf of the Greek Community and by myself on behalf of the Turkish Community before sovereignty was transferred by the British Government to Cyprus. The President will no doubt remember that we had difficult times and long arguments in the preparation of the draft constitution be-fore we could agree on certain formulae which are now embodied in our Con-stitution.

All Reservations Removed by Agreement

Surely if the President had felt that he had certain reservations or doubts on the "draft constitution" he was completely free not to sign it. But quite on the contrary, in April 1959 on the occasion of initialing the draft con-stitution agreed to by both communities the Turkish representative in the Con-stitutional Commission and subsequently I myself made it clear that we would not sign the final draft on the date set for the transfer of sovereignty unless the requirements of 70:30 ratio in the public service were satisfied by that date. The President approached me for an agreement as to the implementation of those provisions within a reasonable time after the coming into operation of the Constitution. I wanted definite guarantee that this would be done. I had a long discussion with the President and finally he agreed in writing that these provisions should be implemented within five months of the coming into op-eration of the Constitution. I then thought that in his signature I had the best guarantee whereupon a committee composed of our Under-Secretaries and representatives of the two Civil Service Associations was set up to prepare a report on the manner of implementation of the 70:30 ratio within five months. This they did and the President, myself and the two Civil Service Associations signed it as an official document which would be honoured by all. It is clear from our conduct that all the way we knew what was happening. We, Turks, were prepared to risk the future and not sign the Constitution until the admin-istrative machinery which was necessary for its full implementation was set up. That was the time for the President to tell us that he felt a great number of points in the Constitution should be changed; that "he had many reservations" as he puts it now. He not only failed to do so but he went to the extent of signing a further document in order to remove from his way our legitimate op-position. Is this compatible with the President's allegation that he had reserva-tions on the workability of the Constitution? In legal matters one reserves cer-tain points for further argument but once these points have been argued about and a settlement reached on them one loses the right to be heard "on his reser-vations". He has signed the agreement. That is what matters in law and in practice. If he had reservations, he should not have signed the agreements.

I do not expect anyone to believe nor to accept the allegation that the Greek community, which was in a much stronger position than the Turkish community, was not in a position to face the consequences of not signing the Agreements or the Constitution while the Turkish community could. On the contrary the Greek side felt so strong and competent that when the negotia-tions on the extent of the British sovereign bases broke down in March, 1960, it was the President himself who suggested to me that we should proceed with the arrangements for Independence on the basis of the draft Constitution without waiting to reach an agreement with the British on the question of sov-ereign base areas and military facilities. I refused to accept this suggestion and negotiations re-started for a final agreement with the British. Surely no one can argue now that the consequences which would have ensued then in case we did not have an agreement with the British over the extent of the sovereign base areas would have been less grave than the consequences which would have ensued if the President had refused to sign the draft Constitution on the excuses which he tries to put forward now. It is difficult to understand how the Greek community could afford to take the risk of refusing to abide by that part of the settlement reached at London on 19/2/59 concerning the question of the bases and defy the power which would transfer the sovereignty to Cyprus, but could not take the risk of refusing to sign the draft Constitution. The argument now put forward by the President that he was faced "with the dilemma either of signing the agreement as it stood or of rejecting it with all the grave consequences which would have ensued" is completely untenable and cannot serve any purpose except to make it clear that the Constitution was accepted and signed with ulterior motives and with the intention (formed prior to the signing) of not implementing it at all. This is obvious from the repeated declarations the President and his colleagues have made since the Republic:

(i) Extract from a speech of President Makarios delivered on the 5th January, 1962:

The noble struggles of the people never come to an end. These struggles, although undergo transformation, are never terminated. The struggle of the people of Cyprus, too, will go on.

The Zurich and London Agreements form a landmark in the course of this struggle, but, at the same time, are a starting-point and bastion for further struggles, with the object of capitalising on what has been achieved for further conquests.

(ii) Extract from a speech by President Makarios delivered on the 1st April, 1963:

As we kneel before the graves of our martyrs, we hear them shout, "Forward, beyond the graves." This voice, which is gushing out of the graves is urging us to strive forward. The struggle did not end. It is continuing. The armed struggle ended, but it is continuing in a different form so that the present may be appraised and the future conquered.

Although this is incomplete, it is still victory. It forms a new epoch and a new chapter in our forward strides. It is a rampart on the course towards conquering the future. It is disclosing the nature of this future, the meaning and conception of the glorious anniversary which we are celebrating to-day.

(iii) Extract from a speech by Mr. Tasos Papadopoulos, Minister of Labour, delivered on the 17th August, 1963:

The President's recent declaration of his desire to abrogate the Treaty of Guarantee and obtain revision of the negative provisions of the Constitution came of no surprise to his entourage. It was the natural and expected confirmation of plan and intention which were born in the mind of the Leader since the day of the birth of the Cyprus Republic. This declaration is nothing more than the natural and inescapable commandment of our Greek history, and is the answer to the challenge of history to our present generation.

All know the negative points of the Agreements. It requires no high intelligence, genius, political experience or patriotism to realize that the Agreements need revision. I am in a position to know that what negators now use as mere slogans were in the mind and heart of our Ethnarch since the very first day of the birth of the Republic.

(iv) Extract from the speech of Mr. Polycarpos Yiorgadjis, Minister of the Interior, on the 29th July, 1963:

With our eyes always turned towards Greece which is the symbol of freedom, we exhibited our civilization and strength to those who maltreated us. Keeping our Greek conscience away from every possible influence, we always remained devoted to our ineradicable goal. This country has always been Greek and will remain so. Even though destiny causes our annihilation, Cyprus will always remind us of Greece. Our ancient monuments will be a proof of Greece. Greek spirit and heroism will push out of this earth, which is watered with blood.

Realizing our responsibilities towards our people, we shall, depending on the strength of right, strive forward without hesitation and with determination, for the materialization of our aspirations, in conformity with the national expectations and dream of the Cypriot Greek people. . . .

It must have been thought by the Greek side that once the big obstacle of British sovereignty was removed they would be free to use the Independence, which they got in return for their promise that ENOSIS would be forgotten, for the purpose of materializing this very aim. Such conduct by any party to any agreement cannot and should not win the support of law abiding and peace loving countries which believe in the Rule of Law. It is significant to mention here that a second conference was held in London on 17th January, 1960, between all the interested parties, to review certain difficulties in the working out of the original settlement arrived at in London on 19/2/59, but none of the principles contained in the present memorandum was raised there, despite the fact that such detailed questions as to whether Akamas range should be used by the British for 10 days or 15 days in a given year was discussed in extenso.

Though the second conference in London in January 1960 was convened by the British Government to consider certain difficulties arising out of the deliberations of the London Joint Committee, yet upon insistence of the British Foreign Minister the draft Constitution was produced to the Conference. If the President had any genuine reservations on the said Constitution that was the finest opportunity for him or any member of his Delegation (which included the Greek Representative to the Constitutional Commission) to raise them. It was clear from the President's conduct and words at the Conference that the draft Constitution which contained the very provisions that he is now complaining was, to use his own words, "satisfactory".

The President's statement in his "suggestions" that "the three years experience since the coming into operation of the Constitution, which was based on the Zurich and London Agreements, has made clear the necessity for revision of at least some of those provisions which impede the smooth functioning and development of the State" is obviously far from being true nor is it convincing. Had the Turkish Community believed that an honest and sincere attempt was made to apply the Constitution and that in that attempt practical difficulties were truthfully encountered, my position as a Vice-President and Deputy Head of the State would have been by the President and not opposite him. But from bitter personal experience over the last three years I know as a fact that this request for a change emanates from Greek political motives and that it is not supported by facts nor is it dictated by necessity. The Greek side is trying to get back from the Turks whatever the latter got out of the compromise settlement; we are being pressed to accept the surrender of our Constitutional rights on cunningly drafted legal arguments which have not got the backing of truthful facts. When dealing with the specific provisions which the President suggests should be amended I shall give sufficient examples in order to prove that this request for amendment arises not because these provisions have in practice proved to be impracticable or an obstacle in the way of smooth functioning of the state but that they were never faithfully applied and that artificial difficulties were created by the Greek side in order to find the excuse of arguing later that they were unworkable.

REAL CAUSES OF FRICTION

The President's statement in his "suggestions" that the consequences of the difficulties created by certain provisions is to prevent the Greeks and Turks of Cyprus from co-operating in a spirit of understanding and friendship etc. is a sweeping statement not born out by true facts. The Greek people of Cyprus have been, deliberately and wantonly prevented from co-operating with the Turks by responsible Greek leadership who have been preaching to them that they are the ruling class in Cyprus, that the Turks are a minority to be ruled, that the rights which the Turks got by the Zurich agreement should be taken away from them by the ruling race, that the fight for union with Greece still goes on and that the Turks, who are an obstacle on their way to Union with Greece must be made to submit to Greek will. As a consequence of this daily preaching through the press and by the Greek leaders the initial approach of the two communities towards each other was stopped. Any Greek who disobeyed the "orders" was either assaulted, threatened or killed. Agitation for ENOSIS which should have been prevented by law has poisoned the atmosphere in the absence of any Law prohibiting its propagation; the war of nerves which has been going on ever since the Republic has not helped the matters either. So, anyone who is "in the know" of Cyprus affairs will immediately grant that it is not the Constitution which prevents the Greeks and Turks from co-operating but the Greek insistence that "the Constitution as it now stands must change and the Turks must give up their Constitutional rights if they want co-operation with the Greeks".

It is true that there is a friction in Cyprus between the Greek and the Turkish Communities but it is equally true that this friction is not emanating from or "as a consequence of difficulties created by certain constitutional provisions" but from the persistent refusal of the Greeks to implement or observe the constitutional provisions; from the refusal of the Greeks to abandon the "Enosis" campaign which is declared prohibited by our Constitution; from the refusal of the Greeks to recognize the Turks as their brothers and partners in the common cause of welfare and betterment of the State; from the persistence of the Greeks to dominate absolutely over the Turks, treat them as second hand citizens and low-down creatures in a manner incomprehensible by ordinary civilized person; from the persistence of most responsible officers of the Republic to look upon the regime "as a bastion for further campaigns" and from the persistence by certain responsible elements "to complete the unfinished victory" etc. In short the friction between the two communities has been fostered by a general lack of sincere desire on the Greek side to collaborate with the Turks in a spirit of good-will and understanding.

NO WILL—NO WAY

It was the common and agreed aim at Zurich that the Cyprus ailment should be cured by the proper administration of a detailed regime. This was carefully worked out and set out in the London Agreement and later, after still more careful attention for 18 months the Constitution was drafted. All that remained to be done was to administer the country according to this Constitution or using a metaphor the time had come to give the medicine to the ailing Cyprus problem. But the medicine was deliberately withheld from being administered and those who are guilty of this neglect are now shouting and saying that "this medicine is useless—we must change it—we want a more drastic remedy," quite realizing that their suggested remedy is amputation— amputation of Turkish rights, the removal of Turkish factor, the creation of a Cyprus which will leave the door open to complete Greek domination of the island and eventually to union with Greece if the rightist Greeks have their say or to becoming a Russian Satellite if the 40% strong Greek Communist factors have their say.

A STATE IS BORN NOT A NATION

The President and indeed the Greek side as a whole agree that the agreements which brought about the Independent Republic of Cyprus "brought about a State but not a Nation", but they all tend to forget this important admission of fact while making suggestions for the amendment of the Constitution. If the President looked upon Cyprus as a State brought about by the agreement of two communities at a settlement then he and his Ministers would immediately stop acting as if the agreements had brought about a Cyprus nation, they (the Greeks) representing this nation. It is because they feel and think that Cyprus is a Greek-ruled island that they cannot afford to treat the Turks as partners in the administration. The moment this mentality *is* changed and Cyprus is accepted as a State created by the will of two communities to be governed under specific conditions embodied in its Constitution then the need for a change will disappear because the Constitution will be put into motion according to its letter and spirit and I am convinced it will work smoothly.

It is noteworthy to mention here, as a further proof of the lack of desire on the Greek side to implement the Constitution, the fact that no municipal legislation was introduced providing sanctions against those who tried to upset the constitutional order. Those who demand the abrogation of the agreements and prepare to resort to armed conflict, if necessary, are "heroes" sitting at top level Government posts. Papers which advocate ENOSIS daily fear no sanctions because no law exists providing for such sanctions. All my attempts and endeavours to provide for such measures as would ensure the security of the regime at its initial steps were of no avail because, I soon discovered, the Greek leadership, from the President downwards, were all determined not to see the continuation of this regime and the application of the Constitution, but to achieve its speedy collapse and the abrogation of the agreements in toto. This determination was so obvious that the illustrated London News of 1st April 1963 introduced the President as "The President of Cyprus started the ENOSIS campaign". No denial came from the Presidential Palace.

Before I start replying to the specific points raised in the "suggestions" I would like to make a few remarks on the wording of the Memorandum.

The use of such words as "at least some of those provisions" and "certain of the difficulties" are clear enough to indicate that the provisions which the President appears to have decided should be removed from our Constitution now are not exhaustive. Therefore, it is quite clear that what he actually wants is to set aside the "order established" by the international settlement of London arrived at after great hardship and sacrifices by all parties concerned and to replace it with an order whereby the Turkish community would remain at the mercy of the Greek community. This is born out by the President's statement that his intention is "not to deprive the Turkish community of their just rights and interests or proper safeguards".

As I have endeavoured to explain above, if the problems of Cyprus were as simple as that, there would have been no need for us to meet at London and subsequently in Cyprus for nearly two years to draft our present Constitution because this same proposal was put forward by the President in the autumn of 1958 just before the Cyprus problem was bitterly fought before the United Nations and was refused by us. It was ruled out by all the interested parties including Greece, which in the words of the President is his "motherland" upon whose King Greeks of Cyprus "look as the King of all Hellenes over the World" (statement in Athens on the occasion of President's official visit in 1962). Here I would like to quote the words of the Greek Foreign Minister as recorded in the proceedings of the London Conference on 17/2/1959. Referring to the Zurich settlement he has this to say:

> We have separated all the matters which ought to be separated, because they are of a completely different nature, as for instance, religious affairs. We have respected the majority, which is overwhelming, and the majority because it is overwhelming, have more part of the administration. But, we have also given

to the minority not only rights but fair parts in the administration. And also the way of the administration is such that the Turks of Cyprus could not feel they are at the mercy of the majority if the majority wanted not to be fair.

Has the majority been fair in the course of the last three years? Is the majority being fair by putting up the present proposals in the manner it is presented? I am sure that all will agree with me that these proposals stand no chance of consideration by the Turks of Cyprus, even if that means for Turks misery and extermination by force and atrocity.

CONCLUSION

What Turks Want

What we want is sincere cooperation with the Greeks and the right of co-existence on basis of justice and equality. Justice is not an abstract matter but is always done according to the rule of Law. I firmly believe that if our Constitution is adhered to, its letter obeyed and its spirit of Greco-Turkish partnership is honoured all causes of friction between the two communities will disappear. In goodwill and harmony we will then bend all our energies and resources to the problems of Cyprus. Trust, confidence and mutual respect will thus be created and the way to happiness and property will be paved. It may be difficult for some Greek extremists to accept the Turks as "partners" and recognize the legitimacy of those rights which have been recognized to them by international agreements. But extremist view will not help us. We would like to feel that those Greeks of goodwill and wisdom will realize that neither of the Turkish rights in the Constitution prevent them from enjoying the full benefits of Independence and communal autonomy. To insist that they should have 100% of what they set out to get in 1955 and leave the Turks to the mercy of the Greek rule is not to face the realities of a very serious situation. I, therefore, suggest that municipal legislation should be introduced forthwith, with a view to ensuring:

(a) that all subversive activity and propaganda directed against the regime and the abrogation of the agreements is stopped;
(b) that all activity and propaganda directed for Union of Cyprus with any other country be made a punishable offence;
(c) that the institutions which were created by the Constitution such as the Public Service Commission be backed up by proper legislation in order to enable them to function smoothly and properly;
(d) that legislation for the municipalities as envisaged by the Constitution be enacted;
(e) that the Election Law proper be enacted;
(f) that the President removes all causes of friction between his office and mine by consenting to take my views on matters of foreign affairs, defense and security and the Turkish Ministers be treated as necessary parts of this government and not as opposition to it;

(g) that adequate subsidies be given to the Communal Chambers at least to the extent of services which they have taken over from the British administration thereby treating them as autonomous public bodies which are running services essential for the country and not treating them as undesirable anti-government institutions the functions of which are alien to government's policy;

(h) that the 70:30 ratio is applied on the basis of our original agreement which bears our signature so that no injustice is done to any serving officer;

I am fully convinced that if there is any intention at all on the Greek side to try out the Zurich regime all the above should be done, and a sufficient time be given to the country to see how things will work. So far nothing of this sort has been done but on the contrary, as explained above, all that is humanly possible has been done in order to prevent the smooth functioning of the Constitution. The goodwill of the Turks has been assailed daily by administrative or other police action. And moreover it is very significant and is a matter for regret that these "suggestions" have been handed to me under the direct and indirect threat that whatever the Turkish Community may do or feel about them, if they are not agreeable to the proposed changes the Greek side will proceed to unilateral abrogation of the Constitution. I need not say anything on the grave consequences of such irresponsible action. With these words I now turn to the specific proposals of the President:

1.   *The right of veto of the President and the Vice-President of the Republic to be abandoned.*

I have set out above the background to the settlement which was reached finally by the signing of the London agreement. The right of veto given to the President and the Vice-President in laws and decisions concerning foreign affairs, defense and security were necessitated having regard to the background of the two communities and to the suspicion that without this safeguard the Greek side would misuse their powers in these fields and achieve political advantages which were alien to the Turks. In other words, if ENOSIS was to be prevented for good the veto in foreign affairs, was a necessity. If the Turkish Community was to be protected against discriminatory actions under the pretext of security measures such power of veto in defense and security was essential. It is obvious that without this safeguard (right of veto) the Turkish Community could not agree to any settlement which in the absence of this right would leave the community at the mercy of the Greeks in these matters. It is inconceivable that this right creates difficulties in the smooth functioning of the State. In three years' practice the veto has been used only in one instance, and that on a decision relating to the Cyprus Army. In that case the Vice-President taking into account the advice of military experts (both Greek and Turk) and believing that the establishment of an Army mixed throughout all units at the initial stage, would mean the provision of opportunity for continuous friction between members of two communities, deemed it necessary to exercise his right of veto in the interest of Cyprus as a whole. He wanted to ensure that further consideration was given to the matter but it is important to note that the matter was never brought up for consideration but treated as a closed case because of the preconceived idea of the President that an Army was not necessary in Cyprus. Indeed, his declaration to the press immediately after the use of this veto by the Vice-President clearly indicates that the State ran into difficulties not because the veto was used but because the Greek side not wanting an Army from the beginning maneuvered things in such a way as to necessitate the use of veto and then turned back and used the veto as a pretext for not establishing the Army. Such powers of veto in the President exist in most countries as a security against the misuse of powers by certain other organs of the State and in order to give the populace a chance to see what is being done on their behalf in matters of grave importance. We must not forget that our regime is a Presidential one and the suggestion that the President's power should be limited to return of laws and decisions cannot be accepted unless the whole regime is changed. The fact that this Presidential regime in Cyprus is ensured by the President and the Vice-President conjointly is the result of the political settlement which all parties signed after due deliberation and this cannot be changed merely because arguments against it have been advanced academically. On this question of right of veto, therefore, we do not see any reason which calls for a change.

The President states that the right of veto should be abandoned and reliance placed instead on the provisions for the return of laws and decisions for reconsideration, and the various other relevant safeguards. In this connection it is interesting to note that out of 3541 decisions which the Council of Ministers has taken since its establishment the Vice-President felt obliged to return for reconsideration 30 decisions but none of these decisions were in any way modified by the Council. The Supreme Constitutional Court (the Greek member dissenting) found, however, in the few cases in which it proved possible to make a recourse, that the arguments advanced by the Vice-President were constitutionally and legally correct. Of the laws passed by the House of Representatives the Vice-President felt obliged to return to the House the following laws:

1) Supplementary Appropriation Law (No. 7), 1960;
2) Supplementary Appropriation Law (No. 4), 1961;
3) The Public Officers (Reinstatement) Law, 1961;
4) The Dentists Registration (Amendment) Law, 1962;

Of the above laws one related to the supplementary subsidy which the Executive wished to make to Communal Chambers at the ratio of 87.5:12.5, two to the payment of nearly £200,000 to dismissed but re-instated public officers. It was expected that Greek Members of the House would not be disposed to make any modification to these three laws on reconsideration, but the attitude Greek members took when the Dentists Registration (Amendment) Law was returned to them for reconsideration leaves much to be desired. This Law was returned to the House for reconsideration of that Section of the Law which permitted professionally unqualified persons to practice dentistry. Though most of the Greek members of the House expressed the view that it was dangerous to allow unqualified persons to practice dentistry, yet the Law was not modified solely for the reason that it would deal a blow to the prestige of the Greek members of the House if they were to accept the warning and recommendations of a Turkish Vice-President. So long as such a mentality exists in Cyprus I wonder what benefit can be derived from the right of return. As to other relevant safeguards, I shall refer to the statements made by the President about the decisions of the Supreme Constitutional Court and to the circumstances in which the President of that Court and his Assistant were obliged to resign when I deal with that part of the "suggestions".

2.   *The Vice-President of the Republic to deputise for the President of the Republic in case of his temporary absence or incapacity to perform his duties.*

        This offer looks generous to the uninitiated but it is unacceptable to the Turkish side because unless the whole structure of elections and the political institutions on which the Cyprus Republic rests are changed it is neither practicable nor scientific. The elections in Cyprus are, by necessity and by the settlement reached in London, on a communal basis—Turks elect the Vice-President and Greeks elect the President. It is not, therefore, possible in law to require the Vice-President to deputize for the Greek President without the consent of the electors and it is of course impossible to get such a consent every time a question of deputising arises. The Turkish side appreciated the situation at the time the settlement was reached and accepted it in return for its guaranteed rights. In order to maintain the present regime which takes cognizance of the existence of two separate communities it is necessary that this form should be kept. In any case the position as it is now creates no difficulties at all and therefore the arguments advanced by the President in calling for this change are only academic. It is noteworthy, however, that by offering this advantage, it is the intention to make consequential or relative amendments. In other words, certain rights and privileges of the Vice-President will be taken away and the structure of the political agreement will be completely destroyed.

3.   *The Greek President of the House of Representatives and the Turkish Vice-President to be elected by the House as a whole and not as at present the President by the Greek Members of the House and the Vice-President by the Turkish Members of the House.*

4.   *The Vice-President of the House of Representatives to deputize for the President of the House in case of his temporary absence or incapacity to perform his duties.*

        The remarks as to the deputizing of the Vice-President for the President apply to this proposal as well. Unless the political structure and the system of election is changed necessitating the reduction of the Turkish Community to the status of a mere minority, these proposals are unscientific and unrealistic and cannot be accepted. Further, we do not consider that a case of hardship or difficulty has been made to warrant a change. The excuse that there is no permanent Vice-President of the House entitled to deputize for the President of the House is a very poor one in view of the fact that the Greek members of the House always know the member who will deputize for the President in his absence.

5.   *The Constitutional provisions regarding separate majorities for enactment of certain laws by the House of Representatives to be abolished.*

This power was recognized as a means for assuring that there would be no discrimination against the Turks. It is essential that it remains as it is, because also of the political structure of the country where the question of taxation by the Communal Chambers has to be considered in line with the power of the State with regard to taxation. In other words, the Communal Chambers have to finance their budget first from State grants and then by levying taxes on members of their community. If the State acts responsibly towards the services which the Communal Chambers render and increases the Government grant in proportion to the services rendered then the question of taxation by the Communal Chambers either does not arise at all or arises in a very small degree. But where Government willfully refuses to give a just grant-in-aid for these services as it has refused for the last three years, the Communal Chambers are forced to impose taxes in order to balance their budgets. In such an event because double taxation is undesirable, the House has to forego its right to impose the same tax as the Communal Chambers have imposed. This, in a normal country, could be achieved by agreement between the Communal Chambers and the State, but where the State creates difficulties for political reasons and in order to wreck one of the most important institutions under the Constitution, namely the Communal Chambers, it is absolutely necessary that the power of separate majority should remain as otherwise the Turkish Communal Chamber may find itself in the position of not being able to impose any tax on members of the Turkish Community. Such a position would mean the bankruptcy of the Chamber.

The whole trend of the submission by the President on this matter seems to be a wrong assumption that the Turkish side presents a danger for willful obstructionism in the way of enacting vital taxation legislation. His fears are not supported by facts as the Turkish members have never misused their power, and it is unlikely that they will misuse it nor do they intend to make use of it as long as fears of discrimination do not arise. If resort to such a power is ever made, the proper step to take is to bring the two sides together and try to ascertain with goodwill and understanding the causes of complaint and find a compromise solution. The example given by the President with regard to the income tax bill does not represent the facts correctly and fairly. The true facts may be summarized as follows:

The Turkish members of the House of Representatives advanced arguments on the above lines and in the end proposed to approve the income tax bill in toto in respect of non-citizens, but in respect of the citizens they agreed to approve the body of Law but make the schedule of rates subject to revision periodically as it is the case in all other countries. The Greek members, however, voted against this proposal of the Turkish members and thus the bill was not enacted. It is clear that Greek members by not agreeing to periodical revision of rates of taxes wished to take away for good from the Turkish members the right of separate majority vote. It would not be out of place to quote here from the speech of the Floor Leader of the Turkish group:

> For example the schedule (rates, etc.) may be approved for a period of two years; if at the end of the two years it is not approved then, in order to solve the disagreement and not to leave the country without a law in the meantime, it may be valid for another three months . . . I shall again request my Greek colleagues at least to accept this proposal and not to leave the country without the income tax law. Thus in the sufficient time given, the future of this law may be discussed and solved. I hope that our Greek colleagues will not follow a line which will cause the non-existence of the income tax law and will therefore accept our proposal.

In this connection it would not be irrelevant to explain here the Greek tactics employed in order to take away this right from Turks. Under para. 2 of Article 188 of the Constitution the laws imposing duties and taxes which were in force before the coming into operation of the Constitution were allowed to continue in force until 31st December, 1960, in order to give time for the preparation and enactment of new laws in accordance with the constitutional provisions. Up to 31st December, 1960, nothing was, however, done and not even a single taxation bill was introduced to the House. Towards the end of December, 1960, a bill entitled "Laws Imposing Duties or Taxes (Continuation of Provisions) Law of 1960, and providing for the continuation in force of all laws imposing duties and taxes until replaced, amended or repealed was submitted to the House. Such a bill was clearly unconstitutional and the real intention behind it was to secure the enactment of the bill under the pretext of necessity and thus deprive Turkish Representatives of their right of separate majority until, at least, such time as a bill imposing a duty or tax had to be introduced to the House. Such a course of action would mean that all taxation laws—including income tax and customs tariff law—would remain in force until amended or repealed. The Turkish Representatives did not agree to the enactment of such a law for an indefinite period and thus a compromise solution was found and the continuation in force of the taxation laws until 31st March, 1961, was approved. Towards the end of the extended period another short bill was submitted to the House to extend the operation of the old laws. The Turkish Representatives agreed to an extension for a further period of two months, urging that the overdue taxation bills as provided by the Constitution should in the meantime be submitted to the House, but Greek members again insisted for an indefinite period. As a result no agreement could be reached and the taxation laws thus expired. It will be observed from this exposition of the true facts that it is the Greek side which misused the right of separate majority and not the Turkish side to which the blame has been unjustly thrown with an ulterior motive which needs no explanation.

The fear that Government has no control over the Communal Chambers in their taxation policy and that if the communal Chambers misuse their power there may be clash of policy between the Chambers and the State is not a valid one. It is a recorded fact that so far the Communal Chambers have acted with due regard to their responsibilities and after full consultation with the Government side on matters concerning general policy. They have accepted constructive suggestions and have maintained an attitude of understanding and cooperation with the Government, in spite of the fact that Government has deliberately let them down by refusing to increase the grant-in-aid unjustifiably. Again I am not convinced that a case has been made necessitating the proposed changes. From the above it will also be clear that the suggested remedy, in case of fear of discrimination, to resort to a Court of Law is not a remedy for the financial and political problems which may arise having regard to the Constitutional structure of the country. I am of the view that in practice the existence of this right of separate majorities has not affected the smooth functioning of the State.

6.   *Unified Municipalities to be established.*

The excuse for this claim is that it serves no purpose to have separate municipalities and that it has proved to be unworkable. The object for the relevant provisions in the Constitution was not to disturb the status quo existing at the time the settlement was reached since separate municipalities had been functioning for more than a year. It was considered it would not be advisable to unite municipalities forthwith and thus create an impression that the implication was to secure for the Greeks the right for political domination over Turks. It was the intention to give the two communities a chance to work their separate establishments on their own, but to co-operate with each other and co-ordinate their work at the level of the co-ordinating committees prescribed in the Constitution. It was a matter for the leaders of the two communities, to decide after a few years of experience whether to unite or not the separate municipalities. In other words, the Constitution made provision for everything in order to assure each side of its rights, privileges and safeguards and to pave the way for full cooperation and understanding once these rights, safeguards and privileges were accepted and settled between the two communities. Had the Greek side approached this problem in this spirit at the beginning the way to unification by mutual agreement and understanding would probably have been paved by now. But instead the Greek side chose to declare unilaterally that there would be no separate municipalities as these according to them were unworkable, unnecessary and uneconomical. It is a paradox that the fact that separate municipalities have existed and continue to exist has consistently and completely been ignored. The geographical areas could easily be defined by one way or other if there was any will at all to define same, but unfortunately all efforts to do so were defeated because of the lack of goodwill on the part of the Greek side.

It is clear from the provision of the Constitution relating to Municipalities that the existence of which areas extend to the Greek or the Turkish Municipality is contemplated and provided for. But when the President declared categorically that he would not allow a single Greek property on, or close on, to remain in a Turkish municipal area he was riding against the Constitution and creating artificial difficulties for non-application of the relevant provisions. In his long exposition of the difficulties which he visualizes will be met if separate municipalities are created, he has completely ignored the basic fact that separate municipalities have been functioning for the last five years. Most of his objections relate to the definition of areas but again he ignores the report of Mr. Surridge who, as an independent authority, fully investigated the matter and submitted proposals to the Government. Our invitation to the President to accept this report as a working paper was declined. As to the financial difficulties of the municipalities it is the Greeks themselves who have been telling us that at the time of the united municipalities they had been paying for our municipal services. So the separation to which they object must have saved them from a great financial burden. On the Turkish side, since separation a marked improvement and development are noticeable in Turkish sectors which were left in a desolate condition by the unified municipalities. The President suggested certain measures which he considered as sufficient in order to appease Turkish fears that Turkish units would be discriminated against. We have two remarks to make on this suggestion:

(_) The Turkish community would have had faith in the President's promises had he kept his past promises and honoured his undertakings which he had given by signing international treaties and agreements. It is the same President who is now trying to take away all the rights of the Turkish community.

(_) It is interesting to note that under the President's proposals an amount proportionate to the ratio of the Turkish population of each town will be earmarked in the annual budget for disposal for municipal purposes recommended by the Turkish Councillors. The offer has no merit for consideration. We are promised to be allocated a sum proportionate to the ratio of the Turkish population of the town. This in fact means that we shall be benefiting to the extent of our contribution to the municipal budgets. In other words, our grossly neglected parts of the towns will be condemned to remain derelict for ever, as it is obvious that the proportion of revenue which we shall be contributing will not be sufficient for necessary developments. A Turkish institution is thus sought to be extinguished in return for nothing. Our proposal on the other hand was just and reasonable. We proposed to establish the Co-ordinating Committees provided by the Constitution, and to increase from time to time their powers and thus bring about the unification (if agreed upon) through a process of evolution. This was also turned down on the plea that the President could not accept to have separate municipalities. It is worth mentioning that in Nicosia and its suburbs there exist several local authorities all working side by side and without presenting any difficulty as to impracticability of defining the areas within which they function. The objection, therefore, to recognize a 5-year old existing Turkish municipalities is merely due to political fanaticism and to nothing else.

7. *The Administration of Justice to be unified.*

    The proposition that the administration of justice should be unified should be examined in its proper perspective. Administration of justice in Cyprus emanates from a unified body, i.e. the High Court of Judicature, which also sits as an Appeal Court for the decisions of the lower Courts. The fact that Turkish cases are decided by Turkish judges, Greek cases by Greek judges and mixed cases by a mixed Court does not give rise to the academic speculation put forward in the President's proposals. The necessity that this should be so arises from a great number of factors; the main one being that of language. Imagine a case where all parties to it and witnesses are Turks and the case to be tried before a Greek judge. Secondly political terrorism at all levels still goes on in Cyprus and in private several judges still complain of attempts made by Greek terrorist organizations to influence them. So long as EOKA Fighters Association continue to exist it is impossible for Greek judges to administer proper justice to Turks. The Constitution has thus saved judges from embarrassment and prevented any doubt being cast upon them as regards their integrity by Greek or Turkish public opinion. It is very easy to claim that the present administration should change and it would be very easy for us to agree to this had we been arguing on an academic issue. But we are arguing on existing facts. We have bitter examples of attempted political interference in the administration of justice, we have the concrete example of the President of the Constitutional Court and his Assistant who were forced to resign because in an important case between Greeks and Turks they did not succumb to Greek pressures. We have the reality which must be faced and accepted as such that the Turkish population has unfortunately lost its trust and confidence in the Greek judges. This should not, however, be taken as an imputation of doubt in the integrity of Greek judges. Had they been free from political pressure this doubt would not have arisen. The fact that we still live in a country where people are beaten and threatened or killed because they chose to disobey the orders of terrorists and traded with Turks or sold immovable properties to Turks should not be lost sight of. We do not want to enlarge upon these unpleasant examples which form the background to our daily experience.

    The Courts as envisaged by the Constitution have been functioning efficiently for the last three years, and it is the first time that we have heard an issue being made of this part of the Constitution. The general Turkish public opinion on the question of Courts is that the acceptance of the agreement as proposed by the President will be tantamount to imperiling personal rights and liberties of the Turkish community in view of the political pressure which is still being exercised on the Greek judges by Greek terrorist organisations. I share this view. All the difficulties which the President sets out in his Memorandum are overcome by the existence of the High Court of Judicature and its appeal jurisdiction, and its power to regulate the work of lower Courts. During the Emergency the British Government was forced to establish separate Courts for the trial of emergency cases not because the integrity of Greek judges was in doubt but because the pressure applied on them from outside was appreciated. Same pressure continues to exist to-day, and it is unlikely that it will diminish as long as the political agitation for reducing the Turkish community to the status of a minority continues in order to fortify ulterior Greek political motives. The President has no doubt not forgotten the case of the monks at Kykko monastery who defied police and fired at them and who upon prosecution before a Greek Assize Court were sentenced to pay the meagre sum of £23 each when the mere carrying of arms was being punished by the Turkish Courts and by Greek Courts (in non-political cases) by heavy sentences of imprisonment. The bitter experience we have had in the exercise of disciplinary powers by the Public Service Commission and the differentiation of treatment they have afforded to Greek and Turkish public officers in matters of discipline should be sufficient to make us dread the consequences for the Turkish community of the unification of Courts. It is common knowledge, and many examples can be cited by way of proof, that for some or even graver offences, Greek public officers are either leniently punished or not punished at all whilst Turkish public officers for same or less minor offences are mercilessly dealt with. A certain Turkish officer who in the exercise of his lawful duties deemed fit to disobey orders given to him by his immediate Greek superior, was so harshly treated that the poor officer has been ruined financially besides losing all prospects for promotion. On the other hand certain Greek officers who defied and insulted their Turkish superior officers have not been punished but rewarded and encouraged in their misbehavior. In the circumstances I cannot agree to any change in this part of the Constitution.

8. *The division of the Security Forces into Police and Gendarmerie to be abolished.*

In all countries the Security Forces are usually divided under different names into autonomous units. The reports on the Gendarmerie indicate that the division has greatly helped in the detection and prevention of crime. The excuse that separation involves increased costs cannot be accepted if we all concede, as we must, that the privileges of independence do necessarily carry with it the burden of additional expenses. This matter has not been raised before and the possibilities of a reorganization for the purpose of reducing costs and stream-lining both forces with a view to bringing about higher efficiency and fuller co-operation between them have not been explored. If there are indeed practical difficulties let us discuss them and see what we can do about settling them. It is very odd, however, that for every difficulty raised the only solution thought of is the amendment of the Constitution and the changing of the whole political structure of the country. When the net outcome of the proposed changes is examined one does not fail to see that it is either a Turkish establishment or a Turkish authority which it has tried to eliminate.

9. *The numerical strength of the Security Forces and of the Defense Forces to be determined by a law.*

The proposition that the increase or decrease of the Security and Defense Forces should be regulated by law is paradoxical because it is conceded that whatever agreement the President and the Vice-President reach between them has to be the subject of the budget on which the House of Representatives eventually decides. The fact that the Constitution gives this right initially to the President and the Vice-President does not in any way impair the smooth function of the State. Having regard to the system of Government which we have, this matter is in my view properly regulated by our Constitution and there is no need for taking away another power of the Vice-President, who, if all the proposals of the President are accepted, will be divested of all power and authority worthy of mention.

10.   *The proportion of the participation of Greek and Turkish Cypriots in the composition of the Public Service and the Forces of the Republic to be modified in proportion to the ratio of the population of Greek and Turkish Cypriots.*

These proportions are an integral part of the overall settlement of the Cyprus problem and were fixed having regarded, inter alia, to the special circumstances of the bilingual State which was being formed. These percentages further guarantee to the state that appointments shall be non–discriminatory of creed or race. It is, therefore, unacceptable that those who advocate the appointment of best qualified persons irrespective of race or creed should also demand, in the same breath, that Turks must not exceed a certain proportion in the Public Service. Having regard to all aspects and interests of the independent Cyprus State, we are convinced that these percentages were, and still are, justified. To quote here the words of Dr. Averoff at the meeting of Cyprus Conference held at Lancaster House, London, on 18th February, 1959:

> We felt, and many Greek Cypriots felt, that as their Turkish brothers of the Island were only 18% it was only fair to give them a bigger part in the administration so that, having its bigger part, they would feel more confidence for the future collaboration with the community with whom they had lived so many centuries on peaceful terms. We felt that this was very small thing that we could give, sacrifice some of our own interests so as to create conditions of collaboration.

The above-quoted statement of the Greek Foreign Minister clearly demonstrates that the architects of the Cyprus Constitution did not regard the participation of Greek and Turkish Cypriots in the public service and the forces of the Republic as a simple mathematical exercise in population statistics. In fixing the ratios they were guided by an important moral significance which, they rightly believed, would lead to the creation of confidence and closer cooperation between the two communities. The President sees the point by conceding that "the fixing of a percentage of participation of a community in the Public Service is for the purpose of securing to the community a right of equal access to the public service of the Country." But his suggestion that the right of such equal participation should be secured by resort to the Court if anyone is discriminated against, is not acceptable. It is unfortunate that the Court which would have looked into our existing grievances was grossly interfered with by certain highly influential Greek personalities in authority and its protection is nullified for the Turkish Community for the time being. Furthermore it should always be born in mind that the administrative machine is for service to the people, and even with the percentages provided for by the Constitution, the Turkish Community is not adequately and satisfactorily served.

The allegation that fixed proportions have created serious problems for the State, as criteria other than qualifications, efficiency and suitability have to be taken into consideration by the appointing authority is completely without foundation. Appointments and promotions are made on the basis of schemes of service which apply equally to Greeks and Turks. At no time the Turkish side has asked or even remotely suggested the appointment or promotion of a Turk who did not possess the qualifications laid down in the Schemes of Service. On the contrary we have concrete evidence that the Greek dominated Public Service Commission has, from the date of its formation, shown alarming laxity in assessing the qualifications and suitability of Greek candidates.

It is our contention that difficulties such as represented were artificially created to hinder the application of the ratio in the Public Service. The President himself had agreed, at the initial stages, to implement the ratio within a period of five months and put his signature to this agreement only to back out of it within a very short time. Had that agreement been implemented, all the points of difficulties mentioned in the Memorandum would have ceased to exist. No injustice would have been done to any public officer, as such officer's interests were guaranteed and provided for. The Greek and the Turkish Civil Service Associations were in full agreement and the implementation of the Report commenced smoothly. It is when they realized that the smooth application of the ratio would show to the world that the Constitution was workable that the Greek side started to create difficulties through the medium of Greek members of the Public Service Commission.

We should, now, revert to other allegations made in the Memorandum, which are designed generally to cast doubt about the quality and availability of Turkish candidates to fill public posts. We assert that Turks have an abundance of University graduates who are still unemployed while posts in their particular field of proficiency are being kept vacant awaiting the arrival of Greek graduates from their studies or filled by less qualified Greek candidates. We shall give examples of such cases further on. Also, an analysis of the qualifications of serving civil servants recorded in the official Staff List, published by the Department of Personnel in July, 1962, will show that of the total number of Greek officers listed (excluding members of Security Forces) only 38.88% have University or other professional qualifications, whereas 50% of the total number of Turkish officers in the same List possess University or other professional degrees. The facts stated above should remove, once and for all, any doubts about the availability and quality of the potential Turkish element within and outside the service.

Touching very briefly on the statement about the exigencies of public business and the pattern of business and professional activity in the Island necessitating the Public Service to contain an adequate proportion of Greek Officers, we should point out that the logic of this statement applies with equal force to the demands of the Turkish Community which is going through a similar process of development in its public and business life. More so, because of the language problems; while Turkish officers, through their knowledge of the Greek language, are generally in a position to serve both communities, very few Greek officers are able to speak or understand the Turkish language.

During the initial stages of Independence, when the Public Service Commission started to apply the ratio in accordance with the recommendations made in the Report, the Greek side was surprised to find that allocation of public posts between the Communities as provided by the Constitution was a workable proposition. It was then that the Commission was brought under the influence of the Executive and the Greek-Cypriot political hierarchy. This was not difficult to accomplish, because the Greek majority in the Commission contained some members whose sole claim for the office they occupied was their earlier close association with the EOKA Movement. In the following paragraphs we propose to expose the confusion which has prevailed in the Public Service Commission, and demonstrate with examples, where necessary, the discriminatory, inconsistent and despotic attitude of its Greek members.

The Greek members of the Commission began their career of discrimination by deciding to discard the Report, which was a document of agreement between the President and Vice-President of the Republic and to interpret the provisions of the Constitution in the way which suited their purpose best. The following ominous statement of the Greek Chairman is recorded in the minutes:

> I have considered whether the report of the Committee appointed to make recommendations on the implementation of the 70:30 ratio in civil service is binding on this Commission. I can find nothing in the Constitution making the Report binding on us. The only articles dealing with the 70:30 ratio is Article 123 sub-section 1 and sub-section 2. The view which I take of these provisions in the Constitution is that all vacancies whether created before or after the 16th of August, 1960, if "promotion post," will be filled by promotion of officers in the service on merits, qualifications and experience, whether such public servants are Greeks or Turks and not by promoting persons inexperienced and unqualified so as to make up the 70:30 ratio. If these vacant posts are "First Entry" posts and if there is no person qualified for promotion in promotion posts then the Public Service Commission will proceed to make allocation of these posts between the two communities. Any deficiency in the 70:30 ratio in the other community will be made up by allocating vacant posts at the lowest grades.
>
> The rights of promotion of serving officers should not be affected by the implementation of the 70:30 ratio. I have no doubt that the procedure followed by the Commission so far is wrong.

In view of the dangerous tendencies displayed by the Greek members the Vice-President of the Republic has pressed for the enactment of a law regulating the powers and duties of the Commission and prescribing the procedure to be followed by them. In spite of repeated representations no such law has been enacted and the Commission has been allowed to function, not being bound by any law or regulations, in a state of complete chaos. For example, it works without an agenda, without up-to-date confirmed minutes, without any right of its members to introduce a subject for discussion, without rules regulating the manner of discussion at meetings, without any right of members to question any omission or error in the minutes or to enquire whether any decision of the Commission has been implemented or not. The Greek members of the Commission do not even feel the necessity to comply with the proviso to paragraph 3(2) of Article 125 of the Constitution, which provides that if a decision regarding the allocation of a post between the two communities cannot be taken in accordance with the provisions of the said Article, the question shall be referred by the Commission to the Supreme Constitutional Court for a decision, and that the decision of such Court shall be final and binding on the Commission. The provisions of the proviso under reference are crystal clear and leave no doubt in respect of their interpretation or application which is a mandatory one. In short the Commission has been working at the whim and wishes of its Chairman.

In matters of appointment or promotion they never follow a consistent procedure, their decisions are, more often than not, affected by racial considerations. In considering the qualification of candidates, they will accept anything offered by Greek candidates, but will, with meticulous care, try to discredit the qualifications of Turkish candidates. For example:

(i) The candidates for the post of Engineer/Hydrologist ought to have a university degree in Civil Engineering. Although the Greek candidate did not have such a degree, a letter given to him by a friendly expert was accepted to qualify him for the job, while the Turkish candidate who had all the necessary qualifications was not appointed. And this is an important post in the Department of Water Development which is expected to play such an important role in the economic development of the Island.

(ii) Of two vacancies in the post of Specialist-Gyneacologist in the Medical Department one was allocated to Turks and the other to Greeks. The Turkish candidate was a Specialist-Gyneacologist since 1955. He was fully qualified under the scheme of service and was serving in the Maternity Section of the Government General Hospital since 1961. Prior to that date he had private gynaecological practice. The Greek members of the Commission disqualified the "Specialist" Turkish candidate and left the post vacant. In turn they filled the vacancy allocated to Greeks by a Greek general practitioner who had some gynaecological experience in the Nicosia General Hospital. It should be noted that the Medical Council of Cyprus did not recognize this officer as a specialist in accordance with Section 26 of the Medical Registration Law. One the other hand the disqualified Turkish Officer was duly recognized as a "Specialist" by the said Council.

(iii) In September 1963, two qualified Turkish doctors were disqualified on the absurd grounds that one of the doctors had "quarantine" experience and that the other was a female.

In the growing inconsistency, the Greek members of the Commission on one occasion insist that merit is the most important criterion for promotion, but on another occasion, should a Turkish candidate have such merit as required, they will turn around and insist on seniority. They alternate in their conflicting views to secure the appointment of Greek candidates. Even in cases where Turkish candidates had both "merit" and "seniority," the Greek members with their perverted justice insisted on the promotion of a Greek candidate with lesser claims for promotion. They did not hesitate to ignore or waive the stipulations of the schemes of service in the case of Greeks candidates, particularly when such candidates were ex-fighters or had the support of such ex-fighters. We give below few examples of scores of such cases:

(i) A vacancy in the post of Forest Officer, Forest Department, was filled by a Greek assistant Forest Officer who did not possess the necessary graduation certificate from the Cyprus Forestry College or similar Forestry Institute as required by the scheme of service for the post. The Turkish Assistant Forest Officer who also claimed the post, and whose claim was disregarded, was a graduate of the Cyprus Forestry College and of the Forestry Training School of Norfolk, England. He was also lecturer and a member of the Examining Board of the Forestry College of Cyprus; he was far more qualified than the Greek candidate appointed.

(ii) A vacancy in the post of postal Officer Grade I, was filled (on 31/1/62) by the promotion of a Greek over the heads of two Turkish officers who were at least seven years senior to him and one of whom had a special report from the Postmaster-General recommending him for promotion. The said Greek officer was an ex-member of EOKA.

(iii) A vacancy in the post of Assistant District Inspector was filled (in June 1962) by a Greek who did not even possess the leaving certificate of a secondary school, which is a basic requirement for the said post. The candidate in this case was also an ex-member of EOKA.

(iv) The vacancy in the post of senior Customs Guard was filled (in November 1963) by a Greek in spite of the existence of *better qualified* and *more experienced Turkish candidates.* In fact the Director-General of the Ministry concerned had strongly recommended the promotion of one of the Turkish candidates.

(v) A vacancy in the post of Senior Commerce and Industry Assistant was filled by promoting, two steps at a time, a comparatively junior Greek officer in spite of the fact that this officer had unfavorable reports in his personal file. The claims of at least two better qualified and more suitable Turkish candidates were ignored.

As opposed to laxity shown in assessing the qualifications and merits of Greek candidates in relation to the requirements of the schemes of service, the Greek members displayed undue severity towards Turkish candidates and always viewed their qualifications with suspicion. In certain cases they went so far as to impose conditions not required by the schemes of service. In certain other cases, where they had no qualified candidates, they left important posts unfilled pending the expected arrival of Greek candidates later on. We give below few examples to illustrate the points made above:

(i)   Five vacancies in the post of Minor Forest Guard, District Administration, had been allocated to Turks. When suitable Turkish candidates were selected, the Greek members of the Commission insisted that these candidates should undergo a period of training prior to their appointment. Although such training was not required by the scheme of service, the Greek members withheld the appointment of the said Turkish candidates until the Minister of the Interior acting in connivance with the Greek members of the Commission declared the appointments unnecessary. Due to this unreasonable attitude of the Greek members of the Commission, 5 Turks were deprived of employment for which they were fully qualified.

(ii)   In the Department of Veterinary Services there are two vacancies in the post of Veterinary Officer, Class II, and the Department concerned is in urgent need of veterinary officers to combat the prevalent diseases. Yet the Greek members of the Public Service Commission have adamantly refused to fill the vacancies with the available qualified and experienced Turkish Veterinary Officers on the grounds that the Turks already had their share of the said posts and that Greek veterinary students studying in Greece were expected to arrive in Cyprus in about six months. Of course, when these students reach Cyprus, they will not have the valuable field experience, which the Turkish Veterinary Officers, who are presently employed in the Service on daily wages, already possess.

(iii) The post of Director, Public Information Office has been vacant since December, 1962. The post was advertised and applications were received from one Turk and three Greeks. None of the Greek candidates was found to have the necessary qualifications. On the other hand the Turkish candidate, who was the Assistant Director of the Public Information Office, had been acting as Director since December, 1962. The Greek members of the Public Service Commission forgetting their cherished principle of selecting, for the post of head of Department, the Assistant Head servicing in the same department, refused to promote the Turkish candidate. The post is still vacant, and it has been readvertised in the hope that a suitable Greek candidate may now be found.

(iv) A vacancy in the post of Storeman was recently filled by a Greek candidate who had only three years' secondary school education. The Turkish candidate who had full secondary education and who had passed several subjects of the London Chamber of Commerce examination was turned down on the excuse that his qualifications were far in excess of those required for the post. This case is a classic example of ludicrous pretexts which the Greek members use when they want to turn down a Turkish candidate.

Mention is made in the Memorandum of instances where vacancies allocated to Turks could not be filled due to non-availability of suitably qualified Turkish candidates. In this respect we should point out that there were more posts claimed for Greeks, which could not be filled due to shortage of suitably qualified Greeks. However, the Greek side was able to get over their difficulty by resorting to the amendment of the relevant scheme of service to suit the qualifications of available Greek candidates. The filling of vacancies in the posts of Director, in the Department of Inland Revenue, Accountant in the Treasury and the Airport Manager in the Civil Aviation were achieved in this manner. Of these, the post of Airport Manager was originally allocated to Turks, but when the Greek members of the Commission insisted that they had a fully qualified Greek candidate, the Turkish members agreed to re-allocate the post to Greeks whereupon the Greek candidate was appointed. But when this appointment was challenged in the Supreme Constitutional Court it was found that this officer in fact was not qualified in accordance with the scheme of service of the post and consequently his appointment was annulled by the Court. But before the ink of the ruling of the Court was dry, the Greek ministers in the Ministerial Council amended the relevant scheme of service to suit the qualifications of the said officer who was immediately re-appointed to the same post. This is another example of so many cases where the Greek members of both the Public Service Commission and the Council of Ministers would resort to any high-handed action in order to serve Greek interests.

Cases cited in the preceding paragraphs are, as stated before, random examples of scores of discriminatory appointments and promotions unconstitutionally made by the Greek members of the Commission. The Turkish members of the Commission regularly reported to the President and Vice-President of the Republic all the irregularities committed by their Greek colleagues. They even requested the Attorney-General of the Republic to refer to the Supreme Constitutional Court disputed cases of allocation, as the Greek Chairman of the Commission had refused to make such a reference as provided by the proviso to Article 125 (3)(2) of the Constitution. Failing to receive satisfactory and positive response, the Turkish members were obliged to refer such cases to the Supreme Constitutional Court thorough their own advocate. More than 150 Turks, whose interests were adversely affected by the decisions of the Greek dominated Commission, have also made recourses to the Supreme Constitutional Court since 1961. These references and recourses made to the Supreme Constitutional afforded ample opportunity to the Greek side to have their difficulties solved by the highest Constitutional Authority of the Republic. However, the Greek side failed to rise to the occasion and the Greek Chairman of the Public Service Commission impeded the progress of these cases by his interminable prayers for adjournments. It is very unfortunate, as we have said earlier, that through malicious interference the Supreme Constitutional Court was made ineffective; consequently more than a hundred Turkish officers are still in suspense.

The Greek members of the Commission were never able to cultivate a friendly disposition towards their Turkish colleagues. They took every opportunity to make disparaging remarks about Turkish candidates and about "qualifications" acquired in Turkey. In the event of any disagreement they immediately accused the Turkish members of intransigence. Moreover, after the collapse of the Supreme Constitutional Court, they became more aggressive and despotic in their attitude. They freely express the view that they will do whatever they like and that the Turkish members may complain to any authority of their choice. In cases of dispute they mockingly counsel the Turkish members to have recourse to the Court which has no judge. The following remark was addressed to the Turkish members at a recent meeting of the Commission:

> You should no longer expect to fill posts according to 70:30 ratio. You represent 18 to 20% of the population. We have abolished the Constitution before the President of the Republic.

All the irregularities and the dictatorial attitude of the Greek members of the Commission and their rude remarks were always reported to the President of the Republic who, however, has failed to take any positive action to improve the conditions obtaining in the Commission or to admonish its Greek member for their unbecoming behavior. This confirms the Turkish view that the President, himself, was to a large measure responsible for allowing the Greek majority to trample upon the Turkish rights in the Public Service Commission.

In the final analysis we do not believe in the sincerity of statements made in the memorandum about the "serious problems created for the State by the implementation of the ratio", about the "universally accepted criteria in matters of appointment and promotion" and about the "efficiency of the public service." Our experience has proved to us that the so-called difficulties were artificially created by the Greek members of the Public Service Commission who were never able to formulate a just and consistent policy in the discharge of their duties. Abusing their majority in the Public Service Commission, the Greek members have, with complete impunity, flouted the provisions of the Constitution and prevented or delayed the appointment or promotion of duly qualified Turks in the Public Service. In view of such bitter experience of the domination of the Greek majority in the Public Service Commission we are unable to agree to the revision of any of the provisions in the Constitution relating to the Public Service. The allegation that the ration of 60-40 in the Army discriminates against the Greeks has to be answered within the meaning of security reasons for the Turks. The whole Cyprus problem arose because of the gross feeling of insecurity by the Turks in a predominantly Greek-ruled State. A balance of power had to be found between the two communities and the balance was struck at 60-40 and this was accepted as a compromise settlement. To raise this issue anew is an attempt to raise the whole settlement which cannot be accepted by the Turkish Community.

11.   *The number of the Members of the Public Service Commission to be reduced from ten to five.*

12.   *All decisions of the Public Service Commission to be taken by simple majority.*

We do not agree that the number of the members of the Public Service Commission is the cause of its working inefficiently. The reason lies in the fact that the Greek members look to the President and his advisers for directions before making appointments and they refuse to accept the relevant provisions of the Constitution as their guide in their deliberations. Furthermore, the State has persistently refused to provide this body with a working machinery, i.e. a Law regulating the functioning of the Commission and has left it loose at the mercy of the Executive. All our insistence that the Law which has been drafted in Bill form should be proceeded with for enactment has not been heeded. There would have been much force in the argument that this body cannot work efficiently in view of its number, had the executive done its share in order to enable the Commission to function properly. As it is, to-day, there are no agendas, members do not know their rights and the Greek members are under orders from the Executive to defy the constitutional provisions. It is very significant that the Greek members do so on the plea which the President himself has advanced in paragraph 10 of his Memorandum. If the number of members of the Commission is reduced and the suggestion in paragraph 12 of the Memorandum that all decisions of the Public Service Commission be taken by simple majority is accepted, a fundamental right and safeguard of the Turkish community will be taken away for no reason whatsoever. All through the Memorandum the President is at pains to show that it is wrong to dwell on the Greek and Turkish aspects of a given case, and he suggests that all those provisions which take cognizance of the existence of two communities in Cyprus should be changed and Cyprus be made into an independent Greek State within which the Turks of Cyprus will have no say at all. This is shutting eyes to reality, and ignoring the whole background which led to Zurich and London settlement. His suggestions, if accepted, would result in the creation of a Greek State looking, in his own words, to "motherland Greece" for all its actions and activities and not in the creation of a Cypriot nation. It is, therefore, a suggestion which stands no chance of consideration by the Turkish side. Moreover, it is a suggestion which revives the bitter causes of friction and struggle between the two communities in pre-settlement days and creates far bigger and numerous problems than it attempts to solve.

13.   *The Greek Communal Chamber to be abolished.*

The proposition that the Greek Communal Chamber should be abolished and the reasons advanced for this suggestion do not stand the test of reason if the present regime is examined in its true perspective.
The Cyprus State is not a Greek State but it is a State brought about by the settlement reached between the Greek and Turkish communities. This is the basic ruling factor which must never be forgotten in approaching our

constitutional problems, but which the President has chosen persistently to forget. If this factor is forgotten then all endeavors for solving our problems lack sincerity and wisdom. The existence of Communal Chambers, when considered in the light of a State resting on Greco-Turkish partnership, is well justified. The attempt to abolish the Greek Communal Chamber and to transfer to Government the services which the Chamber renders is tantamount to making the Cyprus Government a Greek Government and reducing the Turks to the position of a minority in defiance of the Constitution and of the settlement which brought about the Cyprus Republic. All the difficulties of the Communal Chambers can be settled once the Government starts to look upon them as constitutional institutions having charge of services which the Government has a moral obligation to support and finance. In other words, there is nothing wrong in the Government seeing that these essential services are run by elected bodies in the way provided for by the Constitution. Government's economic and social policies once known, can always be made to fit with the services rendered in the field of education provided of course that first a genuine attempt is made to co-operate fully with the two Communal Chambers and to co-ordinate the relevant services rendered by them and the Government. I am not convinced that the existence of the Communal Chambers creates difficulties in the smooth functioning of the State, nor am I convinced that existence of these Chambers places the entire education of the country outside the sphere of Government's economic and social policies. The proposal that the Communal Chambers should be abolished and new system be devised providing for their substitution by appropriate authorities and institutions, is nothing but an attempt to abrogate the Constitution for the sake of abrogation. The fact that education is the responsibility of Communal Chambers should not prevent the Government from treating education as part of its responsibilities and looking upon the Chambers as the appropriate authorities which deal with these matters.

I have considered the President's Memorandum with great care and anxiety. I see in it a pre-determined policy to abrogate the Agreements which brought about the Republic of Cyprus and to create an independent Greek State in which the Turks will be left at the complete mercy of the Greeks. We hope we are wrong in this conclusion, but the net result of the adoption of the President's suggestions is so obvious that it leaves us no room for manouvre and gives us no chance at all to sit round the table and consider practical solutions to any problems which the application of our Constitution is alleged to have brought about. I look upon these proposals as an invitation to us to sit round a table with the Greek side for the mere purpose of signing away all our rights and conceding that we accept the position of a minority in Cyprus. It is in this light that I read the President's concluding paragraphs where he says that it is not his intention to deprive the Turkish community of their just rights and interests or proper safeguards. But all those provisions of the Constitution which the President suggests in his Memorandum should be abolished relate certainly to our just rights, interests and proper safeguards. The President says that his purpose is to remove certain causes of friction and obstacles to the smooth working of the State, but unfortunately he has in mind not a State brought about by Greco-Turkish partnership but a Greek State in which the Turks have no say at all. His allegation that the main object of a Constitution should be to secure within its framework the proper functioning of the State and not to create sources of anomaly and conflict is a statement of a general principle. Our Constitution was prepared having this in mind after long deliberations. Any anomaly which exists is due to the method of approach to the Constitution by the Greek side and the conflict of interest which has arisen is due to the change of mentality from the time the Agreements were signed. The President further says that experience has proved that our Constitution falls short of this object and certain of its provisions have created great difficulties in practice. My reply to this is that the fault does not lie with the Constitution but with the Greek side who has decided from the very beginning not to adhere to the Constitution. When the President says that in the interests of our people we must remedy this I am sure after having studied his proposals in detail that he has in mind the interest of those Greeks who are sworn to annex Cyprus with Greece. Therefore I can state categorically that the Turkish community sees no way at all to accept any of the President's suggestions. I wish to reiterate here that I am ready and willing to consider with our Greek compatriots all the difficulties which they allege they have encountered in the implementation of our Constitution. With a view to finding practical ways and means within the framework of our Constitution and without disturbing the political balance of powers between the two communities which it has maintained and safeguarded. But I cannot agree that the remedy for any real or imaginary difficulty lies in the abrogation of those parts of the Constitution which have recognized rights to the Turkish community.

APPENDIX 75

Turkey's Memorandum Rejecting Archbishop Makarios's Proposals, 16 December 1963

The Memorandum handed by President Makarios to the Turkish Ambassador in Nicosia on November 30, 1963 has been received.

As stated in the Memorandum, it is a fact that the Cyprus Constitution contains "Sui Generis" provisions. The reason for this is that the conditions in Cyprus are equally "Sui Generis", for two distinct national entities with different characteristics as regards race, language, religion, culture and traditions are living in Cyprus.

When the parties concerned had initiated negotiations to work out a solution to the Cyprus problem, they accepted this fact as their starting point. It will be recalled that following lengthy and arduous negotiations, it had been agreed that the two national entities in Cyprus could live together and cooperate only by devising proper constitutional safeguards to protect the legitimate rights and interests of one entity against the eventual violations by the other which because of its numerical superiority would retain the executive and legislative powers in the State of Cyprus.

That is why, the entire Constitution of Cyprus, as stated explicitly in Article I and Article II, has been founded on the existence of two communities and on the necessity to establish a balance ensuring protection and safety for their reciprocal rights and interests.

In the view of the Government of the Republic of Turkey these realities constitute the foundation of the agreements which gave birth to the Republic of Cyprus.

It is maintained in the Memorandum that President Makarios signed the Zurich Agreement during the London Conference to prevent the grave consequences which could have ensued, had he rejected it and that it was a course dictated to him by necessity.

As it will be recalled, the Zurich and London Agreements constitute a compromise which was reached through the common desire of the parties concerned to avoid graver developments and through the renunciation from their respective initial views. And they provide the only solution reconciling as far as it is possible the very complex elements of the Cyprus question. This solution, achieved at the cost of innumerable sufferings and toils, rests upon a very delicate equilibrium between the extremely complex rights and interests of the parties. To remove any element of this equilibrium would create the danger of the collapse of the system as a whole. On the other hand, it is proper to remember that the Zurich and London Agreements have equally not met the aspirations and views of neither Turkey nor those of Turkish Cypriots.

It is true that in the course of the three years which elapsed since the coming into being of the Republic of Cyprus, certain difficulties have been created impeding either the establishment or the functioning of the Institutions of the State of Cyprus. However, these difficulties stem not from the nature of the Constitution, but from the persistent negative attitude of the Greek Cypriot leaders who deliberately are not implementing or are rendering inoperative the stipulations of the Constitution, particularly those concerning Turkish rights and interests.

The Greek Cypriot leaders and the Greek Cypriot Press, ever since the foundation of the Republic of Cyprus on August 16, 1960 have engaged in a systematical and organised campaign of destruction against the Constitutional regime in spite of the explicit existing Treaty commitments. Even the Head of State of Cyprus disregarding the requirements and the impartiality of his high office and his responsibilities towards all Cypriots, has acted solely in his capacity of the leader of the Greek Community and led this Community to take position against the Agreements. The numerous written and oral representations made by the Turkish Embassy in Nicosia to the Ministry of Foreign Affairs of Cyprus pointed out to only a few and the most striking examples of such destructive activities of the Greek Cypriot official and unofficial personalities and of the Greek Press.

These activities have been carried on with an ever increasing violence and intensity despite various friendly warnings made by Turkey. Therefore, the responsibility for the difficulties confronted in Cyprus and the grave and deep unrest resulting from them, should not be attributed to the provisions of the Constitution, but must be sought in the overt activities and undisguised intentions of the Greek Cypriot leaders aimed at the wrecking of the established constitutional regime.

Since the proclamation of the Republic of Cyprus the practice in various fields has given evidence that the Greek Cypriot leaders signed the Zurich and London Agreements with the intention to break them at the very first opportunity. These leaders have not shown the necessary good-will and the spirit of cooperation in the implementation of the Constitution and of the Agreements. They have equally not responded with the same constructive spirit to the reconciliatory proposals made by Turkey and the Turkish Cypriots for seeking in common practical ways and means to solve the difficulties. Moreover, the Greek leaders constantly evaded the application of yet untested Constitutional provisions by alleging that these provisions were unapplicable.

It is not possible to reconcile with good-will the allegation based on a priori and unilateral judgment that certain provisions of the Constitution are unapplicable without even trying to see how the implementation would work out.

Almost all of the Constitutional provisions mentioned in the Memorandum are provisions of vital importance, providing safeguards for the rights and interests of the Turkish Cypriots. Should these provisions be abandoned, the very existence of the rights and interests of the Turkish community in Cyprus would be left entirely at the will and mercy of the Greek community.

It is asserted in the Memorandum that the existence of the Supreme Constitutional Court and furthermore of the "right to return" of the Vice-President on the decisions of the Council of Ministers and the House of Representatives, constitute satisfactory safeguards for Turkish rights and interests.

The past three years' experience has clearly demonstrated that the two above-mentioned legal institutions do not provide sufficient and effective guarantees for the rights and interests of the Turkish Cypriots.

"The right to return" cannot prevent the harmful effects of the decisions taken in disregard of the Turkish rights and interests by the Council of Ministers or by the House of Representatives, in both of which the Greek Cypriot members are in majority, and where practically all decisions are passed by a simple majority vote. At the most, "the right to return" can only ensure a very short delay in their implementation. In the past, decisions of this nature returned to the afore-mentioned organs by the Vice-President, have literally and automatically been confirmed by these organs without even being accorded the benefit of an objective study.

As to the Supreme Constitutional Court, it has unfortunately been rendered incapable of functioning with required speed and effectiveness, due to the negative attitudes adopted by the Greek Cypriot leaders and the Greek judge in the Court. Indeed the fact that Professor Forsthoff, ex-president of the Constitutional Court, and his assistant, who were appointed jointly by the President and the Vice-President, were forced to resign by the Greek Cypriot circles through various threats and blackmail, that many cases submitted to the Constitutional Court could not be settled because of the different dilatory tactics adopted by the Greek judge in the said Court, that the Constitutional Court has been deliberately left in a state of paralysis by the Greek Cypriots, although a period of seven months have elapsed since the resignation of Professor Forsthoff, and that to what extent the Government of Cyprus has complied with the decisions of Constitutional Court concerning the dispute over municipalities are obvious examples of this negative stand.

In the face of these unquestionable realities on the one hand, and the intense activities and campaigns engaged in by the official and unofficial Greek Cypriot circles and personalities aimed at "Enosis" or depriving the Turks of their rights and interests on the other, to ask the abandoning of the Constitutional safeguards of the Turkish Cypriots would be tantamount to demanding a person to put aside the shield which he possesses as the only means of protection against the manifest assaults.

The Government of the Republic of Turkey remain convinced that the constitutional safeguards referred to in the Memorandum are of vital importance.

They cannot, therefore, accept the proposals contained in the Memorandum.

Ankara, December 16, 1963

APPENDIX 76

Cyprus Government's Note, 16 December 1963, Rejecting Turkey's Memorandum

REPUBLIC OF CYPRUS

The Memorandum handed to His Beatitude Archbishop Makarios, President of the Republic, by His Excellency the Turkish Ambassador in Nicosia, to-day, the 16th December, 1963, is unacceptable both in form and in substance and is therefore rejected. Moreover it contains totally unfounded and objectionable allegations.

The said Memorandum purports to reject the proposals of the President made to the Vice-President in a Memorandum dated the 30th November, 1963. These proposals were communicated to the Turkish Government, as they were communicated to the Representatives of other Governments, out of courtesy and by way of information only.

The President's Memorandum of the 30th November, 1963, relates to matters of an internal nature which the President hopes to discuss with the Vice-President. It does not admit of any acceptance or rejection by the Governments to which the text was so communicated.

Nicosia,
16th December, 1963

APPENDIX 77

Statement by the Turkish Foreign Ministry, 17 December 1963

Halkin Sesi, 18 December 1963

STATEMENT BY THE TURKISH FOREIGN MINISTRY

Ankara 17: The Information Office of the Foreign Ministry today issued the following statement in connection with Cyprus:

"The Nicosia Ambassador of Turkey visited President Makarios at 10 a.m. on Monday the 16th December and handed to the President in writing the views of the Turkish Government in reply to the written and signed document, which President Makarios gave to the Ambassador on 30th November for transmission to the Turkish Government, and which concerned the amendment of certain basic articles of the Cyprus Constitution. Hours after this document was accepted by President Makarios and cognizance was taken of its contents, the First Secretary of the Presidency applied to the Embassy, saying that he had an urgent message from President Makarios to be communicated to the Ambassador, and came personally to the Embassy and left an envelope with the Counsellor, about the contents of which he claimed he had no other information, requesting that it should be handed to the Ambassador immediately, and departed. When this envelope was opened, it was found that it contained an unsigned and unsealed short note asserting that the memorandum of the President of the Republic of Cyprus did not necessitate a reply as it was connected with internal affairs and was sent to the other Governments only for information, and that the document handed by the Turkish Ambassador on the 16th December was unacceptable both in its contents and wording, as well as our document in the form of a reply.

As it will be remembered, President Makarios' memorandum concerning the amendment of the Agreements was rejected by our Council of Ministers on 6th December, and this was announced to the public by the Foreign Minister.

The document handed by the Turkish Ambassador simply confirmed in writing the decision of the Turkish Government and exposed the extra-legal strivings and the systematic activities of provocation of the Cypriot Greek office-holders in deliberately not implementing and making unworkable the established and legitimate Constitutional regime and the Agreements, which make possible the co-existence of the Turkish and Greek communities in the Island.

This line of action, which is in complete contradiction with the care shown by us to the international principles of politeness and etiquette when the memorandum bearing the signature of President Makarios, in spite of its contents aiming at the amendment of the Cyprus Constitution and Agreements, was handed to the Turkish Ambassador, and which, as stated above, is found evasive, strange and unnecessary, will, undoubtedly, have no effect whatsoever on the basis of the question.

The Cypriot Greek office-holders cannot free themselves of their responsibilities for these extra-legal strivings, no matter whether activities aimed at exploiting the Cyprus realities and the Constitution and the Agreements, which are an expression of these, are furthered through overt or insidious ways.

Enosis activities or various other activities to deprive the Cypriot Turks of their rights and interests, once again categorically prove the vital importance of the Constitutional safeguards and of the Agreements.

The Republic of Turkey, as has already been repeatedly declared and announced on various occasions, cannot leave the future of the Cypriot Turks and their rights and interests at the mercy and grace of the Greek community through the amendment of the Treaties."

The Turkish Embassy, too, issued the following statement:

"The Nicosia Ambassador of Turkey visited President Makarios at 10 a.m. on Monday the 16th December and handed him in writing the views of the Turkish Government in reply to the written and signed document, which President Makarios gave him previously for transmission to the Turkish Government, and which was connected with the amendment of the Constitution. Hours after this document was accepted by the President of the Republic and cognizance was taken of its contents, the First Secretary of the Presidency applied to the Embassy, saying that the President of the Republic had an urgent message to be communicated to the Ambassador, and came personally to the Embassy and left an envelope with the Counsellor, claiming that he had no information about its contents and requesting that it should be handed to the Ambassador immediately, and departed. When this envelope was opened, it was found that it contained our document in the form of a reply and an unsealed and unsigned short note to the effect that this document, which was connected with internal affairs, was unacceptable. It is found unnecessary to make any other comment on this line of action, which is in complete contradiction with the care shown to the principles of etiquette when Makarios' memorandum, in spite of its contents, was handed to the Turkish Ambassador, and which has no connection with the basis of the question."

APPENDIX 78

Letter from the Permanent Representative of Cyprus to the President of the UN Security Council, 26 December 1963

S/5488

Upon instructions from my Government and in accordance with Articles 34, 35 and 39 and also 1(1), 2(4) and 24(1) of the United Nations Charter, I have the honour to bring to the attention of the Security Council my Government's complaint against the Government of Turkey for the acts of (a) aggression, (b) intervention in the internal affairs of Cyprus by the threat and use of force against its territorial integrity and political independence perpetrated yesterday, 25th December, through the following acts:

(1) Violation of the air space of Cyprus by Turkish military aircraft which, flying very low and circling over Nicosia, made threateningly several passes in a manner calculated on the one hand to terrorise the Greek Cypriot population and on the other to embolden the Turkish insurgents in their persistent attacks against the Police and in their effort to overrun the Greek sector;

(2) The violation of the territorial waters of Cyprus by the appearance and the presence of Turkish warships with the same purpose as above;

(3) The threats of use of force by the Prime Minister of Turkey made on 25th December, 1963, before the Turkish Parliament announcing the despatch of the aircraft and the naval units as above; and also by the threatening movement of paratroopers in the coast of Turkey nearest to Cyprus;

(4) The movement of Turkish troops into Nicosia who joined the Turkish Cypriot insurgents in their fights against the Police and in their efforts to spread out of their sector and attack the Greek sector.

In consequence of the above aggressive actions by the Turkish military units the Greek troops had to move into Nicosia in order to stem the tide of joint attacks by the Turkish Cypriots and Turkish units. Confrontation of the units of the Greek and Turkish armies resulted, with grave and threatening consequences to international peace.

The events which led up to the above described situation are briefly as follows:

In Cyprus disturbances and communal fighting erupted since the pre-dawn hours of 21st December, 1963, as a result of an attack and firing by a Turkish mob against a Cypriot Police unit on patrol. Almost simultaneously attacks by groups of Turkish Cypriots started and also firing from the Turkish into the Greek sector of the town in an effort to drive away the Greek Cypriots from their houses in the vicinity of the Turkish sector forcibly occupying such houses. In fact, at the locality Omorphita the Turks by force occupied Greek houses after killing the women and children found therein, as reported by the international press.

The fighting consequently spread and while efforts were made at a cease-fire the above described intervention by the Government of Turkey had further envenomed and complicated the situation and has caused the present complaint.

In view of the gravity of the situation my Government considered it incumbent upon it in the vital interests of the people of Cyprus as a whole and in the interests of international peace and security to inform the Security Council of this gave violation of the territorial integrity, sovereignty and independence of Cyprus, and to request Your Excellency to be good enough to convene a meeting of the Security Council under Rule 3 of its Provisional Rules of Procedure in order to consider the matter and to take appropriate measures under the relevant Articles of the Charter in order to remedy the situation and to prevent such violations from occurring in the future.

Accept, etc.,

(Signed) ZENON ROSSIDES,
Permanent Representative of Cyprus
to the United Nations.

APPENDIX 79

Letter from Greek Foreign Minister Sophocles Venizelos to Archbishop Makarios, 29 December 1963 (translation)

TOP SECRET

Your Beatitude,

The recent tragic events in Cyprus, as well as past experience, have convinced the Royal Government that, if the Cyprus Government wishes the continuation of the interest of the Royal Government for the solution of the problems of the Republic of Cyprus, this can only be realized in the light of the following.

As is well known, Greece also faces numerous problems, yet it has always been ready for obvious reasons to concern itself also with the handling of the problems of Cyprus. Often, in the past, the handling of these problem by the Greek Government has obliged it to relegate its own problems to a secondary place. Moreover, often in the past the Greek Government, without being notified in advance of actions of the Cyprus Government, has been called upon ex post facto to help the Cyprus Government in facing undesirable situations resulting from such actions of the Cyprus Government on which no prior consultation with the Greek Government had taken place.

It is evident that no Greek Government can continue this practice, namely that, due to actions of which it had not been informed in advance, it be called upon to move diplomatic and other mechanisms to settle matters arising out of actions of the Cyprus Government on which there had been no prior consultation with the Greek Government. In addition to the above, we have at this moment indications that, in the midst of the irregular situation which has been created in Cyprus, the Cyprus Government is conferring, for the solution of the well-known issues, with third Governments with which Greece does not co-operate politically and consequently the Greek Government cannot follow the Cyprus Government in this direction.

The Royal Government wishes to make it clear to our Cypriot brothers and their Government that it is determined to do all in its power for the promotion of the smooth functioning of the Cyprus state and the harmonious co-operation between the Greek population and the Turkish minority, so as to safeguard the future, the progress and the welfare of independent Cyprus.

The Zurich and London Agreements, despite the fact that they may have come into being as a result of political expediency and despite the fact that they may have proved unworkable, can only be improved, by negotiation and not by dynamic means, by stages until the full and unimpeded functioning of the Cyprus state is achieved. For the commencement of these negotiations, the Royal Government is already in close contact with the British Government. The Cyprus Government was right in holding the view that these negotiations should aim, on the one hand, at improving the constitutional status of Cyprus and, on the other, and subsequently, on improving the Treaty of Guarantee. With regard to the latter, the Royal Government has its own views which it will communicate to the Cyprus Government in due course. The course of negotiations, which the Royal Government considers the only possible course for the improvement of the Cyprus regime as well as for the prevention of catastrophic developments, certainly excludes the course of dynamic solutions.

The above stand of the Royal Government may not be to the liking of certain circles in Cyprus. We are even informed that the recent actions of the Royal Government, which have universally been considered wise, and thanks to which irreversible catastrophic consequences for Cyprus and its people have been averted, have been misinterpreted by some such circles which apparently view the solution of the Cyprus problem only in terms of a fatal conflict between Greeks and Turks.

The contents of this letter have been communicated to the leader of the other big national political party in Greece, who has agreed with them.

Please accept, Your Beatitude, the expression of my sentiments of respect and love, and my best wishes that the New Year may bring happier days for our beloved Cyprus.

S. Venizelos.

To His Beatitude the Archbishop of Cyprus
Monseigneur Makarios,
President of the Republic of Cyprus,
Nicosia.

APPENDIX 80

Reply from Archbishop Makarios to Letter from Sophocles Venizelos, 3 January 1964 (translation)

Dear Mr. President,

I am very grateful for your letter dated 29th December last, conveying to me the views of the Greek Government on the handling of the problems of Cyprus and particularly on the situation created by the recent tragic events. I have always been sure of the unequivocal interest of Greece in the fate and future of Cyprus; the instances and manifestations of this interest are continuous. We, the Greek Cypriots, must be truly grateful for this.

I agree absolutely with Your Excellency that we must always be in contact with the Greek Government regarding the handling and the promotion of the problems of Cyprus. I have repeatedly conveyed to the Greek Government through the Royal Hellenic Embassy in Nicosia that I shall be in constant communication with it regarding any action or measure in relation to the Cyprus issue, even if there is not always identity of views. I hereby wish to reiterate this assurance once more.

I do not know, Mr. President, what is the prevailing view in Greece regarding those responsible for the recent events in Cyprus. I very much fear, however, that the Greek Government is under the impression that these events were caused involuntarily or on the basis of a plan by the Greek Cypriot side. I understand from your letter that such an impression is in fact prevalent. This grieves me most deeply. Neither I personally, nor the Government, nor the Greek Cypriot side generally bears the responsibility for these very unfortunate events. I would consider the provocation on our part of such troubles and events in Cyprus, which might also have involved Greece in dangerous adventures, a crime against the whole Nation. I assure you emphatically that there was no instigation of such events on our part.

I now refer to the Conference due to be held in London soon. Personally, I had many doubts and reservations regarding our participation. I entertained, and I continue to entertain, fears that during the negotiations the Greek Cypriot side may find itself under pressure of situations and events to accept hardly satisfactory proposals. I do not exclude the possibility that during the Conference the Turkish Cypriots may provoke troubles in Cyprus and that Turkey, taking advantage of the situation, may threaten intervention, so that we would find ourselves obliged to accept unacceptable solutions of the problems of Cyprus. These fears I have also expressed to the British Government. But in any case, I consider that this Conference constitutes an inevitable procedure and that our participation is imperative. I hope that my fears will be belied and that the Conference will be successful.

I would however particularly request that the Greek Government communicate to me in advance its views or any plans it may have before submitting then to the British or Turkish Government. I would really find myself in a very weak position if the three Governments agreed on a particular plan which is not considered acceptable by the Greek Cypriot side. I am certain that you fully agree on this point.

Thank you again, warmly, Mr. President, for your active interest on behalf of Cyprus. Thank you also for your good wishes for the New Year. Please accept the expression to you of my sentiments of love and esteem together with my cordial wishes.

Archbishop Makarios.

His Excellency
Mr. Sofocles Venizelos,
Athens.

APPENDIX 81

Vice-President Fazil Kutchuk's Appeal to Heads of State, 5 January 1964

Special News Bulletin No. 11

DR. KUCHUCK'S MESSAGE
Appeal to Heads of State

"To All Heads of States,

The Greeks of Cyprus, taking advantage of, and abusing their majority strength in the Government and Security Forces of the Republic, have planned and put into execution an organised armed attack by the Greek Police and civilians on the Turks and Turkish property in towns and villages, including my own residence and office, since the night of the 20th December, 1963.

These attacks continued in a most brutal and barbarous manner until the intervention of the three Guaranteeing Powers. During these attacks Turkish houses in Nicosia and elsewhere have been broken into and many innocent Turks, including women and children, have been murdered in cold blood in their houses or driven away as hostages.

The Greek leaders, who are misrepresenting to the world the true facts have, in complete disregard of our Constitution and Laws, illegally armed with heavy weapons the Greek members of the Security Forces and also thousands of Greek terrorists while Turks holding political posts have been prevented deliberately from exercising their powers and functions and Turkish members of the Security Forces have been disarmed and placed under detention.

At the same time, Turkish citizens have been labelled by the Greek leaders as "rebels" to be shot dead on sight if seen outside their houses or sectors.

Despite the cease-fire agreement, Turkish life and property are still in great and imminent danger in Cyprus.

Even after the cease-fire, Turks have been killed and kidnapped and many Turkish houses have been looted or maliciously set on fire by the Greeks. Turks both in towns and villages are still besieged and all means of communication have been cut off to them. Also, the normal supply of foodstuffs to Turkish citizens is no longer possible.

Reliable reports reaching us indicate that, even now, the Greeks are arming and preparing another onslaught for a general massacre on a larger scale than before.

The Greek leaders have made it abundantly clear that at the impending London Conference they will not back an inch from their policy of complete domination of the Turks and of placing them at their mercy. For this purpose Archbishop Makarios has already made it public that he is determined to abrogate the Treaty of Guarantee. His ulterior motive in so doing is clearly to prevent Turkey from coming to the rescue of the Turkish Community in Cyprus when the ultimate Greek design of complete domination or extermination of Cypriot Turks is finally put into execution.

It is inconceivable that such brutal atrocities could have been committed and that such a state of affairs can be allowed to continue at this advanced stage of civilization.

I, therefore, appeal to you and through you to all peace-loving nations of the world who believe in the inviolability of human rights and liberties and who disapprove of racial discrimination, violence and genocide to give their support, both material and moral, to the Turkish Cypriot Community in their struggle for survival against very heavy odds.

For the Turkish Cypriot Community,
Dr. F. Kuchuk,
Vice-President, Cyprus."

[handwritten] Issued by the Turkish Communal Chamber
Nicosia 5th January, 1964

APPENDIX 82

Green Line Map, 30 December 1963

See Map Supplement.

APPENDIX 83

Green Line Agreement, 30 December 1963

OFFICE OF THE HIGH COMMISSIONER
FOR THE UNITED KINGDOM
ALEXANDER PALLIS STREET
NICOSIA

1.   At a time to be fixed by the Joint Force Commander (General Young) all such Greek Cypriot and Turkish Cypriot posts in the vicinity of the green line from point X to point Y as he may designate shall be evacuated; and he will occupy such evacuated posts as he may consider necessary (subject to the provisions of paragraph 3 and 4 below).

2.   At the same time as the action described in paragraph 1 above, all Greek and Turkish posts in the vicinity of the green line between point Y and point Z, which may be designated by the Force Commander, will be evacuated.

3.   Before the posts on either side of the green line between points A and B are evacuated, the Force Commander will set up such posts as he may consider necessary with the object of creating conditions of security in the blue shaded area (BYCA) to enable the population to return to their homes. As soon as this action has been taken by the Force Commander, all Greek and Turkish posts in the vicinity of the green line between points A and B which may be designated by the Force Commander will be evacuated.

4.   For the avoidance of doubt, the positions to be occupied by the Force Commander will include the flour mill, the cold storage plant, the Roccas bastion and the CYTA building; and the positions to be evacuated, but not occupied, will include the Mula, Barbaro and Loredano bastions.

5.   As soon as the Force Commander begins to take over Greek and Turkish posts he will be entitled, in so far as he considers it necessary, to send patrols at any time without further consultation anywhere in Nicosia and the surrounding area.

30th December, 1963

APPENDIX 84

Agreement Regarding the Restoration of Freedom of Movement and Communications, 6 January 1964

SECRET

POLITICAL LIAISON COMMITTEE

Agreement regarding the Restoration
of Freedom of Movement and Communications
and other important matters

I attach for the information of the Committee the text of an agreement reached last night regarding the restoration of freedom of movement and communications, etc., in Cyprus. I am sure that the Committee will welcome these arrangements which will begin to come into effect from 0600 hours tomorrow, Wednesday, 8th January. When fully implemented, it will do much to bring things back to normality.

Arthur Clark
Chairman of the Committee

7th January 1964

CYPRUS

Agreement regarding the Restoration
of Freedom of Movement and Communications
and other important matters

The Greek side has agreed that with effect from 0600 hours, 8th January, 1964:

(a) the Greek side will remove all offensive and defensive positions at present held by them;
(b) remove all barricades, road blocks, etc.;
(c) disperse all armed Greek Cypriots other than Police and Gendarmerie; and
(d) end all carrying of arms by civilians.

2.   The Turkish side have also agreed that within a period of ten hours of the Greek side implementing their undertaking and in any event before darkness they will fully implement the following measures:

  (a) remove all positions at present held by them;
  (b) remove all barricades, road blocks, etc.;
  (c) disperse all armed Turkish Cypriots other than Police and Gendarmerie; and
  (d) end all carrying of arms by civilians.

3. One exception to the above is that in Lefka and Xeros both sides will act simultaneously as agreed above at a time to be agreed mutually later.

4. Each side has also agreed that they will not request proof of identity, search, arrest or detain persons belonging to the other side; and in particular they will refrain from interfering in any way with normal freedom of movement, transport and communications.

5. The Greek side has given an undertaking that as a result of the above, Turkish Police and Gendarmerie posts now manned by Turkish Regular Police and Gendarmerie will not be taken over by Greek Police or Gendarmerie.

6. Both sides have agreed that in implementing this agreement any minor incident which might occur due to lack of communication will not invalidate the agreement.

APPENDIX 85

Record of Various Meetings Held on 2 January 1964

TOP SECRET

RECORD OF VARIOUS MEETINGS ON THURSDAY, 2nd JANUARY, 1964.

10.00 a.m.

A meeting was held at the Presidential Palace at which the following were present:

His Beatitude Archbishop Makarios, President of the Republic,
Mr. Glafkos Clerides, President of the House of Representatives,
All Greek Ministers, with the exception of Mr. P. Georgadjis who was un-
well,
Mr. Criton Tornaritis, Attorney-General of the Republic,
Mr. Paschalis Paschalides,
Mr. Frixos Petrides.

2. *Mr. Kyprianou* said that he had had a two-hour meeting with Sir Arthur Clark between midnight and 2.00 a.m. that night. Sir Arthur had said that a five-member conference (consisting of the United Kingdom, Greece, Turkey and the Greek and Turkish Cypriots) would have as its terms of reference the creation of a new Constitution for Cyprus without the element of "partnership", the Turks only having some form of self-government in matters of culture and religion. Mr. Kyprianou explained to Sir Arthur the reservations of the Greeks about a five-member conference. Sir Arthur, however, said that we should remember that the United Kingdom would be on our side in any such conference.

3. *Mr. Clerides* said that at 4.00 a.m. that morning he had been called to a discussion with Mr. Duncan Sandys and Sir Arthur Clark. They repeated the same arguments about the five-member conference and said that they had the impression that we no longer had confidence in them since our measures before the United Nations indicated that they were directed against them also as signatories of the Treaty of Guarantee.

4. During discussion, it was suggested:

(a) That we should on principle accept the five-member conference;
(b) Before the five-member conference was convened, we should have a three-member conference (the United Kingdom, Greek and Turkish Cypriots); and

(c)   If there is agreement at the three-member conference then we
      should participate in the five-member conference for the purpose of
      terminating the Agreements.

5.   *Mr. Clerides* produced two drafts suggested by *Mr. Duncan Sandys* if a
five-member conference were accepted.   Copies of these are attached as Annex I.   *Mr. Clerides* explained that he had asked *Mr. Duncan Sandys* what
would happen if the three-member conference failed to reach agreement and
that *Mr. Duncan Sandys* had said that there would then be no question of a
five member conference because there would be no purpose in such a conference.   He said that *Mr. Duncan Sandys* had made this absolutely clear.

6.   The Ministers considered that the following points needed clarification
before a decision could be taken:

(a)   If there is no agreement at the three-member conference will there
      certainly not be a five-member conference? i.e. is the five-member
      conference to be held only if agreement is reached by the
      three-member conference for the purpose of giving effect to the
      agreement so reached?
(b)   If the Turks wreck the three-member conference what will be the po-
      sition of the United Kingdom in case of threat of invasion by Turkey?
(c)   If everything fails and the Turks insist on the Treaty of Guarantee, will
      the United Kingdom support us in any other action which may be
      taken to terminate the Treaty of Guarantee?

11 .00 a.m.

7.   Mr. Clerides left to attend a meeting of the Liaison Committee at
which the question of a five-member conference was to be discussed and returned to the Presidential Palace half an hour later with Mr. Duncan Sandys
and Sir Arthur Clark.

8.   A meeting was then held at which the following were present:

His Beatitude Archbishop Makarios, President of the Republic,
Mr. Glafkos Clerides, President of the House of Representatives,
All Greek Ministers, with the exception of Mr. P. Georgadjis, who was un-
      well,
Mr. Criton Tornaritis, Attorney-General of the Republic,
Mr. Duncan Sandys, Secretary of State for Commonwealth Relations,
Sir Arthur Clark, British High Commissioner in Cyprus.

9.   *Mr. Sandys* said that he had thought it advisable to see the President
and the Greek Ministers before the question of a five-member conference was
discussed at the Liaison Committee, as had been the intention.

10.   *The President* said that there were certain points on which the Greek Ministers wished clarification.   On being asked what exactly would be the "status" of the three-member conference vis-à-vis the five-member conference, *Mr. Sandys* said that it would really be the three-member conference which would be the more decisive and that if there was agreement at this conference then the five-member conference would give its consent to the termination of the Agreements. The purpose of the five-member conference would, in that case, be to get rid of the Treaty of Guarantee in a legal fashion. Mr. Sandys made it clear that the United Kingdom did not like the Treaty of Guarantee either but had had to sign it due to the circumstances prevailing in 1959. It obviously placed Britain in embarrassing positions. Britain did not like interfering in the affairs of other countries. After the three-member conference we would have to judge whether it would be worth going on to the five-member conference. In his view if it were obvious that agreement could not be reached, then there would be no purpose in holding a five-member conference.

11.   *Mr. Sandys* said that the aim of the conference would be a Constitution for an independent Cyprus in which there would be adequate safeguards for the minority. Regarding the present attitude of the Turks, *Sir Arthur Clark* said that he was surprised that the attitude of the Turks was not such as he had feared it might be, i.e. a demand for partition. Both he and Mr. Sandys had the impression that all the Turks were concerned about now was to safeguard their physical security. They mentioned some movement of populations so as to avoid having small numbers of Turks in Greek villages, but nothing which would really alter the "map" of Cyprus.

12.   Discussing the question of possible failure of the conference, *Mr. Sandys* said that the worst that could happen would be that we would end up where we started. "I think", he said, "it would be an awful abdication to start by saying that no agreement can be reached." He said that since an offer of good services had been made by the three Governments (attached for easy reference as Annex III) it would be very insulting to throw it back in their faces and very difficult to avoid a five-member conference. In practice, however, it would be the three-member conference that would be decisive.

13.   On being asked how the safeguards of the minority would be protected, *Mr. Sandys* said that the safeguards would be in the Constitution itself which would not require outside consent for amendment.

14.   *His Beatitude* said that we should separate the Constitution from the Treaties of Guarantee and Alliance. The Constitution was an internal affair and the two Treaties international. He said he was sure that if the Greeks and Turks of Cyprus, with the good offices of the British, came to an agreement then the other powers would also agree. He, therefore, made the following proposal:

"To start negotiations here in Cyprus with the acceptance of the British good offices. No mention of a five-member conference to be made at this stage. The Treaties of Guarantee and Alliance would not be discussed now, but after the constitutional question had been solved".

If agreement were reached then everything would be easy. If no agreement were reached the situation would be as it was now. We from our side would not do anything about the two Treaties without having the final result of the discussion on the Constitution. If we did not agree then we would exchange views with the British Government and would not act without consulting the British Government. We would not, for instance, go to the United Nations without first consulting the British Government.

15.   *Mr. Sandys* said that he wanted an absolute assurance from His Beatitude that until the process of the preparatory conference (meaning the three-member conference) was completed, no steps would be taken by His Beatitude to terminate the Treaties.

16.   *Mr. Clerides* clarified that what Mr. Sandys wanted was—

 (a) An absolute assurance that during the talks we would do nothing about the Treaties; and
 (b) That if everything failed we would still not take any action without consulting the British Government.

Mr. Sandys confirmed that that was exactly what he meant.

17.   During the discussion which ensued it became evident that His Beatitude and Mr. Sandys had been talking at cross purposes in that His Beatitude did not want to accept even the principle of a five-member conference whereas Mr. Sandys thought that this had been accepted. *Mr. Sandys* then clearly and emphatically said that unless the principle of a five-member conference was accepted nothing could be done and the British would not be able to help at all.

18.   *Mr. Clerides* suggested that we should now say that talks would be held between the Greek Cypriots, the Turkish Cypriots and the British Government.

19.   *Mr. Sandys* explained that the position was that an offer of good services had been made by the three Governments of Britain, Greece and Turkey to the Cyprus Government and the two communities and that an answer had to be given. This answer was already overdue. He said, though with reservation, that what we could perhaps say would be that, before considering the proposal of good offices by the three Governments, "we think it would be wise for the two Cypriot communities to have [exploratory] talks with one another and that we would like the British Government to facilitate the talks by offering its good offices."

20.   *Mr. Sandys* went on to suggest that if that were agreed, he might issue a statement which need not be signed by either side as follows:

> "Mr. Sandys has had consultations with the Representatives of the Greek-Cypriot and Turkish-Cypriot communities regarding the offer of good offices made by the British, Greek and Turkish Governments. The Representatives of the two communities have informed him that before giving a reply to this offer they would like to hold meetings with one another on the problems involved. In order to facilitate these talks they have invited the British Government to nominate a representative to take the chair."

Attached are Annexes IV, V and VI showing the amendments subsequently made to the above draft, Annex VI being the draft finally agreed.

21. *Mr. Sandys* again stressed that he would have great difficulty in persuading the Turks to agree to this.

22.   *His Beatitude* was adamant that he would accept nothing else, whereupon *Mr. Sandys* made the following warning:

> "I must warn you with solemnity that if the impression is given that the Greek community does not wish to have talks we shall have no option but to pull out. I have already had great difficulty in persuading the Prime Minister and my Government about the thankless "Police" role which the British are playing in Cyprus."

23.   *Mr. Sandys* elaborated by saying that British troops could not be kept here indefinitely to do "Police" duties and it was imperative that on his return to the United Kingdom he should be able to state that there was a definite indication for settlement of the difficulties. Otherwise the British troops would be removed.

2.00 p.m.

24.   *Mr. Sandys* and *Sir Arthur Clark* then left with the draft at Annex VI to see the Turkish side. They returned shortly afterwards (at 2.00 p.m.) with the Greek Ambassador (Mr. Delivanis) and the Turkish Ambassador (Mr. Ozkol) and the Turkish Counsellor (Mr. Shahimbash). Everybody else was present as before, with the exception of Mr. Tornaritis.

25.   *Mr. Sandys* said that after a short talk it was clear to him that the Turks would not agree to anything so radically different from what was the original offer of good offices. He had, therefore, thought it necessary to return with the two Ambassadors to make a formal appeal to His Beatitude to accept the offer made.

26.   Asked what the difference was between what was suggested earlier on (as at Annex VI) and the proposal for good offices, *Mr. Sandys* said that the latter proposal was one for joint consultation to try to help to bring about a solution. He added that if he were to go away with a refusal of the Greek Cypriots to accept the offer of the three Governments then he was sure the next step would be that his Government would convene a meeting of the three Governments to discuss the present emergency in Cyprus. He then repeated: "What we have come to do is to formally repeat to you the offer of the three Governments to try and help the two communities to reach a settlement and to ask for your reply."

27.   *His Beatitude* said that he could not give an answer to the proposal without first having an indication as to whether there was any ground for common agreement.

28.   *The Greek Ambassador* said that his Government's position was entirely the same as that of Britain.

29.   *The Turkish Ambassador* said that a conference with all three Governments must be held the soonest possible. Without participation of his Government no solution could be valid.

30.   *His Beatitude* repeated that he could not say more than he had said earlier that morning.

31.   When it became obvious that a deadlock had been reached, *Mr. Sandys* suggested that two Ministers should be authorized to discuss a formula with him; but His Beatitude did not consider that this would serve any useful purpose.

32.   *Mr. Sandys* then suggested that he and Sir Arthur Clark and the Ambassadors should withdraw in order that His Beatitude might discuss the matter with his Ministers. This they did.

33.   A discussion then took place between His Beatitude and the Greek Ministers present, which did not bring about any change in His Beatitude's attitude.

34.   *Mr. Sandys, Sir Arthur Clark* and *the Ambassadors* then returned.

35.   *The Turkish Ambassador* said that his Government had the same right to take part in a conference as the British and Greek Governments.

36.   *Mr. Sandys* said that it was not so much a matter of rights which, after all, one could overlook, but it was really a question where a practical position had been reached in which the three Governments had made an offer of good offices. That offer had been accepted by the Turkish Cypriots and he saw no

possibility and no particular good reason why they should accept a different proposal.

37. In answer to a question as to whether "good offices" meant a conference, *Mr. Sandys* said that "good offices" did not necessarily mean a conference although it usually ended up in one.

38.   *His Beatitude* said that his objection was one of substance. It was not that we did not want to participate in a conference. The objection was that if a conference failed then there would be nothing left to do after that. That is why it was necessary to have the three-member conference first, in order to ascertain whether there was any ground for agreement.

39.   *Mr. Sandys* said that we must proceed on the basis of realities, i.e. that the Treaties existed even though we might not like them or even if we eventually did get rid of them. He also said that the mere fact that people are talking about a problem gives hope and creates favourable circumstances and that if we refused to participate in a conference, the situation would deteriorate most rapidly. He said that he had formed the opinion that when His Beatitude said he objected to the "substance" of the proposal this was because he did not like the Treaties and he therefore acted as if they were not there. Mr. Sandys, however, was of the opinion that if we could concentrate on working to get rid of them instead of refusing to talk about them it would be much more constructive.

40.   Referring to the "Police" duties of the British troops, *Mr. Sandys* said that Great Britain was willing to hold this burden only provided there was a definite limit to it.

41.   *The Turkish Ambassador* said that the Turkish community had made it clear that it would not accept any conference, whether preliminary or otherwise, without the participation of the Turkish Government. They had expressed this decision to him explicitly and categorically; they had made it clear that their decision had been taken in the light of experience of the past three years. He was also sure that his Government was not prepared to accept any conference, preliminary or otherwise, without the participation of the Turkish Government.

42.   *His Beatitude* said he appreciated the fact that the Turkish community had expressed their views so clearly.

43.   When it became obvious that there was absolute and complete deadlock, *Mr. Sandys* suggested that two Greek Ministers should meet two representatives of the Turkish community and discuss the matter, before His Beatitude's answer could be taken as final.

44.   *Mr. Sandys* added that, in view of His Beatitude's attitude, he thought this was a waste of time; but, "let us have one last try", he said.

45.   Before leaving, *Mr. Sandys* said: "I shall have to say most clearly to the world and to my Government that there has been no co-operation on your part at all although there has been unreserved acceptance by the Turkish side."

4.00 p.m. – 7.00 p.m.

46.   Mr. Clerides, Mr. Kyprianou and Mr. T. Papadopoulos were authorized to proceed to the residence of the British High Commissioner in order to meet the Turkish-Cypriot representatives and see if common ground for agreement could be found.

47.   About an hour later they telephoned to obtain authority to suggest a formula similar to that suggested by Mr. Sandys at Annex I. This authority was given to them by His Beatitude.

48.   After about one more hour they returned with a draft as at Annex VII. As this made no mention of the Government of Cyprus, it was accepted only subject to its being amended to include the Government. This was accepted by Mr. Sandys and the statement was drawn up and signed by His Beatitude. Mr. Sandys later telephoned to say that he had also obtained Dr. Kutchuk's signature. The final statement is attached at Annex VIII.

ANNEX I

DRAFT JOINT STATEMENT SUGGESTED BY MR. SANDYS TO MR. CLERIDES IN THE EARLY MORNING OF THE 2nd JANUARY, 1964.

Representatives of the Greek-Cypriot and Turkish-Cypriot communities accept the proposals that there should be a conference of representatives of the British, Greek and Turkish Governments and of the two Cypriot communities to discuss the problems of Cyprus. To facilitate its work the conference will be preceded by meetings between representatives of the two Cypriot communities and of the British Government the object of which will be to clarify the issues and to find a basis of agreement for consideration by the conference.

ANNEX II

DRAFT STATEMENT BY THE GREEK CYPRIOTS SUGGESTED
BY MR. SANDYS TO MR. CLERIDES IN THE EARLY HOURS
OF THE MORNING OF THE 2nd JANUARY, 1964. TO BE
ISSUED SIMULTANEOUSLY WITH THE JOINT STATEMENT.

In accepting the proposal for a conference the Greek-Cypriot representatives wish to make it clear that it will be their aim to secure an agreement
upon a comprehensive settlement of the Constitution for an independent
Cyprus and upon the termination of the Treaties of Guarantee and Alliance.

ANNEX III

"The British, Greek and Turkish Governments, as signatories of the
Treaty of Guarantee of 1960 jointly appeal to the Government of Cyprus and
to the Communities in Cyprus to put an end to the present disorders. They
appeal to the Cyprus Government to fix a suitable hour this night for a
cease-fire and to call upon both Communities to observe it.
  The three Governments, mindful of the Rule of Law, offer their good
offices with a view to helping to resolve the difficulties which have given rise to
the present situation".

25th December, 1963.

(Delivered verbally by the three Governments of the United Kingdom,
Greece and Turkey through their representatives in Cyprus between 1.45 a.m.
and 2.15 a.m. on the 25th December, 1963).

VI

Before giving a reply to the offer of good offices made by the British,
Greek and Turkish Governments, the representatives of the Greek-Cypriot and
Turkish-Cypriot communities have decided to hold meetings with one another
on the problems of Cyprus. In order to facilitate the progress of these talks
they have invited Mr. Sandys to take the chair.

Nicosia, 2nd January, 1964.

VII

The Representatives of the Greek-Cypriot and the Turkish-Cypriot
Communities accept the offer of good offices of the British, Greek and Turkish
Governments to help in the solution of the problems of Cyprus. For this pur-
pose a conference of Representatives of the three Governments and of the two

Communities will be convened in London at an early date. After the opening plenary session, a working committee will be formed composed of Representatives of the two Cypriot Communities with a Chairman appointed by the British Government and will report from time to time to the plenary conference.

(Signed) F. Kutchuk   (Signed) Archbishop Makarios

2nd January, 1964.

VIII

   The Government of the Republic of Cyprus and the Representatives of the Greek-Cypriot and the Turkish-Cypriot Communities accept the offer of good offices of the British, Greek and Turkish Governments to help in the solution of the problems of Cyprus. For this purpose a conference of Representatives of the three Governments and of the two Communities will be convened in London at an early date. After the opening plenary session, a working committee will be formed composed of Representatives of the two Cypriot Communities with a Chairman appointed by the British Government and will report from time to time to the plenary conference.

(Signed) F. Kutchuk   (Signed) Archbishop Makarios

2nd January, 1964.

APPENDIX 86

Letter from Cyprus Department of Lands and Surveys to Minister of Justice Stella Soulioti, Accompanied by Map (see Map Supplement), 17 September 1964

CONFIDENTIAL

MINISTRY OF THE INTERIOR
DEPARTMENT OF LANDS AND SURVEYS
NICOSIA,
17th September, 1964.

Your Excellency,
[sent by hand]

In compliance with your instructions passed to me over the telephone by your Mr. Stassopoullos on the 15th instant, I have the honour to forward herewith 3 copies of the Administration map of Cyprus showing in red colour the area "controlled" by Turks, as they have been supplied to me by the General's Headquarters.

2.   The total extent of these areas is 60 square miles and constitutes 1.68% of the whole area of the island and 1.72% of the Cyprus Republican territory.

I have the honour to be
Madam,
Your Excellency's obedient Servant,

[signature]

(G. PH. AVRAAMIDES)
Ag. Director

Her Excellency,
The Minister of Justice,
Nicosia.

CONFIDENTIAL

APPENDIX 87

Copy of Envelope Stamped "Kibris Turk Postalari," 6 January 1964

APPENDIX 88

Letter from Representative of the United Kingdom of Great Britain and Northern Ireland to the President of the UN Security Council, 8 January 1964

DOCUMENT S/5508

I have the honour to refer to the letter addressed to the President of the Security Council on 26 December 1963 by the Permanent Representative of Cyprus* which was the subject of discussion in the Security Council on 27 December [1085th meeting].

Your Excellency will be aware that since the outbreak of intercommunal disturbances in Cyprus on 21 December 1963, the United Kingdom Government, together with the co-signatories of the Cyprus Treaty of Guarantee of 16 August 1960 (the Governments of Greece and Turkey), have been making strenuous effort to assist in resolving this critical and highly dangerous situation peacefully in accordance with Articles 33 and 52 of the United Nations Charter. Since the Security Council is seized of the question, my Government, after consultation with the Greek and Turkish Governments and with their approval, have instructed me to supply you with full information on the steps taken within the spirit of the Charter by my Government, in close co-operation with the Governments of Turkey and Greece, to avert bloodshed and to promote a solution.

On 24 December 1963, the Governments of the United Kingdom, Greece and Turkey issued an appeal to the Cyprus Government and an offer of good offices in the following terms:

"The British, Greek and Turkish Governments, as signatories of the Treaty of Guarantee of 1960, jointly appeal to the Government of Cyprus and to the Greek and Turkish communities in the island to put an end to the present disorders. They appeal to the Cyprus Government to fix a suitable hour this evening for a cease-fire and to call upon both communities to observe it.

"The three Governments, mindful of the rule of law, further offer their joint good offices with a view to helping to resolve the difficulties which have given rise to the present situation."

When on 25 December it became apparent that the situation in Cyprus was continuing to deteriorate, the Governments of the United Kingdom, Greece and Turkey informed the Government of Cyprus (including both Greek and Turkish elements) of their readiness to assist, if invited to do so, in restoring peace and order by means of a joint peace-making force under

---

* *Ibid., Eighteenth Year, Supplement for October, November and December 1963*, document S/5488.

British command and composed of the forces of the United Kingdom, already stationed in Cyprus by virtue of the Treaty concerning the Establishment of the Republic of Cyprus,* concluded between the United Kingdom, Greece, Turkey and Cyprus, and of the forces of Greece and Turkey under the Treaty of Alliance* between Greece, Turkey and Cyprus. The acceptance of this offer by the Cyprus Government was announced in a communiqué issued on 26 December, as follows:

> "The Government of the Republic of Cyprus has accepted an offer that the forces of the United Kingdom, Greece and Turkey stationed in Cyprus and placed under British command, should assist it in its efforts to secure the preservation of the cease-fire and the restoration of peace."

The joint peace-making force was accordingly established under the command of Major-General Young, Commander, Cyprus District. On 28 December, the Secretary of State for Commonwealth Affairs of the United Kingdom Government, Mr. Duncan Sandys, flew to Cyprus to discuss the situation on the spot with members of the Cyprus Government (including both Greek and Turkish elements) and representatives of the Greek and Turkish Governments in Cyprus. On 29 December, a Political Liaison Committee consisting of the United Kingdom High Commissioner, the Greek and Turkish Ambassadors and representatives of the Greek and Turkish communities in Cyprus, was established in order to give guidance to the commander of the joint peace-making force.

On 30 December, the Political Liaison Committee concluded an agreement on the creation and patrolling of a neutral zone along the cease-fire line between the zones occupied by the two communities in Nicosia. The agreement also provided for the exchange of prisoners and the right of the patrolling forces to patrol anywhere in the island. Since the conclusion of this agreement, the patrolling activities of the peace-making force have succeeded in reducing tension and in preventing a further outbreak of serious fighting. Good progress has also been made with the exchange of prisoners and the return of refugees to their homes. Certain British reinforcements have been sent to the island with the agreement of the Greek and Turkish Governments to enable the commander of the peace-making force to carry out his task.

Following further discussions in Nicosia, agreement was reached on the holding of a conference in the near future which will attempt to resolve the difficulties which have given rise to the present situation. This was announced on 2 January in the following statement by Mr. Duncan Sandys:

> "I have tonight received from Archbishop Makarios and Dr. Küçük their acceptance of the offer of good offices of the British, Greek and Turkish Governments to help in the solution of the problem of Cyprus.

---

* Signed at Nicosia on 16 August 1960.
* Signed at Nicosia on 16 August 1960.

For this purpose, a conference of representatives of these three Governments and of the two communities will be convened in London at an early date.

"After the opening plenary session, a working committee will be formed, composed of representatives of the two Cypriot communities, with a chairman appointed by the British Government, and will report from time to time to the plenary conference."

Meanwhile, the Governments of the United Kingdom, Greece, Turkey and Cyprus have jointly requested the Secretary-General of the United Nations to appoint a representative to act as a United Nations observer in Cyprus, whose role would be to observe the progress of the peace-making operation, and report on it to the Secretary-General.

Arrangements have now been made for the conference referred to above to convene in London next week. Meanwhile my Government and the Governments of Greece and Turkey trust that the measures taken will assure a return to law and order in Cyprus and prevent further acts of violence. It will be clear to Your Excellency, however, that the steps already taken have largely succeeded in their immediate objective of alleviating the situation for the time being and have contributed towards obviating the very real and grave dangers which were inherent in recent developments in Cyprus.

(Signed) R. W. JACKLING
Acting Permanent Representative
of the United Kingdom of Great Britain
and Northern Ireland to the United Nations

APPENDIX 89

Record of First Meeting of the London Conference, 15 January 1964

RESTRICTED

C.S.C.(64) 1st Meeting   Copy No. 34

CYPRUS CONFERENCE, 1964

Record of First Meeting held
in Marlborough House, S.W.1.
on WEDNESDAY, 15th JANUARY, 1964
at 12.00 Noon

CONTENTS:

STATEMENT BY THE SECRETARY OF STATE FOR
COMMONWEALTH RELATIONS

ANNEX   LIST OF THOSE PRESENT

STATEMENT BY THE SECRETARY OF STATE FOR
COMMONWEALTH RELATIONS

Mr. Duncan Sandys said: "On behalf of the British Government I wish to welcome you all to this Conference. The fact that the Conference had to be convened at such very short notice has, I know, caused difficulties for some, particularly for the Greek and Turkish Governments. We are, therefore, most grateful to their distinguished Foreign Ministers for attending at this early date, and for giving to the Conference the benefit of their counsel.

We are meeting today under the shadow of very tragic events in Cyprus. We in Britain have for some tine anxiously watched the unfolding of this unhappy story.

We have been profoundly distressed to see feelings of growing enmity develop between the racial communities, more especially since their two motherlands are among our oldest and most trusted friends. When the fighting began, we were filled with apprehension at the prospect of civil war and the possibility that Turkey and Greece might themselves be sucked into the conflict.

That is why, three weeks ago, we thought it right to act before the situation got irretrievably out of hand. In accordance with the Treaty of 1960, we consulted the other two Guaranteeing Powers and jointly offered to help in the task of restoring order. Our offer was readily accepted by the leaders of both communities and the Joint Force was created. Britain is now providing over 2,500 troops for this job. They have so far been successful in their peace-keeping task because they enjoy the confidence and goodwill of both races. The British soldier has, I am glad to say, been welcomed with smiles and cheers by Greeks and Turks alike; and I have myself seen, not without pride how the Union Jack has been greeted in town and village as the flag of peace and the symbol of security. But if, for any reason, we were to lose the co-operation of the people of Cyprus, we should no longer be able to discharge our task. Nor would we feel justified in exposing our men to the dangers involved.

Britain cannot, of course, go on acting as policeman in Cyprus indefinitely, nor, I am sure, would you yourselves wish her to do so. The Joint Force has a specific task to perform, namely to help in separating the combatants and to hold the ring—and this is the most important of all—while a settlement is being worked out. Our action has given Cyprus a breathing space, but that must be used for something more than just breathing. It must be used with a sense of urgency to find an honourable and workable solution to the problems out of which the troubles arose.

While this Conference is sitting I appeal earnestly to both sides to use all their influence with their supporters to prevent acts of hostility and violence which might provoke a renewal of the fighting and which could seriously damage the prospects of agreement around this table.

I know that many people believe that this Conference is, in any case, doomed to failure. They say that agreement is impossible in the present state of tension and that there can be no constructive discussion when feelings are running so high and suspicion is so deep.

I was in Nicosia long enough to sense the fears and passions which have been aroused. But I am not sure that this will necessarily make it any more difficult to solve this intractable problem. There could, I feel, be no more compelling argument in favour of agreement than the horror and misery of these past weeks and the memory of those who have died. Should the negotiations in London fail, this will create a feeling of hopelessness which would inevitably tempt each side to try and impose its own solution by force. If the fighting were to break out a second time, it would be very much more difficult to stop it than on the last occasion; and Cyprus would once again be faced with all the dangers, internal and external, which were so narrowly averted a few weeks ago.

The prospect of failure is really too grim to contemplate. Somehow or another, we have just got to find a solution. Each delegation at this table has got an important contribution to make. It is going to be immensely difficult, but if everyone helps, I believe that we can and shall succeed.

Cyprus is, of course, not the only country which is plagued by inter-racial difficulties. We come across this problem in various forms in many parts of the world. But there is an important difference in the case of Cyprus. Many of the other countries in which this trouble occurs have advanced from primitive pagan tribalism to modern nationhood in a single generation. On the other hand, the Greeks and the Turks in Cyprus are each the proud possessors of a cultural and religious heritage which, in different ways, have contributed so much to the progress of civilisation and the upholding of human dignity.

If you, with your centuries-old experience and tradition, should prove unable to live together in peace and tolerance, what hope, I ask, is there for the newly emerging nations in other continents? I am sure you will recognise that you have a special responsibility not only to yourselves but to the rest of humanity. You have an historic opportunity to set an example and to show the way. If you succeed, you will earn the gratitude, not only of the unhappy people of Cyprus, but of all peace loving men and women throughout the world.

Gentlemen, as agreed, we are going to adjourn and our next meeting will be at ten o'clock tomorrow morning. Thank you very much."

Marlborough House, S.W.1,
15th January, 1964.

ANNEX
LIST OF THOSE PRESENT

BRITAIN
The Rt. Hon. Duncan Sandys, M.P.
The Rt. Hon. Lord Carrington
His Grace the Duke of Devonshire
Sir Arthur Clark

GREECE
H.E. Mr. C. Palamas
H.E. Mr. Michel Melas
Mr. A. Pilavachi

TURKEY
H.E. Mr. F. C. Erkin
H.E. Mr. Zeki Kuneralp
Mr. H. Bayulken

CYPRUS
Mr. S. Kyprianou
Mr. G. Clerides
Mr. T. Papadopoulos
Mrs. S. Soulioti
Mr. R. Denktash
Mr. O. Orek
Mr. Halit Ali Riza

And other delegates and advisers

SECRETARY
Mr. J. T. A. Howard-Drake

RESTRICTED

APPENDIX 90

Record of Second Meeting of the London Conference, 16 January 1964

CONFIDENTIAL

C.S.C.(64) 2nd Meeting   Copy No. 38

CYPRUS CONFERENCE, 1964

Amended Record of Second Meeting
held in Marlborough House, S.W.1.
on THURSDAY, 16th JANUARY, 1964
at 10.00 a.m.

CONFIDENTIAL

1.   BUSINESS OF THE CONFERENCE

The Conference agreed to the following arrangements—

(a) Press Communiqués Brief press communiqués would be issued at the discretion of the Chairman.
(b) Minutes The minutes of meetings, except for opening statements, would be confined to recording conclusions and any points which delegations specifically asked to have recorded.

2.   COMMITTEE

The Conference agreed to set up a working committee of the representatives of the two Cypriot Communities under Mr. Sandys' chairmanship. It was agreed that the proceedings of the Committee would be entirely informal. The Committee would report from time to time to the plenary session.

3.   OPENING STATEMENTS

Mr. ERKIN said: "Before going into the present situation in Cyprus it would be useful to recall the peculiarities that the island's geographic position and the composition of its peoples present.

There is no homogeneous people or nation in Cyprus. It is inhabited by the Turkish and Greek communities who are part of the main neighbouring nations. Apart from these two communities, there are on the island some very small groups, such as the Maronites.

The two principal communities of the island, the Turkish and Greek communities, have, all through history, developed separately. Their religion, language, customs, nationality, and, as a result of all these, their political aspira-

761

tions, are different. The Turkish community for instance has developed parallel to the social and political development of the Anatolian Turks and reacts consequently as part of the Turkish nation, as witnessed inter alia, in the celebration of the national holidays.

As the peoples of Cyprus are composed of the Turkish and Greek communities, and are parts of two neighbouring countries, the relations between the two communities cannot be considered solely as a matter of numbers, without taking their origins and national appurtenance into account, and thus to view them solely from the angle of majority-minority. To try to put together things of a different nature is not only contrary to the simplest mathematical rules but is also illogical.

This brief explanation indicates that it is not possible to consider the Cyprus problem as if there exists on the island only one homogeneous ethnic group and to visualize a political regime based on such an assumption.

As regards the strategic importance of Cyprus one should always keep in mind that the island is geographically a continuation of the Anatolian peninsula. Its strategic importance must be considered from two angles.

Firstly, being sufficiently large and with a suitable location in the Eastern Mediterranean, the island constitutes a convenient base and holds the Eastern Mediterranean under its control. In view of progressing world strategy, Turkey is a country within the Western and even the Atlantic area. Actually Turkey's logistics are closely tied up with the sea communication routes which, coming from the Atlantic towards the Eastern Mediterranean, join up at the South Anatolian ports. All these supply routes are under the control of the island of Cyprus, only 40 miles away from the southern coasts of Turkey.

On the other hand, Cyprus constitutes a foothold behind Turkey's, and consequently the West's, defence system which may be used in the direction of the Eastern Mediterranean and North African shores from the Middle East as well as the Balkans.

All these considerations clearly demonstrate that Cyprus has a vital importance for Turkey not merely because of the existence of a Turkish community on the island, but also on account of its geo-strategic bearing.

As I have already said, the Cyprus problem cannot be approached without taking into consideration the fact that two different national entities live on the island and that all along history, their relations showed the same undeniable peculiarities. This fact, which has been pointed out by Sir George Hill, who wrote the most comprehensive history of Cyprus, and which has been confirmed by the distinguished historian Arnold Toynbee, characterizes both periods, before and after Zurich.

Mr. Toynbee says: "In the course of the last 150 years, all the rest of the vast former Ottoman dominions has been partitioned into a mosaic of national successor-states, in each of which some single nationality is now master of the house".

Mr. Toynbee adds: "The mutual animosity of the intermingled peoples has been too strong; the prestige of exotic Western political ideology of nationalism has been too potent. In Lebanon, as well as in Cyprus, a regime requiring co-operation between different ex-Ottoman nationalities is something of a tour de force, as the recent civil war in Lebanon showed. In Cyprus it would be utopian to hope that the lion and the lamb will lie down together, and that a little child will lead them. The truth is that there are no ex-Ottoman lambs; the ex-Ottoman peoples are all lions or tigers".

These facts unfortunately were never taken into consideration by the Greek Cypriot leaders. Actually, following the termination of the Turkish rule in Cyprus, when the efforts of some Greek leaders towards Enosis did not give any result, in order to obtain sympathy in the international scene, these activities were disguised under the cloak of anti-colonialism or the desire for unilateral self-determination. The Greek Cypriot mentality, which never took into account the existence of the Turkish community, let alone recognised it as a partner, and even tried to destroy at every possible opportunity its minimum rights and interests, was known and even proved by historical documents during the period 1923–1960. It was therefore with the desire to restrain such a mentality and to direct it towards better aims as well as to create progressively an atmosphere of co-operation, mutual respect and understanding between the communities, that the Zurich and London Agreements were conceived.

It would be useful to remember here that the Zurich and London Agreements were concluded following the failure of this monopolistic and selfish attitude which is just the opposite of one based on the principle "live and let live" to be sanctioned, from 1954 till 1959, in all international organisations, including the United Nations. In fact no international organisation can, at least ultimately, condone an attitude which has nothing to do with justice and equity. Acting on a different assumption would inevitably lead to frustration. Enough statesmanship has to be shown to deny that international rules or documents are there to be used on the exclusive behalf of one party, one view or one attitude.

The Constitution which settles the internal status of Cyprus, taking into due consideration the characteristics of the peoples living on the island, has established a sort of federal State based on two communities. The communities' own affairs are divided while matters of common concern are run under joint administration. Some provisions of the Constitution such as those concerning separate municipalities were inspired from the experience of past relations between the two communities. As to the other provisions relating to International Agreements, their inclusion in the Constitution is a result of the peculiarities which governed the creation of the Republic of Cyprus.

Heads of State are two representatives elected respectively by the Greek and Turkish communities (Article 1). These communities are described in detail (Article 2). The official languages of the Republic are Turkish and Greek (Article 3). The communities can hoist the flag and celebrate the national days of their respective motherlands, Turkey and Greece (Articles 4 and 5).

The internal affairs of the two communities composing the Cyprus Republic are their own responsibility and there are Communal Chambers established to this effect (Article 86–111). Disputes falling within civil and criminal jurisdiction where all parties concerned belong to the same Community are brought up before the judges also belonging to that Community (Article 159). Furthermore, it is foreseen that in regions and localities where one of the two

Communities is in an overwhelming majority public officers and armed forces shall also belong to that Community (Articles 123/3, 132).

For matters requiring joint administration common organs are set up composed of representatives of both Communities. The executive power (Articles 1, 46), House of Representatives (Article 62), the Supreme Constitutional Court and the High Court of Justice (Articles 133 and 153) are the examples of this system.

As has been previously pointed out, an example of the constitutional provisions inspired from the experience of past relations between the two Communities concern the municipalities (Article 173). The fact that municipalities dominated by Greek majority always neglected Turkish quarters and attempts persisted to use the municipalities as a tool in the pursuit of Enosis, as well as the difficulty in getting the Greeks and Turks to work together, made it eventually necessary to establish separate Turkish municipalities in five major towns of Cyprus and appropriate provisions were included in the Constitution to this effect.

The political Agreements which created the Cyprus Republic and the links which make the peoples on the island parts of the neighboring countries caused some provisions of the international agreements to be inserted in the Constitution. The reference to the Zurich and London Agreements as the origin of the Constitution (Article 180), the Article 181 stating that "The Treaty of guarantee . . . and the Treaty of Military Alliance . . . shall have constitutional force", the unalterability of the basic provisions of the Constitution (Article 182) and the banning of the Enosis and partition (Article 185) are examples of this necessity.

The international status of the Republic of Cyprus is sui generis. This situation is closely linked with the birth of the State. Cyprus was established by an agreement concluded between the three powers. Consequently, two of the contracting powers obtained for their respective communities the right of existence on the island. The third power secured the military bases for the carrying out of strategic duties to the benefit of the West.

These aims were achieved by several ways. According to the Treaty of Guarantee the union of Cyprus, with any other state was prohibited. In doing this the domination of one of the communities by the country to which the other community belonged was prevented. It is for this same purpose that the Constitution of the new state was also guaranteed by the contracting powers. Again for the same purpose additional guarantees were provided in the Treaty of Alliance.

To sum up this paragraph let me stress that it is not possible to consider the State of Cyprus outside the framework of these Agreements.

Now allow me in this connection to return briefly to strategic considerations. Because of the island's geo-strategic position, Cyprus and Turkey's defence has to be considered together. Moreover, from the point of view of the defence of the Eastern Mediterranean, Cyprus in relation to Turkey and to Nato, must be considered as an inseparable component of the defence system of Turkey and Greece. It is as a consequence of this fact that a Treaty of Alliance between Turkey, Greece and Cyprus had to be concluded and the defence of the island guaranteed.

As for Great Britain, which has sovereign areas on the island, although she is not a party to the Treaty of Alliance, her participation in the consultation and co-operation for the common defence was provided by way of Article 3 of the Treaty of Establishment and thus the defence of the island was incorporated within a logical system.

The scope of the Treaty of Alliance, which has a general character was enlarged by the Application Agreement. In this Agreement, the matters of common defence, the composition and organisation of the Turkish and Greek Forces, as well as the tasks and responsibilities of the Tripartite Headquarters, were dealt with in detail, and the use of the Turkish and Greek contingents, in case of subversive activities on the island, was envisaged.

The desire to attract the sympathy of international opinion by pretending that the Treaties were signed under pressure must be attributed to the monopolistic mentality which tends to ignore the facts. Because it is a fact that the basic principles of the Zurich and London Agreements were arrived at, after the argumentation of all parties had been discussed for years in almost every international institution, and after the United Nations had recommended, in view of the complexity of the Cyprus problem, that it should be solved through negotiation among interested parties. In Zurich and London, all participants undoubtedly sacrificed some of their claims in order to get to a common denominator. But this is true for every dispute solved by peaceful means and not something the negotiators of the interested parties of Cyprus had to face exclusively.

I do not want to take up your time by repeating here the speeches made at the London Conference of February 1959. But this much ought to be emphasized, that it is only through mutual sacrifices that any negotiation can ultimately achieve an agreement. Besides, the basic elements of the Zurich and London Agreements were again the object of negotiations, from April 1959 till July 1960, among the five delegations in London and Nicosia. The minutes of the London Mixed Committee show clearly the kind of work that was achieved during these fourteen months of negotiations. Moreover some of our collaborators who are present here to-day took part in these negotiations.

At the London Committee many additions were made to the previously adopted Zurich and London texts. And these additions were accepted by mutual consent. The fact that to-day one of the parties seems to dislike them or wants to ignore the facts does not change anything. The minutes show clearly that the Greek Cypriot delegate at this Committee, Mr. Rossides, among others, made many proposals that were carried out during the negotiations.

As for the discussions on the Constitution the basis which was envisaged by these Agreements was negotiated for more than a year at the Mixed Commission set up in Nicosia. During this period, not only the basic articles of the Constitution but also its minor provisions were accepted only after thorough studies of several proposals made by all concerned. Mr. Bridel, the Swiss Professor of Constitution, participated personally in this work. Some articles of the Constitution, inter alia Article 46 on the "Executive Power", were taken up outside the commission during the negotiations, with the participation of Archbishop Makarios and the Agreements reached in these negotiations were initialled by him. All these facts clearly disprove the allegations of pressure.

I would like now to speak of the implementation or rather the non-implementation of the Agreements. First let me mention the efforts to divert the Council of Ministers from its essential duties.

According to Articles 46 and 54 of the Constitution, the Executive Power has to be ensured by the President and the Vice President and exercised by the Council of Ministers. The purpose of these Articles is to provide the participation of the representatives of the Turkish Community in the joint administration. These clearly defined provisions of the Constitution have been made unworkable by actions aimed at obstructing the participation of the Turks.

In the first place, the procedure used in the preparation of the Agenda made it impossible for the Turkish Ministers to study sufficiently the matters brought before the Council of Ministers. While the Greek Ministers were informed well in advance of the contents of the Agenda, the Turkish Ministers were advised of them only on short notice.

Another manifestation of this attitude was that many important matters were not even presented to the Council when, of course, it is the duty of the Council of Ministers to discuss and take decisions on all the important administrative and political questions.

In accordance with Articles 50 and 57 of the Cyprus Constitution, the President and the Vice-President have the right of final vote, jointly or individually, against the Laws of the House of Representatives and against the decisions of the Cabinet relevant to foreign affairs, defence and security matters as mentioned in Article 50. However, the Greek Cypriot administrators, as has been the case in other state affairs ever since the establishment of the Cyprus Republic, have acted in a most monopolizing way on matters relating to foreign affairs, defence and security. Thus, rights and authority recognised to the Vice-President by the Constitution were in practice denied to him. Moreover, the Vice-President has been left in absolute darkness, particularly on matters relating to foreign affairs.

Reports and telegrams sent by Greek Cypriot Ambassadors posted abroad to the Foreign Ministry in Cyprus were not shown to the Vice-President. Likewise, the instructions sent from the Foreign Office to its Ambassadors abroad were deliberately kept secret from the Vice-President. Several complaints raised in this connection by the Vice-President to the President and the Cabinet had no positive result. In spite of his promises to the Vice-President to give oral explanation at regular intervals on foreign affairs, the Foreign Minister of Cyprus either gave such explanations infrequently or confined them to insignificant matters. The President felt no need to consult the Vice-President on official visits he was to undertake and, in most cases, it was found sufficient to inform the Vice-President a day or two prior to the official visit. Archbishop Makarios decided to participate in the conference of "non-aligned nations" in Belgrade in September, 1961, without consulting the Vice-President.

The attitude taken by Greek Cypriot administrators on matters relating to Foreign Affairs is enough to give a clear idea about the value they attribute to provisions of the Constitution and to their interpretation of co-operation in various fields with the Turks.

Greek Cypriot statesmen, civil servants, private Greek organizations and associations, and the Greek Cypriot Press indulged in an extensively intense vilification campaign against the Cyprus agreements and the Constitution in the months soon after the establishment of the Cyprus Republic. In accordance with articles of the Guarantee agreements, the Cyprus Government, in spite of its obligations to assure the rule of the Constitution took no measures whatsoever to prevent activities of the Greek Cypriots taking a stand against the Constitution. The demands made by the Vice-President to the President to pass a law with a view to preventing activities in favour of Enosis and against the Constitution were disregarded.

To mention only a few of the countless examples showing how the Greek Cypriots vilified the Constitution and indulged in provoking the Turkish Cypriots would suffice to give an idea as to how detrimental this continuous and systematic campaign, maintained with ever-increasing force, turned out to be in intercommunal relations.

Ethniki in its November 23, 1960 issue stated: "The shameful Zurich and London Agreements cannot wipe out Enosis".

Eleftheria in its September 2, 1961, issue stated: "Cyprus continues to be an indivisible part of Greece in spite of the Zurich and London Agreements imposed on Cyprus".

Alithia in its October 30, 1961, issue: "For us Zurich and London Agreements are but a nightmare and they will not last long".

Eleftheria in its October 31, 1961, issue published a telegram sent by OELMEK to the Greek Ambassador which read as follows: "We, Greek teachers, are doing our utmost in order to prevent the Zurich spirit from spreading among our youth".

Extract from an article of the *Eleftheria* of 24th January, 1962: "The people have no longer any confidence in this false regime. If this regime is not revised in such a manner as to secure political and economic stability, the result will be very regrettable for all concerned, especially for the Turks".

From a comment of the *Ethniki* of 28th January, 1962: "Rotten Zurich regime".

From the *Ethniki* of 4th January, 1962: "Post Zurich curse".

From the *Alithia* of 19th February, 1962: "Why are some of our Turkish friends complaining, why are they moaning like slayed pigs? Immediately after the signing of the accursed Zurich agreement, they started to curse, provoke and threaten us".

From the *Ethniki* of the 18th March, 1962: "The Cypriot people will never endure the persistence of the Zurich calamity".

From the *Synaghermos* of 31st March, 1962: "The Zurich agreements are dragging the Greek Cypriots to disaster. It is high time we demanded the abolition of a regime which is leading us to calamity".

Passage from the speech of Mr. Tassos Papadopoulos, Minister of Labour and Social Insurance, published by the Greek press on the 2nd April, 1962: "The Zurich agreements dictated by foreign interests alien to the Greek spirit . . . .".

I think these few examples illustrate the nature of the campaign carried out against the Agreements.

Article 123 of the Cyprus Constitution specifies that the personnel to be employed in the civil service should be composed of 70 per cent Greeks and 30 per cent Turks.

In July, 1960, before the Constitution came into effect, Dr. Kutchuk and Archbishop Makarios countersigned an agreement whereby they agreed that the 70/30 ratio in the public service should be implemented within five months of the coming into operation of the Constitution. Then a Committee composed of the President's and Vice-President's Under-Secretaries and the Representatives of the Turkish and Greek-Cypriots' Civil Service Associations was set up to prepare a report on the manner of implementation of the 70/30 ratio within five months. The committee prepared a report which was signed by the President, Vice-President and the Representatives of the two civil service associations; thus it formed an official document which should have been honoured by all.

However, neither did the Greek Cypriots abide by Article 123 of the Constitution, nor did they honour the said agreement; they wilfully refrained from implementing the agreement by unfounded pretexts. The declaration of the President of the Civil Service Committee formed of seven Greek and three Turkish Cypriot members reveals the negative attitude that dominated Greek members—taken from official minutes, it reads as follows:—"I have considered whether the report of the committee appointed to make recommendations on the implementation of the 70/30 ratio in the civil service is binding on this commission. I can find nothing in the Constitution making this report binding on us. The only article dealing with the 70/30 ratio is Article 123, sub-section 2. The view which I take of these provisions in the Constitution is that all vacancies, whether created before or after the 16th August, 1960, the "promotion post" will be filled by promotion of officers in the service on merits, qualifications and experience, whether such public servants are Greeks or Turks and not by promoting persons inexperienced and unqualified so as to make up the 70/30 ratio". Thus the provision of the Constitution on the 70/30 ratio was not implemented and a subjective system based on merits, qualifications and experience was adopted in its stead. Consequently, not only was the implementation of the 70/30 ratio principle stopped, but the appointments were carried out with discrimination against the Turks.

The Greek Cypriot side has shown from the beginning a reluctance concerning the setting up of a 2,000-strong Cyprus army, the formation of which was required by the Constitution. This reluctance resulted from ill-intentioned motives and excuses such as "the economic difficulties of a small island", in order to prevent the creation of a force other than EOKA and the arming of Turkish youth, even in small numbers.

Despite all this, in the atmosphere of the initial days of the Republic as a result of the efforts of the personnel on the Turkish side and the organisation of the Alliance, the Army of Cyprus began to be established and a cadre of 370 persons was formed. But then the Greek side brought forward a new argument. The argument was that "the composition of the Army should be an entirely mixed one".

But such a composition was technically possible only above Company level and not possible under this level due to the difference of language, tradition and custom existing between the Greeks and Turks living in separate communities. Also, the provision of the Constitution stating that "Forces which are stationed in parts of the Territory of Cyprus inhabited in a proportion approaching one hundred per centum only by members of one Community shall belong to that Community" rendered such an over-all mixed composition impossible. Therefore, the acceptance of the artificial Greek thesis would even mean the violation of one of the basic articles of the Constitution. The Greek side, however, did not take into consideration the well-founded Turkish objections. And after the veto of Dr. Kutchuk the Greek Cypriots gave up the formation of the Army that was exactly what they wanted.

The question of the Army is another typical example of the attitude shown by the Greek leaders in the implementation of the Agreements. This attitude produced the following negative consequences:

1. The Turkish Vice-President was placed in a position where he had no alternative but to use his veto
2. The implementation of the Treaty of Alliance has been wrecked; and
3. The most important Ministry given to the Turks—the Ministry of Defence—has been reduced to a stunted, ineffective organisation.

Another example illustrating the attitude of the Greek Cypriots vis-à-vis the Constitution is the line of action they followed on the subject of municipalities.

Greek Cypriots persistently refrained from implementing the provisions of the Constitution pertaining to the separate municipalities, claiming that they were "impracticable to implement". Nevertheless, since 1958, separate municipalities existed legally and actually in many cities of Cyprus, and they functioned successfully. This proves that the idea of separate municipalities is not "impracticable to implement" as claimed.

However, Turkey and Turkish Cypriots, suggested to the Greeks that once separate municipalities had been established in accordance with the Constitution, they could be reunified through a gradual process. But this suggestion, like all other constructive ones, was rejected without even being studied.

Turkish Cypriots applied to the Supreme Constitutional Court on the question of municipalities and requested that the disagreement be solved through legal procedures.

The President's reaction to this Turkish request, a very normal and common practice in all civilized societies, was an example of his negative frame of mind. Indeed, in the statement he made to the Sunday Express in February 1963, Archbishop Makarios said: "Even if the Supreme Constitutional Court rules that my action is contrary to the Constitution, I shall not respect this ruling".

I think that this statement needs no comment.

Another depressing incident, which is now known by all, was the way in which the President of the Supreme Constitutional Court and his assistant were forced to resign and leave the island just because they abided by legal principles and did not act in compliance with the wishes of the Greek Cypriots. Professor Forsthoff's statement published in "Die Welt" of December 27th, 1963, needs no comment. He says "Makarios bears on his shoulders the sole responsibility of the recent tragic events. . . . His aim is to deprive the Turkish community of their rights".

The basic articles of the constitution give us another example illustrating the unlawful attitude of Greek Cypriot administrators vis-à-vis the Constitution and the Agreements: Article 182 of the Constitution reads as follows: "The Articles or parts of Articles of this Constitution set out in Annex III hereto, which have been incorporated from the Zurich Agreement dated 11th February, 1959, are the basic articles of this Constitution and cannot in any way be amended, whether by way of variation, addition or repeal".

Moreover, the Republic of Cyprus undertook to secure obedience to its Constitution in compliance with Article 1 of the Treaty of Guarantee; finally, Turkey, the United Kingdom and Greece, in Article 2 of the said Agreement "recognized and guaranteed the state of affairs established by the basic articles of its Constitution".

Therefore it was absolutely clear that the basic articles of the Constitution possessed the quality of an international agreement. Yet, Greek Cypriot administrators have continuously attempted to change these basic articles, simply because the provisions in these articles were the only legal safeguards of the Turkish Cypriots' rights. The reasons advanced by Greek Cypriots for the abolition of these basic articles are nothing but pretexts. Their clear purpose is to degrade the Turkish community into the status of a mere minority left at the mercy of the Greek Cypriot community. The truth is that the Cyprus agreements are founded on mutually agreed principles of co-operation between both communities and not on majority-minority relations. This is the spirit of the Agreements. The aim of the Greek Cypriots is nothing less than to reject the basic spirit of these agreements, which were signed with a view to ending the Cyprus dispute. It is a desire to alter the equilibrium against one of the parties concerned.

With the signing of the agreements, EOKA was allegedly abolished and in its stead a supposedly peaceful organization called EDMA was founded. But even in those days, those who went to the Troodos mountains saw written on one side of the bridge leading to Amiantos that the initials of this organization represented EOKA, DIGHENIS, MAKARIOS, and the ANE (EOKA youth organization). This, as well as indications and activities of a similar nature, has shown that EOKA had never been abolished, but that it had, only at the beginning, disguised itself.

Another aspect of the campaign of provocation and the war of nerves which the Greek-Cypriots have waged against the Turks for over three years is their activities in favour of "Enosis".

Despite the provisions of Article 1 of the Treaty of Guarantee stating that "The Republic of Cyprus declares prohibited any activity likely to promote, directly or indirectly, either union with any other state or partition of the Island", and although the attention of the highest responsible personalities of the Cyprus State was drawn by Turkey and the Turkish-Cypriots on several occasions, both in writing and orally, to the activities of the Greek-Cypriots in this direction, the Greek-Cypriot statesmen, far from taking the steps required by their international commitments, encouraged or even took part themselves in "Enosis" activity.

The proposals put forward by Dr. Kutchuk in order to pass a law forbidding the subversive activities against the Agreements and the Constitution were not taken into consideration by Archbishop Makarios.

It is indeed sufficient to mention only a few of hundreds of examples which would clearly show the Greek-Cypriot activities at all levels in favour of "Enosis".

In a speech delivered on 11th February, 1962, the Minister of Internal Affairs of Cyprus, who is the main responsible person for the maintenance of the Constitutional order and legal system, stated: "Ahead lie new struggles, different in character. Everybody is invited to join us. The struggle which was launched for our country in order to regain what was lost will be continued by other means. The aspiration and expectations of pan-hellenism will be achieved".

An excerpt from the speech made by the Minister of Labour of the Republic of Cyprus, Mr. Papadopoulos on 2nd April, 1962: "When the time comes, we will turn our chains we have broken into arms and use these, in bolstering the bridge that will close the gap separating Cyprus from Greece".

Another excerpt from the *Alithia* newspaper dated 26th February, 1962: "The Enosis is not dead. . . . As long as a single Greek remains on this island, the passion for freedom and for our national ideals will go on burning in our hearts".

From the newspaper "Ethniki" dated 25th March, 1962: "Long live the union of Cyprus with motherland Greece".

From the newspaper "Ethniki" dated 1st April, 1962: "We believe that the chains which are unjustly and illegally separating Cyprus from Greece will be broken, and that freedom leading to *enosis* will become victorious".

From the declaration, dated 1st April, 1961, published by the Cyprus-Greek Fighters' Association: "We shall continue our fight until our glorious flag flies over Greek Cyprus. We shall fight till the very end to unite with our homeland, Greece, and, if need be, we shall die for *enosis*".

From posters stuck up in various parts of Nicosia on 1st April, 1962, the anniversary of the day marking the beginning of EOKA's fight: "The chains of Zurich will be broken. Because heroes have not died for Zurich . . . Hoist the flag of *enosis*", "Forward to new fights", and so on.

Faced with an intensive campaign or provocation and threat directed from various fronts by the Greek Cypriots, how could the Turkish Cypriots possibly feel themselves secure and at peace? During the last three years, the Greek Cypriots have prepared the conditions of the present tragic situation in Cyprus, and, finally, have set out to realize their desires by force.

In fact, while the Turkish Government and the Turkish Cypriots went on with their sincere endeavours to look for peaceful solutions to the difficulties in Cyprus, unfortunately the Greek Cypriots launched, just three weeks ago, an all-out pre-arranged armed aggression against the Turkish community in order to attain their goals by force.

Archbishop Makarios declared in a statement made in August, 1963, that 1964 would be a crucial year in connection with the Greek-Cypriot case. The same idea has also been openly expressed by the Foreign Minister of Cyprus, to the Minister of Agriculture who is Turkish. I shall not dwell here on the tragic events which followed this campaign of terror launched against the Turks according to a premeditated plan. To recall those events is really a heart-breaking experience.

The actions taken by the Greek Cypriots against the Turks, which have been referred to above, are not only in contradiction with the explicit provisions of the Cyprus Constitution, but they also violate the general agreements directly protecting the human being as a human being, such as those relating to human rights and to genocide, which all civilized nations feel themselves obliged to observe.

Now as regards the attitude taken by Turkey in the face of these events let me remind you that since the beginning of the crisis my Government has tried all the courses of action incumbent upon the guaranteeing Powers and foreseen in the various Cyprus agreements. Thus, since December 21st, it has repeatedly appealed to the leaders of both communities and to the Government of Cyprus, inviting them to restore peace. Despite a promise made by Archbishop Makarios that he would stop the clashes—murder, arson, atrocities continued, reaching their climax on Christmas night.

The Turkish Government in the meantime requested the United Kingdom and Greek Governments to take the necessary steps in Nicosia to help put an end to the massacre of the Turkish Cypriots.

A tripartite appeal made to the Cyprus Government was unfortunately of no avail. The Turkish Government then asked twice, by virtue of the Treaty of Guarantee, that the two other Guaranteeing Powers join her in securing a cease-fire between the two communities. Our two allies preferred diplomatic approaches to the implementation of the Treaty of Guarantee. The diplomatic moves unfortunately yielded no results. Thus, all means of concerted action having been tried, as the bloodshed went on and the Turkish casualties increased every passing hour Turkey decided to use her right of unilateral intervention on the basis of Article 4 of the Treaty of Guarantee. But she confined her intervention to a single warning flight of 5 jet fighters of the Turkish Air Force at 2 p.m. on December 25th, 1963, over the terror stricken city of Nicosia. The Guaranteeing Powers have been informed in advance of this flight. The next day Archbishop Makarios expressed his readiness to accept a tripartite action suggested by Great Britain, Greece and Turkey, on the basis of the Treaty of Guarantee.

The events and actions which I have briefly underlined before you, the wilful intentions behind these actions, and the aim of all these actions, reveal in the most naked form the situation in Cyprus and the attitude of the Greeks of Cyprus. The instigators and the executives of the acts of violence perpetrated against the Turkish Cypriots are to be held responsible for all these actions on the national as well as on the international level.

The first point to be decided upon is to start collecting evidence in order to ascertain the scope of this responsibility. Normal life should return to the island so that the work of investigation, which will take some time, can be carried out in security, and the life and property of the Turkish Cypriots so far exposed to unlawful actions can be protected. Therefore, order should be fully restored, and normal services of communication movement and transport must be assured. Besides these measures, the primary needs, such as medical treatment and settlement, of the Turks whose lives were wilfully threatened, whose properties were destroyed and who were forced to flee from their homes, should be met.

The sanctions for creating this state of affairs in Cyprus and for actions against the Turkish Cypriots, and compensation for the harm done, concern only the deeds in the past. The sanction for these actions now will not prevent their authors from indulging in them again. The agreements that establish the internal and international status of the Cyprus Republic have not been able to prevent attempts of intimidation or annihilation against the Turkish Cypriot community, the violation of the international obligations, nor the endangering of peace and security on the island and abroad. The inevitable conclusion is that it is an absolute necessity to find for Cyprus a status that will radically preclude a repetition of the tragic events we encounter today and for the Turkish community additional and effective guarantees designed to ensure an absolute security for their lives, their property, their rights and interests in the future."

MR. PALAMAS said:

"I wish to express to you Mr. Chairman, and through you to the British Government, the warmest thanks of my Delegation for their hospitality and the very high appreciation of the Royal Hellenic Government for the British initiative to convene this Conference. This offers to all parties concerned in the problem of Cyprus the opportunity to present their respective views and to try—by confronting these views—to find their way to a peaceful, reasonable and constructive solution.

Furthermore, we feel grateful to the British Government for their action in Cyprus, for the assistance they conceded to the Cyprus Government to restore law and order and to bring back the peace in the hearts and in the minds of the Cypriot population. This has given ample proof of the sense of statesmanship and responsibility our British friends have displayed by assuming, in accord with the Governments of Greece and Turkey, the leadership in the peacemaking operation.

The Royal Greek Government and the Greek people deeply regret the tragic events in Cyprus. They do deplore the loss of life, the destruction of property and the excesses which are responsible for so many victims. We can see no excuse for those who started this round of violence. We are against violence. Violence begets violence and solves no problems. Since the outset of the recent crisis the Royal Greek Government have constantly stood for moderation and peaceful action. They did everything they could to prevent an extension of the conflict. They did avoid any provocation. Facing extensive military measures taken by our Turkish friends—the concentration of warships, troops and aircraft in the areas neighbouring the island—they showed the greatest measure of restraint in spite of heavy pressure from the press and from Greek public opinion. Thanks to this attitude a dangerous escalation of measures and countermeasures was avoided, but it might have been construed as constituting in many ways a challenge to the Greek people and armed forces, and might have led to regrettable developments. May I submit that both Greece and Turkey are interested in avoiding that sort of brinkmanship. I have every reason to believe that this view is shared by our Turkish friends, because while what I have already mentioned happened on the military side, on the political level there has been a valuable reciprocation of goodwill and co-operation from the Turkish Government and personally from President Inonu.

Now having averted so far the worst we are looking forward to the better.

It is not my intention to elaborate at length on the sequence of events which led us to the present critical predicament in Cyprus. It is now too late to discover the deficiencies of the Agreements concluded a few years ago in Zurich and in London and it is too early to pass judgment objectively on what recently happened in that unfortunate island. The day will come, when the responsibilities will have to be weighed and attributed to those who are really responsible.

For the time being, bearing in mind the purpose of this Conference, as defined by the British Government we had better stick to certain fundamental, political facts.

It is a fact that since the Zurich Agreements were signed, peace and co-operation between the Greek and Turkish Communities did not prevail. Instead, intercommunal strife has been constantly stirred up and reached a climax when bloodshed started.

The Zurich Agreements concerning constitutional arrangements were based on the assumption that the two Communities would live together in close co-operation and mutual understanding. Even now, even after the tragic events of these last days we see no alternative to this basic assumption. Any future accommodation or settlement could not be founded on a different basis.

However, though this basic principle is sound the ways and means for its application proved to be impracticable. The constitution created a complicated system of Government, whereby the two Communities were in constant political competition. They were given the power to neutralise each other. In particular, the minority was granted as guarantees for the protection of its rights, the possibility to block the functioning of the State. Instead of creating a unified State in which the two Communities should participate in a reasonable proportion the constitution produced an amalgamation of two distinct and opposing political factors. This resulted in a constant political war between the two Communities within the framework of the constitution. The majority was nurturing feelings of frustration. Any important initiative was under constant fire from the minority.

All these contradictory and self-destroying rights and limitations pushed the Greek Cypriots to the verge of exasperation. They came to the point of seeing in their Turkish compatriots their opponents, their enemies.

On the other hand the Turkish Community felt she was under constant threat from the majority. By using and by misusing their rights and privileges they made the situation even worse. Thus the situation drifted in a dangerous game of competition between a numerically overwhelming majority and the minority.

We all know that facing an extremely dangerous situation, and desirous to solve the Cyprus problem in the interest of the people of Cyprus and of the friendship between Greece and Turkey, the Governments of our two countries tried in Zurich to make a synthesis of the existing opposing views of the two Communities and produced as a compromise the Cypriot constitution.

That was a well-intentioned experiment. But the experiment partially failed. It did not resist the test of everyday life. The system particularly on some points was proved to be unworkable. The new state, the Republic of Cyprus, was founded but its governmental and administrative machinery could not work properly. As we do see it now, its main deficiency rested with the fact that the constitution aimed at creating a unified State through divisive devices.

We should in all fairness add that if the texts were lacking in efficiency their application by the Cypriots did not make things easier.

Having in view this situation and in order to prevent the worst, President Makarios had taken the initiative to present to all parties concerned a proposition to amend on a few points the constitution in order to make it work. Such action by the Cypriot President was well intentioned and taken in a lawful way.

It was unfortunate that that proposal was flatly rejected. In our view the initiative deserved to be considered more closely in the presence of an extremely complicated and explosive problem, and in the light of factual experience it was worth discussing any suggestion susceptible to improve what could be improved. Discussing does not necessarily mean accepting. But it shows goodwill, alleviates ill feelings and keeps alive the hope.

Now I wish to offer a few remarks on another aspect of the problem, that is to say the Tripartite Treaty of Guarantee. What was the purpose of that Treaty? It was to offer to the Turkish Nation an effective assurance that Cyprus, as an independent State, would never become a danger or even a potential threat to the security of Turkey.

I wish to state right away that Greece is very much alive to this Turkish National concern. It was in order to meet the Turkish fears that the Greek Government agreed to sign the Tripartite Treaty of Guarantee and in addition the Treaty of Alliance between Cyprus, Greece and Turkey. Such a complex of conventional guarantees appeared at that time to serve the course of an even closer co-operation between our two countries. Unfortunately experience has proved that this was not the case. The presence of small Greek and Turkish contingents on the Island did not prevent the outburst of violence; on the contrary it did create the danger of a direct clash between Greek and Turkish forces in the atmosphere of exacerbated national passions on both sides. Such an ominous development has been prevented thanks to the wisdom of the three Governments and the contribution of the British Commander on the spot. But the danger is still there and constitutes a potential deadly threat to Greco-Turkish relations; in the same way the Treaty of Guarantee by admitting under certain conditions the possibility of unilateral intervention, opens a new front between Greece and Turkey which could be inflamed at any moment.

Needless to add that the Cypriots, living under the constant fear of possible intervention, are driven to extremist reactions. They also have the feeling that they have been given an independence which is not genuine independence and the structure of a State which cannot function properly.

I had to mention all these deficiencies as deriving from the facts. We think that if the Conference wishes to accomplish constructive work we must see our way to finding sounder and less risky solutions, solutions acceptable to all.

By saying so I do not wish to be misunderstood. We still have to serve the same purpose and to meet the same end. But we should do this in the light of the factual experience we have already acquired. It goes without saying that any change in the existing Constitution must be agreed by all. As long as this does not happen the validity of the aforesaid Agreements cannot be questioned.

I understand that this Conference will have to consider the views of all the interested parties and to study with an open mind every constructive proposal. Our purpose is to explore the ground for common agreement.

However, I wish to stress the following points which in our view belong to the fundamentals:

(a) The people of Cyprus, the two Communities, both Greek and Turkish, have interests which must prevail over the interests of all the other parties, in case a reasonable co-ordination cannot be reached.

(b) Cyprus is internationally recognized as an independent State. It is a member of the Commonwealth and a member of the United Nations. This constitutes a starting point. We are not here to destroy independence in Cyprus but to make it work.

(c) I have to recall that Greece accepted the creation of an independent Cypriot State as a compromise solution—with a view to preserving Greco-Turkish relations from greater strain and as a contribution to international peace. Anything which could affect this compromise would necessarily reopen the problem as a whole.

(d) Peaceful coexistence and co-operation between the two Communities is still the only basis on which it is possible to build a lasting settlement of the constitutional problems of the island.

(e) The Turkish Community is a minority Community. Experience has proved that it is not possible to change numbers by legal fictions. As a minority the Turkish Community is entitled to secure iron-clad safeguards.

(f) We must bear in mind that in any settlement the interests of the Free World and of the NATO Community to which Greece, the United Kingdom and Turkey belong should be given proper importance.

Now, Mr. Chairman, I have listened with great care and attention to the statement made by my Turkish colleague. There are a few points on which you can understand that we cannot see eye to eye, but this concerns in particular the historical background.

I would just say only a few words, so that my silence could not be construed as meaning that we do accept these points of principle. First, geographical proximity: we consider that this is a factor in international issues, but it is not the main factor. We consider that the human factor is the most important factor.

Concerning majority and minority, we consider that this is a democratic principle which works everywhere, and on this principle are founded all the states belonging to the free world.

My distinguished Turkish colleague mentions strategic importance. I have already said that we do recognise that this is a very important factor. Mr. Erkin mentioned the relation between the lion and the lamb. We do not consider that the majority is the lion and the minority is the lamb. Mr. Erkin referred to the articles of the Constitution, which in his view were not implemented as they should be implemented. I am not in a position to offer observations on these points, but I could say that the provisions which were not implemented as he says, they are all belonging to the dividing process of the Constitution.

Mr. Erkin said that Enosis was claimed in the newspapers and was projected by the Greek Cypriots. We have to bear in mind that the agreements in Zurich and London were based on compromise, and this certainly does not mean that it is easy to stifle the national feelings of people; I would say that the Turkish Cypriots also have feelings for their motherland, and if there were manifestations in favour of Enosis there have been even stronger manifestations in favour of Taxin."

Mr. Chairman, that is all I have to say now.

MR. DENKTASH said:

"Mr. Chairman, the case for the Cyprus-Turkish delegation is as simple as its unfolding is tragic. Whatever we say or do at this Conference we have as its foundation, whether we like it or not, the massacred bodies of Turkish women and children, the useless bloodshed by the so-called security forces of the Government of Cyprus, the enmity and unrest which has been fanned by Greek propaganda since the birth of the Republic and our bitter experience in running a Government in partnership with the Greek side "in goodwill and understanding" as envisaged by the London-Zurich Agreements. These Agreements were drafted and signed with a view to assuring both sides that what has just happened in Cyprus would not and could not happen but despite the guarantees worked into the constitution the recent tragic events did take place.

We must now try to find at this Conference a solution to the problems created by the recent events and work out a satisfactory solution which will prevent the recurrence of such tragic events. The Turkish community must be satisfied fully that the lives and properties of its people will never be at the mercy of the Greek population, that its affairs will not be interfered with, nor its rights denied by the Greek community.

It is with those thoughts in mind that we have come to this Conference.

The Greek side has consistently blamed the constitution for all the ills in Cyprus from the very beginning. Without any attempt to apply the constitution they have maintained that it is unworkable and they have used all possible pressures on us in order to force us to agree to such changes which in our view were fundamental and went to the roots of the political structure which was brought about as a compromise settlement at Zurich.

We have been unable to agree to any change in the present regime during the past three years on the insincere Greek pretext that those provisions in the constitution relating to Turkish rights are unworkable, because we have never believed that an honest attempt on the Greek side was made to implement these provisions.

On the contrary, we are convinced from the declarations made by Archbishop Makarios and his Ministers that the true reasons behind such Greek demands for a change were politically aimed at usurping all Turkish rights with a view to enabling Greeks to use the present regime, in the words of Archbishop Makarios, as a springboard for Enosis. As far back as 1960 Archbishop Makarios declared, repeating himself at every opportunity each year, that "the noble struggles of the people never come to an end. These struggles although undergoing transformation are never terminated. The struggle of the people in Cyprus too will go on. The Zurich and London Agreements formed a landmark in the cause of this struggle but at the same time our starting point and bastion for further struggles with the object of capitalising what has been achieved for further conquests". And on 1st April, 1963 he said "The struggle did not end. It is continuing in a different form so that the present may be appraised and the future conquered. Although this is incomplete, it is still victory, it forms a new epoch and a new chapter towards conquering the future. It is disclosing the nature of this future, the meaning and conception of the glorious anniversary which we are celebrating today." Such statements were deliberately sprinkled into our political horizon at frequent intervals while the call for the change of the constitution went on.

All these sentiments were contrary to what we believed the Zurich Settlement had, in fact, achieved. In the words of the then Foreign Minister of Greece, referring to the Zurich Settlement at the London Conference of 1959: "We have separated all the matters which ought to be separated, because they are of a completely different nature. We have respected the majority, which is overwhelming, and because it is overwhelming, it has more part of the Administration. But we have also given the minority not only rights but also fair parts in that Administration; also, the way of that Administration is such that the Turks of Cyprus would not feel that they are at the mercy of the majority, if that majority did not want to be fair."

Our three year experiment has been a constant fight for justice because of the deliberate attempt of the Greek side to leave us at their mercy and to upset the basic grounds on which the Cyprus Settlement was reached. The notion of Greco-Turkish partnership was never admitted and never applied. Majority shall rule, the Greeks claimed, and scorned off every right which was given to the Turks under the Constitution. Greek rule should either be accepted by the Turks as a fact or it would be imposed upon us by brute force. That was the alternative put before us. The purpose of these machinations and subversive attempts was to use the present regime—which was formed on the firm understanding that Enosis and Partition should be forgotten—for the achievement of this very end, as far as the Greek community was concerned.

It was when we said "No" to the proposals of Archbishop Makarios to a change in the Constitution; when we refused to accept his finding that those parts of the Constitution which he had never applied relating to the Turkish Cypriots were unworkable; when we stood firm and refused to give in to international blackmailing tactics by the Greek side and asked Archbishop Makarios to try and apply the Constitution as it was, that the so-called security forces of the Government were unleashed against the Turkish-Cypriots, resulting in an orgy of appalling bloodshed and violence. It is obvious, therefore, that the root of all the trouble was not the Constitution itself, but the Greek decision not to implement it and to founder it for their own political ends. That the Constitution had its difficult provisions we conceded; but we felt that those difficulties could be removed if the Greek political aims were changed. That the Constitution was sui generis we agreed. All Constitutions have to take cognizance of the realities of a given state. Our Constitution had done this in a realistic way. It should have been up to us to start from these realities and proceed, in good time, after establishing mutual trust and goodwill to an evolution of "Cypriot" notion. The Greek side, however, tried to force down our throats this notion while proclaiming themselves Hellenes and declaring Cyprus to be the Greek land which would eventually unite with Mother Greece.

The Zurich Settlement, which was drafted very carefully in order to make sure that we would not be at the mercy of the Greeks, "if they chose not to be fair", was upset by brute force and violence, and we now find ourselves at the mercy of the Greeks. The riddled bodies of Turkish women and children; the bitterness which Turkish refugees, running away from murder and violence, have left behind; and the constant declaration of the Greeks that they will never accept a position in Cyprus where the Turks can have a say as a community, apart from mere minority rights, are stark realities which we have to keep in mind as we seek a solution at this Conference.

We must also bear in mind that promises given were soon forgotten and agreements reached dishonoured as soon as it was convenient for the Greeks to do so.

Mr. Chairman, we have not come here after this bloodbath of innocent Turks to concede to the Greek side that the guarantees worked into the Constitution for the protection of our lives, properties and human dignity are unnecessary; we are not here in London to give in to their demand that we should accept to live at their mercy just because they keep on arming and amassing arms for the second attack. Nor are we here in order to exploit the situation and take away any of their rights. We are here simply to try and find a solution which will give us full security in our own homes and in our own land where we have lived in peace as honourable citizens for centuries past.

With all these factors in mind we propose that this Conference should give its attention to the maintenance of law and order in Cyprus in such a way that the Turkish villagers who live under constant fear of the Greek gunmen should no longer be under such a terrible threat by removing all physical contacts with the Greek side. The Zurich and London partnership having been deliberately destroyed, we must find ways and means of assuring the Turkish side that they do not live at the mercy of the Greeks and that they are not a subordinate community to them. We must find a solution which will be just, no matter how hard it may be to do so and no matter what the difficulties involved may be, because the alternative is to leave the Turks at the full mercy of the Greeks and to force them to leave the island or submit to Greek political pressure. The horrors perpetrated by the Greek side during the last few weeks and their preparation of more to come make this inevitable and urgent.

The sanctity of life and property, human dignity, honour and justice must be maintained at all costs for the two communities separately. The recent events in Cyprus occurred because these rights were violated by the Greek side. Those who have failed to honour the Zurich Settlement and the London Agreement and who have tried to abrogate the Constitution itself, should not be heard to say that democracy entitled them to do what they please in Cyprus when the very lives and the rights of almost one-fourth of the population is at stake. Democracy does not entitle them to that.

In promises we no longer have any trust.

The world Press is being told that the Greek side wishes to see a Cyprus where Greek and Turk live in peaceful co-existence.

The Turks of Ayios Vasilios who were attacked by Greek policemen and EOKA gunmen with hand-grenades, bombs, bazookas and machine guns were fast asleep in their homes, believing that no harm could come to them from the Greek side. They believed in the Agreements, in the Constitution, in the guarantees and in their Greek co-villagers. They were a handful of Turkish families living in a Greek surrounded area of thousands of Greek families. Those Turks were attacked mercilessly. Those who managed to escape with their lives gave an incredible account of this atrocious attack by armed Greek policemen and all shouting "EOKA" and "Enosis". The dead bodies of those who could not escape and the attack on the nearby villages of Skyllona and Dhenia tell a grim story. Twenty-two Turks of these mixed villages, women and children included, were found buried near the villages, in ditches into which they were thrown in twos and threes fully dressed. One body had its head cut off; some had their hands and feet tied with ropes and they were all shot dead from behind. A woman of seventy and a young girl of twelve were similarly shot and killed.

In the village of Dhenia those Turks who tried to escape were shot, the rest were ordered to stay indoors and were informed that they would be shot when orders to that effect came from above.

In Skyllona, another mixed village, the Turks were driven out of their houses with machine guns and hand-grenades. All Turkish houses were burned down.

No Greek was killed or injured in and around this area, and no damage was caused to any Greek property by the Turks—a clear indication of a premeditated Greek plan to strike terror at Turkish hearts at a given signal, as they did.

The manner of attack in and around Nicosia by the so-called security forces had a similar pattern. Women and children were mercilessly killed by Greek policemen, reinforced by EOKA gunmen, all carrying sub-machine guns and other arms of war. The war-cry of the attackers was again "EOKA", "Enosis", and these Turks who believed in the principle of peaceful co-existence were taken by surprise and killed or removed as hostages.

Old and sick women in their eighties as well as young children of all ages were driven out of their beds and taken as hostages. Some of these were shot dead after being lined up while horrified British eye-witnesses looked on from their windows. Out of 700 hostages taken only 563 were returned. No-one knows what happened to the rest.

This is the way in which the promise of peaceful co-existence was applied in Cyprus. But this was not enough. Even after the cease fire, while the British soldiers tried to restore order, Turkish houses were looted, burnt or damaged, so that those who might come back to their homes and make a final attempt to co-exist should never think of it. The Turks have to be silenced and cowed for good, or they should be exterminated. That was the plan. When the Correspondent of a foreign news agency tried to get information from the Presidential palace, Mr. Spyros Kyprianou waved him off, saying that "This is war. Innocents may also be killed".

Yes, the Greek leaders had armed illegally, unconstitutionally, their police and gendarmerie; they had disarmed the Turkish police and gendarmerie. They had armed their EOKA gunmen and had apparently, and without any notice to the Turks, and for no reason, declared war on the Turkish community because this community had stuck to its rights under the Constitution, believing that it had provided a medium for peaceful co-existence in partnership.

All this talk and all these promises now of peaceful co-existence in a majority-ruled Cyprus with no guarantee mean nothing to us.

I repeat that in such promises we no longer have any trust.

We have come here to seek more guarantees; more real and effective guarantees.

In written words and agreements we have no confidence because we have seen how they were dishonoured. The Cyprus Government which refused to implement that part of the Constitution which provided for a Cyprus Army on several pretexts has found the means to organise an irregular Greek force of bandits for attacking the Turks. The guarantees of life and property were thus brought to an end. Means of communication cut off to the Turks. Turkish villages surrounded and stranded without food and without medical help; freedom of speech gagged; even the Vice-President himself cut off from all the world.

These have been the tragic results of our co-existence with the Greeks. We must seek and find a solution which at no time will permit the reoccurrence of the same events.

We are ready to live in Cyprus with the Greeks but we cannot, from henceforth, afford to live within them. We must find a solution so that we can live in peace and security side by side with them as good neighbours. There can be no better real guarantee for us than this after having witnessed these atrocities.

Because of these atrocities and the continuing threat of them, Turkish villages have left their properties and fled into Turkish areas. Each day more

Turks move out of their insecure surroundings while the Greeks ransack their houses and loot their properties. As a first step we must agree to move those terrorized people into safe areas and establish a machinery whereby properties may be exchanged or compensated.

This evil effect of terrorism cannot be obliterated by words and promises. It cannot be obliterated by written Constitution. It can be only obliterated by effective measures of a lasting nature.

Mr. Kyprianou thought it fit to inform the journalists yesterday that Turks and Greeks had lived together peacefully even during the first and second World Wars. He forgot to mention the killing of Turks during EOKA terrorism in 1955 and 1958, and he also forgot to mention that from 1878 onwards every time the Greek side tried to dominate the Turks politically, the Turks of Cyprus objected and took counter measures in order to prevent such domination.

The root of all the trouble in Cyprus lies in this very fact. The Greeks of Cyprus want, on the one hand, to feel as Greeks of the mainland, to think and act as such, and they openly declare that there is no Cypriot nation; while, on the other hand, when it comes to dealing with Turks and Turkish rights they maintain that Cyprus as such is a nation in which the majority should rule supreme and the community which is lesser in number should be ruled as a minority. It is this paradoxical and selfish attitude which has caused all the trouble.

An honest attempt to apply the Constitution might in years to come create the necessary atmosphere in which the notion of Cypriotism might have arisen. But the experience of the last three years prevented this from happening and the last tragic events have completely annihilated all hopes for such an end. This, we know, is no loss for the Greek side, because their aim has been and it has always been union with Greece and the Turks of Cyprus have stood firmly in their way as an impassable barricade and they intend to do so.

It is obvious, therefore, that what Cyprus now needs is peace and security and the events which have been so far unfolded prove beyond any doubt that security for the Turks can only be provided if such realistic steps can be taken for the prevention of the recurrence of those events.

We must save those Turks who are trapped in Greek areas. There must be complete physical separation of the two communities who should undertake to live in Cyprus, I repeat, side by side as good neighbours in peace and harmony on the basis of a political framework to be agreed upon.

But this principle of separation is fundamental and in the light of the three years' bitter experience and of the recent events and the continuing threat of a repetition of the same on a wider scale, it is absolutely vital and urgent that this should be done. This is the minimum requirement for the effective safety of Turks and the security of their lives and properties.

The Turkish contingent in the island, which has played a vital role for the cessation of the massacre of the Turks, should be increased in numbers and immediate steps should be taken to open all means of communications to the Turks effectively. Those who have lost their lives or properties should be fully compensated. An independent inquiry should be held into the recent events by the Guaranteeing Powers with a view to punishing those responsible for the organising, effecting and directing the massacre of Turks and bringing the guilty to justice. All these must be done with due speed having regard to the urgency of the matter.

Now the honourable representative of the Hellenic Greek Government has touched upon some vital points about the Zurich Agreement and about the Turkish position in Cyprus. I should like very much to reply to him so that our silence may not be taken as acceptance of his exposition of those facts.

It has been said that the Zurich Agreements were based on the assumption that the two communities should co-operate in goodwill. We agree that that assumption was there. We agree that unless the two communities sincerely agree to co-operate on the basis of the rule of law that there can be no peace in Cyprus. There was a rule of law Constitution and we were supposed to abide by that Constitution and to live in harmony and peace until by agreement we changed the Constitution. It is because the Constitution was one-sided and not applied that the present trouble arose. Any settlement which we now reach here, any written Constitution, any guarantee will again depend on these assumptions.

Therefore whatever we do, we must know and we must realise that one side, if it backs out of the new settlement, shall not be in a position to put the other side at its mercy. That is why I have dealt with this physical separation of the Turkish villagers from the Greek areas.

That the Zurich Agreement proved to be impracticable we deny. It was never meant to be implemented. In August, 1963, Mr. Papadopoulos said this—

> The President's recent declaration of his desire to get rid of the negative provisions of the constitution came as no surprise to his entourage. It was a natural and expected plan and intention which were borne in the mind of the leader since the day of the birth of the Cyprus Republic. This is nothing more than a natural and intrinsic development to our present generation. It requires no high genius or patriotism to realise that the agreements need revision.

So we have here full authoritative confirmation that the constitution did not prove itself to be unworkable, but it was not worked with the intentions behind Greek minds. I therefore disagree with the honourable representative of the Hellenic Government that the compromise experiment failed in practice. It was never meant to be applied, and any compromise which will give the Turks any rights which will recognise and guarantee their lives and properties, which will recognise them as a community in Cyprus as they have lived since the Turkish occupation, a separate community from the Greeks, will similarly be attacked and not recognised when the time comes. That is why I repeat again that we insist on real guarantees and real safety. Again it has been mis-stated that the Zurich Agreement created a divided community or state. But the Zurich Agreement only took the realities into hand, that is, the existence of two separate communities and that reality is now more acute and made a framework of constitution within those realities.

It has also been touched upon that it was unfortunate that Archbishop Makarios' proposals to amend the constitution were rejected outright. Well, it was unfortunate that Archbishop Makarios made these proposals at a time when he knew full well that the Turkish side was not in a position even to entertain them for a minute because of his declared intentions previously, both by himself and by his Ministers, that what he was aiming at was to make Cyprus a Greek land; and all the amendments which he required were to those parts of the constitution which dealt with Turkish rights and which if amended would immediately make Cyprus a Greek land free to unite with Greece whenever they wished to do so. So it is a fact that as soon as Makarios explained his proposals to Dr. Kutchuk and handed them over to him, he spoke to the Foreign Minister Kyprianou, and told him these proposals are worse than Enosis—they give us entire Greek domination. So it was not surprising nor unfortunate that the proposals were rejected. Makarios was trying to bring the Turk community into that position to say no to his proposal. We believe he had his plans ready to hit the Turks; to make the issue an international issue; to come to the London Conference and then to come to United Nations. I hope I am wrong in that. It is again paradoxical and unfortunate that at the time he handed these proposals to us, he also held over our heads that whether the Turks liked it or not, he would go and amend or abrogate the constitution. These are the realities of Cyprus.

We have lived in fear for the last three years. The majority may think we are an obstacle in their way. We must find ways and means of removing that obstacle, but in such a way as will maintain our independence as a community. Nothing less can we accept. It has also been said that the presence of Greek and Turkish contingents in Cyprus nearly ended with disaster. In our humble submission, and knowing the facts of Cyprus, the presence of these contingents in Cyprus has been an escape from danger. Ever since they arrived in Cyprus the hotheads in Cyprus, knowing they were there, have always abstained from doing what otherwise they might have done, until Archbishop Makarios realised that whatever he did one by one, no-one would take any notice of; and the indulgence shown by the Guaranteeing Powers to his step by step abrogation of the agreements encouraged him at last to believe that these contingents would never move, could never move. That is why the extermination plan was put into effect.

We believe the presence of the Turkish contingent—and I speak for the Turkish community—is the only real guarantee the Turkish Community cannot forgo. In our view the number of the personnel must be increased so that the sense of security is well settled in Cyprus. I regret to see that the Cyprus problem may involve Greece and Turkey in some sort of conflict in the future. I am sorry to hear it nearly did so in the past, if by that it is meant that the Guaranteeing Powers in spite of their guarantees will sit back and see some part of the population massacred by the other—just because the other one has the authority and power to do so, and has the audacity to name the others as rebels and cut off all communication from the population. Then of course justice cannot be done. Democracy and the rule of law cannot be maintained. We look upon the Guaranteeing Powers—Greece, Turkey, Britain all included—as powers which believe in the rule of law, and which would come into Cyprus and interfere if any such massacre started. We hope that this time they will come sooner than they did last time.

Some talk has been made of a Commonwealth guarantee or a United Nations guarantee. I state categorically that such guarantees are no guarantees to the Turkish community. One is an ephemeral one: the United Nations has not worked anywhere yet; and by the time decisions are taken, in our small island, part of the community can easily be destroyed while British armoured cars are still being stolen for the next assault. It has been said that the Turkish community is entitled to iron-cast safeguards. I believe I have outlined in brief what these iron-cast safeguards can mean for us, and I am sure all those present here will give us the benefit of choosing the iron-cast safeguards, because we know who is going to assault us, how they will assault and how we can be prevented from the assault. We have suffered once and do not want to suffer again.

As to the statement that stronger manifestations in favour of partition have been made by the Turkish side, I regret to say this must have been based on some mis-information. That has not been the case. The Turks have consistently tried and managed and succeeded in avoiding the word "taxim"(?) or manifestation in favour of taxim. The time has come when we must set ourselves to see whether we can find any solution to partition, or whether we must now go fully ahead for partition if no other solution is found. We must not shy off from words which some people think are not to their liking. If the lives and properties of the Turkish community can only be saved by that, then we must take it. It is more necessary that we should do that than give ourselves to the same sort of massacre or atrocities as have been done in the last three weeks. We do not insist on names or definitions or anything else; we seek security—final and full security.

Mr. Chairman, in conclusion we would like to thank the British Government for having taken this humane interest in the tragedy of Cyprus as one of the Guaranteeing Powers and for its hospitality in this conference. We also wish to put on record the gratitude of the Turkish Community for the steps taken by the Turkish Government in order to avert the complete extermination of the Turkish Community from Cyprus during the days of massacre. We further wish to express our thanks to the Greek Government for its participation in the Conference hoping that, after listening to our case, it will use its influence, which we know to be great and effective, on the Cypriot Greek leadership for their agreeing to the minimum requirements of our security as explained above.

The task ahead of us may at this stage look formidable, but we believe if we approach the issues involved with tolerance and understanding and with a spirit of give and take, appreciating and evaluating the stark realities of Cyprus, a just and permanent solution will be found."

MR. CLERIDES said:

"Mr. Chairman, I would like to begin by expressing the appreciation of my delegation for all that Her Majesty's Government has done to bring about the present conference. It is indeed proper and fitting that London should be the venue of this conference, because it is the centre of the Commonwealth. I would like to take this opportunity and express on behalf of my delegation our thanks for the hospitality which has been given to us and for all the arrangements made to render our task easier.

It is a matter of great regret to us that discussion of the problems of Cyprus which culminated in the present situation takes place after the recent tragic events which caused pain and suffering to the people of Cyprus. It would have been better if reason had prevailed at an earlier stage and we had had a conference before the events which have preceded it. I fully sympathise with the feelings expressed by Mr. Denktash about the loss the Turkish community has suffered, but I would have liked him with all sincerity to have expressed sympathy for the many deaths and sufferings which the Greeks have also suffered.

I would like to say at the outset of this conference that our intention here is to approach the various problems in a constructive manner. Indeed, this is the only possible approach if the conference is to have any hope of success. I would therefore urge all participants, and I credit them with the same good intentions, not to begin by taking extreme positions merely for the sake of propagating solutions which are intrinsically unworkable and therefore impossible to accept.

I believe that it is better that there should be no misapprehension about what I mean when I state that our intention is to be constructive in this conference. Let not for a minute our constructive attitude be interpreted as willingness to give way on certain fundamental principles which by their very nature admit of no compromise. It is a fundamental principle that the sovereignty and territorial integrity of our country be preserved. On this issue we shall stand firm. It is equally a basic principle which admits of no compromise on our side that a state of true independence shall emerge from this conference by virtue of which the people of Cyprus shall, without the imposition of limitations by treaties of guarantees, be the master of their own affairs.

We are prepared to reach agreement on the form of a democratic constitution, the essence of which must be that, in accordance with all accepted democratic principles, all citizens shall have equal political rights and consequently the government of our Republic shall be controlled by the will of the majority of its citizens. We wish to see incorporated in our constitution universally accepted provisions about the human rights of the citizens of the Republic irrespective of race, religion or creed, and in this respect we are prepared to consider all reasonable proposals with an open mind; but we are not prepared to accept any system whereby rights are conferred on each community separately in the form of checks and balances which create insuperable obstacles to the smooth and effective functioning of the State, raise artificial barriers between its citizens, divide our people and bring about frustration resulting in conflict and destruction.

I do not think it will be a constructive approach to spend valuable time in recriminations, in an attempt to try and shift the burden of blame from the one side to the other for what has happened, and I had intended not to deal with this aspect of the matter. Unfortunately however, His Excellency the Foreign Minister of Turkey, and Mr. Denktash, have decided at this Conference to go into a great deal of detail of alleged violations by the Greek side of the Constitution, of an intention to annihilate the Turkish community and of accusations which were designed to cast the entire blame on the Greek-Cypriot side.

Sir, I think one can be realistic, and one could admit frankly, if we wanted to be constructive, that there have been faults by both sides. Mr. Erkin has devoted a great deal of time to reading statements from the press and from Greek leaflets, trying to show the evil intentions of the Cypriots. I have, Sir, a file here from the Turkish press, from statements made by Dr. Kutchuk, from statements made by Mr. Denktash, but if I were to start reading them it would be quite an interesting proposition. I would like however to read one statement made by Dr. Kutchuk on the 9th January, 1963, in the presence of Mr. Erkin, at a lunch given by him, and I would like to see how much this differs from some of the statements he has read:

> The Turkish Cypriots will have to conduct a new independence struggle and increased help will enable us to carry out a struggle for our freedom and for the protection of peace.

This was on the 1st January, 1963, by the Vice President of the Republic, in the presence of the Turkish Foreign Minister, saying that the Turks would have to conduct a new struggle and that they would require increased help in that respect. There are statements by Mr. Denktash here, telling them many things and if Mr. Denktash would like to hear some of his own words urging the Turkish youth to fight on and to make Cyprus Turkish, I can read them—we also keep copies of what you say, Mr. Denktash, just as you keep copies of what Mr. Papadopoulos says, but I do not think it is necessary to go into this at this conference or to waste time on it, and I would therefore be very short on this point. I have statements made by the leaders of both communities in the press of both communities, which were not constructive, and in a public statement which was made by me about nine months ago or a year ago to the Turkish press I deplored this practice of making such statements by both sides. Unfortunately I did not receive any response from the Turkish side.

Coming to the analysis of the Constitution given by His Excellency Mr. Erkin who took us step by step through the Constitution of the Republic of Cyprus, I think it is sufficient to say that it has proved entirely unworkable; that the rights which were given to the Turkish community because it was thought that they were necessary guarantees, not only were excessive rights, but have been used to prevent the functioning of the State and to bring about almost the economic ruin and prevent the development of our country. This however is not a matter for a plenary session, this is a matter for a sub-committee between Greeks and Turks, who are primarily concerned to go carefully into the Constitution and find ways and means of correcting what is wrong.

A great deal has been said about arming Greek gunmen of EOKA. Nothing has been said about the armed gunmen of TMT. The machine guns which were firing, the Bren guns which were firing from a number of points on the Turkish border, including the roof of the Turkish Communal Chamber, were the machine guns of the TMT gunmen. The machine guns which were firing from Chetin Kaya were again the machine guns of the TMT gunmen. If therefore we are going to go into the question of who has arms, it is quite obvious that both sides have amassed a considerable amount of arms, and that we do not solve the problem by blaming which ever side had succeeded in having more arms than the other, but by removing the causes which brought about this state of affairs whereby citizens thought it necessary to be armed and fight.

I might remind Mr. Denktash of his statement made even in a court of law, that the Turkish side was armed and was prepared to fight. However, Mr. Chairman, I do not want to be provocative, I do not want to be obstructive, and therefore I will not go into the detail of what has happened in the past. What I and my delegation are interested in is: what can we do to safeguard the future?

MR. KYPRIANOU said:

"Mr. Chairman, I wish to thank Her Majesty's Government for the initiative it has taken to arrange this conference, with the object of finding a solution to the problems of the Republic of Cyprus. I hope this conference will bring about a settlement consistent with democratic principles and the claims of justice, and compatible with the status of the Republic of Cyprus as a sovereign and independent state, a member of the United Nations.

Although after hearing what has been said one is tempted to reply to most of the points raised, I do not propose to do it. I do not propose at this stage to make a long statement. I reserve my right to do that on another occasion. I wish to confine myself only to stressing certain material points, which in my view all interested parties round this table should bear well in mind if this conference is to achieve its objective.

The causes for the recent tragic events—and I repeat, very tragic events indeed, tragic to both sides—are to be found in the agreements and the Constitution. The Constitution of Cyprus contains not only unworkable and undemocratic elements, but also, and I want to stress this, it has as its main feature the division of the people, which is the main source of the friction. The people of Cyprus therefore, far from being encouraged to live in full co-operation as citizens of the same state, have been in fact encouraged to live separately, to work separately, to think as separate entities, to work on the basis of community criteria and thus destroy the very basis upon which co-operation and loyalty to the state by all citizens should be based.

I believe that we have learned a lot from the application of this totally unworkable theory of division. Let us not make the same mistake, or a similar one. We must approach the problems of Cyprus in the right manner, in a constructive manner and in an orthodox way. If one wants to secure happiness and prosperity for the whole people of Cyprus, whether Greek or Turk or Armenian or Maronite it is our duty to create the necessary conditions for that and it is not through division that this can be brought about: on the contrary it is by total and complete co-operation and through unification. All Cypriots should have the same rights irrespective of race, creed or religion and all must feel as citizens of one unitary state. Any sovereign and independent state is entitled to be free from any outside intervention or interference, because otherwise its independence and sovereignty could not be regarded as real and complete. But in the particular case of Cyprus both experience and realism can easily convince anyone, any one of us round this table that the treaties of Cyprus with Greece and Turkey containing unacceptable elements which I have quoted is all the more imperative to do away with.

This I believe would not only be in the interests of Cyprus as an independent state, as a member of the United Nations, as a member of the Commonwealth, but in all objectivity we believe that this would be in the long run in the best interest of all three of us, Turkey and Cyprus and Greece.

As from the 16th day of August 1960, when the Republic of Cyprus Order in Council 1960 came into force, an integral independent and sovereign republic of Cyprus was established in the island of Cyprus. The Republic of Cyprus is therefore entitled to have the Constitution of an integral independent and a sovereign state, based on universally recognised and accepted democratic principles, and free from any outside intervention or interference or independence. The fundamental human rights of all citizens should also be fully protected.

Mr. Chairman, I do not propose to reply at this stage to all the points raised by the other delegations. I believe that the work we have to do is in the working committee. Let us hope that they do under your enlightened chairmanship a good work.

There are only one or two points I would like to mention, and this is in reply to Mr. Erkin. I do not want to start arguments, but I feel I must make one or two comments. First of all it is my duty to dismiss outright any accusation that the Government had any premeditated plan. Secondly, I think it is my duty to refer Mr. Erkin to his statement about the actions of the Turkish Government. He asserts the Turkish Government decided to resort finally to unilateral action in accordance with the Treaty.

I do not propose at this stage to start an argument on that but I would like to reserve my position on this particular point.

Mr. Erkin also said that Cyprus is not a homogeneous country; that is true. He said that there are people of Greek origin and people of Turkish origin; that is true. But I do not believe that is the only case in the world, and I am sure that Mr. Erkin knows of other countries in which more or less the same situation exists. He read a list of statements reported to have been made by various people in Cyprus, and another list of examples by which he sought to prove the Greek Cypriot leadership or the Government of Cyprus have failed to implement certain provisions of the constitution or that there again they contravened the constitution. I could take a long time to reply to all these allegations but I am not going to do that today. One thing he mentioned, by way of example, was that the President of Cyprus decided to go to the Belgrade conference and he did that without consulting the Vice-President. One hour after the President had received the invitation I went on his behalf and consulted the Vice-President at his house. Nevertheless, the final participation of Cyprus at the Belgrade conference was a Government decision in the Council of Ministers, and the Vice-President and all the Turkish Ministers were also present.

Another point which has been mentioned is that physical separation is the only way of safeguarding the citizens. Three mixed villages were mentioned, yet there are 250 other mixed villages in which not a single incident occurred. Turks and Greeks in the majority of these villages still live peacefully in spite of some efforts by other quarters to move them forcibly.

Mr. Chairman, our desire is to see this conference succeed. We are grateful to you for all you have done, for all the British Government have done, and all you personally have done, and we are here to help you complete this; we wish every success to the working committee under your enlightened chairmanship."

MR. ERKIN said:

"I should like first to refer to the Treaty of Guarantee. According to the provisions of Article 2, paragraph 1, of this Treaty, Turkey has together with the United Kingdom and Greece guaranteed the state of affairs established by the basic articles of the Constitution of Cyprus. In addition to that, according to Article 181 of the Cyprus Constitution, the Treaty has constitutional force. Therefore on the basis of the Treaty and the Constitution Turkey has a duty to be concerned for acts which violate the basic articles of the Constitution of Cyprus. Mr. Palamas said that the Zurich agreements have been based on the assumption that the two communities will co-operate. From our point of view the truth is that the Greek Cyprus side did not co-operate; on the contrary they tried to achieve their aims first by intimidation and then by using sheer force.

After hearing the statements of the Greek Cyprus delegation, I come back to the suggestion I made during my exposé in which I proposed that an authoritative investigation be made of the tragic events of Cyprus. But now I insist that this investigation be made not only of the tragic events in Cyprus but also of the records of the Republic of Cyprus since the constitution of the state of the Republic of Cyprus, the main accent being on the mutual relationship between the Turkish and Greek community. I hope my English colleagues will accept my motion.

Mr. Palamas said that the human factor is more important than geographic factors. If my dear colleague has enough time to consult the records of the Treaty of Lausanne in the 1922 or 1923 peace settlement between Turkey and the allied countries, he would be interested to read the discussions concerning the resident race question. There the great Greek statesman Mr. Venezelos was claiming the region of Thrace on the basis of geographic reasons. Now I find the standards of the Greek delegation have changed. May I assume that the yardstick will change according to the country and not to the problems which are examined. In the case of Greece he claimed the geographic reasons were prominent; now in the case of Cyprus the human factor is prominent. Mr. Palamas stated Greek Cypriots had claimed Enosis had Turkey claimed partition. I challenge my English colleagues to find one single occasion on which the Turkish statesmen claimed partition. I received Mr. Kutchuk to dinner, but no speeches were exchanged on that night, and I am not aware of the statement of Mr. Kutchuk referred to.

Mr. Chairman, I do not want to take more of your time but before you adjourn I would like to address our thanks to our host Government the British Government and to draw the attention of members of this conference to the remarks made yesterday by you, Mr. Chairman, paying tribute to your statesmanship and to your action in Cyprus and to the words you said yesterday in your inaugural statement. The situation is very grave, very explosive, and no-one can express this explosive situation in a better way than you did by your words yesterday:—"There could be no more compelling argument in favour of agreement than the horror and misery of these past weeks and the memory of those who have died. . . . If fighting were to break out a second time it would be very much more difficult to stop it than on the last occasion and Cyprus would once again be faced with the dangers of external invasion . . . few weeks ago." I agree 100 per cent with your statement. Thank you, Mr. Chairman."

MR. CLERIDES said:

"I fully agree with what you said yesterday, Mr. Chairman, about the difficulties should fighting break out, but I want to make it clear I do not interpret your statement as containing a threat that if the conference were to fail there would be dangers of external invasion. Had it been possible to give that interpretation even if there was the slightest intention of a threat that if we fail to reach agreement there are dangers of external invasion, I would not have agreed to sit at this conference."

MR. OREK said:

"May I say something, Mr. Chairman. Mr. Kyprianou mentioned that he had consulted the Vice President on the question of the Belgrade Conference before a decision was made. The truth is that on Saturday it was officially announced over the radio that President Makarios had already accepted an invitation to attend a conference in Belgrade of non-aligned nations, and Mr. Kyprianou came to see the Vice President on the following Sunday at his residence at Troodos.

I was staying with the Vice President at the time so I know the case at first hand."

Marlborough House, S.W.1.
23rd January, 1964

APPENDIX 91

Record of Meeting of Working Committee at Marlborough House, London, 16 January, and Talks at Chequers, 17–18 January 1964

The Greek Cypriot Delegation was invited for talks at Chequers by the Commonwealth Relations Secretary, Mr. Sandys. Mr. Clerides, Mr. Tassos Papadopoulos and Mrs. Souliotis were present at the talks at Chequers.

In view of the fact that these talks were considered as sub-committee talks it was hinted by the British that it would be better if Mr. Kyprianou did not participate. The talks were between the Greek Cypriot Delegation and Mr. Duncan Sandys with his advisers, who included Lord Carrington of the Foreign Office and the Duke of Devonshire. Sir Arthur Clark was also present. The Turkish Cypriot Delegation was not present, but it had been invited to similar talks at Chequers which were to be held immediately after the return of the Greek Cypriot Delegation to London.

Prior to the talks at Chequers there was on 16th January a short meeting of the sub-committee under the chairmanship of Mr. Duncan Sandys. Both Greek Cypriot Delegation with its advisers and the Turkish Cypriot Delegation were present. During these talks the Turkish side put forward the view that the security and personal safety of the Turks was a matter which required immediate attention before any discussion began on the Constitution, the Treaty of Alliance and the Treaty of Guarantee. They explained their position thus: the only way in which security could be provided for the Turkish inhabitants was by physical separation between Greeks and Turks. This should be done by removal and exchange of populations so that Turks living in isolated villages or Turks living in mixed villages would be resettled in areas near Turkish villages. They also suggested that an exchange of properties and compensation should be arranged and that they were not prepared to consider the constitutional issue before the question of resettling the population was agreed upon. They were pressed by Mr. Sandys to state their views about the Constitution, but at first they were very reluctant to give even a general outline of their views. There was a difference of opinion between Mr. Denktash and Mr. Halit Ali Riza, regarding the movement of Turkish and Greek citizens into separate areas. Mr. Denktash thought that a number of Turkish Areas could be created by resettling the Turks in those areas but Mr. Halit Ali Riza was of the opinion that the Turks should be settled in one area and that it would be better if the Greeks were moved out of this area. When pressed by Mr. Sandys they admitted that they considered that this Turkish area should be administered by the Turkish Cypriots, that it should have a police force of its own. Mr. Sandys remarked that in his view this was partition. He asked the Turks further if this Turkish area would be a separate independent state and whether it would be a state within an independent Cyprus. Mr. Halit Ali Riza explained that this would be a state within an independent Cyprus with its own Government and that the two separate states thus created would have some form of coordinating body in the centre.

The Greek Cypriot Delegation rejected outright the Turkish proposal and stated that there was no need to move the population in order to secure the physical safety of the Turks and that the Turks were in fact using as a pretext their alleged anxiety about their security in order to bring about the creation of separate Greek and Turkish areas so as to be able to argue that partition was possible. The Greek Cypriot Delegation, apart from stating that the question of moving populations and the establishment of two states within Cyprus was unacceptable, went on at great length to show with reference to facts and figures that the removal of the population and the creation of separate areas was impossible to bring about.

In addition, the Turkish Delegation was asked to state its views on the question of the presence of Greek and Turkish troops in Cyprus.

The Turkish Cypriot Delegation stated that in their view whatever arrangement was arrived at, Turkish troops would have to be stationed in Cyprus and asked for the increase of the Turkish contingent and that Turkish troops should be stationed in areas in which trouble was likely to occur.

Mr. Denktash also stated that there must be set up a Committee of the three Guarantor Powers to find out who is responsible for the events in Cyprus and bring the guilty to justice. Mr. Sandys immediately said that he did not think that this kind of investigation served any purpose but only stirred up a lot of feeling and tension.

The Greek Cypriot Delegation was then asked to state its views. We stated that no settlement arrived at which was based on the principle that there would be a Treaty of Guarantee or Alliance or provided for Greek or Turkish troops to be stationed in Cyprus could be accepted. We explained our views on the constitution i.e. that it should be a constitution based on democratic principles, that all citizens will have equal rights and as a result the majority of the citizens will control the Government and that the human rights of all citizens would be safeguarded by constitutional provisions. We further stated that we were not prepared to recognize to any community any political rights as a community as distinct from the rights of the ordinary citizen.

We were asked by Mr. Sandys what measures we could suggest in order to create confidence in the Turks with regard to their physical security. We again elaborated our arguments that the Turkish side was pretending to be anxious about their physical security in order to gain political rights of a separatist nature. Mr. Clerides then stated that we were prepared to consider that foreign observers such as U.N. observers could be stationed in Cyprus for a limited period until confidence was restored, to observe the operations of the security forces. He pointed out that, although we did not think this was necessary, nevertheless this was a matter which could be considered, and that in his opinion this should be sufficient to remove any alleged lack of confidence by Turks. Mr. Clerides pointed out that such arrangement could be considered provided it was clearly understood that it would be purely temporary. Mr. Sandys stated that, in the light of recent events, the Turks had cause to be anxious about their physical security and that for an interim period i.e. until confidence was restored and as a temporary measure, it may be necessary to consider stationing in Cyprus some international troops so that the Greek and Turkish contingents would be withdrawn from the island. The Turkish side rejected immediately this proposal stating that they could not accept either a Commonwealth Force or a U.N. Force because, as they said, the one was of a temporary nature and the other too loose a guarantee and repeated their claims for the increase of the Turkish contingent in Cyprus, stressing that they were not anxious if Greece did not wish to increase its contingent, but that they wanted Turkey to increase its forces in Cyprus.

Mr. Sandys summed up his views in the following words:

"It seems to me that we have to provide some arrangements for the physical security of the Turks. All of us would like to find a solution that would enable Cyprus to go on as a unified country with one administration.

It may be that the Turks think that this will be an impracticable solution and that only separation of the communities will give them adequate safeguards. It may be that this will prove to be the only answer. But I would not like to feel that that this is the only answer because this would tend to keep the communities apart.

I accept that the question of security is a paramount one, but I do not think that the solution proposed by the Turks is the only one.

The Greek side on the other hand should go a little further and accept that you cannot create confidence at present, by simply having a mixed police. It may be that temporary arrangements will have to be made and it may be that the settlement will not come in one step and that transitional steps will have to be taken.

I ask the Greek side to give some thought to the proposal of inviting to Cyprus some form of international policing unit for a transitional period for helping in the creation of an atmosphere of confidence.

I am not thinking of the contingents of Greek and Turkish Army which are a reserve security force but of some other force which will have sufficient strength to stop such clashes as the recent ones."

It became obvious that there was no possible common ground of agreement and as a result Mr. Duncan Sandys adjourned this meeting (which took place on Thursday afternoon, the 16th day of January 1964) for Monday the 20th to give time for private preliminary talks at Chequers, first with the Greek delegation, and then with the Turkish Delegation, during Friday to Sunday.

The meetings at Chequers between Mr. Sandys and the Greek Cypriot Delegation began on Friday the 17th January at 5 p.m. At the beginning of the meeting Mr. Sandys stated that in his view some measures had to be found to satisfy Turkish anxieties about their physical security. He went on to say that if such measures could be found it would be easier to find agreement on the constitutional issue as well as the issues of Treaties of Guarantee and Alliance. Of course, he stated, although we have to begin from somewhere, nothing would be finally settled unless agreement was reached on all the issues.

We again restated our entire argument about the fact that it was not necessary to make any special arrangements for the safety of the Turks in Cyprus reiterating that, once the causes of friction were removed, i.e. the workability of the constitution and its separatistic trends there would be no need for any special security arrangements. We also stated categorically that we were not prepared to consider the question of security measures for the

Turks and that any security measures, if proved necessary, would be for all the citizens of the Republic. We made it clear that, before considering any security measures, we must have discussions on the new constitution of the Republic and reiterated that whatever form the constitution of the Republic was to take, in no event could we agree that there should be guarantees from foreign countries. Mr. Sandys then developed the argument that, although he agreed in principle, the constitution required amendment, yet nevertheless he was convinced that for a limited period until confidence was restored some special security measures would be necessary. He suggested that the normal policing of the state should be carried out by a unified police force consisting of Greek and Turkish Cypriots as in the past, but in his view, for a limited period until confidence was restored, it would be necessary in cases where there was intercommunal conflict to have a small international police force, which could act as anti-riot squad.

He then went on to say that in his view it would be easier to succeed in getting rid of the Treaty of Alliance and the Treaty of Guarantee and the removal of the Greek and Turkish contingents, if the Cyprus Government was willing to agree to the stationing in Cyprus for a limited period of a small police force as described above, but he added this force must be able to be reinforced from outside in the event of serious trouble breaking out in Cyprus. He suggested that if Cyprus joined NATO, arrangements could by made for the reinforcement of the aforesaid small police force from members of NATO excluding Greece and Turkey and on a proportional basis amongst the NATO member countries in accordance with their respective numerical strength in the NATO forces. He explained that if Cyprus were to join NATO the Turkish arguments about the strategic importance of Cyprus to Turkey would no longer be valid since the defence of Cyprus would be the concern of NATO and consequently the lines of communications to Turkey would not be threatened.

We replied that we could not accept the proposition of Cyprus joining NATO and explained that Turkey, being a member of NATO, would be exercising a serious influence in the NATO Council with regard to Cyprus matters. We also stated that if Cyprus joined NATO the possibility could not be excluded, that if there was any serious international crisis, Turkey would be asked to station troops in Cyprus as the nearest military power of the NATO Block. Mr. Sandys replied that these matters could be arranged if Cyprus decided to join NATO so that neither Greek nor Turkish troops could be entrusted with the defence of the area. He also said that there was no question of NATO or any NATO country exercising any influence on the internal affairs of another country. We stated that although there was no need for anxiety about the physical security of the Turks, provided that it was agreed to withdraw the Greek and Turkish contingents, we might consider the stationing of a small international police force in Cyprus operating under the government of the Republic and only for a limited period until confidence was restored, but we stressed that such force should have no connection with NATO.

Mr. Sandys then asked for our views of the Turkish proposal about the movement of populations and the creation of areas within which the Turks would feel safe. He asked us to explain whether such measures were physically practicable as distinct from the desirability of such measures or not. We explained at length, giving facts and figures, the difficulties of the problem showing that it was impossible to undertake. We further made it clear that even if physical separation of the population was possible, politically it would be completely unacceptable. We also stressed that, in our view, the Turkish side was exaggerating their anxieties about their physical security, for the purpose of creating an impression that such separation of the population was absolutely necessary, with the ultimate object of separating the Greeks and Turks in two areas and thus move a stage nearer towards achieving partition of the Island. We also pointed out that in mixed villages Turks have been ordered to move out and that in many instances they were threatened if they refused to comply with such orders, but in spite of such threats many Turkish inhabitants of mixed villages refused to leave their homes. We stated that instructions should be sent to the Liaison Committee and to General Young to stop the Turks who are forced to leave their villages, otherwise a situation may arise in which it will be impossible for us to continue participating in the conference. Sir Arthur Clark informed us that he was sending an urgent telegram to Mr. Pickard in Cyprus on this issue.

Mr. Sandys then asked us to explain our views on the Constitution. We stated again our position that we want an independent Sovereign Unitary State with equal rights for all citizens. We reiterated that we were not prepared to consider a Constitution in which special political rights would be given to the communities, as such, as distinct from human rights given to the individuals. We made the point that we were prepared to have provisions in the Constitution about human rights similar to those contained in the Rome Convention on Human Rights or the declaration of Human Rights of the U.N.

Mr. Sandys then asked what value would there be in having such human rights incorporated in the Constitution if these could be amended at the will of the majority. We replied that, with regard to human rights incorporated in the Constitution, we could follow the examples of other Constitutions where, in order that such rights could be amended, an increased majority of the Members of Parliament would be necessary instead of a simple majority.

Mr. Sandys then asked us what were our views in the manner of electing Members of the Legislative Body of Parliament. We stated that our intention was that we should produce a system whereby there could be no division between the two communities, and that, in accordance with this principle, we would want all citizens, regardless of religion or community, to be elected on one common electoral roll.

Mr. Sandys remarked that this would mean that the majority (Greeks) could elect all Members of Parliament, and therefore a situation could arise where it would not be possible for a single Turk to be elected. He asked us whether this was our intention. We stated that this was not and in so far as the legislative body was concerned, we had no intention of excluding the Turks from holding a reasonable amount of seats proportionate to the Turkish population, provided that they were elected on a common roll and that no separate procedure for the voting of Bills of any kind, such as separate majorities etc., was to be incorporated in the constitution.

We were then asked by Mr. Sandys what were our views with regard to religious, educational and cultural matters. We stated that in these matters we were prepared to find a way of giving to the Turkish Community autonomy. At this stage Mr. Sandys asked us about the 13 points given by Archbishop Makarios to Dr. Kutchuk for consideration (and asked Sir Arthur Clark to produce a copy of the 13 points). We explained that the 13 points were not intended to be a solution of the constitutional problem of Cyprus and that they dealt with some of the difficulties of the Constitution in an attempt to improve the situation without at the same time purporting to be a remedy. We stressed that, even if the 13 points were granted, it would still leave the constitution of the Republic based on the concept of the communities, each one with distinct political rights and that it was this concept which prevented the smooth functioning of the state and the creation of Cyprus as a state in which the interests represented were the interests of the state instead of the interests of the two communities. We, therefore, persisted in the view that a completely new constitutional arrangement was necessary in order to remove the dividing elements of the existing constitution.

At this stage Mr. Sandys again reverted to the question of Human Rights, and asked if it was our intention that in the new constitutional arrangements there would be no room for a Constitutional Court. We replied that this was a matter of detail and that if there was no constitutional court, a view which we favoured was that the jurisdiction of the Constitutional Court could be transferred to the ordinary courts and by way of appeal to the Appeal Court. We also stated that the possibility could be considered to appeal on the questions of Human Rights to an International Court, such as the European International Court of Human Rights. Mr. Sandys then asked us whether the Turks would have an opportunity to participate as judges in the judiciary and as civil servants in the Civil Service of the Republic. We replied that the intention was that the Turkish citizens would have the right to participate as citizens of the Republic both in the Judiciary and in the Civil Service of the Republic in a fair proportion. He then asked what we meant by a fair proportion, and we stated that, although we were in favour of the Turks participating in the Civil Service, fairly, we did not wish to follow the procedure of fixing a certain percentage. Mr. Sandys remarked that it would be difficult to define what fair participation is without fixing a percentage.

The above are a brief synopsis of the salient matters raised at Chequers. Naturally, there were lengthy arguments demonstrating the reasons for each point we were making and at the same time demolishing arguments which we believe that the Turkish side would be putting forward.

CONCLUSIONS

(a) We feel sure that we have convinced the British that we are sincere in our desire to see a unitary state in which the interests of the state would be the paramount concern of the citizens rather than the communal interests.

(b) We feel that the British have not been convinced that there is no special cause for anxiety about the physical security of the Turks. The reason for this may be twofold. Either they believe, in view of the recent events, that the Turks have a reason to be anxious about their physical safety or they may wish to use the question of physical security as a bargaining point in order to offer to the Turks certain measures regarding their security so as to get them to agree to a new constitution which would not be based on the concept of the partnership of the two communities.

(c) We feel sure that our arguments have convinced the British that the movement of population is not necessary and that the creation of two separate areas is not only impossible to realize but also would create dangers of a bigger and more serious conflict. However, we do not exclude the possibility that the British may recommend some small movement of population in mixed villages where Turks are very few, to other Turkish villages.

(d) With regard to the Treaties of Guarantee and Alliance we feel sure that what the British have in mind is to suggest the abolition of the Treaties of Guarantee and Alliance provided that Cyprus has some connection with NATO.

(e) With regard to the form of the Constitution we believe that the British, although they agree with us that the Turks should not have rights as a community similar to those which they have under the present constitution, nevertheless they are not convinced that it is sufficient protection for the minority to be safeguarded by the inclusion of Human Rights in the Constitution. In all probability they will suggest that in the constitution there shall be provision safeguarding the participation of the Turks in the House of Representatives in proportion to the Turkish population, but without any veto rights such as the rights as separate majorities etc. The British also will suggest that some form or provision should be made in the Constitution about the fair participation of the Turks in the civil service and the judiciary, probably along the line of fixing a certain percentage of participation, and certain other measures that we cannot anticipate from now.

(f) The British suggest some form of autonomy for the minority for religious, educational and cultural matters.

(g) It appears that the British find it difficult to believe that it is possible for the Turks to accept our Constitutional proposals which would mean taking away from them many rights now possessed by the Turkish community under the present Constitution and at the same time agree to the cancellation of the Treaty of Alliance and Guarantee without being able to show that they have abandoned all these rights in exchange for some other benefit.

Note: We pointed out that we are not prepared to consider giving the Turks anything which we believe should not be given, in order to persuade them to accept something. We stated that if such procedure was followed, knowing how unreasonable the Turkish demands are, the result would be an agreement of the type of Zurich.

The next meeting of the working committee has been fixed for Monday the 20th at 11 a.m.

APPENDIX 92

Letters from the Leader of the Greek Cypriot Delegation at the London Conference to the Secretary of State for Commonwealth Relations, 21 January 1964

My dear Sandys,

At yesterday's meeting at Marlborough House, you handed to us a paper containing two alternative proposals, one marked "A" described as the Turkish Cypriot proposal, the other marked "B" described as the Points for Discussion.

I observed at the time that, though the Turkish Cypriot proposals were stated in the paper, the Greek Cypriot position was not included.

From the views expressed by us at Chequers the following proposals emanate:

1. The State to be an independent, unitary integral State.
2. All legislative power to vest in a Parliament elected by general suffrage on a common roll.
3. The executive power to emanate from a Cabinet answerable to Parliament.
4. The judicial power to vest in an independent, unified judiciary.
5. The universally accepted human rights, such as those in the Rome Convention, to be incorporated in the Constitution. These not to be alterable except by a specified majority of Parliament.
6. The Turks are to have self-government in matters relating to religion, education and culture.
7. There shall be a right of appeal on alleged violations of human rights to an international tribunal, such as the European Court of Human Rights.
8. It is not intended to exclude the Turks from participating in the Parliament or the Civil Service of the Republic.
9. The Treaties of Guarantee and Alliance not to continue to be in force.

Yours sincerely,

(GLAFKOS CLERIDES)
Leader of the Greek Cypriot Delegation.

The Rt. Hon. Duncan Sandys, M.P.
Secretary of State,
for Commonwealth Relations.

My dear Sandys,

My Delegation thought it might be useful, at the present stage of the discussions, to forward to you the attached memorandum with the hope that it may help to clarify our position on some of the aspects of the problem, and thus contribute in our common effort in search of a just solution.

(GLAFKOS CLERIDES)
Leader of the Greek Cypriot Delegation

The Rt. Hon. Mr. Duncan Sandys, M.P.
Secretary of State
for Commonwealth Relations.

MEMORANDUM

A. PRINCIPLES:

1. The State shall be an independent, sovereign, unitary, integral State with a Parliament elected by general suffrage on a common roll and a Cabinet answerable to Parliament, on the basis of the democratic majority principle.

2. The Constitution should be such as to ensure the above concept in every aspect, and it is therefore essential to view it in its totality and not to discuss aspects of it in isolation, which may create a whole totally deviating from the central concept.

The above is not a mere theoretical exposition. A factual appraisal of events in Cyprus proves that deviation from such principles has resulted in the present unfortunate situation. The Zurich Agreement, by separating the Greeks from the Turks, has prevented the creation of a consciousness of responsibility to the State as a whole, and, by its inequitable and unrealistic provisions, has been the inevitable source of constant friction, and has engendered frustration and bitterness.

The Treaties of Guarantee and Alliance have encouraged the separatist elements and have proved a threat to the independence and integrity of the Republic.

B. Therefore, any suggestion inconsistent with the above principles is unacceptable. Thus,

(1) Any provision creating or safeguarding any fight for the minority beyond the generally accepted human rights and their safeguards, including matters of religion, education and culture, cannot but result in a situation of privilege rather than equality, in denying to the majority of the population the power to have its will reflected into effective government, and will perpetuate and promote separation and friction.

(2) Any suggestion in support of separate communal representation, instead of promoting the development of democratic institutions and eliminating the clash of communal interests, tends to create separate compartments re-

sulting in a lack of homogeneity and of common consciousness which makes unity of purpose impossible.

In this respect, the adoption of two communal rolls is inconsistent with the conception of a unitary integral State. It promotes separation, in that Members of the Legislature feel that their obligations and allegiance are to their community and not to the State as a whole. It has the effect of exaggerating differences and indefinitely delaying the development of unity and a consciousness of service to the public interest. Furthermore, it promotes a tendency to elect representatives who will look after communal interests rather than the public interest, and there is thus a danger of extremists being returned to the legislature.

These dangers have been amply demonstrated in Cyprus in Practice.

Similarly, any suggestion in support of a rigid provision of percentages for Parliamentary representation and other matters is contrary to the conception of a unitary, integral State, the citizens of which should have equal rights without any differentiation on the basis of race, creed or religion.

Such percentages promote separation and foster allegiance to communal interests instead of to the public interest, to the detriment of the progress and development of the country as a whole.

When applied to the Public Service, the fixing of percentages prevents the formation of a good and efficient Public Service because it makes it necessary to use communal criteria instead of the universally accepted criteria of qualifications, merit, suitability and the needs and interests of the Service.

The implementation of such provisions, which necessitate a complicated machinery based on communal checks, has proved impossible to apply, has created intercommunal friction, stagnation, frustration and grievance and has been detrimental to the efficiency and discipline of the Public Service.

When the percentages fixed bear no relation to the ratio of the Greek and Turkish inhabitants of the Island, not only are the difficulties magnified, but such percentages constitute discrimination against the majority of the population and are contrary to the principles of Human Rights, since the majority of the citizens are denied equal opportunity of participation.

These unjust provisions have given rise to feelings of bitterness and discontent amongst the Greek population of Cyprus.

(3) There would be no justification for the organization of any movement or exchange of population which, far from affording any safeguard for the security of the population so moved or exchanged, will create a great social problem, insuperable difficulties in the absorption of the populations so moved and the provision of alternative employment, and will cause untold human suffering to the people of Cyprus.

The pretext of security is untenable for the reason that the danger does not lie in the physical proximity of the two communities but in the causes of friction. Concentration of populations would increase rather than diminish the danger of intercommunal clashes, as is proved by the recent events in Nicosia.

Any so-called voluntary scheme of movement of population will necessarily result in compelling a portion of such population to move from their homes against their will, which is an infringement of a fundamental human right.

The suggested scheme for the movement or exchange of populations, though ostensibly intended for the security of the Turkish minority, has as its sole aim the creation of conditions preparing the ground for partition and paving the way for the preparation of a potential territory of the Turkish State.

(4) Any suggestion for separate local administration and police duties, in respect of any group of villages, is inconsistent with the unitary and integral conception of the State, the administration of which should be uniform under the control of one and the same authority.

Furthermore, any grouping would result in the creation of pockets which would form centres of criminal activity the prevention and detection of which would become very difficult and would create conditions fostering clashes between police forces.

Any separatist tendency would render any scheme of development impossible, and the economy of the Island would thus be seriously affected.

In this respect, the Council of Europe, by Resolution 262 (1963) of the Consultative Assembly, on the economic situation in Cyprus, have pointed out that the tendency of the two communities to organize their economic life on separate lines is a hindrance to the economic expansion of the Republic and suggested that particular attention should be given to the problems of costs and economic infrastructure of a small geographic area characterized by limited resources.

(6) The Treaty of Guarantee is incompatible with an independent sovereign State, and has proved in practice to endanger the independence and integrity of the Republic. Recent experience has established that the stationing in Cyprus of Greek and Turkish contingents under the Treaty of Alliance is an encouragement to intercommunal friction and a menace to peace and order.

(7) Any suggestion for the stationing in the Republic of a foreign force in any form and for any purpose is not consistent with the status of an independent State. It is a different matter if, for a temporary period and with the consent of the State itself, a Police Force composed of expatriate personnel (other than Greeks and Turks) is empowered by the Government of Cyprus to take appropriate action to maintain the peace in case of intercommunal clashes.

(8) Any suggestion for the filling of senior police appointments by expatriate officers or for the creation of a Police Service Commission with expatriate participation, thus taking the control of security out of the hands of the State, would seriously detract from the notion of any Independent State.

APPENDIX 93

Views of E. Lauterpacht Given on 25, 28 and 29 January 1964 and Note, 30 January 1964*

BRIEF SUMMARY OF MR. LAUTERPACHT'S VIEWS AS EXPRESSED DURING A CONSULTATION ON 25/1/1964

I. Recourse to the Security Council.

(1) Mr. Lauterpacht is of the opinion that we can go to the Security Council either under Article 33 or under Article 35 of the Charter. He considers it important that we should take the initiative and we must, therefore, know exactly what we should ask from the Security Council. He considers that we could ask for any or all of the following:

(a) That the Security Council should take note of the declaration of the Government of Cyprus, in view of the circumstances which have taken place since Independence, to regard the Treaties of Guarantee and Alliance as terminated. Another alternative under this would be to argue that the Treaty of Guarantee is not valid and in any case that, even if valid, the Treaty does not give the right to military intervention.

(b) That Greece and Turkey should be called upon to withdraw their forces.

(c) That the Security Council should take note of the intention of the Government of Cyprus forthwith to establish a Constituent Assembly to draw up a Constitution with safeguards for the human rights of all citizens, and particularly of the Turkish minority.

(d) That the Security Council should invite participation of Constitutional experts to observe the work of the Constituent Assembly.

(e) That the Cyprus Government should state that the individual recourse to the European Court of Human Rights will be accepted.

(f) That the establishment of a United Nations Force to take care of the situation during the deliberations of the Constituent Assembly should be asked for.

(g) That Turkey should be asked to give an undertaking to abstain from sending any forces to Cyprus or to threaten to do so and that United Nations Observers to see that the undertaking is complied with should be asked for, as well as Force to act as a buffer against Turkish aggression.

(2) Mr. Lauterpacht's opinion as to whether the recourse to the Security Council already made should be proceeded with is that our position in pursuing such a recourse would not now be so strong, because of the

---

* *Editor's note:* For the text of the note, 30 January 1964, see appendix 22(3).

circumstances which have in the meantime ensued, e.g. the acceptance of the Tripartite Truce Force including the Turkish contingents. The old threat of aggression by Turkey would now only be of background value in demonstrating the intention of aggression. It would, therefore, be better to make a fresh recourse with the aim of averting the danger of aggression.

(3) In case of failure of the London Conference, Mr. Lauterpacht does not think that, under Article 37 of the Charter, the Governments concerned could be *compelled* to go to the Security Council. This would depend on what pressure could be brought to bear on them to join in such a recourse. Furthermore, such a "joint recourse" might have the disadvantage that it would take the initiative out of our hands; moreover, there might be a conflict of objectives, in that we may wish to ask for something different from what the other parties want.

2. Establishment of Peace-Keeping Force:

(1) With regard to the proposal for the establishment of an International Peace-keeping Force in Cyprus, copy attached for easy reference, Mr. Lauterpacht is of the opinion that, as the proposal now stands, it seems to be quite incompatible with the Treaty of Guarantee under which Great Britain has undertaken commitments both collectively and severally.

(2) The proposal appears to be an attempt to sidestep the obligations under the Treaty of Guarantee and to deviate therefrom. The Government of Cyprus is however in a dilemma in this respect, for the reason that, since the Government wants the abolition of the Treaty of Guarantee, it is difficult for it to ask Britain to act under the Treaty.

(3) Mr. Lauterpacht suggests that a note could be addressed to the British Government saying that, in view of the possibility of a Turkish invasion, would the British Government be prepared to honour its commitments (or to act in accordance or in the manner contemplated by the Treaty of Guarantee) in the event of a Turkish invasion. The note could also add that an early reply would be appreciated because the matter would be taken to the Security Council.

Thus, Britain would have to make its position clear. In Mr. Lauterpacht's opinion this course would also give us a tactical advantage in referring the matter to the Security Council.

(4) With regard to the terms of reference of an International Force it is important that the following matters be clarified:

(a) Objective: Such a force should be for the purpose not only of keeping peace within the Island but also of averting intervention.
(b) Duration: This should be limited in some way, otherwise a force might get in, which we would be would be unable to get out again.
(c) Terms of Reference: The exact terms of reference and powers of the Force should be clearly laid down.
(d) Responsibility for the Force: The authority responsible for the Force and its command should be specified.

3. Treaties of Guarantee and Alliance.

(1) As regards, generally, the validity of the Treaties of Guarantee and Alliance, Mr. Lauterpacht considers that both Treaties are valid. He does not, however, consider that the Treaty of Guarantee gives the right to armed intervention.

(2) He thinks that it is easier to get rid of the Treaty of Alliance than of the Treaty of Guarantee and that the former might be terminated by reasonable notice of termination.

(3) Any move for physical separation is, in Mr. Lauterpacht's opinion, contrary to the Treaty of Guarantee, and the Government of Cyprus may ask the Guarantor powers to take action under the Treaty. Similarly the Government of Cyprus could ask the other Guarantors to take action under the Treaty if one of the Guarantors threatens aggression.

The difficulty here would be the dilemma of the Cyprus Government in seeking to rely on the Treaty whilst asking for its abolition.

4. Mr. Rossides' Credentials:

With regard to any question which might arise as to Mr. Rossides' authority in the case of a recourse to the Security Council, Mr. Lauterpacht does not think that Mr. Rossides' Credentials could seriously be challenged. In any case, if a question arose as to his authority, to act in the particular case before the Security Council, it could be argued that it is absurd that in a case of such urgency one should dwell on technicalities.

London, 25th January, 1964.

BRIEF SUMMARY OF MR. LAUTERPACHT'S VIEWS AS EXPRESSED
DURING A FURTHER CONSULTATION ON 28/1/1964

The questions discussed were:

(1) The form which a recourse to the Security Council should take.
(2) The contents of such a recourse.
(3) The manner in which such a recourse should be supported.

(1) Form of a Recourse: The question was discussed again as to whether the recourse should be a new one or should be a continuation of the recourse already made. Mr. Lauterpacht's view is that, if there is any question of Mr. Rossides' Credentials being challenged, then it is better to proceed on the old recourse since his credentials with respect to that have already been filed.

He suggested that we could confirm whether the credentials had, in fact, been accepted by a perusal of the records of the discussion which has already taken place at the Security Council. These records have been obtained from the United Nations Centre. The only "challenge" to "credentials" which appears therein is an indirect one, as per Appendix "A". A copy of Mr. Rossides' recourse to the Security Council on 25.1.1964 is attached as Appendix "B".

If it were decided to proceed on the old recourse, we should ask that the matter be inscribed on the Agenda again on the basis of the old recourse and then either Cyprus itself or a friendly country could ask for the further things we want as part of the resolution.

(2) The Contents of such a Recourse:

(a) A request that an International Force should be sent to Cyprus:
(i) Composition: If Cyprus were to take the matter to the Security Council it is possible that, due to the membership of the Security Council, a composition might be decided which was not acceptable to us. The Soviet Union, for instance, would not accept a force that did not include Eastern Block Troops. On the other hand, the Western countries would not want participation of such troops, and each would veto any composition to which they did not agree. Therefore, a force acceptable to all might either be impossible to set up or, if established, might not be acceptable, from the composition point of view, to Cyprus. One way in which this difficulty might be faced would be, if Cyprus could reach agreement, before making a recourse, with the various countries willing to contribute forces, so that Cyprus would have a composition to suggest to the Security Council which might then accept such composition.
(ii) Cost of the Force: The question of financing of the force is a matter to be seriously considered. In the case of a United Nations Force, the cost would depend on the decision of the United Nations, which is in great financial difficulties. It is, therefore, unlikely that the United Nations would undertake the financing of the Force, especially as the commitment would be of an in-

definite duration, and would probably ask Cyprus to bear such cost, either wholly or in part.

(iii) Terms of Reference of the Force: Mr. Lauterpacht thinks that we must bear in mind that the United Nations will certainly not allow its Force to take part in the settlement of internal disputes. It would, therefore, not be possible to include in the terms of reference that the Force should assist the Cyprus Government in restoring normal conditions, and the force would, therefore, not be able to do anything to prevent the Turks in their efforts to create de facto separatist situations.

The United Nations would also be very hesitant, to set up a Force, to *prevent a threat* of aggression. It has never yet set up a Force in anticipation of aggression, but only after aggression has occurred. The Security Council would be very reluctant to establish a precedent of such a nature, which would create heavy commitments for it in the future, since it would encourage all sorts of claims on the U.N. whenever any country felt that there was any fear or possibility of aggression.

Therefore, the terms of reference which can be expected are "to maintain order"; it might be possible to enlarge such terms as follows: "to maintain internal order and preserve the integrity and unity of the Republic of Cyprus".

Mr. Lauterpacht thinks that the establishment of such a Force, even though its terms of reference did not expressly include the prevention of aggression, would, in effect, prevent aggression, as the prospective aggressor would think twice before attacking a country in which a Force of this nature was stationed.

(b) Restrain from Aggression: The resolution might also ask that all countries shall restrain from acts of aggression.

(3) The Manner in which a Recourse should be supported:

The question might be asked "what has occurred *now* to warrant a recourse the Security Council?"

It would strengthen our position if the British Government were asked for an assurance that they would not withdraw their forces from Cyprus and were to reply that they were unable to give such assurance.

The "evidence" required in support of a recourse at this stage would be sufficiently provided by a history of developments and threats of aggression, either by concentration of troops or in speeches made. The very fact that a proposal has been made that an International Force should be set up would also tend to show that there is danger to peace in the area.

SUMMARY: A recourse to the Security Council at this stage might, therefore, ask (a) that Turkey shall restrain from acts or threats of aggression; (b) that an International Force shall be set up in Cyprus to maintain internal order and preserve the integrity and unity of the Republic of Cyprus.

APPENDIX "A"

EXTRACT FROM RECORD OF THE 1085 MEETING OF THE SECURITY COUNCIL HELD ON FRIDAY, 27th DECEMBER, 1963

"Mr. Kural, (Turkey)

xxx   xxx   xxx   xxx   xxx   xxx   He (Mr. Rossides) is treading on rather dangerous ground when he says that perhaps members of my Government do not think as I do. I represent an entire Government, my Government as a whole. I wonder whether Mr. Rossides is able to speak likewise. After all, whom does he represent here? Probably the Greek members of the Government of Cyprus. But that is not sufficient.

"Mr. Rossides (Cyprus) xxx   xxx   xxx   xxx   xxx   xxx   xxx I am representing the Government of Cyprus and there has been sufficient authority from the President of the Republic to represent him. If Cyprus is such a country that it cannot have a representative here, that is probably one more reason why this Constitution should be revised—if he thinks that the Constitution is such that they can have no representative".

RECOMMENDATIONS ON THE COURSE OF ACTION TO BE FOLLOWED WITH REGARDS TO THE SECURITY COUNCIL

The views which have been expressed by Mr. Clerides under the heading "reasons why the application pending before the Security Council should not be relied upon" are shared also by Mr. Lauterpacht, who agrees that the application pending before the Security Council should not be relied upon in its present form.

A point of difficulty may arise however, if the present application were to be withdrawn and substituted by a new application.

The difficulty which Mr. Lauterpacht envisages may arise in connection with the credentials of Mr. Rossides. Already Mr. Rossides has filed credentials before the Security Council showing his authority, on behalf of the Government of the Republic, to submit an application. If a new application is made, he may be required to file new credentials, in which case a decision of the Council of Ministers would be required with the possibility of a veto from the Vice-President. Mr. Lauterpacht, however, does not consider that this may cause much trouble, because he believes that an objection to Rossides' credentials is not likely to be sustained by the Security Council, either because this is a matter of municipal law, or because the Security Council would not prevent Mr. Rossides from going into the substance of the matter by the mere fact that an objection to his credentials has been raised. There is, however, precedent and the Security Council has in one case gone into the question of the validity of the credentials of a delegate on objections based on the municipal law of the country concerned. But even in that case, although the Security Council heard the objection, nevertheless, it allowed the delegate concerned to proceed to the substance of his application.

Mr. Lauterpacht however suggested that it would be better to avoid this complication by sticking to the original application and by seeking to expand it. This, in his opinion, can be done in the following manner:

(a) when the appropriate time comes, Mr. Rossides should apply to have the pending application placed immediately on the agenda of the Security Council.
(b) he should give at the same time notice that he intends to give further facts in support by stating that despite the attempt to find a peaceful settlement, the threat of an aggression by Turkey against Cyprus continues to exist.

In other words, in the view of Mr. Lauterpacht, the existing application should be used not for the purpose of getting a decision that Turkey has committed an act of aggression, but in order to support the contention that the facts which have occurred prior to the acceptance of the good officers of the three Governments, together with the actions of the Turkish Government since the acceptance of the good offices, show the continuous threat of aggression against Cyprus. The facts before the date of the good offices will be used, if that view is accepted, as background information supporting the contention that the threat of invasion continues to exist.

The question which arises in connection with the application, is the form of the resolution which we should try to obtain from the Security Council. Great care is needed, either for Mr. Rossides to prepare a resolution or if the resolution is to be put forward by a friendly country after Mr. Rossides' speech, that it should be in the form which we desire.

With regard to the matters to be included in the resolution, please see the papers attached to this document:

(a) Brief summary of Mr. Lauterpacht's views as expressed during the consultation held on the 25th January, 1964.
(b) Memorandum marked (Important) dated 29th January, 1964, prepared by us.
(c) Brief summary of Mr. Lauterpacht's views as expressed during a further consultation on the 28th January, 1964.
(d) Copy of the recourse filed by Mr. Rossides to the Security Council obtained by us from the library of the United Nations, in London.

The views expressed by Mr. Lauterpacht during the consultation held on the 25th January, 1964 as to what the application to the Security Council should contain must not be taken as recommendations as to the contents of the application. What should be included in the resolution is a political decision. Mr. Lauterpacht was advising what legally can be asked of the Security Council. He stated, that either all the points mentioned by him in the interview of the 27th January, (copy of which is attached to this document) or any combinations of them can be asked from the Security Council. However, in a subsequent consultation held on the 28th January, 1964 (copy of which is attached to this document) he expressed the view that an application to the Security Council at this stage might be limited to the following:

(a) that all countries concerned should restrain themselves from committing acts of aggression against Cyprus.
(b) that an International Force be set up in Cyprus by the Security Council to maintain internal order and preserve the integrity and unity of the Republic of Cyprus. Again however, he stressed that the question of the contents of the application is a political decision.

We agree with the view expressed by Mr. Lauterpacht that at this stage the application should be limited to the above referred two points. We must however, repeat again what has been said in our memorandum marked "important" dated 29th January, 1964 attached to this document, the essence of which is, that although there is a good possibility of obtaining the resolution from the Security Council on items (a) i.e. a resolution asking all concerned to restrain from acts of aggression against Cyprus, there is little hope, if any, that the Security Council will agree to send forces in Cyprus prior to an actual attack materialising. Equally, there is little hope that the Security Council will agree to include as terms of reference to such force either of the following:

(i) to defend Cyprus from an external attack or,
(ii) to assist the Government to put an end to the separatists de facto situation created by the Turks in Cyprus.

Mr. Lauterpacht however, is of the opinion that should the Security Council decide to create a force to send to Cyprus, a fact which he describes as most unlikely, even if its terms of reference are internal policing, the presence of such force coupled with the resolution, calling on all parties to restrain themselves from committing acts of aggression would be sufficient to prevent an act of aggression on Cyprus.

We are of the opinion however, that even at the risk of not getting a decision in our favour by the Security Council on the points mentioned herein below, they should be included in the revolution asked, on behalf of the Cyprus Government. The points to be included are as follows:

(a) authorization of the force to defend Cyprus from an attack from without.
(b) to assist the Government of the Republic to restore law and order and preserve the internal unity of the State.

It is, of course, doubtful that the Security Council, unless there is preparatory agreement of the composition of the force, that it will be able to reach an agreement on this issue. Both countries of the east and west have a right to veto in the Security Council and neither will hesitate to use it if the composition of the force includes elements or units exclusively belonging to one group.

It is equally certain that the British and Americans will veto a force containing units of the eastern block.

It is obvious from what is stated above, that the question before the Security Council may take some time to resolve, first because it is unlikely that the Security Council will agree to despatch a force to defend Cyprus prior to an attack materializing and second because there will be difficulties to agree on the composition of the force. It may however, be more effective, from the point of getting a quick decision if the following tactics were followed:

(a) the resolution to the Security Council be limited to asking for an undertaking from all countries concerned to abstain from committing an act of aggression.

(b) agreement to be reached on the composition of the force prior to going to the Security Council, informing the Security Council what has been agreed upon, and place the force under the Security Council asking the Council to name a General as its commander. The above suggestion is put forward for your consideration.

This can be coupled together with the request to the U.N. to set up a committee of Greek and Turkish Cypriots under the chairmanship of a representative of Mr. U Thant and with the participation of U.N. observers for the purpose of finding a solution to the Cyprus problem.

In our view, there are grave dangers if an International Force is accepted to establish itself in Cyprus. The advantage to such a force would be that it would prevent the threat of aggression from Turkey from materialising and thus it would assist considerably in finding a solution to the Cyprus problem, since the Turks once they know that the possibility of aggression has been removed, would have to be ready to accept a solution. The disadvantage however, of any force, whether it is a U.N. force or a NATO force, is that since there is no possibility in either case to give as terms of reference to such force, that it should assist the Government to restore law and order and maintain the internal integrity and unity of the State, the de facto situation will be consolidated and if negotiations were to be postponed indefinitely, the existing de facto situation is likely to remain. In such a case, one would not be able to find a solution which would ignore the de facto situation.

All the above matters mentioned, in our opinion, should be considered very carefully and urgently, decisions must be taken forthwith and clear instructions be given to all concerned.

We are now approaching a time when we have two alternatives before us, either to reject the proposals in London with the subsequent break-up of the Conference or, make every possible effort to improve on the offers made in London. It appears that there is very little likelihood that the British Government will accept to go to the U.N. and ask from Security Council a force, without first having reached an agreement as to the composition of this force. This being so, the Conference will break-up within the next two or three days. Equally the Conference may break-up because Turkey may insist that the force should be a NATO force and that it should contain Greek and Turkish contingents in addition to those already stationed in Cyprus. It would, of course, be a political advantage to us if the Conference fails because of the Turkish position. However, we must anticipate that the Turks may give up the point that Turkish troops should be included. In such a case the onus of rejecting the NATO force would be on us, in which case the Conference will fail.

Which ever way one looks at it for all intents and purposes, the Conference in London will break-up in a very short time. It is however, of great importance that we should be clear in our mind of the following:

(a) What are we going to ask the Security Council.
(b) What would be the effect of a Security Council resolution calling on all to abstain from committing an act of aggression on Cyprus, if it is not supported by an International Force to be stationed in Cyprus before any attack materialises in Cyprus.
(c) Equally it is important to bear in mind that even if we assume that Turkey will intervene and that Greece will also intervene, whether in the meantime an area of Cyprus will not be occupied by Turkish forces, in which case the Security Council or the NATO group will intervene and impose a cease-fire on Greece and Turkey and force them to seek a political solution. In such an event it will be impossible to avoid partition.

If the case is to be filed by applying to the Security Council, without having first agreed to the composition of the force, we must be sure that, should Turkey attack Cyprus, there will be involvement of other forces i.e. Greece, Russia etc. so as to make it imperative for Great Britain and the U.S. to exercise serious pressure on Turkey and thus make it impossible for her to take such a step. Particular importance must be attached to the Russian factor. The fact that we have secured such support must be known in advance to Great Britain and the U.S.A.

In stating all the above and in particular the arrangement to be made by bringing about such a situation, one must have in mind that the time left to us at our own disposal is very short and that urgent action along, the directions indicated, is required.

29.1.1964.

APPENDIX 94

Record of Meeting between the Foreign Minister of Cyprus and the Greek Cypriot Delegation and the Secretary of State for Commonwealth Relations, 31 January 1964

RECORD OF MEETING AT MARLBOROUGH HOUSE WITH MR. SANDYS ON 31.1.1964, AT 11.00 A.M.

The Minister of Foreign Affairs and the Greek Cypriot Delegation were invited to attend a meeting at Marlborough House at 11.00 a.m. on the 31st January, 1964. No indication had been given as to whether it was going to be a Conference meeting or not. It transpired that it was not, in fact, a Conference meeting, but that Mr. Sandys and his advisers were having meetings with the various parties separately.

The meeting was attended by Mr. Sandys and his advisers on the one hand and by the Minister of Foreign Affairs and his advisers and the Greek Cypriot Delegation (Mr. T. Papadopoullos absent) and its advisers, on the other.

Mr. Sandys said:

"As we expected, this Conference is going very slowly. All my reports show increased tension in Cyprus, which might lead to further bloodshed and provide a pretext for Turkish intervention. That is why, I thought that the best thing would be the setting up of a peace-keeping force to hold the ring while talks on the solution of the problems of Cyprus are continuing.

It seemed to us that there were two possible sources for such a force: one, the United Nations, and the other the group known as N.A.T.O.—by this I do not mean N.A.T.O. itself.

We did consider very carefully the possibility of a U.N. force but we foresaw great difficulties because one never knows what may come out, i.e. what sort of resolution may emerge. The really awkward thing is that you may get a veto altogether on any kind of force, and secondly we might have a situation where Russia might insist on participating in any force, or thirdly we might have a situation where all members of the Security Council were debarred from participating, in which case neither Britain nor America would participate.

Your suggestion for a Commonwealth force really only boiled down to Canada in the end. India and Pakistan are busy watching each other and China. Malaysia is busy on the frontier with Indonesia. Australia and New Zealand could not even help us with Indonesia, let alone Cyprus.

Therefore, with some reluctance we came to the conclusion that if we wanted a force composed of the same kind of people as the people of Cyprus, and which included the British, there was no other place to look for such a force except Western Europe and the United States. The United States were approached and were very reluctant. With some difficulty we have persuaded them to participate, provided that the countries directly concerned, i.e. the guarantor powers and the Government of Cyprus, agree, and provided that sufficient contributions are secured to make the force worthwhile. We need a force sufficiently large to make it clear to anybody who is thinking of making trouble that it is not worth their while—we need a force to deter. We are thinking in terms of a force of 10,000, in addition to the Greek and Turkish Contingents already in Cyprus. We have taken the view that there should be no increase of these Contingents. The Commander should be a British officer, because we will still have the greatest number of troops there.

The Commander of the force will have to have terms of reference and, generally, political guidance. The overall political guidance may come from a Committee in London, and the day-to-day guidance from a Committee in Nicosia perhaps on more or less the same lines as the present Liaison Committee.

The guarantor powers should undertake not to exercise their power of intervention while the force is there. Therefore, one of the conditions would be that the guarantor powers undertake not to exercise their right under the Treaty of Guarantee.

We are asking the countries concerned to maintain the troops which they contribute for three months. I have no illusions that everything will be settled in three months, but the important thing is to get the whole thing started.

We feel that we cannot keep this Conference going indefinitely, and I cannot give the time that will be needed for this very heavy task or mediation. There is a very wide gap between the two approaches. What we are therefore proposing is that the parties should agree to the appointment of a mediator and that they should agree to help him in his task. By "mediator" we do not mean an "arbitrator", and nobody has to accept in advance what the mediator may propose. His duty will be to help the two sides to reach agreement. The idea would be to find somebody of standing, enjoying the confidence of both sides, to try and bring the two communities together.

We have now put these proposals to the Greek and Turkish Governments formally. When we get their acceptance we will put them formally to the Cyprus Government and when we get their agreement, if we can, we will start approaching the other countries who will be asked to contribute.

We have asked Mr. Pickard to explain the proposals to-day to Archbishop Makarios and Dr. Kutchuk in order to clear up any queries which they may have.

I shall be glad to clear up any points which you may wish to ask me about."

Mr. Clerides said that, even at first sight, there were many objections to the proposal. In fact, we were being asked to accept the principle that a force would be placed in Cyprus without knowing the purpose of the force, and over which the Government of Cyprus would have no control. As to "guidance from a Committee in London", we had been told nothing about this Com-mittee nor even what its composition was going to be. For all we knew, we might not even be members of it. In short, the whole proposal appeared to be the occupation of Cyprus by a foreign force. As to the Security Council, Mr. Clerides pointed out that no mention had even been made of it.

Mr. Sandys said he appreciated the anxieties and points made by Mr. Clerides, but the details of the proposal would be the subject of further discussion. The purpose of the force would be to keep the peace and help to create stable conditions while talks on the solution of the problem were continuing. "Do not put too much emphasis on the point of the precise terms of reference of the force", he said, "this is a matter for discussion". On the question of the Security Council, Mr. Sandys said that they wanted that the very closest contact should be maintained with the Security Council, and the Observer could report to the Security Council what was being done.

Mr. Clerides said that we could not be expected to accept in principle the proposal without knowing the answers to the questions raised by him. This would amount to the occupation of Cyprus by a foreign force.

Mr. Kyprianou said that this sort of arrangement would, apart from all the other objections, provoke criticism that we were keeping the Security Council out. What was needed was some force to assist the Government in restoring normal conditions and to protect Cyprus from aggression from outside. The force that had been sent to the Congo had among its terms of reference the preservation of the unity of the country. In order to be effective, the force must be an international force which should derive its authority from, and be answerable to, the Security Council.

Mr. Sandys said that the force would derive its authority from the Governments concerned, including the Government of Cyprus, which would be able to ask for something to be done, if it so wished.

Mr. Clerides said that one further point which was completely unacceptable was the suggestion that the three guarantor powers should undertake not to exercise their right of intervention under the treaty while the force was in Cyprus. This would imply that they had such a right—which they did not—and also that they would be able to intervene after the end of the period in question.

Mr. Sandys said that he appreciated the point, but that "intervention" did not necessarily mean "armed intervention". It meant whatever right it was that the powers in fact had under the Treaty.

Mr. Kyprianou said that this was a major matter which should be put before the Security Council, and suggested that, otherwise, it might be against the Charter.

Mr. Sandys said that if there was agreement, there was no question of contravention of the Charter. He said that, as he had explained earlier, we could not be sure that the Security Council would yet set up a force at all, because there were countries in the Security Council which would be happy to see everything go up in smoke in Cyprus. The Russians would be happy to make trouble; this was a great opportunity for them, to have two countries in N.A.T.O. at war with each other.

"If the three guarantor Governments accept this proposal", he said, "then we shall formally put this before you".

Mr. Clerides made the further point that it was difficult to understand how Britain and Greece could purport to act under the Treaty of Guarantee in concert with Turkey who, by advocating and promoting partition, was clearly in breech of the Treaty.

Mr. Sandys replied that International Law was rather flexible.

Mr. Clerides said, that, as valuable time is going by, and we may want to go to the Security Council, he wished to mention this now so that there would be no misunderstanding in the future.

APPENDIX 95

Letter from Greek Prime Minister George Papandreou to Archbishop Makarios, 25 February 1964 (translation)

THE PRESIDENT OF THE GOVERNMENT

Athens, 25th February, 1964

TOP SECRET

Your Beatitude,

Having assumed the duties of Prime Minister, I wish by this message to assure Your Beatitude of the infinite affection, admiration and continuous concern of the Greek people and its Government for the heroic and suffering people of Cyprus.

My negative views on the state of affairs created by the Zurich and London Agreements are known to you. But let us not at this moment dwell on the past. Circumstances demand that we dwell on the present and the future of the Island and that we do so as a matter of urgency. That is in fact the object of this message.

For some time now I have been following with agony the events in Cyprus from day to day. Last December my Government, on the recommendation of the late Sofocles Venizelos then Vice-President and Minister of Foreign Affairs, did everything dictated by the national interest so that Cyprus might be safeguarded from certain danger. Later, as leader of the largest political party, I continued to follow developments in Cyprus and to give my advice to the Caretaker Government.

Now, following the assumption by me of the government of the country once more, the whole weight of responsibility is borne by my Government. And I consider it my primary and urgent duty to exchange thoughts with Your Beatitude on the Cyprus crisis.

I start from the thesis that our Nation, Hellenism, constitutes a single entity. Cyprus is a significant part of Hellenism, of the Nation. And I consider that the principles which should govern the relations of the various parts with the entity must be relations in which there is mutual sharing of information, co-operation and solidarity. There must be harmonisation and the setting of priorities of means and objectives. And this *unfortunately is not the case* to-day in the relations between the Greek Government, which bears the more general responsibility for Hellenism, and the Cyprus Leadership. We run the risk of being informed of Your initiatives through the international press, and You to be informed of the Greek Government's decisions in more or less the same way. Furthermore, the dynamic initiatives of the Greeks of Cyprus unfold in an unco-ordinated manner.

Such circumstances of unco-ordinated and senseless action lead to great dangers and are not, in my opinion, worthy of either of us. If the Nation were aware of this situation it would never forgive us.

We consider that the first essential of our national policy must be the full and timely consultation between us, the harmonisation of views, means and objectives.

Within this concept of the unity of Hellenism and the increased responsibility of Athens, as the Centre of Hellenism, I wish to express my strong desire for full and constant contact between us, understanding and harmonisation of views. If circumstances so warrant, we may even agree to disagree.

If You agree, please let us have Your views on the strategy and tactics of the Struggle, as You understand it, the dynamic means and the political objectives You seek to achieve.

I wish to assure Your Beatitude that it is the decision of the Greek Government to give wholehearted support to the new Struggle of the Cypriot People for the attainment of all its rights. But the form of the support must be determined by common agreement.

We wholeheartedly express the wish that the new national struggle of the Cypriot people will have an auspicious conclusion and we hope that this national message will meet with unequivocal response.

Respectfully,
George Papandreou

To His Beatitude the Archbishop of Cyprus
Monseigneur Makarios,
President of the Republic of Cyprus,
Nicosia.

APPENDIX 96

Letter from Archbishop Makarios to Greek Prime Minister George Papandreou, 1 March 1964 (translation)

PRESIDENTIAL PALACE

Nicosia, 1st March, 1964.

Dear Mr. President,

I deeply appreciate the fact that, on the assumption of your duties as Prime Minister, you hastened to show in a practical manner your unwavering active concern about Cyprus. A further expression of this concern is your message to me of 25th February last, by which you express the wholehearted support of your Government to Cypriot Hellenism and you convey certain views regarding the harmonisation and setting of priorities of means and objectives between the Mother Country and Cyprus, and generally regarding the manner of co-operation for the more effective handling of the Cyprus problem.

I am grateful, Mr. Prime Minister, for this message, and I wish to assure you that I have always wanted close co-operation with the Greek Government and advance consultation and co-ordination of actions, because I believe, like you, that the Greek nation constitutes a single entity, part of which is Cyprus which looks to Athens as the centre of united Hellenism.

It is true that, in some cases, for various reasons, actions have been taken, both on the part of the Greek Government and on the part of the Greek Cypriot side, without advance consultation and co-ordination. Reference to these cases serves no useful purpose. I fully agree with you, however, that it is useful, or rather essential, especially in the present circumstances of Cyprus, that there should be exchange of views and consultation before any action is taken on the handling and promotion of matters relating to Cyprus.

Through the Royal Greek Embassy in Cyprus and the Cyprus Embassy in Athens or directly by letter or through envoys I shall share with you my thoughts on the manner of promoting the Cyprus problem, so that I may have your views; there will thus be understanding between us on the handling of the matter, even if our views might not always coincide.

I am sending to Athens the Acting Minister of Foreign Affairs, Minister of Commerce and Industry Mr. Andreas Araouzos, and the Minister of Interior Mr. Polykarpos Georkadjis, to convey to you in person the thanks of the Cypriot people and myself for your generous support and backing and at the same time to brief you more fully on conditions in Cyprus and also to transmit views regarding the course to be followed in our political and dynamic struggle and the objectives we seek. Responding willingly to your message, I am conveying to you through these envoys also in writing certain views of mine on our objectives and the means of achieving them.

Our aim, Mr. Prime Minister, is the abolition of the Zurich and London Agreements so that the Greek Cypriot people may, in agreement with its Mother Country, determine its future. I am the one who signed those Agreements on behalf of the Greeks of Cyprus. In my personal opinion, under the circumstances of the time, there was no other alternative. However, I did not for a moment believe that the Agreements constituted a permanent state of affairs. It was a state of affairs dictated by dire necessity and, in my view, the less evil solution at the time to the Cyprus drama. Since then circumstances have changed, both internationally and locally, and I think that the time has come for us to attempt to free ourselves from the Agreements imposed on us.

I quite realise that it is not an easy task. The Struggle will be long and very onerous. But I am absolutely convinced that justice will finally prevail. Our struggle is now being carried out in the political field and in the military field. We entered the first field on our own initiative. We were led to the second as a matter of necessity. I am not in a position to foretell the outcome of our Recourse to the Security Council. I think, however, that the debate itself is a positive gain for us, irrespective of whether we shall succeed in the adoption of the Resolution we want. We shall set our further course in the light of the outcome of the discussion at the Security Council. The view has been expressed that in the event of an unfavourable outcome we should ask for an extraordinary session of the General Assembly of the United Nations. I do not think that we would succeed in obtaining the required majority of member states for convening an extraordinary session of the General Assembly. Instead of failure in this effort, it is better to wait for the ordinary session of the General Assembly and make a recourse to it if there has not been a solution before then. The view has also been expressed that we should refer the treaties of Guarantee and Alliance for adjudication to the International Court of the Hague. I rather think that the decision of the International court would be favourable for us. But I fear that the case before the Court might drag on and that due to this uncertainty we would not in the meantime be able to resort to other lawful means.

The abolition of the Treaty of Guarantee presents greater difficulty than the Treaty of Alliance. I am of the view that, due to its nature, the Treaty of Alliance can easily be terminated. If Cyprus informs its other allies that it withdraws from this Alliance and Greece subsequently does the same the Treaty of Alliance is automatically terminated. I have asked the Attorney-General of the Republic to study the matter, and I enclose his Opinion. Any action in this direction is probably premature but I am submitting my thoughts now so that I may have the observations and views of the Greek Government in time.

The unilateral abolition of the Treaties otherwise than in accordance with lawful procedures or the agreement of all the signatories might have serious repercussions. We will not however proceed to such action without prior consultation with the Government of Greece.

I now come to the dynamic side of our struggle.

A large section of the international press and public opinion ascribes the responsibility for the violent events in Cyprus and generally for the prevailing abnormal situation to the Greeks of Cyprus and especially to me. Some people connect the proposals submitted by me on 30 November last for the revision of the Constitution with the tragic events that followed shortly afterwards. My proposals may have been the pretext for a dynamic reaction on the part of the Turkish Cypriots. The allegation, however, that it was sought to impose my proposals by force is totally unfounded and untrue.

The submission of proposals for the revision of the Constitution has been considered by some as premature and untimely. As a matter of fact, I had always intended to try to free ourselves from the Agreements by stages. I considered it fit to attempt first the abolition or revision of certain constitutional provisions. I intended to do this in the second quarter of the current year 1964. I repeatedly talked about my intentions regarding constitutional revisions to the British High Commissioner in Cyprus, Sir Arthur Clark, who communicated my views to his Government. Last November I received through the British High Commissioner a message from the Secretary of State for Commonwealth Relations, Mr. Duncan Sandys, that he agreed with the intended revision of certain constitutional provisions which were obstructing the smooth functioning of the State and were the cause of friction between the Greeks and Turks of Cyprus. He advised that I prepare without delay a document setting out the provisions which I considered should be abolished or revised as well as the reasons dictating the constitutional revision. Mr. Sandys also informed me that on 12 December last he would be visiting Kenya and might visit Cyprus on his way there or back so that we could discuss the whole matter. With this advice and instigation from Mr. Sandys I prepared the well known document of my 13-point proposals. I communicated this document to the British High Commissioner who, after consulting his Government as I believe, made certain suggestions on some points. I accepted his suggestions and the final text of the document was prepared in co-operation with him. On the assumption that the initiative, the co-operation and the promise of support by the British constituted a significant element in ensuring success, and after duly informing the Greek Government, I submitted my proposals to the Turkish leadership. That was the reason why I hastened—and at a time when Greece was in a state of political transition—to submit my proposals for constitutional revision. The events which followed unfortunately belied the hopes I had placed in the British Government, the attitude of which has not been at all sincere.

I have referred to the above, Mr. Prime Minister, so that you may know my thoughts and the reasons which dictated the preparation of my proposals for certain constitutional revisions. Whilst I was expecting the reply of the Turkish Cypriot leadership, however, violent events occurred in Nicosia on the morning of the 21 December, which a few days later also spread to other areas of the Island.

I strongly believe that the responsibility for these tragic events and the whole unfortunate situation lies exclusively with the Turkish Cypriot side. It is true that the Greeks of Cyprus and their leadership had for some time been making military preparations so as to be ready to meet any armed attack by the Turkish Cypriots who, we knew, were importing arms from Turkey and were giving military training to many members of their community. But the Greek Cypriot side, despite the military preparation to meet any eventuality, never entertained any thought or had any intention of attacking the Turks. We did not seek a clash and an armed struggle. The struggle was imposed on us. We found ourselves compelled to meet armed violence with the same means. We may have to do the same in the future. For this reason we are continuing our preparation in this field also.

We have a military Organisation the trained members of which exceed 5,000 men and this number is constantly growing. I do not conceal the fact that our Organisation suffers from certain weaknesses, and there have been cases of lack of discipline and damaging initiatives. Efforts have been made for reorganisation on a better basis, and I may say that to-day the situation in this respect has improved to a satisfactory degree. For more effective control and the imposition of discipline we have decided to increase the numbers of the Auxiliary Police and all the members of the Organisation will be enlisted in that force.

I will not omit to mention that the experience of many officers of the Greek Military Contingent serving in Cyprus and the supply of equipment from Greece have been of great assistance in this sector, and Cypriot Hellenism is deeply grateful for this.

In conclusion, I do not consider it irrelevant to refer also briefly to our ideological orientations and our foreign policy.

We, the Greeks of Cyprus, and in particular I, personally, are accused by a number of Western countries of having been drawn, dangerously, into communist nets and that Cyprus may become a new Cuba. This accusation is totally unjustified. The Greek Cypriot people, which is passing through a critical turn in its history, finds itself without assistance—rather, it is confronted by a negative reaction and hostility on the part of the countries of the Western world—in the pursuit of its rights. When it sees its national future at risk, it seeks help from all directions. The West pushes it towards the East. It accepts support from the East, but it does not change ideological camp. Cyprus, historically and culturally, belongs to the West, even though it will continue following a non aligned foreign policy.

The above, in general terms, Mr. Prime Minister, I wished to convey to you in answer to your message.

Thank you again warmly for your concern for Cyprus and the valuable assistance given to us. Please accept the expression of my great esteem for you.

With cordial wishes and love,
Makarios of Cyprus.

His Excellency
Mr. George Papandreou,
President of the Greek Government,
Athens.

MINNESOTA MEDITERRANEAN AND EAST EUROPEAN MONOGRAPHS

Theofanis G. Stavrou, general editor